PRAISE FOR *Women and the Gift Economy: A Radically Different Worldview is Possible* edited by Genevieve Vaughan

Finally! This is the book we urgently need in these neoliberal, destructive, disoriented times. We all know that a profound change in our economy and culture is necessary, that we need to think in another way. But how? The authors of this collection of articles—all feminists, all peace workers, from the North and the South—demonstrate convincingly that "a radically different world view is possible" when we look at the world with Genevieve Vaughan's radically different paradigm: gift giving instead of the coercive and compulsive exchange paradigm of the market economy.

—VERONIKA BENNHOLDT-THOMSEN, co-author of *The Subsistence Perspective: Beyond the Globalized Economy* and *Women: The Last Colony*

Wow, what a great book. If more people could embrace this kind of thinking the world would be a much better place. In the tradition of my people one's status in society in not based upon how much wealth one possesses and displays but rather it is based upon what one gives away. Thus according to our traditions the creators of this volume deserve special recognition as their work is a gift for the rest of us who have the privilege of reading it.

—D. MEMEE LAVELL-HARVARD, President, Ontario Native Women's Association and Vice President, Native Women's Association of Canada

Those of us honoured to know Genevieve Vaughan know that, for at least twenty years, she has been working tirelessly towards defining and describing the "gift economy, presenting it as a workable alternative to patriarchal capitalism. This anthology, *Women and the Gift Economy*, offers the fruit of myriad scholars on the subject, examining the gift economy from nearly every imaginable vantage point—from history, spirituality, sexuality, and matriarchal social structure to language, finance, childcare, and warfare. Moreover, Indigenous scholars working from their own cultures' ways of knowing receive a representation and a respect equal to what is afforded their European and Euroamerican colleagues. *Women and the Gift Economy* is guaranteed to guide the reader into new and invigorating paradigms, clarifying the economic choices facing humanity.

—BARBARA ALICE MANN, author of *Iroquoian Women: The Gantowisas* and editor of and contributor to *Daughters of Mother Earth*

Genevieve Vaughan has for decades been active in progressive causes—generous with her time, energy, and material resources. Now she gives the best gift of all: her elegant, intelligent, and transformative thinking. This is, simply, a visionary book. Read it, let it into your heart and brain—and you will change the world.

—ROBIN MORGAN

The gift economy is prevalent in most ancient Indigenous societies the world over, many still existing today. Gifting operates especially well among people with fewer resources, in rural areas and urban townships. It is through sharing gifts that many of us survive. Genevieve Vaughan's feminist gift economy is a reminder to all of us about this ancient practice still prevalent in many of our societies, especially in Africa and the global South more broadly, and her life's work in this area perfectly epitomizes the philosophies underpinning the book: it is the gift economy in practice.

—BERNEDETTE MUTHIEN, poet and activist, director of ENGENDER, South Africa

This collection, in its critique of patriarchal capitalism and in its call for a logic of gift-giving over exchange, makes possible a new understanding of—and appreciation for—the true economic and social value of mothering. In this, the book is an invaluable contribution to motherhood studies.

—ANDREA O'REILLY, Associate Professor, York University, and author of *Toni Morrison and Motherhood: A Politics of the Heart*

Based on Genevieve Vaughan's theory of the gift economy, this book offers a radically different world view for 21st century feminism with powerful implications for challenging patriarchy and the market economy in building a sustainable, safe, equitable world society. In the introduction Vaughan outlines the logic and impact of the gift economy. Vaughan's approach provides an alternative paradigm in which "mothering" in all the senses of the term is at the foundation of the social model for being human. Together with the articles that follow her introduction, the book provides a unified feminist philosophy in which the logic of social interaction is based on "gifting" that is, giving to nurture growth by satisfying needs in response to which the receiver models the giver by giving to others. This is a must read for feminists in all countries for it provides a coherent philosophical system based on the power of nurturing for rethinking political and economic thought just as the Enlightenment once based its philosophical innovations on the power of human reason.

—PEGGY REEVES SANDAY, Professor of Anthropology, University of Pennsylvania and author of *Women at the Center: Life in a Modern Matriarchy*

Anyone who wonders why a tree giving us oxygen is only profitable when it's cut down, or why a train wreck increases the Gross Domestic Product but nurturing children does not, is on the way to rejecting patriarchal capitalism. Genevieve Vaughan and her collection of essays by activists and visionaries show us an alternate economic worldview that existed for most of human history, and could exist again. This brave and path-breaking book will give you hope—and hope is a form of planning."

—GLORIA STEINEM

WOMEN AND THE GIFT ECONOMY
A Radically Different Worldview is Possible

WOMEN AND THE GIFT ECONOMY
A Radically Different Worldview
is Possible

EDITED BY GENEVIEVE VAUGHAN

INANNA PUBLICATIONS AND EDUCATION INC.
TORONTO, CANADA

Published in Canada by Inanna Publications and Education Inc.
210 Founders College, York University
4700 Keele Street, Toronto, Ontario M3J 1P3
Telephone: (416) 736-5356 Fax (416) 736-5765
Email: inanna@yorku.ca Web site: www.yorku.ca/inanna

Printed and Bound in Canada.

Cover Design: Val Fullard
Interior Design: Luciana Ricciutelli

Library and Archives Canada Cataloguing in Publication:

Women and the gift economy : a radically different worldview is possible / edited by Genevieve Vaughan

Essays originated at a conference, "A radically different worldview is possible: the gift economy inside and outside patriarchal capitalism," held in Las Vegas, Nevada, November 2004.

Includes bibliographical references and index.

ISBN 978-0-9736709-7-4

1. Gifts – economic aspects. 2. Matriarchy. 3. Indigenous peoples – Economic conditions. 4. Sharing – Economic aspects. 5. Mutualism – Economic aspects. 6. Social change. 7. Feminist economics. I. Vaughan, Genevieve, 1939-

HQ1381.W652 2007   306.3'4   C2007-901648-0

Contents

Acknowledgements   v

Introduction: A Radically Different Worldview is Possible
Genevieve Vaughan   1

I. The Gift Economy, Past and Present

Indigenous Knowledge and Gift Giving: Living in Community
Jeannette Armstrong   41

Pan Dora Revisited: From Patriarchal Woman-Blaming to a
   Feminist Gift Imaginary
Kaarina Kailo   50

The Gift Logic of Indigenous Philosophies in the Academy
Rauna Kuokkanen   71

She Gives the Gift of Her Body
Vicki Noble   84

The Goddess Temple of Sekhmet: A Gift Economy Project
Patricia Pearlman   96

Matriarchal Society and the Gift Paradigm: Motherliness as an
   Ethical Principle
Heide Goettner-Abendroth   99

Significs and Semioethics: Places of the Gift in Communication Today
Susan Petrilli   108

The Biology of Business: Crisis as a Gifting Opportunity
Elisabet Sahtouris   121

II. Gifts Exploited by the Market

Capitalist Patriarchy and the Negation of Matriarchy: The Struggle
  for a "Deep" Alternative
Claudia von Werlhof   139

Big Mountain Black Mesa: The Beauty Way
Louise Benally   154

The Tragedy of the Enclosures: An Eco-Feminist Perspective on
  Selling Oxygen and Prostitution in Costa Rica
Ana Isla   157

Real Bodies, Place-Bound Work and Transnational Homemaking:
  A Feminist Project
Mechthild Hart   171

The Rural Women's Movement in South Africa: Land Reform
  and HIV/AIDs
Sizani Ngubane   181

Endangered Species: The Language of Our Lives
Margaret Randall   187

Facing the Shadow of 9-11
Carol Brouillet   193

Heterosexism and the Norm of Normativity
Genevieve Vaughan   199

III: Gifts in the Shadow of Exchange

The Khoekhoe Free Economy: A Model for the Gift
Yvette Abrahams   217

Gift Giving Across Borders
Maria Jimenez   222

The Gift Economy in the Caribbean: The Gift and the Wind
Peggy Antrobus   230

The Children of the World: A Gift
Assetou Madeleine Auditore   235

Solidarity Economics: Women's Banking Networks in Senegal
Rabia Adelkarim-Chikh   238

Women's Funding Partnerships
Tracy Gary   241

Gift Giving and New Communication Technologies
Andrea Alvarado Vargas and María Suárez Toro   248

Trapped by Patriarchy: Can I Forgive Men?
Erella Shadmi   253

Women's Community Gifting: A Feminist Key to an Alternative
   Paradigm
Linda Christiansen-Ruffman   257

IV. Gift Giving for Social Transformation

Indigenous Women and Traditional Knowledge: Reciprocity is the
   Way of Balance
Mililani Trask   293

Supryia and the Reviving of a Dream: Toward a New Political
   Imaginary
Corinne Kumar   301

Reflecting on Gifting and the Gift Economy in El Salvador
Marta Benavides   310

From Forced Gifts to Free Gifts
Paola Melchiori   318

The Gift of Community Radio
Frieda Werden   327

Gifting at the Burning Man Festival
Renea Roberts 353

Activism: A Creative Gift for a Better World
Brackin "Firecracker" 356

Women's Giving: Feminist Transformation and Human Welfare
Angela Miles 364

Position Statement for a Peaceful World 375

Index 381

Acknowledgements

I thank Luisa Teish for her opening of the conference with her interactive performance. Thank you to the Indigenous women, Jeannette Armstrong, Louise Benally, Dotti Chamblin, Mililani Trask, and to Patricia Pearlman, who offered their prayers. I want to thank Kaarina Kailo for the title, "A Radically Different Worldview is Possible," and Mary Nell Mathis for the subtitle, "The Gift Economy Inside and Outside Patriarchal Capitalism." My heartfelt thanks to all the women who worked on the conference, a challenging project indeed because of its international character and because none of the "crew" lived in Nevada. There were endless details to take care of and snags and miscommunications of all kinds, which had to be dealt with and resolved. I particularly want to thank Sally Jacques, Mary Nell Mathis, Lee Ann LaBar, Liliana Wilson, Jessica Evans, Tobey Penney, Chiquie Estrada, Brackin Firecracker, Sylvia Shihadeh, and the many others who gave their time and expertise to making the event a success. Thanks to Lydia Ruyle for her Goddess Banners with which we decorated the Las Vegas Library auditorium and thanks to Luisa Capelli of Meltemi Press in Rome for sending enough volumes of *Athanor: Il Dono/The Gift* so that all those in attendance could have one. Thank you to Frieda Werden of WINGS and Andrea Alvarado of FIRE for their audio recordings of the conference and to Cara Griswold and Becky Hays of Full Circle Productions for videoing the entire event.

Many thanks to Luciana Ricciutelli for her tireless help with the manuscripts and the many versions of the table of contents as well as innumerable details of corrections and revisions.

GENEVIEVE VAUGHAN

Introduction

A Radically Different Worldview is Possible

The conference, "A Radically Different Worldview is Possible: The Gift Economy Inside and Outside Patriarchal Capitalism," was held in Las Vegas, Nevada in November 2004. The conference took place just after the U.S. presidential elections had left people of good will reeling from the re-election of George W. Bush, an event, which some believe was his second theft of the presidency. Even if Bush II had not won however, Patriarchal Capitalism[1] would have continued in its life-threatening course. The conference and now this book are attempts to respond to the need for deep and lasting social change in an epoch of dangerous crisis for all humans, cultures, and the planet. This goal cannot be achieved without a new perspective, a change in paradigm, which brings with it a radically different vision of the nature of the problems, and of the alternatives.

I have been working on the change of paradigms toward a gift economy for many years, both as an independent researcher and as the founder of the feminist Foundation for a Compassionate Society, which had an international scope but was based in Austin, Texas, from 1987-1998, and then functioned in a reduced mode from 1998-2005. When it became clear that the work of the foundation could not continue for lack of funds, we decided to hold two conferences as the last two major projects. This book about the worldview of the gift economy, presents the first of these conferences. The second conference, which was devoted to Matriarchal studies, under the direction of Heide Goettner-Abendroth (her second international conference on the subject) took place in September-October 2005.

I believe that in discussing the gift economy we are naming something that we are already doing but which is hidden under a variety of other names, and is disrespected as well as misconstrued. It is thus an important step to begin to restore its name and acknowledge its presence in many different areas of life. It is also important to re-create the connections, which have been severed, between the gift economy, women, and the economies of Indigenous peoples, and to bring forward the gift paradigm as an approach, which can help to liberate us from the worldview of the market that is destroying life on our beautiful planet.

Over the years as I have participated in the international women's movement I have met many, many wonderful women. Most of those invited to speak came from those encounters. I have been honoured to get to know a number of Indigenous

1

women in this way and thus was able to invite them to speak at the conference, which indeed could not have been held without their participation. All of the speakers, academics, and activists, are gift givers in their own ways. Some had thought deeply about the gift economy, others were new to the idea. I believe that all of them found it enlightening to hear the gift economy being discussed in so many different contexts. Some 35 women from 20 different countries gave presentations. Women and men from across the United States attended the weekend conference, which was held in Las Vegas, Nevada at the Municipal Library Auditorium. The choice of location came both from the desire to take advantage of cheap airfare, and to have access to the goddess Temple of Sekhmet, a Foundation project in the desert near the U.S. government's nuclear test site. Perhaps Mililani Trask gave the best rationale for the venue, however, when she commented, "What better place than Las Vegas to offer an alternative to casino capitalism!"

The conference and this book are attempts to justify the unity of the feminist movement and claim leadership for the values and the work of women in the mixed movement, which opposes patriarchal capitalism. An analysis that links different levels and areas of life on the basis of an alternative paradigm can suggest that much of what patriarchy has put into place is artificial and unnecessary. An alternative paradigm that sees women as the model of the human, and patriarchy as founded on males' rejection of their own (female) humanity, can provide the basis of a political program beyond present divisions. A radically different frame would make different strategies possible, and eliminate some solutions that would otherwise bring us all (women and men) back under patriarchal control in different forms.

In order to make this analysis we make a basic distinction between gift giving on the one hand and exchange on the other as two distinct logics. In the logic of exchange, a good is given in order to receive its equivalent in return. There is an equation of value, quantification, and measurement. In gift giving, one gives to satisfy the need of another and the creativity of the receiver in using the gifts is as important as the creativity of the giver. The gift interaction is transitive and the product passes from one person to the other, creating a relation of inclusion between the giver and the receiver with regard to what is given. Gift giving implies the value of the other while the exchange transaction, which is made to satisfy one's own need, is reflexive and implies the value only of oneself. Gift giving is qualitative rather than quantitative, other-oriented rather than ego-oriented, inclusive rather than exclusive. Gift giving can be used for many purposes. Its relation-creating capacity creates community, while exchange is an adversarial interaction that creates atomistic individuals.

Our society has based distribution upon exchange, and the ideology of exchange permeates our thinking. For example, we consider ourselves human "capital," choose our mates on the "marriage market," base justice on "paying for crimes," motivate wars through "reprisal," and teeter on the brink of nuclear "exchanges." However, Indigenous and Matriarchal cultures, based more on gift giving, had and have very different worldviews that honour and sustain life, create lasting community and foster abundance for all.

Introducing the Gift Economy

In the Americas, before colonization, there were 300 million people, more people than there were in all of Europe at the time (Mann, C. 2005).[2] Although Europeans tended to interpret the Indigenous economies in the light of their own exchange-based mentality, gift economies were still widespread when the colonizers arrived. Women's leadership was important in these so-called "pre"-market economies. For example the Iroquois Confederation, where women farmers controlled the production and distribution of agriculture, practiced gift giving in local groups and participated in long distance gifting circles among groups. (Mann 2000) Though wampum, made of shells, was seen as a form of currency by the Europeans, Indigenous researchers like Barbara Mann (1995) consider it not to have been money at all but a form of character writing in beads based on metaphoric relations of Earth and Sky. Gift economies are typical of Matriarchies. In Africa and Asia as well as the Americas, various kinds of woman centered-peaceful societies existed and continue to exist today. (Goettner-Abendroth 1980, 1991, 2000; Sanday 1981, 1998, 2002).

My hypothesis is that not only were there and are there societies that function according to the direct distribution of goods to needs, non-market gift economies, but that the underlying logic of this kind of economy is the basic human logic, which has been overtaken and made invisible by the logic of the market economy. In spite of this cancellation, gift giving continues to permeate human life in many ways, though it is unseen and has been misnamed and obscured. The worldview of the peoples of the Americas was indeed radically different from that of the Europeans, so much so that the two groups had difficulty understanding one another. Europeans consistently misinterpreted what the Native people were saying and doing, their spirituality, their customs, their intentions.[3]

Colonization by the Europeans destroyed the civilizations of the Americas because the mechanisms of Patriarchal Capitalism, which were developing in Europe throughout the preceding centuries, needed sources of free gifts, which could be transformed into capital. We live in the aftermath of this genocidal invasion, but this should not blind us to the fact that alternative peaceful ways for organizing the economy and social life did exist before colonization. I am not suggesting that we directly imitate those societies now. However, I believe that if we can identify the logic of gift giving and receiving, and see it where it continues to exist within our own societies, we can reapply it in the present to liberate a worldview that corresponds to it, as well as to create new/old ways of peaceful interaction.

At the same time that we begin to see the light of the alternative, we need to use it to illuminate the problem. That is, we have to see how Patriarchy and Capitalism work together to dominate and de-nature the direct distribution of goods to needs and how they turn the gifts toward an artificial system of exchange, not-giving, and property for the few. The radically different worldview that we need now is not the worldview of the gift economy as practiced by Indigenous peoples only, but a worldview that recognizes and derives from the gift economy both in Indigenous societies and, though hidden and misnamed, inside Patriarchal Capitalism itself; we might even say, inside every human being.

In 1484 The Papal Bull of Innocence VIII was published, marking the beginning of the Inquisition, during which, by some estimates as many as 9,000,000 witches, most of whom were women, were killed over a period of 250 years. It is perhaps not coincidental that these two genocides, of Native Americans and of European women, happened simultaneously. (See Mies 1998 [1986]) By finding the connection between European misogyny and European/American oppression of Indigenous peoples, perhaps we can identify the link that will allow us to create the common platform that is crucial for social change.

One of the reasons why a common collective platform does not presently exist is that approaches that are alternative to the status quo appear to have to do only with self-interest, individual penchants, or personal morality. For feminists the critique of essentialism does not allow the construction of such a platform on the basis of a common identity, yet curiously, even if the identity is not common, the problems are, and links among individuals and groups are made on the basis of shared issues and responses to oppression.

In fact, if we look at the way identity is formed through oppositional categorization and how collective identity functions in "democracy" as the competition of self interested groups, we could see the assertion of group identity as just one more way of dividing and conquering the power of the broader collective. However, perhaps it is not from identity anyway that we should try to derive a common perspective, but rather we should trace such a perspective to an economic practice, gift giving, which women everywhere (and non-patriarchal men and cultures) engage in, often without realizing it. This practice is positive but it makes those who engage in it similarly vulnerable to oppression by market economies. It would be important not only to unite on issues sporadically to oppose the oppression in its various manifestations but to link positively and long-term on the basis of the hidden alternative economy and its perspective. In Capitalist Patriarchy the practice of the gift economy has been assigned especially to women though it has been misrecognized specifically under the names of "mothering," "nurturing" and "care-giving." This assignment should at least qualify women as the (non-patriarchal) leaders of a gift economy movement.

A recent re-visioning of Matriarchies sees these societies as having gift economies and power structures different from those of Patriarchy (Allen 1986; Goettner-Abendroth 1991, 2002; Sanday 1981, 1998, 2002). They are not women-dominated societies but rather women-centered societies. They are not mirror images of Patriarchy, but are egalitarian and consensus-based. A number of examples of these Indigenous Matriarchal societies continue to exist worldwide.[4]

With this re-definition in mind, we can look at most societies now existing as a combination of two modes, one of which is a distortion of the other and is parasitically embedded in it. Capitalist Patriarchy, with its drive toward competition and domination, takes its sustenance from the gifts of the many, which are still being given according to the gift giving values and patterns of so-called "pre" Capitalist Matriarchal societies. Claudia von Werlhof's article in this book, discusses the drive of Patriarchy to negate Matriarchal aspects altogether. We can also look at our present societies as the coexistence of two kinds of economies: a gift economy and an exchange, or market, economy. Two value systems come from the two economies. The exchange economy fosters competition while the gift economy fosters cooperation. Moreover, the exchange economy competes with the gift economy in order to dominate it.

The paradox of competition between a competitive and a non-competitive behaviour carries within it the victory of the competitive behaviour unless it is possible to move to a higher logical level and weigh the two as general principles for organizing life.[5] At this higher level it is clear that cooperation, as a better principle, "wins" the competition. The question is how to understand the interrelatedness of the two behaviours well enough to collectively move from one of them to the other. In order to achieve this understanding we need to look at the underlying logics of the two behaviours and the economies in which they are embedded, and at the paradigms or worldviews these economies give rise to.

My proposal for this task draws not only on the idea of economic structures that determine superstructures of ideas and values (Marx 1904 [1859]), but also on the simple consideration that what we do over and over in daily life influences the way we think. The economy of exchange, on which the Patriarchal Capitalist market is built, functions according to the self-reflecting logic of exchange: giving in order to receive an equivalent. It requires an equation of value, quantification, and measurement according to a standard. Gift giving, directly satisfying the needs of the other, functions according to a logical movement of its own but has usually been considered instinctual or illogical. The action (A gives X to B) already carries with it implications, which are not contingent upon an equivalent return: (B gives Y to A). The elementary gesture of gift giving is transitive and it gives value to the receiver by implication. On different scales, from the small to the large, from the family to the nation, when the gift economy and the exchange economy behaviours coexist, the gift economy, consistent with its principle, gives to the exchange economy, satisfying its needs, giving it value and thereby colluding with its own oppression. On the other hand, exchange—giving in order to receive an equivalent in return—cancels gift giving. It is ego-oriented and gives value to the "giver" by implication rather than to the receiver. It is competitive, positions the exchangers as adversaries (Hyde 1979), and creates a relation between products rather than between persons.

Competing with gift giving while coexisting with it, the economy based on exchange exploits and discredits gift giving, often denying its very existence so that exchange seems to be the source of the gifts it has received or taken. In carrying out this cancellation, the logic of exchange, which is self-reflecting and self confirming identity logic, places gift giving in a non category with which (as a category) it does not have to compete. Thus, the two fit together as parasite and host. In spite of this collusion (and all of its variations), I believe the host is much more extensive than the parasite and gift giving remains as a deep hidden alternative, permeating Capitalist Patriarchy at all levels.

Mothering, which is usually socially identified with women, is an example of gift giving in which goods are distributed to needs in a very detailed and continuous way. We can consider this distribution as an example of an economic structure, which as such, has the capacity to give rise to the values of care as its superstructure. By considering maternal practice as instinctive or natural, the ideology of Capitalist Patriarchy has not only fettered women through essentialism, it has blocked the consideration of mothering as economic. By looking at gift giving as a hidden economy, a mode of distribution, which is the host of the economy based on exchange, we can see women's commonality as *economic*, having to do with a way of distributing goods to needs, a practice and a process which are part of a socially determined role, not an essence. Moreover, in societies based on gift economies, men remain mothering. To be a leader for the Minangkabau, a man must be like a good mother (Sanday 2002). Thus, women and men who are not patriarchal have in common not an essence but the practice of a gift giving mode of distribution.

The coexistence of gift giving and exchange is detrimental to gift giving but advantageous to the market system. Many free gifts are fed into the Capitalist machine, which re names the gifts as "profit" and channels them from the many to the few. The 40 percent that would have to be added on to the gross national product in the U.S. and elsewhere if women's free work were counted (Waring 1988) constitutes a gift that women are giving to the system of Patriarchal Capitalism, which does not have to pay for those services. Surplus value, which according to Marx is created by that part of the labour of the worker, which is not covered by the salary, can also be considered as a gift, leveraged or forced from the worker, but free to the capitalist.[6]

Both genders can practice both economies. Men can practice the gift giving mode of distribution and women can practice the mode of distribution of exchange. Mothering requires direct gift giving to children, however and since mothering is socially assigned to women, many women practice the gift mode of distribution during the time they are caring for children, and continue to do so even when they are not (and often practice it even if they never have children). The boy child's male gender identity in Patriarchy is usually constructed in opposition to the nurturing mother, so he has to reject the gift giving mode on which he is actually dependent. Thus, gift giving is usually identified with women (who are socialized to be mothers) while independence and self-assertion or aggression appear to be male behaviours. The male gender identity finds an area of life, the market, in which gift giving (nurturing) does not predominate; indeed it is cancelled and denied. The market is thus open as a field for other "masculine" behaviours of competition and hierarchy.

The values of care can be seen as the superstructure of the hidden economic structure of the gift economy. The values of self-interest can be seen as a superstructure deriving from the economic structure of exchange,[7] especially as combined with Patriarchy. Much ideological confusion arises from the fact that the economic structures of exchange and gift giving taken together are also the structure of a parasitic relation in which one economy gives to the other, while the other economy actively takes from it. Thus the superstructures also reflect this parasitic relation and are difficult to disentangle.

The above considerations suggest that we should take four basic steps to begin to move from the exchange to the gift paradigm:

First: Distinguish gift giving from exchange.
Second: See gift giving as containing a basic transitive logic while exchange functions according to a self-reflecting identity logic of exclusive and inclusive categories.
Third: Look at maternal practice as gift giving.
Fourth: Consider gift giving (and therefore mothering) as economic, a mode of distribution of goods and services to needs.

Summarizing, we can say that the logic of gift giving is a maternal economic logic, the logic of the distribution of goods and services directly to needs. Using this description we can identify this maternal economic logic as expressed in Indigenous societies, especially in matriarchies, where goods and services are distributed to needs, and motherliness and care have a high social value for everyone. By considering mothering as a particularly intense moment of a more widespread gift economy from which Patriarchal Capitalism now parasitically draws its sustenance, we can begin to change the familiar coordinates by which we understand the liberation of women and other oppressed groups as achievable through their more equal participation in the market economy. Indeed in what follows, I hope to show that the market itself is the problem, not the solution and that the gift economy and its values can be liberated *from* the exchange economy, which is unnecessary and pernicious.

I. Extending Mothering

This approach in which mothering is seen as one example of an alternative mode of distribution breaks the mold of maternity as limited to the relation between mothers and children only. In fact gift economies, which embody many variations of gift giving beyond exchange, use maternity as a general social principle, for both women and men, for women who are not mothers as well as for men who are not fathers. Breaking the mold of mothering as relating only to women and small children also opens the way for considering gift economies as economies of extended or generalized mothering.

Although much has been written in the twentieth century about gift giving, mostly by men, its connection with mothering has rarely been made.[8] Moreover, the fear of essentialism has thrown the mother out with the bathwater for many feminists. Instead we need to consider mothering/gift giving as a basic economic logic and process, not an essence, for all humans. The gift economy gives not only mothers but men (and everyone who does not have a small child) a chance to continue to distribute goods to needs socially as well as individually (and without nursing infants at the breast).

On the other hand, women as well as men can and do practice the logic of exchange and participate successfully in the social system based on the market. Capitalist Patriarchy is not exclusive to males, and women can participate in it in roles of the oppressor as well as of the oppressed. Groups and even global hemispheres also take up the roles of parasite and host. For example, the global North takes the gifts of the global South (the gifts of the South are co-opted and redirected toward the North). This takes place even if people in the North may themselves be individually or collectively exploited as members of groups from which wealth is being siphoned.

The colonial conquest of Indigenous territories and cultures may be seen as motivated by the competition of market economies with gift economies, and the extension of Patriarchal Capitalist parasitism over gift sources. Moreover the struggles for territory among nations can be seen as the attempts of one Patriarchal Capitalist parasite to control the gift sources of another.

Abundance is necessary for the successful practice of gift giving. Exchange competes with gift giving by capturing the abundance, channeling it into the hands of the few or wasting it, thus creating scarcity for the many. Gift giving, which is easy and delightful in abundance becomes difficult and even self-sacrificial in scarcity. Women have been read as "masochistic" when they sacrifice themselves for others. In terms of the gift paradigm we can see that they are actually continuing to practice the gift logic in spite of a context of scarcity, which is usually a product of the market and the exchange paradigm.

Looking at exploitation as the capture of free gifts—of surplus value, of cheap resources, gifts of the environment, land, water, traditional knowledges and seeds, connects these captured gifts with the gift labour of housewives and mothers, and thus connects again the women's movement with movements of workers, and peasants, as well as peace, environmental, Indigenous and antiglobalization activists.[9]

II. Disbelieving in the Market

Direct giving-and-receiving has many derivatives and elaborations, which have been misunderstood and divided and conquered by Patriarchal Capitalist ideology. As we have been saying, they have been hidden to avoid competition with exchange. We can bring these gift derivatives back to light by identifying them in the many different areas where they continue to exist. For example, gift giving has been excluded from academic disciplines as an interpretative key for centuries because it threatens academic control over knowledge. In fact, the gift paradigm illuminates many questions that remain opaque for academia. Moreover, the maternal logic and mode of distribution as elaborated and extended in Indigenous gift economies worldwide, give rise to values and spiritual traditions, which are antithetical to those of Patriarchal Capitalist institutions.[10] Indigenous epistemes, as described by Rauna Kuokkanen in this book, can be seen as arising from the practice of the gift economy. As Kuokkanen states, the gift of Indigenous epistemes has not been accepted by academia. However, neither has the gift-based perspective of women who are often living in the very families of these academics—and caring for them—or of the women academics who are bearing double burdens of family care and teaching. It is important to see both the care and the perspectives as gifts and to receive them with celebration rather than ignominy.

Gift giving permeates the social life of both women and men. It can be considered (Vaughan 1997) the cause of communication and community, and can be found at all levels from the biological to the linguistic. Exchange itself is only one variation on gift giving, a gift constrained, turned back upon itself and made reflexive. As the dominant mode of distribution, market exchange necessitates common quantitative assessment, which requires a process of measurement according to a standard. Western economics textbooks identify economics with the market but we are extending the category "economic" to include both the practice of mothering and gift economies. This change in categorization helps to bring forward gift giving as a pan-human behaviour. Moreover, it can help to clarify the relation between exchange and gift giving at the family level, at the level of the colonization of Indigenous peoples' gift economies by market economies, and at the "new" level of globalization in which the gifts of nature and culture, which were previously free for all (such as water, Indigenous plant species, and traditional knowledges), are being commodified. The two logics also often coexist internally to the individual. While it is clear that all of us practice both logics to some extent, we may also hypothesize that the unconscious may function according to gift giving and the conscious more according to exchange.

Rather than seeing the market as natural or as a prime achievement of humanity, we need to look at it as problematic and unnecessary, a mechanism by which we create scarcity rather than abundance by directing the flow of gifts from the many to the few. The market gives gifts a single way of becoming visible, and that is by transforming them into commodities, i.e., ceasing to be gifts. The globalizing market is Capitalism in a stage in which, on a very large scale, it is performing this transformation. By a sleight of hand it is showing that water, air, knowledge, even genes should be considered commodities "by nature."

We need to take a leap of imagination, which allows us to look at the market from the outside or better, from the inside, but taking a position of total skepticism. With the defeat of Patriarchal Communism, it would seem that Patriarchal Capitalism is the only possible economy. However, the perspective of the gift economy allows us to consider the Capitalist economy as unnecessary, transient, harmful. Feminist economists usually work on creating changes for women inside the market. The gift economy perspective sees the market itself as the obstacle, not as something that can be fixed by allowing fuller participation. Nevertheless, it is possible that changes in the market[11] can help create the conditions for a non-violent transition, which will allow us to start over again on a different basis.

It is not just the Patriarchal Capitalist market that is the cause of so many of our problems but the market itself. This is because its logic stands in contradiction to the panhuman logic of direct giving and receiving. The market is parasitic because it absorbs gifts into a relational structure in which gifts are blocked and cancelled though they continue to be given. Since gift giving is denied—not acknowledged or even seen—the flow of gifts toward the market, as profit, is understood as "deserved" or perhaps stolen—but not given. The "host" does not recognize that it is nurturing the parasite. Historically, this relation between gift and exchange can be materialized in different ways, but the market itself is a mechanism for the extraction and accumulation of profit (gifts), whether of the surplus value of salaried labour or of "housewifeized" (Mies 1986, Benholdt-Thomson and Mies 1999) labour, of the low cost natural resources of the Global South or the ecological inheritance of all the children of the future, whether of women or of slaves, of Indigenous peoples or of immigrants, locally and globally. Now the market also extracts the gifts of corporate profits paid by the money coming from the salaries of the many, whose needs have been manipulated by inventions and advertising.

By making the two economico-logical gestures—gift and exchange—and their interactions the starting point of analysis, we can provide a picture that is very different from that painted by economics proper. In fact we might say that the society we live in is founded on a fundamental polar opposition, one pole of which is not recognized as such. The invisibility of gift giving is the result of the hegemony of exchange, while at the same time it is a tool for the maintenance of its patriarchal power. By obliterating the gift or distracting attention from it by naming it something else, by breaking its common thread, or by considering its examples "primitive," infantile or instinctual, the market and with it Patriarchy, keep control over the gifts of all for the provisioning of life. In order to understand and address the immense problems that come from Patriarchal Capitalism, we need to restore the pole of the gift to visibility. I have been working on this project for many years and the conference, which gave rise to this book, was an important move in this direction.

III. A Self-Replicating Logic

Patriarchy and Capitalism have grown up together, twined around each other like two thorny plants with their roots in the humus of gift giving. Capitalism provides the economic system and Patriarchy provides the motivation toward ever-greater phallic[12] possessions of money, knowledge and power. The logic of exchange is self-validating and creates a consensus around its values, while gift giving, in its shadow, appears only as a feeble appeal to morality. Exchange works like a deep magnetic template to influence all our thinking. The logic of exchange can be seen in rewards and punishments, in guilt (psychologically preparing to pay back) and reprisal. Even justice, seen as payment for crimes, is framed according to the exchange paradigm, while identifying and satisfying the needs that give rise to the crimes would be a gift-based approach. The logic of war is the logic of exchange, attack and equal or greater counter-attack. Using exchange as the basic key for the interpretation of the world around us casts exchanges of ideas, of opinions, of love, of glances, (among many others) as events that might better be understood as gift transactions. On the other hand many activities that are framed as gifts are actually exchanges, such as, for example, donor-driven charity and U.S. aid to other countries.

It is important to describe Patriarchal Capitalism negatively on the basis of the gift alternative. Patriarchal Capitalist academia ignores the explanatory power of the gift and thus obscures the parasitic character of the economy and the ideology of which academia is an integral part.

Moreover sexism, racism, classism, xenophobia, and homophobia have issued from the exchange logic that functions according to the standard of the phallus and the phallic standard of the standard, creating categories based on the logic of identity, self-interest, and the exclusion of the gift giving other. This exclusion is a moment of the process of turning the flow of gifts of the "other" toward the standard. Thus the category of the market excludes the non-category of the gift which reappears as profit; the category "male" excludes the gift giving female who gives especially to males; the category "white race" excludes the other races, which are expected to take gift giving "female" positions toward white people.[13] In spite of the immense tragedies Patriarchal Capitalism and the market continue to perpetrate, they have maintained control of the paradigm through which most people see the world, and continue to define reality while disqualifying the gift economy and its perspective. The answers given within the market paradigm to the question of why such tragedies continue to occur do not provide an understanding that would permit radical change.

With the hegemony of exchange, the transitive and inclusive character of gift giving has been lost and the phenomena to which it gives rise have remained mysterious or have been given false explanations that coincide with the ideology of exchange. Bringing forward the paradigm based on gift giving while showing the negative aspects of exchange, the market, and Patriarchal Capitalism, allows us to see that a Radically Different Worldview is Possible. This in turn is a necessary step for showing not only that, as the World Social Forum motto states, Another World is Possible, but for showing that another possible world already exists in the here and now. Then by bringing it forward and giving it value, we can make gift giving define reality and reverse the polarity with exchange, non-violently liberating this other world, which is the world of the gift economy, into the present.

IV: The Implication of Value

In order to look closely at gift giving it is a good idea to see it first in detailed slow motion. Making, procuring, and providing something that satisfies the needs of others is part of a dynamic, which gives not only material satisfaction to needs but also gives value to the other by implication. The receiver is as important as the giver in the gift transaction because s/he must be able to use the gift to bring it to fruition. If the gift is not used, it is wasted, no longer a gift, and contradicts the value of the work of the giver. The recognition of the giver as the source of the gift by the receiver is not a necessary but is a common aspect of the process. By itself this recognition does not constitute an exchange but is simply a response, and is a sign of the completion of the transaction.

The fact that the giver gives to the receiver implies that the receiver is valuable to h/er because s/he does not let the need go unmet, neglect h/er, or give the good to someone else instead. This implication of value can be drawn by the giver, the receiver, or by any onlooker and thus it appears to be not just anyone's subjective evaluation, but a fact. In exchange, using similar reasoning, the opposite implication is the case. One gives in order to procure the satisfaction of one's own need, and therefore gives value to oneself above the other, implying one's own value. In fact, in exchange, the satisfaction of the need of the other is an instrument for the satisfaction of one's own need.

Many have questioned even the possibility of unilateral gift giving.[14] Exchange appears ubiquitous and more real and rational. Western anthropologists read reciprocity in the light of market exchange, rather than in the light of turn-taking, the repetition of a model, as happens when children imitate their gift giving mothers. Giving, receiving and giving back appear very different in the light of the market and in Indigenous gift economy and Matriarchal contexts. While the logic of market exchange, like God, makes everything in its own image, in so-called "pre"-market Indigenous societies the unilateral gift continues to inform reciprocity. In market exchange the unilateral gift is cancelled, so every act of reciprocity is understood as an exchange.

Even if there were no examples of pure, completely unilateral, giving (Caille 1998),[15]—and I believe that such gifts are actually quite commonplace—the logic of the unilateral gift would, nevertheless, continue to carry the implication of value of the receiver and this even when in practice the gift is mixed with exchange. When people insist on the truism "there is no free lunch," I counter that at least part of most lunches is indeed free in that women have been cooking them without payment for centuries. At the same time, the reception of the unilateral gift stimulates a probable appreciative response of the receiver and thus the gift can occasion mutual recognition of value as a basis of positive bonding.[16] In this interaction the gift itself becomes invested with positive value and functions as a vehicle of the value of the other and a mediator of the relation of mutuality. Gift giving, which is not assimilated to exchange, produces a reciprocity in which this relation of mutuality is not cancelled by the return gift, but is maintained and enhanced. Sometimes an additional gift is given, not as "interest," as happens with debts in the exchange mode, but as another unilateral gift, demonstrating that the return gift was not a cancellation but a turn-taking "imitation" or follow-up of the first, by adding more.

The value that is given to the receiver along with the gift may appear to be inherent in the receiver—a mother gives to her child because the child has value—but her giving and giving value to her also maintain the value of the child by allowing h/er to survive. Giving transfers value to the receiver along with the gift, and the value is passed on along with the gift to others. In fact there is a kind of gift syllogism—If A gives X to B and B gives X to C then A gives X to C. Gift circulation allows this transitivity in which the original source participates in the giving process even to the final receiver, and the implication of value flows from person to person as well.

V. Exchange Value

According to Marx, a commodity is made of use value and exchange value. As we have been saying, in the market, gift value is erased. Exchange, and especially the process of exchange for money in the market, alters the character of value in that it is no longer given as gift value to people other than oneself by implication, but it is attributed as exchange value to commodities as expressed in money. The binary process of exchange in which there is a symmetrical interaction of two ego-oriented exchangers also takes attention away from the original source of the goods. (Thus it is easy to deny the importance of mothering or women's work in the home for example, or on another level it is easy for multinational corporations to hide the sweatshop conditions in which their expensive consumer items are made.)[17] Each of the interactors in exchange is implying h/er own value by using the satisfaction of the need of the other as means, and at the same time is evaluating the value of the commodity relative to all other commodities on the market by using money, so that the exchange will be "equal." The value of the other is no longer implied by the satisfaction of his or her need, but at most, a value of identity of the two exchangers is attested by the identity of value of their products. In other words the identity of value of the products (or products and money) implies the identity of the exchangers, their belonging to the same category because of their common "property" of a quantity of exchange value. However this value depends on the logic of identity, on what they have, and therefore what category they belong to, not on an implication of value transmitted by or to them as human givers and receivers of need-satisfying goods.

The value of the other is transmitted by implication in gift giving; as value, it creates and depends upon a dynamic of transitivity between giver and receiver. The value of the other is cancelled in the exchange transaction, and both of the exchangers are taken as equal in their ego orientation, while their commodities are also judged as equal through comparison with money. Thus, exchange value is a kind of transformation of gift value.[18]

The gift transaction and the exchange transaction both confer value through the transmission of goods, though they function in different ways with different results for human relations and psychology. Where unilateral gift giving creates other orientation, bonding, trust and mutuality, exchange creates ego-orientation and adversarial positions, suspicion, and hostility or detachment as each exchanger tries to surreptitiously make the other give more in the supposedly equal exchange. For example, in cheating, the gift reappears in a negative sense and gives value to the ego of someone who has forced or tricked free gifts from the other—for example, by selling h/er overpriced items.[19] This confrontation creates two levels, a purportedly equal exchange and a private agenda of each exchanger to leverage, force or extort unilateral gifts from the other. Moreover, the categorial identity of the exchangers gives rise to their indifference to each other, in that anyone can substitute for anyone else in their roles.

In gift giving, however, the interactors give and receive in a personal way not just according to an accepted capitalist level of production but according to their individual capacities and needs. Thus gift giving-and-receiving is creative and informative while exchange can become repetitive and standardized. The attention of givers to needs creates sensitivity to the other. Emotional responses are necessary to map the needs. Exchange, which instrumentalizes needs, promotes desensitization, and emotional detachment.

In a context of scarcity, hierarchy, competition, and exchange it is easy for gift giving to become manipulative. This possibility causes receivers to become cautious and defensive and makes exchange appear to be a clearer interaction. Sometimes the receiver has more need for respect, and for independence, than for the gift itself, and the giver has to recognize and satisfy that need by not giving. Marketing is manipulative in that it uses the investigation of needs and the stimulation of desires to determine what products people will buy. Although advertisers themselves probably do not realize it, they are selling exchange itself to us as more valuable than gift giving.

Though exchange is a variation on gift giving, it follows a very different logical pattern, which makes the two really "apples and oranges" to each other. Moreover, exchange has become the main basic logical pattern that we see, so that all human reasoning seems to depend upon categorization, identity and evaluation—not on the transmission of value. The equation of exchange even informs our idea of self-reflecting consciousness, which we believe makes us members of a valued category, "human," while in other-directedness we become opaque to ourselves. At the same time needs are ignored in favor of "effective demand," the needs relevant to the market for which the money already exists in the pockets of the buyers. That is, the fulfillment of these needs can already be categorized as pertinent to exchange when they are identified. Needs which are not pertinent to exchange are not categorized as effective demand and are thus ignored. They do not "exist" for the market except possibly as they influence the raising or lowering of prices.

Without a multi-level shifting of attention toward needs as such, the transitivity that comes through the *free* satisfaction of needs cannot be seen. Nor can the wide range of gifts and the implications of value that these gifts confer be recognized. Gift giving is the interpretative key that unlocks the mysteries of transitivity, interactivity, value and community. For example inclusiveness comes through giving to the other, attending to h/er needs, not primarily through categorization—and it is not primarily by being classified as similar to or different from each other that we create community—but by giving and receiving gifts at all levels.[20]

Many new areas of needs are created by human interaction and this is also the case for the interactions of the market. New needs arise according to the ways society is arranged, and thus the possibility for new kinds of gift giving also arises. In fact the gift is such a fertile and creative principle that it can never be completely dominated by exchange and it re-presents itself again and again in different ways. In a market-based society, the need for money also provides the possibility for the gift of money. The need for jobs allows one to think of the job as a gift given by the employer. The needs created by the exploitation of the global South open the possibility for immigrants to send home billions of dollars as gift-remittances. Each of these examples demonstrates gift giving within a market situation and there are many others. These gifts would not be needed of course and therefore would not be gifts, without the market. Many other kinds of gifts exist before, beyond and around the market. In fact the market floats in a sea of gifts.

VI. Mothering and Masculation

Communication, which is an important human capability, begins in each life between mother (or other primary care-giver) and child, and is deeply connected to gift giving. Indeed, giving goods to needs without an exchange can be considered *material communication* in the sense that the bodies (and therefore also the minds) of the receivers are created through this interaction and they become the actual community members. Givers, who are also receivers, are altered and specified by their giving. The receivers are nurtured and brought into social life in specific ways, becoming givers in their turn. The vulnerability and dependence of human children requires others to give unilaterally to them in order to ensure their survival. Mothering, usually done by women, is thus a prime example of gift giving behaviour, readily available to be perceived by all, which is also a necessary (though always historically located) social constant.

Gift giving functions in mothering to imply the value of the child, but it also functions in reverse mode to encourage the mother to give to the child *because* s/he is valuable. In fact, the child may be considered inherently valuable, even if the implication actually comes from the gifts of the mother to h/er. At the same time the mothers, the source of this potential implication of value—and the rest of society as well—do not give value to mothering and to gift giving by women. They do give value to and nurture males. Identity logic regarding gender can thus exclude girls from the category of those to whom the mother will transitively give value by satisfying their needs.[21] Since the mothers are in the same category as their daughters, they devalue both themselves and the gift giving which is the source of the implication of value.

In Patriarchy it appears that in order to achieve their masculine identity, boys must not have the same behaviour as their mothers. When children are small, the free satisfaction of their needs by their mothers is a very large part of their existence. Thus the mandate to be unlike their mothers turns little boys away from a behaviour, which is crucial for them at the time and which carries the logic of the gift. They are required to be non-mothering, non-gift giving in order to fulfill the gender identity, which is imposed upon them by the society at large, the language, the father, other boys and even the mother herself. "Male" becomes a privileged category with the father as its "prototype"[22] or model with respect to "female," which is identified with the gift giving mother. The father, who went through this process himself as a child, replaces the mother as the prototype of the human for the boy child. Then as the child grows up, *becoming* the prototype, taking over the father's position, becomes the agenda for masculine identity. I call this process "masculation" and I believe it is the psychological root of Patriarchy.[23]

In Indigenous cultures, especially matriarchies, which have gift economies, the process of becoming male can be very different from the process in Patriarchal cultures. This is because there is no clean break between the gift giving, which occurs in childhood and the larger scale gift giving that takes place in the society. The transitive logic of the gift is not seen as limited to the relationship between mothers and infants or pushed into the subconscious mind, but it is expressed consciously and explicitly in the social relations within the community. Therefore the boy child does not have to give up gift giving in order to create his masculine identity.

Such circulations of gifts as potlatch (Mauss 1923)[24] or the Kula of the Trobriand Islanders (Malinowsky 1922) can be seen as a kind of social *bricolage*, a way of collectively and ceremonially thinking through the logic of the gift and exploring its implications. Different kinds of gifts and giving create different kinds of bonds between givers and receivers, and value is implied and passed around from person to person or from one group to another, through gift circulation. Giving to and receiving from nature is practiced as sacred communication.

When there is no market based on exchange, but the society as a whole functions by direct giving and receiving, there is a continuity for both males and females with the caregiving-and-receiving that they learn from their mothers from infancy on up. The mothering model of economics—the gift mode of distribution (and distribution also elicits a mode of production (see Marx "Introduction" to *Grundrisse* 1973 [1859])—functions for both genders. The kinds of behaviours and qualities (cooperation, sensitivity, and respectfulness) appropriate to gift economies therefore have a survival value in those economies.

Conversely, the combination of patriarchy and the market creates an altered and alienated world, which is antithetical to mothering/gift giving, de-classifies and exploits it, making it the behaviour of an unvalued or non-category. (Though this non-category is identified especially with women, who give to the privileged category and also give value to it by implication.) The kinds of behaviours and qualities (competition, domination, and greediness) fomented by Patriarchal Capitalism have survival value in market economies. Traditions of food sharing and hospitality that continue to exist inside market economies maintain some of the qualities of the gift mode and provide a sense of significance and community in spite of the general context of exchange.

Gift giving can be enlisted in the service of patriarchy, hierarchy, and the market, and power itself can be understood as the ability to control gifts to one's own advantage. For example controlling the flow of gifts functions in a similar way, whether it takes place in a family, a community, a business, a government agency, a religious or academic institution, or between the Global South and the North. The market mechanism itself is a kind of pump siphoning gifts from one area to another. This pump works because it is invested with the motives of Patriarchy, which promote the masculated agenda of striving to have the most in order to be the prototype, the one at the top. (Like pistons, some go up only because others go down.) The possibilities for achieving this top position vary historically, but typically involve violence, which in Patriarchal Capitalism becomes systemic economic violence. Wars on the large historical scale, cultural violence on the level of class and race (and internationally), and violence against women and children on the intimate interpersonal scale uphold the flow of gifts to the top and impose the market mechanisms.

The interaction of exchange and the use of money as the prototype of exchange value are taken as standards for "right" human behaviour. While equal exchange appears to be a principle of the highest order in our society, it is not only the "cover" for the extortion of gifts, but it is the model for negative interactions like revenge and retribution, which are used as the justification for violence and war. In fact, war is really the replay of the market on another plane. The purpose of war appears to be not only to create the most killing "exchanges" so that more people of other nations will have to "give" their lives for their country, but the reward for winning is to capture the largest amount of resources, including the money standard, and actually to *become* the standard, the prototype country, the Father of the nations.

Other more "civilized" methods for controlling the flow of gifts include art and monumental architecture, as seen for example in ancient Rome or Egypt, where size seems to demonstrate superiority and obelisks show the phallic deserving of tithes and taxes. Skyscrapers in the modern metropolis have a similar function. With Capitalism the rewards for success include the possibility of becoming the masculated human prototype by accumulating stratospheric wealth or by stardom of various other kinds. Hypervisibility of the few is opposed to the invisibility of the many. The position at the top is given by the gifts of the many, whether economic gifts or simply gifts of the groups' admiring attention (which often translates into money).

Human history in the West has not really begun because from the beginning of Patriarchy until now it has been only the history of an artificial parasitic male gender construction, which leaves out the agency of the rest of humanity. In fact, it is the history of patriarchal (and/or market) mechanisms fighting each other for dominance. Perhaps we could say it is the history of a disease, which infects or destroys all the healthy cultures it meets. Western history on the basis of the gift economy will have to begin over again, and try to link with the gift cultures, which have preserved a memory of what came before and an example of what could be. Women mothered by women do not go through masculation and, though they can succeed in the Patriarchal Capitalist system, their capacity for gift practice usually remains more or less intact because it is not nipped in the bud as happens in masculation. Women should therefore be the non-patriarchal leaders of a movement to dismantle Patriarchal Capitalism and replace it with a gift economy.

We may be forced to begin history on a gift basis by a traumatic crash of the market, by environmental devastation or nuclear war. If we start now however, we can try to extricate society from this perilous situation, methodically and carefully like a person climbing down from a tree—instead of falling. We can avoid the impending devastation, satisfying the needs of the future by stepping back from present conditions. It is not enough to consume less in the North however. We have to change the market mechanisms that take advantage of this consumption and of the gifts that feed it.

VII: Controlling the Gifts

By severing the connections between the many instances of the gift logic Capitalist Patriarchy has clouded the picture of what may be done as an alternative, making the gift paradigm unavailable to conscious choice and elaboration as the basis of a social project. It has achieved this also by considering gift giving instinctual, as opposed to the rationality of exchange, or super human, the province of saints and madonnas, while denying its presence in the rest of life. In this way the gift logic appears special, something not for the common people, something that religions can seize as their own. Authority regarding gift giving is turned over to male priests and Patriarchs, who legislate it, and who judge whether people—women (actual gift sources)—are acting in an altruistic way. (This altruism includes giving gifts of obedience and of money to the religious institutions.)

A theory of gift giving that sees it as an economic logic, not a morality of sacrifice or as an other worldly behaviour, can serve to protect this logic and its carriers from cooptation and colonization by religions and right-wing ideologies. Unfortunately, lacking such a theory, this cooptation has already happened extensively and Patriarchal religions' and governments' versions of gift giving are widely imposed. They thus discredit the gift paradigm for many feminists who rightly fear their dominance, the hypocrisy of their motives, and the power of their hierarchies. Because of this justifiably negative assessment however, feminists risk ceding the whole field of other-orientation to religions and right wing ideologies instead of claiming it for women—and for all humans—with the basis in the gift economy and the values of care.

In this book, Paola Melchiori asserts that we have to distinguish between the gift economy and the nurturing role that then Cardinal Ratzinger, now Pope of the Roman Catholic Church, attributes to women. I would counter that authority about gift giving should not be turned over to Patriarchal religions at all, but should be reclaimed by women. If feminists reject other-orientation they fall into the trap of relinquishing its practice and its values to those who have given up the gift economy as part of the construction of their gender identities. Women, who have the social role and experience of gift giving personally and as mothers should be the authorities on this important aspect of human life. It is not by giving up our claim to other-orientation that women can end exploitation or liberate ourselves and others from the authority and control of Patriarchal religions or right-wing governments. Indeed, by rejecting other-orientation we simply fall back into that opposite of gift giving that Patriarchy has invented, the market with its ideology of self-interest, which is the rationale of Capitalist Patriarchy. Even if this is the self-interest of a group, a gender, an ethnicity, a class or a sexual orientation and even if in practice it promotes solidarity—and thus practical gift giving—within the group, it does not raise the logic of gift giving to the meta level at which it may be used as a guideline for creating a radical and far-reaching alternative.

It is not self-interest that needs to be liberated but other-interest and the process of other-interest—the gift process. We get stuck in the formulation: A gives X to B, and do not add a parenthesis. According to the transmission of gift value, we look at B as having value and probably more value than A. But if we put the parenthesis around the transaction itself (A gives X to B), we can pay attention and give value to the process itself, not to say A is more valuable because s/he gives or B is more valuable because s/he is given to, but the process itself (A gives X to B) is more valuable than the process of exchange, which is (A gives X to B if and only if B gives Y to A).

The ego-orientation of Patriarchy and Capitalism has been extended to women by their participation in the market. This has had a positive effect for many women, especially in the North, who have been liberated to some extent from poverty, domestic slavery and psychological servility. However, it is not primarily the claiming of self-interest that will allow women to create deep and widespread social change but the claiming of control over other-interest.[25] Patriarchy takes the values of motherliness, as imperfectly understood and practiced by masculated men, and recasts these values as morality to mitigate the cruelty of its behaviour, to offset the possibility of revolution and to pay for some of the costs the cruelty incurs. By looking at gift giving as an economic structure with an ideological superstructure, we can see the values of motherliness not as morality but as the traces of this hidden economy, of a better world which is not only possible but already exists.

Generalizing exchange-based self-interest creates a collection of isolated individuals. Generalizing gift-based other-interest creates community. Generalizing other-interest not just for personal conduct but for social change, and giving the control of it to women (Give the land to those who cultivate it!) is a necessary step in creating a radically different worldview and therefore making another world possible.

VIII. Gifts and Communication

Those who talk about a moral economy are accessing the idea of the gift economy without discerning the thread of the gift, which unites so many different disciplines and activities. I believe that the logic of gift giving is also the logic of communication and thus of our becoming human. Recognizing this possibility also contributes to breaking the mold of mothering as only concerned with mother-child relations by extending it to a pan-human capacity in an area considered by linguists to be autonomous and biologically-based.

I have been working personally for years to show that language can be considered as a virtual verbal gift economy, the transposition of gift giving onto the vocal/auditory (or visual) plane where words, sentences, and texts function as verbal gifts given by speakers (or writers) to listeners (or readers), satisfying communicative needs. Syntax is not just the governance of rules but a system of gift transactions among words, transferred from the interpersonal to the interverbal plane. Words combine or "stick together" by being given to and received by each other. For example, the word "red" modifies the word "ball" because it is given to the word "ball," which receives it. The two words taken together satisfy the need of the listener for a human relation-creating device (gift) regarding something (the red ball) on the non-linguistic plane. It is not only the creativity of our language capacity that defines our humanity, but our ability to give language gifts that others can receive, and to receive language gifts that others give, using them to satisfy as well as to stimulate and elicit communicative needs. In other words, language is a kind of individual, and collective, nurturing on the verbal level. The practice of a verbal gift economy, which satisfies communicative needs using word-gifts given by the collectivity and by individuals, creating gifts which are not lost but are enhanced by the giving, humanizes us while at the same time we are becoming de-humanized by the processes of exchange. This conception of language puts it back into the women's camp, from which it seemed to have been removed by biologism, Phallogocentrism, and the symbolic order of the Father.[26] Meaning comes from the assertion of gift giving and the recognition of gifts at different levels, the verbal/syntactic level, the material/nurturing and community level as well as the perceptual level, where we receive/perceive the gifts of our experience and environment. By projecting the mother onto nature, considering nature as actively satisfying our needs (though in fact we have become adapted through evolution and culture to the use of the perceptual and material gifts we are given), we can persist in an attitude of gratitude, which will allow us to respond to and therefore know our surroundings as sacred and treat them with respect. In this, the theory of knowledge of the gift paradigm is consistent with the Indigenous epistemes Rauna Kuokkanen describes in her article in this book.

VIII. The Gift of Social Change

Gift giving continues now inside "advanced" Patriarchal Capitalism though it does not have that name. It continues in the U.S. and internationally, inside families and in community groups, groups with a common purpose, feminist, environmental, peace, ethnic solidarity and other activist groups, AA, spiritual and religious groups, therapy groups, social and art groups of various kinds, in the free software and free information movement, in such initiatives as Wikipedia, in movements against privatization and patenting, in online gifting circles, in solidarity economics, in progressive philanthropy, in immigrants' remittances and in alternative communities. Each group grapples with the control of gift giving and the context of exchange and scarcity that surrounds their attempts to give. Their struggle is more difficult because most of them are presently operating without a conscious grasp of gift giving at a meta-level, which would allow them to see the situation in terms of the relation between two paradigms. They frame what they are doing as morality, as cooperation, as family values, as independence or co-dependence, as right livelihood or grace or political commitment—even as revolution. Viewing the difficulties that arise as caused by the conflict of paradigms makes the big picture easier to understand and it also provides the possibility of intervening in different ways, creating feminist leadership and alternative strategies, which do not turn over the gift paradigm to the authority of religions or right- or left-wing Patriarchal politicians.[27]

There are many initiatives now of people trying to find ways of living beyond Capitalism, even in the Global North. For example there is the movement for alternative currencies such as Interest-and-Inflation-Free Money, LETS (Local Exchange Trading Systems), and mutual credit Time Banks, which I believe could constitute a step along the way to a moneyless gift economy, though these currencies are mostly still based on exchange in one form or another.(see also Raddon 2003). Some, like the Toronto Dollar, where a local dollar is traded for a Canadian dollar but a percentage is given to social projects combine giving for social change with alternative local currency. I would like to mention that these and similar initiatives are themselves social gifts in that they are attempts to fill the need for change and they should be understood as such. Some of them come close to viewing gift giving at a meta-level but they do not usually have an understanding of the negativity of the logic of exchange itself. Without a critique of exchange some initiatives, such as micro-credit for example, try to give the gift of social change by extending market participation. While the desire to satisfy needs is certainly operative in this kind of initiative, it is not surprising that extending poor people's participation in the market is not a long-term solution for social change and that it also brings with it many other negative consequences. The same can be said about debt-for-nature swaps, where countries of the South give up ecologically endangered areas in exchange for debt reduction. These initiatives have been discussed critically by Ana Isla (2004) and in her article in the present volume.

The open source technology movement, which provides collaborative development of software (See Andrea Alvarado's paper in this volume) and publishes the source code of new programs, defines itself as a gift economy, but it embraces the reward of recognition, which sets up a dynamic of exchange and Big Man patriarchal privileged categories. Moreover, the exchange economy, which has been put out through the door comes back in through the window, as some of those who have gained recognition for their free software are now being offered, and are accepting, high paying jobs in corporations.

Then there are entire experimental communities where people try to live according to the gift economy. Burning Man is a short-term experiment of this sort (see Renea Robert's article in this volume). Functioning as a week-long festival once a year, it has grown exponentially in many different locations around the world. Based on the work of Lewis Hyde, this festival revolves around the gifts of artistic expression. I believe that the other-orientation that goes with the gift logic requires that we not use it just as an end in itself, to enjoy or improve ourselves or to save our consciences but to create social change for everyone, especially in these apocalyptic times. Therefore, communities that want to be gift economies should find ways to further social change. They can do this to some extent by proposing themselves as models for others but they need to look at the multiplier effects of their actions and also actively work for change. In each case people have to think their initiatives through and figure out how to connect their immediate realities with the wider context.

All of these groups and movements would benefit by looking at the gift economy at as a maternal economy engaged in a paradigmatic struggle with exchange and Patriarchal Capitalism. Reconnecting gift giving and mothering so that we see gift behaviour as motherliness, whether it is performed by males or females—or by groups or governments—can supercede the masculated gender construction and the valuing of hyper-masculinity that has caused and is presently exacerbating so many of our problems.

Gift giving has been discussed a lot in the last 30 years though the connections between mothering and gift giving have seldom been made, nor have they been made between gift giving and language, nor between gift giving and the construction of Western gender. Most writers, as they have described the gift, have not seen the logic of exchange itself[28] as a major problem nor have they made the connection between Patriarchy and Capitalism. In fact most of them are male and they have once again succeeded in occupying a field of research and practice, which by rights would belong to women.

It is important not to allow the confusion arising from the competition between a patriarchal and a gift giving mode to once more eliminate women's non-Patriarchal leadership of the gift economy movement. Men who are conscious of the negativity of Patriarchal Capitalism can acknowledge and support women in their non-Patriarchal leadership. Rather than competing with them, men can follow the mothering model and give authority to women. Women can do this as well, rejecting Patriarchal Capitalism.

In this way the international women's movement together with all the other movements for social change can put together a project for shifting the paradigm, a project to end wars by altering the construction of gender, to heal the economy by restoring and extending the mothering model, to save the environment by revising our epistemology to recognize knowledge as the creative reception/perception of gifts of all kinds coming to us from our environment, thus enhancing our capacity to treat Mother Earth with gratitude rather than with nonchalance or attempts at domination. By shifting the paradigm we can realize that humanity is not an evil self-destructive species but a species that is creating its own devastating problems because parts of it are misconstructing their gender and are acting out this misconstruction on a wide social scale. We can begin to heal ourselves and the planet by recognizing that we all create our common humanity through giving and receiving material and linguistic gifts, co-muni-cating. The gift economy gives us a rationale for radical social change under the non-Patriarchal leadership of women. By giving value to gift giving, we can dismantle Patriarchy and resolve the paradoxes that have been keeping it in place, so that it will not recreate itself or come again.

***

The conference, "A Radically Different Worldview is Possible," was held at the beautiful semi-circular auditorium of the Las Vegas Public Library. The audience was composed of women and men who had traveled from many places in the U.S. and around the world to attend. From the comments afterwards, it was a groundbreaking experience for many.

Because mothering is an important example of gift giving and women's voices have rarely been given prominence in the present discussions of the subject, we decided to claim a space for women in the discourse on the gift by inviting only women to speak at the conference. Some of the speakers were well versed in the ideas of the gift economy, especially the speakers coming from Indigenous societies. The African, Hawaiian, Native American, and Sami contributions to this volume demonstrate the life experience of traditional and present day gift economies, and their survival in spite of the context of scarcity and deprivation imposed by the market economy. For Indigenous women, the struggle between the two paradigms is no mere theory. They have experienced gift economies and have been forced to experience and participate in exchange economies, by the gradual or violent encroachment of Patriarchal Capitalism upon their territories and traditions. It is a tribute to the possibility of women's solidarity that they accepted the invitation to speak at this conference, and for that I particularly thank them.

There were many presenters at the conference who did not know about the work of the others, and a few of the speakers had not thought about the gift perspective in the areas of their competence before. Nevertheless even those relatively new to gift economy thinking found the approach useful in describing what they were doing as gift giving and thus finding their commonality with one another in very different fields.

The conference gave evidence of a variety of points of view regarding gift giving, each of which can be used to frame the others. Each is strengthened because, taken together, the many points of view provide a wider context, and a continuity, which has been lacking for each instance of gift giving taken singly. In fact gift giving may be seen as a widespread phenomenon, which (in the West) has been deprived of its meta-level. Gift giving has been given many names that bring it into the Patriarchal Capitalist fold, names like "profit," "housework," "morality," "charity," "remittances," "solidarity," "political commitment," even "love." By bringing forward the presence of the gift in many different fields, describing it and naming it as such, we can restore it to the primacy in our thinking that is necessary to create deep social change.

Is everything gift giving then, at least everything that is not exchange? (And I have been saying that exchange itself is just a doubled and contingent gift). And doesn't this make it uninformative? I think it may be indeed that everything is gift giving at different levels, in different tempos, transposed, material, virtual, rematerialized, natural and cultural, microscopic and macroscopic, at the atomic level and at the level of galaxies. Obviously only a few of these levels are based on what humans do, except for the fact that what humans do makes up or should make up the lens with which we look at them. The objectivity of the market has broken these lenses and we have tried to look at the universe without the mother. Although this view helps us make more bombs and missiles, more new profit-making products, more genetically modified organisms, more clones, it takes away our view of all the gift aspects that we would otherwise have seen. We become color blind to the gift-color. We lose our understanding, our caregiving and our respect for human mothers and for the mothering environment, which is all around us, even in the ungiving cities—because our perceptive apparata evolved to receive the gifts of nature and culture, which surround us. The Indigenous people's idea of Mother Nature and Mother Earth, is true. That is because it is as mothered children that our perception and perspectives are developed. Unfortunately, as Claudia von Werlhof says, Patriarchy is trying to take over the power to give birth. It is also altering our conception of mothering/gift giving, so that it appears as if all our interactions were disengaged, heartless, ego oriented. It has taken nurture out of our nature, so that we cannot see it in nature outside ourselves or in culture. It is replacing nurture with indifference and violence. What a different sense it has to say, "light hits the retina" rather than "light is 'given' to the retina," which creatively receives it. Why do we say, "Nature abhors a vacuum" instead of "Nature rushes to fill a lack?" We are stuck in the wrong metaphor, and continue to construct a worldview from which gift giving has been deleted.

Thus it is important to take the hypothesis that everything is gift giving and try to put back what has been taken away over the centuries. This means reworking our lens so that we can see the gift again, healing our gift-color blindness. In doing this we may make some mistakes, overgeneralize, see gift giving where it is not there. However, once the point of view is established the mistakes can be corrected.

This volume is divided into four sections according to general themes. All of the presentations necessarily address the themes of the other sections, however because gift giving as we now know it coexists with exchange, which, as part of the dominant paradigm and the paradigm of dominance, necessarily conditions gift-giving and fractures its continuities. Nevertheless, the first section, "The Gift Economy, Past and Present," attempts to provide a glimpse of gift giving beyond and before the context of Patriarchal Capitalism. It includes articles that give us an idea of what living in a gift economy is actually like and what perspectives emerge from gift-based thinking. These presentations give a sense of community life and worldview in the present and the past where Patriarchy and Capitalism were/are not the central focus of society but instead the gift logic orients human beings towards others, the community at large and nature. They help us see the gift economy as the basic human mode of distribution of which exchange is only a (harmful) variation. Unfortunately the worldview based on exchange has made most Euro/Americans distort our perception of gift giving, so that we have rejected out of hand the important model it provides for organizing society. This section presents the gift as it exists not only among Indigenous people but also as part of the European heritage, and as a perspective that can be used in disciplines as distant from each other as semiotics and biology. Wherever Patriarchal explanations have worn thin, malfunction, or do not exist, the logic of the gift shines through as an ever-present life-giving alternative.

In the first article, Jeanette Armstrong (Canada) gives us a brief but clear description of what life in a gift economy feels like and how it can be organized for collective survival, given that her people, the Okanagan Synyx are presently living in a desert environment. Her sense of the importance of the land and the community comes from a way of life that avoids the pitfalls of Capitalism because it is egalitarian and has gift giving as its core principle. She provides examples from her language of conceptual nuances, which are radically different from those to which Euro/Americans are accustomed.

Kaarina Kailo's (Finland) article discusses the ancient European cross cultural imaginary, which is visible in myths based on non masculated life-centered values, prior to the take-over by the master imaginary. Tracing back the roots of the gift to the epochs preceding patriarchy in the West can allow Euro-Americans to recognize their commonality with Indigenous peoples beyond the divide-and-conquer categories of the master narrative.

Rauna Kuokkanen (Samiland/Canada) speaks of the gifts of Indigenous epistemes, which, like the gift paradigm generally, have appeared incomprehensible or even threatening to the academia of Western Patriarchal Capitalism because of their emphasis on non-productive expenditure. She makes explicit the spiritual traditions of the Northern European Indigenous Sami people in which giving to the land is the way of communicating with and honouring nature. She emphasizes the importance of recognition of gifts as part of a network of relations, which are built upon responsibility towards the other and sees this gift-based worldview as an urgently needed alternative to patriarchal global capitalist paradigms.

Vicki Noble (USA) tells us that "the central icon of matriarchal agricultural societies was the Goddess—the abundant and generous Mother of All Things—whose centrality begs to be re-established today along with women in leadership as her ministers." Noble traces the image of the life giving Goddess from prehistoric cave drawings of vulvas through the venus figurines and ceramic vessels discussed by Marija Gimbutas. Ancient Asian women leaders functioned as Dakinis and Yoginis, female shamans in Mongolia and the bakers of bread in ancient Greece were connected with rituals around pregnancy, healing and birthing, while, contrary to patriarchal interpretations, female communal agriculture provided an early model of a peaceful society without private property. Modern witches belong to a long line of powerful women of many cultures who have threatened patriarchy and bourne the brunt of its reprisals.

Patricia Pearlman (USA) is the Priestess emeritus of the Temple of the Goddess Sekhmet in the Nevada desert, a project of the Foundation for a Compasionate Scoiety based on the gift economy. Patricia, a modern witch, describes the project, which has had thousands of visitors over the 15 years of its existence, and gives us the gifts of her wit and her will.

With Heide Goettner-Abendroth's work on Matriarchies, the Gift Economy finds its wider context. Goettner-Abendroth (Germany) tells us that matriarchies are not, as European patriarchal scholars have defined them, based on women's rule. Rather, these societies, many of which still exist worldwide, are egalitarian and consensus based. Products of the experience of millennia, they function according to the principles of motherliness and gift giving. We do not have to invent an abstract utopia but can turn to these societies that function according to the most intelligent patterns of social organization for a radically different perspective. A professor of philosophy who gave up her position in order to concentrate on the study of matriarchies. Goettner-Abendroth demonstrates the gifts of dedication that have been necessary to start her own Akademie Hagia outside patriarchal academia.

Susan Petrilli (Australia/Italy) brings to the women's movement the gift of her work on the semiotician, Lady Victoria Welby (1837-1912), who was an important predecessor for thinking about language and gift giving. "With Welby and beyond Welby," Petrilli sees the direction towards the other, beyond identity logic as "the logic of humanism, the humanism of otherness," Her discussion of global capitalism as communication-production, -exchange, -consumption denounces the present phase of capitalism as alienated from the humanism of otherness and proposes a semioethics as an antidote to this alienation.

Evolution biologist Elizabet Sahtouris (USA) expands the term "business" to include cooperative as well as competitive economic practices, which she finds in the natural as well as the human social world. Darwin's ideas were influenced by Malthus' belief in competition for survival in scarcity, which as Hazel Henderson has said, were projected into social Darwinist interpretations of economic behavior and are still part of the rationale of the institutions of globalization. Instead from Sahtouris' point of view, throughout Earth's history, competition in evolution has been superceded repeatedly by negotiated cooperation at a higher level. Organizing cooperatively and "glocally" can transform corporations away from competitive behaviour and towards collaborative maturity.

At present Patriarchy and Capitalism weigh heavily upon gift giving of which they form the context and from which they draw their sustenance. Other-oriented gift giving is the ground and complement of self interested exchange, which takes from it, exploiting the gifts of the many. This second section, "Gifts Exploited by Exchange," addresses the context in which gift giving is presently embedded, and gives examples of some of its destructive effects, which are legion. Lies and propaganda follow the ego-oriented model of the exchange economy, while the truth is a gift to the receiver. By revealing the truth about Patriarchal Capitalism, the speakers follow the gift model and satisfy the needs of everyone to know.

Claudia von Werlhof (Austria) tells us that "patriarchy is much more than just a word for polemical purposes. It can instead be understood as a concept that explains the character of the whole social order in which we are living today, socialism included." Patriarchy, she says, is a war system based on the negation of matriarchy, which still exists within patriarchies as a second culture. Von Werlhof gives a deep analysis of how Patriarchy crystallizes into Capitalism and advises us how to move towards an alternative.

Louise Benally, Dineh, Navajo (USA), talks about the difficulty of living in a gift economy while the gifts of the community are being taken by the market. The coal from Big Mountain, where her tribe lives, is used to supply the electricity to Las Vegas where the conference was being held. In fact, the waste of electricity on the neon lights of the city of gambling is notorious. In Big Mountain there is nothing—no electricity, no running water.

Ana Isla (Peru) demonstrates the importance of not accepting the false gifts of Patriarchal Capitalism, which are hidden exchanges, Trojan horses of the market. Her analysis shows that micro credit projects and debt-for-nature swaps can be deadly in spite of what may appear to be good intentions. In supporting the gift economy it is important to recognize what is not a gift, as well as what is.

Condemning the glorification of virtual technobodies in corporate cyberspace and the extraction of the life out of real flesh and blood, Mechthild Hart (Germany/USA) describes the parasitism of Capitalist Patriarchy on the gift-giving bodies of women in international sex trafficking and immigrant domestic work. She places hope in the web of reciprocal obligations of care that develop bonds across great distances.

Sizani Ngubane, is a South African HIV/AIDS activist. Before colonization, she tells us, food was produced by individual families but it was not individualized. There was food for all in the great grandmother's house and Mother Earth was regarded as a sacred gift. Colonization took 87 percent of the land for the whites. Now there is widespread poverty, a break down of the community, and a widespread AIDS epidemic.

Margaret Randall (USA) denounces the Orwellian double speak with which the right-wing and the market are raping our language, while "speech that is truthful and beautiful is the currency of the gift economy." She gives us the gift of two true stories—one of the propaganda attempts of the US government and the other a story of human constancy and rebirth in the face of the paramilitary of Argentina.

Carol Brouillet (USA) reveals the background of 9/11, asks us to look at the dark side of U.S. government and question the official story. The Big Lie cannot stand; researchers from all over the world are trying to bring us the truth.

Genevieve Vaughan (USA/Italy) attempts to understand the logical and psychological connections between heteronormativity and the market. The Western construction of gender as heterosexual brings with it the construction of a non-nurturing mode of distribution based on exchange. The norm of heterosexuality, which privileges the "masculated" male engenders the gigantic sorting process of the market and incarnates the value norm, money. The gift economy provides an alternative for living and thinking beyond the norm of normativity.

"Gifts in the Shadow of Exchange," the third section of this book, provides examples of gift giving that sustain and strengthen community in spite of the exploitation and poverty imposed by the system based on exchange. Survival and even thrival are fostered by gift giving at new levels, not only beyond but within and around the market.

Yvette Abrahams (South Africa) speaks of the gifts of the African Khoekhoe stories, which satisfied the community's needs to know and to follow the telling together. She describes the present scarcity imposed by the system and the continuation of gift giving and sharing in spite of the widespread poverty. Sixty-six percent of food is produced by the gift labour of women's subsistence farming in Africa. The "compassion economy," where everyone chips in to help someone in need, survived slavery and colonialism but unfortunately is not surviving the HIV/AIDS epidemic. Khoekhoe spirituality is based on gift giving; hospitality, and ceremonial giving are a spiritual necessity. Abrahams' description of how her people living in abundance in the past, without private property, related to each other is a key for looking at gift giving as communication. Says Abrahams, "When you have enough and I have enough our giving can taken on a symbolic character."

Scarcity in the Global South, already a result of exploitation by the North, has been intensified by globalization. Thus migrants have been driven from their home countries by poverty, and forced to go to work in the North to provide the necessary sustenance to their families. These individual contributions cumulatively form a huge monetary gift to the economies of the South. According to immigration activist Maria Jimenez (Mexico/USA), women and men of the "two-thirds" world have been engaged in gift giving through the one hundred billion dollars per year that they collectively send home in remittances of $100 to $300 every month or two, gleaned from the salaries they earn in the North. Strong networks based on family bonds facilitate this gift giving and maintain community in spite of distance. The migrants transform the experience of exclusion and exploitation into one of liberation for themselves and their families.

As Peggy Antrobus (Barbados) says, there is a community-building solidarity of gifts between those who have emigrated from the "Creole" culture of the Caribbean, who take or send home useful products from the North, and those at home; bonds are maintained in this way over great distances. At the time of the conference, Grenada, the island of her birth, had been devastated by a hurricane, and Antrobus knew that much gift giving would be necessary by the people of the Diaspora to restore the resources upon which the local economy was based. She believes that the gift economy needs to be recognized and affirmed or it will die, negated by the values of neo liberal, capitalist globalization.

The youngest speaker at the conference, Madeline Assetou Auditore, (Ivory Coast/Italy), eleven years old at the time of the conference, gives an impassioned plea for support for the poor children of the world who are suffering due to the selfishness of the rich.

Rabia Abdelkarim (Algeria/Senegal) describes women's economic solidarity networks in Senegal where "the heart of the economy of women is relationship and they don't want to lose the capacity of the circulation of the gift." Calling upon traditional gift-based rituals and relationships of mutuality, women are trying to create an economy for life, in which values other than money, such as dignity, are primary.

The non-profit sector in the U.S. now counts for more than fifteen percent of the Gross Domestic Product (GDP). Tracy Gary (USA) talks from the point of view of a donor and philanthropic organizer. She tells the story of her decades of work in the women's philanthropy movement and describes how she helped to create an exponential leap in women's giving by empowering wealthy women to donate for social change.

Andrea Alvarado (Costa Rica) talks about FIRE, Feminist International Radio Endeavor, which is a women's internet radio station and began as a project of the Foundation for a Compassionate Society. She discusses open source technology as a gift and gives an example of the way FIRE is sharing it with women.

Erella Shadmi (Israel) discusses the importance of forgiving, that is, shifting into a mode that is not one of retaliation/exchange/paying-back. The mode of for-giving concentrates attention on the unmet needs behind the offense, and attempts to satisfy them. Gift giving re-presents itself at many levels, shifting from theory to practice and vice versa. This presentation was given in tandem with a presentation by Palestinian Sylvia Shihadeh, which was not revised in time to be included in this volume. Together the two activists gave an example of peaceful collaboration and mutual respect, which was a much needed gift to all.

Linda Christiansen-Ruffman from Nova Scotia (Canada) looks at the gift economy features of women's community work. She realizes there are millions of unseen gifts that women give to each other and to the women's movement beyond Patriarchal Capitalism's economic fundamentalism and its appropriation of the commons. However she wonders if recognizing these gifts will not make them more vulnerable to appropriation.

The articles in the fourth section, "Gift Giving for Social Transformation," present conscious strategic uses of giving in struggles for a better world, and point to ways of gift giving that can lead to social transformation. Hawaiian sovereignty activist, UN advisor and lawyer Mililani Trask opposes the commodification of knowledge and nature, the theft of intellectual property and bio piracy that are now being promoted by globalization. Traditional knowledge and relationships with nature are sacred for Indigenous people. The bounty of Earth must be part of the commons so that all may share in the gifts of the creator. She makes the important point that Indigenous women should be in the leadership of the movement for a gift economy. In fact, if they come from gift economies they have the experience of generalized social gift giving, which makes up the context in which their roles as mothers and daughters are formed.

Taking the point of view of the other is an important aspect of an other-oriented gift economy. By taking the point of view of our sisters in the South who have been on the receiving end of "our" economic policies of structural adjustment and globalization, women in the North can recognize that we are part of a much larger international movement, which can give us both hope and direction. Corinne Kumar (India/Tunisia) tells us that we need an imaginary beyond the universalisms of the dominant discourse, a new knowledge paradigm, which refuses to accept the one objective, rational, scientific discourse, cosmology and world view as the *only* world view. Kumar looks at the worldview of the future, of women of the South, the people on the margins, the South in the South and the South in the North. In it she finds the voices of radical dissent that can give rise to a new imaginary. They show us that the development models, the models of democracy, progress, human rights, "enduring freedom" that we have been "sold" are deeply destructive. In contrast they give us an alternative vision where people on the margins are subjects of their own history.

Marta Benevides (El Salvador) life-long peace activist, tells us how the right created the fear of losing the remittances in order to influence recent elections in her country. As a strategist she says we have to vision what we want, do discernment and manifest power by being the future now, being peace. We should give the gift of living for the ideals of peace, freedom and justice, not just of dying for them. She believes we should be peace, be the revolution, changing the situation locally, with peaceful actions of the people, appropriate to each place.

Paola Melchiori (Italy) worries about the gift economy bringing back women to their traditional roles as proposed by then Cardinal Ratzinger, proponent of women's complementarity to men for spousal harmony, who is now the Pope of the Catholic Church. She believes that the only way to protect women from this subtle justification of enslavement is that they be freed from forced giving and practice gift giving beyond patriarchal control. Melchiori also finds hope in women mothering each other, creating relationships in the feminist movement as well as in alternative economic experiments, such as those created under women's leadership during the recent crisis in Argentina. Melchiori grapples with questions within the women's movement, which must be resolved in order for it to assume the leadership role that is necessary for the gift economy and paradigm to prevail.

Frieda Werden (USA/Canada) of Women's International News Gathering Service (WINGS), discusses the models of private and public ownership of radio in different countries and time periods, and suggests that non commercial community radio and television can be seen as gifts, not just of information but of *channels* of information for and by the many. These channels run counter to the prevailing capitalist morality of information for sale and present a transformative model of co-muni-cation as "giving gifts together."

Filmmaker Renea Roberts (USA) showed a clip from her film, *Gifting It.* In her article, she describes what the feeling is at Burning Man, the gift economy festival, which is based on the work of Lewis Hyde. There are now many such four-day festivals, where people share their works of art and imagination free, around the world. Participating in this social experiment it is possible to get a glimpse of what a world based on a gift economy might be like. The festivals thus "normalize" an alternative within the capitalist monolith.

Brackin Firecracker gives examples of activism from her own life, including examples of the innovative new genre of radical cheerleading. She describes the "Rhyzome Collective," a group she helped to form of young activists, who are trying to create a living example of an alternative, while they are at the same time helping to build a global movement of resistance to oppression and injustice. She believes it is important to recognize that gift giving is what activists have been doing all along, and that through this recognition, their values are more generally validated, giving them greater power to satisfy impelling needs for social change.

Angela Miles (Canada) makes important points emphasizing the utility of the gift paradigm as a "critical and visionary perspective that is broad and deep enough to speak to all our struggles and move them all forward." It lets us see for example that "in the non-patriarchal world we aspire to, men will not be masculated; their maleness will be lived through and not against their giving human qualities," and "in a feminist movement seeking giving alternatives to exchange rather than escape from giving, remaining women's sub-cultures and matriarchal Indigenous cultures are honoured as precursors of a more human future, not dismissed as vestiges of the past.

The "Feminist Gift Economy Statement" concludes this book. It was prepared by International Feminists for a Gift Economy, a loose-knit group, which began in Norway in 2001 at a meeting of women called by the nascent International Feminist University Network, makes a collective statement, which affirms the gift economy and critiques the market in the context of globalization. Members and non-members of this informal network have presented together at panels on the gift economy at international conferences such as the World Social Forums and Women's Worlds meetings as well as other activist and academic conferences. Some of the authors of the articles in this book are members of the network. This statement was first presented by the group at their workshop at the World Social

Forum in Porto Alegre, Brazil, in 2002. See the website www.gift-economy.com for furthur information and to join the network list serve.

...In the light of the conference and the articles in this book, I invite the reader to seize the time and change the paradigm!

This is only the beginning.

Genevieve Vaughan is an independent researcher, activist, social change philanthropist, and founder of the feminist Austin, Texas-based Foundation for a Compassionate Society in operation from 1987–1998 and in a reduced form until 2005. She is the author of For-Giving: A Feminist Criticism of Exchange *(1997) and* Homo Donans *(2006), and the editor of an issue of the Italian journal* Athanor *titled* Il Dono/The Gift: A Feminist Perspective *(2004). She is also the author of two children's books,* Mother Nature's Children *(1999) and* Free/Not Free *(2007), and has produced a CD of her* Songs for the Tree of Life. *A documentary about her life,* Giving for Giving: Not All Texans Are Like Bush, *coproduced by Cara Griswold and Becky Hays of Full Circle Productions, has just been completed. Showings can be scheduled and copies ordered from www.givingforgiving.com. Vaughan's books and many articles are available free on her website www.gift-economy.com. She is now based in Italy and devotes her time to writing and speaking about the gift economy. She has three daughters.*

Notes

[1] Patriarchy and Capitalism have similar values and motivations: competition for domination and the desire for accumulation in order to be the biggest, the one at the top. Like Capitalism, patriarchy is systemic. I discuss this more in the text and in my article below.

[2] New information has come out about the numbers of Native people killed by diseases brought by the Europeans. In fact the lands seemed uninhabited because the people who lived there had all died due to epidemics of measles and smallpox brought from Europe. So first, the Europeans were carriers of diseases, which destroyed the Indigenous people. They ignored the extent of the Indigenous civilization because they did not know it. Secondly they attacked the remaining Native people ferociously, taking over their land, eliminating them as competitors. They developed a worldview, which hid the rapacity of their behaviour from themselves, and this worldview was added to their original ignorance. Similarly we do not consciously recognize the gift economy, which we are actually practicing and we also attack and exploit it so we are in denial about it, and this denial is added to our lack of recognition of it.

[3] Barbara Mann tells us with her characteristic wit that the word "How" with which Native people typically greeted the Europeans meant "Go away!"

[4] Examples of matriarchies range from the relatively small group of the Mosuo in China (See the television program *Frontline/World 2005*, "The Women's Kingdom") to the Minankabau in Sumatra, who number some four million (Sanday 1998, 2002), from tribes such as the Navajo, the Hopi and the Iroquois in Northern America (Allen 1986; Mann 2000), and the Khasi in Northern India, the Arawak in South America, and the

Cuna in Central America (Goettner-Abendroth 1991, 2000). There are many more such societies but intense polemics have raged around them because of the threat women's egalitarian leadership poses to patriarchy. As Paula Gunn Allen says "The physical and cultural genocide of American Indian tribes is and was mostly about patriarchal fear of gynocracy" (1986: 3). By defining Matriarchal leadership as egalitarian, not "women's rule," Paula Gunn Allen (1986), Heidi Goettner-Abendroth (1991), Barbara Mann (2000), and Peggy Sanday (1981, 2002) have reframed the discussion so that the non-hierarchical and inclusive leadership style of women can be included among the options for social transformation.

5   Studies of cooperation and "partnership" (Eisler1988) propose that a better world can be built on cooperation by diminishing dominator values. The discussion of the gift economy and patriarchal capitalism attempts to find where cooperative (partnership) and competitive (dominator) values and behaviours come from and to use this knowledge in constructing the alternative.

6   The Bielefeld School in Germany, consisting of Maria Mies, Veronika Bennholdt-Thomsen and Claudia von Werlhof among others, considers work beyond wage labour, such as women's life-giving subsistence labour, the source of capital accumulation. I agree with this approach but I look at this labour as gift labour, which I believe establishes a common thread of continuity with other kinds of gift giving.

7   Because exchange is adversarial it creates a focus on the individual and an ideology of the individual as opposed to others or "the masses." In a society based on the gift economy the individual would appear different, more inclusive of others. I am not proposing the end of individuality but that it develop on a very different basis.

8   An early exception making the connection with mothering is Helene Cixous (Cixous and Clement 1975). Among the men writing about the gift economy are Marcel Mauss (1990 [1923-24]), Bronisalw Malinowsky (1922), Lewis Hyde (1979), Alain Caille (1998) Jacques Godbout (1992), Caille and Godbout (1998), the MAUSS Revue publishing since 1982, as well as Jacques Derrida (1992), Pierre Bourdieu (1990) Serge Latouche (2004) and many others. On the other hand some women have written extensively on the "love" economy, the "informal" economy and the commons without connecting them specifically to gift economies. See for example, Hazel Henderson (1991, 1999). Others have theorized the care economy within the framework of the market (Nancy Folbre 1994, 2001).

9   There are important women's organizations in all of these areas and women are also very much involved in mixed gender movements, often doing much of the gift giving work under male leadership.

10 In this they are similar to the opposition and threat to the institutions created in Europe by the Nature religion of witchcraft.

11 For example, initiatives for economic justice, for equal pay for comparable work, for a living wage, for Fair Trade instead of Free Trade, initiatives for community currencies, for socially useful investing, for solidarity economics, and experiments like the Work Less Party, provide alternative models, help to create a less monolithic economy and empower grassroots agency. These attempts at partial change can make it easier to transition to more radical change without violence. I believe it is important not to consider them the final goals but steps along the path to a gift economy.

12 Since the male genitals are the physiological "possessions" by which males are assigned to their category in opposition to females who lack those possessions, it seems that having greater possessions can place them in a superior category generally. More on gender categorization can be found in my article in this book.

¹³   African gift economies as the "other" of European Patriarchal Capitalism were plundered and their members became "property" through exchange, their gifts turned toward the slave "owners."

¹⁴   For example Derrida (1992) sees gifts as almost impossible because if they are done for recognition, and even if they are recognized, they become exchanges. Isn't the lack of recognition of housework then a proof that it is a unilateral gift?

¹⁵   Godbout and Caille assert that it is not necessary for the gift to be pure.

¹⁶   Matriarchal gift giving is egalitarian because it is not invested with Patriarchal motivations. There is less occasion for a struggle for recognition in egalitarian gift economies because recognition is easily given and passed on. (see Trask and Kuokkanen in this volume) We might look at the give-away competition of potlatch of Native Americans of the Northwest as the struggle to be recognized as the prototype however, and similar to the struggle that must have been going on at the time consciously or unconsciously between the Western and the Indigenous prototypes of the human.

¹⁷   Similarly, after the 9/11 attack on the Twin Towers, there were many people on line calling for an investigation of the root causes of the attack in the poverty and injustice the U.S. had helped to create through globalization and wars in the Middle East. It was hoped that by giving aid to impoverished people of Afghanistan these causes could have been alleviated. Instead, a culprit was found to punish, i.e., with whom to "exchange," retaliating for the harm the U.S. had "received." If anything this punishment aggravated the conditions from which the original attack arose. That is, if the attack was not an "inside job" as many suspect.

¹⁸   For Marx (1930 [1867]) this is abstract labour value. We can say it is labour abstracted from gift giving. The concentration on the need of the other and the creativity involved in filing it, including personal details and tastes, along with the value transmitted, are left aside for this abstraction. In the market a product derives its quantity of value from the relation of similarity or difference with regard to the value of all other products within a given branch of production. These are abstract and general relations. The quantity of exchange value that products have depends upon the socially necessary labour time required to produce them (also calculated abstractly) at a given level of technology and productivity of labour. When the exchanger sells the product to another, the return is not a gift but only an exchange value, which s/he then passes on in a new exchange. The "expenditure of living labour" creates value. But unless it has a direct receiver no gift value is transmitted by it because gift value is the implied value of the other. Marx's metaphors, such as the commodity being "congealed labour" show how hard it is to imagine labour materialized as value in something when it is separated from the receiver of the gift. Such labour is the service or gift-production, which does not reach its destination because it is stopped by exchange or privatization. In her article in this book, Jeanette Armstrong tells us about a word in her Okanagan Syilx language that means to "stop the giving, to put an obstacle between the giving and yourself."

¹⁹   Retailers use gift giving to promote sales with gimmicks; this is a gift used for the purposes of exchange. One can of course buy something for someone else as a gift; this is a gift beyond the exchange interaction itself.

²⁰   Women seem to want to include men in their meetings and events while men typically do not include women. This perhaps shows that the women are practicing the gift logic, which is inclusive. They identify a possible need of men to be included and try to give them that gift while the men are practicing the identity logic, which is categorical and exclusive and does not stimulate them to perceive a need of women

to be included. Even in the cases where they do perceive the need, they usually do not feel compelled to satisfy it. By including men, women run the risk of embracing those who are practicing an opposing and oppositional logic.

21 The practice in some countries of allowing girl children to starve while boy children are fed demonstrates how gifts and the implication of value can be withheld. The girl dies because to her parents and the wider society she is valueless and unvalued (and *because* she is allowed to die she is valueless).

22 The idea of a prototype or best example of a kind for the formation of categories can be found in the field of cognitive linguistics. See George Lakoff (1987) and John Taylor (2003).

23 I have discussed this process extensively in my books *For-Giving* (1997) and *Homo Donans* (2006), and the reader can find more about it in my article in this volume. The Freudian mythical murder of the father by his sons can be read as the overtaking of the prototype position by boys, which, seen in this way, is a moment of the early concept forming process in the child's gender development, not a real historical murder. Even if he overcomes the father as the prototype however, the boy still does not have the access to the gift economy he had when he was identified with his mother. In matriarchies and gift economies he never loses this access.

24 Where male chiefs compete to be the greatest gift givers—the most mothering men.

25 For example, look at the gift perspective and the issue of abortion rights. The idea that women can choose not to undertake years of maternal gift labour demonstrates that gift giving (or not) is a rational choice, that not giving birth, choosing not to give, can be based on other-orientation (recognition of one's own limitations as a giver in a context of scarcity for example), thus giving value and authority to the person who considers or takes that alternative. The ability to choose abortion gives back to women some of the authority over gift giving that Patriarchal religions have taken away from them for centuries. Moreover if the masculated male gender identity rejects the mother and imposes an identity based on not-giving, the ability of women (mothers) not to give, challenges the male gender construction by removing its oppositional cornerstone. The question of abortion is not so much a question of the right of the fetus to life (a right, which seems to end at birth anyway) but the right of the mother to give or not to give, and her authority over the gift logic itself. If religions (and governments) lose their authority over gift giving, what authority do they have left?

26 Though much has been written on women and language the writers have mostly taken their points of departure from within linguistics, semiotics, the philosophy of language as provided by Patriarchal academia. Similarly feminist economists have continued to work within the market paradigm. Writing about language, feminists discuss for instance how women use language differently from men (Lakoff, R. 1975; Tannen 1990) or how to produce an *ecriture feminine* (Cixous and Clement 1975). What is needed is a different conception of language itself in tandem with a different conception of the economy, reformulating both in terms of the gift paradigm.

27 Initiatives as widely divergent as the Bolivarian Revolution of Hugo Chavez, which provides free health care and education to the poor and free petroleum products to poor countries and the Bill and Melinda Gates Foundation, demonstrate gift giving being practiced by men "at the top." I would say that even when men do gift giving at this elevated level they are still practicing the economy of mothering (and Chavez was probably positively influenced by his Indigenous heritage) although the fact of being men in the prototype position again obscures the mothering model. For

masculated men this is perhaps an apotheosis of what they gave up as children, the "return" of what in the Freudian sense has been "removed." This "return" in which the men as philanthropists, become even more gift giving than the mothers whose identity they had to relinquish, paradoxically becomes the reward for acceding to the "one" position. It is in this sense that Patriarchal Capitalist philanthropy should be read. See the excellent book *The Better Angels of Capitalism* by Andrew Herman (1998). This also is the moral veneer of such organizations as the World Bank, the International Monetary Fund (IMF) and World Wildlife Fund (WWF). Patriarchal control of gift giving is normalized once more.

28   The group of the *MAUSS* (Mouvement Anti-Utilitariste des Sciences Sociales) *Revue* critiques what they call "utilitarianism" but they continue to talk about "gift exchanges." An important critique of "economics" can be found in the writing of Serge Latouche (2004).

29   The idea for the temple had its beginnings in in the 1960s when I went to Egypt on vacation with my husband. The tour guide showed us the statue of the goddess Sekhmet, and said that she was the goddess of fertility, and that by making her a promise, a woman could get pregnant. I did that, promising her a temple and that very week became pregnant. I knew I had to keep the promise and finally bought land near the nuclear test site in the Nevada dessert where the was temple built in 1992, and after which I gave the land back to the Western Shoshone. Cynthia Burkhardt was the temple priestess for the first year, and Patricia Pearlman was the second, from 1993 to 2004. Statues of Sekhmet and Mother Earth, by Indigenous sculptor Marsha Gomez, grace the temple along with smaller images of goddesses from many cultures. The temple and its guest house are free to visitors according to the principles of the gift economy. The present priestess is Anne Key (see www.sekhmettemple.com). Patricia Pearlman died of cancer in March 2006. We mourn her passing.

Selected Bibliography

Allen, Paula Gunn. 1986. *The Sacred Hoop*. Boston: Beacon Press.

Bourdieu, Pierre. 1990. *The Logic of Practice*. Trans. R. Nice. Cambridge: Polity Press.

Bennholdt-Thomson, Veronika and Maria Mies. 1999. *The Subsistence Perspective: Beyond the Globalized Economy*. London: Zed Books.

Caille, Alain, 1998. *Il terzo paradigma. Antropologia filosofica del dono*, Torino, Bollati Boringheri.

Caille, Alain and Jacques Godbout. *The World of the Gift*. Montreal: McGill-Queen's University Press.

Cheal, David. 1988. *The Gift Economy*. New York: Routledge.

Chodorow, Nancy. 1978. *The Reproduction of Mothering: Pscyhoanalysis and the Sociology of Gender*. Berkeley: University of California Press.

Chomsky. Noam. 1966. *Cartesian Linguistics, a Chapter in the History of Rationalist Thought*. New York: Harper and Row.

Cixous, Helene and Catherine Clement. 1975. *La jeune nee*. Paris: Inedit.

Derrida, Jacques. 1992. *Given Time. 1. Counterfeit Money*. Trans. Peggy Kamuf. Chicago: University of Chicago Press.

Eisler, Riane. 1988. *The Chalice and The Blade: Our History, Our Future*. San Francisco: Harper and Row.

Folbre, Nancy. 1994. *Who Pays for the Kids? Gender and Structures of Constraint*. London: Routledge.

Folbre, Nancy. 2001. *The Invisible Heart: Economics and Family Values.* New York: The New Press.

Gilligan, Carol. 1982. *In a Different Voice.* Cambridge, MA: Harvard University Press.

Godbout, Jacques T. 1992. *L'Esprit du don.* Paris: Editions La Decouverte.

Goettner-Abendroth, Heide. 1980. *Die Goettin und ihr Heros.* Munich: Verlag Frauenoffensive.

Goettner-Abendroth, Heide. 1991. *Das Matriarchat I: Stammesgesellschaften in Ostasien, Indonesien, Ozeanien.* Stuttgart, Germany: Kohlhammer-Verlag.

Goettner-Abendroth, Heide. 2000. *Das Matriarchat II, 1: Stammesgesellschaften in Amerika, Indien, Afrika.* Stuttgart, Germany: Kohlhammer-Verlag.

Goux, Jean-Joseph. 1990. *Symbolic Economies: After Marx and Freud.* Ithaca: Cornell University Press.

Gregory, C. A. 1982. *Gifts and Commodities.* London: Academic Press.

Henderson, Hazel. 1991. *Paradigms in Progress, Life Beyond Economics,* Indianapolis. Indiana: Knowledge Systems, Inc.

Henderson, Hazel. 1999. *Beyond Globalization, Shaping a Sustainable Global Economy.* West Hartford, Kumarian Press.

Herman, Andrew. 1998. *The Better Angels of Capitalism: Rhetoric, Narrative and Moral Identity Among Men of the American Upper Class.* Boulder, Westview Press.

Hyde, Lewis. 1979. *The Gift, Imagination and the Erotic Life of Property.* New York: Random House.

Lakoff, George. 1987. *Women, Fire and Dangerous Things: What Categories Reveal about the Mind.* Chicago: University of Chicago Press.

Lakoff, George. 2004. *Don't Think of An Elephant.* Chelsea Green Press

Lakoff, George and Mark Johnson. 1999. *Philosophy in the Flesh: the Embodied Mind and its Challenge to Western Thought.* New York: Basic Books.

Lakoff, Robin. 1975. *Language and Women's Place.* New York, Harper Colophon Books.

Latouche, Serge. 2004. *Altri Mondi, Altre Menti, Altrimenti: Oikonomia vernacolare e societa'conviviale.* Soveria Manelli, Rubbettino Editore.

Malinowsky, Bronislaw. 1922. *Argonauts of the Western Pacific.* London, Routledge.

Mann, Barbara. 1995. "The Fire at Onondaga: Wampum as Proto- Writing." *Akwesasne Notes* 26th Anniversary Issue1 (1) (Spring): 40-48.

Mann, Barbara. 2000. *Iroquois Women, the Gantowisas.* New York, Peter Lang.

Mann, Charles. 2005. *1491, New Revelations of the Americas before Columbus,* Alfred A. Knopf, New York.

Marx, Karl. 1930 [1867]. *Capital in Two Volumes: Volume One.* London: J. M. Dent and Sons, Ltd.

Marx, Karl. 1904 [1859]. *A Contribution to the Critique of Political Economy.* Chicago: Charles H. Kerr and Company.

Marx, Karl. 1973 [1859]. *Grundrisse: Foundations of the Critique of Political Economy.* New York: Vintage Books.

Mauss, Marcel. 1990 [1923-24]. *The Gift: The Form and Reason for Exchange in Archaic Societies.* London, Routledge.

Mies, Maria. 1998 [1986]. *Patriarchy and Accumulation on a World Scale.* London: Zed Books.

Mies, Maria and Vandana Shiva. 1993. *Ecofeminism,* London, Zed Books.

Mies, Maria and Veronika Bennholdt-Thomson. 1999. *The Subsistence Perspective: Beyond the Globalized Economy.* London: Zed Books.

Raddon, Mary-Beth. 2003. *Community and Money, Men and Women Making Change.*

Montreal: Black Rose Books.

Rossi-Landi, Ferruccio. 1983 [1968]. *Language as Work and Trade, A Semiotic Homology for Linguistics and Economics*. South Hadley, MA: Bergin and Garvey, Publishers.

Ruddick, Sara. 1989. *Maternal Thinking: Toward a Politics of Peace*. New York: Ballantine Books.

Sanday, Peggy Reeves. 1981. *Female Power and Dominance: On the Origins of Sexual Inequality*. New York: Cambridge University Press.

Sanday, Peggy Reeves. 1998. "Matriarchy as a Sociocultural Form: An Old Debate in a New Light." Paper presented at the 16th Congress of the Indo-Pacific Prehistory Association, Melaka, Malaysia, July 1-7. Online: http://www.sas.upenn.edu/~psanday/matri.html.

Sanday, Peggy Reeves. 2002. *Women at the Center: Life in a Modern Matriarchy*. Ithaca: Cornell University Press.

Saussure, Ferdinand de. 1931. *Cours de linguistique generale*. Charles Bally and Albert Sechehaye. Paris: Payot.

Schrift, Alan D. Ed. 1997. *The Logic of the Gift: Toward an Ethic of Generosity*. New York: Routledge.

Shiva, Vandana and Maria Mies. 1993. *Ecofeminism*. London: Zed Books.

Shiva, Vandana. 1997. *Biopiracy: The Plunder of Nature and Knowledge*. Boston: South End Press.

Tannen, Deborah. 1990. *You Just Don't Understand: Women and Men in Conversation*. New York: William Morrow.

Taylor, John R. 2003. *Linguistic Categorization*. Oxford: Oxford University Press.

Vaughan, Genevieve. 1980. "Communication and Exchange." *Semiotica* 29 (1-2). The Hague: Mouton.

Vaughan, Genevieve. 1981. "Saussure and Vygotsky via Marx." *ars semiotica, International Journal of American Semiotic* 4: 57-83.

Vaughan, Genevieve. 1997. *For-Giving: A Feminist Criticism of Exchange*. Plainview/Anomaly Press, Austin.

Vaughan, Genevieve. 2006. *Homo Donans*. Online: www.gift-economy.com.

Vaughan, Genevieve. 2004. "The Exemplar and the Gift. *Semiotica* 148 (1/4): 95-118. Berlin and New York: Walter de Gruyter.

Vaughan, Genevieve, ed. 2004. *Il Dono/The Gift: A Feminist Analysis*. 15 (8) *Athanor: Semiotica, Filosofia, Arte, Letteratura*. Roma, Meltemi Editore.

Vygotsky, Lev Semenovich. 1962. *Thought and Language*. Cambridge: MIT Press.

Waring, Marilyn. 1988. *If Women Counted: A New Feminist Economics*. San Francisco. Harper and Row.

Watson-Franke, Maria-Barbara. "The Lycian Heritage and the Making of Men, Matrilineal Models for Parenting." *Women's Studies International Forum* 16 (6): 569-579. New York: Pergamon Press.

Weatherford, Jack. 1988. *Indian Givers: How the Indians of the Americas Transformed the World*. New York: Fawcett Columbine.

Werlhof, Claudia von. 2001. "Losing Faith in Progress: Capitalist Patriarchy as an 'Alchemical System'." *There is An Alternative: Subsistence and Worldwide Resistance to Corporate Globalization*. Eds. V. Bennholdt-Thomson, N. Faraclas and C. von Werlhof. London, Zed Books.

Wright, Kenneth. 1991. *Vision and Separation, Between Mother and Baby*. Northvale, NJ: Jason Aronson, Inc.

I. THE GIFT ECONOMY, PAST AND PRESENT

JEANNETTE ARMSTRONG

Indigenous Knowledge and Gift Giving

Living in Community

I would like to share my language with you, and give you greetings from all of my family and my community and my people, the Syilx. I give thanks that I am able to share some words with you.

I'm from an oral culture, and so that's how in this article, I share some of my ideas about giving—the concept of gift—and some ideas about my own people's understanding of giving, in terms of land, community and family, as well as the individual, because I believe something is really wrong in the world today. The only thing that I can offer is my thinking. How it might be put to work, how it might be incorporated, or how it might be thought of in terms of the change that needs to happen, is all up to those who hear and read these words.

I come from a small community in the southern interior part of British Columbia, about 200 miles inland and parallel to Vancouver. My people are sometimes referred to as the Okanagan people, but the Okanagan is actually the geographic valley that we live in. We are the Syilx people, and that is how I refer to myself.

The area that I come from has a lot to do with what I'm going to talk about. It is one of the only areas in Canada that is considered to be a desert. It means we have very little rainfall. This is because of the two mountain systems on both sides of our valley. The ecology is very harsh and dry in the summertime, and therefore the learning that our people have had to accomplish and achieve over many generations, in order to survive, has a lot to do with scarcity. In a land where there is not a lot of abundance, where the fragility of the eco-system requires absolute knowledge and understanding that there must be care not to overextend our use of it because it can impact on how much we have to eat the following year, or years after in terms of your coming generations, we have developed a practice, a philosophy and a governance systems are based on our understanding that we need to be always vigilant and aware of not over-using, not over-consuming the resources of our land, and that we must always be mindful of the importance of sharing and giving.

We must also be aware in everything that we are doing that the same possibilities must be available to our children, our grandchildren, and our great-grandchildren, and so it is an immense responsibility. I think of it in terms of our direct connection to how the land operates, how the land gives life, and how, as human beings, we are a part of that. I think losing that connection has a lot to do with some things that are wrong today in the world. From my perspective, the land is a body that gives continuously, and we as human beings are an integral part of that body.

What Indigenous means to me is that everything that exists on the Earth is interdependent, an interdependence that must be understood. As an Indigenous person, I must have knowledge about it and I must be able to cooperate with all the other living things on the planet, on this land, so as not to make any one of them extinct or remove any one of them for my own need. In other words, to cooperate and to collaborate with every living thing so that they can live and I can live at the same level of health. To cooperate so that they can continue giving to me and to my children and my children's children, the health that they deserve, in being a life form of the land. Indigenous, to me, means you can't be without that knowledge and that level of cooperation with the land. Without this cooperation, you cannot call yourself Indigenous. For example, a plant we may have in our home is indigenous to somewhere because it could live there on its own in an interdependent relationship with its climate, within its land and its topography. But once removed from there, we have to do all kinds of other things to allow this plant to live in our environment. All kinds of energy and work has to be expended to help it live, as this plant, in its pot, is no longer indigenous in a room in anyone's house. If we took it out of the house and put it in the desert, where we live, this plant would not survive a day.

I think of Indigenousness in that way. I think of the paradigm shift that's required to recover the ability for human beings to live on the land without the immensity of destructive support systems that are required for the plant, for us, to live. I think of it in terms of the way that all the systems have been changed in my community in a forced way.

When I think about my life, I think about how the land gave me my life. Without the Okanagan land, without the Syilx people and all the relatives that live and lived on this land, without every single thing that sustains my people such as food, medicine, clothing and shelter, without all of those things that surround us, surround me, I would not be. I can only express in my language the meaning this has for me, and for me to be unable to protect the land, unable to stand between those things becoming extinguished from the land and the depth of love and understanding that's required for us to continue to receive that gift and to continue to honour and respect that gift, is profoundly significant. It's like family members being assaulted while your hands are tied. It is the same feeling with community, and it is the same with all of the generations of relatives that have sustained each other, interacted with each other, in really specific ways to be able to continue life.

I want to give you some idea of how our community thinks of itself and how it thinks about what community is. To us, our community is a living system. Like the land, it's a living diversity of beings and that diversity is immensely necessary, like the diversity on the land is immensely necessary. There's not one thing on the land that isn't necessary, there's not one person within community that isn't necessary, in our understanding of it. It would be like saying I don't need my fingernails or toes just because I don't use them every day. Each person in the community fulfills a part of the community that may not be understood, in their generation or in the next generations. Like each diverse being on the land, we have no way of determining which is more important or which is less important. We have an understanding in our community that no person is superior to another.

I look at how society outside of our traditional community operates with the understanding that some people have more rights than others, that some people have more of a priority to things than others, and that some people not only are born with priority, but are born with the control over who has priority. They live and die within that idea of privilege, control and exclusion of others.

I think that part has always been, for me, a very difficult thing. I relate to people in a really different way because it is how my community relates. I can't recognize hierarchies. I don't recognize hierarchies. People are people in terms of how they relate to me. I notice it on an everyday level when I go into the community that I live next to. Depending on how much money you've got, and how much money you're going to spend, the amount of respect—and I don't like to use that word because that's a problem for me, but I will use the word anyway—the amount of respect paid is really related not to the person, but to their money, their power and to their ability to spend. This is so false and so inhuman and so against community and so very different from our understanding of what respect is within community.

In my community the chief—we do have chiefs in our community, women and men—the idea of "chief" has to do with how well that person hears everyone, and how well that person understands what is going on that might be wrong, that might cause conflict, and so might cause danger to the people. Our word for chief means to be able to take the many strands that are moving outward and twine them into one strand. One strand meaning one people and unification and a re-balancing with the land. It means that person must have an immense ability to feel what the community is saying, an immense ability to listen to the things that have been said, and to know the things that are happening, and to put it all together and say it back to the people. So it's about communication, and it's about being able to listen and being able to put it together so everyone understands and says, "Yeah, that's it!" It's not about telling people what to do, or leading people, or forcing people; it's being able to verbalize and communicate what everybody feels and knows and understands and remembers, and being able to put that together to create a movement forward. So our system relies on that kind of inter-relationship and communication in our community.

There is a process that I am just going to describe to you, briefly, as an example. I helped to establish an educational program to recover our traditional practices on the land within our community and within our families, called En'owkin. I've been working at it for 25 years. The idea for En'owkin comes from *Enowkinwixw*, a word that comes from our language. It is a word that describes how communities should operate, in terms of deep communication as a community process. In our minds, the way communities should operate is to be able to include everyone. The concept of *Enowkinwixw* is that it is an inclusion-seeking process. Rather than exclude minorities, we actually try to find ways to help the minority articulate what they are saying, because minorities usually are saying something really different from everybody else. They are the ones who are experiencing something that really differs from others' experience in the community. Whenever there's an issue or a problem, it's that voice that's most needed, and it's the understanding of that voice that's most necessary towards resolution of conflict. If that voice can't find a way to articulate what the issue is, it can't be heard and can't be listened to, so then the whole community is in trouble. The minority voice is, therefore, a really an important factor in terms of how our community communicates and listens. Listening is the biggest part, and with that, finding ways to bring forward the ideas expressed by that minority voice.

Enowkinwixw describes that process within our community. It describes a process that makes that happen. We use it in our governance process and we now use it in our community dialogues. We use it in our family circles and our extended family meetings. The idea isn't to make decisions, the idea is to hear all of the different aspects, all of the different views, but in *Enowkinwixw*, we actually set up a dynamic in which decisions can happen. It is a dynamic in which we understand that there are always polarities in community, because there is diversity. We try to take the polarities in their larger sense and we give them context in the community. We give the polarities authority in terms of their context within the community, authority which can't be usurped by any other area of community. There are four general polarities we utilize in our community to create a dialogue.

The first of these polarities can be described in our language as something similar to the idea of elders, although that term is not really a correct in our language. It is a word that really refers to those who have had long experience. It doesn't mean in years; it really means to have teachings from generations and generations past. You could therefore be a part of this group even if you are 20 or 30 years old. It's about the knowledge that has been passed on to you and that you express and stand for that makes you an "elder" in our language. As an elder, your thinking and your concerns and your responsibilities are directed toward making sure that everything is remembered that is necessary to make things continue on in a healthy way. This group is usually directly polarized against a group that can be described as the youth, or the young people. We think of these in our language as people that have a really great urge for innovation and creativity, new ideas and new concepts. This is a dynamic that is always needed in any community and any society, and encouraged, just as the elders, in their bringing forward of all their teachings and immense knowledge, is encouraged. But these are two aspects of society that usually are a source of oppositional dynamics. So one part of our *Enowkinwixw* is to create a very clear process in which the people in those two groups speak to and listen to each other to inform each other, and to clarify for each other, their views.

Our process for discussion in *Enowkinwixw* is simple. We start with the concept that if there is a problem or a crisis, or something that we are trying to resolve that we don't understand, if anybody already has the answers and already knows it all, they should have resolved it. So, why haven't they? Therefore, it means, that nobody has the answers and no one person should be arguing for their view, their position, their rightness. What it means is that each should be listening to try to understand what the other is saying, and to try to incorporate into the overall solution what each person is saying, so that what is brought together will make more sense than what one person is saying. Obviously, it means that as an individual, if I didn't resolve it, then what I'm saying isn't important by itself, it is important only in the context of the rest of the community.

The premise is to begin in a way that creates "dialogue." We tell people: "*You're not here to debate or to enforce your own agenda. You're not here to convince me of what you think. You're here to listen, and to hear the most diverse and opposite view to yours, and to understand where it's coming from and why it's there, and why that opinion is important in terms of how we find a solution. You are responsible for doing that. You are responsible for hearing what is the most opposite to your opinion, and finding a way to try to incorporate the other's diversity, the other's difference, and embrace that in terms of what we collectively come up with as a solution, so the difference will no longer be a difference, it becomes part of what we are and who we are.*"

In terms of the other two polarities that exists in community, there is a word for one of these in our language that means "maleness." In our language, in our pronoun structure, we don't use words like "he" or "she" that are used in English. It is quite a difficult thing to think in the English language, because everything is gender-based in that way. I talked with my mother about it, and my Aunt Jeanette, whom I am named after, and both are medicine women, and I said, "*How come we don't have that idea?*" And my aunt looked at me and she said, "*Well, it has to do with being a person.*" I asked, "*What does it have to do with being a person?*" She replied, "*If you were to say 'he' or 'she' in our language, you would have to point to their genitals, you would have to point to what's between the legs, and why would you talk about a person and point between their legs?*" She said, "*It doesn't make any sense.*" And it doesn't—people are what they do and who they relate to and how they relate to the world. It has nothing to do with gender, except that there are males and females. So there are words like "maleness and femaleness."

The word "maleness" actually has to do with our understanding in our philosophy about how things work in the world—the cosmology of things. The way the word is constructed for "male" is about the spreading outward of our life form as human, the spreading outward of the diversity of life on the land. The meaning of the word "male" has to do with the idea of humans being able to dream and be able to spread outward in the life form of the human. And so the aspect or idea of procreation as "male," and the energy behind that, is understood as "maleness."

The word for "femaleness" is a really an interesting word in our language. The idea of separating part of the skin of the community, as a separation into family, is contained in our word for "femaleness." The understanding of "femaleness" means "a separating out from within the covering which is community" or "the skin of the community," that is, from the whole of the people into family systems.

So when family systems, represented by the dynamics of "femaleness" and "maleness", together representing how the land operates, intersect as community, work has to be done to create balance, to make sure that there is clear understanding between those two dynamics.

How the people in the family are related to each other is based on how they feel about each other, how they treat each other. Society is really about feeling. It is about how we care for one another, how we love another, and how we protect one another. How we need to make sure there is food for everyone, that everyone has warmth and shelter, how everyone is nurtured emotionally and how people are made to feel good, and how to celebrate—all these things are what is understood and expressed by the word/concept of "femaleness."

Another aspect of *Enowkinwixw* is the understanding that all of the things that we need, to make shelter, to give food, and to develop in all kinds of ways, requires organizing. Doing so is really about "how" things get done. In other words, it takes actions. That's why "spreading out" is in that word of the "maleness" aspect of society. Everything becomes an action that is to be undertaken and when actions are undertaken there are consequences. In other words, what we do always impacts people. If we do things without thinking and without understanding or knowing how it impacts people, we can and will do a lot of things that are destructive, even though we may think that we are doing these things in the name of good, or in the name of providing, or in the name of prosperity.

If the male aspect of society gets its way that is what it will do. It will just keep doing that. That's what, in this society, we think of as "patriarchy." The patriarchal model is a model in which it does not matter that there are people starving, it does not matter that there are people hurting, it does not matter that there are minorities that are voiceless, that are not being included, that are being excluded. As long as this model is kept going, only some of the people can get good out of it and only some of the people can get privilege out of it, and that is really one of the dynamics that we're talking about here.

The dynamic of the male and the female aspects of community must be balanced. The nurturing, caring and providing for "feelings," for the well-being of the generations to come, must be part of the "doing" continuously, with clear understanding, cooperation and collaboration between both.

The dialogue we call *Enowkinwixw* means that we cannot sit down in our community and have any kind of rational decision, or any kind of rational action, unless we include all four aspects of community in dialogue, in a deep listening process. Without doing so, we are endangering the whole community. We are excluding parts of the community, and in doing so we are taking a vast risk for the next generations. I think that is something that really resonates for me. We need to think about how we can continuously include our view, our diversity, our most opposite opinion, and having to listen to the "other," and how we must be responsible in putting these together.

In terms of the family systems, there are two things that operate within community that I think are important to mention. One is the idea that a family system, like community, is a living organism. We think of it as a body. The whole family system as one body that is incomplete if that whole family system isn't intact. The nuclear family isn't what I am talking about. Family means extended family. Three or four generations of aunts, uncles, cousins, grandmas, grandpas, great grandmas, great granddads, and so on, as the repository of many skills in terms of how to do community, how to be community, and how to be community on the land; in terms of how we treat the land and how we take care of it and how we take care of each other without destroying the land, and how we move that along.

Family systems have become fragmented into non-family systems, and in this society this system is now just a mother and father and children. But, even the mother, father and children don't stay together in this society. There is a diaspora of family because of the market economy. We have to move to get jobs, here and there, around and around, to the other end of the world, and so family really doesn't exist. It does not exist and there is a yearning for it and a hunger for it, and a need for it. A much deeper need than we think we know.

In terms of our Indigenous community, family is the basis of survival. We cannot operate community without family. Community does not exist without extended family systems. Otherwise community is just a collection of strangers. People that are not cooperating, not collaborating, not loving each other, not taking care of each other over generations and generations of learning how to do that on the land they occupy. So there are no communities either.

Our family systems in our communities are like clan systems, and each extended family system usually has a role in the work of the community, maybe something like the long-ago guilds in Europe, where you had the bakers, and the millers, and so on. Huge families passed down those skills and they used those skills to contribute to the whole community. In our system, extended families are the repositories of different kinds of skills. There are medicine families, there are healer families—medicine families and healer families usually are similar, but we could say that one are ethno-botanists, while the healer families are the psychologists or psychiatrists, and usually part of a chief's family belongs to these families, because they have to be psychologists and psychiatrists to do the work that is required of them. There are chiefs' families, hunter families, fishermen, basket-makers, and so on. All these families have people in them that are conversant with different tools that our community needs to continue on its life cycle.

In our tradition, gift giving in our society is very similar to the West Coast traditions in that we too have a huge number of feasts during the year. Feasts are held by extended families. As an example, my mother had a role similar to the West Coast Long House leader. A "winter dance leader" we call it in our community, because we don't have big cedars like the West Coast so we have short houses. We have winter dances in the wintertime. Winter dances, like the smokehouse, big house dances on the West Coast, are big give-aways.

I grew up with my uncle being a medicine man and my mother being a medicine woman and the winter house dance leader. Our extended family—cousins, aunts, uncles, brothers, sisters, children, grandchildren—spent all year long gathering and making and putting aside things that are to be given away during that winter dance. And every year, during that winter dance, our mother gave away everything she owned, without question, without deciding how or to whom it is to be given; it is simply given in a ritual of dance. And I saw this giving all my life, and I was brought up this way all my life. We were told by my mother, my grandmother, my aunts, my uncles, that giving is the only way to be human, that if you don't know that giving is essential to survival, then you don't know how to be human yet.

We are told this, once we can understand it, when we are growing up. When we're two or three years old, the very first thing we are taught is to give. In our families, we are shown how to give. We learn that when we receive something that we really cherish and we really care about, that it is the first thing we should give up, because our community is to be cherished on that level. Our people and our land is be cherished on that level. And if we don't know how to give like that, we are poor. We are in poverty. We might hoard all the things that we think our family or our business needs, but we are poor.

We used to drive through some of the cities, and my mother would look around her and she would say, "Those poor rich people! Those poor, poor rich people!" And she meant it. She wasn't being ironic or sarcastic. She was pointing out what they were missing out on. She was pointing out what they were hungry for and what they were trying to find, in accumulating and hoarding and being selfish.

She was pointing out what is really, really given to us when we reverse that, and what we feel when we give. We all know the feeling we have when we give out of purity. We all know how good it makes us feel. This is a natural feeling to us as humans. It is the real feeling of being human. And we all feel this when we give. For example, at Christmas time everybody is so excited about getting things and giving and giving—and some people go overboard. Where does this feeling come from? When we give to our loved ones (we're used to giving just to our favourite, chosen loved ones in this society), we sometimes do it without realizing that we would feel the same way whether we are giving to a direct blood relative or to a stranger, absolutely not known to you. The feeling is the same. In one of our laws we are told that when we start understanding that principle, and we start working with that principle, and we source that principle, we prosper.

In other words, if we lead our lives by giving continuously, never ever thinking about what we might get back from it or using it as an exchange for something that we want somebody to do for us (which, in fact, is not called "giving" in our language) our needs will never go unmet. In our language, giving to someone in order to get something back, is called something else. There is no word for "greed" in our language that I could find. What I found instead was a word which is used to describe a person that is expecting to get something back, or is expecting to have more than another, mostly desiring or expecting to eat more than another. We describe people that become this way with this particular word in our language. What this word means is "swallower or destroyer of giving."

In our traditions we found a way to describe this condition because it means to stop the giving. To stop the giving you put an obstacle between the giving and yourself. And so we describe a person that way if they want more for themselves, or they want more for their family, or if they in some way act as an obstacle, by being selfish, that prevents everybody else in the community being given what is necessary and needed and deserved.

My language is one of the languages that are on the brink of extinction. I want to make clear that these words that I am defining and describing for you are immensely important words that belong in the understanding of our humanity, and are necessary and needed in the understanding of what needs to be done to make change happen.

In our way we are always told not to ask for anything. We are always told in our community, as a practice, that when we have to start asking for something, that's when we're agreeing that people be irresponsible. Irresponsible in not understanding what we're needing, irresponsible in not seeing what's needed, and irresponsible in not having moved our resources and our actions to make sure that need isn't there, because this is the responsibility that we, and the people that surround us, mutually bear. So in our community we cannot go to a person and say, "I want you to do this for me." All we can do is clarify for them what is happening and what the consequences are for our family, or for our community, or for the land. We must clarify for them what needs to be done and how it needs to be done, and then it is up to them and if they fall short of that responsibility, at some point they will face the same need themselves.

We are told on a spiritual level that when we give freely without asking for anything back, whatever it might be, especially the things that are really difficult to give, that you receive back the equivalent of four times whatever it is that you gave.

The simple exercise my mother taught me was: "Whatever amount you work for, keep a small amount, enough to put food on the table, enough to get you back and forth to work, and give all the rest away. You make sure you continue to do that every year, and you'll never have to worry for finding work. You'll never have to worry about all the things that you need." And I never have. I do this every year of my life, all the time. I give to my community, to my people, to strangers; everything that I do is with this way of living in mind. This is something that is needed in terms of how we are doing things in the world today. And this is something that needs to be understood deeply at the personal level.

It comes down to each person embodying this concept and practicing it without letting-up. It comes down to each person being human in this way.

It is my hope that in sharing these thoughts, that I share with each of you a part of the gift that I was given through community, family, and the land that I am from. I wish to extend my gratitude to those whose ideas, work, and resources were given to the idea of a gift economy.

Jeannette Armstrong is Syilx (Okanagan) from Penticton, British Columbia, Canada and is the Director of En'owkin Centre dedicated to the revitaliztion of the Syilx Language and Culture.

KAARINA KAILO

Pan Dora Revisited

From Patriarchal Woman-Blaming to a Feminist Gift Imaginary

The article revisits the myth of Pandora's Box as the source of mankind's scourges and foregrounds Pan Dora as a pre-patriarchal All-Giver and Guardian of Giving and Abundance. After addressing the gendered assumptions about "human nature" underlying neo-liberal economic thought, I present an example of a Nordic/Finnish Pandora variant with her gift–related aspects. I suggest that the naturalization of a masculated worldview behind the "human norm" needs to be exposed. It is merely one among many possible ways of ordering human life and understanding human nature. In the alternative gift imaginary and logic, instead of *homo economicus*, the norm may well have been *femina donans*, the giving human, *Kave*.

The goal of my engaged research consists in reclaiming gynocentric imaginaries with their implicit ecological economics and sustainable worldview, one that also honours women and nature. In this paper, I will revisit the Greco-Roman myth of Pandora as a cross-cultural motif and its Finnish variant. This master narrative of humanity's creative origins consists in transforming women's gift labour into a woman-blaming narrative of male superiority. I introduce at the same time the gift imaginary with its philosophical tenets based on giving back to nature the goods it bestows on humans. Both patriarchal and gynocentric variants of "Pan Dora" as All-Giver, the goddess of abundance and life-centered values can be found across the world. My discussion of the fate of Pandora in Finnish, and more broadly Nordic mythology, is an example of how we can draw on local, situated mythologies to rediscover and make more visible the submerged and symbolically non-masculated (Vaughan 1997) ways of relating to and ordering the surrounding world.

I call the dominant western paradigm and worldview to do with human nature and values the master imaginary, which echoes aspects of the exchange economy on which Genevieve Vaughan (1997) has elaborated and what eco-feminist scholars have labelled as either the master identity (Plumwood 1993) or consciousness (Warren 2000: 48). The concept condenses the artificial and arbitrary dichotomies that have allowed mostly white heterosexual elite men to dominate nature, women, Indigenous populations, and people of colour as well as men defying the hegemonic gender contracts. The master imaginary refers to the totality of cultural customs, etiquettes, gendered divisions and processes of labour, attitudes, behaviours, activities and gestures that lend legitimacy and inner strength to patriarchy's asymmetrical gender system. Among the central elements of this logic are assumptions and projections of non-egalitarian and hierarchically constructed difference (e.g. men vs. women, humans vs. animals, mind vs. matter or spirit, rationality vs. emotionality). This includes a gendered segregation of "male" and "female" realms of reason, influence, prestige, power or social activities and a relegation of the less prestigious "emotional" labour mostly to women. This imaginary rests also on a perceptual pivot which privileges a worldview of strict boundaries to ground ownership rights, competition and social hierarchies. Establishing society's moral boundaries via the female body is an effect of asymmetrical power relations, not of a categorical logic within social structures.

Women can and do, at different locations of power and privilege also embrace the master imaginary and its logic of mastery over the "other." Many women embrace themselves a system of boundaries projected on the (female) body, on territory and society that marks and defines female corporeality in its "open and vulnerable stage" (menses, pregnancy) as polluted and polluting (Douglas 1996 [1966]). However, it is necessary to distinguish between the internalization of patriarchal societal values and conscious, informed consent to sex/gender systems that subjugate women through a misleading politics of idealization/denigration of the "feminine." If one does not grow up knowing of alternatives to a patriarchal social order, one cannot really claim that women willingly embrace asymmetrically constructed social systems.

Although the master imaginary in its current, markedly economistic form can be embraced by whites, non-whites, men and women, its roots are in the asymmetrical sex/gender systems of patriarchies and thus it contains gendered and gendering as well as class-related processes. David Korten (1996) has provided a succinct and useful summary of the current master imaginary, i.e. the neo-liberal visioning of human nature and worldview.[1] Competitive behavior is believed to be more rational for the individual and the firm than cooperation; consequently, societies should be built around the capital-hoarding, non-giving motive. Also, human progress is to be measured by increases in the value of what the members of society own and consume (Korten 1996: 20). These ideological doctrines assume according to Korten that:

> People are by nature motivated primarily by greed, the drive to acquire is the highest expression of what it means to be human, the relentless pursuit of greed and acquisition leads to socially optimal outcomes, it is in the best interest of human societies to encourage, honour, and reward the above values (1996: 70-71).

These neo-liberal ideas, although a form of extreme capitalistic ethos, fit to some extent what Vaughan (1997) labels as the patriarchal exchange economy and the hegemonic belief system of today.[2]

The mythologies and patriarchal epics of the western world reflect the tenets of the master imaginary, a gaze where women are defined in relation to men and where war, conquest, hero-worship take priority over narratives of life-sustaining events, collaboration and peaceful co-existence. Mythologies are powerful means of mind colonization, and stressing humanity's capacity for good is itself a revolutionary and mind-altering process. Many scholars studying archaic societies ignore the gender-molding cultural processes and refer simply and in a gender-neutral way to a society's social order. Few comment on how the various social contracts are established and consolidated through explicitly patriarchal mechanisms and values where women's views are not as a rule solicited. The socialization through patriarchal myths and grand narratives explains in part why women more than men have internal glass ceilings and self-limiting attitudes regarding power, leadership, authority and other attributes associated positively with men.

The gift imaginary contrasts with the masculated ethos in terms of its goals and values; it is a worldview, an alternative imaginary and ideology that one can perceive dominating pre- and non-patriarchal societies. Although it is important to heed historic and culture-specific variations, generally speaking in such communities economic life is built on balanced human and environmental relations, a recognition of our interconnections and interdependencies and a forward-looking use of resources to ensure future cycles of abundance, fertility, and rebirth of all species. Its logic consists in the rationality of care and responsibility to ensure collective survival and well-being (eco-social sustainability). Giving and sharing the Commons is at the root of this worldview and the norm of the human is best embodied by the care-circulating individual whose logic of action and ethics is like that of the ideal mother, not a distant, absent and judgmental father (see Ochs 1977). Today westerners in particular need to become aware of the white mythology and worldview that has been naturalized as the universal and desirable one. This is one precondition for the kind of ethnosensitivity required for us in the West to become open to alternative, more eco-socially reliable styles of knowing and living (Meyer and Ramirez 1996). The gift and give back economies of by-gone eras appear not to have been as dualistic and based on strict hierarchies of being, knowing and wielding power. Modern westerners have been so conditioned by the dichotomous worldview, however, that it takes a special effort for many of them, as well, to re-imagine the more integrated, holistic model of cognition, perception, and *beingknowing*. The gift imaginary, rooted in the ethos of group cohesion, circulation of a community's resources is not pure utopia (although we also need utopian visions to help chart us towards a more justice-oriented world). Heide Goettner-Abendroth (1987, 1995, 2004) has found evidence of such societies even in the contemporary world[3] and provides much evidence of matriarchal societies having combined sustainable green economics and a worldview of balanced/complementary gender relations beyond the hierarchical and asymmetrical dualisms of western sex/gender systems. In these societies the social imaginary is not rooted in the idea that self-interest and fierce competition are natural or desirable; in contrast, their social rituals serve to guarantee collective survival and not to ground private accumulation.

The myth of Pandora's box epitomizes patriarchy's historical appropriation and reversal of the gift-circulating and woman-friendly mythologies and economies. By re-owning this myth in the North and elsewhere, we can trace our steps back towards the more sustainable view of the human and of communal life that we sorely need today's world of global warming and the green house effects.

On Pandora and Spirit Guardians of the Gift

The myth of Pandora's box is an appropriate "case" for making visible the attributes and values to do with women, gift giving and nature that have been overwritten to make way for the master imaginary and politics. Although our knowledge of pre-patriarchal times is uncertain, there is sufficient scientific data to allow us to speculate that a gift circulating and more gynocentric socio-cosmic order has existed. If matriarchy refers to "mothers at the beginning," and not "maternal domination" as Goettner-Abendroth argues (see her article in this volume), the Pandora myth refers precisely to the world's first woman and beyond the story's patriarchal rewriting to social systems where the primal mothers were honoured as gift providers. There are innumerable versions of the story particularly in Greek and Roman mythology.[4] I will introduce first some patriarchal versions of the myth before elabourating on their feminist reinterpretations. According to *Encyclopædia Britannica*, "Pandora" refers to "All-Giving" and the first woman:

> After Prometheus, a fire god and divine trickster had stolen fire from heaven and bestowed it upon mortals, Zeus, the king of the gods, determined to counteract this blessing. He accordingly commissioned Hephaestus (a god of fire and patron of craftsmen) to fashion a woman out of earth, upon whom the gods bestowed their choicest gifts. She had or found a jar—the so-called Pandora's box—containing all manner of misery and evil. Zeus sent her to Epimetheus, who forgot the warning of his brother Prometheus and *made her* [my emphasis] his wife. Pandora afterward opened the jar, from which the evils flew out over the earth. According to another version, hope alone remained inside, the lid having been shut down before she could escape. In a later story the jar contained not evils but blessings, which would have been preserved for the human race had they not been lost through the opening of the jar out of curiosity by man himself. (*Encyclopædia Britannica* 2002).

In another, more recent encyclopedia version we read:

> … in Greek mythology, first woman on earth. Zeus ordered Hephaestus to create her as vengeance upon man and his benefactor, Prometheus. The gods endowed her with every charm, together with curiosity and deceit. Zeus sent her as a wife to Epimetheus, Prometheus' simple brother, and gave her a box that he forbade her to open. Despite Prometheus' warnings, Epimetheus allowed her to open the box…. (*The Columbia Electronic Encyclopedia* 2005)

One finds the earliest extant (patriarchal) Greek text of Pandora in 700 BC in Hesiod's *Works and Days* with the classic image of Pandora and the box; the latter however is really a "jar," and the story does *not* specify exactly what was in the box Pandora opened. The idea of humans as giving beings (*femina donans*) epitomized in the giving, creative and procreative mother, the first woman, is far removed from the above variants of Pandora. As in today's archi-capitalist ethos of marketization, commodification and structural violence, men and male gods wage war between each other with women merely as trophies, objects, beauty queens or screens on which to project the weakest links of dysfunctional patriarchy itself. In the patriarchal versions of Pandora, a natural impulse—the desire to understand one's surroundings, one's life, one's gifts—is turned in the case of the subaltern—women—to a sin, a transgression. This is no doubt an attempt to keep the lid on women's mental, psychological, spiritual and cultural authority. Both Genesis and the myth of Pandora's Box are among the primal myths that serve to manipulate women to distrust their own impulses, instincts and epistemic desires, and, at worst, to perceive the critical, probing, question-ing mind as evil. Both types of narratives of course help keep women obedient, flexible, and malleable—and humble enough to internalize the master imaginary in its various historical manifestations. In patriarchal mythic narratives, blame for the most unimaginable wrong-doings have been passed on to the female sex, and this is one way of producing free-floating collective guilt as a precondition for submissiveness. Of course, many women can negotiate their gender script and disown parts or even all of it. Yet, the performative repetition of the pri-mal story and woman's role in it does lend dubious support to society's other woman-blaming mechanisms.[5] The bringing of gifts to the first woman echoes another story of divine creation, the birth of Jesus, to whom gifts were brought from near and far. Could it be, then, that even this incidence is an appropriation of the historically more remote gift-bestowing to the Goddess? It is particularly dis-empowering for women to be told that Pandora as first woman was created as a curse and as revenge for the theft of fire by Prometheus. This epitomizes the patriarchal notion of woman as mere currency of exchange in relation to men and male interests. On the other hand, Pandora was fashioned as a bewitching beauty endowed with gifts from all the gods and goddesses. Pandora's beauty, instead of representing the inherent beauty of creation, nature and humanity becomes a pawn of power in the struggle between men for dominance. Indeed, the rapes of women during wars serve precisely the same function of projecting shame on victims rather than the perpetrators of violence. It is a means of dishonouring men and entire nations by depriving their women of honour (sexual "purity"). Woman is honourable only as male property. Pandora's box is a proto-narrative of domination-submission and "power-over" relations beginning with Zeus's power over men and ending with men's power over women's nature, female beauty, and the female body. The story and its many variants epitomize how the ancient mystical vessel—the womb, female blood, and related myths have been turned to their opposite. Philosophically, in Vaughan's terms (1997), the story epitomizes how the gift economy as a particular quality of other-orientation and metalogic has been replaced by a more ego-oriented exchange economy, although both imaginaries continue to co-exist in more or less visible and complex gendered and culture-specific forms. In many variants cited by feminist scholars and numerous research articles, Pandora's mythic origins are foregrounded to reveal the transformative politics of the master imaginary. Sandra Geyer Miller (1995) for one refers to Anesidor as one of the Earth Goddess avatars that the writers of master narratives have sought to replace. Jane Harrison (1975) sees in Hesiod's story evidence of a shift from matriarchy to patriarchy in Greek culture. As the life-bringing goddess Pandora is eclipsed, the death-bringing human Pandora arises (283-85). The above-cited patriarchal variants also hint at a historical and narrative shift from a more peaceful to a more violent and militaristic male order, whereby men are turned into each other's enemies. Eros is replaced by logos, an all-pervasive and positive sexuality transformed into a denigration of women, corporeality, matter, earth, even physicality.

Non-Patriarchal Reinterpretations of Pandora as Pan-Dora

Patriarchal and feminist versions of Pandora differ significantly, and one way to epitomize the transformation is to view them as expressions of the gift and exchange or master economies and the worldview to which they belong. An important point revealed by male and female scholars critical of the hegemonic version is that the very notion of a "box" may have been nothing less than a mistranslation, if not an intentional effort to rewrite mythic herstory. Evidence suggests that indeed, Pandora herself was the "jar"—the creative/procreative womb, the holy vessel or grail. In Ancient Greece jars commonly bore images of women's uterus. The mistranslation is usually attributed to the sixteenth-century Humanist Erasmus of Rotterdam.[6] Various feminist scholars claim that in an earlier set of myths, Pandora was the Great Goddess, provider of the gifts that made life and culture possible.[7] The Greek and Judeo-Christian versions of both the Eve and Pandora myths serve above all now to propagandize the message of early patriarchy about the status of women at that time and Hesiod's tale is seen as part of a propaganda campaign to demote All-Giver from her previously revered status (Geyer Miller 1998). A very different definition is provided by Barbara Walker (1983) who notes, regarding "Vase" that as:

> Forerunner of the funerary urn in Old Europe [it] was the large earthenware vase representing the Earth Mother's womb—of rebirth. When cremation was the chosen funerary rite, reducing the body to ashes, small vases were created to contain these remains and still serve as womb symbols. The uterine shape of the vase so often bore the connotation of rebirth, that even when corpses were no longer stuffed into actual earthenware vases like the funerary *pithoi* of early Greece, a vaselike shape persisted in various receptacles for dead bodies. The sacrophagus seems to take the shape of the uterus in many

societies…. *In pre-Hellenic Greece, a title of Mother Rhea as the Womb of Matter was Pandora, the All-Giver* [my emphasis]. Her symbol was a great vase, originally signifying the source of all things, like the great cauldron of the Mother Goddess in northern Europe. Hesiod's antifeminist fable converted Rhea Pandora's womb—vase into the source of all human ills and evils. Centuries later Erasmus mistook *pithos* (vase) for *pyxis* (box) and mistranslated Hesiod into the now-conventional story of Pandora's Box. The vase retained its uterine symbolism in alchemy, where the Womb of Matter was called *vas spirituale*. A vase containing the Water of Life remains the symbol of the Chinese Great Mother Goddess Kwan-Yin. (160-161)

Among other data, the reference to female imagery, rebirth, and procreation allow us to speculate that Pan Dora as the gift-giving human, the human norm refers back to matriarchal worldviews; of course, more research is also needed to specify and identify the local itineraries and processes of transformation from a more gynocentric[8] to a more patriarchal social order. The stories and myths of the first woman, the Sacred Feminine and primal gift givers have been overwritten across the patriarchal world, in alignment with the values of patriarchy and the master imaginary. The hope that this provides—like Pandora's box itself—is that behind these layers of the myth, we can re-discover, unearth and reintroduce the more originary, woman-friendly versions. I will next elabourate on the Finnish Pandora variant.

Kave and Louhi: From Panarctic Gift Givers to the Origin of all Evils

As there has been a conscious and non-conscious suppression of the gynocentric dimensions and layers of Finnish culture, the female goddesses in their broad spectrum are practically unknown in Finland. Many of them have simply been split along the axis of good/evil, plus replaced and condensed into a monomyth—Virgin Mary or her demonic counterpart. It is therefore empowering to make visible and to re-circulate the gynocentric stories and images, representations and fragments relating to archaic Finnish goddesses, *haltias,* female spirit beings and guardians. This is important because they are the matrix of a different worldview and can be seen to preside over the gift imaginary.

The Finnish *Kalevala*, the canonized epic of the Finnish Golden Past was compiled and put together by Elias Lönnrot, a folklorist and country doctor, in a patriarchal framework and according to nineteenth-century Christian and nationalistic ideas and values. It does contain reflections of the archaic worldview that stressed ecological balance and the philosophy of thanking nature for the gifts it bestows. The give back- based worldview is reflected in numerous poems in the Finnish Folk Poetry collections where the sauna, guardians of game and animal life as well as the forest, among other beings and things, are greeted and thanked as part of a cyclical world order based on bonds rather than an ethos of unilateral mastery over nature. The bear ceremonials and other festivities (Honko 1993)[9] were occasions for sharing rituals and for both establishing and transgressing boundaries of the sacred as a way of reconfirming them (Anttonen 1992). Much has been written about this ancient system of combining economics, religion and socio-cosmic order. Less, however, has been written about the role of the realm labelled as "feminine" or of the gift circulating ethos from a gynocentric point of view. The goddess tradition allows us to foreground prepatriarchal representations of female power, not as "power over" but as creation-power. I look upon the goddess guardian of Bear and game, Mielikki as one such non-patriarchal manifestation of an imaginary beyond the split female psyche, the whore-madonna dualism, for Mielikki as a benign *haltia* need not be pitted against a separate negative goddess. Rather, she contains in herself her shadow aspect; Kuurikki as do all mortal beings. She withholds game if she is not respected and the balance of nature maintained. In the patriarchal order, however, the first woman, the mysterious Kave linked also with Ilmatar, goddess of the Air, is clearly split from the destructive feminine dimension, following the patriarchal imaginary. Good and evil become absolute, rather than shifting dimensions of a single goddess which of old reflected the waxing and waning moon or cycles of nature's death and rebirth. In Finnish mythic herstory, the transformation of Pan Dora, "the all-giver" has been replaced in prominence by the "procreator of scourges," Louhi. The Finnish goddesses of nurturance, fertile nature, sexuality, and rebirth are often linked with or embodied in a figure called Kave, which Irmeli Nieminen (1985) defines more narrowly as just the typical epithet of female *haltias* or goddesses (Mäkinen 2004: 60). A study of the *Suomen Kansan Vanhat Runot* (*SKVR*) (a collection of ancient Finnish folklore and poetry) reveals that Kave is indeed the attribute of a host of different goddess or *haltia* figures. However, she is above all linked with *haltias* associated with healing, midwifery and the enhancement of nature's gifts of plenty. Most importantly, she is the mother of Luonnotars, the daughters of Nature that echo the Roman Parcea, the Nordic Norns, the Sami Uksakka, Sarakka, Juksakka. Finnish mythology commands closer attention in light of comparative mythological studies that allow us to reveal affinities between Finnish/Finno-Ugrian, Nordic and Greco-Roman mythologies. It is challenging both for the renewal of our imaginaries and for scientific reasons to recreate the archaic gynocentric worldview from the fragments and more complete folk materials that have failed to inspire even female scholars identified with mainstream folklore methods and schools of thought. European and Euro-American scholars consider Demeter, Hecate and Persephone to be the proto-types of the three ages of women, personifying virginal youth, sexually mature middle-age and the menopausal age of the Crone. These figures in the culture-specific constellations are part of the continuum of the cyclical worldview and its system of time measurement; the ages of women and of all growth cycles, the waxing and waning of the moon. Kave has obvious affinities with the birth-giving and omni-creative aspect of the primal Guardian/*haltia* just as Louhi is her death-wielding aspect is comparable to many Greco-Roman and international mythic figures from Kali to Hecate. Although myths take on local form, expression and color, the notions of women's puberty, pregnancy, reproduction, coming-of-age and "ripening" are likely universal land-marks of women's life. As an instance of cultural translation of mythic material, the myth's variant is located spatially in the most holy site of Finnish traditional culture, the sauna.

In Finnish folk poetry, Kave, as the principle of nourishing nature and creativity is linked with the material abundance of nature (*Luonto*). John Abercromby, in his two-volume, *Magic Songs of West Finns* (1898), reveals the links between the mysterious Kave—transformed into Virgin Mary in later periods—and Louhi, both of whom are put forth as principles of life protection and creativity:

> The recuperative power of nature would naturally occur to exorcists and wizards when healing the sick, and in a more objective form would be appealed to for assistance. Old mother Kave (the woman), the daughter of nature (*luonto*), *the oldest of womankind,* [my emphasis] the first mother of individuals, is therefore invoked to come and see pains and remove them. Almost in the same terms she is implored to help an exorcist. And under the same title she is invited to allay the pains of child-birth because *she formerly freed the moon from imprisonment in a cell, and the sun from a rock.* [my emphasis] But the original idea is on the wane in a charm for relieving pain, in which it is related that three Luonnotars sit where three roads meet and gather pains into a speckled chest or a copper box, and feel annoyed if pains are not brought to them. And the old idea of her functions is missing where the woman (*kave*), the old wife Luonnotar, the darling and beautiful, is asked to point out the path to a bridal procession. Or when she is invited to bewitch sorcerers and crush witches; to weave a cloth of gold and silver, and make a defensive shirt under which an exorcist can live safely with the help of the good God. (Abercromby 1898: 307-8)

In this passage, Kave's role is that of a midwife, helping women give birth through imitative magic. She is referred to also as *einesten emä*, a dispenser of nature's provisions (*Kalevala* 38:82 and The Birth of the Snake 26:707).[10] In the patriarchal epic, this type of a variant of Kave is replaced with the one-sidedly negative goddess variant, Louhi, now the mirror image of the midwife: no longer the giver or promoter of the gift of life, she is turned into the symbol of spiritual darkness, greed, avarice, denial of life.[11] In Abercromby's (1898) above description of the role of Kave, she is referred to as freeing the moon from imprisonment in a cell, and the sun from a rock. In the *Kalevala* the same motif is found in reverse: Louhi is depicted as imprisoning instead of releasing the luminaries. The birth-giver and creator/releaser of new life is transformed or split into a figure, Lemminkäinen's mother, who can recreate life, and the Pandora-like source of disease and chaos. The goddess with her temporally and situationally changing aspects is thus split into the classic patriarchal dualism of nameless, idealized mother and the whore so labelled because she transgresses the acceptable female role. The copper box in which pains are gathered in the above description, can also be related to Sampo, the Finns' magic mill of prosperity and endless riches (Kailo 1987). A multilevel, overdetermined and mysterious symbol, it has been interpreted as a mythic mill of immaterial and material goods. However, in connection with the Lapp matriarch, it is turned into a metaphoric source of greed and treason. As patriarchy gets stronger, primal woman-blaming increases while the role of female goddesses is replaced by the ascendancy of male gods (cf. Kemppinen 1960: 276-277).[12] To foreground Louhi over Kave epitomizes the Finnish version of Pandora's role and fate from an All-Provider to the Christian projection of All-Evil.

The Finnish Goddess/*haltia* galaxy in its gynocentric form consists of numerous shape-shifting complex characters and spirit guardians with overlapping and context-specific symbolic functions associated with Life and Creation. They include Ilmatar, Rauni, Akka, Maaemo and Suonetar, to name the most common ones.[13, 14] The Finnish concept of *luonto* or nature is also their essential quality and has very different associations from the kind of human nature to which Freud, among others, ascribes aggressive and ego-oriented drives. In her form as Kave, the goddess is her own excuse for being, the graceful materiality and ground of existence, beyond the priority to trade and exchange, or horde and monopolize spiritual power as a way of ensuring mastery over the other. Kave is a complex, yet clearly beneficial energy force of nature in its procreative, fertile and autonomous manifestation. Like all goddesses, she is part of a circle or web of interconnections, not comparable to the solitary hero or autonomous hero-god of patriarchal lore. Kave condenses associations to do with mother, matter, nourishment, food and is related to the Golden Woman, a mysterious archaic being in Finnish and Finno-Ugric oral tradition, referring to honey and the magic meady ("golden") substance giving and maintaining life.[15] She is a condensed Akka/Maderakka (the latter being the Sami variant), with Louhi as her patriarchal version—Hag of the North, Mistress of the North Farm.[16]

I foreground Kave as an appropriate role model and embodiment of the worldview honouring nature, women and the Gift or Give back imaginary. This attribute of the feminine divine allows us to retrace the historic steps back towards the more "originary"[17] meaning of Pandora or the Finnish version of the All-Giver in a worldview based on abundance rather than scarcity and the creation of false needs serving the master imaginary. Since traditional Finnish folk poetry has been above all functional and performative—it was meant to be performed and hence was communal rather than textual—it is misleading to posit anything like a Finnish pantheon of gods and goddesses separate from such a performative function.[18] However, just as patriarchy has created its own would-be-national pantheon of significant male gods, the representations of a gynocentric imaginary can be reintroduced into the collective consciousness. The fact that it is impossible to posit and prove a matriarchal or matristic imaginary beyond the constant give-and-take of cross-cultural influences does not prevent such a goal. It has not prevented the male elite of the nineteenth century from creating an imaginary male order to reinforce male domination in cultural and political matters. If such an epic was used to help Finland achieve its independence, why not use folk poetry also to ensure women's independency from the master imaginary?

In nineteenth-century folklore there are numerous descriptions of the sauna as a sacred site becoming a demonic place in the presence of Louhi—the midwife and "post-menopausal" crone associated with disease and pollution. Louhi as the Finnish Pandora variant is represented as giving birth to various child-monsters and ailments, and transgressing the holiest of societal rules by naming the offspring herself—without the sanctifying intervention of Christian priests or pastors. Both in folk poetry and the Finnish *Kaleval*a, Louhi is described in numerous variants as a harlot or demon, giving birth to a variety of illnesses and evils. Instead of Kave embodying the life and reproductive force, however, the folk poetry is full of references to the Finnish Virgin Mary, Marjatta, helping a male god cure ailments in the sauna.[20] Sauna itself can be seen as a kind of primal pithos or originary womb of rebirth. The sauna is also where Marjatta gives birth to a child echoing the story of Jesus. The sauna has traditionally been a symbolically feminine place—not unlike a bear's den, which is the site for Spring-time rebirth, it is also womb-like in its darkness and warmth. One key recurrent attribute of Finnish folklore is honey. In many folk descriptions Louhi is portrayed as a whore copulating with the wind and producing, for example, nine sons as embodiments of gout and other diseases. Thus the role of the divine midwife is turned to its opposite (*SKVR* 470, Source 2834. Ilomantsi. Eur. H, n. 178. 45. Hattupää) (Kailo 2005b). Not only has Louhi in many representations been made to evoke otherness, blackness, old age, animality and asexuality, but she has been represented in many films and books even of today as the classic dispenser of disease and destruction, pollution and black storms threatening human life.[21]

Emil Petaja (1966, 1967), an American-Finnish science fiction writer has resurrected the character of the dark and "evil witch of the North" in many of his science fiction stories based on the Finnish *Kalevala*, providing a good illustration of the ongoing misogynous myth-making going back to the myths of Pandora and Eve. His repetition of mythic woman-blaming underlines the need to interrupt and transform the master imaginary as the psychological anchor of asymmetrical gender relations. In Petaja's novels the northern witch, Louhi's resurrected spirit is referred to as a black-faced Lapp. In *Kalevala* Louhi requires the Sampo as booty, in exchange for her daughters which the *Kalevala* heroes coveted and desired as their wives. She is represented as a matriarch who breaks her promise and keeps the goods and the magic mill all to herself. At the end of *Kalevala*, the Sampo is finally lost to both the men and Louhi, and it is broken into pieces in the bottom of the sea. Petaja makes Louhi[22] return to the scene where she manages to pick up a few fragments of its mystical cover. This echoes the lid of Pandora's box which represents hope in the story reported by Geller Miller (1995). In Petaja's (1966) retelling, Louhi makes the Sampo grind goods in reverse, i.e., she is depicted as the root of the ecological destruction the book dramatizes. Thus Louhi's avatar is identified in *The Star Mill* as the "Mistress of All Evil" (200):

Sorcery and cunning were the Witch's watchwords. Louhi's evil nature was so strong that it soaked up all of the other evil in the universe like a sponge, and had done so for thousands of years. Her pacts with alien creatures who were inimical to man had given her immense power. (Petaja 1966: 196).

In light of Petaja's science fiction stories where the "Louhi stereotype" is again made to embody pollution, evil, destruction (Petaja 1966: 66x), the question imposes itself as to the reasons for such stability of the oral tradition and their literary offspring—and for the psychological meaning of such projections across time and space, from Finland to North America. Louhi, something of a feminized *alter ego* for the male heroes of *Kalevala* is as a woman of science and innovation/power made to carry all the negative attributes of knowledge as mere black magic. The Sampo, the major symbol of material and immaterial wealth in the Finnish epic could also be related to Pandora's box as the perverted mill of abundance. Whereas a gynocentric story might portray the mill as a womblike pot of honey, source of life and material/immaterial riches, the patriarchal imaginary has made of it a mill of economic prosperity and a source of conflicts between two warring groups, the matriarchal "man-eating Lapps" or their historically ambiguous equivalent, and the patriarchal forefathers of the Finns. This epitomizes the contrast between the master and the gift imaginaries. As is the case with the pithos-pyxis translation mistake in the Greco-Roman stories, the woman-positive meaning of which has been most intentionally re-interpreted, Sampo, too, can be rethought through the word's earthy, ecospiritual and gynocentric interpretations. Sampo's etymologies and possible linguistic variants have provided scholars with a wealth of opportunities for creative speculation. Many of them somehow express the ideas of connection, spirituality and community. It is possible to read into them the most diverse meanings, for at the deepest level, the Sampo is the symbol of symbolism itself. "Symbol" derives from Greek and means "Sun" (together) and "ballein" (to throw). *Symbolon* originally referred to a concrete token of recognition for an object which had been separated from its other half, evoking original oneness and its loss. On one level the symbol means whatever meaning a particular object or phenomenon has been endowed with by a particular society through a social contract. The Sampo can be seen as a condensation of all the etymological theories that scholars over the centuries have given of it; it is a *samovol* (Slavonic), a selfgrinding signifier capable of endless new meaning proliferations; it is also a god-image (*sam bog* – Russian) for it can represent the metaphysical "nail of the North Pole" around which an individual's quest for metaphysical meaning revolves and it is also *summum bonum* (Latin), the highest good, if, as a symbol, cymbal-like, it allows a reader to enter into aesthetic ecstasy or expand his or her perceptual horizons (Kailo 1987). Comparetti associates the Sampo even with the Swedish *sambu* with its archaic meaning of living together (today one's living partner). These interpretations based on linguistic terms believed to lie at the word's root differ greatly from the economic reductions to which Sampo has given rise today (Sampo as the name of an influential major banking institution in Finland).

Conclusion

The myth of Pan Dora when linked with matriarchy is a powerful example of how the world view of gift circulation has in the course of patriarchal history been transformed into its opposite—gift deprivation or an exchange economy-related interpretation of the very concept. It epitomizes how women as creators and reproducers of humanity have been turned into representations of impurity and pollution (Douglas 1966)—the scourges flowing out of Pandora's box. The widely-spread patriarchal narrative summarizes how power elites operate; among other strategies by reverting/recoding/renaming symbols of power and by vilifying those that threaten their monopoly on Truth, Justice, Good and Evil—totalitarian, class-related, gendered and dualistic notions of the patriarchal master identity. The dominant form of the human norm—the neo-liberal pseudo-autonomous individual with his competitive and non-giving ethos—is not a natural reflection of "human nature" and worldview, but one that has developed as elite male hegemony and the master imaginary have deepened.[23] On the other hand, we need the pre-patriarchal myths of Pan Dora myths in order to instill hope and trust that the norm of the human can well be a caring immanent and life-preserving mother rather than an abstract, feared, judgemental father-god. The myth matters also in terms of women's renewed trust in their own power and authority. When a dominant culture insists that power lies only outside the individual, in hierarchical organizations, people eventually cease to believe in their own inner power. This may be another reason why Pandora's Box was "invented." The sense of union with the larger powers of life is tremendously empowering. Hence, the connection between inner wisdom/strength and outer power is one that patriarchy does not want women to make (Iglehart 1982: 294).

Over millennia, mythology has developed narratives about universal human conditions. The gift imaginary represents for me a return to myth making of a more holistic and eco-socially sustainable variety. The validity of a theory and practice might be measured by the extent to which it enhances human/woman rights, wellness and ecological sustainability, and how strongly it advocates the rights of all to spiritual and other basic modes of self-determination and expression. The feminist self-reflection has further ensured a constant process of realignment and assessment of one's own collusion with abusive ethnopolitical politics and ways. As Audre Lorde (1984) notes, the erotic is manifest in everything that binds us, as the eros and magic of everyday life. This is for me an essential quality also of the gift imaginary where we can also give expression to utopias of gift-based communities, equality and justice, the raw materials for change. As Vaughan (1997) sums this ethos, it is based on listening to the sign-gifts of individual and collective needs, and being able to respond to them. For an American writer on ecospirituality, Cynthia Eller (1990), the creation of a feminist spirituality is a logical extension of other feminist premises. The interest in reclaiming the female body as a positive image and as an intrinsic and celebrated part of women's existence through the other imaginary, moves simultaneously with the desire of uniting spirit, body, and mind into a more holistic, resisting or empowering lifestyle. In this context, healing becomes a metaphor for any form of self-transformation, whether physical, emotional, or mental; it is the name given to the overall effort to gain self-knowledge and marshal personal power (Eller 1990: 110).[24] Finnish folk healing also contains the notion that in order to heal one must know the words of origin (*synnyinsanat*), something that applies also to collective balance. To know, cherish and honour one's roots is to stay or become whole, what the fragmented, atomistic modern self suffers from is loss of soul, loss of rootedness and connectedness with the extended family of sentient beings. According to old folk beliefs, people can only be healed by healing them together with the environment and broader cosmic spirits and forces. After all, they all form one, and hurting nature means hurting oneself.

The gift imaginary as the radically other worldview is, as I have tried to suggest, a way of going back to the ecologically and socially sustainable roots of our being and earth communities (the etymology of "radical" has to do with "roots"). Feminists are among the groups today that are trying to make a difference through their engaged politics and consciousness-raising. They are the transgressive women opening Pandora's Box, prying into patriarchal secrets and exposing the roots of the inequities and structural inequalities making the world an unsafe and unstable place for women and men alike. Social activism is also a form of traditionally feminine gift and to such an extent feminists are the modern kinfolk of Pandora, opening the lid on the scourges created by the modern corporate world with its politics of unsustainable accumulation. They remind society that it is the corporate elite, not women that have released the evils that plague us today—global warming, the bird flu, the mad cow disease. Today's scourges unleashed by the neo-liberal fundamentalist globalization are indeed gene manipulation and terminator seeds, terminator technology, computer viruses, nuclear proliferation, a deepening digital divide, and an increasing wedge between the haves and have-nots between the industrial and overexploited countries. In sum, then, the other imaginary means returning to Pan Dora her role as gift giver, not as an enemy of patriarchy. In concrete politics, this also means listening and voting for gift-ed men and women—for a change. And reminding us all what Pan Dora's original vase contained—honey. Not missiles and woman-blaming tales. In Geyer Miller's (1995) view:

> In mythology, gifts are symbols of power and authority. Pandora received many gifts and thus came down to earth well equipped. The patriarchal overlay on the myth has robbed the feminine descendants of Pandora of their birthright, the knowledge of the meaning of the gifts and the power and authority to utilize them effectively. It was the Horae who enhanced Pandora's attractions by embellishing her hair with floral garlands and herbs to awaken desire in the hearts of men (golden grace). Thus Pandora wore the fruits and flowers of the seasons, bedecked with nature's finest perfumed offerings. She is, herself, the most delectable offering in perfect timing, a "natural" gift. She

is the first earth woman, with her cyclic nature and ability to move in tune with the tides and seasons. Pandora is the symbol of birth and death. By her, a man enters and leaves the physical world. Like the Horae, she is the keeper of the gates. Her gift is that of having an integral sense of timing.... The Greek word for grace, "charis," means the "delightfulness of art." Aglaia, the youngest of the Graces, was the wife of Hephaestus. Her name means "the glorious" or Brilliant. Thalia (Flowering) and Euphrosyne (Heart's Joy) were the other two Graces. Older names were Pasithea, Cale, and Euphrosyne which was actually a title of Aphrodite (Pasithea Cale Euphrosyne) meaning "The Goddess of Joy who is Beautiful to All." (9)

The gifts of gynocentric mythology and imaginary remain to be unearthed. Ritvala's Helka festival is one strong gynocentric ritual remaining of the pagan past in Finland. As a women's spring and fertility ceremonial going far back through the oral tradition, it is one of the most promising gateways towards the other imaginary, despite its strong Christian-patriarchal overlay (Kailo 2007). It is not only possible to reconstruct the woman-friendly and ecosocially sustainable imagined communities of the past, it may well be that without a radical change in our worldview, there is not much of a world left to defend. Patriarchy as institution and the master imaginary as its psychological order have let so many scourges out of its arsenals of violence and destruction that hope is indeed the only thing we now have left of a sustainable future.

Kaarina Kailo, senior researcher at the Finnish Academy, has held various women's studies positions in Canada and Finland (1991-), ranging from interim director of the Simone de Beauvoir Institute, Montreal, Canada to professor at Oulu University. She has published numerous co-edited books on topics from postcolonialism (Sami people) to feminist views on folklore, storytelling, literature, gift economy/gift imaginary, neoliberal economic philosophy, honour-related gender violence, mythology, ecofeminism, bear myths, sauna and sweatlodge as gynocentric ritual spaces. Her current research compares Northern/Indigenous women's writings on trauma and healing. She is active in local, national and international Green-Left politics. Her edited anthology, The Gift Gaze: Wo(men) and Bears *will be published by Inanna Publications in 2007.*

Notes

---

1   He exposes the norm of the "human" behind the current value system; it is, I believe, also the invisible Eurocentric norm, linked with a notion of "autonomous" subjectivity that does not fit women's and many non-European cultures' values or perceptions. We are, after all, all dependent on each other—and men particularly so regarding the care work that women provide.

2   Vaughan (1997) believes that the current western norm of the human is, to use a heuristic description of men as a group, a masculated male ego in the "exemplar" position,

reflecting the outcome of a male-specific upbringing and conditioning to become the non-gift giving gender entitled to receive rather than bestow nurture. The individual, cut-throat ethos of neo-liberalism is for educational and socialization-related reasons less expressive of the values and behavioural mores with which women are brought up. It is clear that the greater responsibilities and societal expectations regarding carework fall mostly on women's shoulders. My point in this paper is that the underestimation of female contributions to society through reproductive, emotional and care labour and the concomitant overevaluation of men's realms of influence have their mythic, psychological roots in the primal myths that circulate in and with which children are conditioned in patriarchal Western societies. Hence the importance of exposing and rewriting such myths operating in our deep unconscious.

3   See www.gifteconomy.org and www.akademia.Hagia for information and videoclips of the Peaceful Societies past and present conferences organized by Akademia Hagia.

4   According to William E. Phipps (1988,1976), the myths of Pandora and Eve are similar in that both attempt to explain why woman was created. Hesiod's poetry, entitled *Theogony* (507-616) and *Works and Days* (West 1985: 47-105), provides the only Greek source pertaining to woman's creation.

5   Pandora is in some versions portrayed as the product of Hephaestus' craft and Zeus's guile. Geyer Miller in "What is the Pandora Myth All About?" (1995) offers a version of Pandora in which she is clearly a trophy between warring male gods, providing an illustration of the "exchange economy" as an ideology adopted by men to trade in women and other resources (Vaughan 1997): "Prometheus (fore-thought) and his brother Epimetheus (after-thought) were Titans. Prometheus had remained neutral during the revolt of the Titans against the Olympians and thus had been admitted to the circle of Immortals by Zeus. Seeing that the race of men had been destroyed in the deluge, it was Prometheus who fashioned another prototype man, into whom Athena, the favored daughter of Zeus, breathed soul and life. As long as Cronus had reigned, gods and men had lived on terms of mutual understanding. In the cool of the evening the gods might wander down to earth and sit down together with men to partake of the supper. With the coming of the Olympians, everything changed. Zeus asserted his divine supremacy. Although Prometheus was now an Immortal he harboured a grudge against the destroyers and favoured mortals to the detriment of the gods. He tricked Zeus into choosing the fat-covered bones as the part of the sacrifice for the gods, leaving the best meat for mortals. Zeus, in his anger, withheld fire from man. Prometheus stole the forbidden fire and gave it to the mortals. Zeus, enraged, called for Hephaestus the forger. He bade him make a virgin woman of dazzling beauty equal to the Olympian goddesses. He requested all of the gods to bring her their especial gifts. *Her name was Pandora (anciently called Anesidor, which was one of the names of the earth-goddess), rich in gifts, the all-gifted* [my emphasis]. Zeus also ordered a large Pythos (casket) to be made in which were placed the Spites: Old Age, Labour, Sickness, Insanity, Vice, and Passion to plague mankind upon their release. Delusional Hope was placed in the jar to keep men from killing themselves in despair and escaping their full measure of suffering" (Geyer Miller 1995).

6   See also Kramarae and Treichler (1985), "Pandora."

7   The honey vase of gifts has indeed been transformed into the pot of poison, as even the etymology of the word Gift suggests (it has both meanings of gift and poison in German) (Vaughan 1997).

8   For an alternative view of Pandora, see Spretnak (1978) and Stone (1976).

9   To quote Goettner-Abendroth (2004): "Matriarchal women are managers and ad-

ministrators, who organise the economy not according to the profit principle, where an individual or a small group of people benefits; rather, the motivation behind their action is *motherliness.* The profit principle is an ego-centred principle, where individuals or a small minority take advantage of the majority of people. The principle of motherliness is the opposite, where altruism reigns and the well being of all is at the centre. It is at the same time a spiritual principle, which humans take from nature. Mother Nature cares for all beings, however different they may be. The same applies to the principle of motherliness: a good mother cares for all her children in spite of their diversity. Motherliness as an ethical principle pervades all areas of a matriarchal society, and this holds true for men as well. If a man of a matriarchal society desires to acquire status among his peers, or even to become a representative of the clan to the outside word, the criterion is "He must be like a good mother (Minangkabau, Sumatra)" (3).

10 Lauri Honko (1993) has elaborated in The Great Bear on Finno-Ugric festivities and reflects the Maussian view that behaviour at a feast was characterized by some element of competition between families and communities for whom the maintenance of good relations was important: "The act of hospitality central to festivals and feasts had two functions. On the one hand, it emphasized one's own social position and the status of guests in relation to it. On the other hand, acceptance of hospitality also assumed reciprocity and the guest inevitably had in mind his own forthcoming duties as host, while the host did not forget that it would soon be his turn to act as guest. In this social exchange, not only bonds between individuals but, above all, between groups were defined and strengthened. The host demonstrated his perception both of his own standing and that of his guest by his behaviour and the scale of his hospitality. Sometimes a host might deliberately use the occasion to enhance his own prestige and humble his guest either by exaggerated largesse or by deliberately offering less hospitality than custom required" (259).

11 The poems have been primarily collected from Juhana Kainulainen from a spell used in bathing a sick person: "Kaveh eukko, Luonnotar,/kaveh kultainen, koria" (*SKVR* VII 4, 1758: 90-91). Kave woman, golden, beautiful is implored with other forces to help the one to be bathed be relieved of his or her problem. Luonnotar sometimes also manifests as one of Tapio's daughters (Haavio 1967: 68; Krogerus 1999: 131).

12 Tuulikki Korpinen (1986) reveals through her study of Louhi's etymologies that her name has both the meaning of "flame" (Swedish låga) and lux (light), suggesting how patriarchy has turned this fiery bringer of light into a figure of death and darkness.

13 Iivar Kemppinen (1960), for example, analyzes the history of Finnish mythology and spiritual life and views the gradual replacement of the goddesses with the one god of resurrection as the Finn's heightened maturity and "development" towards a higher form of religion.

14 On Nordic mythology and goddesses from a feminist perspective see Sjoo (1985).

15 In Christian dualistic mythology women are not generally represented as belonging to the sky-world but are kept associated with the inferior "other" of the "masculine" mind (matter), spirit (body), or culture (nature). In the pre-patriarchal representation of the creative spirit women are images both of nature and culture, where such a dichotomy does not exist. The Luonnotar daughters can be associated with an alternative social order and alternative sex/gender system; after all, they create the products of "culture" such as iron out of maternal milk, expressing thereby an imaginary where maternity and the female breast are not restricted to their patriarchal functions: nurturing babies or being objects of the male erotic gaze, the fetishized breast. This

is one telling example of an alternative worldview or way of endowing prestige to social contributions. The above representation of the feminine is not dependent on an approving male order but is defined in relation to itself and its own values, e.g. the inherent value of women creating both life and technology.

16 "Using clay and water, he fashioned the beautiful artifice. The forges and fires of the earth are the artificial womb from which Pandora is born. This Hephaestian passion for creative expression is deeply of the mother. Pandora was not the product of a union with the masculine but through Hephaestus, the most primordial feminine influences of nature are mimicked and made real. In addition to the gift of life, Hephaestus fashioned a golden crown, which was placed on Pandora's head by Athene. On this shining masterpiece were carved all of the creatures of the land and sea. They were complete with voices and movement, an animated world of instinctual and natural energies. It was a crown for an earth goddess (Rhea Pandora), the first woman, Queen of nature, and a symbol of fertility and seasonal life" (Geyer Miller 1995: 2). As this quotation suggests, the earth goddess may well have affinities also with the Finnish Golden woman or Kave. In patriarchal lore, for instance the *Kalevala*, the Golden Woman is turned into a mere fantasy of the eternal smith and hammerer, Ilmarinen. Echoing the Greek Hephaistos, he is the prototype of the engineer-innovator-scientist who tries to reproduce through technology what he cannot own in a flesh-and-blood woman (Kailo 2002). Ilmarinen hammers for himself a kind of primitive cyberlady and exemplies the male effort to create through mechanistic means and machinery what men cannot bring to life in a womb. These efforts of "artificial insemination" or possible womb-envy projected into technological innovation and projected to the level of the nature/culture split and myth fail. The Golden Woman remains lifeless, as indeed are classic dualistic male fantasies of women. They are projections and hence cannot give life to women as complex humans beyond the restricting and unrealistic whore/madonna dualisms.

17 "The givers of gifts were living there and the old wives that give game lay just in their working dress, in their dirty ragged clothes. Even the forest's mistress too, the cruel mistress Kuurikki was very black in countenance, in appearance terrible; bracelets of withes were on her arms, on her fingers withy rings, with withy ribbons her head was bound, in withy ringlets were her locks, and withy pendants in her ears, around her neck were evil pearls. The evil mistress then, the cruel mistress Kuurikki was not disposed to give away, or inclined to helpfulness" (Abercromby, 1898: 179-180). As this description of Kuurikki and its broader context by Abercromby reveal, Mielikki and Kuurikki are not a separate good and bad goddess but two aspects of the same game-giving female haltia. For studies of Louhi see Nenola-Kallio and Timonen (1990); Siikala and Vakimo (1994) and Kailo, in English (e.g., 1996, 2000). Siikala (1986) discusses the connections between Louhi and words or etymologies connoting trance states, addressing the chthonic projections on Louhi as the mistress of the domain of death, the North and the otherworld

18 By "non-imaginary" originary meaning I refer to the postmodern insight that ultimately any one primal version is unknowable. To refer to origins is a "no-no" of postmodernism because such a quest presupposed unified origins and a linear history. While I embrace the constructivist nature of postmodern theory, I refer to originary meanings as part of a conscious strategic essentialist claim to a founding mythology aimed at empowering a group, in my case, women.

19 My source for the analysis of Kave/Louhi is the vast collections of folk material in the archives of the Finnish Literature Society in Helsinki, primarily the *Suomen Kansan*

Vanhat Runot (*SKVR*), plus the Finnish national epic, *Kalevala.*

[20] The sauna is at its best when bathed in meady vapours, and there is a *haltia* of beer, Osmotar, associated with the drink that raises spirits and energies (Kailo 2005a).

[21] She is best known through the Finnish *Kalevala*, an epic that is an appropriate *mise-en-abyme* of the tendencies persisting in literature on the North. The striking feature about these stories is that their representations of femininity and masculinity, male heroes and female anti-heroes could not be further removed from reality, in light of historical facts or contemporary developments (Kailo 2005b).

[22] See Sawin (1998) for an excellent feminist analysis of Louhi.

[23] As Myram Miedzien (1991) has demonstrated, there are numerous peaceful cultures, among them Indigenous nations that have been able to heal from a violence-based social structure. Goettner-Abendroth (2004) has also gathered proof of existing matriarchal social systems with little or no violence. It may be idealistic and naïve to argue that archaic societies or matriarchies were either peaceful or that aggression did not characterize humans at all times. However, it is necessary to distinguish between worldviews that have or have not sought to naturalize giving and a sustainable cultural, economic and biological order. If the peoples labelled as "noble savages" have never been simplistically noble, it is still of great significance that their worldview, if not all individuals, have more humane cooperative values built into their visions of life and way of living than is the case in today's dominant ethos of "each for his own."

[24] However, it is important to stress that feminist approaches to power emphasize power within and empowerment for all rather than power over.

References

Abercromby, John. 1898. *Pre- and Proto-historic Finns. Both Eastern and Western. With the Magic Songs of the West Finns.* London: np.

Anttonen, Veikko. 1992. "Interpreting Ethnic Categories Denoting 'Sacred' in a Finnish and an Ob-Ugrian Context." *Temenos* 28.

The Columbia Encyclopedia. 2001-05. Sixth ed. New York: Columbia University Press.

Douglas, Mary. 1996 [1966]. *Purity and Danger. An Analysis of the Concepts of Pollution and Taboo.* London: Routledge.

Eller, Cynthia. 1990. *Living in the Lap of the Goddess: The Feminist Spirituality Movement in America.* New York: Crossroad.

Encyclopædia Britannica 2002.

Geyer Miller, Sandra. 1995. "What is the Pandora Myth All About?" Online: http://www.support4change.com/general/women/pandora/myth.html.

Geyer Miller, Sandra. 1998. "Did Pandora Bring Trouble or Transformation for Women?" Online: http://www.learningplaceonline.com/change/women/pandora/myth.htm.

Goettner-Abendroth, Heide. 1995 [1980]. *The Goddess and her Heros.* Stow, MA: Anthony Publishing Company.

Goettner-Abedroth, Heide. 2004. "The Relationship between Modern Matriarchal Studies and the Gift Paradigm." Paper presented at the conference, "A Radically Different Worldview is Possible: The Gift Economy Inside and Outside Patriarchal Capitalism." Las Vegas County Library, Nov. 14-17. Online: http://www.gift-economy.com/athanor/5.html/ Date Accessed: 2 July 2005.

Goettner-Abendroth, Heide. 1987. *Matriarchal Mythology in Former Times and Today.* Trans. Heidi Goettner Abendroth with Lise Weil. Freedom, CA: Crossing Pamphlet.

Haavio, Martti. l967. *Suomalainen mytologia.* Helsinki: WSOY.

Harrison, Jane. l975. *Prolegomena to the Study of Greek Religion.* New York: Arno Press.

Hesiod. *Works and Days. 700 B.C.*

Honko, Lauri. 1993. "Festivities." Eds. Lauri Honko, Senni Timonen, Michael Branch. *The Great Bear: A Thematic Anthology of Oral Poetry in the Finno-Ugric Languages.* Pieksämäki: Suomen Kirjallisuuden Seura. 259-284.

Iglehart, Hallie. 1982. "Expanding Personal Power Through Meditation." *The Politics of Women's Spirituality. Essays on the Rise of Spiritual Power Within the Feminist Movement.* Ed. Charlene Spretnak. New York: Doubleday.

Kailo, Kaarina. 1987. "Emil Petaja's *Star Mill* and the Sampo's *Shifted Axis.*" *Ural-Altaic Yearbook/ Ural-Altaische Jahrbücher* 59: 107-117.

Kailo, Kaarina. 1996. "The Representation of Women and the Sami in the Finnish *Kalevala*: The Problem with the "Overlap(p)." *Simone de Beauvoir Institute Bulletin/Bulletin de l'Institut Simone de Beauvoir* 16: 33-49.

Kailo, Kaarina. 2000. "Monoculture, Gender and Nationalism: Kalevala as a Tool of Acculturation." *Ethical Challenges for Teacher Education and Teaching. Special Focus on Gender and Multicultural Issues.* Eds. Rauni Räsänen and Vappu Sunnari. Oulu: Acta Universitatis Ouluensis. 13–37

Kailo, Kaarina. 2002. "Sukupuoli, teknologia ja valta. Nais- ja miesrepresentaatiot Kalevalasta Ööpiseen." [Gender, Technology and Power: Female and Male Representations from Kalevala to Ööpinen]. Tieto ja tekniikka. Missä Nainen Toim, Riitta Smeds, Kaisa Kauppinen, Kati Yrjänheikki, Anitta Valtonen. Tekniikan Akateemisten liitto: TEK. 241-259.

Kailo, Kaarina. 2005a. "The Helka Fest: Traces of a Finno-Ugric Matriarchy and Worldview?" Paper presented at the World Congress on Matriarchal Studies, Societies of Peace. September 29-30, Austin, Texas.

Kailo Kaarina. 2005b. "Mythic Women of the North: Between Reality and Fantasy." *Northern Dimensions and Environments. Northern Sciences Review* Eds. Lassi Heininen, Kari Strand and Kari Taulavuori.Oulu: Thule Institute, University of Oulu. 2005b. 173-223.

Kailo, Kaarina. 2007. *The Gift Gaze: Wo(men) and Bears.* Toronto: Inanna Publications and Education.

Kemppinen, Iivar. 1960. *Suomalainen mytologia.* Helsinki: Kirja-mono Oy.

Korpinen, Tuulikki. 1986. *Sammon ainekset.* Helsinki: Heinola.

Korten, David. 1996. *When Corporations Rule the World. Towards a Green Revolution.* San Fransisco: Kumarian Press.

Kramarae, Cheris and Paula A. Treichler. 1985. *A Feminist Dictionary.* Boston: Pandora Press.

Krogerus, Tuulikki. 1999. *Kalevalan Hyvät ja Hävyttömät.* Eds. U. Piela, S. Knuuttila and T. Kupiainen. Helsinki: SKS.

Lorde, Audre. l984. *Sister Outsider: Essays and Speeches.* New York: Crossing Press.

Lönnrot, Elias. 1985 [1845]. *Kalevala, The Land of Heroe*s. Trans. W. F. Kirby. Intr. Michael Branch. London: Athlone Press.

Mäkinen, Kirsti. 2004. *Sammon sanat. Kalevalan sitaatteja.* Helsinki: Otava.

Meyer, Leroy N. and Tony Ramirez. 1996. "'Wakinyan Hotan'–The Thunder Beings Call Out: The Inscrutability of Lakota/Dakota Metaphysics." *From Our Eyes: Learning from Indigenous Peoples.* Ed. Sylvia O'Meara and Douglas A. West. Toronto: Garamond Press.

Nenola-Kallio, Aili and Timonen Senni. l990. *Louhen Sanat. Kirjoituksia kansanperinteen naisista.* Helsinki: SKS.

Miedzien, Myriam. 1991. *Boys Will Be Boys: Breaking the Link Between Masculinity and Violence.* New York: Anchor Books.

Niemi, Irmeli. 1985. "Kvinnorna i Kalevala." *Tr. J. O. Tallqvist. Nya Argus* 4 (April): 75-80.

Ochs, Carol. 1977. *Behind the Sex of God: Toward a New Consciousness: Transcending Matriarchy and Patriarchy.* Boston: Beacon Press.

Petaja, Emil. 1966. *The Saga of Lost Earths* and *the Star Mill.* New York: Daw Books, Inc.

Petaja, Emil. 1967. *The Stolen Sun* and *Tramontane.* New York: Daw Books, Inc.

Phipps, William E. 1988. "Eve and Pandora Contrasted." *Theology Today* 45 (1) (April). Online: http://theologytoday.ptsem.edu/apr1988/v45-1-article3.htm. Accessed August 10, 2006.

Phipps, William E. 1976. October. "Adam's Rib: Bone of Contention." *Theology Today* 33 (3) (October). Online: http://theologytoday.ptsem.edu/oct1976/v33-3-article5.htm. Accessed August 10, 2006.

Plumwood, Val. 1993. *Feminism and the Mastery of Nature.* New York: Routledge

Sawin, Patricia. 1988. "Lönnrot's Brain Children: The Representation of Women in Finland's *Kalevala.*" *Journal of Folklore Research* 5 (3): 187-217.

Siikala, Anna-Leena. l986. "Myyttinen Pohjola." *Kirjokannesta Kipinä. Kalevalan Juhlavuoden Satoa.* Helsinki: SKS.

Siikala, Anna-Leena and Sinikka Vakimo. 1994. *Songs Beyond the Kalevala: Transformations of Oral Poetry.* Tr. by Susan Sinisalo. Helsinki: SKS.

Sjoo, Monica. 1985. *The Goddess/es of the Northern Peoples.* Part I and II. London: Arachne.

Suomen Kansan Vanhat Runot (SKVR). Vol. I–XVIII. Suomalaisen Kirjallisuuden Seuran kansanrunousarkiston kokoelmat. Suomalaisen karhuperinteen primaarilähteet [Finnish Peoples' Ancient Poems and Foklore]. Suomen Kirjallisuuden Seura. Eds. Kaarle Krohn and V. Alava. Helsinki: SKS.

Spretnak, Charlene. 1978. *Lost Goddesses of Early Greece: A Collection of Pre-Hellenic Mythology.* Boston: Beacon Press.

Stone, Merlin. 1976. *When God Was a Woman.* New York: Barnes and Noble.

Vaughan, Genevieve. 1997. *For-Giving: A Feminist Criticism of Exchange. Foreword by Robin Morgan,* Texas: Plainview/Anomaly Press.

Walker, Barbara. 1983. *The Woman's Encyclopaedia of Myths and Secrets.* New York: Harper and Row.

Warren, K. J. 2000. *Ecofeminist Philosophy. A Western Perspective on What It Is and Why It Matters.* Rowman and Littlefield Publishers, Inc.

West, Martin Litchfield, ed. 1978. *Works and Days/Hesiod.* Oxford: Clarendon Press.

West, Martin Litchfield. 1985. *The Hesiodic Catalogue of Women: Its Nature, Structure, and Origins.* Oxford: Clarendon Press.

RAUNA KUOKKANEN

The Gift Logic of Indigenous Philosophies in the Academy

In this paper, I discuss how the logic of the gift embedded in Indigenous philosophies relates to the prevalent ignorance and benevolent imperialism of the academy. I suggest that there is a pressing need for a new paradigm in the academy; a paradigm based on the logic of the gift as understood in Indigenous thought. With the help of the notion of the gift, I argue that it is possible to envision alternative ways of perceiving and relating to previously marginalized epistemes in the academy. In short, we need to conceptualize a new logic that would make the academy more responsible and responsive in its pursuit of knowledge.

The logic of the gift articulated here foregrounds a new relationship characterized by reciprocity and a call for responsibility toward the "other." Thus far, much academic attention with regard to Indigenous peoples has focused on seeking to "acclimatize" Indigenous students to the university environment and academic culture. This approach is based on an implicit assumption that Indigenous people are in need of help. Further, these assumptions are premised on externalizing responsibility. Those who are ultimately responsible are always somewhere else.

Sami Worldview and Gift Practices

In Indigenous worldviews, the gift extends beyond interpersonal relationships to "all my relations."[1] Put another way, according to these philosophies, giving is an active relationship between human and natural worlds based on a close interaction of sustaining and renewing the balance between them through gifts.

Instead of viewing the gift as a form of exchange or as having only an economic function as many classic gift theories suggest, I propose that the gift is a reflection of a particular worldview characterized by a perception of the natural environment as a living entity which gives its gifts and abundance to people if it is treated with respect and gratitude (i.e., if certain responsibilities are observed). Central to this perception is that the world as a whole is constituted of an infinite web of relationships extended to and incorporated into the entire social condition of the individual. Social ties apply to everybody and everything, including the land. People are related to their physical and natural surroundings through genealogies, oral tradition and their personal and collective experiences pertaining to certain locations.

According to the traditional Sami perception of the world, like in many other Indigenous worldviews, the land is a physical and spiritual entity which humans are part of. Survival is viewed as dependent on the balance and renewal of the land, the central principles in this understanding are sustainable use of and respect for the natural realm. The relationship with the land is maintained by collective and individual rituals in which the gift and giving back are integral. The intimacy and interrelatedness is reflected in the way of communicating with various aspects of the land which often are addressed directly as relatives. The close connection to the natural realm is also evident in the permeable and indeterminate boundaries between the human and natural worlds. Skilled individuals can assume the form of an animal when needed and there are also stories about women marrying an animal (Porsanger 2004: 151-2).

An interesting, almost completely ignored aspect in the analyses of Sami cosmology and "religion" is the role of the female deities in giving the gift of life (to both human beings and domestic animals, mainly reindeer) and the connection to the land. One could suggest that the Sami deity Máttáráhkká with her three daughters signified the very foundation in the Sami cosmic order. Máttáráhkká could be translated as "Earthmother" (the root word *máttár* refers to earth and also to ancestors). Moreover, words for "earth" and "mother" in the Sami language also derive from the same root (*eanan* and *eadni* respectively). The role of women and female deities in Sami cosmology and the world order of giving and relations is a neglected area of study. Máttáráhkká and her three daughters are the deities of new life who convey the soul of a child, create its body and also assist with menstruation, childbirth and protection of children. In spite of the fact that the most significant gift or all, a new life, is the duty of these female deities, they have, in ethnographic literature, often been relegated to a mere status of wives of male deities. This reflects the common patriarchal bias of ethnographic interpretations of cultural practices.

Traditionally, one of the most important ways to maintain established relations and the socio-cosmic order has been the practice of giving to various *sieidis*. *Sieidi* is a sacred place to which the gift is given to thank certain spirits for the abundance in the past but also to ensure fish, hunting and reindeer luck in the future. Although the several centuries' long influence of Christianity has severely eroded the Sami gift-giving to and sharing with the land by banning it as a pagan form of devil worshipping, there is a relatively large body of evidence that the practice of *sieidi* gifting is still practiced (Kjellström 1987; see also Juuso 1998: 137).

I argue that contrary to conventional interpretations, giving to *sieidi* cannot be completely understood through the concept of sacrifice. Even if *sieidi* gifts do have aspects of sacrifice, they are not and should not be regarded solely as such. They may have other dimensions that can be as significant—if not more so—as the aspect of sacrifice. Bones are given back, the catch shared and reindeer given to the gods and goddesses of hunting, fishing and reindeer luck represented by *sieidi* sites as an expression of gratitude for their goodwill and for ensuring abundance also in the future. In this sense, giving to *sieidis* appears involuntary as it is done for the protection and security of both the individual and the community.

The Academy and the Reproduction of the Values of the Exchange Paradigm

The university remains a contested site where not only knowledge but also middle-class with its eurocentric, patriarchal and (neo)colonial values are produced and reproduced. As Althusser and others have exposed, the academy is one of the main sites of reproduction of hegemony. Not surprisingly, then, the studied silence and willed indifference around the "Indigenous" continues unabated in most academic circles. In the same way as Indigenous people remained invisible in shaping and delineating of the nation-states in the "New World" (see Hall 2003, 66), Indigenous scholarship remains invisible and unreflected even in discourses of western radical intellectuals. The politics of disengagement rooted in hegemonic forms of reason combined with the corporatization of basic values—accumulation of intellectual capital, competitive self-interestedness—deter many self-identified critics of hegemonic discourses from seriously committing themselves in elaboration of alternatives or engaging in the slow and demanding process of "ethical singularity" (Spivak 1999: 384). In the spirit of the times, they count upon the revolution—a sudden rupture that appears from nowhere without much effort. Val Plumwood (2002) has pointed out the critical but usually hidden relationship between power and disengagement:

> Power is what rushes into the vacuum of disengagement; the fully "impartial" knower can easily be one whose skills are for sale to the highest bidder, who will bend their administrative, research and pedagogical energies to wherever the power, prestige and funding is. Disengagement then carriers a politics, although it is a paradoxical politics in which an appearance of neutrality conceals capitulation of power. (43)

The reality remains, as Gayatri Spivak reminds us, that mind-changing requires patience and painstaking attempts of learning to learn: "The tempo of learning to learn from this immensely slow temporizing will not only take us clear out of diasporas, but will also yield no answers or conclusions readily" (Spivak 1990). "Instant fix" models or reductionist sloganeering are simply not going to deliver the transformation. "Feel-good" transformation that does not address complexities or multiple realities and challenges will not get us very far. We must be able to see how cynicism and nihilism are not only counterproductive but serves the interests of power. Cynical attitudes particularly common among male intellectuals that suggest that envisioning alternatives is too idealistic only serves the hegemonic structures by creating new and sustaining old hierarchies and relations of power. Peter McLaren (1995) urges intellectuals and educators to deprivilege cynicism "in favor of a will to dream and act upon such dreams" (56).

Another contemporary reality is that, as the pervasive economic globalization has painfully demonstrated, sites of separatism are no longer possible. In a way or another, all societies and communities are affected by the forces of globalization that eliminate borders of all kinds. The pervasive nature of neoliberal corporate mentality is also reflected in the (willy-nilly) adopting much of its values. Particularly relevant in this context is the externalization of social responsibility. It seems that the corporate ethos according to which social responsibility is considered a distortion of business principles (Bakan 2004) is also increasingly influencing the academy, where even "revolutionary scholars" prefer to point fingers and disavow their own personal social responsibilities. One repeatedly hears that we need alternatives and that we have to start creating them, but very few in fact get beyond that point.

Why, then, more academics are not envisioning alternatives? A brief visit to recent conferences in numerous fields and disciplines show that most scholars, including some Indigenous intellectuals, are content to limit their thinking within existing, hegemonic paradigms and become satisfied in asking complacent questions such as "minimum requirements" for our participation in current structures. Ironically, those who do not limit themselves to telling others to create alternatives and new visions but attempt to elaborate them are ridiculed as utopian and idealistic even by those who call for alternatives. Maria Mies (1998) suggests:

> The difficulty of even thinking of an alternative in our industrial societies is due partly to the concept of linear progress which dominates Eurocentric thought. People cannot understand that "going back" and looking for what was better in the past, or in non-industrialized societies, might be a creative method of transcending the impasse in which our societies are stranded.... They are also reluctant to step out of their given mindset and dream of another paradigm, unless they are offered a fully fledged model of another economy. They fear to join a process, which is already under way, and contribute their own creativity and energy. They want security before they step out of their old house. (xvii)

The reality is that we have to have the courage to start from the scratch and participate in an on-going, unfinished process. Suggesting, as some academics have done, that we need to learn from the New Right because their strategies seem to work is not going to get us anywhere. One quickly learns that fabricating lies, manipulating fear, manufacturing myths and hostility toward the other in the name of uniting the nation and at the end, believing in these myths themselves is not going to teach us very much else than how utterly corrupt, savage and unconscionable the New Right is. It is impossible build viable alternatives with these tactics. Moreover, considering how the general spirit of distrust and disillusionment generated particularly by the Right appears to have affected also the spirit of much of the Left, it is clear that we do not need to learn from the Right. In our search for teachers and sources of learning, we need to look elsewhere, scratch the surface deeper and broaden our horizons beyond the Right and Left. We need to start learning from the Gift. As Spivak (1999) states:

> There is an alternative vision of the human: those who have stayed in place for more than thirty thousand years.... Yet here too lies the experience of the impossible that will have moved capital persistently from self to other—economic growth as cancer to redistribution as medicine: *pharmakon*. (402)

Scholarly "Give Back"

A central principle of Indigenous philosophies, "giving back" also forms the backbone of current research conducted by many Indigenous scholars and students. It expresses a strong commitment and desire to ensure that academic knowledge, practices and research are no longer used as a tool of colonization and as a way exploiting Indigenous peoples by taking (or as it is often put, stealing) their knowledge without ever giving anything back in return. After centuries of being studied, measured, categorized and represented to serve various colonial interests and purposes, many Indigenous peoples now require that research dealing with Indigenous issues has to emanate from the needs and concerns of Indigenous communities instead of those of an individual researcher or the dominant society. Indigenous research ethics assert the expectations of academics—both Indigenous and non-Indigenous—to "give back," to conduct research that has positive outcome and is relevant to Indigenous peoples themselves (e.g., Battiste 2000: xx; Smith 1999: 15)

The principle of "giving back" in research—whether it is reporting back, sharing the benefits, bringing back new knowledge and vital information to the community, or taking the needs and concerns of the people into account—is part of the larger process of decolonizing colonial structures and mentality and restoring Indigenous societies.

Besides generating respectful and responsible scholarship, the recognition of the gift of Indigenous epistemes also provides it with a deeper, more informed understanding of contemporary Indigenous-state (or the dominant society) relations manifested in numerous and complex ways as well as of the different perceptions of the world which emphasize the relationship between human beings and the natural environment. Considering the destructive agendas of unlimited economic growth based on prevailing neoliberal, global capitalist and patriarchal paradigms labelled as "free trade" and commodification of all life forms is yet another reason for the academy and the mainstream society at large to recognize and become cognizant of the main principles in Indigenous philosophies.

At the same time, we need to remain vigilant of patriarchal, masculinist mechanisms of control that also exist within contemporary Indigenous scholarship. As a young Indigenous woman and junior academic, I have experienced the old boys" network functioning in most unexpected academic spaces and learned that in some cases, male-bonding and solidarity with other male academics is far greater than the unity of "Indigenous peoples' front" in working towards transformation and decolonization of our peoples and societies. Here of course lies the irony of the double standard—this is the very same front that is considered threatened when Indigenous women concur with feminist analysis and build alliances with non-Indigenous women and feminists. Yet more than once Indigenous women scholars have been faced with the male mechanisms of control which seek to silence and keep women, including young Indigenous women, in their place and stop them stepping on the toes of the authorities. These incidents have made it clear that if we adhere to these male mechanisms of control, we as Indigenous female scholars are allowed and can be critical only within carefully defined parameters.

The Future of the Academy and the Recognition of the Gift

I contend that the future of the academy is dependent on the recognition of the gift of Indigenous epistemes—recognition as understood within the logic of the gift that foregrounds the responsibility in the name of the well-being of all. As in Indigenous epistemes, the future of the academy is dependent on its ability to create and sustain appropriate reciprocal relationships grounded on action and knowledge. In other words, recognizing the gift requires acquiring and adopting a new logic that is grounded on the responsibility toward the other that is defined as the ability and willingness to reciprocate at the epistemic level, not only at the level of human interaction. The call for the recognition of the gift of Indigenous epistemes is a call for an epistemic shift grounded on a specific philosophy and as such, a more profound transformation than efforts toward the inclusive university seeking to "democratize" the traditionally Eurocentric curriculum and the canon. In the discourse of inclusion, the paradigm—the mode of thinking and relating, the relationship—remains unchanged as a one-way relationship where the flow of knowledge is always unilateral (and thus hegemonic), whether from Indigenous people to the academy (the scene of the native informant) or from the academy to Indigenous people (the scene of Eurocentric, hegemonic intellectual foundations of the institution).

The gift logic necessitates mind-changing—opening up to a new way of seeing and conceptualizing knowledge as well as our relationships and responsibilities. As such, it also exceeds analyses put forth by advocates of critical pedagogy. Cultivating critical thinking and social responsibility, critical pedagogy emphasizes the political and emancipatory nature of education. Many also advocate "revolutionary critical pedagogy" that foregrounds the social class and is informed by Marxist theories. For the most part, however, critical pedagogy is a white, male discourse and thus, not necessarily emancipatory for many other groups and individuals (Ellsworth 1989). In its articulation of the primacy of the social class or the processes of democratization, revolutionary critical pedagogy also usually ignores the fundamental question of expropriation of Indigenous peoples lands and territories (see also Grande 2000: 51). Scholars of critical theory and pedagogy are apt to note how capitalism would not be possible without the unpaid work of slaves, people of colour and women, but there is again a studied silence about the usurpation of Indigenous lands. Perhaps it is strategic forgetfulness to ignore "the historical facts which are for many hard to swallow"—that at best, the Anglo-American is a guest on this continent, and at worst, the United States of America is founded upon stolen land" (Silko 1980: 215).

The concept of revolution is inconsistent with the logic of the gift. Revolution is always predicated of violence of some sorts, whether physical, overt violence or more subtle forms such as structural, symbolic, or even epistemic. Revolutions take place to overthrow oppressive, hegemonic regimes. Further, observing the recent discourses of revolution by both the Right and the Left has left me somewhat wary of the potential of revolutions. If the neoconservatives can view themselves as revolutionary in their myth-making and battle against the evil in the name of saving the "nation," revolution has literally come too close to terror and hegemony. In such revolution, there simply can be no liberation for the majority of the world's population. Revolutions are also marked by the gender bias which merely reproduces patriarchal, hierarchical models as the ideals for new sovereignty (see Spivak 1985). As Maria Mies and Veronika Bennholdt-Thomsen note, "[a]fter so many failed or abrogated revolutions, we no longer have confidence in the power which comes out of barrels of the guns of the international warriors" (1999: 120).

Yet another reason for not having faith in revolutions is because no transformation takes place if we are incapable of getting beyond the language of aggression. As we know, language mirrors but also constructs our reality and thus our values. We do not need replication and reinforcement of the language of violence, we need a language of new possibilities. Instead of opposition, we need participation and commitment. The logic of the gift that compels us to reconsider concepts such as responsibility, recognition and reciprocity. This does not mean that Marxist analysis and critique is no longer needed. There is no doubt that epistemic ignorance is sanctioned in the interest of global capitalist relations. But instead of relying on one theory and expect it to do all the work, we have to recognize that no theory alone can deliver change or do the job single-handedly. This is also where our intellectual maturity may begin—when we stop engaging in wholesale dismissals of useful tools called theories without first doing our homework.

I have also called attention to the fact that Indigenous epistemes cannot be recognized as a gift within the prevailing neocolonial, global capitalist system. The language and values of exchange market economy and male rationality have permeated all spheres of life, including the way academics view their responsibilities. Moreover, universities are increasingly run like corporations and are marked by the values of neoliberal ideologies. This directly and indirectly affects to what is considered important and relevant in teaching and learning. By counting on the wealth and profit the gift or aspects of it such as "traditional knowledge" can generate for the advancement of the academy, this system only exploits and commodifies the gift by perceiving it as part of the exchange economy. In this system, knowledge is being commercialized—a trend reflected, for example, in the view of Joseph Stiglitz for whom knowledge is a global public good capable of producing benefits and "one of the keys to development" (1999: 320). The idea of the recognition of the gift challenges this ideology embedded in the current trend of universities on the road of "becoming corporate institutions motivated by profit-thinking" along the lines "[t]he more money one attracts, the more one is "excellent" (Kailo 2000: 65; see also Findlay 2000: 312).

Further, the concept of epistemic ignorance seeks to pave way to a new language that exceeds cultural discontinuity theories and analyses. Epistemic ignorance refers to the predominant, general resistance to, indifference and lack of recognition and knowledge of Indigenous worldviews and discursive practices in the academy. The concept assists to expose practices of active and passive "not-knowing" and mechanisms of exclusion in the academy which ensure that the gift remains impossible. However, it is clear that academy is not only benevolently ignorant but also in many ways, adamantly opposes Indigenous epistemes because they do not conform their learned views about the world, knowledge and rationality. Therefore, epistemic ignorance does not only refer to innocent not-knowing but also structures of power, ideologies that seek to maintain status quo, consolidate native informants and keep them in the academic reservations.

Instead of focussing on the question of what needs to be done for Indigenous people in the academy, we need to hold the academy responsible for its ignorance and therefore, for its homework. Creating Indigenous spaces and asserting their voices in the academy is an insufficient measure because these gestures do not guarantee that Indigenous people can speak or are heard and understood by the academy. The historic, cultural and social foundations of the academy continue to be informed by patriarchal and colonial discourses and practices, resulting in a situation where "[t]he conditions of intellectual life are circumscribed by these assumptions and practices" (Green 2002: 88). In addition to the conditions of intellectual life, also what is being heard is confined and defined by these parameters. Due to the selective, rarefied intellectual foundations of the academy, those coming from other epistemic traditions are either forced to "transcode" their systems of knowing and perceiving the world into the dominant ones or simply remain "unheard" or misunderstood.

What is urgently needed is an unconditional welcome and openness to the "other" epistemes in such a way that "translation" of these epistemes is not a prerequisite to be welcomed to the academy. The questions that we need to ask include: how to move beyond the pervasive and widely sanctioned benign neglect? How to transform mere tolerance to engagement and to active participation in the logic of the gift?

Epistemic ignorance, however, is not only an "Indigenous problem." It is also a problem of higher education at large for it seriously threatens and limits "free and fearless" intellectual inquiry and pursuit of knowledge. Beyond the academy, it is a problem of entire society. With the current suicidal economic priorities and destructive values, what is at stake is the long-term survival of everyone. Therefore, the problem of epistemic ignorance in the academy or elsewhere in society is not solved by adding "Native content" in curriculum or incorporating the "Indigenous" in critical pedagogy. Calls for raising awareness and increasing knowledge are not new—they can be found in almost any list of recommendations dealing with education and Indigenous peoples. In Canada, for instance, they are among the core recommendations in the *Report of the Royal Commission on Aboriginal Peoples* in 1996 and reiterated in the more recent report, *Learning About Walking in Beauty: Placing Aboriginal Perspectives in Canadian Classrooms* in 2002.

I argue that in the academy, Indigenous epistemes need to be recognized as a gift according to the principles of responsibility and reciprocity that foreground the logic of the gift. The recognition called for here, however, is of a specific kind. It is not limited to the often fleeting moment of recognizing diversity in terms of "other" identities and cultures associated with multiculturalism but as I propose, it stems from an understanding grounded in the logic of the gift. This recognition requires knowledge but also commitment, action and reciprocity—one must take action according to responsibilities that characterize that particular relationship. As the various gifts of the land cannot be taken for granted in this logic—if they are, the balance of the world which life depends on is disrupted—the gift of Indigenous epistemes cannot be neglected. If they are, the university has failed its profession. As the gifts of the land have to be actively recognized by expressions of gratitude and giving back, the gift of Indigenous epistemes must be acknowledged by reciprocating which includes the ability to understand not only the gift itself but also the logic of the gift behind it.

Changing our mindsets to the logic of the gift is a challenging, interminable process that requires a strong commitment to hospitality and a sense of responsibility toward the "other" on the academy's part. Rather than simply comprehending otherness, it is a matter of recognizing agency of the other (see Spivak 1995b: 182). Knowing (about) other cultures or epistemes will never alone erase systemic inequalities and disparate relations of power and privilege in the academy or elsewhere in society. This is why the academy must be called into action by an unfaltering commitment to responsibility and reciprocity as discussed above. Echoing Spivak's words, my work makes "a plea for the patient work of learning to learn from below—a species of "reading', perhaps—how to mend the torn fabric of subaltern ethics..." (Spivak 2001: 15).

This plea is not romanticizing: "What we are dreaming of here is not how to keep the tribal in a state of excluded cultural conformity but how to construct a sense of sacred Nature which can help mobilize a general ecological mind-set beyond the reasonable and self-interested grounds of long-term global survival" (Spivak 1995a: 199). This mobilization, however, does not imply taking the easy but irresponsible step across the threshold of embracing a "land ethic" or the logic of the gift, for that matter, without addressing the contemporary realities of Indigenous peoples. Nor it involves viewing Indigenous peoples as "nature folk" and picking and choosing aspects of Indigenous cultures according to the personal preference and need. It is not a call for simply paying tribute to Indigenous peoples and their land-centered practices or for merely employing them as inspirational symbols without knowing and acting upon one's responsibilities as required by the logic of the gift.

Superficial cultivation of short-lived references to Indigenous peoples' relationship with the land has nothing to do with the logic of the gift. Rather, they only romanticize and perpetuate persistent stereotypes with regard to "tradition" versus "contemporary." The gift has to be read in its various contexts and one of the sites is the academy. Neither various gift practices nor the logic of the gift can be rendered as belonging only to "archaic" or "traditional" societies. The logic of the gift remains central in Indigenous epistemes. We are all contemporaries although some of us may have different ways of perceiving and relating to the world.

A commitment to openness and learning to learn will hopefully also assist people in the academy to see the links between issues such as the logic of the gift and contemporary land rights of Indigenous peoples—a question that, from the perspective of the dominant, often appears controversial, problematic and above all, political. The gift is a reflection of a worldview that emphasizes the maintenance of good relationships with the land. If there is no land to have a relationship with—that is, if the land is expropriated or used for other, more "profitable" purposes, whether in the name of civilization or globalized economy—not only the gift is made impossible but also the survival of the people is impossible. In other words, the subordination of the rights of peoples to the global "imperatives" of capital and profit does the same job as the earlier anti-potlatch law and other policies and measures of banning cultural practices of Indigenous peoples. The Bretton Woods institutions effectively continue the legacy of colonization and assimilation by making the conditions of the gift and other practices impossible. To turn Pierre Bourdieu's theory of gift practices upside down: it is not the gift, but WTO, that is the most effective form of symbolic violence. The WTO *is* the new "anti-potlatch law" (see, for example, Bracken 1997; Cole and Chaikin 1990). Therefore, the bottom line is to change the values and thinking behind these values because—as Indigenous people in particular know—otherwise we kill the planet and ourselves with it.

The gift is a wakeup call to the academy and society at large. It is a collective vision for a common future that is more reasonable—if we recall, the non-hegemonic form of reason implies the ability to receive—as well as a more sustainable and just society. The gift is not only about applying new tools for teaching as sometimes suggested. The logic of the gift is not merely settling with minimum requirements within existing paradigms, nor is it just about "Indigenous voices" in the academy. It is a much more fundamental transformation of mindsets and values with a measure of creativity and radical break with previous practices. This transformation goes beyond incorporation of subjugated knowledge in the margins of an intact core of the knowledge. It is a radical change in the way academics, students, administrators and others in the academy perceive the role and nature of "other" epistemes. As Luce Irigaray (1985) contends, there cannot be change in the real without a concurrent change in the imaginary. As long as the mainstream western society is dominated by a destructive imaginary, change is simply impossible.

The heart of the logic of the gift lays in the conceptual push to reimagine the academy as a site of responsibilities where epistemic reciprocation occurs. There is no single mode how this can be done. Rather, the logic of the gift is embedded in a practice that takes into account the multiplicities and specificities of each individual context. The very core of the gift logic is that there is not a single set of practices—this is evident in the multiplicity of gift practices of Indigenous peoples. The logic is shared but the practices vary from a context and situation to another. The intellectual maturity starts when we recognize that there is no one magic way, only the on-going active participation of everybody and endless ways of reciprocating, receiving the gift and taking responsibility. The logic of the gift cannot and should not be reduced "to a congerie of prescribed methods and techniques that sacrifice theory and reflection at the altar of high priests and prophets of practice" (McLaren and Farahmandpur 2005: 7). Advocates of "concrete solutions" who separate practice from theory are misguided in their dualistic mindsets and hyperseparation that reflects the ingrained modern consciousness, only reinforcing the politics of disengagement. As we can see in the relationship between the philosophy and the multiplicity of practices of the gift, theory and practice are inseparable and overlapping, one informing the other. For those, who are not sure how to practice the logic of the gift, one place to start looking is the gift giving practices themselves. Another place is self-reflection: How can we collectively and individually start transforming our values so that they would better reflect the basic principles of the gift logic, participation and reciprocation—the conditions of being human? How can we practice these principles in our work, research, teaching and daily academic life? What do we need to learn to ensure that Indigenous epistemes "can speak'? At the same time, we need to continue critiquing the patriarchal global capitalism and its values in the academy and engage in lesser used strategy of social justice—practising and living our alternatives—the gift logic, for instance—also in the academy.

This article is based on my forthcoming book, Reshaping the University: Responsibility, Indigenous Epistemes and the Logic of the Gift *(University of British Columbia Press, 2007).*

Rauna Kuokkanen is Associate Professor of Pedagogy and Indigenous Studies at the Sami University College, Guovdageaidnu/Kautokeino (Norway). She holds a Ph.D. on Education from the University of British Columbia (Vancouver, Canada) and an MA on Comparative Literature (University of British Columbia) and on Sami Language and Literature (University of Oulu, Finland). She has published articles on Indigenous research paradigms, education and critical theory, Indigenous literature, the gift paradigm, and globalization and Indigenous women. Her current research examines the intersections of autonomy, violence, and political economy in the context of Indigenous women. She was the founding chair of the Sami Youth Organization in

Finland, established in 1991, and has served as the Vice-President of the Sami Coun-cil. Currently she is a member of the Board of Directors of Terralingua, International Organization for Protection of Biocultural Diversity, and a member of the Call of the Earth Circle, Indigenous Peoples' Initiative on Intellectual Property Policy.

Notes

1   The expression "All my relations" (or "all my relatives") is commonly used as a way of concluding a prayer, speech or piece of writing by North American Indigenous people, reflecting the underpinning philosophy of the interconnectedness of all life (e.g., Vine 1996). In the introduction of an anthology of the same name, the editor Thomas King writes that besides reminding us of our various relationships, it is also "an encouragement for us to accept the *responsibilities* we have within this universal family…" (1990: ix). Moreover, as Deloria contends, the phrase "describes the episte-mology of the Indian worldview, providing the methodological basis for the gathering of information about the world" (Deloria, Foehner and Scinta 1999: 52).

References

Bakan, Joel. 2004. *The Corporation: The Pathological Pursuit of Profit and Power.* Toronto: Viking Canada.

Battiste, Marie. 2000. "Introduction: Unfolding the Lessons of Colonization." *Reclaim-ing Indigenous Voice and Vision.* Ed. Marie Battiste. Vancouver: University of British Columbia Press. xvi-xxx.

Bourdieau, Pierre. 1997. "Selections from the Logic of Practice." *The Logic of the Gift: Toward an Ethic of Generosity.* Ed. Alan Schrift. New York: Routledge. 190-230.

Bracken, Christopher. 1997. *The Potlatch Papers. A Colonial Case History.* Chicago: Uni-versity of Chicago Press.

Cole, Douglas and Ira Chaikin. 1990. *An Iron Hand Upon the People: The Law Against the Potlatch on the Northwest Coast.* Vancouver: Douglas and McIntyre.

Deloria, Barbara, Kristen Foehner and Sam Scinta, eds. 1999. *Spirit and Reason: The Vine Deloria, Jr., Reader.* Golden, CO: Fulcrum.

Deloria, Vine, Jr. 1996. "If You Think About It, You Will See That It Is True." *ReVision* 18 (3): 37-44.

Ellsworth, Elizabeth. 1989. "Why Doesn't This Feel Empowering? Working Though the Re-pressive Myths of Critical Pedagogy." *Harvard Educational Review* 59 (3): 297-324.

Findlay, Len. 2000. "Always Indigenize! The Radical Humanities in the Postcolonial Canadian University." *Ariel* 31 (1&2): 307-26.

Grande, Sandy. 2000. "American Indian Identity and Intellectualism: The Quest for a New Red Pedagogy." *International Journal of Qualitative Studies in Education* 13 (4): 343-60.

Green, Joyce. 2002. "Transforming at the Margins of the Academy." *Women in the Cana-dian Academic Tundra: Challenging the Chill.* Eds. Elena Hannah, Linda Paul and Swani Vethamany-Globus. Toronto: McGill-Queen's University Press. 85-91.

Hall, Anthony. 2003. *The American Empire and the Fourth World.* Montreal: McGill-Queen's University Press.

Irigaray, Luce. 1985. *This Sex Which Is Not One.* Trans. C. Porter and C. Burke. Ithaca:

Cornell University Press.

Juuso, Inga. 1998. "Yoiking Acts as Medicine for Me." *No Beginning No End. The Sami Speak Up*. Eds. Elina Helander and Kaarina Kailo. Edmonton: Canadian Circumpolar Institute/Nordic Sami Institute. 132-46.

Kailo, Kaarina. 2000. "From Ivory Tower to Menstruation Hut: How Women's Studies Challenges Academic Culture." *Simone De Beauvoir Institute Review* 18/19: 61-74.

King, Thomas. 1990. "Introduction." *All My Relations. An Anthology of Contemporary Canadian Native Fiction*. Ed. Thomas King. Toronto: McClelland and Stewart. ix-xvi.

Kjellström, Rolf. 1987. "On the Continuity of Old Saami Religion." *Saami Religion*. Ed. Tore Ahlbäck. Åbo: The Donner Institute for Research in Religious and Cultural History. 24-33.

Learning About Walking in Beauty: Placing Aboriginal Perspectives in Canadian Classrooms. 2002. Ottawa: The Coalition for the Advancement of Aboriginal Studies and the Canadian Race Relations Foundation.

McLaren, Peter. 1995. *Critical Pedagogy and Predatory Culture. Oppositional Politics in a Postmodern Era*. New York: Routledge.

McLaren, Peter, and Ramin Farahmandpur. 2005. *Teaching Against Global Capitalism and the New Imperialism. A Critical Pedagogy*. Lanham: Rowman and Littlefield Publishers.

Mies, Maria. 1998. *Patriarchy and Accumulation in the World Scale: Women in the International Division of Labour*. London: Zed Books.

Mies, Maria and Veronika Bennholdt-Thomsen. 1999. *The Subsistence Perspective: Beyond the Globalized Economy*. Trans. Patrick Camiller, Marie Mies and Gerd Weih. London: Zed Books.

Plumwood, Val. 2002. *Environmental Culture. The Ecological Crisis of Reason*. New York: Routledge.

Porsanger, Jelena. 2004. "A Close Relationship to Nature—the Basis of Religion." Trans. Kaija Anttonen and Linna Weber Müller-Wille. *Siiddastallan. From Lapp Communities to Modern Sámi Life*. Eds. Jukka Pennanen and Klemetti Näkkäläjärvi. Inari: Siida Inari Sámi Museum, 151-4.

Royal Commission on Aboriginal Peoples. 1996. *Gatheirng Strength: The Report of the Royal Commission on Aboriginal Peoples*. Ottawa: Canada Communication Group.

Silko, Leslie Marmon. 1980. "An Old-Time Indian Attack Conducted in Two Parts: Part One: Imitation 'Indian'; Part Two: Gary Snyder's 'Turtle Island'." *The Remembered Earth*. Ed. Geary Hobson. Albuquerque: University of New Mexico Press. 211-16.

Smith, Linda Tuhiwai. 1999. *Decolonizing Methodologies. Research and Indigenous Peoples*. London: Zed Books.

Spivak, Gayatri Chakravorty. 1999. *A Critique of Postcolonial Reason: Toward a History of the Vanishing Present*. Cambridge, Mass.: Harvard University Press.

Spivak, Gayatri Chakravorty. 2001. "A Note on the New International." *Parallax* 7 (3): 12-16.

Spivak, Gayatri Chakravorty. 1995a. "Afterword." Trans. Chakravorty Gayatri Spivak. *Imaginary Maps. Three Stories*. Ed. Mahasweta Devi. New York: Routledge. 197-205.

Spivak, Gayatri Chakravorty. 1995b. "Teaching for the Times." *The Decolonization of Imagination. Culture, Knowledge and Power*. Eds. Jan Nederveen Pieterse and Bhikhu Parekh. London: Zed Books. 177-202.

Spivak, Gayatri Chakravorty. 1985. "Three Women's Texts and a Critique of Imperialism." *Critical Inquiry* 12: 243-61.

Stiglitz, Joseph. 1999. "Knowledge as a Global Public Good." *Global Public Goods: International Cooperation in the 21st Century*. Eds. Inge Kaul, Isabelle Grunberg and Marc

VICKI NOBLE

She Gives the Gift of Her Body

The archetype of selfless or altruistic giving—without attachment to outcome or any concept of "reciprocity"—belongs originally and most fully to the Goddess, the Great Mother of All Things. Whether we see it in the bountiful harvests of the agricultural fields of Mother Earth, or the life-giving nurturance of a mother's body supporting a pregnancy and nursing her baby, "the feminine force is active and life-producing" (Gimbutas 1999: 8). The female body in ancient times was perceived as "parthenogenetic, that is, creating life out of itself" (Gimbutas 1999: 112). As creator of the universe, known scientifically as the "Big Bang," her boundless creativity gave rise to the endless and diverse forms found in Nature whose beauty is impossible to replicate and whose primary expression is unceasing, dynamic, cyclic growth—birth, death, and regeneration. I see the Goddess as a great spider spinning the world from her center, patiently reweaving the web of life again and again, through eons and ages. This cyclic continuity should be enough to give us hope in our current situation, no matter how bad it gets.

First Woman and the Gift of Life

Since the first vulvas were inscribed on cave walls and rock outcroppings tens of thousands of years ago, the female has been formally imaged as gift-giver par excellence. In Australian rock art, she is known as "First Woman." The gift she gives, of life and all that sustains it, made a lasting impression on early humans coming to consciousness, beginning to express themselves through language and art. So-called "Venus" figures from the Eurasian Paleolithic period, with their huge breasts and buttocks emphasized over any distinguishing personal features, demonstrate the acknowledged gift-giving capacity of the ancestral matrix figure later to be called Great Mother, Mother Earth, Pachamama. The vulva—that sacred doorway—was the original glyph of the human species becoming literate as far back as 30,000 years ago. It is a sign expressing gratitude, reverence, and awe toward the female body and its marvelous ability to create life, sustain it, and even—in death, as Mother Earth—to receive it back. Vulvas carved in rocks and painted on walls all over North and South America are known to have been used for female blood mysteries and "puberty rites" since the most ancient times (Marshack 1991). Images of females dance among the pregnant animals that predominate in caves and rock shelters used by humans during the Ice Ages (Bahn 1997 [1988]). The female mysteries of periodicity and nature were at the center of whatever religious rites were practiced by early humans, whose lunar menstrual calendars document their interest in cyclic reality (Marshack 1991). Upright, our ancestors walked out of Africa and journeyed east and west, bringing their metaphorical "Dark Mother" with them, and eventually peopling vast continents (Birnbaum 2001). The first acts of human worship appear to have been in honour of this original ancestress, the Mother of Life, inside of whose mystery we had awakened to ourselves. Tens of thousands of years later, clan structure is still organized around the mother of an extended household in modern matriarchal societies, such as the Mosuo in China or the Maninkabau in Indonesia, where she is perceived as the central "pillar" of the home (Sanday 2002).

At the end of the last Ice Age, the weather warmed over much of the planet and our ancestors left their caves. Many of them developed the ability to settle, grow food, and domesticate animals. Cultivation, rather than being a sudden "revolution" as once thought, apparently unfolded in a fairly natural way from the sophisticated gathering that had gone on for millennia. (Harris 1996) The development of agriculture marks the beginning of the Neolithic period around 10,000 years ago. One important center of agriculture ("Nautufian") emerged in northern Africa, the Sinai Peninsula, and the Middle East, from which it later was carried to other places, including the female-centered early civilizations of Greece and Anatolia (ancient Turkey). Archaeologists, linguists, and biologists have tracked the spread of agriculture eastward beyond the Caspian Sea and along the trade routes that would much later be known as the Silk Road (Harris 1996). Centers of agriculture also arose—perhaps independently or maybe through diffusion, this is currently still being debated—in China as well as in the Americas (Diamond 1999).

Women and Agriculture

Women are usually credited with having invented agriculture, particularly the deliberate cultivation of plants and the various complex processes that accompanied it, such as cooking, processing, and food storage—extending to basketry, pottery, and other forms of vessels, as well as granaries allowing for a surplus of food for whole populations. The granary is a metaphor for the womb of the mother, as well as representing the literal ownership by the communal female group of the property in agricultural societies. The Dogon of Mali equate the Sirius star system with the "granary," seeing it as a "reservoir and source of everything in the world" (Temple 1976: 43). Egyptians called the same star "Sothis" ("to be pregnant") and represented it as the Great Goddess Isis (Temple 1976: 71). At Catal Höyük, a seventh-millennium town in ancient Turkey, an important female figure, perhaps pregnant herself, and sitting enthroned between two leopards, was found in the granary (Gimbutas 1989: 107). Ceramic vessels crafted with breasts or in the shape of a female body emphasize the biological functions of pregnancy and lactation, womb and breast—the female's concrete gift of life. Breasts on ceramic vessels used in ritual emphasize the female body "and by extension the body of the divine female, as a vessel of nourishment or renewal." (Gimbutas 1999: 7)

Shamanism Was Originally Female

The common equation of women with "hearth and home" links to the evolutionary act of harnessing fire for cooking and warmth, as well as referring to the sacred nature of the hearth as altar and the woman as shaman-priestess. Portable offering tables or altars have been found in female burials since the beginnings of civilization, documenting the ongoing function of the sacred woman. By the first millennium BCE, portable altars were buried with every priestess in central Siberia, and these altars or offering tables, along with certain other predictable items such as mirrors, are among the defining features of shaman priestess burials across Central Asia (Davis-Kimball 2002).

"Among several tribes traditions exist that the shaman's gift was first bestowed on women. In Mongolian myths goddesses were both shamans themselves—like the Daughter of the Moon—and the bestowers of the shamanistic gift on mankind" (Czaplicka 1914: 244). A Russian ethnographer from the early twentieth century states that "Neo-Siberians" all have different (later) words for "male shaman," but a common (original) word for female shaman from the most ancient times which has etymological links to the words "bear," "earth-goddess," "housewife," and "wife" (Czaplicka 1914: 244). Shamanism is understood to be a sacrificial (or "gift") vocation, in which one heals the sick, dispenses wisdom, performs magical rituals and communal ceremonies, and is generally available to the community in beneficial ways. Although male shamans are more often featured in contemporary ethnographic studies and shamanism is generally equated by scholars with maleness, Czaplicka's 1914 book suggests otherwise.

> Among the Kamchadal [in Kamchatka] there are no special shamans… but every old woman and *kockchuch* (probably women in men's clothes) is a witch, and explains dreams…. [T]hey used no drum, but simply pronounced incantations and practiced divination. (171)

Female Biological Mysteries and the Baking of Bread

Birthing, ritual ceremonies, and the baking of bread happened more or less side-by-side in the early Neolithic temples of northern Greece. Ovens were created in the shape of a womb with an umbilicus, and pregnant female figurines were found nearby (Gimbutas 1999: 16). Evidence of bread offerings are found in most sacred sites in Europe, from as early as 12,000 BCE in the Ice Age caves of France, down through the Neolithic, and into the classical period when Dianic priestesses baked crescent-shaped cakes for the Moon Goddess. Today it is the Catholic nuns who still bake wafers for communion, and we still say "she has a bun in the oven" when a woman is pregnant (Noble 1991: 24) Before this altruistic and communal nature of women was colonized and exploited, it functioned for the good of the whole and society was able to sustain itself for several thousand years in peace. Even now remnants of these ancient practices exist all over Europe, as I witnessed recently at Lepinski Vir in Serbia where a village man brought a freshly baked loaf of bread to show the assembled group of scholars. The bread was decorated with Old European symbols of the Goddess and formed in the shape of a mandala not dissimilar from those used for meditation by contemporary Tibetan Buddhist practitioners.

Mandala-shaped loaf of freshly baked bread, brought to Lepinski Vir archaeological site by local Serbian man the day author visited with tour group sponsored by the Institute of Archaeomythology. Photo: Vicki Noble

Paradise Lost

It is a fatal error to assume, as many people do these days, that the development of agriculture itself was the beginning of private property and domination of nature (Noble 2004). Ancient female-based agriculture was practiced in harmony with nature and presents us with an almost utopian model of sustainability and peace on earth, compared with everything that has occurred since these civilizations were first disrupted during the fourth millennium BCE. At that time—with the introduction of male-dominance, kingship, war, slavery, and private property—the peaceful agricultural societies began to disappear (along with their languages, scripts, art, and rituals). The incredibly beautiful artwork of a society like Sumer, for instance, which in the opinion of art historians has never again been equaled (Giedion 1962), was quickly replaced by mass-production and the values of the economic bottom line, while images of women dancing and performing rituals diminish and were eventually replaced by men (Garfinkle 2003: 269).

Organic and biodynamic farmers today are instinctually groping their way back to what was once an intact system of complex and intelligent relatedness with all of life. Our ancestors (and ancestresses) left us many images, artifacts, and physical signs of the successful continuity of culture, which they created and in which they existed successfully for several thousand years. Their central icon was the Goddess—the Mother of All Things—whose centrality begs to be re-established today along with women in leadership as her ministers. If progressives could begin to look at this legacy with open eyes, we could stop confusing the agribusiness of today with the agriculture of the past, and instead recognize matriarchal agriculture as the holistic model it is. We would then be forced to stop claiming, ignorantly, that "there has always been war, and there will always be war, it's just the human condition." Perhaps this realization would give us the impetus to refuse and reject the efforts of powerful corporations like Monsanto currently involved in dangerously altering our food at the DNA level, as well as taking out patents (private ownership) on life.

Womb as Tomb: She Gives the Gift of Death and Rebirth

As mentioned earlier, I had the good fortune to visit Lepinski Vir, the oldest Neolithic site in Europe, which was originally situated on "an inaccessible" terrace overlooking the Iron Gates region of the Danube River separating Romania from Serbia (the former Yugoslavia). The site, on the Serbian side and once facing a "tumultuous whirlpool" (Gimbutas 1999: 56), had to be moved when the river was dammed in recent years. Dating from the mid-seventh to the mid-sixth millennia, and composed of "tombs and shrines in the shape of the female body" (Gimbutas 1999: 55), the site was "not meant for habitation, but for rites of death and regeneration" (Gimbutas 1999: 57). The trapezoidal shrines, which clearly represent vulvas (the sacred pubic triangle of the Goddess), were accompanied by enigmatic rock sculptures that archaeologists have called "Fish Goddesses," but which are also undeniably an expression of the much later "Sheela-na-gigs" found all over the British Isles. The sculptures, many of which were covered in red ocher, show a wide-eyed (entranced) female figure with legs spread and hands pointing to (or opening) her triangular vulva. And like the earlier paleolithic period, some of the rocks at Lepinski Vir had only a vulva incised—referring in the most abstract and refined way to the Great Goddess in her dual manifestation of life and death, death and rebirth.

Because the human skeletons found at the site were mostly "disarticulated" and the skulls "set aside for special care, often protected with a box of stones," we can assume that the people practiced secondary burial rites in which they "laid out their dead in front of the shrines for excarnation." After the defleshing of the human

Fishlike female stone deity ("Ancestress") found at Lepinski Vir (6000 BCE). Reproduction. Courtesy Iron Gates Archaeological Museum on the Danube in Serbia. Photo: Vicki Noble

bones by carrion birds, whose bones have also been found at the site, the remains were buried in the shrines (Gimbutas 1999: 59). The earliest images of such "sky burials" are found in wall murals from Catal Hüyök in Turkey dated to the seventh millennium BCE. One painting shows two towers—one where the headless body has been placed, and one with a head—with vultures approaching each. A second painting shows vultures "with 'human' legs and a headless corpse" (Mellaart, Hirsch and Balpinar 1989: 59-60). Rites of excarnation ("secondary burial") were practiced all over Old Europe and the Mediterranean region for millennia, and in Central Asia as well, and remnants of this practice are carried on in some places today. Marija Gimbutas (1991) documents such practices in Italy, the Near East, Anatolia, Greece, and even as far north as the Orkney Islands, with skulls routinely buried separately and skeletons "disarticulated" (283). The famous hypogeum of Malta, for example, contains the remains of 7000 human skeletons that were deposited there over a period of 1500 years. The site was simultaneously used as a gathering place for funerary rites and communal rituals, a widespread custom of ancient prepatriarchal people.

Frequently these finds (skulls and disarticulated bones, some with cut marks) have led archaeologists to conclude that "cannibalism" and "human sacrifice" were practiced. Yet in Tibet the ancient rite of "sky burial" is still practiced, where a corpse is taken to a "specially designated area outside the town or village, often at the top of a mountain," and "bodybreakers" (*domdens*) chop the body into pieces and feed it to the vultures who are considered to be incarnate *dakinis*. Recent films about Tibet (e.g. *Seven Years in Tibet, Kundun,* and *Himalaya*) show graphic representations of these funerary rites, where pieces of flesh are laid out as a banquet and the giant screaming birds come to feast ravenously on the remains. We in the West tend to view such practices with alarm, judging them as primitive, barbaric, unnatural or gruesome. Tibetans, on the other hand, view a three-day-old corpse as lifeless, "its purpose fulfilled. The manner of disposal is considered as *a final act of generosity*, enabling other animals to be nourished by one's remains" (Batchelor 1987: 65, my emphasis). This funerary gift-giving seems to reflect a remnant of the ancient matriarchal understanding of our embeddedness in nature, quite counter to the dualistic phobia of death we have cultivated in the modern West.

A pre-Buddhist rock painting at an important site in Tibet sacred to the Goddess Tara shows a bird-like female identified as a "khyung," a mythical figure sacred to Tibetans and perhaps a precursor to contemporary "sky women" or dakinis. (Bellezza 1997: 185) This harks back to megalithic sites all over Old Europe where excarnation was the main burial rite, "skulls received special attention" (Gimbutas 1999: 66), and birds of prey were associated with the megaliths (Gimbutas 1999: 71). Bird Goddesses and shamanistic "sky-walking women" (dakinis) are ubiquitous in the matriarchal strata in Europe, Africa, Asia, and the Americas, suggesting a particular function of the female. The function of flight is widely celebrated, perhaps pertaining especially to funerary rituals but also generally related to the spirit journeys of shamanism. Valkyries were winged "corpse choosers" who carried the souls of the dead off the battlefields, and Ovid describes Scythian women as rubbing their bodies with flying ointments just like later European witches were purported to do.

Miranda Shaw (1994) reports on the "siddhis" (powers) of famous yoginis, who "could become invisible, had mastered the ritual gazes, and had the power of fleetfootedness, the ability to traverse vast distances in a matter of minutes" (79). As I wrote about Medea of Colchis, a Bronze Age shaman woman or "sorceress" known for her regenerative magic (Noble 2003), her lineage may continue even today in a group of mostly women and girls living in the Caucasus who are "called *messulethe* and described as sorceresses" according to a report by Jeannine Davis-Kimball (1997/98). They live among tribes considered to be descendants of Scythians and Sarmatians, and they "fulfill a role very similar to that of Altaic shamans, falling into trances, escorting the dead to the underworld, or reincarnating them" (42).

Dakinis and Yoginis Carry on the Tradition of the Gift

Shamanism is a service vocation. Once exclusively a women's province (Czaplicka 1914), shamanism is a sacrificial practice in which the shaman uses her body as a vessel for powerful energies to flow through her for healing and magic. In the most ancient times, women performed this function collectively in ecstatic rituals and communal ceremonies involving (and on behalf of) the whole community. Female Buddhas and high-ranking shaman priestesses are pervasive in the artifacts and images from female-centered civilizations of Old Europe (6000 BCE). [illustration] Later during the Bronze Age (3500-1200 BCE), as agricultural civilizations were disrupted and scattered by violence, a special African-European-Asian amalgam of the shaman priestess emerged in the Mediterranean region (known as "Maenads") with counterparts in the Indus Valley and northern Tibet (China's Tarim Basin).

Possession is the norm in "women's religion" around the world, as elucidated in I. M. Lewis's classic text, *Ecstatic Religion* (1989 [1971]). Just as a pregnant woman gives over her body for the duration of her incubation, a shaman gives over her body for the temporary use of an incarnating spirit or ancestor. Denigrated today as "merely mediums," descendants of these special women are still able to make way for more powerful healing energies to inhabit and work through their bodies. Female shamans are officially still active in the contemporary societies of Japan and Korea, as well as in isolated regions of Russia and Mongolia. They can also be found in Nepal, India, Indonesia, and Central and South America, to name only a few places.

The ability to become "empty" is a formal goal of meditation practice, highly valued in Tibetan Buddhism, and embodied by the Tibetan Dakini (sky-going woman). Her selflessness is said to be "compatible with activity in the world … with, or for, the sake of others" (Klein 1995: 123). The Wisdom Dakini is described as "fully awakened and acts to awaken others." (Simmer-Brown 2001: 64) Although it mostly goes unrecognized, Dakinis are believed to take human form as women, so any woman could potentially be acting as a Dakini at any time. As Judith Simmer-Brown puts it in her book, *Dakini's Warm Breath* (2001), human "women are the display that emptiness takes when it expresses itself in form" (40). The dakini gives "the blessing of her own body," referring especially to the "subtle yogic body" with its "vital breath, channels, and essences." In a tantric sexual encounter, the dakini blesses her partner "with her empty and radiant body, a direct transmission of her nature" (Simmer-Brown, 2001: 249). But the dakini's "empty and radiant body" can also be given in bodywork, healing, and other forms of interaction that are sacred, magical, and nonsexual.

According to scholar John Vincent Bellezza (1997), the Medicine Buddha ("*sman lha*") has a female precursor in Tibet, a pre-Buddhist group of Tibetan female deities who "often form sisterhoods." He describes them, sadly, as "no longer popular and nearly extinct in the region." The Tibetan word ("*sman*") pertains to "both medicine and women," is "defined as benefit, use or beneficence" (111), and is also "an honorific term for women." (Bellezza 1997: 130) Put simply, women embody the gift. Bellezza states that, "Women and the sman share the same qualities … [and] sman also came to mean medicine by virtue of its connection with the feminine qualities of nurturer and healer" (1997: 111). As in Siberian shamanism, the female "sman mo" ("benefactress") predates the later "sman pa" or male doctor (111). Recognizing the long continuous female lineage that runs like an underground stream through Tibetan Buddhist literature and territory, Bellezza states that, "Though the appearance, theology, and culture of the great goddess could be altered, she was never eliminated" (1997: 117).

Today Dakinis and Yoginis are treated mainly as abstract deities or "yiddams" in the texts, interiorized into Indian and Tibetan Buddhist tantric visualization practices. Nonetheless, their historical reality is strongly attested to. Bellezza and others mention references to "Eastern and Western Kingdoms of Women," where "women held dominant social and political roles in the autocracy and authority that was matrifocal" (Bellezza 1997: 134). The area to the immediate west of Tibet was once known as Oddiyana, the "Land of the Dakinis." This is the place from which the great guru, Padmasambhava, arrived in Tibet in the eighth century. Dudjom Rinpoche, a high Lama and head of the Nyingma Lineage, is quoted as saying in the twentieth century that "the women of the region belong to an ancient race of dakinis and still 'have power over the arts of magic gaze, transformation of objects by means of certain gnostic spells, and some minor sorcery'" (Simmer-Brown 2001: 55). "Bodily offerings appear to be the province of all dakinis," says Simmer-Brown (2001: 247).

In India, the so-called "cult of the Yoginis" embodied many of these same concepts. In tantra, the transformative quality of the female fluids was perceived as source and nourishment for the tribe. "(W)hen she is not a mother, its excess is discharged as menstrual blood; when she is pregnant, it becomes the 'uterine milk' that feeds the embryo in her womb; when she is a mother, it becomes the milk that feeds her child" (White 2003: 92). Women's blood is described in tantric texts as the "supreme fluid" and the "font of life itself" (White 2003: 93). "Female [menstrual] discharge is the 'milk of the vulva,' and a Yogini's menstrual blood, which has its origins in her breast, is nourishing" (White 2003: 91).

The Yoginis, also known as Matrikas or "Circles of Mothers" (White 2003: 136), were famous for their "eight siddhis" or supernatural powers. They represent an ancient lineage going back to the Indus Valley and Central Asia, continuing in some form to the present day in self-proclaimed shaman women ("Devi") like Ammachi. In our day, Ammachi embodies the feminine ideal in her gift-giving expression of divine love. People come to her by the thousands for "darshan" (blessings) which consists of standing in line and getting hugs from this giant of a woman who performs her hugging function for many hours at a time without (apparently) becoming tired. People describe her energy transmissions as powerfully electric, emotionally moving, and consciousness-altering.

Much of my research in the last decade has been to document the unbroken lineage of female shamanism across Afro-Eurasia, from ancient times to the present. The continuity of practices, rituals, and artifacts identifying the sacred women who have functioned as religious leaders in their communities all across the Silk Road for thousands of years is a main theme in my 2003 book, *The Double Goddess: Women Sharing Power*. A major subtext of the book demonstrates direct links between Greek Maenads, Central Asian Amazons, Indo-Tibetan Dakinis and Yoginis, and European Witches. All of these assemblies of women were known for their abilities to fly through the air, heal the sick, resurrect the dead, brew sacred intoxicating fermented beverages (such as Soma), and perform sexual and divination practices for which they have been misunderstood, maligned, peripheralized, and demonized in the modern world.

A timely example of this negative bias is a Russian article describing a rich female burial recently excavated in the Crimea. The Sarmatian woman, who died in her mid-40s, was buried with symbols of great wealth or rank, including her "lavish dress, massive golden earrings decorated with garnets, golden necklace, and golden medals sewn to her dress." But it was the "occult inventory" ("nine bronze rings, the same number of bells … [and] a whole array of different amulets" and beads) buried with her that caused the archaeologist to jump to the incredible conclusion that she must have been a "witch" (in the pejorative sense). Because "all the relics date back to a much earlier period than the woman's corpse," he imagines: "The witch must have dug out those accessories from ancient burials in order to intensify her magic powers." ("Archaeologists discover witch burial in Crimea"). In fact, heirloom artifacts are commonly found in important female burials from all over the ancient world, and were most likely passed down as "cult" items from one priestess in a lineage to the next, or from mother to daughter—another form of the gift.

The Patriarchal Transition: Stealing the Gift

The shift from a gift economy to a commodity culture can be seen in the transition that occurred from matriarchal cultures to patriarchal ones everywhere. Under patriarchy, shaman priestesses became "witches," "ogresses," "demonesses," "sacred Harlots," or "temple prostitutes," and what was once freely given became a commodity controlled by male authorities in male-dominated social structures. Just as the Earth has been harnessed by modern agricultural methods to produce without pause, women's natural gift-giving capacities have been exploited and colonized for the use of men and male society.

Most recently the transition can be seen in India where the Devadasis ("temple dancers") were still—until the 1950s—giving the gift of their bodies by dancing for the deity in temples, cooking food to be shared communally with the worshippers in attendance, and performing the sacred sexual rites to benefit all beings. Because the British conceived of them as "prostitutes," the Devadasis were outlawed and forced to stop practicing their ancient rites (Marglin 1985). The visible outlawing of this ancient female tradition of gift-giving goes hand-in-hand with the further colonization of women as witnessed in the systematic use of rape in war, as well as the catastrophic rise of sex work and female sexual slavery around the world in recent decades. In 2004, Amnesty International decreed these pervasive crimes against women to be the worst human rights violations in the world—a pandemic of domestic violence being the number one contemporary global problem named in their report.

When research scholars in the women's spirituality movement plead for a return to the Goddess, it is not a frivolous or peripheral issue as compared with some supposedly "larger" issues of the day. It is a call to remember the core model of gift-giving that belongs innately to the human species—our evolutionary birthright—which has been gradually diminished and forgotten over several thousand years of patriarchal domination. As Genevieve Vaughan (2004) often reminds us, we all received the gift of life from a mother—she who gives the gift of her body. The memory of gift-giving exists within us, individually and collectively, and needs only to be remembered and reinvigorated.

Vicki Noble is a healer, artist, scholar, and writer, co-creator of Motherpeace, author of Shakti Women and the Double Goddess. *She teaches in the Women's Spirituality Program at New College of California in San Francisco.*

References

Amnesty International. 2004, January 1. UN Commission on Human Rights. Online: http://web.amnesty.org/library/Index/ENGIOR410012004?open&of-ENG-373.

"Archaeologists discover witch burial in Crimea." *Pravda* 22 October 2004.

Bahn, Paul G. and Jean Vertut. 1997 [1988]. *Journey Through the Ice Age.* Berkeley: University of California Press.

Batchelor, Stephen. 1987. *The Tibet Guide.* London: Wisdom Publications.

Bellezza, John Vincent. 1997. *Divine Dyads: Ancient Civilization in Tibet.* Dharamsala, India: Library of Tibetan Works and Archives.

Birnbaum, Lucia Chiavola. 2001. *Dark Mother: African Origins and Godmothers.* San Jose, CA: Authors Choice Press.

Czaplicka, M. A. 1914. *Aboriginal Siberia: A Study in Social Anthropology.* London: Oxford University Press.

Davis-Kimball, Jeanine. 2002. *Warrior Women: An Archaeologist's Search for History's Hidden Heroines.* NY: Warner Books.

Davis-Kimball, Jeannine. 1997/98. "Amazons, Priestesses and Other Women of Status: Females in Eurasian Nomadic Societies." *Silk Road Art and Archaeolog: Journal of the Institute of Silk Road Studies 5.* Kamakura, Japan.

Diamond, Jared. 1999. *Guns, Germs and Steel: The Fates of Human Societies.* New York: W. W. Norton and Company.

Garfinkle, Yosef. 2003. *Dancing at the Dawn of Agriculture.* Austin: University of Texas Press.

Giedion, Siegfried. 1962. *The Eternal Present: The Beginnings of Art, A Contribution on Constancy and Change.* New York: Bollingen Foundation/Pantheon Books.

Gimbutas, Marija. 1999. *The Living Goddesses.* Edited and supplemented by Miriam Robbins Dexter. Berkeley: University of Calilfornia Press, 1999.

Gimbutas, Marija. 1991. *The Civilization of the Goddess.* San Francisco: Harper and Row.

Gimbutas, Marija. 1989. *The Language of the Goddess.* San Francisco: Harper and Row.

Harris, David R., ed. 1996. *The Origins and Spread of Agriculture and Pastoralism in Eurasia.* Washington, D.C.: Smithsonian Institution Press.

Klein, Anne Carolyn. 1995. *Meeting the Great Bliss Queen: Buddhists, Feminists, and the Art of the Self.* Boston: Beacon Press.

Lewis, I. M. 1989 [1971]. *Ecstatic Religion: A Study of Shamanism and Spirit Possession.* London: Routledge.

Marglin, Frederique Apffel. 1985. *Wives of the God-King: The Rituals of the Devadasis of Puri.* Delhi, India: Oxford University Press.

Marshack, Alexander. 1991. *The Roots of Civilization: The Cognitive Beginnings of Man's (sic) First Art, Symbol and Notation.* Mt. Kisco, NY: Moyer Bell Limited.

Mellaart, James, Udo Hirsch and Belkis Balpinar. 1989. *The Goddess of Anatolia.* Milan: Eskenazi.

Noble, Vicki. 2003. *The Double Goddess: Women Sharing Power.* Rochester, VT: Inner Traditions/Bear and Company.

Noble, Vicki. 2004. Forthcoming. "Brewing, Baking, and Bleeding: The Womanly Arts of Agriculture." Paper presented at the Archaeomythology Conference at Rila Monastery in Bulgaria, June 2004.

Noble, Vicki. 1991. *Shakti Woman: Feeling Our Fire, Healing Our World (The New Female Shamanism).* San Francisco: HarperSF.

Sanday, Peggy Reeves. 2002. *Women at the Center: Life in a Modern Matriarchy.* Ithaca, NY: Cornell University Press.

Shaw, Miranda. 1994. *Passionate Enlightenment: Women in Tantric Buddhism.* Princeton, NJ: Princeton University Press.

Simmer-Brown, Judith. 2001. *Dakini's Warm Breath: The Feminine Principle in Tibetan Buddhism.* Boston: Shambhala Publications, Inc.

Temple, Robert. 1976. *The Sirius Mystery.* New York: St. Martin's Press.

Vaughan, Genevieve. 2004. "Gift Giving and Exchange: Genders are Economic Identities and Economies are Based on Gender." *Il Dono/The Gift: A Feminist Analysis. Athanor: Semiotica, Filosofia, Arte, Letteratura* 15 (8). Roma: Meltemi Editore.

White, David Gordon. 2003. *Kiss of the Yogini: "Tantric Sex" in its South Asian Contexts.* Chicago: The University of Chicago Press.

PATRICIA PEARLMAN

The Goddess Temple of Sekhmet

A Gift Economy Project

First a prayer and then a pledge of allegiance. Here's the prayer:

I will fly; I know barbed wire, [thumb tacks], bare halls. I've seen the white walls of slavery, and I can transform them, too. Each thing examined regains beauty. I will fly into colour itself, red as the fiery robes of huge women, blue as the veins in her breast, green as her hair trailing on the sea, purple as her most sacred self. I will fly like a plant flies, invisible in small seed pods, borne on the friendly goddess winds, touching endless possibilities. Someday, the sod of rich land, where to sprout, knowing I will fly again, I will be rich weighted by a hundred flying women, gold flashes from caring, and as they fly by my window, wearing images of the goddess next to their skin, I'll fly in a rising mist of desire, I'll touch the smoke, taste the wet air, fly above, fly below, infinite acrobat. I will fly, fly in dreams, fly working, break out of the shadow flying, skywrite letters and invocations, fly lonely as purple dipping sun, or fly in clouds of beautiful women, or drifting into the [warm dress] of the Mother herself. I'll see as I fly; my eyes will fly, I am simple and splendid in flight. Like all natural things, a simple miracle, a woman in flight.

A pledge of allegiance:

I pledge allegiance to the Earth, and to the flora, fauna, and human life that it supports, one planet, indivisible, with faith, air, water, and soil, economic justice, equal rights, and peace for all.

The Sekmet Temple is a product of the gift economy. It's a gift to all that go to visit it. It was the greatest gift for me. Living the gift is very unique. It has been wonderful living the gift economy. At the Temple, there are no member-ship dues. We don't pass the hat because we don't wear one. And we don't have a donation box. People will say, "Well, what if I want to donate?" We reply, "if you want to give a gift, that's fine. But it's also important to give others the gift of receiving." So when people offer me a gift I never say no, because even if I

The sand-coloured stucco Temple opens to the elements of nature, with archways to the four directions and an open roof to the sky. Photo: Anne Key

may not have a use for it, I know I'll find somebody who does. And this way it's a gift that keeps giving.

If we deny some of those things, like all the gifts that the Goddess or the Creator provide, it would be like denying what our Mother wants to give us. At the Temple, we do weddings, christenings, hand-fasting, legal weddings, and all the rites of passage. I also give lessons, instructions, and there is never a charge or fee for any of these things. Some of my colleagues or acquaintances in the area say, "Oh, you've got to charge, or people won't appreciate it." But as soon as you put a fee on these things, that's all they're worth. And so you can't charge for anything like this. And then they would say, "Well, for instructions you have to charge, because they have to make a commitment."

Anybody who drives to the Temple has made a commitment. We have a guesthouse that can accommodate twelve people. The guesthouse has all the conveniences, kitchen etc., and women from all over come and visit. The guesthouse is also a gift to the women visiting. That's no charge for that, no fee.

Most of the things that I have, have been gifts from people visiting the Temple. When people come to visit, if they aren't going to stay, I will serve them tea and chocolate. That's what witches do. That's how you know them. It has been a wonderful experience all these years, and the hundreds and hundreds of women that I have met from all over, not only appreciate the gift economy, but practice it as well.

I would like to pass one little thing on that I learned from someone once. No matter what your budget is, you can hold onto a few extra dollars a week that you can carry around with you. I started this practice a while ago, and I use it for people who I see begging out in the streets. I always have x amount of dollars that I can give to them, so when somebody comes up to me and is in need, I don't have to say "no." Just couple of dollars here or a dollar there. I learned this from a woman who was practicing the gift economy. And this is a really great thing, because you don't feel like you're being used, but you've got this special little extra, this special something for somebody who really needs it, and I like to encourage people to give what they can.

Let me tell you about how I got to be at the Temple. When I moved to Las Vegas, I didn't know where I was going to live, or what I was going to do. I as doing a radio show for awhile but I wanted to move outside of the city. I wanted to be in the desert. It was a full moon, 1993; it was on Samhain, which is our special day, and it also was on a Sunday that the clock had turned back, so it was a 25-hour day, full moon, and Samhain. Three things. So I wrapped myself in a white sheet and went out under the moon and told the Goddess, "I want to lose this life, it's coming out of the closet, the broom closet. I want to be in this community and live it 25 hours a day." A year to the day is when I took over as Priestess at the Goddess Temple.

We have the power to do things, to put out our energy, and to make changes. I would like quote Sojourner Truth. She was speaking at the National Women's Suffrage Convention in 1852 when she said, "If the first woman God ever made was strong enough to turn the world upside down all alone, these together ought to be able to turn it back and get it right side up again."

And now we are asking to do this, and men, you better let us!

Patricia Pearlman was the Priestess of the Temple of the Goddess Spirituality Dedicated to Sekhmet in Cactus Springs, Nevada, for more than ten years. She established the Temple as an institution, giving it a foothold in an unlikely environment, between a nuclear test site and the airforce base, not far from the adult Disneyland that is Las Vegas. She created and sustained a community of people who visited the temple for rituals, healing and counselling. She passed away on March 24, 2006.

HEIDE GOETTNER-ABENDROTH

Matriarchal Society and the Gift Paradigm

Motherliness as an Ethical Principle

The extent of a society's development is most clearly reflected in the freedom women enjoy, and in the extent to which they are able to express their creativity. The way we live today, as members of society, is influenced by a worldview, and a sense of history, that are based to a large extent on male principles: an ideology of male dominance and universal patriarchy, the foundations of which are underpinned by structural and physical violence. The principles of matriarchal societies contradict this worldview.

The emerging subject of Modern Matriarchal Studies is the investigation and presentation of non-patriarchal societies, both past and present. Even today there are societies that exhibit matriarchal patterns in Asia, Africa, America, and Oceania. None of these societies are, however, a reversal of patriarchy, where women are perceived to rule over men—as it is often commonly believed. Instead, they are all egalitarian societies, without exception. This means that hierarchies, classes, and the domination of one gender by the other are unknown to them. This is what makes them so attractive to those looking for a new philosophy to create a just society. Nevertheless, while they are societies free of domination, they still have guidelines and codes of conduct that govern relationships and community.

Equality in matriarchal societies does not mean a mere levelling of differences. The natural differences between the genders and the generations are respected and honoured, but they never serve to create hierarchies as is common in patriarchy. The different genders and generations each have their own honour, and through complementary areas of activity, they are geared towards each other.

This can be observed at all levels of society: the economic level, the social level, the political level, and in the areas of their worldviews and faiths. More precisely, matriarchies are societies with complementary equality, where great care is taken to provide a balance. This applies to the balance between genders, among generations, and between humans and nature.

The differentiated patterns of existing matriarchal societies have been researched in detail. But history alone will not reveal how matriarchal people thought and felt, how they conducted their politics, and how they lived out their faith. To be able to observe this is an advantage of anthropology. Over the past few decades, my major work has been to research, describe, and present a wide range of matriarchal societies throughout the world. Based on cross-cultural examination of case after case, I have outlined in my work the structures and regulative mechanisms that function across all levels of matriarchal societies (see Goettner-Abendroth 1988, 1991, 1995, 2000).

I call all non-patriarchal societies "matriarchal" despite of the word's various connotations. But I believe the term should be redefined. This redefinition would be a great advantage especially because, for women, *reclaiming* this term means to reclaim the knowledge about cultures that have been created by women.

Philosophical and scientific re-definitions of words mostly refer to well-known words or terminologies. After these words have been re-defined, scholars can work with these new interpretations, but the words do not lose contact with the popular language of the people. In the case of the term "matriarchy," we are not obliged to follow the current, male-biased interpretation of this word as signifying "domination by the mothers." The only reason to understand "matriarchy" in this way is that it seems to parallel our understanding of the word "patriarchy." However, the Greek word *arché* has a double meaning. It means "beginning" as well as "domination." Therefore, we can translate "matriarchy" accurately as "the mothers from the beginning," while "patriarchy," on the other hand, translates correctly as "domination by the fathers."

The word "patriarchy" could also be translated as "the fathers from the beginning." This nevertheless leads to its meaning as "domination by the fathers," because not having any natural right to "beginning," they have to enforce it through domination! By the same token, since the mothers clearly *are* the beginning by their capacity to bring forth life, they have no need to enforce it by domination.

Defining "Matriarchal Society"

Up until recently, scientific research in the field of matriarchy has lacked clear criteria for defining matriarchal societies and a scientific methodology to prove their existence, despite several competent studies and an extensive data collection.[1] This absence of scientific rigour opens the door to the emotional and ideological entanglements that have been a burden to this research from the beginning. Patriarchy itself has not been considered critically and stereotypical views of women, as well as a neurotic fear of women's alleged power, have often confused the issues.

The definition of matriarchal studies that I present below has has been derived from my cross-cultural studies of matriarchal societies that continue to exist worldwide. I will present the various criteria for matriarchal society on four different levels: the economic level, the social level, the political level, and on the cultural level.

On the *economic level,* matriarchies are most often agricultural societies, but not exclusively so. Goods are distributed according to a system that is identical with the lines of kinship and the patterns of marriage. This system prevents goods from being accumulated by one special person or one special group. Thus, the principles of equality are consciously kept up, and the society is egalitarian and non-accumulating. From a political point of view, matriarchies are societies with perfect mutuality. Every advantage or disadvantage concerning the acquisition of goods is mediated by social rules. For example, at the village festivals, wealthy clans are obliged to invite all inhabitants. They organize the banquet, at which they distribute their wealth to gain honour. Therefore, on the economic level they produce an economy of balance, and I thus call matriarchies *societies of economic reciprocity.*

On the *social level,* matriarchies are based on the union of an extended clan. People live together in big clans, which are formed according to the principle of *matrilinearity,* i.e., kinship is acknowledged exclusively in the female line. The clan's name, and all social positions and political titles, are passed on through the mother's line. Such a *matri-clan* consists at least of three generations of women: the clan-mother, her daughters, her granddaughters, and the directly related men: the brothers of the mother, her sons, and grandsons. Generally, the matri-clan lives in one big clan-house, which can hold anywhere from ten to more than 100 persons, depending on size and architectural style. The women live there permanently as daughters and granddaughters never leave the clan-house of their mother when they marry. This is called *matrilocality.*

What is most important is the fact that women have the power of disposition over the goods of the clan, especially the power to control the sources of nourishment: fields and food. This characteristic feature, besides matrilinearity and matrilocality, grants women such a strong position that these societies are distinctly "matriarchal." (Anthropologists do not make a distinction between merely matrilineal, and clearly matriarchal societies. This continues to produce great confusion.)

The clans are connected to each other by the patterns of marriage, especially the system of mutual marriage between two clans. Mutual marriage between two clans is not marriage between individuals, but rather a communal marriage. The married people do not leave the houses of their mothers, but practice visiting marriage. That is, a husband will visit his wife in the clan-house of her mother, where she lives, only in the evenings, leaving at dawn to return to his home, the clan-house of his own mother. Due to additional patterns of marriage between all clans, everyone in a matriarchal village or a matriarchal town is eventually related to everyone else by birth or by marriage. Therefore, I call matriarchies *non-hierarchical, horizontal societies of matrilineal kinship.*

On the *political level,* even the process of taking a decision is organized along the lines of matriarchal kinship. In the clan-house, women and men meet in a council where domestic matters are discussed. No member of the household is excluded. After thorough discussion, each decision is taken by consensus. The same is true for the entire village: if matters concerning the whole village have to be discussed, delegates from every clan-house meet in the village council. These delegates can be the oldest women of the clans (the matriarchs), or the brothers and sons they have chosen to represent the clan. No decision concerning the whole village may be taken without the consensus of all clan-houses. This means that the delegates who are discussing the matter are not the ones who make the decision. It is not in this council that the policy of the village is made, because the delegates function only as bearers of communication. If the council notices that some clan-houses are of a different opinion, the delegates return to the clan-houses to discuss matters further. In this way, consensus is reached in the whole village, step by step.

A population living in the region takes decisions in the same way: delegates from all villages meet to discuss the decisions of their communities. Again, the delegates function only as bearers of communication. In such cases, it is usually men who are elected by their villages. In contrast to the frequent ethnological mistakes made about these men, they are not the "chiefs" and do not, in fact, decide. Every village, and in every village every clan-house, is involved in the process of making the decision, until consensus is reached on the regional level. Therefore, from the political point of view, I call matriarchies *egalitarian societies of consensus*. These political patterns do not allow the accumulation of political power. In *exactly* this sense, they are free from domination: They have no class of rulers and no class of suppressed people; i.e., the *enforcement bodies* that are necessary to establish domination are unknown to them.

On the *cultural level,* matriarchal societies do not know religious transcendence of an unseen, untouchable, and incomprehensible all-powerful God, in contrast to whom the world is devalued as dead matter. In matriarchy, divinity is immanent, for the whole world is regarded as divine— a feminine divine. This is evident in the concept of the universe as a goddess who created everything, and as Mother Earth who brings forth every living thing. And everything is endowed with divinity—the smallest pebble and the biggest star, each woman and man, each blade of grass, each mountain.

In such a culture, everything is spiritual. In their festivals, following the rhythms of the seasons, everything is celebrated: nature in its manifold expressions and the different clans with their different abilities and tasks, the different genders and the different generations, believing in the principle of "wealth in diversity." There is no separation between sacred and secular; therefore all tasks, such as sowing and harvesting, cooking and weaving are at the same time meaningful rituals. On the spiritual level, I thus define matriarchies as *sacred societies as cultures of the Goddess.*

The Relationship between Matriarchal Societies and the Gift Paradigm

In order to explore the relationship between matriarchal societies and the gift paradigm, we need first to examine the guidelines and codes of conduct that govern relationships and communities in matriarchal societies.

There is no private property and there are no territorial claims. The people simply have usage rights on the soil they till, or the pastures their animals graze, for "Mother Earth" cannot be owned or cut up in pieces. She gives the fruits of the fields and the animals to all people, and therefore the harvest and the flocks cannot be privately owned; instead they are shared equally.

The women, and specifically the oldest women of the clan, the matriarchs, hold the most important goods in their hands, for they are responsible for the sustenance and the protection of all clan members. The women either work the land themselves or organize the work on the land and the fruits of the fields, and the milk of the flocks are given to them to hold and distribute equitably among the community.

Matriarchal women are managers and administrators, who organize the economy not according to the profit principle, where an individual or a small group of people benefits; rather, the motivation behind their action is *motherliness*. The profit principle is an ego-centred principle, where individuals or a small minority take advantage of the majority of people. The principle of motherliness is the opposite, where altruism reigns and the well-being of all is at the centre. It is at the same time a spiritual principle, which humans take from nature. Mother Nature cares for all beings however different they may be. The same applies to the principle of motherliness: a good mother cares for all her children in spite of their diversity. Motherliness as an ethical principle pervades all areas of a matriarchal society, and this holds true for men as well. For example, among the Minangkabau in Sumatra, if a man desires to acquire status among his peers, or even to become a representative of the clan to the outside word, the criterion is: "he must be like a good mother."

This is not a romantic idea of motherliness, as it has often been portrayed by the patriarchy, which has has lead to the concept of motherliness being devalued as a merely sentimental cliché. This is the way in which patriarchy systematically obscures the caring and nurturing work done most often by mothers, by women. Without this work of daily care, there would be no help for the sick, no aid in crisis situations of any kind, no assistance for the elderly. In particular, there would be no children, which means any society would cease to exist in a short while. Motherly work is the most important work of all; it is work for life itself, work for our future. It is because of its great importance, that this work is intentionally made invisible by patriarchy.

Matriarchies consciously build their existence on this work, which is why they are much more realistic than patriarchies, not to mention the fact that they have much more vitality. They are, on principle, need-oriented. The guidelines on which their societies are based aim to meet the needs of each with the greatest benefit for all.

Gift giving is, therefore, not a coincidental, arbitrary act in matriarchal societies, something confined to the private sphere. On the contrary, it is the central feature of their society. In matriarchal societies, goods, nurturing, care, cultural creativity in ritual events, all circulate as gifts. These gift are manifest in the festivals which are at the core of these cultures and which drive their economies. Matriarchal societies celebrate the festivals of the agricultural year, along with the lifecycle festivals of the individual clans, festivals that are also celebrated together with the whole village or town. During these festivals the goods and food, nurturing and care, and cultural presentations are "moved around": not in the sense of exchange with the expectation of something in return, but as an unconditional gift. For example, a clan that has had a bumper crop and is able to collect a great harvest will give this fortune away at the first opportunity. At the next festival, this lucky clan will overextend itself by inviting everybody in the village or town or district, will lavishly care for their well-being, feed them and give them cultural presents like music, dancing, processions, rituals, which everybody participates in according to their religious traditions. The clan hosting the festival will not hold back anything. In a patriarchal society, this would be considered suicidal behaviour and would ruin the giving clan. But in matriarchal societies these festivals work according the maxim: "those who have shall give." At the next big festival another clan, one that is by comparison better off than the rest of the community, will take on this role. Now the others are invited and gifts are lavished upon them. Round and round it goes in the community, and it is always the well-off clans who have the responsibility for the festivals.

It is apparent that in this system an accumulation of material or cultural goods, with a view to personal gain and enrichment, is not possible. Matriarchal societies are not based on accumulation, as are patriarchal societies. The opposite is the case: the economic and cultural actions are geared towards a levelling of the differences in living standards, and to the joy of everybody participating together in the cultural performances.

A generous clan never gains any claim to material or cultural goods from the other clans; rather, it wins honour. "Honour" in matriarchy means that the altruism and pro-social action of this clan gains great admiration from the other clans, and that this act verifies and strengthens the relationships between the clans. Honour means priceless and invaluable human contact and cooperation. It sets free the most honourable human feelings such as unreserved giving, true devotion, benevolence, and friendship. It enables love to grow. Such a clan will always be supported by the other clans should it have need of anything or even fall on hard times. This reciprocity is also a question of honour.

The Matriarchal Model as Guiding Principle for the Future

It should be clear from this outline of matriarchies that these cultures demonstrate knowledge of non-patriarchal, egalitarian patterns of society that are urgently needed in this late phase of globally destructive patriarchy. During their very long history, as well as in the societies that continue to exist today, matriarchies have maintained and sustained themselves without domination, without hierarchies, and without wars. It is particularly important to stress that the violence against women and children that characterizes patriarchal societies all over the world is, in these matriarchal societies, completely unknown

I have begun to consider that knowledge of the *matriarchal model* can have enormous significance for present and future society. Indeed, compared to philosophically constructed futures that could never be implemented, matriarchal societies are not abstract utopias built on ideas. These societies have been developed over long historical periods, embody practical experience and thought gained over millennia, and belong indispensably to the cultural store of knowledge of all of humankind. Their precepts show how life can be organized in such a way that it is based on needs: peaceful, non-violent, and simply human.

Together we can glimpse what this *matriarchal model* could mean for the situation our present day world is in.

On the *economic level* it has become impossible to further increase industrial production—and so-called living standards—without risking the total destruction of the of the planet's biosphere. An alternative to this kind of destructive growth are the communities that use a subsistence perspective as an economic strategy for smaller units of organization, such as at the regional level. These communities work frugally and self-sufficiently, stressing the quality of life over the quantity of production. On a worldwide scale, it is urgent that we strengthen and enlarge the still-existing subsistence societies, where production and trade are usually overseen by women. We must not, under any circumstances, let them be sacrificed to the process of globalization. Establishing regionalism in which the economy is guided by women is a matriarchal principle.

On the *social level* the task is to prevent a further fragmentation of society, which drives people deeper and deeper into solitary living and loneliness, becoming increasingly ill and destructive. In the end, this is the matrix in which war and violence grow. To counteract this, the goal is the formation of diverse communities. They might be intentional communities or networks or neighbourhoods. Elective affinity does not come about by merely shared interest; interest groups come and go very quickly. Elective affinity only comes into being if there is a spiritual-intellectual common ground. On this basis, a symbolic clan comes into being that is more committed than any interest group. The matriarchal principle here is that these clans are usually initiated, carried, and led by women. The measuring stick is the needs of women and children who are the future of humankind, and not the power or potency wished for by men that has led to patriarchal extended families, such as the big political, economic, and religious men's clubs, which have suppressed and excluded women. These new matri-clans will integrate men totally, but with a value system based on mutual care and love instead of power.

On the *political level,* the matriarchal consensus process for making decisions is indispensable for an egalitarian society. This is the most important principle for matriarchal community formation as it prevents the establishment of domination by individuals or groups in newly organized symbolic clans of various designs. A consensus decision-making process establishes the balance between men and women, but also between the generations, because both older and younger people have their say. Furthermore, it honours the promises formal democracy makes but never keeps.

According to matriarchal principles, well-ordered groups of the new matri-clans are the supporting social unit and the actual decision-makers at the regional level.

Flourishing self-sufficient regions based on susbsistence economies are the aim, not nation states, nation-alliances or super-powers that grant more and more power to the ruling classes and in which human beings are reduced to numbers and have become merely human "resources."

This kind of regionalism does not mean people are limited to connecting spiritually and culturally within just the one region, because this would lead to the narrow mind of provincialism. The regions will have symbolic connections with each other as sister-regions, and these connections will be realized through cultural exchange in the celebration of joint festivals. In this way a free, horizontal network comes into being between the regions. This network-based paradigm is completely different from a centralized, hierarchical state control. In the age of the Internet, this network is not limited to neighbouring regions, but can span the globe. Why should a matriarchal region in Europe not have sister-regions in India, Africa, the Americas, and yet another one in Polynesia? Such connections are limitless, but they are totally different from the global structures and hierarchies of exploitation that patriarchal states have with each other.

On the *spiritual-cultural level,* we will bid farewell to the various fundamentalisms that are associated with hierarchical patriarchal religions and their claims to absolute truth. With their claims to moral superiority they have debased and vilified the earth, humankind, and especially the half of humankind who are women. Now we have the opportunity for a new sanctification of the world in accordance with the matriarchal imagination: the whole world, and everything in it, is divine. This gives rise to celebrating and honouring all life on the planet—creatively and freely: nature with her multitude of beings and phenomena, and her great diversity of peoples, each with their own special capabilities. All this diversity is celebrated to the full. In this way, matriarchal spirituality permeates everything and once again becomes a central and integral part of everyday living.

It is evident that destruction of nature, sexism, and racism are not possible in a future matriarchal culture. According to the matriarchal principle, *diversity is the true wealth of the earth, humankind, and culture.* The values of the matriarchal ethos are: balance, reciprocity on all levels, and the loving connection with all living beings and phenomena of nature.

In all of this matriarchal spirituality is central. Matriarchal societies have always been sacred societies. Their entire structure has been developed in accordance with their spiritual beliefs. For this reason, establishing new matriarchal patterns in our societies is not possible without an all-permeating matriarchal ethos.

To sum up, this new research called "Modern Matriarchal Studies" has presented us with a rich spectrum of knowledge and practice that can be useful in our work toward the development of a just and peaceful future based on a matriarchal model. The gift economy/gift paradigm as presented by Genevieve Vaughan (1997) also offers us a vision of what is possible, and demonstrates how, every day and everywhere in patriarchal society, gift giving is practiced, and is, in fact, what these matriachal societies are based on. Matriarchal societies demonstrate that gift giving indeed embodies *the highest value* and the *practical reality of whole societies*, past and present. We need not invent an abstract utopia to find social structures that embody motherliness as an ethical principle and that practice gift giving, because they have existed over the longest eras of human history, and they still exist today worldwide. The social organization of matriarchal, gift giving societies can inspire us, and teach us how to develop a future based on a matriarchal model that will result in just, well-balanced, and peaceful societies, in which women do not rule, but in which motherliness as an ethical principle provides the foundation for life, for living, and for giving to satisfy the needs of each for the benefit of all.

Heide Goettner-Abendroth was born in 1941 and is the mother of three children. She has published various books on matriarchal society and culture and has become the founding mother of Modern Matriarchal Studies. In 1980 she was visiting professor at the University of Montreal (Canada) and, in 1992, at the University of Innsbruck (Austria). In 1986, she founded the International Academy HAGIA: Academy for Modern Matriarchal Studies and Matriarchal Spirituality in Germany. The results of her research have been the basis for further studies and projects in many different countries. She is one of the 1,000 "Peace Women" all over the world who have been nominated by the Swiss Peace Initiative. Visit her website: www.goettner-abendroth.de.

Notes

---

[1]   For an extensive bibliography, see Goettner-Abendroth 1988, 1991, 1995, 2000.

References

Goettner-Abendroth, Heide. 1988. *Das Matriarchat I. Geschichte Seiner Erforschung.* Stuttgart: Kohlhammer-Verlag.

Goettner-Abendroth, Heide. 1991. *Das Matriarchat II,1. Stammesgesellschaften in Ostasien, Indonesien, Ozeanien.* Stuttgart: Kohlhammer-Verlag.

Goettner-Abendroth, Heide. 1995. *The Goddess and Her Heros: Matriarchal Religion in Mythology, Fairy-Tales and Literature.* Trans. Lillian Friedberg. Stow, MA: Anthony Publishing Company.

Goettner-Abendroth, Heide. 2000. *Das Matriarchat II,2. Stammesgesellschaften in Amerika, Indien, Afrika.* Stuttgart: Kohlhammer-Verlag.

Vaughan, Genevieve. 1997. *For-Giving. A Feminist Criticism of Exchange.* Austin, TX: Plainview/Anomaly Press.

SUSAN PETRILLI

Significs and Semioethics

Places of the Gift in Communication Today

> Woe to those who lie upon beds of ivory,
> and stretch themselves upon their couches,
> and eat lambs from the flock,
> and calves from the midst of the stall;
> who sing idle songs to the sound of the harp,
> and like David invent for
> themselves instruments of music;
> who drink wine in bowls,
> and anoint themselves with the finest oils,
> but are not grieved over the ruin of Joseph!
> Therefore they shall now be the first to go into exile,
> and the revelry of those who stretch themselves shall pass away.
> (Amos 6, 4.7)

Gift Giving and Significs

What is significs? Significs is that discipline, or better, theoretical orientation that consists in obstinately asking the questions: "What does it signify? What does it mean? What's the sense?" It is not surprising that this discipline should have been invented by a woman, Victoria Lady Welby (1837-1912). Nor is it surprising that this woman has never entered the Pantheon or genealogical tree of the "Fathers" (of course!) of the science of signs and language, in spite of the influence she exerted on scholars such as Bertrand Russell, Charles S. Peirce, Charles K. Ogden, George F. Stout, John M. Baldwin, Ferdinand S. Schiller, Ferdinand Tönnies, Frederik van Eeden, and many more.

"What does it signify? What's the sense?" These are questions that Welby induces one to ask in the face of any form of expression, verbal and non-verbal, any piece of human behaviour or social practice, in the face of all languages in ordinary life and in the professions, in intellectual life, in the face of scientific languages, the languages of artistic discourse, religion, politics, economy, etc. As a significian, Welby (see 1983 [1903], 2006[1], and unpublished mss.) focused on the relation between the signs and values that go to form languages and behaviour. This led to her invitation to interrogate the sense of words, human practices, in the ultimate analysis of the worlds human beings contribute to constructing for themselves. What does a given discourse, text, behaviour mean? What's the sense of a given social program? What does education imply? Why poverty? Why exploitation? What are the implications involved in the progress of science? What's the use of definition? Dogmatism? Why keep the different at a distance? What's the sense in isolating that which is different? The disobedient with respect to dominant ideology? What is the sense of war? How must we respond to all this? These are examples of the questions that significs teaches us to ask.

With a focus on the dignity of the human person, Welby (1881, 1887, 1910, 1983 [1903], 1985 [1911], 2006, unpublished mss.) promoted and theorized the development of critical consciousness and interpretive capacity from infancy (see also, Petrilli 1997, 1998a, 1998b, 2004, 2005, 2006; Petrilli and Ponzio 2005: chp. 2). Such themes are accompanied throughout her writings by reflection on the inevitable connection of signs and values with responsibility and freedom and, therefore, with the capacity for hospitality and listening to the other alien to self. According to the logic of significs, which is in line with the logic of a new form of humanism, the humanism of otherness, to take responsibility for the other is inextricably connected with creative love for the other, care for the other, and therefore with the capacity for proposing new and better worlds with and for the other.

Proceeding with Welby, and beyond Welby in the world of globalization, we propose to work for the construction of worlds which are no longer founded on difference understood in terms of the logic of identity. Thus understood difference means to construct worlds on the basis of identity separations—whether these pertain to gender, ethnic group, religion, ideology, etc. Such logic inevitably involves the need to defend rights and interests connected with difference as subtended by the egocentric logic of identity and belonging, even to the point of accepting the logic of war, which, impossible to deny, characterizes the global world today.

In contrast, from the perspective of significs or what we propose to call "semio-ethics," it is possible to work for a world that is founded on difference understood in terms of otherness and dialogism, rather than of prevarication and dominion of one difference over another. Such logic involves the capacity to stay together on the basis of intercorporeal dialogue and co-participation among differences, even when they clash. Global peace and freedom cannot be separated from the relation of global involvement with the other—without identities, barriers, or alibis—from the relation of responsibility for the other, of dialogic responsiveness towards the other. And according to this logic, to be committed to human rights means to be committed, always and without reserve, to the rights of the other.

The gift is a constant theme throughout Welby's writings both as the object of discourse when she predicates such values as love and care for the other, and compassion, justice, and patience as the guiding values for social practice. But even more significantly, she identifies gift logic as a constitutive component in the relation among signs, in the generation of signifying processes and practices. Otherness and excess, overflow with respect to identity logic, are recognized as determining factors in the dynamics of interpretive processes and therefore in the development of expressive systems, including verbal language. This is all one with the dynamics of the constitution of subjectivity, the development of interpersonal relations and experience of the world.

The Problem: The Logic of Identity and Global Communication-Production

The expression "global communication" refers to the capitalist, or postcapitalist, system in its current phase of development. It may be understood in at least two different senses. In fact, the term "global" in the expression "global communication" indicates: 1) the *extension of communication over the entire planet*; and 2) *the realistic tendency of communication to accommodate the world as it is* (see Petrilli and Ponzio 2000).

Globalization implies that communication pervades the entire productive cycle. That is to say, communication not only enters exchange relations, as in earlier phases of socio-economic development, but also relations of production and consumption.

Globalization involves interference of communication, understood as communication-production, not only in human life, but in all life over the planet. Therefore, the expression "global communication-production" indicates the fact that the communication network with the market based on equal exchange logic has extended worldwide. But even more radically, it also refers to the fact that life in its globality, including human life, has been englobed by the communication-production system.

The capitalist system today in its global communication-production phase is characterized by the industrial revolution in automation, globalization of communication, and universalization of the market. That the market has been universalized implies not only a quantitative fact of expansion, but also a fact of quality. This is represented by the translatability of anything into goods and by the production of new goods-things. Communication today does not just concern the intermediate phase in the production cycle (production, exchange, consumption). Far more extensively, it has also become a constitutive modality in production and consumption processes. In other words, not only is exchange communication, but production and consumption are also communication. This means that the whole productive cycle is communication. For this very reason, it follows that the current phase in capitalist production may be characterized as the "communication-production" phase.

Communication understood as communication-production is *global* communication in the sense that it has expanded over the entire planet (of course, the planet of the privileged!), but also in the sense that it is communication of the world *as it is*, of *this* world. Communication-production relates to the world, it accommodates the world as it is, it is appropriate to *this* world. In this socio-economic context, the capitalist or post-capitalist production system, communication and reality, communication and being coincide. Communication *is* reality. Realism in politics must keep faith to ontology, to being, and even goes as far as to accept the *extrema ratio* of war, the crudest and most brutally realistic face of being, dictated by the inexorable law of the force of things. Realistic politics (and if it is not realistic, it is not politics) is politics that fits global communication, the being of communication-production. Today, the relationship between politics and ontology is the relation of politics with the ontology of being-communication, which is global communication, that is, global communication-production.

Perseverance in communication-reproduction is *perseverance in one and the same social system*, the capitalist. Capitalist society, with its continual adjustments and transformations functional to its own maintenance, has not yet ceased to set, has not yet finished ending, in spite of the signs of its ending, in spite of its having emerged only at sunset (Hegel's "noctule" [see Hegel 1819-20]). Ideology that is functional to maintaining capitalism identifies *being, the being of communication-production,* with the *being-communication* of social reproduction in general. The being of communication-production identifies so closely with the being of social reproduction in general that it seems natural, indeed the only possibility for human beings, an inherent part, as it were, of human nature. In other words, once high levels have been reached in the economic, cultural, and scientific-technological spheres (according to the logic of linear development), *being-communication-production* is passed off as structural to human beings, as a necessary and unchangeable modality of existence for the human species.

World planning for the ongoing development of communication and for control over communication itself goes together with the reinforcement and reaffirmation of the being of communication-production. This approach to world planning is based on awareness of the productive character of communication and of the fact that communication and being identify in capitalist communication-production society. This socio-economic plan also knows that control over capital can only be achieved by controlling communication.

Communication-production ideology is the ideology of total control over communication. Communication-production ideology is so realistic, coherent, and consistent with the being of things as they are, that it would seem to be the logic of communication-production more than its ideology. Nor does communication-production ideology hesitate to flaunt the good news of the end of ideology. In relation to *global communication-production*, we propose the expression "*ideo-logic*" rather than *logic* or *ideology*. Ideology functional to maintaining this particular social system passes itself off, in good or bad faith, as the ideology that subtends social reproduction in general.

On the contrary, social reproduction must escape the established order, that of being-communication, in order to reinvent and re-organize social relations. Indeed, social reproduction must get free of social systems such as that represented by global communication-production given that the latter obstacles and endangers social reproduction itself.

To preserve the being of communication-production is destructive. Reproduction of the *productive cycle* itself is destructive. The reproductive cycle destroys: (a) machines that are continuously replaced with new machines—not because they are worn out but because they are no longer competitive; (b) jobs, thereby making way for automation which contributes to increasing unemployment; (c) products on the market, where new forms of consumerism are ruled by the logic of reproducing the reproductive cycle itself; (d) products that once purchased would otherwise exhaust the demand (which means that products must be designed so as to become immediately outdated and obsolete; in this way similar but new products may be continuously proposed and introduced onto the market; (e) commodities and markets unable to stand up to competition in the global communication-production system.

The European Commission has devoted special attention to the problem of inventiveness and innovation functional to profit, to "immaterial investment" and "competitivity," as dictated by equal exchange market logic. In the context of this logic, the "ideo-logic" of capitalism, it is not surprising that the European Commission (1995) has identified "*innovation*" with "*destruction.*" The innovative character of a product coincides with its capacity for destruction: new products must be able to destroy products that are similar and already present on the market, which would otherwise prevent the circulation of these new products. In today's world the capacity for innovation coincides with the capacity for destruction, therefore the criteria for evaluating innovation are adjusted to equal exchange market logic.

The *conatus essendi* of today's communication-production system destroys the natural environment, the life-forms that inhabit our planet. It also destroys difference among economic systems and among cultures. Equal exchange market logic activates processes of homogenization, which eliminate difference. Global communication-production renders habits of behaviour and needs identical (although the possibility of satisfying them is never identical). Even worse, communication-production society levels desires and the imaginary at a worldwide level. The *conatus essendi* of communication-production destroys traditions and cultural patrimonies considered a threat to the capitalist logic of development, productivity and competition, or that in the light of capitalist logic are simply useless or nonfunctional. The communication-production system destroys any forces or expressions of humanity that tend to escape the logic of capitalist production. Intelligence, inventiveness, and creativity are subject to "market reason" and as such are penalized (especially when production forces invest in "human resources"). Today's communication-production system is also destructive because it produces underdevelopment as *the condition for development,* pushing human exploitation and misery to the point of non-survival. This is the logic behind the expanding phenomenon of *migration*, which "developed" countries are no longer able to contain because of objective space limitations. No doubt this problem has reached greater proportions today than ever before.

To globalize the market is destructive. The global market means to globalize the status of merchandise which is applied indiscriminately to anything, including relationships; this too is destructive. In today's world, the more merchandise is illegal, the more its economic value increases and the more it is expensive—think of the traffic in drugs, human organs, children, uteruses, etc. To exploit the work of other people is destructive. The more work produces profit the less it costs: with the aid of a powerful support system as is global communication-production, developed countries are ever more turning to low-cost work in underdeveloped countries ("stay where you are, we will bring work to you"). The disgrace of the communication-production world is manifest in the spreading exploitation of child labour, which is mostly heavy labour and dangerous. Much needs to be said and done about children as today's privileged victims of underdevelopment, children living in misery, sickness, and war, on the streets, in the work-force, on the market.

The destructive character of worldwide communication-production is made obvious by war, which is always a scandal. Global communication-production is also the communication-production of war. War calls for new markets for the communication-production of weapons, conventional and unconventional. War must also be acknowledged as just and necessary, as an inevitable means of defense against the growing danger of the menacing "other": from this point of view war is used as a means of imposing respect for the rights of "identity" and "difference." However, identities and differences can neither be threatened nor destroyed by the "other." The real menace today is a social system that encourages and promotes identity and difference while undermining them, rendering them *fictitious* and *phantasmagorical*. This is why we tend to cling to such values so passionately, so unreasonably, according to a logic that fits the logic of the communication-production of war to perfection.

The spread of "biopower" (Foucault 1988) with the controlled insertion of bodies into the global production-communication system is supported by the idea of the individual as a separate and self-sufficient entity. The body is conceived as an isolated biological entity that belongs to the individual. Such a conception has led to the quasi-total extinction of cultural practices and worldviews based on intercorporeity, interdependency among bodies, the exposition of bodies, and opening to each other. What we are left with are mummified residues studied by folklore analysts, archeological remains preserved in ethnological museums or in the history of national literatures—the expression of a generalized situation of museumification.

Think of how the body is perceived by popular culture as discussed by Mikhail M. Bakhtin (1963, 1968), of the various forms of "grotesque realism." According to the logic of grotesque realism, the body or corporeal life in general are not conceived individualistically, that is, separately from the rest of life on Earth, indeed, from the rest of the world. However, only weak traces of the grotesque body have survived in the present age. Examples include: rites, ritual masks, masks used during popular festivities, masks used for carnival. Before individualism was asserted with the rise of the bourgeosie, the body was presented by "grotesque realism" ideology in popular culture during the Middle Ages as undefined and unbounded, as flourishing in symbiotic relations with other bodies. In the Middle Ages, the body was related to other bodies in relations of transformation and renewal that transcended the limits of individual life. On the contrary, present day global communication-production reinforces the individualistic, private and static conception of the body.

As evidenced by Michel Foucault (1988, see also Foucault *et al.* 1996), division or separatism among the sciences is also functional to the ideological-social necessities of the new cannon of the individualized body (Bakhtin 1968). (On this point we must also remember the work of the Italian philosopher and semiotician Ferruccio Rossi-Landi (1975) and his sharp analyses of the 1970s.) Separatism among the sciences associated with ideological and social individualism favour control over bodies and their insertion into the reproductive cycle of the communication-production system.

A Way Out as Indicated by Global Semiotics and Semioethics: The Logic of Otherness

We propose an approach to the signs of life and to the life of signs that is global and at once detotalizing. This approach is connected with the logic of otherness. It implies a high degree of availability for the other, readiness to listen to the other, a capacity for hospitality, and for opening to the other both in qualitative and quantitative terms (global semiotics is omni-comprehensive). Semiotic interpretation must not prescind from the dialogic relation to the other. Dialogism and the condition of intercorporeity are fundamental conditions for an approach to semiotics that is oriented globally and at once open to the local, which is not simply to be englobed. The approach we are theorizing privileges the tendency toward detotalization and otherness rather than totalization and englobement according to the logic of identity.

As Emmanuel Levinas (1961) demonstrated, otherness obliges the totality to reorganize itself ever anew in a process related to what he calls "infinity." This process may also be related to the concept of "infinite semiosis" (or sign activity), as understood by Charles S. Peirce (1931-1966). The relation to infinity is more than a cognitive issue. It involves co-implication with the other, responsibility beyond the established order, beyond convention and habit, and beyond the alibis these provide to keep a clean conscience. The relation to infinity is the relation to *absolute otherness*, that is, a relation to that which is most refractory to the totality. The relation to infinity implies a relation to the otherness of others, to the otherness of the other person. We are alluding to the other understood as the other that is alien, the extraneous other, and not the other understood as another self like one's own self, another *alter ego*, another "I" belonging to the *same community*. The other we are theorizing is understood in the sense of strangeness, diversity, difference toward which we must not be indifferent, toward which we must tend in spite of all the efforts made by self to the contrary, in spite of guarantees offered by the identity of I, of self.

This approach to semiotics is not ideological. On the contrary, our focus is on the human being understood as a "semiotic animal," therefore on human behaviour in the light of a unique capacity specific to human beings for responsibility. The expression "semiotic animal" indicates a responsible agent capable of producing *signs of signs*, of suspending action and of meditating and reflecting: the semiotic animal is capable of responsible awareness with respect to signs over the entire planet. From this perspective, "global semiotics" does not imply a cognitive approach alone to semiosic processes. Global semiotics is sensitive to another dimension beyond the theoretical, that is, the ethical. Given that this dimension concerns the ends toward which we must strive, we have also designated it with the terms "teleosemiotics" or "telosemiotics." Now we propose the term "semioethics."

Semiotics and, therefore, the semiotician, must inevitably make a commitment to the "health of semiosis." The capacity for responsive understanding toward the entire semiosic universe must be cultivated. To do this, semiotics must be ready to improve and refine its auditory and critical functions, its capacity for listening and critique. Semioethics can provide semiotics with adequate instruments for a critique of signs and sign systems. We believe that semioethics can provide an interpretation of sign processes in transition, that is, an interpretation in terms of the dynamics of shift, rupture, and flux that regulate sign processes, in contrast to signs and sign systems fixed and crystallized into objective entities and conceived in terms of being instead of becoming.

Places of the Gift from a Semiotic Perspective

As I have stated elsewhere (2004), semioethics may contribute with gift theory (see Vaughan 1997) to a better understanding of today's world and of the subjects who inhabit it. Ultimately, they may contribute to radical social change according to the logic of "social agapism" (from "*agape*" = love). This is a happy expression proposed by Genevieve Vaughan in a letter to me commenting on my 1997 paper, "Subject, Body and Agape."

As Vaughan says in the book *For-Giving* (1997), gift giving exists "*in many places*" but is made invisible by patriarchal capitalism. In reality, gift giving is effectively the basis of communication, including communication-production in the present day phase in capitalist production. Traces of gift-giving are in fact visible on a large-scale in the capitalist system: for example, in economies of Indigenous cultures, in such phenomena as women's free housework, or the remittances sent by immigrants to their families in their home countries. As Vaughan also demonstrates, even linguistic work, or "immaterial work" (as we now call it), is inseparable from gift giving and, in effect, is itself gift giving, linguistic gift giving. What we also need to underline is that in the global communication-production system, linguistic work or immaterial work is now acknowledged as a fundamental "resource," a basic "investment" (that is, an "immaterial investment"), indispensible to that system.

As a contribution in a semiotical key to the gift giving paradigm conceived by Vaughan (1997, see also Vaughan 2004), the following may be indicated as further places of the gift and may also be considered as susceptible to development in the direction of semioethics (and significs).

A *place of the gift* is *creative inference,* which the American semiotician Charles S. Peirce (1931-1966) has contributed to emphasizing with his concept of *abduction.* In the language of inference and inferential processes abduction indicates innovative argument, creative reasoning. Abduction is the name of a special type of argumentation, the development or transition in reasoning from one interpretant to another, which is foreseen by logic but supercedes the logic of identity. Abduction develops through argumentative procedures that may be described as eccentric, innovative, and inventive, especially in its more risky or creative expressions. In abduction, in contrast to induction and deduction, the relationship between the interpreted sign, i.e., the premise, and the interpretant sign, i.e., the conclusion, is regulated by similarity, attraction, and reciprocal autonomy. Grounded in the logic of otherness, abduction is dialogic in a substantial sense. Therefore, abduction belongs to the sphere of otherness, of substantial dialogism, creativity; it proceeds through a relationship of fortuitous attraction among signs and is dominated by similarity. As anticipated, abductive argumentative procedure is risky, which is to say that it advances mainly through arguments that are tentative and hypothetical, leaving a minimal margin to convention and mechanical necessity. Insofar as it overcomes the logic of identity and equal exchange between parts, abduction belongs to the sphere of excess, overflow, exile, *dépense,* of giving without profit, of the gift beyond exchange, of desire. It proceeds, more or less always, at the level of the "interesting" and is articulated in the dialogic and disinterested relationship among signs. This relationship is regulated by the law of creative love. Therefore, abduction is an argumentative procedure of the *agapastic* type.

Another place of gift giving that is strictly connected with creative inference, is what Victoria Welby (2006, unpublished mss.; see also Petrilli 1998b, 2006; Petrilli and Ponzio 2003, 2005: chp. 2) calls "primary sense." Welby proposed the term "mother-sense," or "primary sense," for a capacity that is common to men and women as much as it may be sexually differentiated in our patriarchal-capitalist society. Mother-sense is commonly referred to with a series of stereotyped terms including "intuition," "judgement," "wisdom." In any case, mother-sense is common to men and women even though it may be particularly alive in women owing to the daily practices they are called to carry out in their role, for example, of mother or wife. The allusion is to practices oriented by the logic of otherness and responsibility, practices based on giving, and responsibility for the other, care for the other. Welby also underlined women's responsibility, as the main custodians of mother-sense in the development of verbal and nonverbal language and, therefore, in the construction of the symbolic order. With the concept of "mother-sense" or "primary sense," Welby also signals the need to recover the human capacity for criticism, for gift logic subtending inferential procedure (in particular abduction), otherness, and dialogism, for unprejudiced thinking, for shifts in the orientation of sense production, for prevision and anticipation, for translation (understood in the broadest sense possible of this term, that is, for translation across space and time, across the order of signs and the axiological universe with which the latter are interconnected).

Finally, *individual identity* itself may be indicated as a place of the gift. The individual may be described, as does Welby (2006; see also Petrilli 1998b; Petrilli and Ponzio 2005: chp. 2) as a dialectical, indeed dialogical, relationship between the "Ident" and the "Self." The Ident is a generative center of multiple *selves* and at once a multiplicity inhabiting each one of our selves. The Ident is a dialectical and open unit with respect to the sum total of its parts, its multiple selves. With respect to the self, the Ident represents an overflow, an excess value, a gift:

> In order to Be—and really to Be is to be Given—what is impotent for fertile being *is* not; there *must* be overflow, there must be in some sense gift. True that in the arithmetical sense the bare unit may be added to and may multiply. But that is just because it has no content and no identity, as it has no fertility. Full identity is generative, is a Giver of its very self. (Welby 2006 [1907]).

The Ident is an orientation toward the other, toward the self insofar as it is other; a continuous transcending and transferral of the limits of the subject as it is, of the *hic et nunc* of subjectivity. The self represents that which to a certain extent can be identified, measured, calculated; instead the Ident can only be approached by approximation, tentatively and hypothetically—but never captured—and only by working through the means at our disposal, that is, our selves.

In Welby's description and similarly to Peirce, the human being is a community of parts that are distinct but not separate. Far from excluding each other, these parts, or selves, are interconnected by a dialogic relation of reciprocal dependence. In other words, they are founded in the logic of otherness and of non-indifference among differences, which excludes the possibility of non differentiated confusion among the parts, of levelling the other on to self. As says Welby (2006), to confound is to sacrifice distinction. Therefore, to the extent that it represents an excess or an overflow with respect to the sum of its parts, the I or Ident is not the "individual" but the "unique" (Welby 2006 [1907]). What Welby understood by "unique"—which has no relation to the monadic separatism of Max Stirner's (1844) conception of the unique, of singularity—may be translated with the concept of "non relative otherness," as understood by Levinas (1961), or with his concept of "significance," which is also theorized by Welby (1983 [1903]; see also Petrilli 1998a, 1998b, 2004; Petrilli and Ponzio 2005) in the context of her own theory of meaning. In fact, she proposed a meaning triad that distinguishes between "sense," "meaning," and "significance":

> ...for we may represent the Unique. That is the word which might well

supersede the intolerably untrue "individual." It is in fact just our dividuality which constitutes the richness of our gifts. We can, but must not be, divided; we must include the divisible in the greatest of Wholes, the organic Whole, which as risen to the level of the human, may crown each one of us as unique. (Welby 2006 [1907]).

From Welby's (1910) theoretical perspective, the self is also described as a way and not as an end; and in this sense it may be considered as "individual," that is, a way without interruptions to life and knowledge.

The ether, as science is revealing, is the unfailing way, the medium, whereon and whereby the light itself reaches us. Now "Self," again, is properly a Way, a Medium through which we energize and act, though alas, with our unconscious selfishness, we turn it into an End and identify Man with that. Yet, even as it is, we do not praise a man when we call him selfish. One who knows his self not as end but as means alone understands the highest form of identity. For the true Man is first and last the way through truth to life in a mentally Copernican sense, and through consciousness and tested observation, to knowledge. In such a way there must be no flaw, no slit, no gap or chasm. In this sense Man as a way is individual, that is, not divided or broken. (431)

According to Welby (1887), the secret of life is the concept of life as the gift, which means also the gift for truth, knowledge and interpretation. In her own words from her early papers: "The power of the Gift ... was vitalizing all truth, interpreting all problems, unifying all nature" (1). The gift is described as the human capacity to perceive life in all its expressions, to experience nature, the world at large, the universe in their dialogic relations of interconnection and vital interdependency; the capacity to experience, to know and be conscious of the existent in a Copernican or heliocentric perspective, indeed, even more broadly, in a cosmic perspective. And to live and experience the relation among signs and senses in their dialogic and intercorporeal dynamism and interdependency, in their capacity for change, transformation, and continuous development, in their capacity for creative interpretation, also means not only to recognize but also to enhance the human capacity for critique and radical change.

Susan Petrilli is Associate Professor of Semiotics at the University of Bari, Department of Linguistic Practices and Text Analysis. Her principal areas of study include sign theory, subject theory, theory of meaning and language, communication theory, problems of ideology, translation theory. She has edited three collective volumes of the series Athanor *(1999, 2000, 2001) on theory and semiotics of translation, another dedicated to the theme* Nero *(2003), and the most recent dedicated to Ferruccio Rossi-Landi entitled* Lavoro immateriale *(2004). Her major publications include:* Su Victoria Welby. Significs e filosofia del linguaggio *(1998);* Teoria dei segni e del linguaggio *(1999);*

and with Augusto Ponzio, I segni e la vita. La semiotica globale di Thomas A. Sebeok *(2002); Semioetica (2003); and* Views in Literary Semiotics *(2003).*

Notes

1   Includes writings by Welby and writings on Welby by Susan Petrilli. The volume also includes her correspondence with important figures of the time, and a small reader in significs with papers by significians influenced by Welby.

References

Bakhtin, Mikhail. 1963. *Problemy poetiki Dostoevskogo.* Moscow: Sovetskij pisatel. Published in English as: *Problems of Dostoevsky's Poetics.* Trans. and Ed. C. Emerson. Minneapolis: University of Minnesota Press, 1984.

Bakhtin, Mikhail. 1968. *Rabelais and His World.* Trans. and Ed. Krystina Pomorska. Cambridge: Massachusetts Institute of Technology.

European Commission. 1995. *Green Book on Innovation.* Typescript.

Foucault, Michel. 1988. *Technologies of the Self. A Seminar.* Amherst: The University of Masschusetts Press.

Foucault, Michel *et al.* 1996. *Biopolitica e territorio. Millepiani* 9. Milan: Mimesis.

Hegel, Georg Wilhem Friedrich. 1932 [1819-20]. *Grundlinien der filosofie des Rech.* Ed. G. Lasson. Leipzig: Meiner.

Levinas, Emmanuel. 1961. *Totalité et Infini.* The Hague: Nijhoff. Published in English: *Totality and Infinity.* Trans. A. Lingis. Dordrecht: Kluwer Academic Publishers, 1991.

Peirce, Charles Sanders. 1931-1966. *Collected Papers of Charles Sanders Peirce.* Eds.Charles Hartshorne, Paul Weiss, and Arthur W. Burks. 8 Vols. Cambridge, MA: Belknap Press of Harvard University Press.

Petrilli, Susan. 1997. "Subject, Body and Agape. Toward Teleosemiotics with Peirce and Welby." *Working Papers and Pre-publications* 261-262, Series A (February/March): 1-39. Centro Internazionale di Semiotica e di Linguistica, Università di Urbino.

Petrilli, Susan. 1998a. *Teoria dei segni e del linguaggio.* Bari: Graphis.

Petrilli, Susan. 1998b. *Su Victoria Welby: Significs e filosofia del linguaggio.* Naples: Edizioni Scientifiche Italiane.

Petrilli, Susan. 2004. "Gift-Giving, Mother-Sense and Subjectivity in Victoria Welby. A Study in Semioethics." *The Gift/Il Dono: A Feminist Analysis. Athanor: Semiotica, Filosofia, Arte, Letteratura* 15 (8): 179-198.

Petrilli, Susan. 2005. *Percorsi della semiotica.* Bari: Graphis.

Petrilli, Susan, ed. 2006. *Introduction to Victoria Welby's Significs Through a Selection of her Writings Presented and Commented by Susan Petrilli.* Toronto: University of Toronto Press.

Petrilli, Susan and Augusto Ponzio. 2000. *Il sentire nella comunicazione globale.* Rome: Meltemi.

Petrilli, Susan and Augusto Ponzio. 2002. *I segni e la vita: La semiotica globale di Thomas A. Sebeok.* Milan: Spirali.

Petrilli, Susan and Augusto Ponzio. 2003. *Semiotica.* Rome: Meltemi.

Petrilli, Susan and Augusto Ponzio. 2005. *Semiotics Unbounded: Interpretive Routes through the Open Network of Signs.* Toronto: Toronto University Press.

Rossi-Landi, Ferruccio. 1975. *Linguistics and Economics.* The Hague: Mouton.

Stirner, Max. 1972 [1844]. Der Einzige und sein Eigentum. Ed. Ahlrich Meyer. Stuttgart: Reclam.

Vaughan, Genevieve. 1997. *For-Giving: A Feminist Criticism of Exchange.* Austin, TX: Plainview/Anomaly Press.

Vaughan, Genevieve, ed. 2004. *Il Dono/The Gift: A Feminist Analysis.* 15 (8) *Athanor: Semiotica, Filosofia, Arte, Letteratura.* Roma, Meltemi Editore.

Welby, Victoria. 1883. Links and Clues. London: Macmillan and Co.

Welby, Victoria. 1887. *The Secret of Life.* Grantham: W. Clarke.

Welby, Victoria. 2006 [1907, June]. "I and Self." *Introduction to Victoria Welby's Significs Through a Selection of her Writings Presented and Commented by Susan Petrilli.* Ed. Susan Petrilli. Toronto: University of Toronto Press.

Welby, Victoria. 1910. "Jesus or Christ?" *The Hibbert Journal* 8(2): 430-433.

Welby, Victoria. 1983 [1903]. *What is Meaning? Studies in the Development of Significance.* Amsterdam: J. Benjamins.

Welby, Victoria. 1985 [1911]. *Significs and Language: The Articulate Form of Our Expressive and Interpretative Resources.* In *Foundations of Semiotic.* Vol. 5. Ed. H. Walter Schmitz. Amsterdam: J. Benjamins.

Welby, Victoria. 2006. *Introduction to Victoria Welby's Significs Through a Selection of her Writings Presented and Commented by Susan Petrilli.* Ed. Susan Petrilli. Toronto: University of Toronto Press.

Welby, Victoria. Unpublished Manuscripts. Welby Collection, York University Archives and Special Collections, York University, Toronto, Canada.

ELISABET SAHTOURIS

The Biology of Business

Crisis as a Gifting Opportunity

As an evolution biologist, it is obvious to me that we humans are part of Nature and that Nature has been doing business for billions of years, if we take a broad definition of business to be the economy of making a living, of transforming resources into useful products that are exchanged, distributed, consumed, and/or recycled. So, to talk about the biology of human businesses, I could simply point out that all our businesses are systems made up of people, who are living beings, and that therefore businesses are living systems or biological entities. However, to say something more useful I need to go back through history to show why most human businesses, despite being made up of people, do not function like living systems, at least not like healthy living systems. Those few that do are swimming upstream against the norm, usually with great difficulty, and that just should not be, need not be, and must not continue to be.

Our businesses, unlike those of other species, are organized and run in a socio-political cultural context, and that context has a history. Historical context has a great deal to do with what we believe about ourselves and our world, and when I sort through that socio-political history looking for the most salient influences on contemporary business from my own perspective, I am naturally drawn to the history of science.

Four very important publications by two great nineteenth-century scientists have so strongly shaped our beliefs about our world that they affect everything about human culture including our definition of human nature and the way we do business. They are: Rudolph Clausius' *On the Motive Power of Heat, and on the Laws Which Can Be Deduced from it for the Theory of Heat* (1850); Charles Darwin's *On the Origin of Species* (1859); Clausius' (1865) paper on Thermodynamics reformulating the fundamental laws of the Universe as energy constancy and entropy; and Darwin's *The Descent of Man* (1871).

I will argue that Clausius' model of a universe running down by entropy and the Darwinian model of biological evolution as an endless competitive struggle for scarce resources both give us half-truths about Nature that seemed appropriate in their historical context, but are now seen to be fundamentally flawed, thereby seriously misleading us and holding up our own natural evolution. The full truth—including the other half of a more holistic view in physics and biology respectively—reveals that Nature is on our side in role-modeling the evolutionary leap that would rapidly bring about an energy efficient and globally beneficial human economy that functions like a truly healthy living system.

The bottom line of human experience is that it all takes place within our consciousness and that our minds form the beliefs on which we act by collectively creating a uniquely human world. Change those beliefs and that world changes accordingly.

How could science have *failed* to rectify hugely important flaws in nineteenth century science even in the twenty-first century? I believe the answers lie in the fact that science, for all its protestations about being value-free, has never been an independent cultural endeavour free to pursue unbiased inquiry into Nature. Science was raised to the status of a secular priesthood—in the sense of being given the mandate and power to tell us how things are in our universe and who we are within it—by an even more powerful political economy, in turn for the great power of science in its engineering applications that keep that political economy in power.

Our world is now in sufficient crisis that transparency in all our endeavours is critical to our survival. Light shed on the relationship between science and political economy can, I believe, show us the way to true freedom and a healthy economy for all the world's people. It is Business that will lead the way, providing it, too, adopts transparency and belief in the mission of creating value for all stakeholders from people to planet.

Science and Political Economy: in which God Gives Way to Man

Only a few centuries ago in Europe, a new alliance of industrial entrepreneurs and scientists forged the industrial revolution, bringing the modern age successfully into being and replacing the prior cultural hegemony of the alliance between Church and State. Let me address a few details of this process, while noting here the current attempt to reinstate the Church/State alliance in the U.S. at present.

Over the past few centuries, science became far more than a vast research enterprise that gave us an advanced technological society with more commercial products than any previous culture could possibly have imagined, along with "progress" at a breakneck pace that leaves us breathless and wondering if we can even hope to catch up with our own children and grandchildren. Science, in addition to spawning that technological society, also became the cultural priesthood appointed to give us our cultural worldview: our beliefs about How Things Are in this great universe of ours, and on our planet Earth in particular. This is a relatively new and very important historical phenomenon in the history of civilization, as the priesthoods of most previous civilizations (large organized sociopolitical entities with urban centers), with notable exceptions such as China, were religious, getting their worldviews more from revelation than from research.

The scientific worldview founded by Galileo, Descartes, Newton, Bacon, and others was of a non-living, non-intelligent mechanical universe—a clockworks projected from human mechanical inventions to God's as the "Grand Engineer's" Design of Nature in which humans were just complex robots, the males alone imbued with a piece of God-mind, according to Descartes, so that they, too, could invent machinery. As models of celestial mechanics, the Newtonian motion of stars and planets, became more elaborate, social institutions as well were increasingly seen and modeled on mechanism, and expected to run like the well-oiled machines of factories. Time/motion efficiency studies of workers turned people themselves into machines as Charlie Chaplin movies so well caricatured. Most of today's businesses are still conceived, organized, and run as hierarchical mechanics.

As men of science had come to feel increasingly competent and knowledgeable about the physical world, and in consequence felt themselves to be in control of human destiny, they had formally abandoned the "hypothesis" of God, thereby removing any notion of Nature, including humans, as existing through sacred creation. Rather, Nature was redefined as a wealth of natural resources to be exploited by Man, the pinnacle of accidental, natural evolution.

One of the most pervasive and persistent cultural beliefs we have been given by science is the concept of this godless universe as non-living, accidental, purposeless, and running down by entropy, with life defined as a transient "negentropy" opposing this force of decay, yet never overcoming or even balancing its inevitable slide into heat death. To me, this is like describing the life of any one of us as a one-way process of decay toward death, with a negdecay process of birth and growth opposing it, though overall unsuccessfully.

This dreary view of life made me wonder deeply about the very concept of non-life, realizing in the process that it was invented by western science. All cultures have understood life and death, but non-life is something that never was or will be alive—a concept that came into human culture with the invention of mechanism in ancient Greece and resurfaced some dozen centuries later in a new era of mechanics. Was it really appropriate, I asked myself, for science to force life to be defined within a context of non-life? Could one really explain the existence of living things as accidentally derived from non-living matter? Could one derive intelligence from non-intelligence, consciousness from non-consciousness as I was consistently taught in the graduate science departments of several universities and research institutions?

Entropy Reconsidered

It was German theoretical physicist Rudolph Clausius, who first formulated the two basic laws of Nature in 1865—exactly halfway between Darwin's publication of *The Origin of Species* in 1859 and *The Descent of Man* in 1871—as:

> *The energy of the universe is constant.*
> *The entropy of the universe tends to a maximum.*[1]

Clausius' work on the thermodynamics of entropy, openly acknowledged by Maxwell in England, was based on Sadi Carnot's experimental work with energy transfer in the closed mechanical systems of steam engines and applied (by Clausius) to the universe as a whole with no evidence that the universe was a closed system in which such extrapolation might be valid. Yet these two "inviolable laws," along with the more basic conceptualization of the universe as purposeless non-life, have persisted since as absolute dogma in physics and all other areas of science.

But this model is a less satisfying conceptualization from scientific observation than the ancient Taoist, Vedic, and Kotodama model of a universe built on fundamental dualities within the Oneness of Cosmic Consciousness. Dualities are essential to the process of creation and the primary duality is often described as outward/inward, centripetal/centrifugal, expansion/contraction, translating in contemporary western science to radiation/gravity as the most fundamental forces or features of Nature.

Elsewhere (Sahtouris 2001), I have cited Walter Russell (1994 [1947]), as well as Nassim Haramein and Elizabeth Rauscher (2004), for their models of a universe in which entropic radiation and *centropic* gravity are in a perfect dynamic balance of expansion and contraction that constitutes a unified field. Haramein and Rauscher's theory is so conceptually and mathematically elegant that universal forces are reduced from four to two and the need to postulate hypothetical dark matter and energy in the universe is eliminated. In short, the work has been done to show that a universe of unified opposites satisfies our observations better than a one-way entropic universe, and shows that the universe is *not* running down at all.

The still "official" entropic universe, conceptualized after Einstein as beginning with a Big Bang and deteriorating ever since, is in sharp contrast to previous worldviews of Nature as alive and vibrant with intelligent creation and purposive direction—a view closer to my own model of a self-organizing, living universe in which planetary life is a special case of extra complexity, now actually measurable as being halfway between the microcosm and the macrocosm, where "upwardly" and "downwardly" spiraling energies collide on physical surfaces where such life can evolve (Sahtouris 2003).

Historically, the social consequences of the proclamation of an entropic universe by the scientific establishment were enormous, giving rise, for example, to belief in the Malthusian struggle for existence in a world soon to end (see below), interpretations of Darwinian evolution theory as a "dog eat dog" world, and a philosophy of existentialism extending this view of the purposeless and hopeless human struggle into psychology, art, and western culture at large. Such beliefs fostered the growth of our current consumer society with its "get what you can while you can" outlook in which advancing in the "job market" to increase power to consume became the driving force of modern and post-modern western civilization. Humanitarian social values and morals were left to religions with lesser persuasive clout than science, which came to openly pride itself on being value-free, and therefore even more *scientific* (read: unassailable in its conclusions about How

Things Are.) Small wonder that businesses carried out the competitive struggle justified as "social Darwinism" and deemed inescapable.

Darwin, Global Conquest and Evolution

Darwin himself had concluded with great elaboration in his magnificent opus on *The Descent of Man* (1871), that humans must exercise their evolved capacity for moral behaviour, as David Loye has so beautifully pointed out in his book *The Great Adventure* (2004), but this aspect of Darwin's work was not promoted by the science that took up his theory of evolution, focusing rather on his explanation of struggle in scarcity as the driver of evolution, which is best understood as rooted more in Darwin's historical context than in Nature itself. Had Darwin been able to see beyond that context, he might have noticed that highly evolved natural systems evolved long before humans display cooperation, mutual support, altruism and other features we define as ethical, but that is getting ahead of my story.

Columbus' voyages in the late fifteenth and early sixteenth centuries had inspired commerce between Europe and the New World, including such feats as Pizarro's plunder of 24 tons of treasure collected for the Andean Inca Atahualpa's ransom before his murder—exquisite art works of master craftsmen that were melted into gold bricks for transport to Europe—and trade in African slaves that were used to build colonial infrastructure, care for the colonists, etc. The American colonies were, in fact, settled by a corporation—the Massachusetts Bay Company, chartered by King Charles in 1628 for the purpose of colonizing the New World and its commercial ventures (Debold 2005).

Magellan's global voyage in the sixteenth century had established that all the world's territories were finite and could be owned, and the East India Company was founded in 1600, Queen Elizabeth granting it monopoly rights to bring goods from India to challenge the Dutch-Portuguese monopoly of the spice trade. Eventually the East India Companies of eight European nations functioned as the world's first great multi-national corporation or multi-national cartel of corporations. Though it incited American colonists to riot in the Boston Tea Party rebellion of 1774, Betsy Ross was commissioned in 1776 to sew the circle of stars representing the first thirteen states of the new union over the British emblem in the top corner of an East India Company flag to create the first U.S. flag. To this day we retain its thirteen red and white stripes with a blue corner field.

In Darwin's day, Thomas Malthus had been commissioned to inventory the Earth's natural resources as head of the Economics Department vof the East India Company's Haileybury College. Malthus concluded from his work that the world would end soon because human populations would overwhelm food production, causing an inevitable dying off of humans. This prediction justified the East India Company's "us or them" policy of assaying and acquiring all the Earth resources possible for Europeans so that they, at least, could survive.

Darwin, after doing his own Earth inventory work as a young shipboard scientist, could find no better way to explain the driver of evolution for his theory than simply to adopt his family friend Malthus' theory of human competition in scarcity and apply it to all of nature. This came to give scientific validity to our socioeconomic vision of scarcity and fierce competition for resources, of humanity doomed permanently to win/lose economics and warfare. As Darwin put it in *The Origin of Species* (1859):

> ...Nothing is easier than to admit the truth of the universal struggle for life, or more difficult ... than constantly to bear this conclusion in mind. Yet unless it be thoroughly engrained in the mind, I am convinced that the whole economy of nature, with every fact on distribution, rarity, abundance, extinction, and variation, will be dimly seen or quite misunderstood.... As more individuals are produced than can possibly survive, there must in every case be a struggle for existence.... It is the doctrine of Malthus applied with manifold force to the whole animal and vegetable kingdoms; for in this case there can be no artificial increase of food, and no prudential restraint from marriage.

Thus, Darwinian theory as Darwin *himself* established it, not just through later misuse as "social Darwinism," was very essentially rooted in political economy, which was itself rooted in a scientific worldview of a godless, mindless, coldly mechanical universe ever running down.

From Competition to Cooperation

My own work as an evolution biologist shows a very different picture of How Things Are in Nature and in our human world. Once I adopted Francisco Varela, Humberto Maturana and R. Uribe's (1974) definition of life as *autopoiesis*—that a living entity is one continually creating itself in relation to its environment—and Vladimir Vernadsky's (1986 [1926]) definition of life as a disperse of rock (which I paraphrased as "life is rock rearranging itself"), I quickly recognized that the Earth itself qualifies as a living entity. Its crust continually creates itself from erupting deep magma and recycles itself back into that magma at the edges of tectonic plates; its pervasive biological creatures are continually formed from and recycled into that same crust—all this in relation to Earth's Sun star, moon, other planets and greater galaxy.

Further, oceans, atmosphere, climate, and weather are all global systems, while biological creatures from bacteria to mammoths and redwoods are created from the same DNA, the same minerals and largely from the same proteins. Therefore, evolution is better understood as the biogeological process of Earth as a whole and the changing species patterns, both physiologically and behaviourally, over time within that larger context.

This leads me to include in my view of evolution the observations that the process of biological evolution goes well when individual, species, ecosystemic, and planetary interests are met simultaneously and reasonably harmoniously at every such level of organization, and that human behaviour is as much a part of biological evolution as is the behaviour of other species.

Nested levels of biological organization were called holons in holarchy by Arthur Koestler (1978), and are a useful contrast to the hierarchies humans have tended to model in machinery and build into socio-cultural organizations. In a healthy holarchy, no level is more important or powerful than any other; rather, all are vitally important, so none can dictate its interests at the expense of interests at other levels. All levels must continually negotiate their interests with other levels. In our bodies, for example, cells must negotiate their interests with their organs, organ systems, and the body as a whole, just as families (the next level of holarchy beyond individuals) must negotiate family interests with family members. A clear violation of healthy holarchy occurs when cancerous cells cease to negotiate and consider only their interests in proliferation at the expense of the body as a whole. This is, of course, a self-defeating strategy on their part.

The process of evolution is universally recognized as leading from the simple to the complex. Early Earth was a homogenized mass of mineral elements and evolved to the extremely complex planet of which we are part. Its first organisms were invisibly tiny archebacteria, while we ourselves are vastly more complex multi-celled creatures. Multi-celled creatures are relatively huge cooperative enterprises that could never have evolved if individual cells had been doomed to a struggle in scarcity, so they cannot really come about at all by the Darwinian hypothesis. Even the single nucleated cell—the only kind of cell other than bacteria—is now known to be a cooperative enterprise evolved by once hostile bacteria.

Note that I said, "once hostile." Indeed it seems that the first half of Earth's life in which bacteria had the planet to themselves, was for much of its existence indeed a Darwinian world of stiff competition, great crises caused by the archebacteria themselves and wonderful technologies they invented in the course of it, not at all unlike the human world's current situation. In fact, the archebacteria harnessed solar energy, invented electric motors (now coveted by nanotechnologists), and nuclear piles. They even invented the first World Wide Web in devising their very productive and universal information exchange in the form of DNA trade, as I have described in great detail in my book *EarthDance: Living Systems in Evolution* (2000). Eventually, however, as we know through the work of microbiologist Lynn Margulis (1993), they created the collaborative nucleated cell, turning these very technologies to good use in cooperative ways and streamlining themselves, as well as committing to community, by donating some of their DNA to the collective gene pool we call the nucleus.

What (r)evolutionary learning process made this shift from competition to co-operation possible? The key to answering this question and developing a complete model of biological evolution is suggested by the standard classification of natural ecosystems into successive Type I, II, and IIIs. A typical description of succes-sion—defined as the replacement of species with other species—is as follows:

Ecosystems tend to change with time until a stable system is formed … pio-

neer organisms modify their environment, ultimately creating conditions...
under which more advanced organisms can live. Over time, the succession
occurs in a series of stages which leads to a stable final community called a
climax community. This community may reach a point of stability that can
last for hundreds or thousands of years.[2]

Type I ecosystems are populated by aggressive species establishing their niches
through intense, sometimes hostile, competition for resources and rapid population
growth, while the species in Type III ecosystems tend toward complex cooperative
or collaborative systems in which species feed or otherwise support each other to
mutual benefit. Type IIs generally lump together various "transitional" ecosystems.
It seems reasonable to ask where the "more advanced" species that can "build
stable final community" come from? How did they evolve? Logically, there must
have been a time when only pioneer species existed, yet somehow evolution led
to the existence of mature, cooperative species. It would seem there had to be
some kind of evolutionary learning process in which species discovered through
their experience that cooperation pays!

Why *not* recognize the evidence for this ancient learning process revealed in the
different types of ecosystems? We are certainly familiar with learning and matura-
tion processes human life, especially the transition from immature adolescence,
so often feisty in its competitive stance, and socially cooperative maturity in
adults, who at their best become wise elders role-modeling the finest in human
behaviour. The ancient adage "as above, so below" has proven itself again and
again in seeing the similarity of patterns at different levels of Nature from simple
to complex, from microcosm to macrocosm. It is in the similarity of its patterns
that we see the true elegance of Nature.

We know the stages of evolution in the archebacteria, from intense competition
to their huge leaps in cooperation forming nucleated cells. We also know *these*
cells' collaborative process in evolving multi-celled creatures, all the way to our
own highly-evolved bodies containing up to a hundred trillion cells, each of which
is more complex than a large human city, each containing some 30,000 recycling
centers just to keep the proteins of which they are built healthy.

Again and again our close looks at Nature show this sequence from intense
competition to the discovery that peacefully trading with competitors, sharing with
them, feeding them, providing homes for them, even helping them reproduce, all
the while collectively recycling resources and ever enriching the shared environment,
is the most efficient and effective way to survival, and even thrival, for all.

It is in this mature cooperation that we find the ethics Darwin thought could
only be evolved by humans. Indigenous tribal peoples learned such ethics by recognizing them in Nature, copying reciprocal gifting and insuring food and shelter
to all tribal members, even working consciously to ensure tribal and ecosystemic
well-being seven generations hence. Like most Indigenous peoples, ancient Greeks
advised cooperating with Nature by giving back as much as we take from it, yet
our advanced civilization seems to be the last to learn this. We seem stuck where

Darwin was stuck, believing we are doomed to remain in hostile competition forever. How fond we are of repeating, "you can't change human nature" without ever really looking clearly at the nature of Nature itself.

Glocalization as an Evolutionary Leap

For some eight to ten thousand years up to the present, much of civilized humanity has been in an empire-building mode that is immature from the biological evolution perspective. From ancient empires ruled by monarchs we progressed to national expansion into colonial empires and more recently into multi-national corporate empires. All these phases have increased our technological prowess while also increasing the disparity between rich and poor that is now devastating the living system comprised of all humans, as well as the ecosystems on which we depend for our own lives.

As we have seen, healthy, mature, living systems are dynamically cooperative because every part or member at every level of organization is empowered to negotiate its self-interest within the whole. There is equitable sharing of resources to insure health at all levels, and the system is aware that any exploitation of some parts by others endangers the whole. Clearly, internal greed and warfare are inimical to the health of mature living systems, and humanity *is* now forced to see itself as the single, global living system it has become, for all its problematic, yet healthy, diversity.

Therefore, I see the formation of global human community—including but not limited to economics—as our natural evolutionary mandate at this time. We are actually achieving quite a few aspects of this process in positive, cooperative ways; for example, in our global telephone, fax, postal and Internet communications, in air travel and traffic control, in money exchange systems, in the World Court initiative and international treaties on environment and other issues, in most United Nations ventures, through ever more numerous and complex collaborative ventures in the arts, sciences, education, and sports, among religions and the activities of thousands of international NGOs. Yet the most central and important aspect of glocalization, the glocal economy, is still following a path that threatens the demise of our whole civilization.

Let me draw once again on the historical context of the alliance between science and industry. Hazel Henderson (2005) points out that Adam Smith related his famous theory of "an invisible hand that guided the self-interested decisions of business men to serve the public good and economic growth," as set forth in his 1776 book *An Inquiry Into the Nature and Causes of the Wealth of Nations,* to Newton's great discovery of the physical laws of motion. Also, that economists of the early industrial revolution based their theories not only on Adam Smith's work, but also on Charles Darwin's,

> … seizing on Darwin's research on the survival of the fittest and the role of competition among species as additional foundations for their classical eco-

nomics of "laissez faire"—the idea that human societies could advance wealth and progress by simply allowing the invisible hand of the market to work its magic.... This led economists and upper-class elites to espouse theories known as "social Darwinism:" the belief that inequities in the distribution of land, wealth and income would nevertheless trickle down to benefit the less fortunate. Echoes of these theories are still … propounded in mainstream economic textbooks as theories of "efficient markets," rational human behaviour as "competitive maximizing of individual self-interest," "natural" rates of unemployment and the ubiquitous "Washington Consensus" formula for economic growth (free trade, open markets, privatization, deregulation, floating currencies and export-led policies). (Henderson 2005)

All these theories, as Henderson points out, underpin today's economic and technological globalization and the rules of the World Trade Organization, the International Monetary Fund, the World Bank, stock markets, currency exchange and most central banks.

When the Bank of Sweden's economics prize, incorrectly but widely considered as one of the Nobel prizes, was awarded in December 2004 to economists Edward C. Prescott and Finn E. Kydland for their 1977 paper purporting to prove, by use of a mathematical model, that central banks should be freed from the control of politicians, even those elected in democracies, there was a wave of long-building protest. Scientists, including members of the Nobel Committee and Peter Nobel himself, demanded that the Bank of Sweden's economics prize either be properly labeled and de-linked from the other Nobel prizes or abolished on the grounds that economics is not a science, but a set of increasingly destructive policies.[3]

It seems high time for our dominant western culture, especially the United States, to learn the economic lessons that were learned by many an other species in the course of their biological evolution. In human economic terms, Henderson (1981) long ago made the analysis of the relative costs of destructive wars and constructive development, showing clearly how making war to destroy enemy economies was vastly more expensive than peaceful development of economies.[4] More recently, Ben Cohen of Ben and Jerry's beloved ice cream company made an animated video for the web-based organization True Majority using stacked Oreo cookies to show the amount of money the U.S. Pentagon requires for its military and the comparatively trivial amount it would take to feed all the world's children, build adequate schools, and provide other basic services at home and abroad.[5]

The unsustainability of present economics has now become widely discussed around the world, but it is still not clear we understand deeply that the word *unsustainable* means *cannot last*, and therefore, *must be changed*. Knowing how and why current economic policies are unsustainable is not enough; we must become more conscious participants in the process I call *glocalization*, rather than letting a handful of powerful interests and players lead us all to doom.

Capitalist free markets can only succeed in the long run if a) they really are free, which is not currently the case; and b) if that freedom leads more and more towards friendly (rather than hostile) competition and increasing collaboration—not as exploitative cartels, but as ventures consistent with global family values. Profits *can* be increased by treating people well and forming cooperative ventures such as Business Alliance for Local Living Economies (BALLE), a scheme I helped pioneer in the Social Venture Network (SVN) that is dedicated to building alliances among locally networked businesses for the common good.[6]

Reclaiming human communal values and acting upon them in ways that renew our economies while reversing the ravages of colonialism, and what John Perkins calls the "corporatocracy's" more recent predations as he so horrifically describes them in his new book *Confessions of an Economic Hit Man* (2004), is absolutely necessary if we are to turn our economies from unsustainable paths of destruction to sustainable paths leading to thrival.

Fortunately life *is* resilient, and we are witnessing a growing tide of reaction and dialogue on the present nature of economic globalization. These natural and healthy reactions have in common the recognition that communal values have been overridden in a dangerous process that sets vast profits for a tiny human minority above all other human interests. For a World Trade Organization to dictate economic behaviour that does not meet the self-interests of small, struggling nations, as it is increasingly discovering, would be like trying to run a body at the expense of its cells. We *are* living systems, whether we like it or not, and the only way to build a healthy world economy—to *glocalize* successfully—is Nature's way. (I use the terms *glocalize* and *glocal* economy to indicate all levels of economic holarchy from local to global.)

Economic success has so far been measured in monetary terms rather than in terms of well-being for all, focusing on GNP/GDP accounting rather than on quality of life accounting such as that pioneered by Henderson (2005) and now taken up by many progressive economists and at least one nation—Bhutan—by decree of its king, while others, notably Brazil, are leaning in that direction.

The Biology of Business

In my book *EarthDance* (2000), as well as in my article "The Biology of Globalization" (1998), I set out the Main Features and Principles of Living Systems, as:

1. Self-creation (autopoiesis);
2. Complexity (diversity of parts);
3. Embeddedness in larger holons and dependence on them (holarchy);
4. Self-reflexivity (autognosis—self-knowledge);
5. Self-regulation/maintenance (autonomics);
6. Response ability—to internal and external stress or other change;
7. Input/output exchange of matter/energy/information with other holons;
8. Transformation of matter/energy/information;
9. Empowerment/employment of all component parts;
10. Communications among all parts;

11. Coordination of parts and functions;

12. Balance of Interests negotiated among parts, whole, and embedding holarchy;

13. Reciprocity of parts in mutual contribution and assistance;

14. Conservation of what works well;

15. Creative change of what does not work well.

This list was derived from my observations, as a biologist, of living systems from single cells to complex multi-celled creatures, and of healthy ecosystems. These features should also be present in any healthy human system from family to community, business, government or other social system up to our global economy. But it became quickly clear that few businesses show these features.

Note that numbers 9, 10, 12 and 13 on the list, in a business that functioned like a healthy living system, implies the active empowerment and participation of every employee of that business in what it does and how it is run, with open communications among all. This, in short, means full inclusion and transparency, features totally abused in recent cases brought to public light, such as Enron and WorldCom, which glaringly highlighted what happens to businesses that see themselves in fierce competition rather than as healthy, collaborative aspects of their greater (stakeholder) communities. In sharp contrast, Bill George, former CEO of Medtronic and author of a book called *Authentic Leadership* (2003), once made headlines by boldly declaring that shareholders came third, *after* customers and employees. In his address to the World Business Academy annual meeting in 2004, George expanded on this, saying, among other things, he had told all employees on becoming CEO that none of them would be fired on his watch. In a time of unprecedented job insecurity at all levels of employment up to the top, this was bold leadership toward a very healthy company, whose shareholders had no complaints on his watch either.

The Internet, which is playing a huge role in business now, is a vast boot-strapping, self-organizing system that, however young and chaotic, shows all 15 of the features in one way or another and must therefore be considered a real living system. One of the big problems remaining to be worked out on the Internet is its ethical self-governance. A *Wired Magazine* article on Wikipedia, the phenomenal self-organizing web-based encyclopedia that rapidly outstripped—in numbers of articles—existing encyclopedias fashioned by experts over very long periods of time, showed it to be an exciting example of how this self-governance is now coming into practice. While anyone with web access is free to initiate, amend, or extend articles at any time, fleets of dedicated contributors monitor the changes and quickly catch malicious insertions. As reported in the March 2005 issue, the average time it took to detect attempts to sabotage Wikipedia's integrity was 1.7 minutes!

Cooperation, collaboration, and community empowerment are, as Nature role-models them and as I cannot repeat too often, more efficient and effective ways of doing business than living in fear of drowning in a competitive race or wasting energy and resources on beating down the competition.

Tachi Kiuchi, former CEO of Mitsubishi Electric, and Bill Shireman, an ecologist, put it this way in their important book, *What We Learned from the Rainforest* (2001): "There is no problem ever faced by a business that has not been faced and solved by a rainforest." A rainforest is a Type III ecosystem in which mutual support among all species has proven more efficient and effective than spending energy to make war among species. (Note that predator/prey relationships are actually cooperative when seen from the ecosystem level of holarchy because prey feeds predators while predators keep prey species healthy.) The rainforest (like a prairie or coral reef) creates enormous new value continually by very complex production and trading systems as well as by recycling its resources very rapidly.

Kiuchi (2003) has proposed a clear program for corporate accountability that he calls "The Eightfold Path to Excellence." The eight steps of this path, related to the rainforest lessons, are:

1. Adopt a bold and visionary *corporate mission*, one that envisions how your company will
2. Conduct a regular *assessment* of your success in maximizing return to stakeholders, and
3. Develop *incentive structures* that reward the creation of real stakeholder value on behalf of the corporate mission.
4. Adopt *management systems* to help you manage the company toward maximum stakeholder return, and measure your step-by-step progress.
5. Establish a *stakeholder engagement system*, to monitor and solicit feedback from
6. Create value for the *poorest* in the world, the stakeholders through whom the greatest mutual benefit can be delivered.
7. Issue an *annual report to stakeholders* that is as systematic as your annual report to shareholders.
8. *Live* the mission of your business. Make *that*—not your 90-day earnings report—the map to guide your course.

From an evolution biology perspective, glocalization is a natural, inevitable, *and* desirable process, much broader than economics and already well on its way—the latest and greatest evolutionary instance of cooperative collaboration in a living system. Consider all the collaboration required for global communications from telephone and fax to television and the Internet, for money exchanges across all cultures, for international travel, scientific cooperation, world parliaments of religion, the many global activities of the United Nations, and so on. All these instances of cooperation remind me of the formation of the nucleated cell a few billion years ago, when the technologies invented by archebacteria in their hostile competitive phase were put to cooperative use in building the new communal cell. This glocalization process is not reversible, though it certainly could fail, with the consequent destruction of human civilization as we know it. The critical link will prove to be how we change the way in which we carry out our economic, business activity as a global species.

As we have seen, unopposed universal entropy and Darwinian evolution through struggle in scarcity, presented as official scientific Laws of Nature, have prevented us from seeing them as half-truths requiring completion from a more holistic perspective. The entropy of radiation balanced by gravitational "centropy" is, at the biological level of Nature, the life/death recycling process that creates overall abundance—on Earth some 4.8 billion years of value creation despite huge accidental extinction setbacks. Darwin's struggle in scarcity is, therefore, not permanent for any species, because young pioneering species can and do learn to share, recycle, and support each other. We humans are such a young, pioneering species, and I believe we now stand on the brink of our own evolutionary maturity, ready to do business as it is done in the rainforest.

Once we convert our economies to more natural ones showing the features of healthy living systems, it will not be so big a step to move into the ultimate economic phase of the gifting economies proposed by Genevieve Vaughan (1997).

Elisabet Sahtouris is an internationally acclaimed evolution biologist, futurist, and author who teaches sustainable business and globalization as a natural, evolutionary process. She is a fellow of the World Business Academy and a member of the World Wisdom Council. Her venues include the World Bank, Boeing, Siemens, Hewlett-Packard, Tokyo Dome Stadium, Australian National Government, Sao Paulo's leading business schools, State of the World Forums (New York and San Francisco), and the World Parliament of Religions. Her books include EarthDance: Living Systems in Evolution; A Walk Through Time: From Stardust to Us *and* Biology Revisioned *with Willis Harman. Visit her websites: <www.sahtouris.com> and <www.ratical. org/lifeweb>.*

Notes

1 See Rudolf Julius Emmanuel Clausius,1822-1888. December 2000. Online: http://www-history.mcs.st-and.ac.uk/history/Mathematicians/Clausius.html
2 See http://regentsprep.org/Regents/biology/units/ecology/ecological.cfm
3 Op-Ed in Sweden's main newspaper, *Dagens Nyheter*, December 10, 2004.
4 Henderson co-created the *Calvert-Henderson Quality of Life Indicators;* see www.calvert-henderson.com and is Executive Producer of the new financial TV series, "Ethical Marketplace," airing on PBS stations in March 2005.
5 See BenCohen's animation video for True Majority Action. Online: http://www.truemajorityaction.org/oreos.
6 See BALLE, online: http://www.livingeconomies.org

References

Darwin, Charles. 1859. *On the Origin of Species.* Online: http://www.literature.org/authors/darwin-charles/the-origin-of-species.

Darwin, Charles. 1871. *The Descent of Man.* Online: http://www.literature.org/authors/darwin-charles/the-descent-of-man.

Debold, Elizabeth. 2005. "The Business of Saving the World." *WIE Magazine* 28 (March/April).

George, Bill. 2003. *Authentic Leadership: Rediscovering the Secrets to Creating Lasting Values.* New York: Jossey-Bass, Warren Bennis Series.

Haramein, Nassim and Elizabeth Rauscher. 2004. "The Origin of Spin: A Consideration of Torque and Coriolis Forces in Einstein's Field Equations and Grand Unification Theory." Online: http://theresonanceproject.org/research/scientific.htm.

Henderson, Hazel. 2005. "Economists as Advocates." Online: http://www.ethicalmarket-place.com/articles/ed1002.htm.

Henderson, Hazel. 1981. *Politics of the Solar Age.* New York: Doubleday.

Kiuchi, Tachi. 2003. "The Eightfold Path to Excellence in Corporate Accountability." Online: http://via-visioninaction.org/Kiuchi-Eightfold_Path_to_Excellence.mht

Kiuchi, Takashi and Bill Shireman. 2001. *What We Learned in the Rainforest: Business Lessons from Nature.* San Francisco: Berrett-Koehler.

Koestler, Arthur. 1978. *Janus: A Summing Up.* London: Pan Books.

Loye, David. 2004. *The Great Adventure: Toward a Fully Human Theory of Evolution.* New York: SUNY Series in Transpersonal and Humanistic Psychology.

Margulis, Lynn. 1993. *Symbiosis in Cell Evolution: Microbial Communities in the Archean and Proterozoic Eons.* 2nd edition. New York: W. H. Freeman.

Perkins, John. 2004. *Confessions of an Economic Hit Man.* San Francisco: Berrett-Koehler.

Russell, Walter. 1994 [1947]. *The Secret of Light.* Waynesboro, VA: The University of Science and Philosophy.

Sahtouris, Elisabet. 2003. "A Tentative Model of a Living Universe." Online: http://www.via-visioninaction.org/Sahtouris–TentativeModel-1.pdf.

Sahtouris, Elisabet. 2001. "A Tentative Model of a Living Universe," Parts I and II. Online: www.via-visioninaction.org.

Sahtouris, Elisabet. 2000. *EarthDance: Living Systems in Evolution.* Lincoln, NE: iUniverse Press.

Sahtouris, Elisabet. 1998. "The Biology of Globalization." Online: http://www.ratical.org/LifeWeb/Articles/globalize.html#p8.

Varela, Francisco, Humberto Maturana, and R. Uribe. 1974. "Autopoiesis: The Organization of Living Systems, its Characterization and a Model. *Biosystems* 5: 187-196.

Vaughan, Genevieve. 1997. *For-Giving: A Feminist Criticism of Exchange.* Austin, TX: Plainview/Anomaly Press.

Vernadsky, V. I. Vladimir. 1986 [1926]. *The Biosphere.* Oracle, AZ: Synergistic Press.

World Business Academy. Online: www.worldbusiness.org.

II. GIFTS EXPLOITED BY THE MARKET

CLAUDIA VON WERLHOF

Capitalist Patriarchy and the Negation of Matriarchy

The Struggle for a "Deep" Alternative

In her important book, *For-Giving: A Feminist Criticism of Exchange,* Genevieve Vaughan states: "In order to reject patriarchal thinking we must be able to distinguish between it and something else: an alternative" (1997: 23). I fully identify with this statement as I, too, have tried "to think outside patriarchy" although being inside it most of the time. At the "First World Congress of Matriarchal Studies," held in Luxemburg in 2003, where Vaughan and I first met, she stated, "If we don't understand society in which we live we cannot change it; we do not know where the exit is!" Therefore, "we have to dismantle patriarchy." In this article, I would like to add to Vaughan's analysis of capitalist patriarchy and tackle the task of dismantling patriarchy.

"A Different World is Possible!"

This has been the main slogan of the worldwide civilian movement against globalization for years. I have to add: "A *radically* different world is possible!"—it is not only possible but also urgently needed. But without a *vision* of this radically different world we will not be able to move in this direction. Therefore we need to discuss, first of all, a radically different worldview. For this purpose we have to analyze what is happening today and why. Only then will we be able to define a really *different* world, worldview and vision.

"Globalization:" An Explanation

A radically different worldview is necessary because today we are observing global social, economic, ecological, and political developments that are completely different from what they should be. "Globalization" is obviously not a movement toward more democracy, peace, general welfare, wealth, and ecological sustainability, as its propagators are pretending everywhere. On the contrary, the opposite is true. Never in history are so many people dying from hunger and thirst, environmental destruction, and war, most of them women and children. Never in history have so many people been confined to poverty, income reduction, expulsion, expropriation, and extreme exploitation, again, most of them women and children.

Never in history has technological progress led to such intense and threatening destruction of the environment globally. Never in history has the nuclear threat been so acute. Never in history have the political systems been changing so clearly in the direction of authoritarian, if not despotic rule in many parts of the world. And never in history has such a tiny minority on the globe been so incredibly rich and powerful. For transnational corporations and their "global players" today, we, and the planet, are nothing but their "play material."

This situation can be called the "development of underdevelopment" (Frank 1978). But this time underdevelopment is not only taking place in the South, but also in the North. It is the result of a "new colonization of the world" (Mies 2004) that did and does not happen inexplicably, but is actively and aggressively promoted by governments as their general and apparently "normal" policy, beginning in the 1980s of the twentieth century. This policy consists in a "continuing process of primitive accumulation" (Werlhof 1988) that leads to a forced economic growth through the direct expropriation of the peoples of the globe and the globe itself. The name of this policy is "neo-liberalism." This new liberalism serves exclusively the interests of the corporations. For the rest of humanity it means just the opposite, totalitarianism.

Is this "New World Order" (Chomsky 1999) the "best of all possible worlds" that western civilization pretends to develop? Or is the current development of western civilization better defined as the peak and turning point towards its final decline (Wallerstein 1974)?

Capitalist Patriarchy: A Historical Concept

Many people have provided descriptions of globalization as global crisis and its dynamics (Chossudovsky 1966; Hardt and Negri 2000; Wallerstein 2004; Ziegler 2002). There seems to be "no future"—astonishingly enough even for the global players themselves. I call this situation *west end*: western civilization is in its final decline globally (Werlhof 2002). With the self-given "licence to loot" (Mies and Werlhof 2003; Werlhof 2000), the resources of the earth will come to an end. The decline of resources is already underway. With the resulting "resource wars" (Klare 2001)—the new global wars for oil and water—we are witnessing the beginning of the end of the "modern world system," as a logical consequence.

But, there is almost no deeper analysis of the causes of this extraordinary situation or the dynamics that seem to exclude any alternative. There is no real, no deeper explanation of the world's dilemma and its causes. For example, is the profit motive alone sufficient as an explanation? Why do most people believe that human nature is nothing but ego-centric? What about control and domination of nature? In what is it rooted?

I suggest the reason why most people do not know why this crisis is happening is due to the fact that the left as well as the right, and the sciences in general, have never really analyzed patriarchy. And not having analyzed patriarchy also means not really understanding capitalism, because the two not only share a time of being together on this earth for 500 years now, but are deeply related to each other in a way that has not been understood by most people, even feminists. Therefore, it is time to take the necessary step of analyzing capitalist patriarchy from its roots and as a theoretical concept for the subsequent analysis of society. Only then can it be seen that patriarchy is much more than just a word for polemical purposes. It can instead be understood as a concept that explains the character of the entire social order in which we are living today, socialism included (Werlhof 2007).

Patriarchy: The Development of a "War System"

Recent studies of matriarchal societies and the development of patriarchy (see Göttner-Abendroth 2005) suggest mainly four things:

The Genesis of Patriarchy

Patriarchal society as we know it, did not exist "as such" and independently from, or even before, matriarchal society, but began to develop after the armed invasion, violent conquest, and systematic destruction of matriarchal societies by armed hordes that had lost their own originally matriarchal culture after having been exposed to "catastrophic migration" (forced migration due to climatic changes and other catastrophes). This process is reported from the fifth millennium B.C. onwards—concerning the "Kurgan" people and the Indo-European migrations in general—and it occurred in China, India, the Middle East, North and Central Africa, Europe, and the Americas as well (see Gimbutas 1994; Mies 2003). As patriarchal society, "as such," did not exist, we need to examine the conditions that led to its development.

The development of patriarchal society is related to the invention of something that from then on has been called "war," and since then patriarchy has been dependent on the ongoing existence of war(s) even in so-called "peace times." Without war, the people of conquered communities and societies could easily liberate themselves from their conquerors' rule. The logic of patriarchy is thus the *logic of war,* which means that all the social institutions invented by patriarchy are principally drawn from war experiences.

1) Patriarchy invented a *political system* based on the invention of the state, which meant the hierarchical dominance of armed men over the conquered people and the dominance of men over women, because women were at the centre of pre-patriarchal society and were responsible for the maintenance of its egalitarian principles.

2) Patriarchy invented an *economy* based on the the plunder of other peoples' property, since then called "private" property (*privare* = to rob), and on an always more systematic exploitation of the conquered, especially the women, because women in matriarchal society had control over the means of production, were the producers and distributors, the providers of concrete wealth—life, food, and security—and were responsible for the integration of everyone into the com-

munity (Vaughan 1997).

3) Patriarchy invented a *society* split into social classes, "races," generations, and "sexes." This means, especially since then, that women were regarded as being subject to men *by nature,* a belief fabricated by the patriarchs in order to prevent women from ever again being able to re-establish a matriarchal society.

4) Patriarchy invented a "*God-Father*" or "male creator-religion" based on the "great warrior," plunderer, proprietor, or "big man" (Godelier 1987), who was considered able to give life and was legitimized to take it. The Great Mother or Goddess was replaced by the idea and the ideology of an omnipotent, violent, and jealous single God, an abstract patriarchal "mother-father."

5) Patriarchy invented a *technology* based on "war as the father of all things," namely by beginning to transform the pre-patriarchal philosophy of *alchemy* into a patriarchal one. This means that since then men have systematically tried to use existing (female) knowledge about life and nature in order to appropriate it, to pervert it into a means of control over life and nature, finally, trying to *replace* life, women, and nature themselves through "technological progress" (Werlhof 2004a), the project of a "*second creation.*"

6) Patriarchy invented a *psychology* that defined the ways men could develop their "masculation" (Vaughan 1997), and their competitive, ego-logical patriarchal individuality (Girard 1992), opposing community, women, and nature.

The patriarchal order of society thus involves a total break with the matriarchal or gift giving social rules, traditions, and taboos, which had existed from time immemorial, and the development of a "war system" (Werlhof 2004b). And even if there have been times and places that did not at all fit this picture, the development or "evolution" of patriarchy has, nevertheless, been continuous, and women could not prevent it from happening. This can be seen more clearly today than ever before.

The Negation of Matriarchy

In patriarchal societies we can always find vestiges of former matriarchal societies—matriarchy as "second culture" (Genth 1996)—left over or newly re-organized after the patriarchs had started to deny the reality and quality of matriarchal society (Werlhof 2004b). This matriarchy as second culture can be observed everywhere, for example, in mother-child relationships, and other love relationships, and in gift giving generally (Vaughan 1997). It contradicts the patriarchal order, but also helps it to exist, because a society without *any* matriarchal relations could simply not survive. Therefore, patriarchies are always somehow "mixed" societies, whether to a higher or lower degree, and they are hiding this fact as much as they can—for obvious reasons. But today it is clear that patriarchy is trying to complete its negation of matriarchy in order to replace it with itself, a "pure" patriarchy, as much as possible. This destruction and the fading away of the second culture in patriarchy, and of much of the still existing gift paradigm within it, is one of the main reasons for the depth of the crisis of in contemporary civilization.

The negation of matriarchy consists in presupposing that there have never been any matriarchal societies; that patriarchal society has existed from the beginnings of human life on earth; and /or pretending that a violent and evil "rule of women" had to be broken before patriarchal society could develop so-called "civilization" and "progress." Due to this patriarchal mythology, most people today still think that matriarchy never existed, or that it meant "rule of women" instead of "rule of men," which indeed was never the case in matriarchal society, but may be so in patriarchal society instead. Most people, therefore, do not understand that the terms "matriarchy" and "patriarchy" are not just referring to men and women, or "male" and "female," but to the character of the whole social order, so that both men and women living in matriarchy have to be considered "matriarchal," and likewise men and women living in patriarchy have to be considered as principally "patriarchal" in their thinking, acting, and feeling.

The negation of matriarchy furthermore consists in:

•*Destroying* matriarchal society as a social order on its own.
•*Appropriating* everything from matriarchal society that seems important to the patriarchs, robbing and usurping these things, especially the image and the abilities of the mother (and the goddess), because patriarchy does not have an original culture of its own and can destroy but cannot originate life on its own.
•*Perverting* everything matriarchal into its opposite, which is the way "patriarchal" is defined.
•*Transforming* the original matriarchal society into a patriarchal one by developing policies of "divide and rule," by dissolving and abstracting the interconnectedness of people, communities, genders, generations, culture, commons, and nature in general; and by
•*Replacing* these and the entire matriarchal order with a "purely" patriarchal one.

The crucial significance of especially this last process of the transformation and substitution of nature and women has almost never been recognized.

The "Gnostic" Worldview of Patriarchy

Peoples' experiences with patriarchal society, war, despotic rule, and ceaseless violence logically led to a complete change in the general worldview, too. The Gnostic worldview thus appeared (Sloterdijk and Macho 1991). Gnosis means recognition: It is recognized that the world is "bad," "evil," "low," primitive, violent, sinful, and not worth living in. A better, "higher," more developed, "noble" and civilized world, therefore, is the ideal for people living in patriarchy. However, this "higher" world cannot be found on earth, even less so in the matriarchal past or presence elsewhere. The "higher world" is thus perceived as a metaphysical world that can only be envisioned through the imagination.

A metaphysical world beyond physics was not thought of in matriarchal society. So, the words *mater* and *arché* together do not mean "rule of mothers," but instead mean, "in the beginning the mother," life stems from mothers. *Arché* is beginning and "uterus" (Markale 1984: 207). Therefore, life, death, the mother, and the goddess, are always *here* in this world, and they all belong to each other, so that there is neither the need for, nor the idea of, another (metaphysical) world than the one in which we live every day (Chattopadyaya 1973).

In patriarchal society, on the contrary, another world beyond the existing one had to be invented, because the words *pater* and *arché* together do not simply mean "rule of fathers," but, instead, "in the beginning the *father*"—a word unknown in matriarchal times. Or, rather, life stems from "fathers" instead of from mothers; fathers are men with uteruses who are able to give life without needing women at all! (The Pharaoh Echnaton, for example, had himself painted as a pregnant man [see Wolf 1994]). Only on the basis of this fantasy would men be legitimized to rule over those who are not "fathers," the people, and especially the mothers. The "father," therefore, is defined as somebody who is a ruling man and as such not only able to take life, but also to give life.

In patriarchy the word *arché* thus did not only mean "beginning, origin, uterus," but also "rule" and "domination," too. This second meaning of *arché* did not exist before patriarchy, therefore, in matriarchy *arché* could have never meant domination, much less mothers' or women's rule. There simply was no domination, and therefore there was no word for it. Etymology shows that 1) a matriarchal society in which women were in power the way men are in patriarchal society never existed, and that 2) the "father" in patriarchal society has to be related to power as a *system of domination*, at least as long as he cannot replace the mother.

This means that the political system of patriarchal society can be regarded as a first step in the direction of the development of a *pure*, fully elaborated patriarchy, in which the fathers would really be "men with uteruses" or with something like "uterus-machines," who would then no longer need to dominate, because they would be able to do without nature, women, and matriarchal society. The political system of patriarchy would only be needed for the period in which patriarchy moves toward its final realization, toward a "full patriarchy," conceived of as the end of history. From this point of view, history is only the time in which patriarchy appeared and "evolved" until it became one hundred percent reality.

The patriarchal usurpation, destruction, and perversion of the mother and the wish to replace her thus led to an early sort of "science fiction": to the idea that what is only—and absurdly—*supposed*, namely that life stems from the father and *not* the mother, is considered even *more real* than what is experienced every day, namely the opposite. This *credo quia absurdum*—I believe in the absurd—of the early church-patriarchs, began from then on its nearly uninterrupted career on earth.

Gnostic metaphysics and the belief in another, "higher" reality appeared everywhere, in every theological as well as philosophical tradition until today. Since then the belief in metaphysical assumptions has become much more important than knowledge about the world in which we live, even more so in the secularized modern sciences of today, as we shall see below.

The historically new concept of the "father" is a triple fiction: it imitates the fiction of a powerful patriarchal "mother" and/or "goddess" and imagines to have successfully replaced her. This way the "father" is defined as a "patriarchal mother," the god as patriarchal goddess, who—as a contradiction in itself—could never have been thought of before.

This shows that the father originally is not regarded to be a man who relates to a woman with whom he has a child. This type of a father, as we normally define him today, is much less the "idea" of the father than the early fiction of a man with a uterus. The reason for this "loss" in defining the father is very simple: It has until now really been impossible to have new life without women.

But we know that biotechnology and genetic engineering are working hard to resolve patriarchy's main problem: the desire that only men should be the creators of life. Having to be born from women seems to be the biggest disgrace for patriarchal men and society (see Anders' 1994 description of the "shame of being born instead of being made"). Our actual "soft" understanding of the father who is still dependent on a mother proves every day that patriarchy in reality *does not* yet exist at all the way it is supposed to. The world—at least in this respect—basically still functions in a matriarchal way.

From Idealism to Materialism

But the fiction is the program. The *idea* of patriarchy has become its political and technological project. Patriarchy as a society in which life stems from fathers and not from mothers has to be artificially produced, or it will never really exist. The project is this: life—or what is considered to be life—should be born from or be made by men. And, only what men produce is considered to be "real life" and to have a "value," *as if* patriarchy had been realized already.

This way patriarchy becomes not only a *theory* (vision of God), but also a *theology* (the logic, the true words of God, his creation by the word that was "in the beginning"), a *theo-gnosis* (proof of the existence of God), and a *theophany* (God is appearing), and structurally *theo-morphical* and *theocratic*. Furthermore, patriarchy seems to prove its *entelechy* (its capacity to evolve its "naturally" given form to its perfection) and its potential for *eschatology* (end and new beginning of the world, death, and rebirth).

Once all this is the case, even the system of domination is imagined to eventually be abolished, because there would *really* be no alternative to patriarchy any longer.[1] Only if/when men become "real" fathers, will patriarchal society—in the long run—not have to fear women and matriarchy or the gift economy as an alternative any longer (Sombart 1991).

Since Aristotle, patriarchs not only pretended that their theory about life was true, even if they could not prove it, but they started to do something about it. This is how the Gnostic view became practical and "materialistic" in the patriarchal sense of the word. From the patriarchal viewpoint material is *mater* (matter), "mother-material," generally called "raw material," which is given by God/nature in order to be transformed into patriarchal "life," being a "resource" for "value-" or life-production, for something like a "mother-machine" (see Corea 1985).

From this perversion stems *fetishism* as the confusion between dead things and living beings.

This materialistic becoming of the Gnostic worldview, nevertheless, did not mean a return from metaphysical adventures. On the contrary, it meant trying to realize on earth what had been imagined beyond it; Plato's "ideas," for example. The Gnostic view, therefore, was not abolished. It became *the* program for patriarchal society, instead.

It is as if today, for example, the electronic production of the "virtual world" were considered to be the only "real world," and the real world were considered to have already been replaced by the cyber world, continuing its existence as the former real world only in imagination—so to say as a new "metaphysical" world "beyond" the virtual world. But this time metaphysics are no longer welcome. On the contrary, they appear outmoded and old-fashioned, if not reactionary, because they remember the natural world. This would be the real patriarchal perversion! And it has entered the thinking of women as well, even if they did not care much for the invention of machine-technology (Genth 2002). But this form of so called "post-materialism" can be found in many "gender-studies" that criticize, for example, the discourse on "nature" as being "essentialist" which means being metaphysical, because nature is supposed not to exist in reality - any more! (Werlhof 2003; Bell and Klein 1996).

In short, the Gnostic view, which is so typical of all the other patriarchal ideologies until today, did not work against patriarchy, though it correctly "recognized" many of the evils that it brought to the world. For the conclusions drawn from of this recognition were no longer oriented toward a matriarchal world. The evils recognized by the Gnosis were not considered to be those of a patriarchal society. They were considered, instead, to be of society in general, of "the world," of people, and even nature everywhere. The difference between a matriarchal society and a patriarchal one, or between society and nature, or between the ruling and the ruled, was no longer thought of. At that time, patriarchy was already taken for granted.

The Gnostic view had accepted the State. It did not question it any more, and those who could afford it tried to flee its consequences and its ugliness. In this way, the two main tendencies in thinking about patriarchal society came about: *idealism* and *materialism.* The two should not therefore be regarded, as usual, as pure contradictions, but as two sides of one coin, the "Siamese twins" of patriarchy: the "materialistic" side fighting actively against the lasting importance of "matter," the mater-mother, nature, the goddess, and life, in order to get them under control, and the "idealistic" side propagating the ideal of a motherless world, a purely patriarchal utopian paradise that seems peaceful because it appears to have finally resolved the contradictions with the material, matriarchal world or what remains of it. Idealism thus proves to be no less violent than materialism, because it is formulating the *idea* that became the project of a *material realization,* which cannot be other than radically violent.

From then on nature and women were no longer respected in their own subjectivity, beauty, truth, goodness, and strength, their inventions, abilities, products and culture, their *gifts* to the world since time immemorial. They were seen, instead, as representing the "chaos," the "sin," and the "evil" that had to necessarily be subjugated *under* and transformed *by* the socio-economic-political-ideological-religious-technological project of patriarchy. From this point of view, women and nature had to be oppressed, exploited, expropriated, transformed, and destroyed in a way that could be used as proof of male superiority, strength, and creativity.

Capitalism: The Latest Stage of Patriarchy

Having defined patriarchy, what does this mean for defining capitalism? From my analysis of patriarchy it follows that capitalism and modernity, including so-called socialism, far from being or becoming independent from patriarchy, are the latest stage of patriarchy. My hypothesis is that patriarchy crystallizes into capitalism. Capitalism is the period in which patriarchy becomes really serious. *Homo faber* is supposed to be finally replaced by "homo creator," a sort of secularized God.

This means that with capitalism there is a break as well as a continuation in patriarchy. But both tend in the same direction, namely fostering patriarchy. The logics of patriarchy led straight to the modern epoch, because capitalism is the promise to finally realize the futuristic Gnostic utopia materially and on earth. It consists of the intent to produce a purely patriarchal society, "cleaned" of all its matriarchal vestiges, and propagated as a male-created second paradise, including the invention of a finally "good" patriarchal "mother."

Metaphysics are to become the new physics. This is the propaganda of modern society as a whole, its politics, economy, religion—especially in the form of Protestantism—and technology.

Gnosticism becomes secularized. The content is the same, but the program has become one of action. The times of mere contemplation are fading away, the *vita contemplativa* is followed by a new kind of *vita activa* (Arendt 1987).

Since the Renaissance, the always increasing numbers of inventors and colonizers, scientists and soldiers, entrepreneurs and explorers, settlers and missionaries, merchants and money lenders are the modern activists on their way to the proposed, second, man-made and final paradise on earth (Rifkin 1998).

This is the beginning of the "Great Transformation" (Polanyi 1978) for which modern Europe became so famous. The new epoch was for the most part *not* seen as a continuation of an earlier one. It seemed, instead, to be the birth hour of a totally new society, not bound to history any more, a society that would be able to solve all the problems of mankind (indeed, not of womankind) for ever—like the U.S. today.

From the point of view of patriarchy, capitalism is the epoch in which women, nature, and life in general are finally successfully replaced by the artificial products of industry: gifts by exchange; subsistence goods by commodities; local markets by a world market; foreign cultures by western culture; concrete wealth—gifts by money, machinery, and capital—the new abstract wealth; living labour by machines; the brain/rational thinking by "artificial intelligence"; women by sex-machines and

147

"cyber-sex"; real mothers and/or their wombs by "mother-machines"; life energy by nuclear energy, chemistry, and bio-industry; and life in general by "artificial life" like genetically modified organisms (GMOs). The only problem that remains today consists in how to "replace" the elements and the globe itself.

Therefore, technological progress, through the development of modern sciences and the invention of the machine as a totally new techno-system, is the logical backbone of the modern patriarchal epoch. Patriarchy itself is progress, and all "progress" today is patriarchal. It serves the project of a materialization of metaphysical images via an industrial "life"-production which I call the "alchemical system" in development, because the idea behind it is as old as patriarchy and its first attempts to progress used the methods of a patriarchally-modified "alchemy" (Werlhof 2001).

The invention of profit that could be drawn from this adventure of the whole world's transformation convinced always more people, mostly men. But many people, especially women, had to be violently forced to participate in the new game. The political means consisted in processes of "original accumulation," which deprived the peasants of their means of production, and the women, through "witch"-hunts, even of the control over their own bodies, leaving nearly no way to survive beyond capitalism (Federici 2004).

Through all this progress mother earth will be more and more destroyed. Some of this rapidly increasing devastation is already irreversible, especially if caused by nuclear and the genetic modifications (Anders 1995; Chargaff 1988). Artificial death and artificial wealth—the violent "nothing"—a lot of money, is all that is left. The earth is on the way to being transformed into dead "capital," full of empty holes on the one side, and trash-hills for the next billion years on the other.

That all this is possible shows that most people believe in the violent nihilism of patriarchy and its dangerous delusion that has become "real." This astonishing fact can only be understood when one considers that the "alchemical wonders" patriarchy is promising, do not stem just from modern times, but are prophecies already 5,000 years old. Therefore, the destruction and desertification of the global ecology, including the human one, has not led to a general panic. On the contrary, it seems that, at least in the West, it is believed that only when the natural world has gone, can the patriarchal one finally be constructed, in all its glory, in its place.

Capitalism—as well as socialism— with its activism, optimism, positivism, rationality, and its irrational belief in patriarchy, world domination, money, science, technology, and violence, is not just capitalism, but has to be defined as "capitalist patriarchy" (and, by the way, not as "patriarchal capitalism" because there is no non-patriarchal capitalism). This epoch is still on the march because it has not yet reached its destination. Therefore, there is no post-capitalist, post-industrial, post-modern or post-materialist epoch in sight—unless capitalist patriarchy is stopped by a breakdown of its resources, technologies, markets, and money systems, by huge natural and or social catastrophes, or by an upheaval of the people who do not want to lose their lives, their planet, and the future of their children. If the "matter" of capitalism, its *mater*, its mothers, its women, and its matriarchal remains do not "obey" any more, and if nature fails to as well, only then will capitalist patriarchy disappear. And as capitalist patriarchy is obviously not a society for eternity, all this may well be happening today already.

The "Deep" Alternative

What Has to be Recognized

The alternative to capitalist patriarchy has to be a "deep" one, or it will fail. First of all, the "roots" of this war system will have to be recognized at all levels of society, individual life, history, and the globe. This will occur like a huge transdisciplinary research-project of and for the people. Out of this experience, the alternative will be a systematically non-capitalist and non-patriarchal one. It will be based on the remains of the "second culture" of matriarchy and of the gift-paradigm within patriarchal society, because they offer a body of concrete experiences people have been familiar with ever since humankind began on earth. Even though they have been underestimated, hidden and made invisible to most of us, they can be made conscious again, and this is happening already in many parts of the world (see Bennholdt-Thomsen, von Werlhof and Faraclas 2001)

Even if it appears overwhelming to overcome not only 500 years of modernity, but 5,000 years of patriarchal traditions, this is actually very little in comparison to the hundreds of thousands of years of human experiences outside patriarchy that we have to draw upon.

On the other hand, partial change/reform that maintains features of capitalist patriarchy will most probably, and quickly, lead back to the system that must to be overcome if we want to continue life on earth. Whether the alternative/s that can be found on this basis will again be matriarchal ones or not, cannot be foreseen. At least they will be *post-patriarchal.* At the moment it is historically open if matriarchy can be re-invented, and/or what a matriarchal society and a gift-economy would mean today.

What Has to be Done

What is needed is a re-version of a perverted parasitic society and (wo)mankind. The patriarchal "mother-father" as a "cyborg," which is the alchemical materialization of a metaphysical fiction has to fade away as soon as possible. We can accomplish this in a number of ways, mainly:

- de-constructing patriarchal institutions, policies, economies, technologies, and ideologies;
- making visible matriarchy as the second culture and the gift paradigm and recognizing their importance in every day life;
- giving up the metaphysical Gnostic worldview, including the belief in patriarchal religions and the patriarchal philosophy of idealism-materialism;

•re-gaining a matriarchal spirituality that leads again to a recognition of the interconnectedness of all life;

•not defining technology/progress any longer as having to produce a substitute for life, women, and nature in general;

•not defining economy any longer as having to produce a "value" and a profit;

•recognizing that the paradise which is supposed to be invented, is already here: It is the earth as the only planet in the known universe that is full of life and the only one on which human beings can survive;

•taking action to save the earth from further human destruction;

•liberating ourselves from the idea that "material" [physical] life on earth is unimportant, sinful, humble, and something that has to be overcome;

•liberating ourselves from the delusion and the hubris that there can ever be a substitute for life and nature on earth;

•learning the lessons of nature again, recognizing that the destruction of nature for the purpose of its transformation does not lead to a better world, but to its destruction;

•giving up war, believing in violence, and seeking to rule over others; learning instead to live in commonality and organizing around egalitarian principles;

•taking seriously what we are doing in and to the world, and accepting our responsibility for the maintenance of life on the planet;

•learning to rehabilitate and love life, including our own, and the life of the earth;

•seeking creative ways for the maintenance and culture of life on the earth; acting in favour of and not in contradiction to them;

•giving up "masculation" (Vaughan 1997), "egotism" as the search for competitive "identity," and identifying instead with gift-giving and the traditions of men and women in matriarchal cultures;

•learning that women can teach us a lot;

•giving up belief in patriarchy and joining with others in order to stop it; listening instead to the joyful song of mother earth.

We need to be able to perceive an alternative to capitalist patriarchy and see that this alternative is already in the making. Soon we will not be able to understand how or believe that men and women supported and even admired such a destructive delusion for such a long time!

The Struggle

Many alternative movements in the whole world are *already* in this process, for historical reasons most of them initiated by the global South (Kumar 2007) and most of them guided by women. This is the case because the South and women have and had to bear most of the negative consequences of patriarchy and especially capitalist patriarchy. This is why they are at the forefront of the new movements. Additionally, for women it is still much easier to remember matriarchal society and culture, and gift giving, because the remains of matriarchal culture and practices have for the most part been maintained by them. The way into a post-patriarchal society, therefore, is much more logical and visible for women than for men. The thinking, acting, and feeling of women, especially of poor women in the South, often shows a high level of dissonance with western globalization and culture. They defend life on "two fronts" of the conflict: against the war system of capitalist patriarchy and in favour of a new society (Bennholdt-Thomsen, Werlhof and Faraclas 2001; Werlhof 1985, 1991, 1996).

At the University of Innsbruck a new international research project is planned, the title of which is "On the Way to a New Civilization? Examples Of.... " For this research project, current alternative movements worldwide will be compared. Movements that are active on only one of the "two fronts" we are facing today, or that do not address the most important aspects and dimensions of life under patriarchal attack, will find themselves in crisis, sooner or later. This is still the case with many movements in the North and of those traditionally guided by men (Werlhof 2007).

It seems as if a larger and deeper movement in the North will only be possible when the illusions of moving upward within the system have been lost and the daily conditions of life have worsened further. But, in the meantime, extremists of the far right and "religious" fundamentalists everywhere are preparing their field of action, too.

Nobody knows what will be left of alternative movements and "deep feminism" in North and South when the patriarchal system and order of society is imploding and dissolving itself, and when the conflicts within it become increasingly violent. But if anybody has a chance to move in the right direction, it is the truly alternative *post-patriarchal* groups, communities, and movements worldwide.

Claudia von Werlhof is a women's studies professor in the Department of Political Science and Sociology at the University of Innsbruck, Austria. She has published numerous articles and books on a feminist theory of society, critiques of and alternatives to capitalism, and on globalization and patriarchy. Her most recent publications are There is An Alternative: Subsistence and Worldwide Resistance to Corporate Globalization *(2001), "Using, Producing and Replacing Life? Alchemy as Theory and Practice in Capitalism" (2004), and "The 'Zapatistas', the Indigenous Civilization, the Question of Matriarchy and the West" (2005), and "No Critique of Capitalism Without a Critique of Patriarchy! Why the Left is No Alternative" (2007).*

Notes

---

[1]   Compare, for example, the discussion about the "abolition of the state" and the idea of a "communist" society in Marx (Marx and Engels 1970: 415).

References

Anders, Günther. 1995 [1956]. *Die Antiquiertheit des Menschen*. München: Beck.

Arendt, Hannah. 1987 [1967]. *Vita Activa. Oder Vom tätigen Leben*. München: Piper.

Bell, Diane and Renate Klein, eds. 1996. *Radically Speaking: Feminism Reclaimed*. London: Zed Books.

Bennholdt-Thomsen, Veronika, Claudia von Werlhof and Nicolas Faraclas, eds. 2001. *There is an Alternative: Subsistence and Worldwide Resistance to Corporate Globalization*. London: Zed Books.

Chargaff, Erwin. 1988. *Unbegreifliches Geheimnis. Wissenschaft als Kampf für und gegen die Natur*. Stuttgart: Klett Cotta.

Chattopadyaya, Debiprasad. 1973 [1959]. *Lokayata: A Study in Ancient Indian Materialism*. New Delhi: Peoples Publishing House.

Chomsky, Noam. 1999. *Profit Over People. Neoliberalism and Global Order*. New York: Seven Stories Press.

Chossudovsky, Michel. 1996. *The Globalization of Poverty*. London: Zed Books.

Corea. Gena. 1985. *The Mother Machine*. New York: Harper and Row.

Federici, Sylvia. 2004. *Caliban and the Witch: Women, the Body and Primitive Accumulation*. New York: Autonomedia.

Frank. André Gunder. 1978. *Dependent Accumulation and Underdevelopment*. London: Basigstoke.

Genth, Renate. 1996. "Matriarchat als 2. Kultur." *Herren-Los. Herrschaft—Erkenntnis—Lebensform*. Eds. Claudia von Werlhof, Anne Marie Schweighofer and Werner Ernst. Frankfurt: Peter Lang. 17-38.

Genth, Renate. 2002. *Über Maschinisierung und Mimesis. Erfindungsgeist und mimetische Begabung im Widerstreit und ihre Bedeutung für das Mensch-Maschine-Verhältnis*. Frankfurt: Peter Lang.

Gimbutas, Marija. 1994. *Das Ende Alteuropas. Der Einfall der Steppennomaden aus Südrussland und die Indogermanisierung Mitteleuropas*. Innsbruck: Innsbrucker Beiträge zur Kulturwissenschaft Sonderheft 90.

Girard, René. *Das Heilige und die Gewalt*. Frankfurt: Fischer.

Godelier, Maurice. 1987. *Die Produktion der Großen Männer*. Frankfurt: Campus.

Göttner-Abendroth, Heide, ed. 2003. "Gesellschaft in Balance. Dokumentation des 1 Weltkongresses für Matriarchatsforschung in Luxemburg. Stuttgart: Kohlhammer.

Hardt, Michael and Antonio Negri. 2000. *Empire*. Cambridge, MA: Harvard University Press.

Klare, Michael. 2001. Resource Wars. *The New Landscape of Global Conflict*. New York: Henry Holt and Company.

Kumar, Corinne, ed. 2007. *Asking, We Walk: The South as New Political Imaginary*. Bangalore: Streelekha.

Markale, Jean. 1984. *Die keltische Frau*. München: Dianus-Trikont.

Mies, Maria. 2003. "Über die Notwendigkeit. Europa zu entkolonisieren." *Subsistenz und Widerstand. Alternativen zur Globalisierung*. Eds. Claudia von Werlhof, Veronika Bennholdt-Thomsen and Nicolas Faraclas. Wien: Promedia. 19-40.

Mies, Maria. 2004. *Krieg ohne Grenzen. Die neue Kolonisierung der Welt*. Köln: Papyrossa.

Mies, Maria and Claudia von Werlhof, eds. 2003 [1998]. *Lizenz zum Plündern. Das Multilaterale Abkommen über Investitionen—MAI—Globalisierung der Konzernherrschaft und was wir dagegen tun können*. Hamburg: Rotbuch/EVA

Polanyi, Karl. 1978 [1944]. *The Great Transformation. Politische und ökonomische Ursprünge von Gesellschaften und Wirtschaftssystemen.* Frankfurt: Suhrkamp.

Rifkin, Jeremy. 1998. *The Biotech Century.* New York: Tarcher/Putnam.

Sloterdijk, Peter and Thomas Macho, eds. 1991. *Weltrevolution der Seele. Ein Lese und Arbeitsbuch zur Gnosis. 2 Bde.* Gütersloh: Artemis und Winkler.

Sombart, Nicolaus. 1991. *Die Deutschen Männer und ihre Feinde. Carl Schmitt. Ein deutsches Schicksal zwischen Männerbund und Matriarchatsmythos.* München: Carl Hanser.

Vaughan, Genevieve. 1997. *For-Giving: A Feminist Criticism of Exchange.* Austin, TX: Plainview/Anomaly Press.

Wallerstein, Immanuel. 1974. "The Rise und Future Demise of the World Capitalist System. Concepts for Comparative Analysis." *Comparative Studies in Society and History* 16 (4): 387-415.

Wallerstein, Immanuel. 2004. Interview at the World Social Forum, Mumbai 2004. *Netzwerk gegen Konzernherrschaft und neoliberale Politik.* Info brief Nr. 15. March 2004. Köln: Demokratie von unten statt Post-Demokratie. 8-10.

Werlhof, Claudia von. 1985. *Wenn die Bauern wiederkommen. Frauen, Arbeit und Agrobusiness in Venezuela.* Bremen: Peripheria/CON.

Werlhof, Claudia von. 1988. "Women`s Work: The Blind Spot in the Critique of Political Economy." *The Last Colony: Women.* Eds. Maria Mies, Veronika Bennholdt-Thomsen and Claudia von Werlhof. London: Zed Books. 13-26.

Werlhof, Claudia von. 1991. *Was haben die Hühner mit dem Dollar zu tun? Frauen und Ökonomie.* München: Frauenoffensive.

Werlhof, Claudia von. 1996. Subsistenz. Abschied vom ökonomischen Kalkül?. *Herren-Los. Herrschaft—Erkenntnis-Lebensform.* Eds. Claudia von Werlhof, Anne Marie Schweighofer and Werner Ernst. Frankfurt: Peter Lang. 364-393.

Werlhof, Claudia von. 2000. "'Globalization' and the 'Permanent' Process of 'Primitive Accumulation.' The Example of the Multilateral Agreement on Investment (MAI)." *Journal of World-Systems Research* 6 (3) (Fall/Winter): 728-747.

Werlhof, Claudia von. 2001. Losing Faith in Progress: Capitalist Patriarchy as an 'Alchemical System.'" *Subsistence and Worldwide Resistance to Corporate Globalization: There is an Alternative.* Eds. Veronika Bennholdt-Thomsen, Nicolas Faraclas and Claudia von-Werlhof. London: Zed Book. 15-40.

Werlhof, Claudia von. 2002. "Go West End." *Der Tag. an dem die Türme fielen. Symbolik und Botschaft des Anschlags.* Ed. Christine Stecher. München: Droemer/Knaur. 274-280.

Werlhof, Claudia von. 2003. "Haus. Frauen. 'Gender' und die Schein-Macht des Patriarchats." *Widerspruch* 44 (23, Jg./1 Halbjahr): 173-189.

Werlhof, Claudia von. 2004a. "Using, Producing and Replacing Life? Alchemy as Theory and Practice in Capitalism." *The Modern World System in the Longue Durée.* Ed. Immanuel Wallerstein. Boulder, CO: Paradigm Publishers.

Werlhof, Claudia von. 2004b. "Patriarchy as Negation of Matriarchy: The Perspective of a Delusion." Paper presented at the First World Congress of Matriarchal Studies, Luxemburg 2003.

Werlhof, Claudia. 2007. "No Critique of Capitalism Without a Critique of Patriarchy! Why the Left is No Alternative." *Capitalism, Nature, Socialism* 18 (1) March: 13-27.

Wolf, Doris. 1994. *Was war vor den Pharaonen? Die Entdeckung der Urmütter Ägyptens.* Zürich: Kreuz.

Ziegler, Jean. 2002. *Die neuen Herrscher der Welt und ihre globalen Widersacher.* München: Bertelsmann.

LOUISE BENALLY

Big Mountain Black Mesa

The Beauty Way

I am Dineh (Navajo) from northeastern Arizona. I come from a community, Big Mountain Black Mesa, where our principles and foundations are based on a matriarchal society, and I was raised that way among my people by my mother and father. I come from a large family. I have seven brothers and three sisters, and so, in my life, gift, the beauty way, means not just human relations with one another, but rather, a recognition of universal interconnectedness. They say that the sun is our father; without the sun, there is no life on earth. The mother is the Earth, and in this way we try to remember that there is a balance because there is a female and a male in all our systems. We try to walk this beauty way of life being mindful of this balance, which is difficult right now because there is no longer harmony with this very government that we live under. We have been oppressed for the last 30 or more years in my community because of greed that is lighting up Las Vegas. We have a coal mining operation on our land that has devastated our community for many, many years, and even though our situation may be pleasant at times, our life ways are not the greatest. We still value the gifts of our sun, the gifts of the earth such as food, air, water, and the environment, all of which are being devastated right now because of greed that has no limit and that is affecting everybody everywhere.

How can we get this superpower, this country, to stop this? We don't really know exactly how. Maybe we should show them that just as mothers give un-conditionally to their children—a mother's love is the gift we mothers give to all our children, our people, all people, young and old alike—we must give back, unconditionally, to the Earth. Yet, there is greed, there is hatred, there are people that do not understand this world and are going in a direction that depletes and destroys the Earth, never thinking about the next person, never thinking about the future generations.

How we, as the Black Mountain people, live is not recognized in this day and time. We continue to communicate with the earth, with the sky, with the sun, with the atmosphere, with the different seasons, and all the life that is here. Because we feel that we have no control, it does not matter if George Bush is the president. We still have to eat, drink, raise children, and live. In our community we try to exist now by denial; denying that there are all these policies that are affecting our lives. If we let these policies affect us all the time then we are imbalanced because we are concerned, we are worried, and we may be depressed. So, in my world, I deny that this is happening to our people. The reality of my life is that I have to live, I have to provide, I have to in some way give back to the earth, to the air. I travel to different places speaking and encouraging young people to understand these ways and to value them.

Today it is very challenging because our atmosphere is deteriorating, and in our part of the country, our water is being privatized. There is a very little bit of good drinking water left and all these different companies are after our resources; they want to privatize them, for greed. What do they give back in return? Pollution. And pollution is affecting all the life on earth today. The air is not pure anymore, the water is not pure anymore. This is of great concern to me, and my community.

I feel for the mothers on the other side of the world that are being frightened by terrorists. How are we going to change this? Will it have to be the women who step up and say, "No! We need to stop this!" If this is what it takes, then we must do this, the sooner the better, because there are children, there are mothers, there are brothers, and sisters that are being killed, that are dying, for no reason.

And in Big Mountain the situation is the same. We are not literally being killed, but we are being oppressed, we are denied our human rights, we are denied religious rights, we are denied the right to grow our own food, and we are denied the right to gather a load of wood so we might stay warm through the night. Our life is being denied.

I have lost a lot of people—my elders, my children, my brothers, my sisters—as a consequence of this situation. My people are heartbroken. They don't know what to do. They don't speak English, so there's no comprehension of why others would want to destroy the land. We don't understand this at all. Why do they want to control the air, the water, and how we live?

As children of the earth we should share what we have. If we can give, we must give. If we cannot let go of all of it, we can break a piece of it and still give. That's what "gift" is to me, to my people. Our struggle has always been difficult, because we are up against great odds all the time. But if we pray, if we sing, if we eat, if we grow our food, if we harvest our firewood—that's what our life was like before colonialism—we can continue to walk the beauty way. And we teach this to our children, so that they will have hope to walk in these hard times.

Right now many, many of our children are sent overseas to commit huge crimes against humanity. We, as mothers, have to say something, as sisters we have to say something, as aunties we have to say something. We cannot stand by and allow this to continue, allow our children to be killed, and to kill others. Somehow we have to stop this. We need to unite locally and globally and say, "No! Stop this! Correct this!"

In the end—and we don't have very much time left, with the way things are going now—the greedy want to destroy everything, they want to take everything, but they don't know what lies beyond. Their scientists don't know either. I know because my grandpa used to say: "Don't let them take all the resources from the earth, because the moon controls the water wave. If we lose a lot of the resources on the earth, it will unbalance the earth and the moon, and then we are going to be in real trouble." And that is where we are headed.

The Las Vegas lights, the power to light the city up, comes from my community, Big Mountain Black Mesa. We have no running water, we have no decent housing, we have no electricity, we have no school roads for our kids, we have nothing, but our resources light up Las Vegas. We are outcasts in our own country. But that doesn't stop us. It encourages us to walk the beauty way and heed the cries of Mother Earth to heal the planet before it is too late.

Louise Benally is a 46-year-old Dineh mother and grandmother. She is a human rights activist, an environmental activitist, a traditional educator/counsellor, and an herbalist. Currently, she is working for the Northern Arizona University on health promotion, diabetes prevention, and healing gardens. This is one way she teaches about a "healthy living world" for all the living beings.

ANA ISLA

The Tragedy of the Enclosures

An Eco-Feminist Perspective on Selling Oxygen and
Prostitution in Costa Rica

This paper develops the premise that patriarchal capitalism, which understands
conservation in terms of enclosure, uses it as another instrument for colonization of Third World resources, women's work, and nature. This paper connects
two aspects of this process: the first is the enclosure of the forest for as an oxygen
generator/carbon sink; and the second is the enclosure of women's labour through
prostitution. As the forest and women's non-wage labour comprise the support
system that local communities use for survival, selling oxygen and prostitution
have become a war on subsistence and, consequently, an expansion of poverty.
Presenting a case study of the interactive socio-economic-ecological-gender impact of land management on local communities in Costa Rica, I conclude that
Costa Rica's foreign debt crisis provides grounds for restructuring accumulation
in the industrial world by selling oxygen/carbon sink capacity as the technological
solution to environmental destruction, and for repairing masculine anxiety, or
"masculation" (Vaughan 1997) by selling its women's and children's bodies as a
result/consequence of the inequality crisis.

Introduction

Since the Industrial Revolution humans have greatly increased the quantity of
carbon dioxide found in the Earth's atmosphere and oceans. The major sources
of these gases are being emitted by industrial processes, fossil fuel combustion,
and the modification in land use, such as deforestation. If emissions continue at
the present rate, current projections suggest that there will be a global increase in
temperature of between, approximately, 1°C to 5°C by 2100 (PhysicalGeography.
net; Pew Centre on Global Climate Change). Forest vegetation stores carbon
that otherwise might trap heat in the atmosphere, driving up temperatures and
speeding up climate change.

Selling oxygen from the rainforest to act as storage of carbon sink has become
part of the sustainable development agenda as outlined in the Kyoto Protocol.
Governments first agreed to tackle climate change at the Earth Summit in Rio
de Janeiro in 1992. The Kyoto Protocol was the follow-up to the United Nation
Framework Convention on Climate Change (UNFCCC), which set a non-bind-

ing goal of stabilizing emissions at 1990 levels by 2000. This goal has not been met overall (Forbes 2003).

The World Bank (WB) defines sustainable development as the management of the entire cycle of life (humankind and nature) with the intention of expanding "wealth." This definition of sustainable development allows for the management of a nation's portfolio of assets. These assets include built infrastructure, natural resources (minerals, energy, agricultural land, forests, etc.), human capital, and social capital. According to the World Bank (1997), many of the critically important ecological and life-support functions provided by natural systems are not yet measured as part of the wealth of nations. Among those not yet captured is the forest. The forest must be embedded in the economic system as natural capital to become a resource for sustainable development. This is very problematic for rainforest dwellers that are not embedded in the market economy.

As forests become commodities for selling oxygen/carbon sink provision, the sexual division of labour and women's oppression is affected in powerful and serious ways. Evicted from a forest, peasant families are forced to migrate toward cities to look for employment. Rural women and men need to find resources to assure subsistence and emotional support for themselves and dispossessed family members. In the exchange logic, according to Genevieve Vaughan (2004), those who do not succeed in the market, are seen as "defective," less human, and therefore more exploitable (17). In this context, the gender relations of patriarchal capitalism have constructed peripheral women as cheap labour—cheap sex. In Costa Rica, patriarchal males find a place to practise their quest for domination. Their domination is expressed through their ego-oriented individual psychology, that Genevieve Vaughan has called "masculation." Masculation expresses dominance of men over women's bodies. Some males need to confirm their superiority through the use of sexual violence; this is done by degrading anyone in the position of other. In this paper, prostitution and sexual slavery are the enclosure of women's and children bodies, because they no longer have decision-making power over their own bodies.

The advantages of selling oxygen/carbon sink capacities has been articulated by mainstream environmentalists. Environmentalists from the industrial world have adopted a political stance that sets them and the environmental movement above and beyond class struggle, gender oppression, colonialism, and imperialism. Practicing this narrow form of environmentalism has reinforced the dominant relations of power in global capitalism (Foster 1994). They are oblivious to exploitation, poverty, and the inequalities facing local communities, thus contributing to the displacement of communities on a global level through ill-conceived conservation strategies. In their view, the rainforest and its dwellers are seen as spectators only (Hecht and Cockburn 1990). As a result, the sustainable development agenda has defined the forest as "natural capital," while rural women have been constituted as "cheap human capital." Since capital has converted the sensuous world into an abstraction for the purpose of profit, the forest and women come to express alienated ways of being. The double enclosures of the forest and women's labour have become another war on the subsistence capacity of rainforest dwellers. This paper will connect the selling of oxygen/carbon sink capacities and prostitution of women and children in Costa Rica.

Capitalist Patriarchy in Costa Rica

Ecologists have provided evidence of the natural limits of the planet to industrial growth (Foster 1994) and consumerism (Wackernagek and Rees 1996), and rejected the belief in unlimited economic growth (Daly 1996). The natural limit is already expressed in the destruction of resources and absorptive capacities for wastes (Alvater 1994), and in irrefutable global warming. As economic growth continues to be central to sustainable development, two Earth Summits— one in Rio de Janeiro, Brazil and the other in Johannesburg, South Africa— to reduce emissions of greenhouse gases, air pollution in the form of carbon dioxide, dust particles, and carbon monoxide have failed, making clear that traditional environmental movements are inadequate, and even dangerous in their propositions on how to confront the environmental crisis.

Ecologists and feminists plea for the reorientation of economic development to the goals of maximal reduction of energy and material throughputs for local self-sufficiency as opposed to export-oriented trade competitions—and for consumption norms that recognize "enoughness" (Sachs 1992; Shiva 1989), "sufficiency" as a good life (Bennholdt-Thomsen and Mies 1999), subsistence economies (Bennholdt-Thomsen and Mies, 1999), and gift economies (Vaughan 2004). Genevieve Vaughan (2004) argues that patriarchy fabricated an economy based on *private* property (in Latin *privare* = to rob) (see also Claudia von Werlhof on page 141 of this volume). Patriarchy artificially created scarcity in order to erase the gift economy, practiced generation after generation, because most labour in the world is still gift giving. These gifts are women's non-waged household work; peasant and Indigenous people's labour; industrial workers' forced gifts (in Marx's theory, surplus value is an unpaid portion of the worker's labour, which is a gift); voluntary work; child labour; and nature.

Costa Rica has an export-oriented economy, however, due to its foreign debt, it is an example of export pressure on resources (Guha and Martinez Alier 1997). In terms of land ownership, United Fruit, a U.S. multinational corporation, enclosed the southern part of the country with banana plantations; the local business community enclosed the central valley for coffee plantations; and foreigners and local businesses enclosed the northwest for cattle ranching. These land grabs by foreign and local businesses deeply divided Costa Rica in terms of land control and power. Excluding the owners of one hectare parcels of property, 83.4 percent of land owners with less than a 100 hectares control 1.12 percent of the national territory, while 0.71 percent of the owners with more than a 100 hectares own 70.3 percent of the country's territory (*El Estado de la Nacion* 1996: 68).

The sustainable development agenda has aggravated this unequal access to resources by intensifying earlier enclosure of the land through the Conservation

Area System created in 1989 by the then Ministry of Natural Resources, now the Ministry of Environment and Energy (MINAE). Through Sistema Nacional de Areas de Conservación (SINAC), the conservation area model was implemented to manage the country's wildlife and biodiversity. SINAC divided the country into eleven Conservation Areas, which incorporate wildlife, privately-owned land, and human settlements, and placed them under the current Ministry of Environment and Energy's supervision. In enclosing 24.8 percent of the national territory, SINAC expanded the enclosure model. The expropriated land has been organized along the lines of national parks in North America from which people are excluded and denied any role in sustaining the ecosystems contained therein (Hecht and Cockburn 1990). These expropriated lands are linked to transnational and political networks to forge local and global "stakeholders" through categories of management such as human patrimony, national parks, wet land, biological reserves, protected zones, forest reserves, and wildlife refuges. At the same time internal boundaries are established, separating local people who share volcanoes, waterfalls, rivers, hot springs, congo-monkeys, and turtle-spawning havens. The separated lands then become sites for mining (Isla 2002), research (Isla 2005a), ecotourism (Isla 2005b), and the selling of oxygen.

Enclosure of the Rainforest: Selling Oxygen/Generating Carbon Sinks

In the sustainable development framework, forests have become natural capital. But the forest, in the rainforest, is an essential mechanism for flood control. In the forest, trees are connected directly to each other through the multitude of creatures that relate to them as food, shelter or nesting place; through their shared access to water, air and sunlight; and through an underground system of fungi that links all the trees as a super-organism. Rainforest people are also members of this super-organism.

The Kyoto Protocol commits industrialized nations to reducing emissions of greenhouse gases, principally carbon dioxide, by around 5.2 percent percent below their 1990 levels by 2007. In the Climate Change Convention held in Kyoto in 1997, industrial countries agreed to create mechanisms to reduce the emissions of gases responsible for the greenhouse effect. Among these is carbon dioxide (CO_2), largely discharged by the industrial world. However, reducing gas emission implies high costs for industries that the industrial world protects. Thus, it was easier for the major emitting corporations, with the backing of their governments, to propose a self-interested "solution": create a global market in carbon dioxide and oxygen, focused on the forest of indebted countries. According to the scheme of the Climate Change Convention, countries or industries that manage to reduce emissions to levels below their limits will be able to sell their "credit" to other countries or industries that exceed their emission levels. Following the Convention, the Clean Development Fund thus evolved into the Clean Development Mechanism (CDM), an arrangement under the Kyoto Protocol that allows industrialized countries with a greenhouse gas reduction commitment to "invest" in emission reducing projects in developing countries as an alternative to what is generally considered more costly emission reductions in their own countries.

With the introduction of the Kyoto Protocol, the rainforest is valued economically through the securing of CO_2 strategies. Carbon emission became subject to trading in an open market. The use of the absorption of CO_2 by the forest to compensate for other countries' emissions developed easily in indebted Costa Rica.[1] Through international covenants, Costa Rica organized conservation, management of forests and reforestation, and sells environmental services to Norway, Germany, Holland, Mexico, Canada, and Japan (*El Estado de la Nacion* 1996: 129). During Jose Figueres' administration (1994-1998), the Forestry Law (7575) and the decree DAJ-D-039-98 were signed to regulate payments for environmental services. Certification for forest conservation is legislated by Forestry Law, Art. 22, which is under the jurisdiction of MINAE. Under the Forestry Incentive Programs (FIP), MINAE receives, evaluates, and approves the terms of the program and promotes and compensates owners of forestry plantations. The decree recognizes the forest and forest plantation owners, small farmers (*finca* owners), and Conservation Areas (CA) as providers of environmental services eligible to receive payments for the environmental services they provide. MINAE also developed a law of expropriation, which outlines the limits placed on initiating any project on small and medium-size farms.

Since the industrial world is not held responsible for mitigating its own level of emissions, this "solution" has allowed the industrial world to continue polluting by means of the purchase of carbon credits from the indebted rainforest, while energy-related emissions produced by the increase in the amounts of coal and oil burned mainly in the industrial world, the leading cause of climate change, proceeds unimpeded.

Selling CO_2, to mitigate carbon emissions, is a colonial, class- and gender-biased practice that impacts on the nature of indebted countries, subsistence production, and on women.

Paying the Price of the Kyoto Protocol: Crisis of Nature

The selling of oxygen is transforming the rainforest. Forest farms have been established. Reforestation is particularly promoted among large-scale agricultural entrepreneurs in association with international capital, which also benefits from tax relief under Fiscal Forestry Incentives (FFI). FFI reforestation involves international capital, which uses foreign forest species of high yield and great market acceptance, such as *melina* (used by Stone Forestall, a United States corporation), and teak (used by Bosques Puerto Carrillo and Maderas). Big projects related to the planting of forests in general are also connected to the interests of big mining corporations. For instance, in Arenal-Huetar Norte Conservation Area, Industries Infinito S.A, a subsidiary of the Canadian company Vanessa Ventures, which obtained permits to operate Mining Crucitas over an area of 1,000 hectares, also has a reforestation project on 32 hectares where it planted 20,000 trees to profit from the Forestry

Incentive Plan (FIP). The corporations are allowed to log the trees after ten years of growth and transform them into wood for floors and/or paper.

Between 1996 and 2001, around 121,000 to 147, 000 hectares of foreign trees were planted; 50 percent percent of the species are *melina* and teak (MINAE 2001; Sage and Quirós 2001; De Camino, Segura, Arias, and Pérez1999), and the rest are eucalyptus. The government had enthusiastically promoted converting forest ecosystems into sterile monocultures by planting homogeneous forests, despite the fact that *melina,* teak and eucalyptus are not indigenous to Costa Rica's rainforest. In order to plant homogenous species, if the owners want to manage recurrence (return), the first step is to remove all the native trees and vegetation, which increases the extraction of nutrients, and with it the devastation of the productive capacity of the soil. Thus, chemical fertilizers are massively spread throughout the area targeted for the plantation. This choice was clearly dictated by industry (flooring wood and paper). This has negative effects on soil fertility, water retention, and on biological diversity.

The consequences of planting teak has been explained by Sonia Torres (2001), a forestry engineer, who explains how foreign trees produces erosion on flat lands. In the rainforest, biodiversity means a great number of leguminosae with differently sized leaves, which lessen the impact of rainfall and prevent erosion. She used the example of teak to illustrate the problem.

> *Since the planting of these foreign species, I have observed that teak has a root system that grows deep into the soil, but in the rainforest the systems of nutrient and water absorption are at the surface. In general, nutrients and water are concentrated between 70 and 100 centimetres deep. As a result, teak trees are encircled by flaked soil. In addition, when it rains, the size of the leaf accumulates great amounts of water that then pours violently onto the soil. A drop of water, at a microscopic level, forms a crater; when water falls from 15 metres or more it forms holes. Water descending on soft soil destroys the soil. The far-reaching spread of the roots and the shade produced by the leaves obstruct the vegetative growth on the lower forest layer, which could prevent the soil damage from the violent cascades.*

Torres advocates the planting and protection of indigenous tree species that can also feed the indigenous population, animals, bacteria, etc.

Crisis of Rainforest Dwellers

The selling of oxygen scheme has also transformed local communities. In Costa Rica, the state's project of selling CO_2 expropriated the small- and medium-sized landholders without compensation to the owners has been exposed:

> A symbol of pride of Costa Ricans, the national parks constitute a unique model in the world, which offer innumerable benefits to society in particular

and the planet in general, but they are in a critical situation due to the lack of resources to give them sustainability and cancel the debt to the former property owners whose lands were expropriated or frozen for the sake of protection. (Odio 2001: 2)

By August 1999, the government owed US$100 million to evicted *campesinos/as* (peasants). Around that time, it offered to pay US$6,703.45 per hectare to the dispossessed families (Vizcaino 1999). However, by 2001, 14,917 hectares of land were still not paid for, affecting approximately 745 families that have been made landless and impoverished by the conservation areas system.

Large projects related to the planting of forests in general are also connected to the interests of international mining corporations, large environmental NGOs, and government institutions (MINAE in Costa Rica). For instance, in the Arenal Conservation Area, organized by the World Wildlife Fund-Canada, national parks such as Arenal Volcano and Tenorio Volcano National Park, and forestry reserves such as Cerro Chato, sell oxygen. But to put the oxygen on the market, in 1994, the Arenal Volcano was declared Arenal Volcano National Park. From five hectares, the park was extended to 12,010 hectares. As a result, entire communities were forcibly evicted. While the majority of the land around the volcano was not arable or adequate for cattle ranching, small farms had existed in the area. *Campesinas/os* who had organized their lives by clearing land for agricultural production and pasture around the Arenal Basin were expelled by (MINAE). An injunction brought to Costa Rica's Supreme Court (Division IV of the judicial system), reported heavy losses by *campesinas/os* who lived in the Basin area of the Arenal Conservation Area. They lost land, pasture, houses, dairies, and roads. Former property owners have become hut renters (*ranchos*) or slum inhabitants (*tugurios*). The personal effects of the *campesinas/os*, such as cars and small electrical appliances, were taken by the commercial banks when they could not afford to repay their loans acquired for economic development (Monestel Arce 1999). When, in desperation, some of them returned to their land to plant yucca, beans, maize, and other subsistence foods, they were declared to have broken the law and some of them were thrown in jail (Siete Dias de Teletica 1999).

In 1996, La Cuenca de Aguas Claras was also declared a forestry reserve. In 2001, I attended a public Town Hall meeting in La Cuenca de Aguas Claras at which more than 200 farmers, men and women, arrived ready to be interviewed. Since they were too many to each be interviewed, the farmers chose Abel Fuentes and Luis Guimo[2] to speak on their behalf. They declared themselves witnesses of the following accounts. According to Fuentes (2001), MINAE had stated that:

our survival way of life is producing deforestation and pollution, and reducing the water level of La Cuenca de Aguas Claras. [But] MINAE exaggerated the level of deforestation to oust almost all the inhabitants because it is reforesting our land in order to sell the oxygen to other countries and get "donations."

MINAE's argument for expropriating their land was based on the claim of water reduction in the area. Water scarcity has been converted into a strategy to convince *campesino/as* to let MINAE reforest while the owners of the land are evicted. Fuentes had witnessed the forced eviction of rainforest dwellers.

Until 1996, in La Cuenca de Aguas Calientes, 200 families lived and the land was organized as follows: 70 percent percent was pastureland, holding around 2,000 cows; 10 percent primary forest; and 20 percent combined secondary forest, which was used for beans and pig production. By 2001, we were only three families; the majority were forced into exile. And the land has been re-organized as follows: 90 percent is primary and secondary forest; 10 percent is pastureland with less than 200 cows; and land to produce beans has been extinguished.

Fuentes believes that his rights and his community's rights have been violated under the law of expropriation of 1995. As soon as the expropriation law was passed, some of the *campesino/as* went to MINAE's office to get more information about the law, but were purposely misled by the government. Fuentes declared that:

the government denied our right to know the law. When we requested a copy of it, a representative of MINAE showed us a giant book, saying that he couldn't give us a copy, because of the volume of the decree. However, later, one of our members found the legislation on the Internet and printed it on just one page.

Martin Guimo (2001), also a small landholder who still lives within the expropriated land, added:

When we ask MINAE officials for information, they decide when and where we can get it. When we propose a meeting, they decide when and where we can meet, then they change the hour, the date, or they cancel the meeting without telling us. Many of us live far from the meeting place and sometimes we have to ride a horse for three hours to go to a meeting and it is disappointing to arrive and learn that the meeting has been cancelled.

The snatching of the forest from local communities who use it to sustain themselves has become a death sentence for small and medium-size landholders. As a result, their needs are dismissed, and community members who used to live off the forest are declared enemies of the rainforest.

The eviction of the rainforest dwellers is justified by claims they will find employment in the cities. Rural community members know opportunities for well-paying jobs and upward mobility in Costa Rica's cities is a myth. They know that there is a surplus of people in the cities whose basic human needs cannot be met and whose human rights are violated (Robinson 2003; Bennholdt-Thomsen and Mies 1999). Maria Mies (1986) argues that community members in the Third World dispossessed from their livelihood cannot expect to become dependent on wages. Peripheral landless women and men will not have the good fortune of their peers from the core countries to find a job and share the wealth extracted from colonies, because they themselves are the colonies.

Crises of Women and Children: Impoverishment and Prostitution

The power of the industrial world to re-design the forest as oxygen producer exacerbates inequalities. As a new structure of accumulation emerges, the disintegration of the ecosystem that supported the means of survival of local communities has powerful effects on the sexual division of labour and women's oppression. When families are violently disintegrated or displaced and impoverished, rural women are encouraged to migrate to San Jose and tourist areas in the hope of earning an income for themselves and their dispossessed families. Introduced into the cash base economy, impoverished women earn all or part of their living as prostitutes. Prostitutes in Costa Rica are women at work supporting children and family members. They are in the market not by choice but out of necessity. Along with them, there are an astonishing amount of children who are bought, sold, and mistreated by society (Casa Alianza 2001a). By complying with the desires of the so-called developed men, these women contribute to the global production of the tourism industry, and to the wealth of businesses and states, as we will see.

Pressured by the global institutions (the International Monetary Fund [IMF] and the World Bank), indebted Costa Rica has become the premier eco-tourism and sex tourism destination since the early 1990s (Isla 2005b). Eco-tourism promotion links conservation areas with tourism, and promises a world of leisure, freedom, and safe risk; while sex tourism portrays an image of women and children as exotic and erotic. This image of the country entangles the economic relations of domination between creditors (the industrial world) and debtors (the indebted periphery), and the psychological relations of hypermasculinity or "masculation" of fragile male egos that the exchange system develops. As Costa Rica becomes impoverished by its foreign debt, manufactured by the U.S and England in 1982 (Roddick 1988), we can see the marks of these changing international power relations on the bodies of Costa Rican children and women (Pettman 1997). Rich, white men move across borders for racialized sex tourism. Male sex tourists, in their 40s and 50s, come mainly from the creditor countries, such as the U.S, Europe, and Canada. In Costa Rica, most pimps that profit from sex-tourism are men from the patriarchal industrial world—U.S, Canada, Spain, and others. They bring with them the political economy and culture, material relations, and particular perceptions of how the world works (Pettman 1997: 96). On the Internet, there are currently more than 70 websites selling Costa Rican women.[3]

Costa Rica is also indebted to Canada; from 1992 to 1996, 313,525 Canadians visited Costa Rica. In 1997 alone, 36,032 Canadians (ITC 1999) visited Costa Rica, while by 2002 this number had grown to 50,000 (Malarak 2004). A 2004 CBC report by journalist Victor Malarek, made it clear that Canadian males engage in sex-tourism. According to his report, these men can be found at the

El Rey Hotel in San Jose, where secret videos for sex and teenagers are waiting to be bought and women are sold for $10 or $20 dollars. Prostitution in Costa Rica has become widespread; in San Jose alone 2,000 girls are working in the sex-trade (Casa Alianza 2001a). Trafficking is a growing problem. Many of the teenagers being sold into the sex industry in Costa Rica are victims of trafficking from Nicaragua, Guatemala, and Honduras. Traffickers threaten to kill their parents and siblings if they are identified. The "wealth" generated by those women goes back to the IMF and the World Bank as interest payment on Costa Rica's outstanding foreign debt.

As the country slides into a more subordinated position, the entire country has become a paradise for pedophilia. Men interested in young girls, and gay male tourists (and so-called straight male tourists) who want to have experiences with boys travel to Costa Rica to engage in sex with or take pornographic pictures of children. Child pornography has become an established industry in Costa Rica (EFE News 2003).

> More than a million tourists go to Costa Rica every year, and at least 5,000 are pedophiles....Women and children involved in sex work commonly contract sexually transmitted diseases or die of AIDS-related illness. (Casa Alianza 2001b)

By 2001, international groups put Costa Rica's government under intense scrutiny for its lack of action against the sexual abusers of children, most of them tourists. In an economy increasingly based on enclosure of the Commons, complicit Costa Rican governments do not want to stop the sex-trade industry because they know that this is the only way left for women and children to earn a living. As a result, the government's attitude is one of general indifference to recognizing and reporting the criminal activity. Ex-president of Costa Rica, Miguel Angel Rodriguez stated on an American television program in 2001 that there were only "20 or 30" children being sexually exploited in Costa Rica, even though the U.S. Department of State estimated 3,000 children were victims of commercial sexual exploitation in Costa Rica (see Casa Alianza 2001c). The Costa Rican government also protects the sex industries because it generates hundreds of millions of dollars per year that the state uses to pay its foreign debt.

Although prostitution is prohibited in Costa Rica by law, there is no enforcement to stop this oppression of the poor and marginalized members of society considered disposable. To endure their misery of sexual activity with five or six men daily, many of the enslaved women and children turn to drugs and alcohol. In 2001, three young street girls went missing and were eventually found dead, cut into pieces and strewn around San Jose (Casa Alianza 2001c) with seeming impunity. By 2001, there were only five people in jail (four U.S citizens and one Costa Rican) awaiting trial for the sexual exploitation of children, despite the 230 criminal complaints that Casa Alianza (2001a), a U.S. nonprofit organization in Central America that works with homeless children and kids at social risk, presented to the Costa Rican authorities. In addition, the police are often part of the problem. On August 10, 1999, the Costa Rican Special Prosecutor Against Sex Crimes received a judge's order to raid "The Green Door," a private club operated by a U.S citizen that offered female "escorts" and minors for sex to businessmen and foreign residents in Costa Rica. Helped by the Minister of Public Security, Rogelio Ramos, the U.S criminal escaped (see Casa Alianza 2001b). Further, when young girls are arrested, the victims are punished by police who demand oral sex (Malarek 2004).

In Costa Rica, women are also sex tourists. Rich U.S, Canadian, and European women sex tourists take advantage of their superior class and race status to lure young boys and men. There are reports that young boys and men engage in "romance tourism" with these women, usually well-off, single, professional women who travel to resort areas and provide a willing male with drinks, dinners, shopping sprees, jewellery, and other luxury goods in exchange for sex and companionship. In this criminal environment, women can be as exploitative as men (Sanchez Taylor 2001), but women can also be endangered by their "romantic companions."

Resisting Narrow Environmentalism

The definition of forest as oxygen generator actually destroys sustainable ways of living, thus creating real material poverty, or misery, by expropriating or diminishing the capacities of the forest to sustain its dwellers. *Campesino/as* know that their human rights have been violated by MINAE and other organizations that call themselves environmentalist. Referring to these "environmentalists" organizations, Luis Guimo (2001) stated:

They used to come to us for information, and we provided it. I personally boarded people and allowed them to use my horses to move about comfortably. Things are changing; we cannot collaborate anymore. MINAE told me that I have to sell my finca to the state and at the price the state decides. We are not leaving. They have to kill us if they want our land.

Further, the creditors' power relations that encourage selling oxygen are written on the bodies of the forest, the women, and the children of indebted Costa Rica. As dwellers are evicted from their land, dispossessed and vulnerable women and children turn to the sexual tourism industry for survival, forcing them into sexual slavery. First world white males, with the complicity of local governments, thus exploit the economic hardships of the inequality crisis created by global capitalism with impunity.

The messages of power from the industrial world and its privileged males deem Costa Rican women and children, and nature inferior. Consequently, the enclosure of the Costa Rican forest, for capital accumulation, has condemned Costa Rica's rural women and children to destitution, prostitution, and/or death. Ironically, the situation of Costa Rica as country is the same as the situation of its prostitutes—both are kept in financial debt by their pimps: the IMF, the World Bank, commercial banks, and powerful countries in the first case and brothel owners in the second. They live in debt bondage where the arrangements are such that neither the country nor the sexual slave can ever earn enough to pay off their debts or become autonomous beings.

But, Costa Rican women and men, with the support of local municipalities, are no longer silent. They are defending their rights to a secure livelihood. In their battle against losing livelihoods, men and women have uncovered the class, gender, and colonial relations of the sustainable development agenda in the alliances between their "national" government and international capital. At the same time, women and children's battered and enslaved bodies have shown that the Kyoto Protocol that uses the rainforest as carbon sink is not separated from their subsistence and everyday life.

By pressuring investors around the world and by exposing the fallacy of "sustainable development" that does not acknowledge its class, gender, colonial, and imperialist bias, women from all over the world can join their Costa Rica sisters in their struggle for a just and healthy world. No blank cheque to the Kyoto Protocol! The women's movement needs to support the Kyoto Protocol only if it is committed to reducing greenhouse gas emissions by imposing limits on the gases produced by the factories and lifestyles in the North. It cannot be endorsed if it will continue with the expropriation of the rainforest that represents the basis of the survival economy of its dwellers.

Ana Isla's current research specialty and interests are feminism, eco-feminism, women in development, Third World women, women's micro-enterprises, political economy, political ecology, the Commons, enclosure in the twenty-first century, debt crisis, globalization and global issues, social justice, racism, economic development, sustainable development, debt-for-nature swaps, poverty issues, community organizing, the gift economy, bio-piracy, Indigenous knowledge, eco-tourism, mining and environmental NGOs. She is assistant professor at Brock University and a member of Toronto Women for a Just and Healthy Planet.

Notes

1   Costa Rica had a small debt, US$ 4,000,000 in 2000, but it is one of the highest indebted countries in the world due to its reduced population.
2   These names are psdeudonyms.
3   See, for example, the website of U.S citizen Alan Seaman, who organizes prostitution tours from a website called "Dream Getaway: Fantasy Resort Adult Vacations." In his advertisement, Costa Rican women are constructed as a "body-for-others," as body object of desire, or bodies for men's use (Pettman 1997): "Dream Getaway Packages or Adult Vacation Packages can be mixed-and-matched to suit your most exotic, erotic dreams and budget. The packages here are merely suggestions. Dream Getaway works with you on a personal basis to truly make your dreams realities...."

Please note that some people think these prices include companions. They do not.... The companions set their own prices, varying from $200 to $600 per day. If that is not what you want, we can offer a City Tour (in a nice casino hotel) and a Private Beach Club where you can stay in safety and pick your own girls by the hour or day. The cost is $100/day."

References

Bennholdt-Thomsen, Veronika and Maria Mies. 1999. *The Subsistence Perspective.* London: Zed Books.

Casa Alianza. 2001a. "Man Charged in Costa Rica for 'dishonest abuse' of children." January 9.

Casa Alianza. 2001b. "Costa Rica policeman convicted for helping child pimp escape." January 31.

Casa Alianza. 2001c. "Third Street Girl goes Missing in Costa Rica." March 14.

Clean Development Mechanism (CDM). Online: http://unfccc.int/kyoto_protocol/ mechanisms/clean_development_mechanism/items/2718.php. Accessed February 14, 2007.

Daly, Herman. 1996. *Beyond Growth: The Economics of Sustainable Development.* Boston: Beacon Press.

De Camino, Ronnie, O. Segura, L. Arias and I. Pérez. 1999. "Forest Policy and the Evolution of Land Use: An Evaluation of Costa Rica's Forest Development and World Bank Assistance." Online: http://www.wrm.org.uy/english/tropical_forest/WorldBank.html.

Dream Getaway: Fantasy Resort Adult Vacations. Online: http://1dreamgetaway.com/packages.htm. Date accessed: June 15, 2005.

EFE News. 2003, April 10.

El Estado de la Nacion en Desarrollo Humano Sostenible. 1996. Primera Edicion 1997. San Jose, Costa Rica.

Forbes. 2003, December 9. "Factbox–What is the Kyoto Protocol?" Online: http://www. forbes.com/home_europe/newswire/2003/12/09/rtr1175321.html. Date accessed: June 15, 2005.

Fuentes, Abel (pseudonym). 2001. Personal interview, July 22.

Foster, Bellamy John. 1994. *The Vulnerable Planet. A Short Economic History of the Environment.* New York: Monthly Review Press.

Guha, Ramachandra and J. Martinez-Alier. 1997. *Varieties of Environmentalism: Essays North and South.* Delhi: Calcutta Chennai Mumbai.

Guimo, Luis (pseudonym). 2001. Personal interview July 22.

Hecht, Susana and Alexander Cockburn. 1990. *The Fate of the Forest: Developers, Destroyers and Defenders of the Amazon.* New York: Penguin Books.

Instituto Costarricense de Turismo (ITC). 1999. Unpublished internal paper. Isla, Ana. 2002. "A Struggle for Clean Water and Livelihood: Canadian Mining in Costa Rica in the Era of Globalization." *Canadian Woman Studies/les cahiers de la femme* 21/22 (4,1): 148-154.

Isla, Ana. 2005a. "Conservation as Enclosure: An Eco-Feminist Perspective on Sustainable Development and Biopiracy in Costa Rica." *Capitalism, Nature, Socialism.* 16 (3) (September): 49-61.

Isla, Ana. 2005b. "The Tragedy is Enclosure: An Eco-Feminist Perspective on Eco-Tourism in Costa Rica." Paper presented at Women's Studies Paper Series, Brock University, St. Catharines, Ontario, Canada, September 21.

Kyoto Protocol. Online: http://unfccc.int/resource/docs/convkp/kpeng.html. Accessed February 14, 2007.

Malarek, Victor. 2004. "Prostitution in Costa Rica." Canadian Broadcasting Corporation.

Mies, Maria. 1986. *Patriarchy and Accumulation on a World Scale: Women in the International Division of Labour.* London: Zed Books Ltd.

Ministry of Environment and Energy (MINAE). 2001. *Plan Nacional de Desarrollo Forestal 2001-2010.* San Jose, Costa Rica.

Monestel Arce, Yehudi. 1999. "Campesinos Precaristas en su Propia Tierra." *Eco Catolico* January 17: 11.

Odio, Elizabeth. 2001. "Modelo Unico en el Mundo." *Al Dia* August 24: 2.

Pew Centre on Global Climate Change. "Global Warming Basics." Online: http://www.pewclimatc.org/global-warming-basics. Date accessed: June 15, 2005.

Pettman, Jan J. 1997. "Body Politics: International Sex Tourism." *Third World Quarterly* 18 (1): 93-108.

PhysicalGeography.net. "Introduction to the Biosphere." Online: http://www.physical-geography.net/fundamentals/9r.html.

Robinson, William. 2003. *Transnational Conflicts: Central America, Social Change, and Globalization.* London: Verso.

Roddick, Jackie. 1988. *The Dance of Millions: Latin America and the Debt Crisis.* London: Latin American Bureau (Research and Action).

Sachs, Wolfgang. 1992. *The Development Dictionary: A Guide to Knowledge as Power.* London: Zed Books.

Sage, Luis and R. Quirós. 2001. *Proyección del volumen de madera para aserrío proveniente de las plantaciones de melina, teca, y otras fuentes. Proyecto Mercadeo e industrialización de madera proveniente de plantaciones forestales.* TCP/COS/006(A)-FAO. 25.

Siete Dias de Teletica. 1999, January 19. Newscast.

Sanchez Taylor, Jacqueline. 2000. "Tourism and 'Embodied' Commodities: Sex Tourism in the Caribbean." *Tourism and Sex: Culture, Commerce and Coercion.* Eds. Stephen Clift and Simon Carter. London: Pinter, Biddles Ltd., Guildford and King's Lynn. 41-53.

Shiva, Vandana. 1989. *Staying Alive: Women, Ecology and Development.* London: Zed Books.

Torres, Sonia. 2001. Coordinadora Frente Nacional de Oposicion a la Mineria, Personal interview.

Vaughan, Genevieve, ed. 2004. *Il Dono/The Gift: A Feminist Analysis. Athanor: Semiotica, Filosofia, Arte, Letteratura* 15 (8). Roma: Meltemi Editore.

Vizcaíno, Irene. 1999. "Deuda millonaria por las expropiaciones." *La Nación* August 29.

Wakernagel, Mathis and William Rees. 1996. *Our Ecological Footprint: Reducing Human Impact on the Earth.* New Catalyst Bioregional Series. Gabriola Island, BC: New Society Publishers.

World Bank. 1997. "Measuring the Wealth of Nations." *Expanding the Measure of Wealth: Indicators of Environmentally Sustainable Development.* Environmentally Sustainable Development Studies and Monographs Series No. 17. 19-39.

MECHTHILD HART

Real Bodies, Place-Bound Work and Transnational Homemaking

A Feminist Project

In this paper, I walk on "hope's edge." I first focus on what has been "pushing our little planet closer to hope's very edge" (Lappé and Lappé 2002: 11) by looking at the way migrant domestic workers or trafficked women are being used, abused, or used up. The second part of the essay looks at the radical political message that migrant domestic workers and trafficked women give us. They push our understanding of what Genevieve Vaughan (1997) refers to as "gift labour" a bit further by laying bare its physical, bodily, place- and earth-bound grounding, and how that can be, must be the grounding for transnational, global political connections. Their stories tell us that we need to be both place-bound and nomadic.

For the past three decades my main political interests and concerns have been with international and sexual divisions of labour around the notion of "subsistence work." Because raising children, or motherwork, is primarily oriented towards sustaining life, it is a prime example of subsistence work. Within Vaughan's framework subsistence work is paradigmatic for gift labour. Moreover, and that is my main emphasis here, it is place-bound work, and it is tied to the physical necessities, the blood, guts, and gore of real, messy life.

I previously investigated how this place-bound work is inserted in a political economy of race-class segregation in the inner city of Chicago, where I live (Hart 2002). Here mothers do place-bound work in a confined, sectioned-off space.

The "welfare debate" of the 1990s—culminating in the 1996 *Welfare Act* in the U.S.—did not criticize any racial-economic segregations or confinements. Nor did it criticize the relocation of jobs to cheap labour countries, jobs most inner city residents held in the steel or car industry.

It did, however, "criticize" by vilifying the place-bound nature of the work "welfare mothers," also referred to as "welfare queens," were doing. The government had to pay for work that made women get stuck in one place. They clearly had to become mobile, had to get away from their children—or disappear between the cracks of a punitive welfare system, and of economic realities that offered jobs only to some, and only for non-living wages.

It is not difficult to see a link between this enforced mobility and the growing internationalization of domestic and cleaning work. In order for the state to reduce its expenses, or to receive remittances badly needed to pay back loans to the International Monetary Fund (IMF) or World Bank, mothers have to be torn from their children. The children then become the invisible and never-talked-about little figures being pushed around in an abysmal or non-existing childcare system, or being taken care of "back home" in the nether-land of a private household.

At the current stage in the patriarchal-capitalist game trafficking in women and the movement of migrant women across the globe are part and parcel of the overall transformation of national economies.[1] Motherhood and sexuality are an integral, logical part of import/export schemes that are typical for this new economy where poor countries export, or send, and rich (or richer) countries import, or receive. Mobile motherhood and mobile sex are intricately tied to capital mobility, and to the extractive nature of a predatory finance capitalism.

There are often tremendous cultural differences and geographical distances between so-called sending and receiving countries, and all countries have their own variation of patriarchal cultural practices.[2] However, it is the patriarchal-capitalist underbelly that provides the connective tissue of all—paid or unpaid—versions of a kind of labour that has always supported a capitalist interior infrastructure of service and servitude, one that has now simply gone global.

It is only logical that the U.S. military was the institution that introduced organized prostitution to the Philippines. Here ordinary guns are joined by hard (erect) penis-guns. We can add to this arsenal of guns the gene gun, and what Vaughan calls "the phallic-father-money"(1997: 219) of the financial money gamblers. These guns are all pointed at real, organic, imperfect bodies or organisms. They blast DNA coated particles into live, not-yet modified organisms, they make bodies do what is profitable (or pleasurable), penetrate them, and dispose of them once they are no longer useful, or they simply bomb them out of existence.

Global trafficking in women's bodies, sex home-delivery to American GIs, and rapes of live-in "maids to order"(Hondagneu-Sotelo 2001: 92) in the privacy of individual households are all variations of the same greedy contempt for women's sexuality and birthing capacity.

Real life is extracted from real bodies by trading them as disposable sex toys (that get shipped back once American GI's infected them), or disposable domestic workers. Extraction is part and parcel of keeping in check such real life, or real life capacity.

Profitable capitalist-patriarchal assaults on migrant women's bodies often result in death. For instance, as reported by GABRIELA, a U.S.-Philippine women's solidarity organization, one coffin per day is sent back to the Philippines with the body of a woman killed as a domestic or a sex worker.

Foreign domestics are aliens from a different culture, and they are non-citizens that marks and regulates them as bonded or enslaved labourers. Or they are undocumented illegals desperate enough to put up with any kind of abuse. Pierette Hondagneu-Sotelo (2001) lists various agency names in the Los Angeles area, which she studied: Mama's Maid to Order, Domestic Darlings, Maid in Heaven, or Custom Maid for You. She also observed that the name the maids themselves give to all of them is "Domestic Desperation" (92).

In the United States, the worker's immigrant status provides the most powerful axis of inequality, especially with respect to live-in domestic workers (Hondagneu-Sotelo 2001: 13). The informal privacy of individual, isolated households deliberately invites keeping desperate undocumented immigrants in slave-like conditions. Live-in jobs, the typical point of entry for Latina immigrants, are therefore described as prisons, where *te encierras*—you lock yourself up (63). Moreover, the *Fair Labour Standards Act* (Sec.14(b)(21)) completely exempts live-in employees from overtime coverage.

There exist some limited protective labour laws. Not surprisingly, those who "work as personal attendants—for example, baby-sitters, caregivers to young children, or companions of the elderly and infirm" "are explicitly *excluded* from the right to earn minimum wage and overtime pay." The laws cover "those who clean and care for material possessions." If those who do private care work want to have the same legal rights they must show "that they devote at least 20 percent of their work time to housekeeping duties"(Hondagneu-Sotelo, 2001: 212-13).[3]

Officers of international money lending institutions such as the IMF or World Bank directly benefit from cheap, bonded, or enslaved labourers, especially in the U.S., the most powerful Minority World country. The provisions of special visas (A-3, G-5, and B-1) allow foreign nationals, diplomats, and IMF or World Bank officials to import domestic help. The State Department does keep records of the whereabouts of A-3 and G-5 domestic workers, but "this information is classified as confidential, for the privacy of the employer." B-1 is a catch-all business category, and the State Department keeps no records of domestic helpers imported under its provisions. It not only allows foreign nationals but also American citizens with a permanent residence abroad to bring along domestic help when visiting the United States. The workers suffer some of the most blatant abuses, from having to sleep outside with the family dog, being sexually harassed, or working for sixteen hours per day, all week long, for $100 a month. In contrast to A-3 and G-5 visa holders, workers employed under the auspices of a B-1 visa do not have the legal right to transfer to another employer which makes the women "live as prisoners in the homes they clean" (Zarembka 2003: 145-47).

All forms of hyperrelgulation, indentured servitude or enslavement are interwoven with seemingly endless variations of racialization practices, abetted by an equally diverse array of immigration policies, government-sponsored labour import or foreign contract labour programs, national regulatory regimes, and the actions of placement or employment agencies, brothel owners, or sex traffickers.

The "racialness of alien labour" may be camouflaged by labour importation or employment schemes by hiding behind terms such as "foreign" (Cheng 2003: 183) or by using the ability or inability to speak English as a code for national and ethnic-stereotypical preferences. When employment agencies advertise their "Malibu Mamas" or "Nannies By Design" by listing various important steps in the screening progress (Hondagneu-Sotelo 2001: 93), linguistic criteria are used to hide, or de-racialize, hiring selections that employ certain cultural or national stereotypes. An employer may have a racial preference for a Latina applicant precisely because she does not speak English so she cannot understand what her employer family is talking about, thus making her presence more invisible (102). Filipinas may therefore be rejected because they are more educated, and thus more "uppity." As reported by Wolfgang Uchatius (2004), formerly unemployed teachers, accountants, or veterinarians may have taken a course at Manila's Women's University on how to fold, tug, or line up the sheets when making a bed in an Italian household in order to find paid domestic work. Especially in English-speaking countries, their educational background and the fact that they also speak and thus understand English directly undermines their classification as subordinates who are incapable of doing anything but physical domestic labour.

Sex-touring and trafficking in women likewise feed off the notion of sex workers' special proclivities. European companies' brochure designers, or Internet advertiser on The World Sex Guide do not see any need to camouflage racialized attributes. In Germany or the Netherlands, for instance, they become advertising turn-ons that praise "slim, sunburnt, and sweet" wares because "they love the white man in an erotic and devoted way," or as "little slaves" they "give real Thai warmth" (Bales 2002: 226, 227).

There is an alarming structural continuity between "taking a girl" as easily "as buying a package of cigarettes" (as advertised by Kanita Kamha Travel in the Netherlands), and turning the export of cheap prostitutes to Japanese brothels into a "robust business." Businessmen who dwell in the stratosphere of pure financial calculations here join virtual hands with the body handlers by discarding a girl once most of the profit has been drained from her and she is no longer "cost-effective," replacing her "with someone fresh" (Bales 2002: 227, 226, 220). The Internet adds additional stratospheric qualities to the sex industry. As Donna Hughes (1999) reports, geographic and cultural distances become as "virtual" as any effective barriers for regulating the global free trade on women and children, thus greatly benefiting the industry's growth and profitability.

The free trade in women's bodies is only part of the worldwide patriarchal script. The other part includes the patriarchal need to severely monitor and control women's sexuality. In the case of foreign domestic workers' sex life various national regulatory regimes or allocation systems are set up to fulfill this important function. A work permit may only be given if the imported domestic worker agrees not to marry a native-born man (Yeoh, Huang, and Gonzales 1999). She also has to be, or at least pretend to be, single (Lan 2003), or where she has children these have to remain in the invisible nether-land of her own private household back home where other invisible women are taking care of them.

It is rather ironic to see how pimping joins hands with Christian church imperatives that women give in to the body's reproductive power rather than take control of it. As Ninotchka Rocha from GABRIELA told me in a personal conversation (May 8, 2004), the children of prostituted women workers in American military bases are treated as disposables, like their mothers. They grow up in severe poverty and without education or any other social services. When I asked her what the women can do to protect themselves from becoming pregnant, she said they are discouraged from doing so because the Catholic Church does not allow any form of contraception.

As Claudia von Werlhof (2001) points out, at the core of the capitalist-patriarchal system lies its quasi-religious belief in "the power of money to force all of life into prostitution," which "makes our system out to be a kind of Christian pimping" (34). We are here dealing with a rather dense knot of contradictions which, when unraveled, illustrate the perverse logic of the capitalist-patriarchal desire to control or do away with impure female bodies. According to this logic these bodies may need to be kept in a confined, tightly supervised space where they care for and clean after the products of higher-ranking female bodies' reproductive capacity. The state, the church, or father-husbands may also mandate that women's bodies keep reproducing. Where these bodies are prostituted, their reproductive capacity becomes entirely irrelevant in the overall scheme of control and exploitation, at least as long as it does not interfere with their primary purpose of serving male sexual desires.

It is now time to look down the other side of hope's edge.

Instead of joining the capitalist "Stratos dwellers" (Korten 2001) by speculating on the utopian possibilities of a cybertechnology they created,[4] I rather look at the fate of millions of people all over the globe. Most of humankind neither surfs the net nor has access to the disembodied experiences of a virtual reality. Women's reality of being cut or penetrated is not a simulated version of cybersex, nor is it that of women who have their breast size reduced or enlarged. Both groups are at opposite ends of the patriarchal pole that nevertheless unites them. Both groups live the patriarchal script. How can we then move, I ask, from a (global) culture that glorifies virtual techno-bodies in corporate cyberspace and extracts the life out of real, flesh-and-blood bodies who keep moving from place to place, and who are picking up after the lords of cyberspace, the Stratos dwellers, and after their children? How can we stay grounded in our physical, bodily, place-bound reality *and* reach across vast geographical and cultural distances? Where is our anchor?

As an "alien resident" in the United States I have been studying various writings on diaspora living. "Home" is a recurrent motif in these writings. Some writers focus primarily on the "Big Home" (Magat 1999) and describe the anguish of national relocations or displacements, of living in exile or in a diaspora, of transnational migrations. There are, of course, also analyses of the "Little Home." They address the presumably mundane tasks and experiences associated with daily living in a small place and space. As many if not most women know experiences in the Little Home are fully embedded in problematic normative assumptions and larger social power relations. Some writers such as bell hooks (1990), however, emphasize that a physical homeplace can also be the only place that provides safety, especially in a hostile social environment, and how homemaking therefore includes work that benefits the well-being of an entire community. The collection of essays in This Bridge We Call Home is exemplary for revealing the many hidden social, cultural, and political connections between the Big Home and the Little Home (Anzaldúa and Keating 2002).

I believe that replacing "domestic" with "home" can ignite a flare of radical political sparks. The very word domestic conjures up images of narrowness, smallness, docility, or violently enforced captivity. On the other hand, home can link the smallness of a concrete place with the largeness of a wide open space.

Gloria Anzaldúa (2002) writes that "'home' is that bridge, the in-between-place of nepantla, and constant transition, the most unsafe of all spaces" (574). She refers to the struggles of a traveler in transition to a new way of seeing herself, and herself in relation to others and to the world. Migrant domestic workers' experiences speak more directly, and more brutally of home as not only the most unsafe of all spaces, but also of all places.

Yet these workers are also messengers of an embodied, grounded *nepantla*. They are walking hope's edge. Many Filipina migrant workers, for instance, have shown that it is possible to develop "transnational bonds" or "transnational family ties" (Parreñas 2001). In other words, they live possibilities of transnational homemaking. At the same time, the work of migrant nannies/housekeepers[5] also shows us that hope "isn't clean or tidy," that it has an edge, that it is "messy" (Lappé and Lappé 2002: 11) as it is woven into place-bound care work. Walking on hope's edge therefore means more than being able to form transnational bonds. As many nanny/housekeepers have shown they not only take care of the foreign employer's children but often also form emotional attachments to the children in their care. These attachments are certainly enmeshed in the pain, anguish, and longings for their own children who are far away, and whom they can see only once in a blue moon. Regardless, however, of the multi-layered complexity of experiencing loss and attachment the very ability to form strong emotional bonds with a foreign employer's children demonstrates that it is nevertheless possible to walk on hope's razor-sharp edge.

Despites cuts, bruises, and open wounds these women live a life-affirming hope, thereby touching the very core of the meaning of home: letting the children in their care be loved, be taken care of, be safe. They therefore also give a message to global feminism: We can, or should be, place-bound as well as moving, anchored in the body's and the land's multiple needs and gift offerings but also transmigratory, or nomadic. In other words, we can be at home both in our own place and space, and in the world at large by constructing a nomadic home.[6] Such a transnational homeplace links the recognition and affirmation of a concrete solid place to the recognition and affirmation of many other concrete solid places in different social, cultural, and political spaces that together build the foundation of our world.

Sex workers, maids, and nannies have to navigate between many kinds of violently imposed norms and expectations regarding servicing employers' or clients' needs and desires. However, both care and sex work are inseparable from primary bodily events, that is, birth and sexuality. At the same time, there are fundamental differences between cleaning a house, servicing male sexual desires, and taking care of children's well-being, whether corresponding norms and expectations are self-imposed or forced upon the actors. Caring for children is of a different order than cleaning a house, and whereas sexuality can be experienced as a powerful life force that may or may not be linked to the creation of new life, celebrating that life force is nevertheless fundamentally different from the actual, physical giving of life. Likewise, assuming responsibility for one's own sexual or a sexual partner's well-being is also quite different from assuming responsibility for the care of new life. Once born a child reminds us daily and nightly of the bodily, messy grounding of life, of being alive. Care work is not simply about "reproducing" humankind. It is about sustaining life by making and letting it grow in a way that affirms its physical, material, bodily grounding.

My claim here is that if we want to not only be critical of neoliberalism and neo-patriarchy but also eager to advance new ways of understanding, we must foreground the existence and needs of children both in our theory and our practice. Regardless where they live and under what circumstances, children's need for care is universal. How we greet, carry out, and ultimately transform this universal need into work that sustains life in general is a question that points to larger, all-embracing responsibilities. The African American migrant women in the United State's East Bay community made that point quite clear by considering children as "the freshest link in the web of reciprocal obligations"(Lemke-Santangelo 1996: 146).[7] It is these universal, collective, and reciprocal obligations that provide the concrete, physical-spiritual foundation for making connections between people and places that may be separated by vast geographical, geopolitical, and cultural distances. These connections can be expanded, translated into reciprocal obligations to safeguard, repair, or rebuild the conditions of life, that is, our future. In other words, they can become core elements of planetary homemaking.

Planetary homemaking means creating a life-affirming Big Home that is attentive to the universal yearning for being grounded, for being safe, for belonging, and for finding shelter, rest, and physical, psychological, and spiritual nourishment. It means caring for the foundations of life, for the air we breathe, the water we drink, and the land on which we grow our food. Safeguarding biodiversity and the integrity of individual life forms are therefore integral components of making the world a home for all.

Planetary homemaking is a transnational feminist project. It requires to journey across intellectual-categorical and experiential divides, and across often vast cultural and geographic distances. These travels to other places need to be fuelled by the desire to better understand and change a fragmented and interconnected world. They need to be based on the knowledge that it is possible to make translocal connections to local, place-bound, life-affirming actions. This desire, this knowledge anchor nomadic journeying and practical engagements in the shared commonality of living in a body as well as on and from the earth, the great giver, and in the willingness to not only take but continuously to give back to her.

Migrant domestic workers are travelers in constant transition. It is not their desire to cross a political and spiritual life threshold but brutal economic necessity that brought them to a place where their lives are regulated, controlled, and supervised in bearable or unbearable ways. They do not engage in gift giving due to political convictions, but due to the fact that living bodies need physical attention and care. That's why the workers are messengers of an embodied, grounded *nepantla* that speaks of a future where diasporic and place-bound living are conjoined in dignified, life-affirming ways. In other words, they speak of the possibility of creating a nomadic home. They teach us that no matter where we are located, where we are at home collectively and individually, the universal need for physical, bodily place-bound care work firmly anchors our desire to turn home into a life threshold, thus enabling us to engage in political nomadic journeying to other far-away places.

Portions of this article also appear in my article, "Women, Migration, and the Body-Less Spirit of Capitalist Patriarchy" (Hart 2005b).

Mechthild U. Hart is Professor at DePaul University's School for New Learning. She moved from Germany to the United States in 1972, worked in a number of women's and community organizations, and has been teaching and mentoring at the School for New Learning since 1987. She has published several articles, book chapters, and two books on international and social divisions of labour, with special emphasis on poverty and motherwork.

Notes

1   The term "patriarchal" certainly deserves some specification. Although I hope that its meanings unfold in this essay, I also refer the reader to "Women, Migration, and the Body-Less Spirit of Capitalist Patriarchy" (2005B) where I elaborate on the term within the context of neoliberalisms and modern Western patriarchal thinking.

2   Migrant domestic workers have many different cultural and national backgrounds, and they always experience their own variations of national or cultural stereotyping, as do, for instance, Indian or Thai women in Singapore (Yeoh, Huang, and Gonzalez, 1999); see also Munira Ismail (1999), who writes about Christian, Muslim, or Hindu Sri Lankan women in the Middle East. Their stories are unique *and* they illustrate the universal fate of being super-exploited.

3   Laws regarding wages and working hours are also quite different. Some states "mandate higher hourly wages than does federal law. Others specifically expand the labour rights of domestic workers. New York, for example, extends overtime protections to live-in workers. Still other states, among them Alaska, Delaware, Hawaii, Idaho, and Kansas, exclude domestics from state minimum wage laws and from other protections" (Hondagneu-Sotelo 2001: 213-214).

4   See, for instance, Susan Hawthorne and Renate Klein (1999).

5   In Hondagneu-Sotelo's (2001) writings the term "nanny/housekeeper" is deliberately used in order to capture the fact that the paid domestic worker is doing the job of two for the pay of one.

6   I elaborate on this notion in my article, "The Nomad at Home" (2005a).

7   In my book, *The Poverty of Life-Affirming Work* (2002), I elaborate on this point, especially with respect to mother-activists.

References

Anzaldúa, G. 2002. "Now Let Us Shift … the Path of Conocimiento: Inner Work, Public Acts." *This Bridge We Call Home*. Eds. G. Anzaldúa and A. Keating. New York: Routledge. 540-578.

Anzaldúa, G. and A. Keating, eds. 2002. *This Bridge We Call Home: Radical Visions for Transformation*. New York and London: Routledge.

Bales, K. 2002. "Because She Looks like a Child." Eds. B. Ehreneich and A. R. Hochschild. *Global Women: Nannies, Maids, and Sex Workers in the New Economy*. New York: Metropolitan Books. 207-229.

Beasley, C. 1994. *Sexual Economyths: Conceiving a Feminist Economics*. New York: St. Martin's Press.

Cheng, S. J. A. 2003. Rethinking the Globalization of Domestic Service. *Gender and Society* 17 (2): 166-186.

Ehrenreich, B. and A. R. Hochschild, eds. 2003. *Global Woman: Nannies, Maids, and Sex Workers in the New Economy*. New York: Metropolitan Books.

GABRIELA Network. Online: http://www.gabnet.org.

Hart, M. 2002. *The Poverty of Life-Affirming Work: Motherwork, Education, and Social Change*. Westport, CT: Greenwood Press.

Hart, M. 2005a. "The Nomad at Home." *Journal of Prevention and Eds.tervention in the Community* 30 (1/2): 127-141.

Hart, M. 2005b. "Women, Migration, and the Body-Less Spirit of Capitalist Patriarchy." *Journal of International Women's Studies* 7 (1) (November): 1-16. Online: http://www.bridgew.edu/SoAS/jiws/Nov05V2/Hart.pdf.

Hawthorne, S., and R. Klein, Eds. 1999. *CyberFeminism: Connectivity, Critique and Creativity*. North Melbourne: Spinifex Press.

Hondagneu-Sotelo, P. 2001. *Doméstica: Immigrant Workers Cleaning and Caring in the Shadows of Affluence*. Berkeley: University of California Press.

hooks, b. 1990. *Yearning: Race, Gender, and Cultural Politics*. Boston: South End Press.

Hughes, D. 1999. "The Internet and the Global Prostitution Industry." Eds. S. Hawthorne and R. Klein. *CyberFeminism: Connectivity, Critique and Creativity*. North Melbourne: Spinifex Press. 157-183.

Ismail, M. 1999. "Maids in Space: Gendered Domestic Labour from Sri Lanka to the Middle East." Eds. J. H. Momsen.*Gender Migration and Domestic Service*. London and New York: Routledge 229-241..

Korten, D. C. 2001. *When Corporations Rule the World*. San Francisco: Berrett-Koehler.

Lappé, F. M. and A. Lappé. 2002. *Hope's Edge: The Next Diet for a Small Planet*. New York: Jeremy P. Tarcher/Putnam.

Lan, P. C. 2003. "Among Women: Migrant Domestics and Their Taiwanese Employers Across Generations." Eds. B. Ehreneich and A. R. Hochschild. *Global Woman: Nannies, Maids, and Sex Workers in the New Economy*. New York: Metropolitan Books. 169-189.

Lemke-Santangelo, G. 1996. *Abiding Courage: African American Migrant Women and the East Bay Community*. Chapel Hill: The University of North Carolina Press.

Magat, I. N. 1999. "Israeli and Japanese Immigrants to Canada: Home, Belonging, and the Territorialization of Identity." *Ethos* 27 (2): 119-144.

Parreñas, R. S. 2001. "Transgressing the Nation-Sate: The Partial Citizenship and 'Imagined Global Community' of Migrant Filipina Domestic Workers." *Signs: Journal of Women in Culture and Society* 26 (4): 1129-1154.

Uchatius, Wolfgang. 2004. "Das globalisierte Dienstmädchen." *Die Zeit* Aug. 19: 17-18.

Vaughan, G. 1997. *For-Giving: A Feminist Criticism of Exchange*. Austin, Texas: Plain View Press.

Werlhof, C. von. 2001. "Losing Faith in Progress: Capitalist Patriarchy as an 'Alchemical System.'" Eds. V. Bennholdt-Thomsen and N. Faraclas and C. von Werlhof. *There Is an Alternative: Subsistence and Worldwide Resistance to Corporate Globalization*. London: Zed Books. 15-40.

Yeoh, B. S. A., S. Huang and J. Gonzalez. 1999. "Migrant Female Domestic Workers: Debating the Economic, Social, and Political Impacts in Singapore." *International Migration Review* 33 (1): 114-136.

Zarembka, J. M. 2003. "America's Dirty Work: Migrant Maids and Modern-Day Slavery." Eds. B. Ehreneich and A. R. Hochschild. *Global Women: Nannies, Maids, and Sex Workers in the New Economy*. New York: Metropolitan Books. 142-153.

SIZANI NGUBANE

The Rural Women's Movement in South Africa

Land Reform and HIV/AIDS

The Rural Women's Movement (RWM) is a land-rights grassroots women's organization based in South Africa, in the province of Kwa Zulu Natal. The RWM is
working with Indigenous, poor, rural, farm dwellers, and landless women whose
communities were forcibly evicted from their ancestral land as a result of 1913
Land Act and other Acts that followed. RWM is currently made up of 500 community-based grassroots women's organizations, with a total membership of about
35,000 women between the ages of 16 and 78 years. RWM advocates for women's
economic emancipation, land and property independent rights.

Faced by a legacy of apartheid systems, the districts we work in are characterized be a deep rural consciousness and social conservatism evidenced in strongly
held traditional social values, including around gender roles and relationships.
For the most part the women are located within patriarchal households. When
we interviewed one of the chairpersons of the community land trust in one of the
districts, he said, "I'm the manager of my household. I have knowledge about a
number of things. Therefore I don't want my wife getting involved because she
might fumble and mess things up. A woman will do things a woman's way and
make things worse. She may even sell our land to her boyfriends, and the man
will be held responsible. She would then be a problem in the community. When
the police come, they ask for the man, so women should follow their husbands."
This was very sad for us because when the land reform program began in 1995,
the government made it very clear that women must be represented in all land
reform projects and structures and their voice must be heard. But this chairperson,
who was supposed to be assisting the project in his community, was against having
women participate in the decision-making process.

The social and agrarian history of some districts in the province is marked by
extreme social divisions in which land conflicts have played an important part.
The deeply scarred patterns of contestation over land, territorial boundaries, and
labour stretch back to the mid-nineteenth century. These patterns enforce not
only conflict between black, landless, or land-hungry communities and white
landowners, but also clan-based violence within black communities.

In one magisterial district where labour tenancy was abolished, more than 20,000
people were forcibly evicted from white-owned farms between 1969 and 1972.

Many of the people were dumped in resettlement camps close to their former land. The province I come from is one of the poorest provinces with more than 70 percent of its inhabitants living in rural areas, which are significantly worse off economically than urban areas. More than 30 percent of households in this province are headed by women, and women-headed households, in terms of poverty, are worse off compared to households headed by men. Their access to arable land, on which to live and grow food, is severely limited and this contributes significantly to women and children's increasing poverty in South Africa.

But it wasn't always like this. Pre-colonization, individuals could not own land. Land was regarded as a sacred gift from *Umvelinqangi* (The Creator). For example, traditionally, when a baby was about to be born, the Grandmothers, symbolizing Mother Earth, would be the first people to take care of the newly born baby. While the mother is in labour, the grandmothers would dig enough soil outside to make mattress of earth in the hut. They would place blankets and sheets over the mound of earth and then have the woman in labour lie down on that earth-mattress. That earth would be kept in the hut for one week and could only be removed by the Grandmothers in the early hours of the morning while everyone was still sleeping. The Grandmothers would dig a big hole in the earth and bury it. The umbilical cord would be buried in the same way. The earth used for the mattress was regarded as sacred and only the Grandmothers know where it is buried after its removal from the hut.

Mother Earth was also regarded as a sacred home for our people who had passed on, and as the sacred source of food for the nation. Food was produced by individual families but shared with everyone in the community. When it was time for supper at night, the women, each bearing a bowl of food, would gather in the Great-Grandmother's house. Everyone—children, women, and men—would sit in a circle and each of the mothers would pass around their bowls, and everyone would eat from these bowls of different foods. In this way, there were no people suffering from starvation, because even if a family did not have enough food to bring to the Great-Grandmother's supper, they could come for supper without having to bring anything, and eat with the rest of their extended family, and neighbours.

In the past, communities stayed together and shared whatever resources they had. Mother Earth was regarded as a sacred gift and no one owned the land. People ploughed and tilled the land communally. The food that was produced from the land was shared among the families. If a woman had to visit her parents' home for a couple of days or weeks, she didn't have to go to someone and say, "Please look after my children while I am away." She could just let all the members of the extended family know that she would not be around, and her children could go to anyone's house and be fed.

When the youth who are looking after the livestock came back from the fields, they didn't have to go to their mother's kitchen to have their meals. They could go to any house in the community and find food ready for them. The heads of the households, usually men, were regarded as managers, but they could not make any decision without consulting their extended family, including the children (girls and boys). Even the children had a voice in how the cattle could be kept, and their voices were respected by the elders. Women had access to property and they were treated with respect.

In order for communities to build houses, the people in the community would perform what used to be called *Ilima*. This is when the community would come together in support of a community member who needs to be assisted to carry out bigger tasks, like building a house. One week they would build one person's house and the week after it would be another person's house. This practice still exists in some communities but its beginning to disappear. The principle behind it, however, continues to exist in events like weddings, burials, and credit unions.

Colonization left women without access to land. It took away communities' togetherness. People became individuals, and land became privately owned; Mother Earth was carved into small pieces. About 87 percent of this land went into the hands of the few white men, and the majority of the nation was left with only 13 percent of barren land on which to survive. The tilling of the land was the only means of survival for our communities. To force our men into migration, the colonizers made it illegal for people to have more than five cattle. People had to reduce the number of cattle they had, on which they also depended for survival. With migration came the breakdown of communities and also the breakdown of family values. As Africans we began to look at our households as individual households.

This is when we began to see orphaned children, street children. In 1991 alone, there over 100,000 children in South Africa living in the streets of major cities like Durban, Johannesburg, Cape Town and some other small towns like Pietermaritzburg. Boys and girls had to sell their bodies in order to survive.

Before the land was taken away from the communities, the communities did not need to have money. People could survive without money. My mother told me that my grandfather sometimes worked for money for six month periods. Then he would come back and work at home, and it would be his brother's turn to earn money. They would negotiate among themselves who was to go and work for money that year, while the others continued to work at home on the land and take care of the livestock. The money earned by the person who had volunteered to work was not his own, because the others were at home looking after his cattle, after his family, and ploughing and tilling his fields. So the money my grandfather or his brother earned and brought back was for the entire extended family.

All of this is gone now because of the scarcity of resources and the scarcity of land. The breakdown of extended families is seen as the main cause of poverty, especially women and children's poverty in the rural areas. Women and children, 60 percent of the population, live below the poverty line in rural areas. As a nation, we are witnessing vast numbers of women evicted from their marital homes after the death of their husbands, and from their parents' homes after the death of their fathers and mothers, because of the scarcity of food and economic resources. A woman cannot inherit land because she is considered a minor. Traditional leaders are turning a blind eye on this physical and psychological eviction. An example is a woman from Mbulwana in Greytown whose husband died of AIDS. After the burial, anonymous people threw stones at her window and roof until she was forced to leave the area and return to parents' home.

South Africa is currently experiencing one of the most severe HIV epidemics in the world. By the end of 2006, there were more than five million people living with HIV, according to UNAIDS estimates (www.avert.org/aidssouthafrica.htm). A recent study by the South African Department of Health, based on its sample of 16,510 women attending neonatal clinics across all nine provinces, estimated that 30 percent of pregnant women were living with HIV in 2005. Our province, KwaZulu Natal, recorded the highest rates, with a prevalence of 36 percent where the national prevalence is 30 percent.

The breakdown of family values and communities has also led to a high rate of teenage pregnancies. More than one-third of births in South Africa are to mothers under the age of 18. This is one of the highest teenage pregnancy rates in the world. Sexually transmitted diseases such as syphilis are commonplace among sexually active teenagers, and despite some public education efforts over the past ten years, condom usage among teenagers remains at around ten to fifteen percent. But there are many interrelated factors contributing to this environment of increasing sexual promiscuity. Abuse and violence among young South Africans, poverty, the of breakdown of family structures, political liberation, and men no longer acting as role models are shaping the attitudes of our African youth.

The Rural Women's Movement recently established an HIV prevention program for youth in the district of Greytown. Our dream for this program was motivated by realizing that the HIV/AIDS pandemic, especially in KwaZulu Natal province where I come from, would affect labour turnout in agriculture and manufacturing, and mining which is predominantly migrant labour sectors of our economy. This would result in increasing malnutrition, adding to the problems of rural women, especially female-headed households, arising from division of labour, land rights and scarcity of resources, and deepen the debt crisis with increasing medical expenses for sick family members, and the increasing number of funerals.

The Rural Women's Movement main strategy is to get South African youth, particularly the youth between the ages of eleven and nineteen, to speak more openly about sexually transmitted diseases and the impact of HIV/AIDS. We strongly believe that this strategy will work because there is substantial evidence from different countries that HIV prevention programs work, but to be successful, prevention programs must be strategically targeted and sustained over many years in order to bring about lasting transformation. In South Africa, land reform organizations have not until recently needed to take into account of issues such as HIV/AIDS. However, it is becoming increasingly clear that HIV/AIDS is likely to present one of the greatest challenges to land reform and capacity building of community.

It is estimated that, as the nation, we will lose 600 loved ones every month to AIDS-related diseases, like tuberculosis and pneumonia. It is also estimated that every day there are 1,500 to 1,800 new infections. More women than men are infected. Some of the reasons why are clear and can be traced to deeply held traditions that give men sexual authority in relationships. HIV infection among South African women has increased dramatically, especially among women aged 20 between and 39, and especially among poor African women.

Women who are poor are doubly vulnerable because they have no economic or social power. In a situation where gender inequality is culturally entrenched, women's poverty is frequently associated with violence and abuse, and this is further advancing the spread of HIV. In one of the workshops we held, more than 50 percent of the HIV-positive participants were married and were faithful to one partner all their life. Infected women in abusive relationships remain in those relationships for financial support, especially for their children. AIDS is also putting more pressure on women in other ways, as we have to make hard choices in allocating time between household needs, rearing and caring for children, and caring for the sick. When we lose valuable team members, our productivity is reduced, and we also find we are often depressed. Not one of us is untouched by the rising incidence of illness and death rapidly engulfing our nation. We are carrying a heavy burden of grief.

I would like to share a short story about four children who lost their mother a couple of weeks ago. This woman was dying of AIDS after all her family members, including the grandmother and the grandfather of her children, had already passed on. She was the last one to pass on in the family and because she was the last, she resisted. She didn't want to die. In order for someone to enter her room, they had to have a broom because there were worms crawling on the floor and her bed was dripping with body fluids, her body finished. Four children, the youngest, a little girl four years old, had to witness this situation. She refused to die until she realized that her children will be taken care of even after she is gone. She said to the caregivers, "I have remembered, I can still die and my children would not suffer this much. I can remember that someone from somewhere would come and take care of my children." And she asked four women if they could please look after her four children. And they said they would be happy to assist her. A week later she passed on and four women came to collect the children and took them to their homes. Within a week's time the children had run away from their foster homes and returned to their mother's house. It was two days before the community members noticed that the children were back. The Community Health Worker telephoned me to tell me the children were in their own in their home and it seemed they hadn't eaten for four days.

In South Africa, about 29 percent of the productive active population is unemployed. As activists we know that 29 percent does not accurately reflect what we are seeing in the rural areas where we have people who haven't been employed for the last decade. While the government argues the 29 percent of the population is unemployed, civil organizations maintain that the unemployment rate is actually 43 percent. Perhaps government statistics refer to people who are still looking for jobs; and these statistics do not include those who have given up looking for work. So, the community did have anything to share with these children. The Community Health Worker who called me did not even have enough food for her own children, and because we had a bit of money in our organization's account, I asked the chairperson if we could use some of that money to buy food for the children. The money in that account was not raised to buy food but rather to buy school uniforms and pay school fees for the children. We had to do something we were not supposed to do, in order to feed the children.

AIDS thus poses challenging questions to existing approaches for development, which is part of the reason why, as a lands rights organization, we decided to integrate HIV prevention programs into our work. In some situations, the epidemic has exposed the failure of previous development intervention to address persisting gender inequalities. In many cases existing inequalities have been exacerbated by the epidemic, such as widows being evicted from their homes.

Our work has shown that the impact of HIV has also raised the importance of inter-household entitlement to food and other resources, partly because of the number of orphan children being taken in by different families. Gender sensitive and entitlement-based approaches are now more urgently needed than ever before. The situation is scary, especially in the rural areas, and we need to do something about it now.

Sizani Ngubane is the founder and director of the Rural Women's Movement in KwaZulu Natal-South Africa. She worked for ten years as a gender specialist for the Association for Rural Advancement in KwaZulu Natal. Prior to that, she worked for the South African Women's National Coalition as a provincial coordinator. Her skills and abilities were recognized when she was appointed the first organizer in the Northern Natal Region by the Africa National Congress (ANC), which has recently been legalized. She has been an activist for women's rights for 40 years, and is particularly passionate about women's independent rights to land, property and inheritance. She has two grandchildren and currently lives in Winterskloof. As a Zulu-speaking child, she grew up in the rural areas just outside Pietermaritzburg. She was unable to complete high school because of her family's financial situation, but has made it a priority to educate herself.

MARGARET RANDALL

Endangered Species

The Language of Our Lives

Democracy. Once upon a time the word evoked access, fairness, participatory representation. Once upon a time we could think of the United States as a democracy; and defenders of its policies proposed it as an example to nations around the world. This hasn't been true for decades, of course, but the cartel, which less than two weeks ago succeeded in grabbing control of this country for the second time, has managed to radically change the meaning of the word. Today "the greatest democracy" describes drastic curtailment of freedom and opportunity here at home and a politics of coercion, destruction, and death globally.

Democracy is not the only word or combination of words that criminals in high office have twisted beyond recognition. Others that come to mind are revolution, right to life, family values, sanctity of marriage, compassionate conservatism, health care, no child left behind, healthy economy, jobs for everyone, impartial journalism, weapons of mass destruction, freedom and liberty, count every vote and make every vote count. This discourse from an administration whose president boasts that he says what he means and means what he says is Orwellian doublespeak at its most outrageous.

As someone who expresses herself primarily with words, I find misleading or cowardly turns of speech particularly annoying, often dangerous. In a true gift economy speech that is truthful, courageous, filled with holistic vision, rich in linguistic beauty, and useful in that it offers choices and encourages positive change, is the most valuable currency there is.

We used to think of lesbian as the "L" word. Now it is liberal. One more in a long list of co-opted words. The neo-conservative patriarchy currently exerting its power over our lives—and over so many lives across the globe—has paid special attention to language and its influence. Repeating the lie is referred to as "staying on message." Sound-bite shorthand replaces in-depth discussion. Spend enough money imbuing words and concepts with meanings different from—often diametrically opposed to—their original definitions and people assimilate a language of lies. The unacceptable becomes acceptable.

My generation of feminists paid indignant attention to how language was used. Early on we demanded a discourse in which the pronouns "he" and "his" would no longer be common denominators, meant to represent all humankind.

We invented the generic "Ms" so that women wouldn't have to define ourselves by whether or not we belonged to a man.

We urged that language assume responsibility for its acts: not the passive "I was raped" but the more explicit "so-and-so raped me." Names. Places. Dates. Accountability. A feminist and egalitarian use of language spread throughout the world. Women from different cultures and with different linguistic codes made innovative contributions to this reclamation of self. Speaking the truths of our lives helped us understand who we had been and could become.

For many years I lived in Latin America, working for social change in Mexico, Cuba, and Nicaragua. There I learned that all the peoples of the continent call themselves Americans, a word long monopolized by the United States. In Mexico, *qué padre!* (in praise of the father) is an exclamation denoting excitement or approval, while *está de madre* (quite literally, "how mother-like") describes something ugly or wrong. An advertising for a popular beer displays the words, *la rubia de categoría*: the high-class blonde. Prejudice reveals itself in speech in so many more ways than we are aware.

Latin American feminists have also righted some of these wrongs and returned denigrated images to their rightful meanings. An important example is La Malinche, the Indian woman whose family gave her to the Spanish conqueror Hernán Cortéz. Because she represented the mixing of the races—an Indian woman who "slept with the enemy," i.e., the Spanish invader—the term *malinche* was used to signify betrayer in contemporary Latin American Spanish. A feminist rereading of this history pointed out that it was in fact La Malinche who had been betrayed: first by her family who gave her away, then by the Spaniard who raped her and kept her enslaved. For many of us La Malinche is a symbol of dignity and courage.

Today a fundamentalist reading of several different scriptures turns words and concepts inside out. We live in a time of redefinition and backlash. A powerful corporate media draws on unlimited financial resources and sophisticated psychological manipulation to make sure we go along with the game plan. A punishing system of injustice makes sure we don't rebel.

Fear and hatred of others is sold as Keeping America Safe. Policies advertised as repelling terrorism only increase the anger other nations and peoples feel when faced with U.S. belligerence; such policies do not keep us safe, they provoke future attacks. Severe curtailment of citizen rights is described as a necessary sacrifice in The War on Terror. Invasion is sold as liberation. An environmental policy that is poisoning the air we breathe, the water left for us to drink, and the earth that is our home bears the name Clean Air Act.

How can we fight this rape of language? Even with a new and creative use of the Internet our resources are meager compared to those the system is able to muster against us. I believe in preserving and nurturing memory, in restoring language to its original meaning and, most of all, in the power of our stories.

I offer two examples. In the first I call your attention to an underreported event that illustrates—better than many—the ways in which our government usurps and attempts to control our lives by usurping and controlling the authentic storylines of these times.

The National Endowment for the Arts (NEA), a government agency established to support the art that sustains us, recently announced its latest project launched in conjunction with the Pentagon and funded almost entirely by Boeing Corporation. Military men and women, returned from Afghanistan and Iraq, will have the opportunity of attending workshops with professional writers. In these workshops they will presumably learn the skills that will enable them to write about their experiences of war. The best of this writing will then be published in an anthology. One can only imagine the promotional efforts that will catapult the volume to best-seller status. Along with embedding journalists with contingents of fighting troops and the treatment of misinformation as entertainment, this project will help construct the official stories of the wars being fought in our names.

At first glance this might seem to be a laudable endeavor. As in the case of the embedded journalists, won't these veterans be writing about what they've experienced on the ground? Isn't the protagonist always the most authentic storyteller?

But look more closely. Rather than use public monies to send these veterans to legitimate writing programs, where they may be able to gain some distance from their trauma, learn from mentors and peers, and eventually produce a literature tempered by time and self-reflection, the NEA's hurry-up approach takes men and women who are still living on military bases, still under military orders, and uses them to produce propaganda pretending to be art.

Veterans of America's war in Vietnam, who were able to write after years of struggle and healing, have denounced this project as the worst sort of language control. The very men and women in a position to share the pain and horror of today's "preemptive" wars are being forced to regurgitate that pain and horror undigested, unexamined, and removed from context. It will take years for us to disentangle the real stories from this constructed storyline. The NEA project is one of many examples of how the Bush administration takes our language, twists it to serve its interests, and uses it against us in its assault upon our lives.

The second story is a tender gift. I offer it here because it exemplifies the worst and best of our humanity, the horrendous crimes and power of resistance that have defined our lives. This is a true story.

In Latin America during the 1970s brutal dictatorships ravaged hundreds of thousands of lives. In Argentina, Chile, and Uruguay paramilitary forces captured young rebels, torturing and murdering them in clandestine prisons. "Disappearance" was a new type of state terrorism, designed to punish revolutionaries and instill fear and uncertainty in their communities. These revolutionaries' small children were often stolen and given to childless couples involved with the criminal regimes. In many cases pregnant women prisoners were kept alive only until their babies could be harvested. Then they were murdered, their offspring adopted by the very men and women against whom they'd struggled. These are Latin America's lost children.

The Grandmothers of the Plaza de Mayo in Buenos Aires is a tireless group of women who for years they have demonstrated for the return of their grandchildren. With determination, hope, and DNA technology, some 60 lost children have been identified to date. Many wish to reconnect with their families of origin. Others—raised in a culture of hate—have been poisoned by an ideology that doesn't allow for them to reclaim the identities they never knew they had.

This is the story of Sara Méndez and her son Simón. Sara and her husband were Uruguayans, captured in Buenos Aires, Argentina on July 13, 1976. Like so many others, they disappeared. Their 22-day-old son Simón was taken and never seen again. But unlike most of the tens of thousands of disappeared, Sara and her comrade Mauricio Gatti survived years of torture and imprisonment. In May 1981 Sara was freed. Like all such survivors her process of reentry and healing would be difficult. She made finding Simón her life-long goal.

The Sara Méndez / Simón case became a popular cause. For years in Montevideo lampposts and walls bore flyers asking, "*Dónde está Simón?* Where Is Simón?" Sara was obsessed in her quest. Human rights organizations worked on this case along with hundreds of others. As months became years and years decades, some began to refer to Sara as "that crazy woman looking for a son who won't be found." Tenaciously she appealed to governments and international institutions. Mostly they promised help but did nothing.

Several years ago a Uruguayan senator named Rafael Michelini decided to take up Sara's quest. His father and also senator, Zelmar Michelini, had been gunned down in the streets of Buenos Aires many years before—by the same criminals who had taken Simón. Sara Méndez was his friend. He didn't think she was crazy. He believed she had a right to find her son.

Michelini asked himself what he would have done with a 22-day-old infant had he been a paramilitary operative in Buenos Aires all those years before. It occurred to him that he might have delivered the baby to the nearest police station. Based on this hypothesis, he located the precinct closest to the scene of the crime and set about to identify the men who had been on duty the night Simón was taken. Four names surfaced, all belonging to officers now retired.

The self-proclaimed detective decided to call these men, one by one. As a member of parliament in neighboring Uruguay he had some prestige. A brief introduction was enough to convince the first man on the list to meet him at a bar. As Michelini told the story of Sara and Simón, the man's eyes filled with tears. "*Recuerdo la noche como si fuera ayer* ... I remember that night as if it was yesterday," he said; and went on to describe the protocol they were ordered to follow when paramilitaries brought these children in. "We did the necessary paperwork and then sent them to a nearby orphanage," he explained. It was clear that this man had been an honest policeman doing his job, not someone aligned with the dictatorship or who shared in the responsibility for its crimes.

The retired policeman went on to describe how he had gone home and told his wife about the "orphaned" child he had processed at the end of that night's shift. Childless herself, she told him "*Ay, Viejo ... son tan fríos esos lugares.* Those orphanages are such cold places! Couldn't we adopt that baby ourselves?" And so it was that the policeman now telling his story to Michelini had gone and retrieved the child. He and his wife had raised him as their own.

They had never told their son he was adopted. He said. "He's a good boy. We've had such a happy life together." But Michelini could tell the story wouldn't end here. The retired policeman promised to go home, talk to his son, and leave it up to the boy—now 26—whether he wanted to meet his birth mother. He promised he'd be back in touch.

A week later Michelini got the call. Simón's adoptive father said the truth had come as a shock to his son. Upon learning of his origin, he'd left the house in confusion and gone to stay with his girlfriend. "It was she who calmed him," the man said, "and convinced him to find out more." He wanted to talk to Michelini, who assured him he would travel to Buenos Aires the following day.

And this is why, on March 8, 2002, as Sara Méndez emerged from a Montevideo radio station where she'd participated in an International Women's Day program and was making her way through the heavy traffic of Avenida Artigas, she heard her cell phone ring. Unaware of how her life was about to change, she reached into her bag, retrieved the phone and said hello. On the other end of the line a young man's voice asked, "Mother?"

The lamppost flyers in Montevideo now read "Welcome Home Simón." This story and others like it, from many different cultures and profiling the human experience in its broad array of tragedy and hope, give us back our language freed from the distorting manipulation that would use it against us.

This is not a story told in isolation. Obsessed as we in the U.S. were with our own 2004 election, we may have missed hearing about the election in Uruguay. In that small South American country the stories of repression and struggle had been kept alive, passed from mouth to mouth, from generation to generation, even when uttering certain words was forbidden by law. Few families do not have victims on one side or the other. Many of the torturers remain free.

The dictatorship in Uruguay had been defeated when, in a 1980 plebiscite designed to perpetuate its power, 57.2 percent of voters spontaneously wrote the word "No" on their ballots. Slowly, steadily, people worked to revive an opposition movement. The Frente Amplio is made up of communists, socialists, Tupamaros,[1] social democrats, environmentalists, and others. For 31 years, through a succession of elections, they gained in strength. In 2004, with 51 percent of the vote, the Frente Amplio finally came to power. In the same election, Uruguayans resisted a sinister measure to privatize water.

The vote is obligatory in Uruguay. And there is no absentee ballot. Between 40,000 and 50,000 citizens who live in other countries came home to participate in this national decision. People danced in the streets.

This shows what can happen when real issues are discussed, honest dialogue is encouraged, and language has not been successfully co-opted; when people refuse to put up with doublespeak, pharmaceutical companies are not allowed to advertise on television, diet commercials do not follow on the heels of commercials featuring fast food, and grandparents and parents keep alive the stories that inform their and our lives.

We must not let the power-greedy rip meaning from our words. We must not let them usurp our stories. Memory and stories are among our most precious tools for life. We cannot allow them to be turned into weapons of death.

Margaret Randall lived for much of her life in Latin America: Mexico, Cuba, and Nicaragua. She returned to the U.S. in 1984, only to face a deportation order due to the opinions expressed in some of her books. She won her immigration case in 1989 and has resided in her native Albuquerque, New Mexico since. Author of more than 100 books, among her most recent titles are When I Look Into the Mirror and See You; Terror and Resistance; Into Another Time: Grand Canyon Reflections, *and forthcoming from the University of Arizona Press,* Stones Witness, *a multi-genre volume which includes poems, personal narrative, and photographs. She lives with her lifetime companion, artist Barbara Byers.*

Notes

---

1   The Tupamaros (MLN or National Liberation Movement) were an armed struggle organization active in Uruguay during the 1960s and '70s. Many of its members later transitioned into a political organization which is now an important part of the Board Front (Frente Amplio).

CAROL BROUILLET

Facing the Shadow of 9-11

After a second stolen election and another murderous assault upon Iraq, the dark side of the U.S. government should be obvious. Yet, when confronted with news of a terminal illness, or disaster, individuals experience a range of emotions, the first being denial. Behind denial lies fear. Fear destroys rational thought; "war" itself is recognized as "collective insanity." Wars, however, are not spontaneous, they are planned. They serve powerful interests. Aggressors are generally trained mercenaries, following orders. Historically, wars are engineered, benefiting the merchants of death and financiers. In Yugoslavia, the International Monetary Fund (IMF) and the World Bank prepared the way for the dismemberment of the country. Victors claim the spoils, while victims pay the price. The most lucrative business on earth is war.

The World Wars were marked by the rise of national fascism. This millennium is witnessing the rise of transnational fascism, where imperial powers share in the looting of conquered nations. In the era of "globalization," new alliances pit corporate interests against the vast majority.

Aung Sung Suu Kyi wrote: "It is not power that corrupts, but fear—fear of losing power and fear of the scourge of those who wield it" (see Abrams 1997).[1]

Behind the trappings of wealth, in limousines and mansions, are a frightened group of people who fear losing power and control in an increasingly "unmanageable" world. Protesters converge on significant gatherings where global policies are "decided." The shutting down of the World Trade Organization in Seattle in 1999 was one of a series of global protests. A major protest was scheduled for Washington, DC in September 2001, but was cancelled in the wake of 9/11.

The surreal attacks upon World Trade Centre and the Pentagon on September 11, 2001, were desperate acts by a frightened few, trying to cling to power, using their traditional methods of war and terrorism to frighten people into silence and submission. The *Patriot Act*, passed into law after the 9/11 attacks, mirrors the *Enabling Act* that Adolf Hitler passed after the Reichstag Fire; both were designed to dismantle democracy. Similar legislation has been passed in other countries to re-label dissenters "domestic terrorists." Recently, in India, people rescinded their anti-terrorist legislation. In the U.S., four states and 357 cities and counties have passed resolutions against the *Patriot Act*.

The War on Terrorism benefits the arms, security, surveillance, and oil industries. Bogus terror alerts, war, have terrorized people, but no one can remain in "panic mode." When people "come back to their senses," and think critically about the War on Terrorism, they should be able to see that it really is a War of Terrorism against Americans and the world. The Big Lie cannot stand.

Vice President Dick Cheney believes (as did Napoleon) "You don't have to suppress the truth forever, just until it doesn't matter anymore." The truth does matter now; the sooner people recognize it, the greater our chances of getting humanity off the war path.

Rachel Corrie's father told a story about Rachel after she died. She was the young American peace activist crushed by a bulldozer as she stood in its path to prevent the demolition of a Palestinian home. As a very young child, just two-years-old, Rachel had posed a question to her father: "Is being brave part of growing up?"[2]

Many Americans have no idea of how much violence the U.S. government has sponsored, and do not know how to stand up against it. Rachel understood this. She stood in solidarity with the people of the world and stood for the values that America is supposed to stand for, inspiring a new generation of activists.

At the International Citizens' Inquiries into 9/11, we[3] showed that the government lied about 9/11, destroyed evidence, engaged in a major cover-up, and was complicit in the attacks. Our largest obstacle in getting out the facts to the press and the public has been fear and denial. However, each day more people are coming to the conclusion that "9/11 was an inside job" (see Hargrove and Stempel III 2006).

In brief, Al Qaeda was created by Saudi Arabia and the Central Intelligence Agency (CIA) through Pakistan's Inter-Services Intelligence (ISI), and remains a CIA asset. The Money Man behind 9/11, the head of the ISI, General Mahmoujd Ahmad (who ordered $100,000 be sent to Mohammad Atta, the alleged lead pilot of the attack) was meeting with top U.S. officials during September 2001, including Congressman Porter Goss and Senator Bob Graham, Chairmen of the Joint Inquiry on 9/11, on the morning of the attacks (Chossudovsky 2003). Those in charge of the official inquiry were people who should have been investigated. The so-called "Independent Commission" was worse than the Warren Commission, and the Commissioners had major conflicts of interest, particularly oil; they failed to address most of the key questions (Lynn 2004).

The failure of the military to intercept the hijacked planes was explained by the multiple war games being conducted that morning. One deployed fighter resources to Northern Canada and Alaska, another placed false blips on radar screens; the CIA was conducting a drill to respond to the simulation of a plane crashing into the National Reconnaissance Office, and a "live fly hijack drill" was underway.[4] The multiple exercises combined to make it impossible for fighter jets to interfere with the attacks. Cheney was in command that morning. The book, *Crossing the Rubicon: The Decline of the American Empire at the End of the Age of Oil*, by Michael C. Ruppert (2004), and the documentary, *The Great Conspiracy: The 9/11 News Special You Never Saw*, by Barrie Zwicker (2005), detail Cheney's role in 9/11 and key facts that should have been headline news years ago.

Individually and collectively, Americans need to "be brave, to grow up," to overcome fear, to think, to face the harsh realities that the rest of the world has witnessed. There is a disparity between American ideals and American policy.

People are rising up in the United States, and around the world, against war and the dominant institutions, the IMF, the World Bank, the World Trade Organization, transnational corporations, that clearly benefit a global elite, at tremendous human cost, and threaten the planet.

The Project for a New American Century,[5] the neo-conservative cabal occupying the White House, wrote in detail of their imperial desires and the likelihood of resistance from the public, "The process of [military] transformation is likely to be a long one, absent some catastrophic and catalyzing event—like a New Pearl Harbor" (*Rebuilding America's Defenses* 2000).

To pursue the militarization of the country and world conquest, 9/11 was the event they needed. It was also a gamble, and depended upon an acquiescent media to pull it off. John Galtung, peace activist, when asked about the differences between the Americans and the Russians, said, "In Russia when people hear the Party Line; they know it's the Party Line. In America, they don't."[6] In war, the first casualty is truth.

The quick passage of the *Patriot Act*, the rush to war against Afghanistan, Iraq, counter-terrorist wars against other countries, the construction of Homeland Security, the revamping of the intelligence agencies, the construction of a "Global Security State," are being hurried through Congress as quickly as possible. The speed of the changes, the psychological war directed against the public has formed a crucible that is forging a vast resistance movement.

The craziest conspiracy theory of all was linking Iraq to 9/11, which Cheney used to sell his war. 9/11 is the Achilles' heel of a failing paradigm, already suffering from loss of credibility and legitimacy.

Children can see "the Emperor has no clothes." It was logistically impossible for a lone gunman to assassinate John F. Kennedy in 1963; 19 guys with box-cutters couldn't possibly have outwitted the multi-trillion dollar U.S. defense department and brought down all those buildings.

What has happened is that people have raised questions that officials cannot answer. Through a vast cooperative effort, researchers from all over the world, activists in a multitude of cities, filmmakers, writers, artists, musicians have challenged the Big Lie. The spotlight on the darkness has exposed the secrets, the crimes, the treason committed at the highest level of government.

The 9/11 Truth Movement was nurtured by a free flow of information, analysis, thousands and thousands of people helping one another to put together the pieces of a vastly complex puzzle (see *Aftermath; The Great Conspiracy* 2005; Griffin 2004, 2005; Lappé and Marshall 2004; Thompson and the Center for Cooperative Research 2004). Truth and courage are needed to overcome fear and recognize the deeper problems we face, which are beyond left and right, beyond rich or poor, beyond gender or race.

Our current debt-based monetary system concentrates wealth and power, while destroying the planet; it is only supported by belief in the current system. When faith in the U.S. government collapses; dollars are likely to collapse, as well, with far reaching effect. Fear paralyzes people who cannot imagine a better alternative to the dysfunctional, criminal, financial system that surrounds us.

Money, next to brute military force, has been the most powerful tool of empire, but money is little understood, how it is created, how it works. The antithesis of the gift, debt-based money relies on fear and scarcity to maintain its value and power. The war economy fails to recognize the value of life. The failure of the financial system, the totalitarian corporations, the institutionalized violence, however, is giving new life to a more powerful force. Mahatma Gandhi, Martin Luther King, Cesar Chavez, Rachel Corrie, and others, are beginning to awaken to the power of truth, non-violent resistance, solidarity with others; recognition that respect and cooperation are essential survival skills, and bring joy, meaning and hope to our lives.

We are grappling with the Big Lie versus truth, fear versus courage, war versus peace. We must stand up to the frightened necrophiliacs[7] that believe that if they cannot own or control something; they have the right to kill it. There is a rising consciousness that the hope of the world is to acknowledge and respect all people; that real security means healthy relationships between people, between people and planet, not the military domination of the many by a dysfunctional few. Americans should rein in their own government and call for compassionate impeachment, the lifting of the American boot off the throat of the world. Imagine redirecting the world's resources away from killing and controlling the planet, to healing.

The time for a Global Truth, Peace and Justice Movement is now. To help others overcome fear, we must help light the path, and encourage the emergence of genuine community that comes from the free exchange of gifts.

Carol Brouillet is a longtime activist. She has organized three gatherings on "Strategies to Transform the Global Economy," with an emphasis on money. She also organized (the first) marches on her Senators and Congresswoman in January 2002 to "demand a congressional investigation of 9/11." She has published Deception Dollars *(over 6,000,000 in print), and co-founded the 9/11 Truth Alliance, and the Northern California 9/11 Truth Alliance. She also produced the musical comedy/benefit and film,* Behind Every Terrorist There is a Bush *and organized the San Franciso International Inquiry into 9/11. She is the mother of three boys, and ran for Congress in 2006 on the Green Party ticket on a 9/11 Truth, Peace and Impeachment platform. www.communitycurrency.org.*

Notes

[1] The title essay in her collection, *Freedom from Fear* (edited and published by her husband, Michael Aris) begins, "It is not power that corrupts but fear. Fear of losing power corrupts those who wield it and fear of the scourge of power corrupts those

who are subject to it." In conclusion she writes that "truth, justice and compassion … are often the only bulwarks against ruthless power" (see Aris 1991).

2   Craig Corrie told this story at the Herbst Theater in San Francisco at the Annual Veterans for Peace National Convention in 2003 when Rachel was honoured post-humously as a member of Veterans for Peace.

3   I organized the San Francisco International Inquiry into 9/11 in cooperation with Canadians who organized the Toronto International Inquiry into 9/11. We worked with activists, organizers, researchers, and victims' family members who were filing suit against the government for their role in the attacks. The Inquiry in San Francisco brought together the major authors, researchers, filmmakers, and activists—those active in alerting the public to the facts about 9/11 and the disparity between the official narrative and reality—together physically for the first time. 9/11truth.org, an international network to nurture the 9/11 Truth Movement, was basically born out of the Inquiry, and the Truth Movement continues to grow since then. "We" here means the 9/11 Truth Movement which became the 9/11 Truth Alliance. Physical meetings organized by the Women's International League for Peace and Freedom (WILPF) members—Premilla Dixit and myself—launched the local New York and San Francisco groups that continue to spearhead visibility actions, events, marches, rallies, and produce films.

4   See Michael Ruppert's address at the Toronto International Inquiry, and at the Commonwealth Club, August 31, 2004. Online: http://www.fromthewilderness. com/PDF/Commonwealth.pdf.

5   "The Project for the New American Century, is a non-profit educational organization dedicated to a few fundamental propositions: that American leadership is good both for America and for the world; and that such leadership requires military strength, diplomatic energy and commitment to moral principle." Online: http://www. newamericancentury.org/.

6   As told to me by my mentor Bill Moyer, author of *Doing Democracy* (Gabriola Island, BC: New Society Publishers, 2001).

7   Psychologist/philosopher Erich Fromm (1964, 1970) believed that the lack of love in the western society and the attraction to mechanistic control leads to necrophilia. Expressions of necrophilia are modern weapon systems, idolatry of technology, and the treatment of people as things in bureaucracy.

References

Abrams, Irwin. 1997. "Heroines of Peace: The Nine Nobel Women." Antioch University, September 22. Online: http://nobelprize.org/nobel_prizes/peace/articles/heroines/index. html.

Aftermath: Unanswered Questions from 9/11. Guerrilla News Network.

Aris, Michael, ed. 1991. *Freedom From Fear and Other Writings by Aung San Suu Kyl.* New York: Viking.

Cheney, Dick. Online: http://www.ajr.org/Article.asp?id=788.

Chossudovsky, Michel. 2003. "Mysterious September 11 Breakfast Meeting on Capitol Hill." Online: http://www.globalresearch.ca/articles/CHO308C.html/.

Fromm Erich. 1964. *The Heart of Man.* New York: Harper and Row.

Fromm Erich. 1970. *The Anatomy of Human Destructiveness.* Austin, TX: Holt, Rinehart and Winston.

The Great Conspiracy: The 9/11 News Special You Never Saw. 2005. Prod: Barrie Zwicker.

Griffin, David Ray. 2004. *The New Pearl Harbor: Disturbing Questions About the Bush Administration and 9/11.* Northampton, MA: Olive Branch Press.

Griffin, David Ray. 2005. *The 9/11 Commission Report: Omissions and Distortions.* Northampton, MA: Olive Branch Press.

Hargrove, Thomas and Guido H. Stempel III. 2006. "Was 9/11 an 'inside job'?" Scripps News Service, August 3. Online: http://seattlepi.nwsource.com/national/279827_conspiracy02ww.html.

Lappé, Anthony and Stephen Marshall. 2004. *True Lies.* New York: Plume.

Lynn, Jocelyn. 2004. "The 9/11 Cover-Up Commission: How the Foxes are Guarding the Chicken Coop." March 27. Online: http://www.communitycurrency.org/joycelynn.html.

Patriot Act. Online: http://www.aclu.org/safefree/resources/17343res20031114.html.

Rebuilding America's Defenses: Strategy, Forces and Resources for a New Century. 2000, September. A Project for the New American Century. Online: http://www.newamericancentury.org/RebuildingAmericasDefenses.pdf.

Ruppert, Michael C. 2004. *Crossing the Rubicon: The Decline of the American Empire at the End of the Age of Oil.* Gabriola Island, BC: New Society Publishers.

Thompson, Paul and the Centre for Cooperative Research. 2004. *The Terror Timeline: Year by Year, Minute by Minute: A Comprehensive Chronicle of the Road to 9/11—and America's Response.* New York: ReganBooks.

GENEVIEVE VAUGHAN

Heterosexism and the Norm
of Normativity

In the 2004 U.S.presidential election, one of the issues used by the right wing to divide and conquer the electorate was the issue of gay marriage. If we can understand homophobia and heterosexism in terms of their connections with Patriarchal Capitalism and the market, perhaps we can strengthen ourselves for further political struggles, as well as clarifying our thinking regarding the gift and the exchange paradigms. In order to do this we need to go back to the social construction of gender as the basis not only of the division of labour but of the division of economies.

The construction of the male gender in opposition to the mother and the consequent denial of mothering gift giving as the main human principle and process, creates a norm of heterosexuality *and* an economic norm of the distribution of goods through exchange (not-giving), both of which are artificial and pernicious. The denial of gift giving and the privileging of not-giving blight the individual personality as well as the economy. The constructions of "male" in this deeply mistaken way and of "female" as its opposite and complement, are motivating privileged Euro/Americans[1] to destroy everything we would otherwise celebrate and love. Heterosexism becomes a way of affirming the Patriarchal Capitalist market. That is, it affirms the primacy of not-giving except according to the *upward* flows established by the market and male dominant heterosexuality. And conversely, Patriarchal Capitalism affirms this norm of heterosexuality, not only in its use of sexualized images for advertising and propaganda but also in its parasite/host structure, in its motivation towards competition and economic domination, and in its privileging of identity and penalization of difference, which is the logical and emotional matrix of homophobia. The values of heterosexism and the market promote each other, and this is made more powerful because the two derive from a common root in "masculated" not-giving.

Despite the gift giving done by lesbians and gay men to each other and to the LGBT movement as well as to the peace and social change movements at large, and despite the challenge to biological gender determinism that we offer, neither the movement nor most of the individuals in it have so far taken their true political positions as opponents of a destructively heterosexist economy. Recognizing a common derivation of the artificial constructions of heterosexuality and of the capitalist market shifts the emphasis from the politics of the defense of personal preference to a much more general socio/economic/political engagement.[2] It can constitute a step beyond issue-bound identity politics to a deep commonality with the other progressive social movements. At the same time, thinking about heterosexism and its connection to Capitalism can serve as a new perspective for feminist and progressive thinking in general.

Masculation

An early change of categories for boys from the model of the mother to that of the father and thus from female (mother-identified) to male, makes masculinity a lifetime mandate or behavioural agenda (see Vaughan 1997 for a more complete discussion). In itself this change of categories, which I call "masculation," seems innocuous enough, but I believe the projections and paradoxes to which it gives rise are now destroying the earth and all her creatures. We do not have much time left, if any. Yet in order not to worsen the problems we need to calmly understand them so that we can create change in the right direction.

Patriarchies place little boys in a category that is opposite to that of their mothers. Since in infancy and childhood mothers are doing most of the caregiving (gift giving) for their children, and this is the most important experience for the children at the time, it appears that in order to achieve a masculine identity little boys have to give up a model of behaviour, which is life sustaining and all encompassing. The rejection of the model of the mother becomes the rejection of the behaviour of unilateral gift giving, and in its place not-giving and domination are offered as "male" characteristics. The not-giver receives gifts without acknowledging them, on the basis that he deserves them because he is in a privileged (male) category. In fact, the mother continues to give to the child even if he will never be a mother, and she encourages him to behave in the not-giving ways of his father (or other significant males) to whom she also gives.

An alternative to gift giving is available to the boy child: hitting. Like gift giving, hitting is transitive. By hitting, one person touches another and establishes a relation, though this is a relation of domination rather than one of mutuality and trust. I realize that this description of the boy child's socialization is an abstraction—but actually he is abstracted,[3] his motherliness, his gift giving humanity, is held in abeyance indefinitely—as he is extracted psychologically from the mothering context. For the boy child, the norm of the mother is replaced or cancelled by the norm of the father (or other masculated male model) and this cancellation itself becomes part of the male identity as does a mandate for the boy to become the overtaking and canceling norm. This gender construction is Oedipal as well as economic. The privileging of the phallus, patriarchal law, and the norm of normativity all take place through an artificial construction of masculinity over and against a prior mothering, gift giving model. The pre-Oedipal stage is not just *jouissance*, a symbiotic merging between the child and the mother but an economically primary stage of gift giving-and-receiving, a proto and (in Capitalist

Patriarchy still) just nascent gift economy.

The Norm of the Norm

Recently there has been a current in cognitive psychology and linguistics called "prototype theory" (Rosch 2000 [1978]; Lakoff 1987; Taylor 2003 [1989]). Concepts are seen as organized around a best example of a category, the prototype or exemplar. So, in experiments in the U.S., in a mid-level category such as "birds," the robin is taken as the prototype by most people. This current implicitly recalls an early (1920s) experiment on concept formation by the Soviet psychologist Lev Vygotsky (1962), in which he provided exemplars of experimental categories and asked children to select members of those categories by comparison with the exemplars. By tracking the various ways in which they accomplished this task, he was able to identify and describe different strategies of concept formation. I noticed (Vaughan 1981) the similarity of this process with the process of the market as seen by Marx (1930 [1867]) and his identification of money as the general equivalent—the prototype of value with regard to the many commodities which are related to it. Jean Josef Goux (1990 [1973]) wrote about the one-to-many form of the general equivalent as incarnated in social structures, for example, the relation of the king to his many subjects, of the general to his army, the patriarchal father to his family, and the phallus to the other parts of the male body. The exemplars or prototypes are the "ones" in the one-to-many structures and may be seen as norms or standards. People take on these roles, which also often permit them to impose legal norms and standards of behaviour. What I derive from looking at this proliferation of similar patterns is the startling conclusion that the form of a thought process, the concept, has become mistakenly embodied in human social structures.

In the area of the market, money is the standard or prototype of value and functions as "one" with regard to "many" commodities. This one-to-many structure is repeated over and over in our society. Chief Executive Officers (CEOs) and Mafia lords, film stars and rock stars, popes and presidents are all examples of one-to-many "prototypicality" and are used as behavioural norms by the many who serve or emulate them. There is a somewhat similar relation also between the owner of private property and the many items that are owned by h/er. Perhaps property relations are more similar to one of Vygotsky's (1962) "complex" stages, which he sees as steps in the development conceptualization proper. In the case of property, this would be the "family name" complex[4] where each item relates individually to the one exemplar, but this does not imply a common quality among the items. Similarly a person can own many different kinds of items (chairs, a sack of tomatoes, a reproduction of the Mona Lisa, a car), which do not have anything in common with each other beyond this property relation to the one owner. In the patriarchal family the "complex" of property includes people among the items, the "chattel," which are related to the "one" *pater familias*.

Antonio Negri and Michael Hardt (2004) have recently written a book,

Multitude, in which they describe the "swarm," which is their conception of the "many" beyond the relationship to the "one." Unfortunately they leave aside heterosexist gender relations, which nevertheless condition the members of the "swarm" internally. Even if the multitude were to succeed in detaching itself from political one-to-many power structures altogether, these structures would still exist within individuals, families and among the masculated (one-to-many) males and correspondingly femized (many to one) females who make up the many.

The one-to-many norm, of which there are so very many instances in our society, self replicates at a higher logical level and becomes the norm of normativity itself (whatever is not normative is not normal). Being normal is being a "one" or being related as one-of- many to a "one," as a star is related to her fans or fans are related to a star. This kind of relation is so commonplace that it seems natural. In the U.S. we use it in selecting our presidents, where the many choose which person (of two) will be the "one" and the candidate with the greatest number of votes of the "many" becomes the "one" for all.[5] We derive our (normal) sense of identity from being in these relationships, playing one or the other role, as well as from being in one-to-many family or property relationships.

Patriarchal institutions such as the law, the prisons, the police and the military, schools and businesses, are all set up according to the norm of one-to-many normativity and they determine behaviour both within and outside their own hierarchical structures. However, in a strange twist in an already unwarranted use of the concept form, the market itself has displaced the concept of value from human beings to objects, and has incarnated the one-to-many norm of value in money. Thus the market broadcasts normativity to us in a transversal way, which is difficult to recognize and remains largely unconscious, though it is part of our daily behaviour.

In fact the market is a gigantic sorting mechanism, which includes commodities and excludes gifts, at the same time evaluating the commodities according to the quantities of the monetary prototype. Quantification, measurement, and the judgment of value according to the monetary norm become normal behaviour for everyone and people judge each other and even themselves in this way. The existence of this social sorting process influences the other one-to-many structures and vice versa, so that all of them become "natural," "objective reality," the way things are. Gift giving and receiving, which imply the value of the other, are left out of the picture and sorting by evaluation in terms of the norm, takes their place.

Those who cannot relate themselves to the monetary norm because they are unemployed or their (gift) work is not monetized, are sorted out, and they become irrelevant, beyond the pale. Similarly, those who are themselves neither the one nor one-of-the-many related to the one, as modeled in the patriarchal family, for example, are also beyond the pale, irrelevant. Anyone who does not accept the norm of heterosexuality can be seen as dangerous and socially deviant by those who do. In fact homosexuals step outside the norm of normativity itself, beyond the one and the many, challenging that structure in much the same way that the gift economy challenges the structure of the market and Capitalist Patriarchy. Of course, many homosexuals and transgendered people performatively repeat the power relations they find in the society around them (Butler 1990). But being beyond the norm of normativity brings with it a revolutionary potential, which could be empowered if the connections between heterosexism and the economy of the market were made more explicit. Unfortunately the market and heterosexism validate each other in many different ways, which we may not identify as such, and it is easy to be trapped in a hall of mirrors without seeing the connections.

Those who are geographically and ideologically beyond the pale are now being considered as potential threats to the security of those within it, whether they are a many related to a "one" who is different from "our one": another real or invented leader such as Osama Bin Laden, or an "other" monotheistic God, or whether they are simply "disaffected" individuals. Such individuals appear to be capable of immense destruction, given the level of development of arms technology (see my discussion of the "one" character of guns in my 1997 book, *For-Giving*). In fact, with this technology, it only takes one to kill many. The fear that many will avail themselves of this option drives the decision-making of the ones at the top who (in order to solve the problem!) are continuing to provide the model of national patriarchal aggression of one against the many on a grand scale.[6]

Since women have not been masculated, we are somewhat outside the one-to-many structure, unless we are placed in a relation of gift giving to a one. Thus perhaps we have a chance to do things differently especially if we do not cling to (home or homeland) security. However, young heterosexual women are socially encouraged at every turn to find the "one" to whom to relate themselves, and to whom they will give long term. Without this "one" they remain in an outsider position. Although this outsider position is made to seem inferior and women who are not married or in relationships are often punished with isolation, there is a revolutionary potential here as well.

I do not believe women should imitate masculated violence in order to change the system. We have to find other ways of dismantling the structure, or shall I call it syndrome, of patriarchy. There is no reason why the "one" prototype of a concept should be invested with special value or why someone in that position should be able to make decisions and act aggressively "for" all. Or receive the gifts of the many. Or fight against the prototype of others, the "one" related to other manys. We have misconstrued and misvalued this part of the way we think. Knowing that this is what we are doing can allow us to strategize to collectively change it in nonviolent ways.

I believe that by promoting the radically different worldview of the gift economy we can undermine the power structures of Patriarchal Capitalism. The attribution of reality and normality to these power structures constitutes one of the cornerstones of the edifice of the "master's house" (Lorde 1984). We can challenge and dismantle the norm of normativity by which positions of power are validated. The values of the gift economy, espoused by the many, could reabsorb the exacerbated and over emphasized "ones" into the midst of the many—given that this reiterated one-to-many structure is actually a collectively constructed psychosocial artifact. That is, though forming concepts is perhaps the human, species specific, development of a modeling capacity shared by all life (Sebeok and Danesi 2000), using a part of this process as a structure for social organization and individual ego formation, is a mistake and an unnecessary and aberrant form. Indeed the fact that there are many people beyond the norm of normativity (neither many nor one) shows that this use of the one-to-many form is not a biologically determined aspect of the human species. The general crisis to which these norms have led us must deeply trouble both the ones and the many and signals the need for radical change. In fact the swing towards Fascism that we have recently been experiencing may be a reaction to this crisis, a mistaken attempt to solve the problem by intensifying its cause.

On the other hand, beginning to practice the gift economy consciously and recognizing the many ways in which we have already been practicing it unconsciously, gives an accessible inroad into the alternative. It is not by behaving according to norms that we create community and live in peace and harmony with one another, but by satisfying needs, by giving and receiving at many levels. These levels are material, and perceptual as well as linguistic and semiotic; they are levels of gifts and services of all kinds as well as signs and signals, pheromones and colour changes, tones and gestures, all of which can be seen as gifts that satisfy our needs to know about one another. Our identities do not come from being assigned to a category or from being related as one of many to a "one" or even from becoming or having the potential to become a "one." There is a whole other fabric of giving and receiving, which makes us who we are regardless of whether or not at the same time we are continually categorizing and being categorized according to a norm.

Our thinking has become excessively categorical due to the exchange-based economy, which excludes gift giving and thus (1) serves as a model of categorical inclusion and exclusion, with money as the prototype and (2) places gift giving on the outside where it is invisible. By (3) evaluating everything quantitatively, the market creates abstract quantitative categories of similarity and difference, which again serve as models for categorization. Then 4) the normativity of money and the market resonate with the other one-to-many normative forms, setting up a reciprocal validation.

The concept formation process functions by comparison and contrast, including each item of the many in a category by virtue of its similarity with the one, and finding the common quality among the many which are related to the one in this way. In the relation between commodities and money the same process takes place, as each product is evaluated quantitatively in terms of an amount of the money standard. Each person confronts the other either as holder of the "one" or as holder of an item of the many, as holder of money or of a product. The exchangers often change roles as sellers and buyers.

The exercise of evaluation according to a norm becomes commonplace. Not-giving to satisfy the need of the other and therefore not-implying the value of the other, also becomes normal behaviour. Instead we give in order to receive either a product or the incarnated value norm (money), giving value to ourselves by implication. The exchangers are all similar to each other in this way. They thus belong to the same category and only differ according to the quantity of exchange value they own and exchange, while the transitivity of gift giving is excluded from the process. What has been put out at the door comes back in through the window as profit—what people "deserve" for having participated in the process—gifts reframed as rewards, i.e. exchanges. The forcing of the gifts upwards as profit seems to prove the superiority of those who have them and the race to the top, to be a human "one" through the accumulation of gifts (capital, which can then be reinvested) proceeds. The exchangers are placed in adversarial positions, and are detached from the needs of others, which their products might satisfy. Rather than creating community they create isolation by enacting these ego-oriented patterns of inclusion and exclusion over and over again. The man who is the "breadwinner" of the family, can be in a position of giving to the family in exchange for nurturing of himself and his property. This creates a situation of debt, dependency, and responsibility regarding his intimates, which is different from the relations created in (egalitarian) mothering gift giving. The nuclear family itself is fostered by market-based adversarial relations among families.

The compare-and-contrast thinking processes, which people engage in regarding the norm of whatever category concerns them at the moment, is repeated in the compare-and-contrast process of commodities and money in the market, which feeds back into the thinking processes, and the categories people form regarding themselves and each other. Judgment according to a norm seems to be the most important process in community and communication, while transitivity and needs are set aside. We are really barking up the wrong tree.

In spite of their seeming ubiquity, however, this tangled collection of normative structures is actually rather fragile and therefore needs to be protected from the possible alternatives. Think of the "threat" communism was supposed to pose—though in fact communism (as State Capitalism) was also set up according to one-to-many structures. We do not need these psychologically invested norms[7] and the norm of normativity is false. Rather we need to allow and value processes of giving and receiving which will let us all become completely human. And we need to understand our thinking as based in these processes not just on categorization.

In the construction of heterosexism, imposing the male prototype of the category human actually leaves out the female as a category altogether. Canceling the female prototype leaves females as uncategorized, seemingly *pre-categorical* and thus "childlike"! It thus appears that not-giving and prototypicality go together while gift giving implies irrelevance to categorization. Gift giving seems simply not important enough to be categorized. While males have been taken away from, abstracted from the gift context, and the patterns of abstraction have themselves been abstracted and used for understanding the world, the patterns of gift giving have not been abstracted and used for understanding. This leaves large lacunae in what we think of as knowledge. Why do we not know how words relate to the world, for example? Too many explanations for experience and for human relations are still being stuffed into the black box of biology because gift giving/mothering is not being used as an interpretative key.

The Binary Norm of Heterosexuality

The norm of normativity is the norm of over valued prototypicality, a "one" invested with special significance, with regard to which the many are related as similar members of a category. This relation is binary (or polar)[8] as an item is either the "one" or one of the many. The norm of exchange is either money or commodity; and the binary relation of property is similar with two aspects: either object or owner and either mine or others' (not-mine).

Heterosexuality is a common example of normativity but it is imbalanced towards the male "one" since part of the character of maleness in our society lies in being the "one." Of course oneness cannot actually stand alone, but is relational. The heterosexual norm requires at least two of which one is *more* one than the other. It has binary poles of which one pole, the male, is the "one" while the female functions as the eclipsed norm and eclipsed giver, sorted out, but giving to the one, who dominates. She can function as a giver of many things but, more importantly, she herself is one-of-many when, having been cancelled as the original prototype, she is grouped together with her children (or with property) as "many" with regard to the "one" husband/father. She can also be one-of-many women regarding a Don Juan male figure. In a way, in masculation, the privileging of the category "male," functions to make all women "many," to whom every male is (or "deserves" to be) related as "one." On the other hand the male "one" is nothing without the many, and he also needs the eclipsed gift giver in order to maintain his position. Following this model, playing these roles, in the family, in the media and in the market, people unknowingly help maintain a norm of dominance and privilege, which subjugates gift giving. Homosexuals as the third or fourth sex, both/and and neither/nor, form a plurality, which destabilizes the distorted binary heterosexual norm.

Once established, the psycho-logic of heterosexuality can be turned around so that regardless of biological gender anyone who takes the "one" not-giving position appears as "male," while anyone who takes the "many" or gift giving position is "female." Since in patriarchy the many serve or give to the male one, the position of the many appears to coincide with "female" gift giving. In fact what we call "power" is the ability be the "one" and to force others into the femized gift giving position, whether the "one" is biologically male, female or an abstract entity such as a corporation. The power of the corporation over the many can therefore be seen as male, or masculated power, even though the corporation itself is not a human being but a legal entity, which does not have physiological genitals. The "male" one and the "female" many are thus relational positions that are imposed as stereotypical sexual and economic roles.

Power relations make egalitarian gift giving and receiving difficult. However, positive communication and community depend on human beings treating each other as (communicative) givers and receivers. In our linguistic communication we construct our variegated similarity ad hoc through the gift process, having in common an egalitarian point of departure as speakers of the same language. As speakers and writers we exercise a gift giving agency that has its fruition in the understanding of listeners or readers whose communicative needs are both elicited and satisfied by our linguistic gifts. They are able to receive these gifts because they themselves are also communicative agents who in their turn construct similar gifts for others, using the common verbal virtual gift mode of a particular language.

The performance of the masculated and femized roles beyond biological gender might be considered a social bricolage, a game of exploration—here of the one-to-many relation and of the relation between gift and exchange, in the intimate interpersonal arena. Since, in Capitalist Patriarchy it is possible for women[9] to achieve the "one" position, as a rock star or a prime minister or in the family as the (usually economically disempowered) single mother of many children, it is clear that the capacity to be the prototype is not biologically determined as male, nor is the capacity to be gift giving and one-of-the-many only female. Creating these roles as conscious performance and even as parody calls the roles into question; the ability to relate to one another outside the norm can be an assertion of the generic human. It can also provide the kind of egalitarian relations that are necessary for the liberated practice of the gift economy. Though heterosexuals do also often relate to each other beyond the stereotypical roles, the roles themselves in their case still seem deeply embedded in biology. It is perhaps a special gift of the LGBT movement to show the way to the unmasculated gift giving human.

The Norm of the Un-Normative, Beyond The Pale

We could dismantle the binary norm of heterosexism, *first* by extracting gift giving from it. That is, we would recognize that gift giving is of a different order, a different logical status, in that it is a human process already the possession of everyone, whether male or female, one or many—an "operating system" put into the "computer" very early on—and therefore it is pertinent to everyone beyond the binary norm, not an aspect of gender. Looking at language as transposed gift giving (as I have been trying to do for many years), confirms the pan-human character of gift giving because the capacity for language itself is not determined by gender.

Second, if we could restore gift giving to the concept of "human" we would no longer construct maleness in opposition to gift giving in a binary way, and therefore would not misuse an exemplar of a not-giving father in opposition to the gift giving mother, to construct the accepted masculine identity for boys. If the prototype of the father did not take over and cancel the prototype of the mother, the "one" position would be less emphasized and the father himself would be seen as less dominant. He and like him, his sons, would also not be expected to replace gift giving with hitting. As happens in matriarchies, the mother would be seen as the model of the human practice of gift giving for *both* males and females. However she would not need to be dominant, as her capacity to be the model would not have to cancel a polar opposite model. Moreover, since gift giving is other-oriented, it is not a self-centered dominant model, not focused on being "one." It includes others, and therefore is a link in a similarly constructed gift giving "many" (which does not exclude males who in a gift-based society would not be masculated anyway).[10] We could do away with the norm of normativity altogether, constructing ourselves and each other through gift giving-and-receiving processes at many different levels. In this way we would produce a kind of subjectivity and agency very different from those we are now creating under the dictates of the norm and the logic of exchange. Constructing ourselves and our genders differently would allow us to defuse the motivation towards domination and accumulation. It would also help us recognize the deeply dysfunctional configurations of our institutions and would clarify the ways to change them.

Relations

The process of gift giving and receiving allows each person to influence and participate in the other's development. It creates relations of mutuality and reciprocal recognition while exchange creates relations of competition or mutual indifference (in which recognition is only "given" through a struggle). In the gift process, needs are valued, not considered in terms of effective demand as the means for making a profit. New needs develop according to the specific satisfaction of old needs. The agency of each person develops during the process in which s/he, as a giver is able to recognize the needs of the other and fill them creatively. Then the giver also becomes a creative receiver in h/er turn and is able to use the gifts of others, as well as to see the others as the source of the satisfaction of h/er need. S/he is also able to know specifically the object or the service s/he has been given, often by actually incorporating it. In fact I believe that the response to the gift, which at a conscious level is gratitude, may be considered at a less conscious level as knowledge. It is this giving and receiving interaction, this mode of distribution, that socializes us as human, rather than the more abstract and adversarial interaction of exchange, with the equations and categories of which we continue to identify and which we over-value as self-reflecting consciousness. In fact I believe we should be called *homo donans*[11] instead of *homo sapiens* or we should realize that the two are really the same thing, that we cannot know anything without first receiving and beginning to learn to give the gifts that satisfy our physical, perceptual and emotional needs and those of others.

Actually, the process of giving and receiving *is* the process of knowledge. Our perceptual needs are satisfied by our experience of the world around us, and this experience also brings us the methods and means for satisfying our more complex needs for knowledge. Thus *homo donans* and *recipiens* come before categorizing *homo sapiens* and should be recognized as more descriptive names for our humanity. We have been projecting the objectification we have learned from the market onto the universe rather than projecting the mother as Indigenous gift-based societies have done. Just as the male we have invented cancels female humanity, exchange cancels gift giving, and the market economy cancels the gift economy.

The Market and Masculation

The logical contradictions in the constitution of binary heterosexism derive from the misuse of the concept formation process in masculation. Logically there can be only one "one" but there are many people, especially masculated males with the same mandate to achieve that position. Social hierarchies are created so that at least some of the contenders can achieve the top position. The one-to-many aspects of concept formation are externalized, and transferred onto the plane of interpersonal relations and the construction of gendered subjectivities.[12] Lived out, these artificial and mistaken heterosexist constructions of gender, which are also re projected into group relations and institutional structures, cause huge social problems, yet perhaps because of their similarity to aspects of the concept formation process, they seem to give meaning and structure to the lives of the individuals who are their bearers. The market as one of the projections of masculation, provides a field in which the not-giving masculated identity of individuals can exercise its mandate to get to the top. Corporate entities also act out a disembodied masculated agenda though they have not gone through a gender construction as such. Competitive capitalism is motivated by masculation.

In Capitalism, goods and services are produced by labour, which for Marx (1930 [1867]) is abstract (not-gift) labour. The common relation of commodities to each other is quantitatively assessed in money. If something cannot be assessed in money it is irrelevant to the market, uncategorized. It is as if the market replays the moment of transition from the gift giving mothering (non) category to the category "male," with the commodity playing the part of the boy. The money standard/norm plays the part of the father norm, the one to which all commodities are related as many, and to which "female" gifts are or appear to be irrelevant. It is in this sense that the market appears to be a replay of the construction of heterosexism. It repeats and rebroadcasts its mistaken logic into our minds and behaviours from a different, object-based dimension—one that seems to have very little to do with gender. The market also seems to be neuter or neutral because women can participate as well as men in its not-giving (or gift-canceling) mode of distribution. The emphasis on objects that the market promotes, objects from which gift value has been deleted through the process of exchange, leaves us with the idea that the market is objective, giftless, and "fair." Nevertheless many gifts of profit are channeled through the market, and value is thus surreptitiously given to the ego-oriented exchangers and to the market itself. Moreover, since gift giving is hidden or misnamed, the market appears to be the only mode of distribution, and therefore also production for the market appears to be the only mode of production. Similarly patriarchal heterosexism seems to be the only mode of gender construction possible. The two social constructions back each other up in such a way as to make both seem natural and unavoidable. It follows that challenges to the market disturb the masculated identity and challenges to masculation disturb the market.

It is part of the market's seemingly neutral and independent dimension that there is an emphasis on equality after the fact. That is, after gift giving has been sorted out, the equation of value between different commodities and different kinds of productive labour or services becomes a moment of a process in which all the market participants engage on a daily basis. The value given to, and seemingly by, equality with the (money) standard becomes itself a model for human relations. Unfortunately this is an equality, which is established after gift giving has been excluded from the picture. Thus the fact that someone works harder and longer than someone else for the same pay is not interpreted in the light that h/er extra work is a gift to h/er employer. Rather it is seen as deriving from the fact that h/er job is less important or that s/he is less skilled or less educated—or the wrong gender. In fact the jobs which have most to do with gift giving such as housework, childcare, and teaching, are notoriously poorly paid—as if to emphasize their inferiority and irrelevance to the masculated market. The extraction of gifts is treated as "injustice" because the payment does not reach the standard of quantitative equality, while the gifts that permeate the market, and are extracted at every turn, are invisible. Even if the wrongs are righted in some cases, justice cannot solve the problem in general because the market itself is a mechanism for gift extraction. It is not by giving value to equality from which gift giving has been removed that we can create better selves or a society where the needs of all are satisfied. Instead we need a shift from a market-based to a gift-based society.

Politics

There are two main opposing views in the U.S., as demonstrated by the two-party system. These views very generally retrace the opposition between the gift paradigm and the exchange paradigm, which retrace the construction of heterosexuality, which we have been describing. However our understanding does not go far enough to allow us to take a radical gift giving standpoint, because those on the "Left" typically think that women are equal to men according to the male (masculated, giftless) standard, and those on the "Right" think that women should be femized, nurturing men in their masculated roles. The femized woman is the one the Right sees as gift giving. The masculated adult man protects her as he protects his property (and his country). The gift giver has not been seen or recognized as the human standard, the human prototype, though s/he pervades the society. That is why the Right says that the Left does not have values—and the Left believes the values of the right are false and based on cruelty, greed, deception—and the stereotypical roles of heterosexism.

If we cannot find a radically different point of view from that of the masculated men of the Right wing, we cannot hold back their rush to domination. But we on the Left also need to go beyond the equality with the masculated norm of the equation of value from which gift giving has been removed and beyond normativity itself. We are *all* wearing the eyeglasses of Capitalist Patriarchy. To find the alternative we need to reveal gift giving as something that has a status and logic of its own, which is (at least) as important as the logic of the market. We need to understand and embrace gift giving as autonomous, not see it as an adjunct to exchange.

We have appealed to the legal system devised by Patriarchy to restrain some of the worst aspects of masculation. However, law and justice are based on crime and payment by punishment, on the logic of exchange, and do not offer a real alternative to exchange. The perspective of the gift, where we actively investigate needs in order to unilaterally fill them in an effective way, is more basic and is as powerful as the perspective of exchange. Reprisal, vengeance, exacting payment for a wrong done ("bringing the perpetrators to justice") are part of the exchange paradigm reasoning of balancing the accounts, and they leave aside gift giving. War with its attacks and counter-attacks is the logic of exchange played out large. The cold war arms race was also a replay of exchange, in which the equation between weapons systems was repeatedly established, re "valued" and re established. By unilaterally giving way Gorbachev at last broke through the escalation and satisfied an impelling need for peace. Unfortunately Patriarchal Capitalism immediately extended its parasitic tentacles to the former Soviet Union to take the gifts that had been made available by many years of socialism.

We are playing out the masculated syndrome large, causing worldwide devastation. We need a point of view that is radical enough to offer a real alternative. The gift paradigm can satisfy that need. Instead what we have now is the Patriarchal dominance model and the market equality-and-justice model.[13] We need to go farther than that, to the gift paradigm. The reason for this is that the dominant father model and the market model are really part of the same paradigm. Money has the place of the norm in the market, while the father has the place of the norm in the family.[14] Heterosexism is the imposition of the masculated norm bolstered by the norm of normativity, while femization is the casting of gift givers—women and men—in the roles of the many who adapt to and nurture the masculated norms. (These norms are both individuals in top positions and the one-many structures projected into society at large. Masculated men and ideologies of course attempt to keep women, and other men in gift giving roles, roles of the many, which they control and dominate.) We need to imagine and construct ourselves outside the norm(s), recognizing and validating gift giving, the unmasculated and unfemized gift giving of women, of men, of the many.

For the transition to a gift economy we need to take the mother as an easily available prototype of the gift giving human, but not the only one—disestablishing the hegemony of the norm of normativity. We can do this by showing how widespread gift giving is in society at large and by considering normativity not as important in itself but only as an element of the process of concept formation. In this way we can create a gift economy, in which boys are not required to reject mothering, and the economy of adulthood is nurturing. In gift economies, where there is no market based on the (mis)construction of the male gender, sexual orientation is sexual and affectional, not economic.[15]

Genevieve Vaughan is an independent researcher, author of For-Giving, a Feminist Criticism of Exchange *(1997) and* Homo Donans *(2006). A documentary on her life,* Giving for Giving, *has just been released. Her books and many articles are available free on her website www.gift-economy.com.*

Notes

1   Heterosexism exists of course in many other groups but it is presently in the European/American culture that the structures of dominance at many levels have united to form a collective non-nurturing mechanism of power over the many. There are alternative constructions. Discussing the continuation of matricentric structures in a number of African societies, Ifi Amadiume (1997) says, "The presence of these fundamental matriarchal systems generating love and compassion also means that we cannot take the classical Greek Oedipal principle of violence as a basic paradigm or given in the African context... (156).

2   The same may be said for the feminist movement and abortion rights. See that discussion in the Introduction. In fact the exchange economy pushes us into hyper individualistic positions.

3   I think this is similar to what Alfred Sohn-Rethel (1965), talking about commodities, called a "real-abstraction."

4   Vygotsky's (1962) discussion of complexes in the '20s is probably prior to Wittgenstein's (2001 [1953]) conceptualization of meanings as family resemblances or strands in a rope, and both came long before Lakoff's (1987) discussion of similar categories. Vygotsky sees complexes as developmental stages of thinking coming before conceptual abstraction.

5   This U.S. election process is strikingly similar to the way the model of the father is "chosen" over the mother as the prototype of the human, for boys and eventually also for girls who accept their secondary status. The president and the party that win the election are thus "male" while the ones who lose are "female" and give way.

6   It is just the paradox of the mandate of masculinity that in order to achieve their gender ideal males have to become the "one." The patriarchal family provides this possibility at an individual level and a number of hierarchies are available for this purpose at a societal level. In fact by separating fields of activity from each other and creating vertical hierarchies, the possibility is given to some of the many to become "ones" even though logically there should be only one "one." With the break down in the patriarchal family and the present scarcity of jobs in the system, there are not enough "one" positions available. Thus people enact the one-to-many activity of group killing, as when schoolboys shoot their classmates. They do this to become normal. Nations do it as well.

So we can see a kernel of "truth" in the contention of the Right that feminism "causes" male violence by challenging male dominance, ie, not allowing males to take this "one" position in the family. However the construction and belief in this "one" position, masculation and the norm of normativity are what are actually causing the problem. It is not surprising that the "one" pope of the "one" church of the "one" God would promote such a belief.

7   Judith Butler (2004) thinks we do need norms for community though she would like to change the ones we have. I believe that while we may need prototypes for developing concepts, the investment of the prototype with normativity, and with a special value and the power to elicit or force gifts from others, is unnecessary and unwarranted. Categorization itself is only half of the picture of thinking, to which the transitivity of gift giving needs to be restored as the other half. Giving-and-receiving creates relationships of mutuality and trust from which community as co-*muni*-ty and communication as co-*muni*-cation arise. (*Muni* means "gifts" in Latin).

8   Marx (1930 [1867]) discusses this configuration when he is discussing money: "the character of being generally and directly exchangeable is, so to say, a polar one, and is as inseparable from its polar opposite, the character of not being directly exchangeable, as the positive pole of a magnet is from the negative" (41).

9   Or corporate entities or nations.

10   The very characteristics of gift giving, which penalize it in a context of exchange: for example its inclusiveness and lack of a drive towards domination become functional in a context where exchange and masculation are not dominant.

11   See my book by that name (2006). In her essay in this volume Kaarina Kailo suggests instead using the term *femmina donans*.

12   The prototype is not "better" than any of the other items of a category. However masculation *invests* it with value. The people who use the prototype and aspire to be a "one," attribute value to it and the many who are not the "one" give value to it by giving to it.

13   George Lakoff (2004) has proposed the Dominant Father and the Nurturing Parent models as typical of the Right and Left in the U.S. Significantly he does not identify the female mothering model as such.

14   We seem to be looking for a nurturing dominant father, trying to make Patriarchal Capitalism nurturing look at Dr. Phil, Bill Gates, perhaps even the Bushes themselves The creation of nurturing males to be done by socially dismantling masculation, however, and not by including the nurturing father in the package of masculation. A more truly gift giving male leader is Hugo Chavez. Not surprisingly he is of Indigenous heritage.

15   Even where there is a market, but women are in control, heterosexuality is less oppressive. For example, see Veronika Bennholdt-Thomsen's (1994) work on Juchitan, Mexico, where women are in control of the market, the queer *muxes* are highly respected and considered a blessing for the family in which they are born.

References

Amadiume, Ifi. 1997. *Reinventing Africa: Matriarchy, Religion and Culture*. London: Zed Books.

Bennholdt-Thomsen, Veronika, ed. 1994. *Juchitan-Stadt der Frauen*, Hamburg, Rowohlt Taschenbuch Verlag.

Butler, Judith. 1990. *Gender Trouble: Feminism and the Subversion of Identity*. New York: Routledge.

Butler, Judith. 2004. *Undoing Gender*. New York: Routledge.

Goux, Jean-Joseph. 1990 [1973]. *Symbolic Economies: After Marx and Freud*. Ithaca: Cornell University Press.

Lakoff, George. 1987. *Women, Fire and Dangerous Things.* Chicago: University of Chicago Press.

Lakoff, George. 2004. *Don't Think of an Elephant.* White River Junction, VT: Chelsea Green Publishing.

Lorde, Audre. 1984. *Sister Outsider.* Freedom, CA: The Crossing Press.

Marx, Karl. 1930 [1867]. *Capital.* Trans. E and C. Paul, London. J. M. Dent and Sons.

Negri, Antonio and Michael Hardt. 2004. *Multitude, War and Democracy in the Age of Empire.* New York: Penguin Press.

Rosch, Eleanor. 2000 [1978]. "Principles of Categorization." *Concepts: Core Readings.* Eds. E. Margoulis and S. Laurence eds. Cambridge: MIT Press. 189-207.

Sebeok, Thomas A. and Marcel Danesi. 2000. *The Forms of Meaning. Modeling Systems Theory and Systems Analysis.* Boston: Mouton de Gruyter.

Sohn-Rethel, Alfred. 1965, April. "Historical Materialist Theory of Knowledge." *Marxism Today* 114-122.

Taylor, John R. 2003. *Linguistic Categorization.* Oxford: Oxford University Press.

Vaughan, Genevieve. 1980. "Communication and Exchange." *Semiotica* 29 (1-2): 113-143. The Hague: Mouton.

Vaughan, Genevieve. 1981. "Saussure and Vygotsky via Marx." *American Semiotic* 4 (1): 57-83.

Vaughan, Genevieve. 1997. *For-Giving: A Feminist Criticism of Exchange.* Austin: Plainview/Anomaly Press.

Vaughan, Genevieve. 2006. *Homo Donans.* Online: www.gift-economy.com.

Vaughan, Genevieve, ed. 2004. *Il Dono/The Gift: A Feminist Analysis. Athanor: Semiotica, Filosofia, Arte, Letteratura* 15 (8). Roma: Meltemi Editore.

Vygotsky, Lev Semenovich. 1962. *Thought and Language.* Cambridge: The MIT Press.

Wittgenstein, Ludwig. 2001 [1953]. *Philosophical Investigations.* London: Blackwell.

III. GIFTS IN THE
SHADOW OF EXCHANGE

YVETTE ABRAHAMS

The Khoekhoe Free Economy

A Model for the Gift

The Khoekhoe are Indigenous South Africans. South Africa, Nairbobi, Southern Angola, Botswana, Zambia, Zimbabwe, and southern Mozambique are historical homes of Indigenous populations. The word "Khoekhoe" means "people of people" as opposed to "animal people" or "clod people," thus the English translation would be "humans"—we are then South African human beings.

The topic of this paper is the social structure of the historical Khoekhoe as a model for the gift economy. I am writing about the historical Khoekhoe because after 350 years of colonialism, 250 years of slavery, 48 years of apartheid and ten years of structural adjustment, there is not much that has survived.

The foundation of the Khoekhoe free economy is our spirituality. Fundamentally we give because we are given to, and the biggest thing that we were given, of course, is creation. The sign of our creator is the circle, sign of wonders; the open hand, which is obviously a giving hand. Engravings of the circle are one of the most frequently observed in Khoekhoe rock art. What the circle means is blessedness. It symbolizes that the divine is within each of us. When I give, I am giving from the divine in me to the divine in you. We are one creator, one world. The two of us, as aspects of the creator, are sharing in a joint creation.

We give because we are created. We are all aspects of the creator. The Khoekhoe used to think of us as being part of each other, of all being aspects of one creator. The Khoekhoe tradition of rock art and cave drawings is a tradition of story-telling, and storytelling is a gift. The Khoekhoe paint their stories on cave walls and rocks for all the world to see. This is the very opposite of capitalist art. The art on cave walls and rock art are out in the open; they cannot be bought, they are given, there for any passerby to enjoy. One of the most celebrated things in rock art is motherhood, and there are many paintings of mother and child, of a child suckling, which is one huge aspect of gift giving.

Only a mother can suckle her child, but other than that, mothering was not really a gendered act in Khoekhoe society. The broader aspects of mothering, taking care of children, was not considered a gendered task; it was something everybody did. Everyone watched over the children. The Khoekhoe people are non-gendered. If there is task specific to men, you will always see that it is a man in paintings about hunting, and if it is a task specific to women, like suckling, you will always be able to see a woman. But by far the majority of figures in the art rock are non-gendered, they are just human beings, the Khoekhoe.

One thing the Khoekhoe love to give as well is thanks. With a spirituality based on gifting, when the men used to hunt, they would say, "Give your life that I might live." The taking of a life indiscriminately was just not done. It is probably one of the reasons we were so easily colonized. It took about 150 years for the Khoekhoe to get over killing one colonist. It just wasn't part of our culture. It was only around the mid-nineteenth century that the Khoekhoe began to understand the capitalist idea of taking life, as opposed to sharing life.

In all the stories, and rock paintings, of hunting, when the hunters come home with the meat, thanks are given to the buck that gave its life so that we could live. There would be drumming and dancing, more storytelling, people changing into cats and bucks, dancing in a circle, in a double circle, the celebrated and sacred sign of spirituality.

One of the interesting aspects of the Khoekhoe gift economy is that men and women are separate but equal. While there were things that only the men did, like hunting, and there were other things that only women did, like gathering of plants, and suckling children—different spiritual tasks—this did not transform into any form of gender inequality. The reason for this is quite obvious. It is because the Khoekhoe society did not have private property, and therefore never developed a hierarchical, class society. The means of production were never privatized. The Khoekhoe put it this way: the land cannot be ours, it is God's, it is given to us by God to take care of and pass on to the next generation. It is not something that you actually can give; it is not yours to give in the first place. If you cannot give it, then you cannot sell it, you cannot buy it, you cannot own it.

And to me, this really important when we look at modern-day versions of the gift economy. Not having private property or owning land was a basis for the Khoekhoe gift economy because if I have enough and you have enough, then the gifts take on a social symbolism. I don't need to give you anything to eat, because you have enough to eat. You don't need to give me anything to eat, because I have enough to eat, so we can start thinking of gifts as something that is not necessary, something that we do because we want to, not because we have to, and that's really different from today. Today, I cannot give away my labour. I have to work in order to eat. In the old days, gift giving used to symbolize social exchange. The Khoekhoe consider it very rude to refuse a gift, because what it means is, "I don't want to know you. I don't to accept you as part of my particular social structure." When you give me a gift, it's saying you want to be part of me. Me giving you a gift is saying, "Yes, I like you. Let's be in a community together."

Today I cannot do this. I will pass somebody in the street, a person starving, and it's raining, and I have to give them food. It is not a choice on my part, but an imperative. At some point one might have to stop giving because they ran out of food, and this has a different social meaning in a situation of landless-ness and privatized property. In South Africa, the whites used to own 87 percent of the land. Ten years after the implementation of structural adjustment programs, they still own 85 percent of the land. The politics may have changed, but the economy has not. The power of gifting is thus diminished. It is beautiful when gifting is choice, but not when you are forced to do it. These are the kind of things we grapple with today.

What do we do today to manage to exist, now that we are divorced from the gifting economy on which our society was based? What still survives of the old traditions? The first thing we give each other is respect and recognition. And people in many parts of the world do not do this. We say, "Hello, how are you?" meaning, I see you, I recognize you, and I care how you are. If we are in the rural areas, then people will go on forever, "how's your mother, how's your father, how's your grandmother, how's your uncle, how's your aunt?" We give each other that recognition. When we ask, "how are you?" we speak to the divine in the other person. We care.

We have many rituals around food that have survived quite well, even through the years when we were slaves and we didn't have much food. Still today, the Khoekhoe will never dish out the last portion of food in the pot. They always leave a little bit of food in the pot. And this may seem strange, as many people today do not have enough food. But that remnant in the pot symbolizes leaving some food for God, and if a stranger knocks on the door and needs food, you will be able to feed that stranger. When you share food for the family, and leave some for whoever might need it, a gift giving social system is reinforced. There may be some of our people sleeping on street corners, but they have got certain families that they can regularly go to for food: one on a Monday, another on a Tuesday, and so on. That last portion of food in the pot, the last piece for God, you're giving it to God in this other person.

Sharing food is fundamental. Many people do this all over the world. I am not suggesting it's specific to the Khoekhoe, but just sharing with you how we do things. When you visit a Khoekhoe house, you cannot leave without eating a dish of something. It would be rude to not offer a guest, a visitor, or even a stranger something, even if there is nothing but water in house. Water is also a precious resource. I was brought up this way. When you walk into my house, you will not be able to leave without having had some tea or coffee and something to eat. It was quite surprising to me when I visited in Europe and I discovered that some people do not do this, as we do.

There are also all kinds of ceremonial giving. Giving is a symbol of relatedness. There are many ceremonial gifts around courtship and marriage. To share your *karosse* (shawl) with somebody is a symbol of engagement. You might ask, "are you cold?" and then lay the shawl over the other person's shoulder. You are sharing warmth, but you are also making a statement, "do you want to share my *karosse*?" Gifting between the two families involved in courtship and marriage has survived. In the nineteenth century families would each exchange a cow or a sheep; it was a symbol of the joining of bloodlines. Today we cannot afford cows or sheep. Today we exchange DVDs or TVs. But the symbolism is still there.

Storytelling continues. We will give you poetry at the drop of hat, and in fact we will continue to read poetry after everybody falls asleep.

Women give a huge amount of free labour. Male responsibility for childrearing remains, in some cases. There should be social recognition of male mothering, though in practice, the more the men are colonized, the less and less they do of it. But if we studied the gift givers, we would see that they are all women. I raise this because Genevieve Vaughan (1997) talks about ways in which the exchange economy still uses the gift economy, and in many ways could not survive without it. If women's free labour is 40 percent of the economy, then it is certain that the market economy could not survive without it.

Also in Africa, it is the women who farm the land. About 66 percent of the food that feeds the continent comes off this land, it comes from women's subsistence farming, yet this food production never makes it into Africa's economic figures. This is because this food is not bought, is not sold, it is given. But we could not survive without this. Women's non-waged labour provides two-thirds of all the food that Africans eat each year. In a way, it leads to greater independence, but in another way, it is a huge subsidy of the globalized capitalist economy. Imagine if African wages went up by two-thirds. It would do all kinds of interesting things to the economy.

We also have a compassion economy. During colonialism and during slavery, we would not have been able to survive without a compassion economy, meaning that when somebody gets into trouble, everybody chips in, we all help. This has been under a lot of strain now because of the HIV/AIDs epidemic. We've seen it breaking down in various parts of the country. This gift, this compassion economy survived slavery, it survived colonialism, but it's not surviving HIV/AIDs.

The compassion economy is about the self. I give because I am human, because I am Khoekhoe, it's not because I want to impress you, it's not because I want you to love me, and I know there may be heaps of psychological studies on the gift demanding attention, but in our culture it's not like that. Giving is about me, it's about who I am. I is the way I was brought up. I do it not for you, but for me, and for the sake of the divine in me.

But gift giving is based on access to land and on a certain level of self-sufficiency. Access to land means I can give. What we are working on inside Africa primarily is simply access to land. Compulsory heterosexuality and the bearing of sons is necessary for African women to have access to land. If you are not married to a man, if you are barren, if you have only given birth to girls, you are barred from accessing land. In Africa, it is not so much that women want to have all these children that they have to look after, so they don't have time to spend on the struggle, it's that they must. If they don't, they, and their children, are not going to eat. So, that's what we're looking at for the next ten years or so, is just getting some of that 85 percent of land back and feeding ourselves.

Yvette Abrahams was born in 1963, in Crawford, Cape Town, South Africa. She grew up mostly in exile, in Scandinavia. She is a historian and spends most of her working hours researching gender in different forms. She dreams of laying a pathway that will lead young Black women securely towards freedom in the new millennium. From January to December 2002, she was a visiting scholar at the African Gender Institute. Her articles have published in a number of edited anthologies, including Black Women in White Institutional Cultures (*Indiana University Press, 2003*) *and* Discourses on Difference, Discourse on Oppression *(Centre for Advanced South African Studies, 2001).*

References

Vaughan, Genevieve. 1997. *For-Giving: A Feminist Critique of Exchange.* Austin, TX: Plainview/Anomaly Press.

MARIA JIMENEZ

Gift Giving Across Borders

I am challenged by the many issues and ideas and conceptions of the gift economy and its concrete expression throughout history and society. For someone like me, whose time is spent in the practical realm of forming social movements (aimed at establishing institutions that support the development of the human potential by protecting, promoting, defending and practicing the principle that all human beings are equal in rights and dignity), reflecting on the different theoretical constructs of how we interpret the practice of a gift economy is an important part of what long-term activists have known as the relationship between theory and practice.

The relationship between theory and practice guides my political work and the work that we do in the formation of these social movements. Theory gives us direction and practice gives us the movement, and it is the learning from theory that enables us to actually move these movements forward in their development in a way that will benefit people, but it is also the practice that *retroalimenta* (in Spanish)—provides feedback—and enhances theoretical development.

In this article, I look at the immigrant rights movement, the human rights movement, and the communities where I do my political work, to try to understand what this theory of a gift economy is in its practical expression. And certainly one of the most important aspects of gift restructuring and integration into the global economy is the human right to mobility. The right to mobility is important because it affects how gift giving is being integrated at the global economic level. Human mobility is about the interdependence of social, economic, and political relationships in the human family. Thus, in its current phase, which is being restructured by economic and political elites worldwide, human mobility conditions the way people live within countries, as well as those that cross borders.

The wealth created millions of people worldwide has enabled, more than ever before in human history, the technology, the communications and the ability to move easily across borders, a historical experience recreated within the configuration of civilizations and countries throughout the globe. But that increased capacity, given the current strategy of economic global development, has made mobility safely and legally across borders a right for only a very few—the global economic and political elite.

This mobility is easily seen when we observe the movement of CEOs (chief executive officers) of corporations all over the world; the meeting of political elites without any problem, safely and legally, across borders, to also discuss issues of global dominance and exploitation and control; and also the movement of so-called "refugees" such as, for example, the Marcos (Ferdinand and Imelda) of the Philippines, Carlos Salinas de Gortari (ex-President of Mexico), and all others who are considered the "wealthy refugees." All of these elitist groups move legally and safely across the world without any problems, so that their role is sustained and maintained in the re-creation and construction of this globalization from above.

When we look at the development of immigration policy in nation states throughout the world, and how these define who is allowed to enter, who is allowed to stay, who is allowed to become a member of the nation state, it becomes very clear that immigration policy and border enforcement policy is about the restriction of mobility of the international working poor and the internationally displaced, who are also poor.

Borders, barriers, border agents, and militarized institutional violence to restrict mobility are some of the mechanisms used to reinforce on a global scale the social, political, gender inequalities of the very few against the very many. Institutional violence is necessary to sustain these inequities. Therefore, those that must sustain these inequities, like any other type of human activity, will define the movement across borders without government inspection as a crime. A crime that has no violence and has no victim, but that permits the construction of institutions both internally and externally, which ensure that the strategy of economic development of these elites persist, and that this strategy will continue to produce high profits by maintaining low wages.

It is a mechanism that also assists in the implementation of the structural adjustment policies of a scorched earth policy that results in the creation of havens for speculative capital investment circles, while curtailing investments in social infrastructure and in human development. It is a policy that then forces millions to opt for incorporation into a global labour market, their only option for survival. Thus, the movement of people becomes an important aspect of challenging the very policies that want to restrict its conditions according to plans for increasing profits.

So when communities and families, faced with structural adjustment policies of scarcity, opt to move to another country, the decisions to do so are made by families in consultations to determine who must emigrate and who must stay. These family decisions are made in communities that have a tradition of moving across international borders, and that have established networks to receive the migrants in the destination countries. These networks also help the migrants move across the borders, and the migrants, in turn, help to sustain the families and communities in their countries of origin.

The decision, in that sense, is a decision made by families to regenerate their survival, forming strong emotional bonds that will respond to the needs, fundamental basic needs, to sustain their development as families and as humans. And yet it is this very act, the act of migrating across international borders, this timeless transnational network that operates in the context of exploitation and policies of plundering countries of origin that actually form the networks of resistance and rebellions to those maintained by the powerful economic elites.

These family networks facilitate migration; the family networks ensure reinstatement of community needs, and family networks allow the instant conveying of resources, information, and even affection. It is interesting to note the growth and the use of, for instance, cell phones in communities of origin and reception. There are even communities that install computers in the community so that families can then see each other from places, for instance, as far as New York, to places in tiny villages in Mexico or in Ecuador.

Thus, in the current global configuration, the movement of people is a strategy of survival, and actually a strategy of "thrival." And this strategy of thrival is based on an economy of "giving" that sustains economic prosperity and interconnections between people moving North and resources coming from the South in the midst of unbridled free trade policies that threaten the sustainability of communities and economies, and particularly the development of human beings.

Understanding that international migrants invest in their families and community so generously, it became clear that there *is* a gift economy in this project of transnationalization, of movement of communities. And what is this gift? People who live outside their countries of origin are responsible for moving a hundred billion dollars globally every year between the so-called "developed countries" and the developing countries. This is the money sent back home by millions of immigrants worldwide; 30 billion of those dollars go to Latin America, 15 billion, half of that, to Mexico. And then there are also many unrecorded gifts in resources to communities. It is estimated that half of the unreported and the free labour given to development in communities has actually out-edged net, direct foreign investments in countries of origin ("All in the Family" 2004; Orzoco 2003; Suro 2003; Alarcón 2000).

As often proposed to Mexican immigrants, we might as well form a co-op and buy Mexico. So what is the gift? The gift is the at least $190 sent back to families seven times per year. In cases it is $100, and in some cases it is $300. In some cases immigrants will send back 15 percent of each paycheque, and others will send 50 percent of each paycheque, so the range is 15 to 50 percent of salaries in labour markets of exploitation that go back to sustain the families ("All in the Family" 2004; Suro 2003; "Importance of Remittances to Household Incomes" 1998).

Who are the senders? They tend to be migrants (emigrants), selected and agreed to by the consensus of families, to move out of the country to seek economic opportunity. They are the socially excluded who transform the experience of migration as an experience of liberation for themselves and for their communities. If we look at Latin America, some six million immigrants send money back home on a regular basis. Six million sent 30 billion dollars. Of these, one-half have been in the U.S. for less than ten years. Who are the senders? In a national employment survey conducted in Mexico, it was discovered that out of 5,896 individuals who migrated to the United States between 1997 and 2002, 70 percent had sent money back home, 89 percent were married, 60 percent were less than 30 year old, 48 percent were of homes that also have other senders of money, and 79 percent of these are people who entered the United States without documents ("All in the Family" 2004; Suro 2003).

Two-thirds of these senders have been in the United States less than ten years, and they send money once a month. When you look at migrants that have been in the United States less than five years, three-fourths send once per month. And when we look at the income range of the senders in the United States, we find that of the people who earn $50,000 or more a year, nine percent (this is talking about Mexico) send money back home. Of the people who earn $30,000 to $50,000 a year, 32 percent send money back home. And of people who earn less than $30,000, 46 percent send money back home ("All in the Family" 2004; Suro 2003).

So, in effect, 78 percent of the 15 billion dollars sent back to Mexico is sent back by people who earn less than $50,000 a year, and who send 15 to 50 percent of their paycheque back to relatives in Mexico.

Who receives? In Mexico, it is 18 percent of the adult population. Of those who receive, the majority are women. What impact? How many households? In Mexico, 4.4 percent of the households, or 4.3 million people receive these gifts. Forty percent of those receiving the gifts depend on them to sustain themselves and to not slip into dire poverty. Three to four people per household benefit from receiving and spending. And 73.6 percent of the recipients are under the age of 15 and over the age of 65 ("All in the Family" 2004; Suro 2003; "Importance of Remittances to Household Incomes" 1998).

As a community/family consultation strategy and method of survival, people decide which family, and which family member, migrates, and while the majority are men, 40 percent of those who migrate (emigrate) are women, and they support brothers and sisters, not necessarily just parents. Yet, when we look at who receive, we see that recepients are primarily family households of women, children, and the elderly. In the case of Mexico, these senders probably constitute those who send remittances that, according to many sources, are not really not taken into account by any financial institution, because these gifts are not transferred through banks, but are taken to the communities directly through clubs and their representatives (Orzoco 2003; Alarcón 2000). These tend to be immigrants who have settled longer within the United States, but who sustain a large number of new immigrants every year. The clubs, or hometown associations, are volunteer, structurally organized, collective entities that consult with the community they are from to decide on how to develop projects and mutual obligations for the well-being of the town. Some of these projects are in response to crises, such as a natural disaster, but others are a continual and developed interchange between the hometown and the hometown association, or clubs, in the United States.

And what do they do? They collect money through simple activities, such as dances and bake sales, very grassroot types of activities, and they invest in the community, but they also send goods. There are certain goods that they will buy in the United States and then transfer to the community. For example, ambulances, medical equipment, school buses and supplies, machinery for the development of the town well, equipment that may lead to the construction of a particular hospital. They invest in social projects, scholarships for students in the town, health clinics, childcare facilities, homes for the elderly. And they even invest in job creation such as supporting vocational schools that permit the youth to acquire skills necessary to operate in the economy.

How many of these are there? We really do not know. It has been estimated that there are approximately 600 associations in 30 U.S. cities; 218 in Los Angeles alone (Alarcón 2000). Many groups also form state federations. Some of the strongest in different states are La Federación de Clubes del Sur de California (the Federation of Clubs of Southern California), the Federation of Clubs of the State of Michoacan, and the Federation of Clubs of Jalisco.

And how do they collect the resources and the monies to be able to invest in the town? This is done through membership dues, through quotas, through fundraising activities, donations, and sometimes, in the case of the oldest and strongest, like the Federación de Clubes del Sur de California, they even enter into arrangements with local and state governments. Some of the federations have even entered into arrangements with the North American Development (NAD) Bank in order to create pools of resources to increase support for their communities (Orzoco 2003).

For instance, the Federation of Clubes of Zacatecas, in 1995, convinced the governor of the state that if they invested one dollar, the municipal government should invest one dollar and the state government should invest in another dollar. And thus was created the program known as "Dos por Uno" (Two for One). Among the Federation clubs they gathered $600,000, which they took to Zacatecas, and with the investment of municipal and state governments, were able to fund 56 projects in 34 towns. Four hometown associations of the Mexican state of Michoacan, based in Illinois, also raised $650,000 for projects in their localities around the same time.

There are concrete examples of this kind of support also being provided by individual clubs. There are 100 families in Anaheim, California that formed a club called El Club Tomás Titián that has organized various health projects in Tomás Titián because there is a sanctuary in the town, El Señor de los Reyes, which many people throughout Mexico visit in the hopes of being healed. The townspeople observed that visitors seeking the spiritual healing of El Señor de los Reyes would often experience a health crisis, and there was no infrastructure in the town to care for the sick. The club, therefore, invested in building a house to serve as a heath center that medical schools around Mexico could send student doctors to who could then practice and train in the town. The club bought surgical equipment, and even installed a water pump to assist the clinics of the area.

Another example is Club Pesqueros. One of the inhabitants of Pesqueros died because there was no ambulance, so the families of Pesqueros, Jalisco in the U.S. joined together and bought the ambulance. Now the club has a fund that provides scholarships for middle and high school students, a strategy they implemented to prevent drop-outs, and to support 57 children with developmental problems. Every year one of their fundraising activities in the United States is to hold a banquet, a *baile* (dance), and a rodeo, where they crown a Reina of the Club Pesqueros (Queen of the Club Pesqueros). This young woman, however, is not the most beautiful young woman, but the one that can raise the most funds for the collective fund that pays for work in the town. I have been thinking of suggesting to the Club Pesqueros that instead of "Queen" they call that young woman "The Goddess of Gift Giving."

These are examples, then, of community; the poorest of the poor on the international global scales, the most exploited, the women you see cleaning our rooms, the people cutting our lawns, the people working in the restaurants, these are the ones who are gift giving, despite the conditions of exploitation.

What are the impacts? There are impacts within many spheres. First, these remittances are not actually considered to be "good" investments. While remittances might bring 15 billion dollars into the country, it is money that is not invested in productive projects, or capital-generating projects. The money simply supports families. And this goes to the heart of some of the theories put forth in the gift economy of how the sustaining of families and the sustaining of communities, like the infrastructure projects that many of these clubs have undertaken, are not considered valuable from the capitalist point of view, although they are a valuable form of gift giving to the community.

I came across a paper presented by John B. Taylor, the Under Secretary of Treasury for International Affairs at the Federal Reserve Bank of Atlanta, in which he states: "In my remarks I would like to discuss, number one, why the Bush administration cares so much about remittances." Why does the Bush administration care so much about remittances? That is, as the capitalist financial establishment and corporations begin to understand the volume of gift giving that is being sent back by individuals and communities, the question becomes, "How do we take advantage of it? How does this gift giving contribute to our own interests and developments?" The Federal Reserve Bank now needs to find ways to facilitate easy wire transfers between immigrant communities and countries of origin, and a way to profit from this.

Immigrant communities, faced with increasing problems around the ability to move across borders because of tougher enforcement measures and the lack of programs to legalize their status in recipient countries, find it much more difficult to transfer money now because it was once done by family members and persons going back to the community. The financial institutions are currently positioning themselves to see which can offer the better program, and at the same time, charge for the transfer of these funds. Even a fee of one percent for the transfer, or a lowering of the cost of transfers that is now in many cases done through Western Union or Moneygram, could actually contribute one more billion dollars to sustain families in the countries of origin.

The governments have other interests, the Fox administration particularly. It is interesting how the current President of Mexico, Vicente Fox, has begun congratulating the people in the United States for what now has become the largest source of foreign exchange to Mexico, beyond petroleum, beyond tourism, and again, like in other countries, has edged the net direct capitalist contribution and foreign investment in Mexico. The Fox administration has developed several government programs so that these funds are invested in productive projects, which again mean capital-making projects. One of people in Fox's administration recently stated in a public speech, "Our economy is doing great. We have had so much success in oil, in trade, and by the way, in remittances sent by the *paisanos* (countrymen)," as if they had anything to do with earning these funds and/or sending them back.

But certainly the phenomena of remittances is being seen by the capitalist establishment as having become a gold mine, formerly invisible—as is most gift giving—and only recognized by those that receive these remittances and the communities that have had the experience of the projects paid for by the many clubs that exist in the United States. This is the impact of the movement of people, and the sending back home of money, on the global economy. The very small ant-like savings of migrant people have a tremendous aggregate effect upon the economies that are being fed.

It is interesting to note that studies with the sophisticated analysis that economists can now do, have shown that even those micro-gifts that become aggregate sums have a tremendous impact on the well-being of the economies, such as the Mexican economy. For instance, in one study it was shown that the injection of two billion dollars, as a result of remittances, increased the output of production in Mexico by four billion dollars and increased income in Mexico to approximately 2.2 percent of total income, and resulted in the creation of 325,225 potential jobs ("All in the Family" 2004). In other words, there can be one job created for every $4,400 of the money sent back home by immigrants.

Remittances have a definite impact on economies and well-being, and the capitalists are ready now to capitalize on this. When I look at the issue of gift giving and where progressive movements are in the theoretical development of such experiences, what we see is that the experience of gift giving comes from homes that send, comes from decisions of consensus, comes from decisions in which men and women decide who emigrates and who makes the decisions as how to invest when that money is received. These good people who give have the values associated with a gift economy, which are the values of mothering, nurturing and giving, but their actions are meaningless unless they are infused with the experience of those who are exploited and oppressed, because that is what gives us direction. It is the difference between the mothering and the nurturing described by the Cardinal Ratzinger in Rome (see Paola Melchiori's article in this volume), that characterizes women, and the nurturing and caring that is being done by immigrants all over the world of their families and which is a direct result of the experience of exploitation and oppression, and how to resist, how to construct communities, how to really live in the practical terms of globalization from below.

Maria Jimenez lives in Houston, Texas and has worked with the Latino community in the non-profit sector over the past 20 years. She has developed human rights monitoring and documentation methodology and trained community groups in human rights monitoring and documentation. She has also written numerous articles on international migration issues. She has received many awards for her work including the Humanitarian Award from the Mickey Leland Centre, Texas Southern University in 2004, and the Community Leadership Award from the Houston Peace and Justice Centre in 2005.

References

Alarcón, Rafael. 2000, September. "The Development of Hometown Associations in the United States and the Use of Social Remittances in Mexico." Departamento de Estudios Sociales, El Colegio de la Frontera Norte. Online: http://www.thedialogue.org/publications/alarcon.pdf.

"All in the Family: Latin America's Most Important Financial Flow." 2004, January. Report of the Inter-American Dialogue Task Force on Remittances. Online: http://www.thedialogue.org/publications/country_studies/remittances/all_family.pdf.

"Importance of Remittances in Houshold Income." 1998. Newsletter of the National Board on Population of Mexico.

Orozco, Manuel. 2003, September. "Hometown Associations and Their Present and Future Partnerships: New Development Opportunities(?)" A Report Commissioned by the U.S. International Development Bank. Online: http://www.thedialogue.org/publications/country_studies/remittances/HTA_final.pdf.

Suro, Roberto. "Remittance Senders and Receivers: Tracking the Transnational Channels." 2003, November 24. Pew Hispanic Center Reports and Factsheets. Online: http://pewhispanic.org/reports/report.php?ReportID=23.

PEGGY ANTROBUS

The Gift Economy in the Caribbean

The Gift and The Wind

In the search to redress the deepening of unequal access to economic resources
there is a major call for a new politics and new ethics building on our collective
responsibilities. Such new ethics would be founded on values that embrace diversities yet reject the deepening fractures of racism, religious intolerance, ethnic
violence, and unthinking individualism. Within this search there is a need to find
innovative analysis and new methods that de-center neoliberal global capitalism as
all encompassing and highlight the many ways we love, live and work together.

> [An] important contributions to this search—the gift paradigm—aims to put in
> place a new theory, vision, and way of life founded on solidarity or *convivencia*
> (conviviality). This vision aims to transform the current rules of the game,
> going beyond market economics and rejecting a world where people's time,
> energy, and hope, and Commons of all kinds, are turned into commodities
> and sucked into a hugely unfair market system. (Harcourt 2003)[1]

In this paper, I would like to put that experience of the gift economy in the
Caribbean in the context of the natural disasters—the hurricanes—that each
year stalk our islands, placing them in great jeopardy and reminding us of the
fragility of material conditions (the market economy) and the importance of
relationships (the basis of a gift economy) that endure and enable us to survive
the worst of circumstances.

In September 2004, the island of my birth, Grenada, experienced one of the
worst hurricanes in recent history. Hurricane Ivan, almost completely destroyed
the country: the beautiful capital of St. Georges was devastated; 90 percent of the
homes throughout the country lost their roofs; most of the schools and churches
were destroyed; and the entire market economy shattered. The main elements
of Grenada's economy are tourism, bananas, and nutmeg—all resource-based
and particularly susceptible to the destruction wreaked by hurricanes. And this
setback was not just for the short run: a nutmeg tree takes thirteen years before
it will bear fruit again.

The principles and the values that speak so powerfully to the concept of a gift
economy come from our people, a very modern people who emerged after the

Europeans had killed, decimated, and sent into exile the Indigenous people of the Caribbean—the Caribs and the Arawaks—who were inhabiting these islands of the West Indies when Christopher Columbus lost his way and happened upon them.

I'm speaking of the experience of a "creole" people. In the Caribbean we use the term "creole" to describe a people who are not Africans, Asians, or Europeans, but all of those combined, with a bit of mixture from the Middle East, the Lebanese and even from China. I am speaking of the experience of a people who have survived the extreme exploitation of market forces through enslavement, displacement, indenture, and colonialism to create and sustain new families and new communities.

And I am talking about a small island "developing" state where, in a sense, people really had to start all over again. But the only way to understand how we have survived in the Caribbean and how the people of Grenada have survived is to understand our history.

Hurricanes are destructive but they also help to strengthen our sense of solidarity with each other—including with our brothers and sisters in the wider Diaspora that stretches from North America and Europe, from Asia to Africa. For the Caribbean (and for other countries as well) the Diaspora is important because it allows us to reflect on the strength of the relationships of family and friendship that help sustain us in times of crisis.

For people in the Caribbean, part of the creation of new families and new communities after slavery and indenture was the creation of a family that is not just a family based on kinship. In the Caribbean, when we say "family" we go beyond kinship, to include deep and enduring friendships. Women are the center of that sense of family: women establish and maintain the ties that link us to the people of the Diaspora. The people of the Diaspora are extremely important, because although they have physically left the Caribbean to live in North America or Europe, in search of income and a better life, in another sense, emotionally, they never leave. And communications technology allows us to keep in very close contact with each other. There is, therefore, reciprocity between who live in the islands and those who live overseas.

I want to describe some of the ways in which the gift is manifested in the way that we survive. Imagine a young woman leaves the Caribbean in search of work. She goes to North America and maybe she leaves behind her children with her parents. She buys a barrel and she puts that barrel into the center of her room, in Brooklyn, or in Toronto, and every time she shops, or every time there's a sale, she buys things and puts them into that barrel. And when the barrel is full, she sends it back to her home in the Caribbean. This is known as the "barrel trade."

Imagine people who've gone from Jamaica, from Barbados, to Europe, to work in the transportation sector or in the hospitals in England. They send remittances, and these remittances amount to substantial sums of money. Figures really do not capture what those remittances mean to families, and to the economies of our countries, but in the 1950s, when Britain introduced its first *Immigration*

Act, the remittances that were sent from Jamaicans working in Britain to their families in Jamaica in one year were more than the entire Colonial Development and Welfare grant[2] to the entire region for four years. In short, remittances are not marginal to Caribbean economies; they make a very significant contribution to the economies, and not just to the families who receive them. At that time I was a student at a British university, reading for a degree in economics, and this information left an indelible mark on my thinking about economics.

But there's another kind of gift inherent in the relationship between the Diaspora and our home countries. Caribbean people who have migrated, who send remittances and barrels back to their family and friends in the islands, also go back to the islands, and they receive from the islands the gift of friendship, appreciation, and recognition, which allows them to live and work in what are often very hostile environments in the cities of North America and Europe. So there is that reciprocity: the material gift and the gift of friendship and appreciation that gives people a feeling of connection. And there is also the gift of acceptance and affirmation these Caribbean people receive when they return to their islands.

There are also associations of Caribbean people in the North that collect money within their community to support communities, schools, scholarships, hospitals and clinics, medical equipment, daycare centers, etc. in their home communities.

In the aftermath of hurricanes, the communities of the Diaspora are the first to come to the assistance of their countries. On receiving the news they immediately mobilize to send supplies and money to sustain families and communities, to rebuild homes and to enable children to continue their education.

And it is these gifts that make it possible for us, not just to survive, but to really thrive, and as people experience joy in our lives despite the hardships and the annual ravages of hurricanes and other natural disasters.

However, over the last few years, because of the relentless spread of neoliberal capitalism throughout the world, it has become increasingly difficult for people to survive. Increasingly people have fewer options for survival. There is a sense that as soon as you try to do something to earn a living, it's destroyed. More and more people, especially young people, out of despair and a sense of hopelessness, are resorting to drugs, to money laundering, to all of these criminal activities.

In this context it is more important than ever to recognize and affirm the gift economy. As Wendy Harcourt (2003) puts it:

> The insights of Gen Vaughn's work on "the gift paradigm" allow us to move analytically and practically beyond the dominance of neoliberal global capitalism and the hegemony of patriarchal competition and hierarchy. It reverses the apparent given that the logic of the market and competition are the only way to live life "we have to be in it to win it." Instead another paradigm is offered—that of gift giving. It is by freely fulfilling others needs that we sustain and nurture life, and it should be this logic—the logic of gift giving that so many women within capitalist economies and non capitalist

economies practice—rather than the logic of the market and exchange of equivalents that guides our transformative vision for the future.

By making visible the gift paradigm, and valuing it for itself, we can foster economic and social relations based on an other-orientation that aims to satisfy needs, creates bonding and cooperation rather than egoism, isolation, and competition. By recognizing and restoring the gift paradigm in the innumerable places where it has been taken away, we can build on new/old values to bring about the transformations that our world so desperately needs in these days of fracture, fear, and insecurity.

If we do not recognize and affirm the gift economy, it will die. It will get negated, as we are drawn increasingly into the notion that the market is the only thing that contributes to livelihoods and the economy. Indeed, we are drawn increasingly to the idea that we must commodify everything; that everything must have a price.

The gift economy is to be found everywhere. We need to document it in different cultural settings, and to politicize it, to use it as way of understanding what we have and what we must defend against: the spread of the ideology of the market. Ultimately, the gift economy could become a way of countering the spread of globalization, the spread of the idea that only the market is important in people's lives and livelihoods.

The gift economy reminds us of the existence, and the power, of another kind of economy. We need this as we try to imagine a different world. We need this more than ever today because we can easily feel defeated and helpless in the context of neoliberal, capitalist globalization. I am amazed that working-class people, black people, and women in the United States can vote against their interests. The implication is that people lack the analysis to show them the links between all of those forms of oppression and exploitation, indeed, the links between patriarchy and capitalism.

More than ever we need to strengthen that kind of work, not just the documentation, the politicizing, but the analysis that will allow people to see the links between U.S. policy and what happens to people in the rest of the world.

To return to the question of the disaster: Sometimes a crisis can provide a particular kind of opportunity for innovation, creativity, and resilience. We have to see disasters as opportunities to really intensify our efforts at documenting and affirming the gift economy. I have no doubt that in the case of Grenada, Hurricane Ivan was an opportunity to start all over again, to do something differently.

I had already decided that Grenada would be one of the countries where I would do some of that documentation of the gift. The hurricane gives me an opportunity to put that into a completely different context. We are very fortunate, I think, that we actually have the networks, we have the analyses, and we have the technology that makes it possible to link the efforts that are going on in our own country to the efforts that are also going on at the global level. And it is in that sense that I find the optimism to continue.

Born in the Caribbean, Peggy Antrobus has worked for the advancement of women's rights and development, starting with her post as Advisor on Women's Affairs to the government of Jamaica on the eve of the UN Decade for Women (1974). She is a founding member of many feminist organizations including the Caribbean Association for Feminist Research and Action (CAFRA), DAWN, and the International Gender and Trade Network. She was General Coordinator of DAWN from 1991-1996, and currently serves on the Steering Committee of DAWN Caribbean. Her book, The Global Women's Movement: Issues, Strategies and Challenges, *was published by Zed Books in 2004.*

Notes

---

1   Personal communication with Wendy Harcourt, editor of *Development,* the journal of the Society for International Development (SID) following the meeting on the gift economy held at Stone Haven in 2003.

2   Colonial Development and Welfare grants were the equivalent of foreign assistance or foreign aid today. They were the sums of money given by the British government to the British colonies in recognition of Britain's responsibility toward its overseas territories.

ASSETOU MADELEINE AUDITORE

The Children of the World

A Gift

All mothers and fathers have the right to love and care for their children, and would do well to love the children of others too! This was not possible for my mum and dad in Africa. And not because they did not love me and my brother, Kalif, but because they lived in a world which did not let them be healthy, did not let them live and stay with us. Indeed, they loved us so much that they entrusted us to our new parents so that we could live in safety, love each other and continue loving them. We children want a world where not one more mother has to cry because she cannot feed her children or protect them from people who want to exploit them, a world where children can laugh, sing, and play without suffering famine, violence, exploitation, solitude, war.

In the world today there are more than 600 million poor children, the children of the Third World. But poor children can be found in the rich people's world too.

The children of the Third World are easily exploited and treated badly. They are often forced to work, to go to war, to leave their mothers. In some cases mothers are even forced to sell their children, to get money and maybe be able to provide food to their other children. Such a disaster occurs because of the poverty and exploitation of the people in countries such as Africa, South America, and Asia.

The United Nations was born in 1945 with the aim of ensuring peace, freedom, justice, and respect for human rights. In 1959, the United Nations approved a Declaration of the Rights of Children. Rules were written that had to be followed by the parents of the child and by all other adults. For example: the child has a right to food, to a home, to play and to health care. If in a situation of physical, mental, or social inferiority, the child must receive psychological treatment and education and all the special care required.

Even in developed countries like Italy, there are poor people and poor children who are already working by the age of ten, and sometimes younger. Italy is the country in Europe with the highest number of children who leave school to go to work.

Some poor children don't get affection, attention, and understanding from their parents, either because they don't have parents or because these children were sold, like the hero of a true story that I am about to tell you. This really happened.

235

There was a twelve-year-old boy by the name of Iqbal who lived in India as a slave in a factory of carpets with many other children. He started working at four years old and stopped when he was ten. Iqbal met a union worker who denounced the exploitation of minors, of children in slavery. Iqbal and the union worker became great friends. Iqbal reported the system of exploitation of minors to the whole world. But because of this, our dear friend Iqbal did not live long. He died early, too early, he was assassinated.

Iqbal threatened the interests of the industrialists who were losing profits because of him. He was shot from a car while he was playing on a bike with his friends. It was on Easter Sunday in 1995. And that was the end of Iqbal's life, the end of a hero who became a martyr.

In today's world, which is the world of globalization, as my mummy says, children are becoming poorer and poorer and exploitation is growing. Even in Italy, and in Bari too, where I live, I see children in my neighbourhood who do not go to school, but spend their day on the streets. Some of them work and some of them just hang around. Isn't there a law, at least in Italy, that says that children must learn to read and write? Aren't there laws that protect children from criminals who also spend their time on the streets? Where is their space to play with other children, that is not on the streets?

If all of us help children and their parents, we wouldn't have people begging. You and I, have we ever asked why children come up to wash our cars when we are on the road? And this is Italy, a rich and first world country, as adults say! Have you ever asked yourself why these children are forced into "jobs" of that kind or why they beg? I can answer all this because there is only one explanation: because some people have lots of money and they spend it only on themselves, for their clothes, for too much food, for cars like limousines or Ferraris. And why are all these things we don't need on the market? I can answer this question too: so that the rich people can buy them, because they think these things are important, and not the children, people, who are in difficulty. The truth is that these things are not worth anything at all, because, as my friend Gen says, they have no value beyond market exchange value!

What can we do for the children? First of all, we must be aware of the problem, know that many children live in poverty, that they are exploited, that they don't go to school, and that they live in danger. We must know the dangers and the violence that threaten them. Many poor children live like slaves, nobody loves them, they don't have food, they don't have a mother, not even a place to sleep. We have to talk about this with our schoolmates, in our families, in our cities, with all the children of the rich countries. We must report these injustices. Internet and the email can help us do that, too. When we recognize the problem, it means that we can make plans and do something to help our friends, close or far away, but always close to our hearts.

There is enough food for everyone on the earth, but children die of famine. Have you ever asked why? I know. Because there are a lot of selfish people who don't think about the children, who don't care if they are healthy or not, whether they have food or not, whether they go to school or not, whether they are happy or not, whether they can play instead of gathering garbage or living in the sewers. Many people think of money, of making money grow, only for themselves. Many people want power and think only of accumulating material things, of getting richer, and I bet they are not even very happy!

Children can help other children on the planet Earth, for example, by not buying products on the market that are made with child labour. These products are very many.

Luckily, there are some people who care for others and help people, including children, who know how to spend their money for others, showing the way to a better world.

All children want to be loved, protected, and welcomed into the world with joy. All children are a gift.

Bari, 31/5/2004
Translated from Italian by Amelia Rossi-Landi

Assetou Madeleine Auditore (or simply Madou) was born in Yaou, Ivory Coast on 14 December 1993 from parents who had migrated there from Burkina Faso. She now lives and studies in Bari, Italy, where she is currently doing her first year middle school. She takes piano, sax and singing lessons at the Conservatorium Niccolò Piccinni in Bari. She enjoys playing sports, dancing, and good food!

RABIA ADELKARIM-CHIKH

Solidarity Economics

Women's Banking Networks in Senegal

In this paper, I write about the experiences of women in Senegal and the Economy and Solidarity Network. These experiences have to do with banking, in particular women's banking networks, one of the initiatives that women developed to fight the impact of structural adjustment policies on our country, on our lives. This was a terrible experience for people in Senegal and all West Africa because we woke up one morning and the value of our currency had been cut by half, drastically reducing our capacity to purchase or sell products for our subsistence. This devaluation was a very big violence against our people so the women started coming together to see if they could find a way to deal with the impoverishment caused by structural adjustment.

When I learned about women's banking networks they had been in existence for about ten years. I read many evaluation reports on the banking networks written by "experts" and economists from the academe, and sometimes also by feminists, that said the model had to change. These evaluations, by so-called experts, compared the success of women's banking networks to formal banking institutions, using the same indicators to measure "success:" the amount of money in the bank to the amount of money generated by the women in the banking networks. These "experts" all recommended training to improve women's management abilities.

My disagreement with this kind of approach is that, as usual, it prefers to focus on "teaching" women how to do things, rather than attempting to understand the skills these women, who are not part of the dominant economic discourse, bring to the initiative. I decided to see for myself how the networks worked, so I joined a group and went there to learn and to listen the women in these networks. And I am going to share *their* views and *their* way of thinking and *their* way of analyzing the results, because for them, the banking networks have been a great success, not only in their daily lives, but also at the level of community.

These networks are about the mutuality of saving and credit. To be part of the network each woman is required to deposit very small amounts of money with the network. The rule is that the access to the funds must be absolutely open to each woman, even if what they can manage to contribute is only 25 cents of the dollar. This is the first rule. The second rule is that the network is a space for women, by women. No men. I asked them, "Why don't you accept a poor man or men?" They told me, "Rabia, you are a feminist. We are not feminists but we know that there is a problem of power. If we accept only one man and we are 300 women, all the rules are going to be changed." They started with 100 women and now these networks have connected over 30,000 women.

The words that they used to evaluate their success did not refer to money. They measured their success in terms of values. They said, "We are not richer, we are not bourgeoisie, we don't have a lot of money, but we have won our dignity. We have won the right to speak, to participate in decision-making, and we are very proud because our success at the community level is absolutely recognized. We do not accept men inside our space, but we train them and they learn from our experience." Their analysis of the network's success thus focused on values such as the dignity they felt operating as a collective that could ensure women's equitable access to credit. I asked if their success was also due to being able to generate the money needed for the network to extend credit, wondering whether the "banking" networks were actually working or not. They told me, "yes, it works well but it is only about relationships, it is not about money."

I was surprised by this response because to be able to acquire material things you need to have money. What did they mean about relationships? They told me there is no guarantee of capital accumulation or profit in the network; the success of the network is based only the relationships between the women themselves. "Our success is not only measured by our rate of repayment. We have the highest rate of repayment because of our women's honour [which in Woluf is *kersa*]. For instance, men do not have kersa. If they are in debt, they are not ashamed. That's why even when they are learning from our experiences, their networks of credit fail." The women never want to remain in debt to the other women. And thus success comes as a result of the relationships between them, and not in the exchange, or circulation, of money. The starting point is the relationship among the women, which they emphasize with a ceremony dedicated to relationship and friendship.

In the ceremony the women come together and each one will propose to another, and ask, "Would you like to become my friend?" And in Woluf, the word for friend is *xaarit*, which means "you are part of me." It is a simple ceremony in which they give each other little gifts. If you have nothing that you can give, you can give a piece of wood. The gifts are not given for the value they have, they are given at the symbolic level. So these women mobilized all their knowledge and the experiences they have had to help each other, and what they value is their solidarity. The networks are not based on a market economy model. The women do not try to change the scale of their intervention, they do not want to change the rules they have put in place, they do not want or need to accumulate more money. They simply need enough money to solve the concrete problems of daily life. The women told me they need to have time if they are going to run after more money, and this would mean they would lose their social time for ceremonies, for friendship, and for families. What is also important then is their perception of the value of money.

They said they don't even have a lot of money in the so-called "bank." "The women's bank is poor," they tell me laughing. It is a joke between them. They said that in the Woluf language there is a saying that money that is sleeping, not moving, kept in the bank, is like a dead body. They prefer that the money is circulating and moving, and if the money is shared it will make the relationships grow.

The heart of the economy of women is their social relationship and they don't want to lose the capacity of circulation of the gift. I have learned about the gift economy and gift giving and I talked to the women about this when they spoke about the economy. From this experience I can say that theirs is "an economy for life, an economy of life against the model of the war economy," in which values other than money, such as dignity and solidarity, are primary.

We have to link economy for life with the gift economy and challenge the global market economy, which has forced many countries, like those on the African continent, into debt, so that we must fight for debt relief.

Maybe, instead, it is the world market economy, concentrated in the hands of the white, male, anglo-saxon Protestants, the dominant economy, that has contracted a huge debt vis-a-vis the women of the world, and the African countries. I hope we will change this paradigm.

Rabia Abdelkarim-Chikh is an Algerian, living and working in Senegal as a researcher in social sciences for the international NGO, Environment Development Actions Third World. She is a feminist activist involved with the African Women Forum for Economy in Solidarity (FAMES) and has facilitated a number of different workshops and panels at World Social Forums.

TRACY GARY

Women's Funding Partnerships

In this paper, I offer a few stories of audacity. If we want to feel hopeful about what we can do for the world and for women and through women, we might look back. We have only to look at one moment in history, toward the end of the twentieth century, to see the advances women made, at least in the United States, briefly, during the 1970s.

If someone had told me how much progress we might make simply by advancing women's knowledge, education, and giving women a broader perspective about what needed to happen for the world, giving them certain tools, financial education, philanthropic education, and some analysis, certainly, of their place of privilege in the world, I would have said, "You must be dreaming."

I recognize my place of privilege and want to share with you my journey.

For the past 31 years I have worked full-time as a feminist donor organizer within the context of the social change and women's funding movements. As a young inheritor in 1973, I graduated from a privileged institution, Sarah Lawrence College, with a degree in mythology. This is a study of cultures and of spirits across those cultures. I was a seeker for justice and the promise of democracy during the 1960s' tragedies and multiple slayings of John and Robert Kennedy, Martin Luther King, Malcom X, and many others. I was ignited by these incidents, and fueled by the injustices I had witnessed for African Americans in the civil rights movements, as well in the halls of my own family's residences. I knew nothing about what was going on globally.

Raised mostly by African American caregivers and household workers, I knew what community and family could be. I was determined to change the economic injustice that I discovered existed when I learned what weekly wages these beloved family members received, relative to my golf-playing and charitable parents, who were part of a conspicuous wealth movement in the 1960s and 1970s. At age nine, I learned that most of those who cared for me were being paid $75 a week, or $350 a month, plus room and board, relative to the $10,000 a month in cheques or stocks that my parents received via inheritance, or simply, as wealth holders.

This was a gap in a household partnership that I could not tolerate, and have worked to change ever since. Nelly, my primary caregiver, to her death after 55 years of service to my family, simply said, "Tracy, just love people, and they will

241

heal over time, and so will you." Nelly embodied the gift economy and will always be my first role model for giving and sharing. But Nelly also exposed me to the realities of my class and race privilege and its responsibilities, and she was diligent, diligent in her way as a woman with a third-grade education, about being sure that I knew that I would have opportunities with the wealth I had. She said that I should think carefully about how to use any influence as a white inheritor that I would have with people and communities outside the elitism and the illusions of my own class upbringing. I was truly blessed.

I was propelled toward a vision of a just society and fueled by the social and very personal injustices that I had witnessed of people I loved. Nothing has taken me off that track since. I had moved from New York, and various other places that my family had their five homes in, to San Francisco, and was so glad to find a diverse and political community that was ripe for growth. In 1973, San Francisco was burgeoning in its need for women-led projects and institutions, the product mostly of women-only schools, I knew well the benefit of women's voices and fell quickly into both my own preference for working with and loving women. My feminism was sparked during my own job search in my early 20s and bolstered by the growing visibility of more and more women leaders and artists making their voices heard and perspectives clear.

I can remember thinking that I had found heaven when in 1977 I attended a "Women on Wheels" concert, with women musicians donating their time to advocate prison reform for women prisoners. Given the interplay between the artists, the passion of the music, and the poets in the room, with the hope that was uncorked, and the mission to build a just society, I had found my tribe. I was sure I had fallen into heaven prematurely. It was a time of utopian partnerships. I loved and valued women and had total freedom to do so. How unusual this was!

For 25 years I worked and lived in the idealism of the Bay area, starting with a team of others, all women, women's building, women's music, funding cultural projects, local and global women's foundations, battered women's shelters, women's health clinics, children's impairment programs, women's leadership efforts, women and people of colour projects, and countless projects that have protected the civil rights of women and the disenfranchised. All in all, I have participated in the emergence of some 400 new projects or organizations led by women, 90 per cent of which stand across the United States and elsewhere. And I have heard annually about at least 500 new projects for over 30 years. This represents more than 15,000 projects that women have birthed, at least in ideas for creating change. And there are millions more.

I bring you optimism. At the age of 35 in 1986, after going on over 350 site visits to explore the viability or health of various projects, or just to learn about the creative capital, the courage capital, and the wisdom capital of the leaders in those organizations, I was inspired to give away my full inheritance, a million dollars, to build a movement of more engaged donors willing to fund similar projects and leaders who were building feminist or social change organizations.

I had a change strategy. I had a theory of change, but it had taken me ten or twelve years to figure out what that was. It was very clear. We needed more donors and effective leaders who saw social change philanthropy and socially responsible investing as key leverage points in building a world that would work for more people, and who would redistribute their wealth and power and be active partners in that new and more civil society. I had no idea how, but I knew we needed to dismantle patriarchy and we needed to dismantle capitalism.

We needed more women and women leaders who understood how to use their money and their influence, and who could articulate a vision for a more just society and influence people to get there. Clearly women would be the ones to shape and leverage the changes ahead. We looked to the women's spirituality movement for our history, to give us the courage to go forward. We deepened our spiritual practice to tool ourselves.

As I traveled in the service of that mission, I soon saw how many people wanted, in fact, to make a difference, and who were eager and were already on path of at least part of this mission. Little did I know that millions of women were moving simultaneously globally to bolster and propel more change. They are with us now.

We knew in the 1970s that we needed culture and we needed hundreds of women's recordings, theatre, publishing, bookstores, radio programs, community centers, and cafes to assure that we could find each other. We knew we needed a magazine, or a way to communicate with each other on a more regular basis. *Ms.* Magazine was one place to exchange ideas, and when it failed by being too mainstream, we were sure to publish more radical material, or to tune into our favourite public radio stations and hear the voices recorded by Frieda Werden, Dorothy Abbott, Maria Suarez and others who have diligently documented our movement over the years. Worldwide women's voices were coming forth

We had won *Roe vs. Wade* in 1973. We were on a roll to advance the new generation of women who wanted to work, or who needed to work in better-paying jobs. And we knew we needed policy changes. We needed women lawyers, doctors, politicians, and we made sure that they had opportunities. We looked globally at the 1977 Houston International Year of Women; we created a platform, we rolled up our sleeves to join our global sisters. The women's movement felt unstoppable.

Feminist activist, Jo Ruckleshouse, said in 1977, "We are in for a very, very long haul. I'm asking for everything you have to give. We will never give up. You will lose your youth, your sleep, your patience, your sense of humour, and occasionally the understanding and support of people that you love very, very much. In return I have nothing to offer you but your pride in being a woman and all your dreams you've ever had for your daughters and nieces and granddaughters; your future, and the certain knowledge that at the end of your days you will be able to look and say once in your life you gave everything you had for justice, everything."

This was for me, and still is for many of us, a kind of inner refrain that flowed in me like the wave of feminists around me moving women towards our full potential. We knew we needed money for all our efforts and that building women's funds or foundations was the surest way for women and girls to learn and control local and global financial resources. Albeit that many of these funds had only hundreds of thousands of dollars, we knew over time that they would have multimillions, and we wanted to to learn how to fundraise and how to redirect these dollars powerfully. We knew we had to change the body politic to make systems change as well. Funding locally or funding globally women and women's leadership seemed an obvious place to start.

Between 1973 and 1985, some 50 new women's foundations were established, and there are currently over a 125,100 in the United States and 25 emerging internationally. By 2020, I predict we will have a total of 50 women's funds globally. The Global Fund for Women began in 1983 and is now recognized as the premier of these women's funds, and has managed to redistribute some $25 million from over 10,000 donors to a 181 countries worldwide in only 20 years. Women donors began to convene under the Women Donors Network in 1990, through my organizing, and at the first meeting there was $2 billion present in the assets, which the 24 women donors present were stewarding. These 24 donors were giving collectively, although not funding the Network altogether, some $150 million, each a social change philanthropist of some kind.

This was more than all the 85 women's funds at the time were raising and distributing annually. I had the belief that together we could double the dollars and donors who were sparking human generosity, and investing in political leaders, and that with careful shaping we would at least create an alternative to the patriarchy or leverage a crack in its roots through these well-connected women at the top. These women were not just part of the top two per cent of the American population, but at the top one-half percent globally in terms of their income and assets. These women had influence. But did we know how to use it?

What I did not anticipate was the lack of exposure and analysis that many women donors had, and how burdened they would become with the growing needs of their local communities and families. Few of them had ever worked or given internationally. We moved them in funder tours internationally on the subject of sex trafficking, on the subject of international media, on trying to get them to understand and see through the conference at Beijing and other global opportunities. They are still moving out and moving forward.

The more visible these women became, the harder it was for most of them to forge and maintain a giving strategy or their theory of change. Feminism and its theories were not fully understood by this generation, and I was, with a few others, a minority in our more socialist commitment. Each of these women donors, as they become public, were besieged by thousands of requests annually, sending most of them into greater reflection and often retreat into anonymity again. They needed staff, but were by and large ill-equipped to manage, along with children, their enormous responsibilities, and were resistant to their public roles in the face of the demands of their private roles. And yet they found ways to strategize together, and continue to find ways to move their money out.

This group is now made up of a hundred women that contributed over $12 million to the last political election in an attempt to overthrow the current regime in America. We take no pride in the fact that we were not successful or that the other side managed to manipulate the final figures.

Women have always been leaders in the gift economy and women donors reject the exchange model of philanthropy, although unfortunately philanthropy has become more of an exchange model as men have gotten more involved. But those who do reject to this exchange model of philanthropy are liberated by the simple joy of giving, of purely giving.

The question is, shall we keep developing alternative communities and economies? How then shall we influence men and boys and others to make systemic change? And what are the leverage points? Women's shelters first appeared with the anti-violence movement of the late '70s. Programs for perpetrators were aimed at violence prevention, but those men who truly stepped up to change the conditions of violence in America are few and far between.

Women have always managed to convene and express their passions for justice. In the nineteenth century, women came forward at the time of the underground railroad when the slaves were moving from the South to the North in the U.S. A white woman would place a quilt upside down on her clothesline to signal that food and water would be waiting in the basement for slaves seeking freedom to the North. This often happened in the face of many of their husbands being part of the KKK, no doubt.

Women have convened in the public sector and helped each other in partnerships and non-hierarchal formats from quilting bees in the nineteenth century to childcare cooperatives, book clubs, sports teams, ladies church groups, business and professional groups, investment groups, micro-loan groups, and then women's foundations. In the twenty-first century, women's giving circles are emerging as the preferred model of women's collectivity. These giving circles are headed by women with shared monies going generally to women serving or women-led community-based organizations. Women give anywhere from $5 to $25,000. It is up to them how much they contribute.

There are now hundreds of these in the United States and there will be thousand of them. We must claim and shape them as the evolution of feminism and as ways, just like the twelve-step programs and the women's spirituality circles, that demonstrate the power and collectivity of collaboration, and we must teach and partner with these women to learn more about how to be effective social change activists.

I have been thrilled at the women's giving circles, but I also wanted women to give up control of the decision-making by giving to community-based foundations. The politically powerful model is a community-based model in which donors pool and collectivise their activism with grassroots activists, creating better decision-making, so that the donors wouldn't be the only one making decisions, but rather arrive at decisions through a more community-based process. The more decisions are made with community-based activists at the table, the more we can understand what needs to change. Either way, women learn and understand the power of sharing and engagement. The lessons of giving up class-based control may, for many, take a lifetime. Nonetheless, the gift of the women's funding movement has been a significant move for the democratization of philanthropy. We knew that 70 per cent of women now fill the public sector. They are only 30 per cent of people working in the non-profit sector, the remaining percentage are men. We must expect no less of the women in non-profit sector than to create radical and dramatic change. The best way to do this is to counterbalance that which goes on in government with that which goes on certainly in business. We must deepen and diversify in order to make that critical change.

If someone had told me that my sense of abundance and hope would come from giving all that I inherited and by stepping up to give over 50 per cent of what I earned, I would say "You've got to be kidding."

I know well that mistakes in judgment come with fatigue. I spent half my time working with donors and the other half listening to those needing resources to see how I might best connect them. I know too that making and being called to make so many decisions involves the exploration and challenges of expressing power. Coming from a place of privilege, we were trained to lead and to dominate. When I have fallen short of my own potential as a leader, or better yet as a partner, I have taken spiritual guidance from others who are trying to make similar changes. Our shared difficulty as products of patriarchy with respect to power and domination is natural. We who do want to be seen as dominators, or matriarchs, suffer at times by not having the skillfulness or consciousness needed to broadly redistribute power resources by holding on to our own and others' developing wisdom.

But no one can say that we have not experimented or done everything possible to try to bring justice and feminine values to the table. True audacity is in our midst.

The key is now how to make visible the stories and dreams and work that is going on for countless others. This will take a revolution in the media and our use of it. We need more daring and caring women donors to advance all that had been laid. Younger women demand our politicization and speaking up. We have found our voices, but we are still learning to use our passion and our leadership and our voices effectively. An amazing infrastructure has been put in place in only 30 years. I'm the first to admit that feminist values have been cloaked or dropped during the past 15 years of this revolution. It was intentional. We had a choice to expand the movement and then politicize it, or face the limitations the feminist movement had in the mid- to late-1980s. We chose to expand the movement, and are now busy working very hard to politicize it. Perhaps we made the wrong choice.

Given the fierce present now and the hesitations of so many, I completely agree that we must bring back, front and center, a vision of a just society, and how best to get there. Many agree that women are the guides to lead us to survival. I also agree that language, how we express ourselves, and vision must be inspiring and ignite again the passion and hopes of all citizens. Our time to save the planets is sadly short.

The future of humanity does depend on this strategy and how we unfold it. In the end I do not know if prayer or activism will save the world. I know I am called with you to do both. It is very hard to face the fact that after 30 years of full-time work in this area, the richest 20 per cent have more income, 75 times that of the poorest 20 per cent of the world, 30 times as much as in 1960, and that half the world's population lives on less than $2 a day. But that is where we are, and we must continue to educate and effect the radical change needed to bring capitalism and the patriarchy to its conscience, if not its knees.

Recently in Scotland for a visit to see the physical presence of the Divine Feminine with Margy Adam and other feminist activists, about the time of the Iraqi prison abuses, I was given a message there, as spirits are keen to do. It was a message about the gift economy, not tied up in the complexities of matriarchy or patriarchy, capitalism or socialism. It was simply this: "The world speeds up, but you must infuse your actions with the wisdom, the spirit and hope in the honour practices of Indigenous peoples everywhere. Women and caring men must counterbalance and stop the exponential destruction being perpetrated with their exponential and effective good. Step up and step out, make the dreamers and the dream makers more visible, make your vision for a just society a reality, and get out of the fog."

And so my journey for justice continues. Transformation is a gift delivered through faith and feminism and action. We are on path. Let us simply invite and engage the millions who seek our sharing, our sustainable ways, and our affirming bridge-building to another way, a joyous, giving way.

Our task is not impossible, it is about taking what we have done and becoming more effective spokespeople for the clear changes needed. We shall go forth. We shall inspire others with the tenacity and solidarity of our movement. In the end, as Jeanette Armstrong (see her article in this volume) has said, "giving is the only way to be fully human."

Tracy Gary transforms communities as a donor activist, philanthropic and legacy advisor, and nonprofit entrepreneur. She has been on over 30 boards of directors and has help to start 19 nonprofits and foundations including Resourceful Women and Changemakers. Her latest adventure is Inspired Legacies, which helps to catalyze billions of dollars of the public good through linking of powerful dreamers, dreammakers, and advisors. Tracy is the co-author of Inspired Philanthropy: Your Step by Step Guide to Creating a Giving and Legacy Plan *(Jossey Bass, 2007) with new worksheets for those planning their lifetime legacies. She credits the leadership of the women's movement and mentors like Gen Vaughan for their inspiration of her feminist philanthropy and commitment to the women's funding movement.*

ANDREA ALVARADO VARGAS AND MARÍA SUÁREZ TORO

Gift Giving and New Communication Technologies

The use of new communication technologies has become a growing need for thousands and thousands of people worldwide. The expansion of these technologies into the multiple activities in daily life and the undeniable way in which they make our lives easier, has created this need. However, the satisfaction of this need is a reality only for those who, in making use of the instruments of the market economy, can afford to buy them. It is no secret that it is the poor, especially women, the poorest of the poor, who are at a disadvantage in the increasingly globalized market of new communication technologies.

The possibilities that are opened with the use of new communication technologies are many. Among the most important is the communication process. Another is the capability of interacting with other people from around the world, and expanding our knowledge base. Third, is the way in which new communication technologies facilitate the process of production of knowledge itself.

But global corporations produce this technology and these technologies are located in the developed countries. They are framed in the neoliberal economic model, and thus are designed to further develop capital and capitalism, whose aim is the production and sale of commercial goods.

These corporations are not concerned with the fact that the majority of the population, for example the so-called "Third World," cannot afford the price of their products. And they are not interested in developing forms of uses based on solidarity and cooperation among people that would satisfy the needs of those who have less opportunities and less access to these technologies.

Gift giving is an alternative paradigm that seeks precisely the opposite of corporate globalization. Currently, there are many social movements that are struggling to revert the corporate neoliberal reality by using and developing new communication technologies, that are freely shared to challenge the market paradigm. The gift economy is being applied practically in the use and sharing of these free technologies.

The ways that women are using and sharing new communication technologies are very different from those of corporatization and commercialization. These women's political objectives are focused on sharing information, interacting among like-minded people and building movements for social change within a human rights framework. In the words of Nedelka Lacayo of the Honduran Black Women's Network who participated in a Feminist International Radio Endeavour (FIRE) training workshop: "A web page is not an end in itself. It is an instrument for our objectives, which go beyond instruments themselves, because they are political. The Internet is a multiplier of our political actions. It is also a means to create and recreate our own knowledge. The Internet, especially for us black women, has to allow us to speak with our own voices, to share our experiences and voices or perspectives, instead of waiting for others to do so for us".

Three examples of gift giving in new communication technologies are the open source movement, the community radio movement in Latin America, and third, the experience of FIRE in sharing communication technologies benefiting women.

Open Source Software and Freeware

Open source software (OSS) is software for which the source code is freely and publicly available, though the specific licensing agreements vary as to what one is allowed to do with that code. The free software movement stems from an ethical and political stance that advocates freedom from corporate control, and aims to disseminate information freely, giving the gift of knowledge.

The concept of open source software has become a true technological—and political—revolution. The premise is very simple: computer programmers create and share these software programs at no cost to others, who in turn are able to add or change the characteristics and codes of the programs according to their own needs, and share them further with the user community around the world. Thus, the open source programs are constantly evolving through an open and shared development process.

Open source technology is considered to be more stable, secure, and creative than its commercial counterparts. Open source software is not only much more cost-effective but it distributes technical power democratically. While many leaders of the open source community reside in the U.S., the power that comes with the use of open source technology is very well distributed internationally. In fact, the most famous open source programmer is from Finland, Linus Torvalds.

People in the South who have been utilizing open source software benefit in many ways. Firstly, the actual cost of open source software is usually zero or very inexpensive. Hundreds of billions of dollars can be saved yearly by using open source software. Secondly, the implementation of open source projects does not require in-depth knowledge. Technicians in the developing world are no longer reduced to following instructions handed down to them by global corporations, they can work shoulder to shoulder with their peers in the open source community. Thirdly, the majority of money that is spent on implementing software projects stays in the community and is not concentrated in the hands of a few. Fourth, with local technologists implementing the solutions, these solutions are far more in-tune to local needs than are their foreign corporations. The users of this technology no longer must adapt their organizations to fit software designed for others; they can have solutions that are appropriate for them and which thus greatly increases the effectiveness of the technology (FIRE and Nomadic Solutions 2003: 10).

Due to the fact that knowledge and brainpower are the true movers of open source technology, there are great opportunities for women with basic Internet access, while learning, to be able to adjust software programs to meet their own needs and strategies for action.

New technologies and new movements have emerged in this context. They struggle to keep the structure and flow of information open, despite corporate efforts to revert this gift giving trend. The open source movement and the free software movement are part of the social movements that have been able to become global, precisely because of their use of open source software and free access to the Internet.

Open source software is one of the ways gift giving can be evidenced in the use of communication technology, as a common wealth rather than a commercial product. Thus, gift giving on the Internet is democratizing and signals a paradigm shift in market economics.

Community Radio in Latin América

In Latin América, community radio was conceived as a means of communication whose goals was not to achieve profits. Community radio is a form of media with scarce economic resources and, in most cases, is restricted by legislation that not only impedes the sale of publicity, but also limits the scope of its range to one kilometer around, which is the case in Brasil.

But community radio benefits communities, vindicating the human right to freedom of expression, and promoting the ownership of media in the hands of communities of people, rather than in the hands of of entrepreneurs and/or corporations, which is the case in most countries.

What differentiates community radio from commercial radio is not only the popular nature that characterizes one, versus the commercial motivation of the other, but rather the logic of sharing communication as a human right and not as a commercial product which aims to generate profits.

Community radio is incorporating new technologies in its work, not only in terms of basic digital equipment, like tape recorders, but also by using the computer as an instrument of communication, using email to disseminate information, and as a system for the automization of radio programming. Many use open source technology to do this.

Many experiences in community radio in Central América show gift giving in the form of volunteer work, and the sharing of the microphone with people in the communities who do not expect anything in return. Community radio stations satisfy the communication needs of their audiences, without seeking profits, but rather for the sake of growing and sharing, not gaining, which in essence is gift giving.

FIRE: Open Source Technology and Radio in the Hands of women

One example of gift giving through community radio, among thousands world-wide, is FIRE, or, Feminist International Radio Endeavour, which exists because of its use of free or open source technology.

In November 2003 in Costa Rica, FIRE held a training workshop to share the gift of communication. An Internet server called Apache, using Linux, an open source operating system, was created during the workshop entitled "Internet Technologies for Our Political Action." The server had two functions: to share a non-corporate Internet operating system with the 32 workshop participants from throughout the Latin American and Caribbean region, and to offer these same participants a local server to use for practice during the workshop.

On this experimental server, each participant had their own website, access to e-mail, and a link to the internal server network for the workshop, all free and in a form created and designed for the event itself and the participants. The participants were also able to use a free version of File Transfer Protocol (FTP) to create and modify their websites. By adding their own presence in the Internet, every user in the workshop contributed to the collective knowledge accessible to those already online, another dimension of gift giving.

As a result of the training workshop, female activists from 15 grassroots organizations were able to design and POST web pages for their organizations. The "first time" each of them opened a Pandora's box: a new window to the world that taught them that the Internet is a tool, not only for gathering information, but for making their own voices heard worldwide.

Surrounded by a circle of 24 computers in the conference room of the Comfort Inn Hotel in Santa Ana, Honduran Nedelka Lacayo clutched the computer keyboard as her new "key" to the worldwide web. "I even learned how to put my own voice in the page. Come and see.... Come and hear, as you open the page, I welcome people to the site of my organization. It almost like magic!" exclaimed Nedelka.

As Katerina Anfossi (2003), Co-Director of FIRE, explained in a panel presentation during the training workshop:

> FIRE among others, is addressing the digital divide, both because it is an international channel of communications based in the Global South, but also because it is in the hands of women. FIRE is working to ensure that women are given access to new technologies and that their voices are heard in the world's media. Only by creating international communications venues, appropriating new media venues for diverse voices and connecting multiple voices, strategies and technologies, will a truly democratic media become a reality.

FIRE's experimental open source server during the workshop served to showcase that women's ownership of computer servers is possible and furthermore, it can make the use of the Internet much less expensive and accessible to more women.

These three experiences: one, the movement of free open source technology; two, the gift of community radios; and three, initiatives like FIRE to empower women though community radio, have a lot in common. They show us that technology as such is not an end in itself, but rather an instrument through which we can broadcast and disseminate thoughts, ideas, experiences, and most of all, make the voices of women, and marginalized communities, be heard.

Free and democratic access to new communication technologies is a human right we should promote constantly, instead of the corporate agenda that deepens the digital divide, the breach between rich and poor, and between men and women. One way to further these efforts is to articulate different initiatives to strengthen the search for new paradigms. Voices cannot be bought or sold when in the hands of those who believe that another world is possible.

Andrea Alvarado Vargas is a Costarican journalist, radio producer and audio technician. She has worked as a trainer in radio production, digital edition, and new technologies courses for some years for different social communication organizations. She is an advocate for non-profit communication and communication rights and a feminist activist. She has a strong relationship with community radios in Central America, and is part of strengthening projects for these radios. She works as a producer for Radio Internacional Feminista/FIRE.

María Suarez Toro is a Puertorican and Costarican feminist, women's human rights activist, and communicator. She has been co founder, co director and now producer of Feminist International Radio Endeavour (FIRE) since its birth in 1991. She has also worked as a human rights activist in the Central American Human Rights Commission in the past and also in adult literacy in the region.

References

Anfossi, Katerina. 2003. FIRE's Workshop: New Technologies for Political Activism. Online: www.fire.or.cr

FIRE and Nomadic Solutions. 2003. FIRE's Feasibility Study for a Feminist Open Source Server. Unpublished document.

ERELLA SHADMI

Trapped by Patriarchy

Can I Forgive Men?

Genevieve Vaughan (1997) writes:

> The logic of unilateral gift giving is the logic of transmission, and in satisfying the needs of the other, it gives value to the other by implication.

> The receiver often emulates the giver, giving in h/er turn, but this does not cancel the gift. Rather it enhances it, and passes it on.

> Let us look at predatory behaviour as an aberration and at gift givers not primarily as victims but as positive agents who are momentarily trapped and exploited by a system based on a false and illusory gender construction, which takes their gifts.

> I am trapped. Here is why and how.

Part 1: Mother

I was a young student at that time. I went to visit my mother for the weekend as I did every other weekend since my father passed away. We sat to the Sabbath dinner. My mother lit the candles and served the Jewish food that I like so much and she cooked so well. Then she said something. I really don't remember what exactly she said to me but I clearly recall how furious I became. I was so angry with her that I could not control my mouth. I said many vicious and ugly words to her. I insulted her. She turned silent, just looking at me.

We finished our Sabbath dinner silently. After a while we went to bed. I was lying in my bed but could not fall asleep. I was still furious at her. I sensed that she couldn't fall asleep as well. Slowly I began feeling sorry. After a while I got up, went to her bedroom door and said, "I am sorry, mother." She said, "I forgive you."

Forgiveness is the best gift my mother could give me. Her forgiveness is a way of embracing me, of accepting what I am unconditionally; it is compassionate, loving, and inclusive.

Part 2: Daughter

When my daughter turned 17 she got her first call to the Israeli army. We both looked at the letter not knowing what to do. Throughout the years my daughter spent much time in antiwar demonstrations, in the feminist and civil rights movements; she joined me in my struggle against militarism. And now, this letter.

We had many talks about this letter. I told her unequivocally that I wanted her to refuse, not to join the army. She understood why. Like me she was against occupation, war, militarism, and violence. But she also had her reasons to join the army. We had numerous discussions. One day she asked me, "what will you do if I decide to join the army?"

I said, "it will be a terrible moment for me. I will be sad."

"You know," I said to her, "when my friend's son decided to go to the army, she decided not to support him in any way because supporting him is supporting the army so she decided not to visit him on the base like parents do and not to wash his clothes."

"Will you do the same?" my daughter asked me.

"No," I said. "I will support you because I accept you the way you are even if I disagree with you." I emulated my mother. I circulated the gift of forgiving.

Part 3: Politics

I sit in my home at the outskirts of West-Jerusalem reading the titles of the papers to be delivered at the Las Vegas conference on the gift economy. Some of them are: Solidarity Economics; The Gift Giving Philosophy of Open Source Technology; Women's Gifting Relations and Community Work: Toward a New Public Policy Framework and a New Knowledge Paradigm; Enabling the Gift Logic of Indigenous Philosophies; Gift Giving Across Borders; Ecospiritual and Activist Movements Reviving the Gift Imaginary; Epistemology and the Gift; Women's Giving: A New Frame for Feminist Policy Demands.

I read these titles and others like them and feel the hopes and desires they express. I see women giving everywhere. But I look around me and see the Apartheid Wall being built not far from my safe home. I see the many murdered and wounded Palestinians in Gaza. I hear the warmongers shouting in the streets of Jerusalem. I hear the cries of the traded, raped, and beaten women behind the walls of the homes and the brothels and I wonder: can I, as a feminist, forgive men for the many harms they have inflicted on women? Can I, as an Israeli, be forgiven by the Palestinians for years of occupation and exploitation? Can I forgive and be forgiven?

Fury made me a feminist. This fury has slowly accumulated over the years. I was not aware of the way it accumulated, growing more and more, until one day, when the conditions had ripened, it erupted, and it erupted with a big cry and a lot of joy—a cry against men that treated us, women, so viciously and a joy celebrating the pain that turned into protest and the sisters that I found.

The fury has been translated into demonstrations, politics, organizing, research, teaching, and words. It burst like a dam unblocked: tales of oppression, cases of offences, experiences of rape, reports of evils, exploitations, trampled dignity.

The never ending stream of narratives, incidents, experiences that women began to tell has turned into a demand for men to take responsibility, to recognize the evils they have done, to confess the truth—so as to bring about reconciliation, exactly as the Germans did after the Shoah, as the Africaners did after the Apartheid, as the African Americans demanded of the Yankees: the Truth and Reconciliation Committee in South Africa, the reparations the Germans paid the Jews, the lands given back to the Aborigines in Australia.

In the same way I demand the three Rs from men: Reflexivity, Responsibility and Reparation. But I wonder: perhaps there is an alternative way like my mother taught me, like I am teaching my daughter. Can I give and forgive? Can I forgive the harm done to us, to me? Can I give my forgiveness on a silver plate without asking for truth and responsibility?

I have my doubts: will men understand my forgiveness? Won't they see me like one who compromises, swallowing her pride, giving up, afraid? Will they see it as another of their victories?

On the other hand, these are the excuses Israeli military men are raising against the withdrawal from Gaza and any talks with Palestinians. I know better: forgiving is power. Forcefulness is weakness. If so, does forgiving have a political meaning? Does it promote our struggle to transform the world, to shatter patriarchy, to construct a new world? Does my personal forgiveness, even when some other women join me, rock the ship of patriarchy and construct a new world?

I am not sure yet and therefore I am afraid to forgive.

Add to all this the context in which I live: Jewish tradition insists on remembering Amaleck—the ancient people that defeated Israelites thousands years ago. Muslim tradition puts revenge and honour up on the private and public agenda of every believer. And Israeli modern culture is dominated by the Culture of the Freiher. Freiher is a vulgarism meaning "sucker." The culture of freiher defies a person that is ready to give way, to be used, to forgive. Such a person is viewed as one that does not care for his honour or power. For example: you are a freiher if you yield to other drivers. And especially, you are a freiher if you talk with "terrorists," if you let your wife dominate you. In a culture of the freiher you do not take responsibility for your mistakes, you do not share your ideas lest they be stolen, you are never weak lest you are exploited. So you learn to manipulate, to lie, to exploit people, to hide your feelings.

In a culture of the freiher, in the region and religion ruled by honour and unforgetting, how can I forgive and be forgiven? The issue is how my words, my deeds, my text, will be read, accepted, interpreted. It is an issue of intertextuality, My desire to forgive and be forgiven does not stand by itself, as an autonomous text, but is positioned in the context of other meaning constructing practices, in this case, the culture of the freiher and the practices of honour and unforgetting. My forgiving maintains links with other ideological and cultural systems loaded with their own codes and voices. The context of the culture of the freiher of honour and unforgetting creates a new intertextuality that may distort my forgiveness and make it meaningless.

It is an issue of working and talking within one paradigm and being read and interpreted within a different paradigm. How will my forgiveness be understood by the culture I am living in? Will it make a difference?

I look up to my mother. She forgave me. She taught me the power of motherly forgiveness. I forgave my daughter. But still I am not sure about men. I guess my fury stands in the way, as does the culture I am living in. Being a radical feminist, I am often ahead of my sisters. I am often trying to touch the stars, to reach to my vision. Being a radical feminist I want men to take responsibility. So I am still torn between my fury and my vision, between my motherhood and my womanly experience. I feel I am stuck. I am trapped by patriarchy.

For over 30 years, Erella Shadmi has been a radical feminist, lesbian, peace and anti-racist activist in Israel. She is the co-founder of Kol HaIsha, the Jerusalem women's center, and of the Fifth Mother, a women's peace movement. She is one of the first Ashkenazi Israelis (Jews of western origin) to speak out against the oppression of Mizrahi Israelis (Jews from Arab countries). Dr. Shadmi is the Head of the Women's and Gender Program at Beit Berl College. She is also a criminologist who has published numerous critical analyses of Israeli police. Her book, Contemplating Women: Women and Feminism *in Israel, is forthcoming.*

References

Vaughan, Genevieve. 1997. *For-Giving. A Feminist Criticism of Exchange.* Austin, TX: Plain View Press/Anomaly Press.

LINDA CHRISTIANSEN-RUFFMAN

Women's Community Gifting

A Feminist Key to an Alternative Paradigm

This paper explores the connections between the theoretical and empirical understanding of women's community work that I have developed over thirty years of feminist research, analysis and activism and the other scholarly literature, especially Genevieve Vaughan's thinking about the gift paradigm. It is written with a growing conviction that a radically different world is necessary and that feminist insights hold a key to a viable alternative.

I was on my way to a meeting to commemorate the twenty-fifth anniversary of an historic event in Canada.[1] An emergency gathering of Canadian women on Valentine's Day weekend in 1981 had successfully led to women's inclusion in the 1982 constitutional guarantees of the new Canadian Charter of Rights and Freedoms.[2] In 2006, we were going to Ottawa to reflect on what might be called women's community work or women's community gifting. As my husband drove me to the plane for this second Valentine's Day meeting in the nation's capital, he exclaimed, "Someone should send the Canadian government a bill for your valuable contribution!"

This statement clearly shows that he recognizes the value of women's local and global community work, the mainly unpaid contribution of women to improving their surrounding communities (locally to globally), making them more liveable, equitable, and just, and, in this case, contributing to political change in Canada at the constitutional level. But should we be sending a bill for our unpaid work? Is it in women's interest—and society's public interest—to commodify women's community work and reduce it to monetary value?

Even if I agreed with my husband that sending the government a bill would make an important political point, what would be on the invoice? What would we count and on what basis would we make each of the economic calculations? Would we count only our transportation costs? All our "out of pocket" expenses? Our time there? Our time preparing and afterwards—and whose time and at what price? Would we count only the 1,400 women who jammed into the room on Parliament Hill in 1981? What about all those many women who contributed to the "Butterfly Coalition" that did the organising and local community work across the country which was essential to our success? Do we reimburse and count (as valuable economic activity) only those who bought the butterflies to display on lawns and windows? What about the time involved in mounting them into some form of display, planning that display, and what about those who made their own butterflies and spread the word to others? And what about the many hours doing the analysis, communicating with other women, and lobbying the politicians and other decision-makers? And how much of that? How would we calculate a value of this work: on the basis of what monetary principles and with what calculation of interest? And so far we have only included the time of the meeting until the present. But the event would not have been successful without the many meetings around kitchen tables, park playgrounds, office cafeterias and at women's caucuses, groups, and other gathering places leading to 1981! And what about all the other unpaid work of women that has such social and public benefit? Should not women's helping, caring, and problem-solving work in communities also be counted? If we are serious about an economic reckoning, in addition to the women's community work, should we not also calculate other unpaid women's work in families? And why does work necessary to sustain life, such as mothering and women's community work, not count as valuable in today's "work world," while work associated with premature death, such as weaponry and militarism, has value in the market economy?

In this paper I will outline the intellectual stages through which I came to recognise women's gift-giving community work, to question the translation of this work into the dominant monetary measures, and both the difficulties and need to develop an alternative feminist approach and paradigm. Here I will be using a scholarly approach that is, at the same time, socio-historical, experiential, and analytic. Its multi-levelled and holistic feminist social analysis draws from: (1) my own retrospective reflection as a feminist sociologist within the academy, working in professional associations at the local, regional, national, and international levels; (2) the inductive tradition of participant observation and of C. Wright Mills' (1961) "sociological imagination," combining history and biography; (3) the results of praxis as. what might now be called. a feminist action researcher for social change within the academy; and (4) the results of praxis as a community-based feminist and activist on issues related to progressive social change for "community development" based on principles of equality, social justice, environmental and economic justice, and peace. It also draws analytically from the sociology of knowledge.

I began my work in this area with a new empirical focus on women without any adequate concepts or assumptions. Theories imported from "male-stream thinking" could lead to publications but not to recognizing or valuing women and women's contributions. New insights led first to the questioning of old assumptions and to the discovery of women. Then it led to more complex understanding of the mechanisms of patriarchal syndromes within scholarship and to a deeper recognition of women. Eventually it also led to participating in, and working to rebuild from within, a feminist movement that is advocating radical social transformation and a feminist scholarly and societal paradigm shift. Along the way, this journey brought me to an appreciation of women, community activism, and women's politics, of the women's movement and feminist movement, of alternative ideas about wealth and, most importantly here, of women's community work. Drawing on ideas of Genevieve Vaughan's theorising of the gift economy, what I have call women's community work becomes "women's community gifting," a type of activity which is outside of the paradigm of exchange and monetary calculations.

In addition to the idea of Women's Community Work, the paper uses two other major concepts, feminism and paradigm, which are now present in most textbooks such as W. Lawrence Neuman (2006). Feminism has many definitions, and I use a concept of feminism which is holistic, multi-faceted, change-oriented and transformative. It includes: (1) a focus on the diversity of women's experiences across the globe and across patriarchally-constructed differences; (2) a critique of patriarchy in all its layers and manifestations and the need for fundamental change; (3) an articulation of the collective vision and principles to which we aspire; and (4) the affirmation of a strong and diverse women's movement to lead our societies and cultures into change beyond the patriarchal paradigm which exploits and enslaves all living things (see Sen and Grown, 1987; Miles, 1996; Christiansen-Ruffman, 1998; Antrobus, 2004).

The concept of a paradigm is associated with Thomas Kuhn (1962), and W. Lawrence Neuman (2006) defines a paradigm as "a general organizing framework for theory and research that includes basic assumptions, key issues, models of quality research and methods for seeking answers" (81). Other scholars of the sociology of knowledge have also written about radical shifts in the zeitgeist or paradigms of global cultures over time and space as well as on interrelationships between scholarly and societal paradigms, despite allegedly naive notions of "objectivity" that some scientists still claim.[3] The journey I describe indicates clearly that the dominant paradigms in scholarship and social life do not recognize or value women's community work. Many of the characteristics of paradigm challenge are reminiscent of descriptions by Thomas Kuhn (1962) in his classic book, *The Structure of Scientific Revolutions*. A feminist paradigm would eliminate the existing patricentric syndrome and its patriarchal assumptions of knowledge and its values of hierarchy, dominance, and competition. Feminist values would replace the ancient patriarchal values based on tribalism, violence, and control, replacing them with a worldview which honours, respects, and protects all life, especially biodiversity and social diversity on this planet. A paradigm change would not occur if men were simply replaced by women in the current system. A changed paradigm would transform ideas and assumptions of hierarchy and of "power over" into circles and spirals that convey "power with" and "power to."

This paper identifies some of the difficulties of seeing through and beyond existing paradigms and assumptions. It draws on my research and scholarly writing on women and community in the 1970s and 1980s in the light of new conceptual distinctions Genevieve Vaughan (1997, 2004) offers in her work on gift giving, or community gifting according to need, not exchange. Her ideas are based on a theory developed from her perspective as a mother. A women's focus and knowledge is now in danger of being buried again by the misogyny and new forms of patriarchy which is part of militarism, religious fundamentalism, post-modernist "meism," and neo-liberal globalization, with its individualism and economic fundamentalism. At this critical juncture of the future of the earth's living beings and of humanity, it has been reassuring to realize that the future may be in our midst. Vaughan helped me to understand that features of the transformed alternative futures that I had been struggling to imagine are, in fact, here "in the now." Vaughan's recognition of the powerful, extensive contemporary presence of a gifting paradigm and my own long knowledge and appreciation of the importance of what I now call women's community "gifting" enhances the possibilities of radically different paradigmatic possibilities.

"What's Important About Women?" Discovering Women in Community Work

Initially I had problems even seeing women's community work, even though it interested me. My focus was "citizen participation," and I was interested in conceiving of women as citizens. This desire to "discover," "see," or "conceive" of women was a characteristic of the times.[4] Women were absent in scholarly knowledge and in higher education; it was not exceptional that there were no women in Sociology on the graduate faculty at Columbia University when I was doing my Ph.D. As a young researcher in the early 1970s, I was living in Canada and studying citizen participation in Halifax, Nova Scotia while also working on my Ph.D. dissertation on newcomers in that provincial capital. For a paper presentation in March 1972, I asked a women colleague, Patricia Loiselle (now Connelly), to work with me because she had a different sociological train-ing. It was an unsuccessful attempt to find something interesting for a paper on women relevant to my research on citizen participation. The sociological literature forced me—and us—into what I considered to be the boring scholar-ship of counting people to find "who participates." Comparing women to men using male standards did not allow us to see anything of interest to women, and patriarchal culture at that time had made women's culture invisible. We wrote the paper, but it was not a satisfying intellectual experience.

Two years later, Pat Connelly and I wrote a paper completely and explicitly focused on women. It was a huge improvement because we addressed women's actions and women's perceptions of women's liberation. In the paper we combined the scholarship of two well-known sociologists, applying C. Wright Mills' (1961) conceptualization, "private troubles and public issues," to our data and creating a sociological typology reminiscent of the style of Robert Merton (1957). Even in that paper, which was entirely focused on women and based on qualitative interviews with women, however, we were conceptually crossing the theoretical approaches of two male theorists and not fully embracing alternative assumptions in a way that would lead us (and others) to build an alternative feminist scholarship.

In 1975, as part of a government-sponsored initiative for International Women's

Year, I led a team of five women from my university. We conducted research and wrote a report entitled *Women's Concerns about the Quality of Life in Halifax* (Christiansen-Ruffman, Hafter, Chao, Katz and Ralston 1975). The study used a multi-method research approach, and in retrospect, I am impressed with the data and presence of women in that study. At the time, and with a few exceptions, however, it still did not foster an appreciation or help me to see women's community work in Halifax in a full and conceptually different way. I was still influenced by society's and scholarship's patricentric focus—which did not allow us to conceive of women as fully autonomous individuals but always within the shadow of men's priorities. What I noticed women doing did not seem to be interesting or important or on the "public" agenda. The possible exception was, interestingly, the case of women who were fighting for the protection of their neighbourhoods against the development industry at that time. In one of the only quotes from a male in that report, the developer attributes power to these community activist housewives and to the presence of children, not as priorities but as functional. He is quoted as saying:

> The majority of these groups and the people involved in them are decent, honest and well meaning people. They are concerned first with their own homes, their property values and they are concerned with their community and the quality of life in the area. The problem that we as developers face is that laced through these well meaning honest citizens there are ... the punks and the maoists and the members of the New Left, the bleeding hears and the radicals, the malcontents who operate in whipping up the pressure groups. Sometimes the groups are led by housewives who are looking for a cause and using community involvement as their main social activity to release their frustration. And you know what they say—you learn the wrath of a women's scorn—and I can tell you, you get three or four of these ladies from a neighbourhood and they will effectively organise, sign petitions, whip up the school children, berate the newspapers with letters and they do a very effective job. And this is their life. They are imbued with a cause! They think they mean well; they have a tremendous power and they are very much a cause or a cost factor in the development process. (Christiansen-Ruffman *et al.* 1975: 35)

My Ph.D. education as a sociologist at Columbia University, an institution which claimed to be the greatest university anywhere for sociologists, had not taught me to see the world fully, to recognize women, to value women and to value myself and my ideas. I realized even at the time that it was not only the result of that particular university but of the patriarchal nature of knowledge. It was a systemic fault. It took a few years and experiences with Labrador women, however, for me to recognize a major reason why I could not even begin to "make sense" of women's community work: women were present in scholarly thinking only insofar as they were functional to men. Scholarly training had socialized me into this colonised thinking.

"If It Weren't for the Women, There would be No Community...."
Recognizing Women's Community Work

I could not escape seeing women in Labrador communities when I went there as part of a several year research evaluation study of the Community Employment Strategy (CES) with a consulting firm. At first, however, the women there appeared to be the stereotypical "traditional" women, uninvolved in the "important" politics of life. They stayed at the back of the hall in the kitchen rather than at the meeting—or sat on one side of the room, apart from the men. In my "modern" but misogynist "sophistication," on my first trip to Labrador, I assumed that the men in Labrador were the important ones and discounted the women. After more research in these communities, however, I had to reassess this initial perception. I returned again after CES was finished in order to learn more.

The women of Labrador taught me to see and to appreciate women's community work. They taught me to see that women were, in fact, creating the community. "If it weren't for the women, there would no community," they confidently told me. And I realized that they were correct about their important role, despite the "gloss of patriarchy" on the "surfaces" of Labrador cultures. Years later I read a description which conveys the strength of women's community work by Janice Lawrence of Bridgetown, Nova Scotia, a self-declared "farmer, farm worker, farm wife, farm mother, agricultural activist and community builder." She is quoted by Jo Leath (2001) as comparing "the contribution of rural women to thread in a quilt; present in every inch of the greater community and strong enough to hold it all together"(2).

In 1979, the community strength of Labrador women led me to respond to a call for papers for the annual meting of the Canadian Research Institute for the Advancement of Women (CRIAW) in Edmonton (see Christiansen-Ruffman 1980) on women as persons. Implicitly thinking of women in Labrador, I defined "personhood" as the extent to which an individual's contribution to the community is recognized by that community as important. The personhood of women was analyzed along three dimensions: the extent to which women's activities contribute necessary resources to the community and to the family unit; the extent to which women exercise control over resources in the household and community, and the extent to which women are respected in the household and community. Using these dimensions, I found that many women in rural Labrador had more personhood at this time than women in urban Halifax.[5] This finding challenged a number of assumptions which were (and remain) deeply embedded in contemporary societies and in scholarship. The paper brought together evidence to contradict the following three propositions:

1) Women in rural areas, often called "traditional women" and characterized by relatively rigid sex role segregation, are relatively deprived of personhood compared to their more sophisticated urban counterparts.

2) Progress toward personhood is gradually being made as communities

become more urban and industrialized.

3) Women in rural communities and generally in Atlantic Canada are conservative and are not innovative or politically active in community life.

All three of these propositions were not supported. Each of them was found to be misleading in the context of Atlantic Canada even though it was based on popular conceptions and scholarship. The evidence challenged taken-for-granted assumptions in North American scholarship and life at that time, especially about stereotypical women as well as the currently present belief in linearity and unilinear "progress."[6]

The insights from Labrador women and from the community women in Nova Scotia started me on a whole new course of unlearning and learning, both as a scholar and as a person. This educational process really began after I had a Ph.D! At the time, it was easier to see myself as a sociologist than as a woman, despite the women's movement, because of the levels of societal hatred of women, or misogyny, which I had absorbed. I gradually realized how colonized many of us were—at some level not even recognizing ourselves as women, even as we were engaged in the women's movement. I cast my lot with women once I recognized that there was nothing that I could conceive of doing at the time that would change the fact that I am a woman and would be treated as such. I reasoned that, given the current state of discrimination against women, my only hope was to be part of those making changes with other women. As a social being, I realized that I had to work with others to create alternatives for ourselves, to reformulate our social relationships as more equitable and respectful, and to work for a more equitable, just, environmentally friendly and peaceful new world.

At the time it is not surprising that I was having trouble focusing on women. Women were absent, ignored, or disparaged in both scholarly and everyday life. As I discovered women, I also discovered more fully women's absence in the scholarly literature and in policy. I found, for example, that in Charest's (1973) discussions of development policy in a rural area of Quebec near Labrador, women were so non-existent that only a mention of birth rate and one sentence on inheritance even implies their presence. Yet in small communities adjacent to those studied by Charest, I could not ignore the central role being played by women in the community as well as in its "development."

The almost unconscious treatment of women as invisible by Charest contrasts with that of many anthropologists who did see "sex roles" or what we now call "gender" and characterised these communities as male dominant. The sociologist Ralph Matthews (1976) also saw the communities in this way and used a series of arguments to explain why he did not include any women in his survey sample of rural Newfoundland communities which had resisted resettlement. A woman in Labrador was so incensed with this treatment of Labrador women that she pulled me away from a dinner table when she discovered that I was a sociologist; she wanted to expose me immediately to his discriminatory and invalid reasoning (see my later detailed analysis Christiansen-Ruffman 1985). Matthews (1976) had omitted all women from his sample because he claimed that women were not community leaders in Newfoundland/Labrador or heads of households. Yet, in one of the three communities he studied as case studies, he documents the importance of a particular woman community leader in preventing the relocation of this community.

In the mid-1970s the male standpoint was completely dominant, creating knowledge that was elitist and oppressive to the community and to women. Scholarly paradigms did not allow us to see the world of women or women's culture in its deeper, more complete ways. Women scholars began to understand the ways in which that knowledge needed to change in order for us to begin to look at each other and think with each other, together. We began to interrogate and question the assumptions on which knowledge was constructed within the existing paradigm. Most importantly, we began to see glimpses of alternatives in women's cultures. Interactions between individual academics, especially those influenced by women's movements, allowed for this challenge of patriarchal paradigms and the development of research agenda that was by women, for women, about women, and with women. In Canada a great deal of this thinking led to and then was facilitated by the Canadian Research Institute for the Advancement of Women (CRIAW) which held annual conferences starting (unofficially) in 1976 with a Halifax conference and which was committed to bridging the academic/activist/community divides.

Women's Politics and Women's Community Work: Trying to Understand a Third Part of the Puzzle[7]

In the 1980s, as I worked with other feminist scholars and community activists to discover a world where women's culture and values were central and to reconceive of politics and cultures through women's eyes, I began to see women's community work as a third part of the puzzle. Scholars had used dichotomies for many years to identify production versus reproduction, wage labour versus domestic labour, public versus private, and work versus leisure. These dichotomous analytic concepts, however, ignored, undervalued, and rendered as virtually invisible the important features of community life which many women understood in Labrador and Nova Scotian fishing and farming communities, namely women's public unpaid work. More importantly, through reading and talking with other women, I discovered that this feature of life was not limited to these geographic areas but present in most parts of the world.

It was startling to find these common features of women's cultures because they were identified neither in the relevant scholarly literature nor in public discourse, especially in the urban communities I knew. In the 1980s I embarked on a lengthy search of scholarly literatures in an attempt to discover women's politics and women's community work in both its empirical treatment and its scholarly conceptualization. Leslie Brown and I wrote a paper (Brown and Christiansen-Ruffman 1985) after a thorough search for accounts of women's community work, caring work, volunteer work and political work (broadly conceived). Surprisingly, one of the most complete accounts was not recent but Mary Ritter Beard's 1915 study, Women's Work in Municipalities. This book describes in detail women's activities which changed social life in such areas as education, public health, corrections, civic improvement and racial assimilation. Subsequently the book's conceptualization of women's work in municipalities has been rendered invisible, both empirically and conceptually. As Marilyn Gittell and Teresa Shtob (1980) describe, historical writers of the Progressive Era tend to ignore women's work contributions or include it in with reform work in general. Nevertheless, scattered references to women's community work remain. For example, Susan Mann Trofimenkoff (1984) has discussed the role of women in organizing and providing volunteer relief for the victims of the Halifax explosion in 1917, and Leo Johnson (1974) describes the role of aristocratic women as (volunteer) managers of the welfare system of Ontario in the early 1800s.

Another independently developing literature relevant to women's community work (including women's networking activities) is the still growing body of scholarship on women as caregivers. As Hilary Graham (1983) writes:

> caring is thus experienced as an unspecific and unspecifiable kind of labour, the contours of which shift constantly. Since it aims, like so much women's work, 'to make cohesive what is often fragmentary and disintegrating', it is only visible when it is not done.... A conception of caring-as-women's-work clearly advances our thinking in a number of ways. We can appreciate its economic and ideological nature, as a labour which, although essential for survival, is invisible, devalued and privatised. (26-7)

Leslie Brown and I saw this burgeoning literature as interesting for several reasons. Some of this literature recognizes that it is often inappropriate to treat caring as a commodity on the same conceptual level as shopping, cooking, working and cleaning. Secondly, the idea and praxis of caring does not easily lend itself to a dichotomous conceptualization, but more easily to a continuum—caring has public as well as private components. Thirdly, the literature on caregivers calls our attention to some of the overriding similarities of caregiving within communities, mediating between communities and family, and within the family itself. It also focuses our attention on women as nodal points in family and community.

If we extend the idea of women as caregivers to women's community work, this highlights the work women do such as writing letters/sending gifts to absent family and friends, organizing annual neighbourhood or block parties (while trying to achieve the "right" mix of people), caring for an elderly or incapacitated friend, taking a casserole to a bereaved acquaintance, getting "the girls" together to smooth over conflicts between husbands or children or workers, acting as the family's delegate to the school, the local church, the public library or recreational centre, the doctor or school counsellor. Clearly these activities require conceptualization and, we would argue, must be seen as part of women's work and as incorporating a community work component. The reflections of an Italian community worker, recorded by David Kertzer (1982), remind us that these discoveries, while "new" to the academic literature, are incorporated into the strategies of many women activists. This Italian woman stresses the importance of a locally based women's group which "... keeps the women a little organised, a little prepared for certain activities, as long as they aren't directed to just one single party" (57). That she feels these networks are effective is clear as she asserts, "There isn't much prejudice around here against the immigrants, because we have always conducted local educational campaigns" (58).

Although Brown and Christiansen-Ruffman (1985) discovered evidence of women's community work described by scholars in many places over time, this 1984-5 review of the literature also confirmed that key dimensions of women's work have been and remain invisible to both the public and the scholarly community. We found that women's community work was sometimes invisible by definition, sometimes by implication, and other times semi-visible and not conceived as work. When women's work was included, it tended to be undervalued, subordinated, or functional to male work. Brown and I also found episodic, often idiosyncratic statements about particular examples of women's community work, often described as volunteer activities or the work of "housewives." For example, Meg Luxton (1980) writes, "Housewives have always been active in their communities demanding a whole range of things that make life easier and better—schools, hospitals, paved roads and street lighting, parks and recreation centres. Periodically they organize around issues that are of specific interest to women" (212-213). She points out that such activities change the relations of women to their work and their families. Luxton does not, however, analyze these activities as aspects of women's work itself. Conceptually women's community work remains invisible in spite of the acknowledgement of its empirical presence. Indeed, the scholarly literature at this time was characterized by loose theoretical concepts which uneasily embrace some aspects of this work while omitting others. This lack of theorizing about women's unpaid community work probably accounts for the fact that empirical studies collect data on women's community work but then ignore the data in analysis. For example, Richard Berk and Sarah Fenstermaker Berk (1979) collected time budget data on visiting, church involvements, neighbouring and volunteer work which were unanalyzed although data on time driving to and from work were included in the analysis.

This examination of women's community work enabled Leslie Brown and me to search the literature for new empirical examples and to describe features of this work. Though occasionally present, these descriptive accounts were rarely highlighted or analyzed. Neither the longer term focus on women's volunteer work nor the more recent feminist focus on caring work nor the other sub-types of community work have developed their own theoretical traditions with their own conceptual questions. This is not surprising because these features of women's community work are not consistent with the dominant paradigms. Although this detailed review of the literature needs updating, my on-going reading suggests that the theoretical invisibility of women community work remains. Indeed, a recent survey of the social capital literature confirms this (Bezanson 2006).[8]

In the 1985 paper, Brown and I argued that the sociology of work literature and our understanding of women's community work could benefit from starting with a conceptualization of work as the expenditure of energy. Such a suggestion is reminiscent of physics. A sociological definition of energy expenditure however, would not only focus on physical energy but also on mental energy, social energy and emotional energy and the activities produced. Work would be conceived as the expenditure of social, emotional, mental and physical energy relevant to responsibilities, obligations or values. Interestingly, such a sociological definition of the potential energy and social energy underpinning the concept of work is not inconsistent with the Webster dictionary definition of work as an "activity in which one exerts strength or faculties to do or perform something"; It "may imply activity of body or mind … or it may apply to the effort or to what is produced by that effort"; it "may apply to any purposeful activity whether remunerative or not."

Community Work: Toward Alternative Interpretations

Brown and Christiansen-Ruffman (1985) concluded that the proposed all-embracing, non-institutionalized definition of work was important but not the full theoretical story. In the process of discovery and definition of women's community work, we had also come to a fuller understanding of the fact that women's community work does not fit comfortably into existing theoretical assumptions. Unanswered questions emerged. We encountered difficulties incorporating processes such as networking, mediating, caring, and transforming into a neat set of categories. Could we really draw boundaries between paid, domestic, and community work? We found that components of women's community work are related to other types of women's paid and unpaid work. Figure 1 of the paper pictured women's community work at the core of and interlocking with other types of women's work: community-building/ change work, liaison/ mediating; maintaining household; individual care/ nurturing; reproduction/ socialization; production for use/ subsistence; production for exchange/ formal economy; production for exchange/ informal economy; volunteering (social, service, political organizations). We were also led to question the extent to which volunteer work still has the characteristics of women's community work or has it been transformed? Moreover, we confronted the problem that in showing women's community work to be valuable, there is a tendency to conceptually harness and change apparent caring work into the service of contemporary patricentric institutions.

To fully incorporate women, we had to start from different assumptions.[9] Therefore, we concluded our extensive review of the literature by raising theoretical questions and suggesting the need to develop a whole new puzzle, solidly grounded in women's work experience.

The alternative, transformed conceptualization of women's community work cuts across, permeates throughout and in fact is at the core of the work women do on the job, in the home, and in the community. In this transformed conceptualization, women's community work (public, unpaid work) is networking or the production and reproduction of community. Women's community-building work takes place in the family, in the kinship group, in the neighbourhood, in the work place, and in various arenas within the larger society. The building and nurturing of networks, associations, and interpersonal relationships is, we argue, as much a work activity as the activities or transactions (social and economic consequences) made possible by these processes. Women expend energy, which must be replenished, in carrying out this work. This work does take time, although it is difficult to locate in time-budget analysis.

The 1985 paper focuses on a specific example of women's creative community work in bringing a feminist lecture series to Halifax. The women involved were all university professors and membership on this committee as active community participants was also part of their paid work. The series had previously featured mainly male speakers on topics such as "The Crisis of Modern Man as Seen by Some Contemporary French Writers" and "Man/Animal Communication: Pitfalls and Opportunities." In 1984 the series was entitled "Feminist Visions" and featured Marge Piercy, Sheila Rowbotham and Mary Daly. A capacity audience of over 1,000 people attended each session and the series was one of the most popular in the eleven-year history of the lecture series. The work of the all-woman committee was positively recognized by some members of the university community and by the feminist community, but the usual dinner of thanks to the organizers of the series never materialized. Moreover, such work is not really "counted" in university promotion, pay, or reward structures.

The feminist and social process that led to the success was not rewarded although it took effort and energy to realize and had a number of positive implications for the university and beyond. The proposal was a collective effort among women faculty and had to be of a high quality to be selected in competition with other proposals. Unlike other years, the feminist organizers paid creative attention to lectures as a learning process and held pre-lecture sessions to introduce the speaker's ideas so that audience members would be more knowledgeable and would gain more from the series.

In planning these sessions and later in organizing small seminars with the invited speakers or in sharing time with them over meals, the committee involved not only their own members but those from other universities in Nova Scotia and from the non-university community in Atlantic Canada. Institutional barriers between universities and elitist barriers between the university and "non-university community" were minimized. The needs and interests of the diverse women's community were melded with those of the speakers. For example, in the case of the feminist separatist, Mary Daly, a special time was set aside for her to meet with the Nova Scotia lesbian community. Also the typical "by-invitation-only" reception was replaced by a general invitation to the audience to join in refreshments in the art gallery, in the same building as the lecture hall.

The work of the university feminists in this case shows clearly that feminist work, like women's work is not "just a job" but an effort which creates results by mobilizing, enhancing and renewing networks, and by maximizing community involvement. It requires considerable energy expenditure on work which has been invisible. This example of women's community work cuts across institutional boundaries and permeates women's paid work activities.

Women's community work is also embedded in the "private" work of women. Whether picking up litter and child-minding during a picnic, helping children to meet friends and learn to play with others, caring for her family's nutritional needs, mediating between family and friend's institutions such as school, we see the thread of community work. In fact, women's community may be conceived as being at the core of all women's work activities as they are conceived along a public to private continuum which challenges those very concepts and rigid boundaries created by male institutional imaginaries, dichotomies and hierarchies.

Rather than organize our thinking in dualisms and dichotomies of "public" and "private" work of women, we saw women's valuable community-building and maintaining work as embedded in the relationships and activities of living. The new puzzle illustrated women's way of "making a living" in relation to others. Through caring, provisioning, sheltering, socialization, network building and maintaining, communication and organizing, women create communities necessary to sustain social life.

Moreover, women's community work contributions with their emphasis on mutual caring and the building of community are a reflection and expression of women's culture as it has developed historically. The type of work that is women's work cannot be reduced to commodities because the process and product cannot be separated as they are within the more institutionalized, patriarchal social arrangements. As many studies have shown, and as Myra Marx Feree (1985) emphasizes, women "stubbornly" tend to doubt that the demands of the market place should take priority in determining where one lives, how one arranges one's schedule, and the extent of non-paid commitments in one's life. Women's relationships are an inseparable part of mutually contingent and inter-related life processes. Moreover, women are nodal points in family, neighbourhood, and community networks that take many forms among the diverse cultures of the world. Even within similar cultures, there is a wide diversity of ways in which women engage with their surroundings and these life processes.

Wealth: A Fuller Meaning[10]

What is wealth? How does one value life or women's community work which might be considered invaluable? How does one appreciate something that is pervasive, invisible and that we hardly understand? Rachel Kahn-Hut, Arlene Kaplan Daniels, and Richard Colvard (1982), in an introduction to a section of their edited book, *Women and Work: Problems and Perspectives*, focus on "Invisible Work: Unacknowledged Contributions" and point out:

… the actual importance of much of the work women do, not only in maintaining a family and a home but also in establishing community life, facilitating interaction within and between families and throughout communities, has still not even been systematically studied. In our society, for example, the work of volunteers is given lip service as honorific, but little attention is really paid to how the society would function in its absence. Women assume most of the responsibility for providing linkages between home and school…. Women raise money for the church, welfare, the elderly, and for children's activities, and provide staffing. But the value of that work in our cash-nexus economy and the worth of those who do it are left ambiguous. Like other currently conventional forms of women's work, such as writing family letters, it may be praised but it seldom has exchange value in market terms. (97)

The above quote is interesting here because it suggests two analytic ways to assess the value of women's community work. The most usual way to assess wealth is to translate women's community work into the dominant monied system of evaluation, as my husband had also suggested. Although the calculation requires arbitrary and problematic assumptions as the opening of this essay suggests, for some analytic and political purposes, and with the caveats mentioned above, we may want to highlight the positive economic potential of women's community work. In the example of the lecture series, one might wish to calculate what the university would have had to pay for the public relations benefits and community understanding which was generated by that series: how much high-priced public relations staff time? How many management consultants would generate the same result? Note, however, that such a question leads to another—how does one measure the wealth generation of an increased social vitality, of a more informed citizenry, or higher trust levels, and what are the costs of a society focused only on control rather than empowering each other? Have we not outlived the usefulness of the monied economy as the indicator of wealth in life?

These issues are urgent for everyone in society to consider now. As the world has adopted more economically fundamentalist values and as women themselves are more likely to apply economic reasoning as they move more fully into the paid labour force and mainstream institutions and into exchange-based negotiations with others in their lives, will the rich and varied aspects of women's work be lost? If it is, what are the consequences for everyone in the society and all of life? Is the measure of wealth, based solely on the value of monetized exchange, even valid? Is not the idea of exchange itself a big part of the problem? Must community work be reduced to market criteria (and according to whose criteria?) to be valuable? What about substantive, quality of life criteria? Perhaps the dystopias of writers such as George Orwell are, as much as anything, worlds in which women's work is no longer done.

The second way of assessing the value of women's community work is by the removal design. Effectively, by asking how society would function in the absence of the work of volunteers in the quote above, Kahn-Hut, Daniels and Colvard

(1982) are suggesting this analytic device. If we take away all of women's community work, as well as all of the unpaid work women do, how would the society function? When women get angry enough, it might be an interesting experiment to start with a series of rotating "strikes"—or to start first with-holding women's work for a minute, then for two, then for four, and continue at an accelerating rate. Beginning with an hour or a day, of course, would have a much more immediate impact. In the interim, we could begin to think into the future and to use the removal design to "think through" what communities would be like without women's unpaid work and to suggest changes. In such an exercise which was focused also on policies to eliminate poverty and the production of a special issue of *Canadian Woman Studies/les cahiers de la femme* (Armstrong *et al.* 2004) on Benefiting Women? Women's Labour Rights, Canadian feminist thinkers/activists produced the "Pictou Statement" which is a feminist argument for the need for a Guaranteed Living Income.[11]

Both of these approaches for assessing value show significant differences between what women and some men value through their community work and what is valued by the existing patriarchal paradigm with its measure of money. For a feminist alternative perspective and as the author of a paper re-examining wealth presented in 1985 (Christiansen-Ruffman 1987), I turned to the humanities and literature on the one hand, and to women's organizations on the other hand, to gain insight into conceptualizations of wealth from the standpoint of women. Women's negative attitude to the patriarchal concept of wealth—as money accompanied by greed, corruption, and human slavery—is contained in a brief section of a poem by Peggy Antrobus (1983), a feminist from the Caribbean:

Wealth has always been our greatest enemy;
The price of skin,
The currency of betrayal of our kin.

An alternative feminist vision of wealth, one to which Antrobus would subscribe rather than critique, is contained in a play, Ngaahika Ndeenda (I will marry when I want) from Kenya:[12]

Development will come from our unity.
Unity is our strength and our wealth.
A day will surely come when
If a bean falls to the ground
It'll be split equally among us.
(Thiong'o 1982: 130)

This second, broad definition conceives of wealth as multi-dimensional. It is not limited to economic wealth, commoditized wealth, and monetary wealth. Instead, wealth encompasses all that is valuable.

My examination of women's "development" projects locally and around the globe in the early 1980s indicates a broad variety of types of projects: In Canada there were information generating projects (for example, providing health information and/or women's rights information in Toronto); change-oriented projects (for example, successfully advocating for the participation of women in planning a Halifax maternity hospital and preventing its effective demise); income-generating projects (for example, craft production, and building and operating a museum in southern Labrador); and service-oriented projects (for example, women's initiation of a transit system, a battered women's shelter, and a women's drop-in centre in Whitehorse, Yukon). These projects all create wealth from the perspective of the community and the women who undertook them, even though only one of these ways of wealth-generation is consistent with economically fundamentalist approaches which have spread like cancer since the 1980s.[13]

An examination of almost any project in slightly more detail indicates the multifaceted nature of most women's projects. For example, the mainly service-oriented project in Whitehorse produced several forms of wealth in the community as women identified their problems of isolation and planned a local transit system to serve their needs. The project provided not only a much needed community service but also employment opportunities for women. Moreover, workers' "shifts" were especially designed to minimize conflicts with family responsibilities and thus contributed a new cultural definition of job possibilities. Bus schedules and routes were geared to the needs of women and families. In this instance, wealth was created in the community not only by the service, subsequently taken over by the municipality, but also by networks and organizations including a Status of Women group, a Women's Centre and, in conjunction with other networks and organizations, a Transition Home for Women in need of temporary shelter. These, in turn, acted to increase options for women and to make the community a wealthier place, both at the time and for subsequent generations. In the course of establishing these services, women as individuals gained training, education, skills, insights and ideas, self-confidence, human energy, and increased their human individual resources as well. The community acquired material wealth through new resources such as childcare, transit, and shared labour as well as income and jobs. At many levels, and in mutually generating ways, this community-oriented project provided a full array of gifting activities and generated a wealth of social and cultural resources such as feelings of belonging, caring, networking; education and alternative ideas about of paid-work time and ways in which the community is organized. It also served to develop consciousness of women within individuals, families and communities.

A second project illustration comes from Jamaica and Honor Ford-Smith's (1980) description of the feminist popular theatre group of women from the ghetto of Kingston. Eleven women employed as street cleaners by the government came together to form Sistren. They used "drama as a means to explore and analyze the events and forces which make up their lives; and later, through theatre, share this experience with other groups" (19). The work in building networks, linkages, understanding of common everyday oppressions and problems of everyday life has added wealth to these women and to the working class community of women and has helped pressure for change. As Ford-Smith points out, "By confronting what has been considered taboo, indecent or irrelevant we have begun to make a recorded refusal of the ways in which our lives are thwarted and restricted" (14). Such individual and collective analysis and its subsequent public presentation and discussion add social and cultural wealth; they are important prerequisites if the world is to embark on alternative courses of development. See also Ford-Smith (1986).

Challenges to the Patriarchal Wealth Paradigm

Major challenges to patriarchal scholarship and policy and to its reflections in contemporary societies are raised by taking seriously women's projects which create wealth (see Christiansen-Ruffman 1987). The main challenge is that the formal institution of the economy is built on assumptions that discriminate profoundly against women. What is termed "women's unpaid work" in the monetary economy, by definition, has no value, and this lack of value is socialized into gendered roles and into individual self-esteem and shapes social interaction. The current concept of "rational man" acting in his own self-interests is antithetical to women's community work as well as to mothering. This profound exploitation of women was described in a marvellous article by Claudia von Werlhof (1984), who argues that the housewife rather than the free wage earner is prototypical of capitalist exploitation. She points out that 80 percent to 90 percent of the world's population resembles the housewife more than the proletarian. She also gives great importance to a study of housework, claiming that "if we have understood housework, then we have understood everything.… Women are always 'the ones below'. But only from below, hence at the bottom of the cask, can the whole be seen as the whole. Nothing is more important—actually nothing is more vitally necessary—than to support this tendency of analysis 'from below'" (131).

Maria Mies (1998) describes "the Iceberg Economy." The part that the world sees and economists study is above the water. The remaining 90 percent of the economy, contributed largely by women and subsistence communities, is invisible. Genevieve Vaughan (1997) articulates the ways in which the gift economy supports the mainstream economy and, indeed, how that mainstream monied economy is parasitic on the gift.

Women's community work and mothering challenge the validity of money as a measure of wealth. Moreover, the negative implications of simply extending the existing monetary measures of value to include the informal, (mainly) invisible creation and distribution of goods and services as practiced by women are amply illustrated in Arlie Hochschild's work The Managed Heart: Commercialization of Human Feeling (1983). She demonstrates the dangers of making feelings part of what an employer purchases as part of labour power. Instead, feminist scholars would argue the need for other, women-centred conceptual bases. A focus on women's community work may facilitate this development, and to the extent that it does, therein lies the theoretical and societal importance of women's community work. This type of analysis also helps to question contemporary ways in which women's community work is hindered, changed, co-opted, made impossible or invisibilised by large institutionalised structures aimed at controlling life, including patriarchal capitalism or bureaucratized socialism.

Women's full inclusion in contemporary calculations of wealth violates too many of the patricentric assumptions implicit in scholarship and policy.[14] For example, neither economists nor time budget scholars who calculate women's unpaid work activities use assumptions which treat seriously the 24 hours a day and 365 days a year responsibility of mothers for children. Discussions of this problem with economists, even those who are women and identify as feminists, usually end with their saying something like: "But if you did that, the numbers would not work"; "It would mess things up!" or "Our methodologies [for time budget studies] have gotten better [because women are more apt to multi-task]: we now count three simultaneous activities." It has become clear that the assumptions of contemporary economics and of scholarship and policy do not work for women. It is time for feminists to articulate what different assumptions are necessary and to develop further the feminist alternative.

Implications for a Feminist Conception of Wealth[15]

Analysis of women's culture, women's organizations and women's activities indicates that women's conception of wealth is fundamentally different from the usual patricentric and monied concept of wealth. Components of women's material wealth, social and cultural wealth, and human resource wealth cannot simply be added to economic wealth as easily handled minor and superficial additions. The multifaceted components comprising women's concept of wealth radically affect the assumptions embedded in the existing patriarchal concept and transform the concept itself in a number of fundamental ways. Qualitatively, it becomes a different concept, because it is multifaceted rather than one-dimensional and it is people-centred and relational.

The patriarchally-based monetary concept of wealth rests on assumptions that everything important may be translated into an impersonal and amoral means of exchange (called money), that everything may be reduced to one dimension, the so-called "bottom line," that everything that matters may be placed along a scale of value, that the more money that one has, the more wealthy one is, and that people have an insatiable desire for money.

Women's projects and thinking about wealth reflect a culture in which wealth is determined according to human-oriented assumptions. The many different components of wealth are not reducible to a common denominator and do not operate on the patriarchal principles of reductionism, insatiability, commodification, and unilinear thinking. The calculus that women routinely use takes into account the innate value of human beings and is not oriented toward insatiable accumulation. From woman's point of view, for example, having 10 or 100 or 1,000 times the amount of necessary food is not an indicator of wealth and, in fact, overabundance itself would create further costs and a further burden of labour. Parts of women's wealth calculus, therefore, do not follow the traditional arithmetic rules. Moreover, bottom lines change based on circumstances and are relational rather than absolute. At the present time, wealth for women might be conceived not as presence of commodities but as the absence of the forms of oppression: poverty, hunger, unfilled basic needs, and scarcity. Wealth, for example, might be considered absence of the threats of violence to women and men, children and seniors, and the ability of all peoples to develop their human potential.

The concept of human potential that is central to women's concept of wealth is almost totally absent from traditional concepts of wealth and standards of living. As the economist Raymond W. Goldsmith (1968) points out concerning the GNP, human resources "are omitted because human beings are not considered part of the national wealth unless they can be appropriated. Where slavery exists, the market value of slaves, which in part reflects their training, constitutes a separate category of national wealth" (52). It is perhaps symptomatic of patriarchy that the concept of standard of living is based on an assumption which only includes human potential if it is enslaved.

Women's concept of wealth is also distinguished by its collective and relational orientation. Women engage in the creation and definition of the moral order and hence are oriented to and help to create the collectivity. This orientation to the collectivity involves a commitment of caring and responsibility for others, of making qualitative distinctions, and of contextualising. Women expend energy by networking and creating spiritual, social, and cultural resources; hence, the calculus of women's wealth creation is more likely to involve sharing and maximizing the payoff and potential for all.

Patriarchal concepts are unable to comprehend and fully embrace women's community work because it is not commodified. As Brown and Christiansen-Ruffman (1985) have argued, the products of women's community work cannot be separated as they might be within the more institutionalized patriarchal social arrangements. A key feature is that of the network relations themselves. In essence, women's community work is networking or the production and reproduction of community, and women's community work produces wealth through which women and others are empowered. Unlike exploitative concepts of wealth, where profit is gained by exploiting the labour of others rather than working together for the collective good, all parties gain: the calculus is very different.

Superficially, both the GNP and standard of living are also used as measures of the collectivity or the group. However, as is indicated by an example from Paul A. Samuelson and Anthony Scott (1980), two housewives could add $10,000 to the GNP by exchanging jobs and each paying $5,000 for the other's labour. As this example shows, the traditional concept of wealth is not based on activities within a collectivity. Instead, it is based on artificially formulated monetary principles and an aggregated self-interested individualism. Concepts such as the GNP in fact mask the collective good and principles of equity by aggregating individuals. Because of such assumptions, what looks like development may be an illusion and in fact hide collective deterioration. For example, Sylvia Hale (1985) makes reference to an observation by Irene Tinker about India that "the introduction of grinding mills and oil presses have [sic] been estimated to have raised the national income by nine times the value of jobs lost, but this new technology benefited directly only the large farmers, and the owners of the rice mills. Women, meanwhile, lost their jobs as millers, and could not afford the new rice" (qtd. in Hale 1985: 25). Poverty increased even though "wealth" (measured in patriarchal ways) increased. The averaging feature of the GNP and the current practices of development do not focus attention on increasing inequalities. They mask individual exploitation and the absolute and relative decreases in the poor's standard of living and ability to participate actively in creating a new social order. They are unable to tap the collectivity, the collective good, or the benefit of equal sharing.

The patriarchal concept of wealth is unable to comprehend the collective value of resources. For example, as Goldsmith (1968) points out "natural resources … are excluded [from calculations of national wealth] insofar as they cannot be separately appropriated or sold, as is the case with sunshine and precipitation" (52). During the 1970s the environmental movement focused attention on the wealth of having access to clean air, sunshine, and pure rather than polluted acid rain. Women's concept of wealth is associated with safe and uncontaminated collective environment.

Women's concept of wealth also considers as extremely valuable the public services and community infrastructure which help both to ease women's burdens and to enrich women's lives. In fact, social and community infrastructure tends to be doubly utilized by women both in their own well-being and in their caring for others. To the extent that women do a good job caring, the need for infrastructural support becomes even more invisible to the male decision-makers. Recently throughout the world, governments have been cutting back on social services. As DAWN (1985) points out, "Reduced access to human services such as health, literacy, transport etc. affect women in two ways, first by reducing women's own access to these services, and second, by their having to fill the gap of providing them to others (e.g., children, the aged, infirm or unemployed) because of their traditional roles" (9).

Neo-Patriarchal Attack on Women's Community Work

The period of Structural Adjustment Programs (SAPs) in countries of the economic South and of "restructuring" and "privatization" in countries of the economic North have been difficult for women because it has resulted in reduced human services. The policies cut back on public and social institutions and focus increasingly on economic growth and trade. The scholarly literature on the impact on women of these policies shows that SAPs have "sapped" women's energies and added an increasing burden to the community work needed for family survival[16] (see Antrobus *et al.* 2002). While political leaders of western countries such as Canada's conservative Prime Minister Mulroney were interviewed and jubilantly described the withdrawal of food subsidies in countries of the economic South and former Soviet Union, women's interests everywhere were being harmed by these neo-patriarchal policies which made women's lives around the world so much more difficult.

In Canada, and especially in Nova Scotia, these neo-conservative/ neo-reform/ neo-liberal policies are dismantling the welfare state, undermining rural livelihoods and restructuring the political, economic, and social fabric of Canada. For several years the governmental "spin" took the rhetorical form of an urgent need to tackle the debt and deficit. This governmental "spin" was aided by an increasingly concentrated corporate media and had the effect of dismissing other competing values such as equality, the environment, and socio-economic justice.[17] Values of individualism, competitiveness, greed, and other economic values trumped others. Words associated with political rights such as "citizen" became "customer" and "consumer." Women were dismissed as "special interest groups" while the powerful corporate special interest groups and the government increasingly led by public relations interests were able to "spin" their issues without being challenged or identified as the real beneficiaries of these changed values.

The restructuring throughout this period has not been all spin, and it has been accelerating for some time.[18] The mid-1990s saw massive cutbacks in social programming and a down-sized Canadian government, creating crises in social programs which some Canadians fear was a deliberate way of privatizing these services. Unemployment Insurance, a government supported program to provide a safety net to workers, was also massively cut back and restructured at exactly the time when workers needed support. Higher education was also under siege, and when monies were given back to higher education several years later, the nature of the funding was entirely different; it focused on scholarships for individuals rather than funding for the university system.

Feminist research in Nova Scotia during the 1990s on women in fishing communities and the work of Nova Scotia Women's FishNet provided insights into the ways that the strong social fabric which had supported fishing communities for centuries was being ripped apart by a series of government policies and an environmental crisis of fish stock depletion (see Catano *et al.* 2004; Christiansen-Ruffman 2004, 2002, 1995). The policies were favourable to large corporations and not to small owner-operated boats. Corporate interests and government attempted to implement policies such as individual transferable quotas (ITQs) that were known elsewhere to have shifted fish from being part of "the Commons." Moreover, the policy approach of the government to conservation of the cod stocks was to prohibit the inshore fishers from their livelihood and even from catching fish such as cod for their own subsistence. On the other hand, the large and increasingly concentrated corporate fishery, which used more environmentally-destructive technologies and fished further offshore, continued to catch cod as part of a "by-catch" when they were licensed to catch other new species. Fresh cod continued to be sold in the supermarkets despite the "cod moratorium."

The particular policy choices being implemented were quite literally making people sick, breaking morale because they were considered unfair, and also devastating the social relationships among women and within families and communities. The networks on which women's community work had been created and sustained were being torn apart, sometimes with the help of government policies and corporate manipulations; a way to create dissent and to split apart families and communities was to offer "deals" of licenses or fish quota to specific individuals or corporations if they agreed to new policies or favoured conditions. Other times networks were torn apart because of the power of the economy and the lack of alternatives: community members were forced to close their store because of lower revenues, compelled to leave for work elsewhere, or did not have enough gas money to drive an elderly person to the store for groceries or to the doctors or to pay for a school trip. At the same time that fishing communities were in crisis, the provincial government was cutting back on social programs and was closing down rural health and education facilities, substantially interrupting the networks and support systems on which rural peoples had been relying. The shadow of the economy was so strong that all of the webs and networks supporting the well-being of community members and community wealth were being silently destroyed, without raising a policy alarm. Chains of events hit simultaneously and seriously affected well-being in coastal communities. Rural communities were especially hard hit with loss of both public and private services for transportation, health, and education. Women's community work was out of favour, unappreciated and undersupplied at the same time as it was even more desperately needed. Neoliberal corporate/ neoconservative/ neo-reform agenda brought values associated with rampant consumerism to communities with essentially no money, further depressing community members who could no longer participate in social life, and introducing significant class differentials into relatively equalitarian communities. Moreover, this new agenda imposed an economically fundamentalist value system that intensified an already dominant economic agenda and further marginalized the region and rendered women's community work even more invisible.

As a feminist sociologist, I was particularly dismayed by the overlapping and destructive social processes which I feared might have long-term consequences. I still hope I was not witnessing the social creation of profound impoverishment, a form of destruction of the social viability of these communities that could have negative consequences on future generations. Although these communities were previously on the margins and certainly not rich in monetary terms, they were socially, individually and morally strong, vibrant and more independent before the restructuring. They were very far from the profound, dysfunctional impoverishment which I had experienced in parts of Appalachia in the United States and in some inner city ghettos.

The ingredients of this new impoverishment included the destruction of the social support systems of these communities. Moreover, independent individuals were being deskilled and demoralized. These individuals included not only the men and women who caught fish in boats on the sea but also the "women who were the captains of the shore crew." They had managed the small family business by handling repairs and buying new equipment, keeping the books, monitoring the boat for safety, and knowing the rules and regulations from government agencies. The restructuring of the fisheries deskilled these women of the shore crew who no longer could keep up with the rapidly changing rules and regulations. They were robbed of their self-esteem at the same time as the government policies robbed their families and communities of their ways of making a living. They were robbed of compensation for being put out of work because in many cases their work on the shore crew was not recognized as "work," even for women who put bait on many hooks of the "trawl." Not only were they not eligible for financial compensation, but they were not eligible for training programs and some jobs. At the same time as fishing families were told that they could no longer continue to do the only work they knew, the downloading of governmental responsibility onto individuals and user pay mentality was abolishing their social entitlements. It was also eliminating the public and community institutions on which women relied as part of their community work. I think it took less than six months before the media began to blame the "lazy" fishers—who had just been banned by government regulations from using their boats.[19] Surprisingly, these processes of community destruction and social devastation remain largely unnamed.

From Women's Community Work to Community Gifting

For many years, women's groups and feminist scholars have been expressing the need for new paradigms and alternatives.[20] While neo-patriarchal forces in the last decade in Canada and globally have sapped energy from women and women's movements, they also have made it even clearer that alternatives are urgently needed. The neo-liberal policies are clearly unsustainable for both the planet and its human societies, encouraging destructive behaviours, exacerbating gaps between rich and poor within and between countries, diminishing social and bio-diversity, and threatening the ecosystem. The "Wise Women's Workshop" in Norway in 2001 was a response to the growing urgency about both the neo-patriarchal resurgence and the need to think together with other feminist scholars (see Linda Christiansen-Ruffman, Paola Melchiori and Berit Ås, 2006). We attempted to understand the times and to envisage alternatives. In lengthy discussions about alternative economies, I was introduced to the work of Genevieve Vaughan, the implications of the exchange basis of the economy, and especially the false dichotomy of equal and unequal exchanges that masked the problematic nature of exchange itself. It is a tremendous intellectual shift to recognize that difference.

Discussions at the "Wise Women's Workshop" and subsequent meetings made clearer and more realistic the possibilities of putting forward alternatives based on women's current ways of living in a gifting way. Therefore, rather than envisioning a future without a past or present, we could build upon existing hidden women's cultures and economies which bring forward matriarchal cultures from the past into the present. It was liberating and comforting to envision alternatives and inspiration in our own lives and those living on the margins of the contemporary madness. We discussed rural women's community work in different cultures, Indigenous survival cultures, and the ways in which Aboriginal peoples have lived in contingent inter-relationship with the natural world, respecting nature and its gifts. It is a major achievement to figure out that women's peaceful, caring ways of being in this world, rather than some other magic, invented solution, is a major key to thinking into the future.

To celebrate new insights, emphasize the idea of process, and suggest a new paradigm, I decided to change the name of the central concept from women's community work to women's community gifting. The idea of gifting better represents the visionary and alternative assumptions at the core of women's community activities. It may well be that that women's community work might be its name, bound within strictures of the old paradigm and gifting might be a way to release the creativity of women's community work in the new paradigm. I look forward to "thinking into this concept" in the future and have just started to do so in this paper. I invite others to participate in thinking through the alternative assumptions and conceptualisations which may be useful in further specifying the shape of the new gifting paradigm.

Conclusion

The escalating impoverishment of individual lives and threats to life itself, which are results of new forms of patriarchy, needs to be assessed. This patriarchal world is based on an outmoded system of elitist and abstracted logic. Its measures are false and no longer valid. Money is misleading as a measure of wealth and development. Militarization as a measure of security is not only wrong but dangerous. Patriarchal thinking that leaves human beings, life, and relationships simply as abstract categories to be controlled or ignored is inadequate for a civilized world. Our scholarship needs revamping. Our religious systems, which breed violence and hatred, guilt and sacrifice, are logically based in slavery rather than liberation of spirit and potential. These outmoded patriarchal ideas and myths have taken us and our societies beyond their "limits to growth." We have become lost in Orwellian double speak, or "spin." In this world where the measures of wealth, security and well-being have been increasingly translated into their antitheses, it is time for a radical change. A radical transformation is possible only if we recognize that the old patriarchal paradigm has outlived its years and that we must live into a new approach and paradigm.

This paper has analyzed the history of the emergence of the idea of women's community work as a feminist alternative paradigm. The emergence of any new paradigm, according to Kuhn (1962) has always met with resistance. Thus, perhaps we should not be surprised at the more recent reinvisibilization of women's community work; deepening shadows have again been cast upon it by new forms of patriarchy that have been escalating over the last fifteen years. But I detect a shift. During the period of new forms of patriarchy and patriarchal intensification, surprisingly, the patriarchal inroads were not taken seriously. Perhaps because they did not appear to be gendered. This is now changed. The old paradigm is so full of holes and inconsistencies that its failures to explain and come up with solutions can no longer be ignored. More and more individuals, including Canadians such as Stephen Lewis and James Robert Brown (2001) are vocally recognizing the importance of women's leadership. Lewis noticed the important women's community work of the grandmothers in Africa when he was the United Nations Envoy for HIV/AIDS in Africa until 2007. Brown credits feminist scholarly leadership in shifts towards a new scientific paradigm.

This analysis of women's community gifting shows both the necessity and the potential of a feminist and women-centred approach to create a more humane world for all living beings. It also directs us to the alternative assumptions on which we might recognize wealth and value. The grandmothers of this world still know the importance of women's community work, and we could learn by listening to their wisdom of living life. The young women have declared "the women are angry campaign and will not accept cutbacks and push-backs."[21] Personally, I can think of no better alternative to seeking solutions to world problems than listening to the wisdom of women who are trying to work with non-patriarchal assumptions. What if each of us, in our own spheres, takes up this approach and learns to live with and into these different assumptions? Applying women's community gifting to everyday relations with each other and with the world is probably the best way of creating that radically different world, a world full of new possibilities and hope for all.

Linda Christiansen-Ruffman (Ph.D. Columbia University) is Professor of Sociology at Saint Mary's University. She served as a President of both the Canadian Sociology and Anthropology Association and the Canadian Research Institute for the Advancement of Women as well as their Atlantic counterparts. She has chaired the Research Committee on Women in Society of the International Sociological Association (ISA) and been a member of the ISA executive committee and its representative to the United Nations in New York. In the 1970s she began to conduct local research and to teach, write, and organize some of the "early" research by, for, about, and with women. She became part of the feminist challenge to unlearn biased theoretical and methodological assumptions of disciplines and to invent new ways. She chaired the Taskforce on the Elimination of Sexist Bias in Research of the Social Science Federation of Canada. Her scholarship on feminist theory, methodology, sociology of knowledge and women's movements (local and global) has benefited greatly from feminist praxis. She has helped to found many organizations, committees and caucuses including graduate women's studies in Halifax, Nova Scotia Women's FishNet, FAFIA (Canada's Feminist Alliance for International Action) and the International Feminist University.

Notes

---

[1] This paper incorporates a comment from Alan Ruffman about women's valuable work of constitution building into a paper, co-presented at the November, 2004

Las Vegas conference with Angela Miles. The paper was called "Women's Giving: A New Frame for Feminist Policy Demands" and the conference, "A Radically Different Worldview is Possible: The Gift Economy Inside and Outside Patriarchal Capitalism," was organized by Genevieve Vaughan. Thanks go to Gen for bringing together such interesting feminist thinkers from all other the world, for her feminist generosity and for her fresh and sophisticated feminist intellectual insights. Special thanks also go to Angela Miles, Azza Anis, Luciana Ricciutelli and Genevieve Vaughan for their help with the writing of this paper.

2   In 1981 the Prime Minister of Canada was intent on repatriating Canada's Constitution from Great Britain and including a Charter of Rights and Freedoms in it. A conference had been planned by the Canadian Advisory Council on the Status of Women to focus on Women and the Constitution. When that conference was abruptly cancelled by the (male) Minister for the Status of Women, the head of the Advisory Council resigned publicly, creating a focus for intense women's activism, including a hurriedly organized Valentine's Day conference, which led to the insertion of women's equality rights into the Constitution. See Penney Kome (1983) for a detailed account of the activities, especially as they relate to Ottawa.

Despite the Constitutional victory, feminists recognized that the work was not over. See the results of the Wilson Task Force in the 1990s for an accounting of discrimination against women within the legal profession and the articles in Faraday, Denike and Stephenson (2006) for the ways in which Canadian women, especially those associated with the legal profession, have worked within and outside the Supreme Court at Making Equality Rights Real: Securing Substantive Equality Under the Charter (to use their book's title).

3   See Jill Vickers (1989) and Margaret Benston (1989) for a critique of objectivity as it was naively practiced in positivism. Their accounts do not make the naive assumption that certain elements of both are not possible in scholarship. Moreover, Benston also makes a useful distinction between what she calls "objectivity" and "pseudo-objectivity."

4   This desire to "discover," "see," or "conceive" of women was partly influenced by my personal biography and partly by the growing women's movement during my graduate student days (see Christiansen-Ruffman 1998; Christiansen-Ruffman, Melchiori and Ås 2006).

5   Methods employed in this research were participant observation and interviews. In Labrador I used the same or similar questions, research instruments and sampling techniques as used in the 1975 Halifax study to allow for comparison. The paper's conclusion mentions a suggested historical process and required strategy: "the decreasing personhood which accompanies increases in societal scale and the development of capitalism has given rise to conditions which so undermine the status of women that concerted efforts are needed to institutionalize personhood in society."

6   A retrospective analysis of the Labrador case study illustrates the tremendous power of societal assumptions, namely ethnocentrism, sexism and unilinearity. Even though I organized courses explicitly to challenge ethnocentric attitudes, had conducted research in Africa with a women professor and studied anthropology, nevertheless. this case study illustrates that as a researcher and a young feminist scholar in the mid 1970s, to some extent I shared the taken-for-granted ethnocentric view of progress, especially as a "modern" woman in my first meetings with the stereotypically "traditional" women in Labrador. The comparative research perspective led to the framing of my 1979 paper and allowed me to challenge the dominant social science (and societal) view of linearity.

7   The paper, "Women's Community Work: A Third Part of the Puzzle," was written
with Leslie Brown from Mount Saint Vincent University. She was also a member of the
executive of the Canadian Research Institute for the Advancement of Women in Nova
Scotia (CRIAW-NS) and an expert on cooperatives. After presentation at the conference
"Women and the Invisible Economy" at Simone de Beauvoir Institute of Concordia
University February 21-23, 1985, it was revised for publication in a book of selected
papers from the conference, edited by Suzanne Peters, the conference organizer. Like
many feminist books and other work outside of paradigms, ths book was widely circulated
but never published. (See Spender 1981b and Morgan cited in Christiansen-Ruffman
1985 for an analysis of the difficulties faced by feminist scholars from the gatekeepers
of publishing who tend to support existing, mainstream paradigms.) In this section and
the next, I draw heavily on the argument and quote the 1985 paper extensively (but not
formally as I would a publication). The reader should therefore consider much of these
two sections as being co-written written with Leslie Brown although I am responsible
for its current framing.

8   As suggested previously, however, feminist empirical recognition of women's unpaid
work does not necessarily lead to a search for an alternative paradigm. Bezanson (2006)
is arguing for "applications of a social reproduction perspective to social capital-based
policy" (438).

9   Feminist ideas of starting from different assumptions and developing new paradigms were
part of the feminist intellectual climate at that time. The spirit was evident, for example, in
the title of Dale Spender (1981a)'s edited book, *Men's Studies Modified*. Scholarship, policy,
and everyday life were all considered deeply problematic, and feminist scholars repeatedly
tried to peel back the layers of patriarchy and to discover patriarchal mechanisms. In the
late 1970s and throughout the 1980s, conferences of the Canadian Research Institute for
the Advancement of Women (CRIAW) could be counted upon for new insights into the
nature of patriarchal knowledge, and in 1984 I presented a paper concerned about the
extent to which we were doing a critique and the limited scope for going beyond what I
called the inherited biases within feminism, explicitly the patricentric syndrome and the
dichotomous either/or syndrome (see Christiansen-Ruffman 1989). In the early 1990s I
also added the abstraction syndrome, the tendency of patricentric thought to focus and
embellish the most abstract and generalizable ideas without respect to context. While
such an assumption might work better in natural sciences than in social sciences, over
time the decontextualisation of abstractions has also been challenged in the so-called
natural "scientific" world, thanks to theories of relativity and "chaos."

10   This initial quote and some of the arguments in this section are also contained in the
1985 paper with Brown on women's community work. This section, however, draws
most heavily from a paper which I wrote and presented to the Association for Women in
Development (AWID) meetings in April 1985. It rethinks wealth from a feminist point
of view and was greeted with considerable excitement (see Christiansen-Ruffman 1987).
In that paper I question some of the assumptions underlying the monetary system and
"development" which have been brought to public attention by Marilyn Waring (1988).
Thinking through that paper helped to convince me that it is not useful, in the long run,
to translate women's work into a crumbling, exploitative, controlling and unsustainable
monetary system. The intensified individualism and economic fundamentalism since
then as well as critiques of the money system (see Kennedy 1995) and exchange (see
Vaughan 1997, 2004) have supported that decision and brought me back to that paper.
In many ways my paper on wealth is an example of what I have called "autonomous
feminist theorizing (see Christiansen-Ruffman 1989), using "women's common sense,"

different assumptions and definitions, feminist analysis and grounded theory to think the world afresh.

11 See, also, Angela Miles's article in this volume, and in particular, page 371 for the text of the statement.

12 As Ngugi wa Thiong'o (1982) points out, the play describes "the double oppression of women. As suppliers of labor in colonies and neo-colonies, they are exploited; and as women they suffer under the weight of male prejudices in both feudalism and imperialism." He also points to "the need to look for both causes and solutions in the social system of how wealth is produced, controlled and shared out" (119). The play was put on by the people's theatre at Kamiriithu Community Education and Cultural Centre, Limuru, Kenya, but it was stopped by Kenyan authorities after ten performances. A second play by the Kamiriithu Theatre was denied a license because the government claimed that, "women were being misled into cultural activities that had nothing to do with development" (Thiong'o 1982: 128). The theatre was seen as teaching politics under the cover of culture. Application for a licence was a procedure introduced in British colonies as a method of vetting and censoring natural cultural expression (Thiong'o 1982: 124). The potential importance of this type of activity for women and development is perhaps underscored by patriarchy's violent response, which, in this case, involved the physical destruction of the theatre building.

13 Unlike Buvinic (1984), this analysis of development projects does not consider them "misbehaving" when they deal with items related to women's community welfare.

14 One important bias implicit in much of patricentric thinking is the institutional bias. In my case, it became especially apparent through a feminist study of politics. I eventually developed an alternative, non-institutional women's definition of politics Its broad, non-institutionalized conception of politics (including a dichotomy broad versus narrow and a discussion of a closeted women's political culture) was required to explain the empirical facts that women were political actors even when they were not part of male-defined political institutions. These insights eventually became part of an analysis of women's community work. Once one began to see women's politics, patricentric views and interpretations appeared particularly biased. See, for example, Christiansen-Ruffman's (1982) critique. As Leslie Brown and I began to explore women's community work, we encountered a similar institutionalized definition. The definition of work needs to be taken out of its institutional context for work, not only for women but for everyone in this new century. Indeed all concepts need to be de-institutionalized and reconceptualized to rid them of their antiquated patriarchal bases at the same time as the antiquated and biased assumptions on which all disciplines rest need to be reconceived.

15 A version of this entire section was previously entitled "Implications for a Conception of Wealth" in the Michigan Working Paper (Christiansen-Ruffman 1987).

16 A comprehensive review of the literature on SAPS and restructuring policies and their general effects on women was conducted with Srabani Maitra for (Christiansen-Ruffman 2001). It found that the overwhelming majority of the studies found negative impacts. The few articles that mentioned some positive benefits tended to focus on the positive benefit to women from women's movement mobilizations in protest to the policies.

17 See Christiansen-Ruffman (1995) for a description of these processes. Although I did not use the word "spin" for the onset of the economic fundamentalism which pervaded public discourse over a decade ago, the concept of spin helps to "make (sociological) sense" of the processes involved at that time (*Spin Cycles*, "Sunday Morning (third hour)," February 2007, Canadian Broadcasting System).

18 There is considerable debate about restructuring and globalization: whether or not they

are new and when the processes began. Generally I agree with Antrobus (2004) that 1980 marks an important date with the emergence of conservative governments in Britain and the United States and the so-called "Washington Consensus," a shift in macro-economic development policies which introduced Structural Adjustment Policies. In Canada, even before that period, some serious cutbacks to social programs began in the mid- to late-1970s with the introduction of food banks as "a temporary measure" because interest rates were in the double digits and accelerating inflation was feared. This threat to human entitlements in Canada has intensified with more recent financial and socio-structural cutbacks such as the repeal of the Canada Assistance Plan. The Canada Social Transfer currently has no standards or guarantees for human entitlements. Major shifts in Canada' macro-economic policies began in the late 1980s with the Free Trade agreements, and in 1995 with the cutbacks to social programs. The website of the Feminist Alliance for International Action (FAFIA) hosts an interesting economic analysis of these cutbacks by Armine Yalnizian (2005). Of particular interest is the argument that the cutbacks in social programs were not necessary and that the debt and deficit would have been reduced in a few years because of falling interest rates and debt financing. See also FAFIA's presentation to the United Nations Committee reviewing Canada's compliance with the Convention on the Elimination of All Forms of Discrimination Against Women and its focus on the ways in which women's lives were worsened by these government policies which created poverty.

19   As I write this, another example of policies that violate Canada's social and economic obligations to fishing families is on the news. Earlier this year, the union of a fish plant went on strike, then the plant owners decided to close the plant for good. The workers now seem to have been abandoned with no legal recourse and no clear source of funds to sustain themselves in this crisis. Instead of acting like a safety net, the federal government announced it would take the case of court, continuing the limbo into which these children, women and men are being pushed. A gifting community approach would first support those individuals in need and then work out later how the bill is to be paid among various levels of government and other institutions.

20   Ideas of transformational changes such as Thomas Kuhn's (1962) idea of a scholarly paradigm shift and the vision of radical feminist alternatives have captured the analytic attention of many feminist scholars. They have often started from different interests and such diverse fields as development (e.g., Jain 1983; DAWN 1985; Sen and Grown 1987); feminist methodologies (e.g., Mies 1983; Maguire 1987; Smith, 1987; Benston 1989); the environment (e.g., Mies and Shiva, 1993); human rights (e.g., Kumar, 1998); mothering (e.g., O'Brien 1981; Vaughan 1997); politics (eg., Miles 1996; Ricciutelli, Miles and McFadden 2004); and peace (e.g., Franklin 2006). They all share a vision of an alternative social world and their work is based on assumptions which share many values associated with women's community gifting. Patricia Madoo Lengermannn and Gillian Niebrugge (c1998/2007) in an analysis of fifteen women founders in sociology and social theory from 1830 to 1930 argue that these women founders were not invisible in their times but were actively written out of North American sociological history (especially pp. 1-21). They also found a remarkable similarity among all of these fifteen women theorists: "[T]he women founders created a range of theories. But those theories all share a moral commitment to the idea that sociology should and could work for the alleviation of socially produced human pain. The ethical duty of the sociologist is to seek sound scientific knowledge, to refuse to make that knowledge an end in itself, to speak for the disempowered, and to advocate social reform.... [I]n key respects the sociology of the women founders is guided by

rules similar to those of contempoprary feminist scholarship that theory and research should be empirically grounded and empowering of the disempowered, that the correct relationship between researcher and subject is one of mutuality of recognition, that the social theorist should reflexively monitor herself as a socially located actor, and that social analysis should build from situated accounts to a general and critical theory of society" (Lengermann and Niebrugge 2007: 19). The characteristics of these early thinkers as analyzed have a striking similarity to those scholars I used as examples above. Further research will examine the extent to which they share similar foundational assumptions with each other and with women's community gifting.

21   The campaign, created by young women, is at www.thewomenareangry.org. It was established in response to measures taken by a "new" (minority) conservative government in Canada. Although Canada ratified the Convention on the Elimination of All Forms of Discrimination Against Women (CEDAW) in 1981, in Fall, 2006 it banned the words "equality," "advocacy," and "research" from the mandate of Status of Women Canada and made cuts to staff and budget. The government's tactics have motivated women's actions and a renewed women's movement may be emerging in Canada, which is also part of women's community work. See Temma Kaplan (1982), Peggy Antrobus (2004), and Luciana Ricciutelli, Angela Miles and Margaret H. McFadden (2004) and the many other books and articles on the change-making community gifting of women's movements around the world. This change-making work is important not only for women but for the society and community as a whole.

References

Antrobus, Peggy. 1983. "Beneath These Ashes Lie Important Truths." A poem for Grenada, personal communication.

Antrobus, Peggy *et al.*, eds. 2002. *Women, Globalization and International Trade.* Special issue *Canadian Woman Studies/les cahiers de la femme* 21/22 (4/1) (Spring/Summer).

Antrobus, Peggy. 2004. *The Global Women's Movement.* London: Zed Books.

Armstrong, P. *et al.*, eds. 2004. *Benefiting Women? Women's Labour Rights.* Special issue *Canadian Woman Studies/les cahiers de la femme* 23 (3,4) (Spring/Summer).

Beard, Mary Ritter. 1972 [1915]. *Women's Work in Municipalities.* New York: Arno Press.

Benston, Margaret. 1989. "Feminism and the Critique of Scientific Method." *Feminism: From Pressure to Politics.* Eds. Angela Miles and Geraldine Finn. Montreal: Black Rose Books.

Berk, Richard and Sarah Fenstermaker Berk. 1979. *Labour and Leisure at Home: Content and Organization of the Household Day.* Beverly Hills: Sage.

Bezanson, Kate. 2006. "Gender and the Limits of Social Capital." *Canadian Review of Sociology and Anthropology* 43 (4) (November): 427-443.

Brown, Leslie and Linda Christiansen-Ruffman. 1985. "Women's Community Work: A Third Part of the Puzzle." Paper was presented at the Women and the Invisible Economy conference, Simone de Beauvoir Institute, Concordia University February 21-23.

Brown, James Robert. 2001. *Who Rules Science? An Opionionated Guide to the Wars.* Cambridge, MA: Harvard University Press.

Buvinic, Mayra. 1984. *Projects for Women in the Third World: Explaining their Misbehavior.* Prepared for the Office of Women in Development, U.S. Agency for International Development. Washington, D.C.: International Center for Research on Women.

Catano, Janis Wood, Janet Rhymes, Stella Lord, Ann Manicom and Linda Christiansen-Ruffman, eds. *Good Policy, Good Health: An Information and Action Kit for Women in Coastal Communities.* Updated second edition. Halifax: Nova Scotia Women's FishNet.

Christiansen-Ruffman, Linda. 1980. "Women as Persons in Atlantic Canadian Communities." *Resources for Feminist Research* (Special Publication) 8: 55-57.

Christiansen-Ruffman, Linda. 1982. "Comment on Lawson and Barton's 'Sex Roles in Social Movements: A Case Study of the Tenant Movement in New York City'." *Signs: Journal of Women in Culture and Society* 8 (Winter): 41-44.

Christiansen-Ruffman, Linda. 1985. "Theories of Participation and the Methodological Construction of Invisible Women: Feminism's Call for Appropriate Methodology." *Journal of Voluntary Action Research* 14 (2 and 3): 382-386.

Christiansen-Ruffman, Linda. 1987. "Wealth Re-Examined: Toward A Feminist Analysis of Women's Development Projects in Canada and in the Third World." Working Paper #140, April Working Papers: Women in International Development Publication Series. East Lansing: Michigan State University.

Christiansen-Ruffman, Linda. 1989. "Inherited Biases Within Feminism: The 'Patricentric Syndrome' and the 'Either/Or Syndrome' in Sociology.'" *Feminism: From Pressure to Politics.* Eds. Angela Miles and Geraldine Finn. Montreal: Black Rose Books. 123-145.

Christiansen-Ruffman, Linda. 1995. "Canada, Social Development and the Debt Crisis: A Feminist Revaluing and Reconstruction." *Development* 1: 41-44.

Christiansen-Ruffman, Linda. 1998. "Developing Feminist Sociological Knowledge: Processes of Discovery." *The Global Feminist Enlightenment: Women and Social Knowledge.* Ed. Linda Christiansen-Ruffman. Madrid/Montreal: International Sociological Association, 13-36.

Christiansen-Ruffman, Linda. 2001. "Feminism, Globalization and Inequality." Plenary paper presented at the Equality and Globalization Conference, The First Regional Conference of the International Sociological Association in Latin America, Margarita Island, Venezuela, May 7-11.

Christiansen-Ruffman, Linda. 2002. "Atlantic Canadian Coastal Communities and the Fisheries Trade: A Feminist Critique, Revaluation and Revisioning." *Canadian Woman Studies/les cahiers de la femme* 21/22 (4,1) (Spring/Summer): 56-63.

Christiansen-Ruffman, Linda. 2004. "The Gift Economy in Atlantic Canada." *The Gift/Il Dono: A Feminist Analysis. Athanor: Semiotica, Filosofia, Arte, Letteratura* 15 (8). Ed. Genevieve Vaughan. Roma: Meltemi Editore. 283-291.

Christiansen-Ruffman, Linda, Paola Melchiori and Berit Ås. 2006. *Portraits of Women's Wisdom: Feminists Exploring New Paradigms in Life, Knowledge and Politics.* Milan: Wise Women International Feminist University Network.

Christiansen-Ruffman, Linda, Ruth Hafter, Faith Chao, Wendy Katz and Helen Ralston. 1975. *Women's Concerns About the Quality of Life in the Halifax Metropolitan Area.* Report presented to Canada's Ministry of State for Urban Affairs. Halifax: Saint Mary's University.

Development Alternatives With Women (DAWN). 1985. *Women and Development: An Assessment and Future Visions.* Draft papers prepared for series of workshops in Nairobi, UN Conference on Development Alternatives with Women, Institute of Social studies Trust, New Delhi, India.

Faraday, Fay, Margaret Denike, and M. Kate Stephenson (ed). 2006. *Making Equality Rights Real: Securing Substantive Equality Under the Charter.* Toronto: Irwin Law.

Feree, Myra Marx. 1985. "Between Two Worlds: German Feminist Approaches to Working-Class Women and Work." *Signs: Journal of Women in Culture and Society* 10 (3) (Spring): 517-36.

Ford-Smith, Honor. 1980. "Sistren: Women, the Arts and Jamaican Society." Unpublished paper.

Ford-Smith, Honor. 1986. "Sistren: Exploring Women's Problems through Drama." *Jamaica Journal* 19 (1) (February-April): 2-12.

Franklin, Ursula M. 2006. *The Ursula Franklin Reader: Pacifism as a Map.* Toronto: Between the Lines.

Gittell, Marilyn and Teresa Shtob. 1980. "Changing Women's Roles in Political Volunteerism and Reform of the City." *Signs: Journal of Women in Culture and Society* 5 (3) (Spring Supplement): s67-78.

Goldsmith, Raymond W. 1968. "National Wealth: Estimation." *International Encyclopedia of the Social Sciences.* Vol. 11. New York: Macmillan and Free Press.

Graham, Hilary. 1983. "Caring: A Labour of Love." *A Labour of Love: Women, Work and Caring.* Eds. Janet Finch and D. Groves. London: Routledge and Kegan Paul.

Hale, Sylvia M. 1985. "Integrating Women in Development Models and Theories." Paper presented at Conference on Women and Development, St. Thomas University, Fredericton, New Brunswick, Canada, January 19.

Hochschild, Arlie Russell. 1983. *The Managed Heart: Commercialization of Human Feeling.* Berkeley: University of California Press.

Jain, Devaki. 1983. "Development as if Women Mattered or Can Women Build a New Paradigm?" Lecture delivered at OECD/DAC meeting, Paris. New Delhi: Institute of Social Studies Trust.

Johnson, Leo. 1974. "The Political Economy of Ontario Women in the Nineteenth Century." *Women at Work, Ontario, 1850-1930.* Eds. Janice Acton, Penny Goldsmith and Bonnie Shepard. Toronto: Canadian Women's Educational Press (13-32).

Kahn-Hut, Rachel, Arlene Kaplan Daniels and Richard Colvard, eds. 1982. *Women and Work: Problems and Perspectives.* New York. Oxford University Press.

Kaplan, Temma. 1982. "Female Consciousness and Collective Action: The Case of Barcelona, 1910-1918." *Signs: Journal of Women in Culture and Society* 7:(3) (Spring): 545-566.

Kelly, Joan. "Early Feminist Theory and the Querelle des Femmes, 1400-1789." *Signs: Journal of Women in Culture and Society* 8 (1): 4-28.

Kennedy, Margrit. 1995. *Interest and Inflation Free Money: Creating an Exchangne Medium That Works for Eveybody and Protects the Earth.* Piladelphia: New Society Publishers.

Kertzer, David I. 1982. "The Liberation of Evelina Zaghi: The Life of an Italian Communist." *Signs* 8 (1): 45-67.

Kome, Penney. 1983. *The Taking of Twenty-Eight: Women Challenge the Constitution.* Toronto: The Women's Press.

Kumar, Corinne. 1998. "South Wind: On the Universality of the Human Rights Discourse." Unpublished paper.

Kuhn, Thomas. 1962. *The Structure of Scientific Revolutions.* Chicago: University of Chicago Press.

Leath, Jo. 2001. "World Rural Women's Day: Front-line Feminism in the Village." *Rural Womyn Zone* News November 14: 1-2.

Lengermann, Patricia Madoo and Gillian Niebrugge. 2007 [1998]. *The Women Founders: Sociology and Social Theory 1830-1930, A Text/Reader.* Long Grove, IL: Waveland Press.

Luxton, Meg. 1980. *More Than a Labour of Love: Three Generations of Women's Work in the Home.* Toronto: Women's Educational Press.

Maguire, Patricia. 1987. *Doing Participatory Research: A Feminist Approach.* Amherst, Mass: The Center for International Education, University of Massachusetts.

Matthews, Ralph. 1976. *There's No Better Place Than Here: Social Change in Three Newfoundland Communities.* Toronto: Peter Martin.

Merton, Robert K. 1957. *Social Theory and Social Structure.* Revised and enlarged edition. Glencoe, IL: Free Press.

Mies, Maria. 1983. "Towards a Methodology for Feminist Research." *Theories of Women's*

Studies. Eds. Gloria Bowles and Renate Duelli Klein. Boston: Routledge and Kegan Paul. 117-139.

Mies, Maria. 1998. "Decolonizing the Iceberg Economy: New Feminist Concepts for a Sustainable Society." *The Global Feminist Enlightenment: Women and Social Knowledge.* Ed. Linda Christiansen-Ruffman. Madrid/Montreal: International Sociological Association. 75-90.

Mies, Maria and Vandana Shiva. 1993. *Ecofeminism.* London: Zed.

Miles, A. 1996. *Integrative Feminisms: Building Global Visions, 1960s-1990s.* New York and London, Routledge.

Miles, Angela and Geraldine Finn, eds. 1989. *Feminism: From Pressure to Politics.* Montreal: Black Rose Books.

Mills, C. Wright. 1961. *The Sociological Imagination.* New York: Grove Press.

Neuman, W. Lawrence. 2006. *Social Research Methods: Qualitative and Quantitative Approaches.* 6th edition. Boston: Pearson, Allyn and Bacon.

O'Brien, Mary. 1981. *The Politics of Reproduction.* London: Routledge.

Randall, Melanie. 2006. "Equality Rights and the Charter: Reconceptualizing State Accountability for Ending Domestic Violence." *Making Equality Rights Real: Securing Substantive Equality under the Charter.* Eds. Fay Faraday, Margaret Denike and M. Kate Stephenson. Toronto: Irwin Law. 275-317.

Ricciutelli, Luciana, Angela Miles and Margaret H. McFadden, eds. 2004. *Feminist Politics, Activism and Vision: Local and Global Challenges.* Toronto/London: Inanna/Zed.

Samuelson, Paul A. and Anthony Scott. 1980. *Economics.* Fifth Canadian edition. Toronto: McGraw-Hill Ryerson.

Smith, Dorothy. 1987. *The Everyday World as Problematic: A Feminist Sociology.* Toronto: University of Toronto Press.

Spender, Dale ed. 1981a. *Men's Studies Modified: The Impact of Feminism on the Academic Disciplines.* Oxford: Pergamon Press.

Spender, Dale. 1981b. "The Gatekeepers: a Feminist Critique of Academic Publishing. *Doing Feminist Research.* Ed. Helen Roberts. 186-202. London: Routledge and kegan Paul.

Sen, Gita and Grown, Caren. 1987. *Development, Crises, and Alternative Visions: Third World Women's Perspectives.* New York: Monthly Review Press.

Thiong'o, Ngugi wa. 1982. "Women in Cultural Work: The Fate of Kamiriithu People's Theatre in Kenya." *Development Dialogue* 1-2: 51-64.

Trofimenkoff, Susan Mann. 1984. Public Lecture at Mount Saint Vincent University, Halifax, Nova Scotia.

Vaughan, Genevieve. 1997. *For-Giving: A Feminist Criticism of Exchange.* Austin, TX: Plainview/Anomaly Press.

Vaughan, Genevieve, ed. 2004. *Il Dono/The Gift: A Feminist Analysis. Athanor: Semiotica, Filosofia, Arte, Letteratura* 15 (8). Roma: Meltemi Editore.

Vickers, Jill McCalla. 1989. "Memoirs of an Ontological Exile: the Methodological Rebellions of Feminist Research." *Feminism: From Pressure to Politics.* Eds. Angela Miles and Geraldine Finn. Montreal: Black Rose Books. 37-56.

Waring, Marilyn. 1988. *If Women Counted: A New Feminist Economics.* San Francisco: Harper and Row.

Werlhof, Claudia von. 1984. "The Proletarian is Dead: Long Life the Housewife?" *Households and the World Economy.* Eds. Joan Smith, Immanuel Wallerstein and Hans-Dieter Ever. Beverly Hills: Sage. 131-147.

Yalnizyan, Armine. 2005. *Assessing the Federal Budget 2005: What's In It for Women?* Ottawa: Canadian Feminist Alliance for International Action (FAFIA). Online: www.fafia-afai.org.

IV. GIFT GIVING
FOR SOCIAL TRANSFORMATION

MILILANI TRASK

Indigenous Women and Traditional Knowledge

Reciprocity is the Way of Balance

I. Reciprocity

Reciprocity is a fundamental value of the gift economy. It is also a fundamental cornerstone of Indigenous communities. Reciprocity implies that there is an ebb and flow in relationships, a give and take. Reciprocity infers that there is a mutual sharing, something given for something taken.

In Indigenous societies, reciprocity is the way things work—in society, within the family and extended family frameworks, and in the relationships between human kind and the rest of God's creation. Reciprocity is not defined or limited by the language of the market economy because it implies that more is owed than financial payment, when goods and services exchange hands. Reciprocity is the way of balance—planting precedes harvesting, sowing precedes reaping. In most Indigenous societies there is a common understanding (sometimes referred to as the "original instructions"), that humankind's role in the world is to be the guardians of the creation. Indigenous peoples know that if we care for, nurture, and protect the earth, it will feed, clothe, and shelter us.

II. Market Economics and the Gift Economy

The gift economy is diametrically opposed to the market economy. The Gift Economy is collective, the market economy favours individualism. The Gift Economy thrives when there is a bounty to be given. The market economy increases the price and fiscal value of items that are rare commodities. The values, activities, and outcomes of these diametrically opposed economic systems also conflict.

Capitalism/Globalization

Values: consumption/individualism
Activities: production and marketing/allocation based on ability to pay/buy
Results: profit and debt /polarized development of the wealthy versus the poor
Practice: secularization.

Gift Economy/Indigenous Communities

Values: sustainability, preservation/collectivism, social obligation
Activities: gifting, exchange/allocation based on need
Results: community development and advancement
Practice: spiritualism.

III. Indigenous Women and Traditional Knowledge

In all Indigenous cultures, gender roles and responsibilities flow from and are part of a broader socio-cultural environment. That is to say that Indigenous peoples and societies delineate between the roles which women and men assume based on the cultural protocols and survival needs of their collective society (Cohen 1999). The essential feature of a peoples' socio-cultural environment is "meaning." As Walter Rochs Goldschmidt (1990) states:

> Each culture provides pathways by which individuals may satisfy their needs for positive affect, prestige and meaning. Small-scale, hunting-gathering societies provide several such pathways: excellence in hunting or story-telling or as a healer. More complex societies offer a greater array of "careers." Whatever its size, complexity or environment, a central task of any culture is to provide its members with a sense of meaning and purpose in the world."

"Gender" is a sociological concept that encompasses economic, social, and cultural distinctions between women and men as manifested in their differing roles, authority, and cultural undertaking.

In recent times there has developed an understanding that gender roles in Indigenous cultures establish who in that society (male or female) is the keeper of traditional knowledge. In traditional societies women are the keepers of certain knowledge systems and make use of different resources than those used by men. Where women might gather healing herbs or edible fruits from trees, men would more likely be employed in the timber industry.

For several years, the Food and Agriculture Organization of the United Nations (FAO) has explored the relationship between gender and food security, agro-biodiversity, and sustainable development. FAO's research and development projects have documented the important role that Indigenous women play in these three critical areas. FAO's (1999) findings are as follows:

> 1. Through their different activities and management practices, men and women have often developed different expertise and knowledge about the local environment, plant and animal species and their products and uses. These gender-differentiated local knowledge systems play a decisive role in the in situ conservation, management, and improvement of genetic resources for food and agriculture. It is clear that the decision about what to conserve

depends on the knowledge and perception of what is most useful to the household and local community.

2. Women's and men's specialized knowledge of the value and diverse use of domesticated crop species and varieties extends to wild plants that are used as food in times of need or as medicines and sources of income. This local knowledge is highly sophisticated and is traditionally shared and handed down between generations. Through experience, innovation, and experimentation, sustainable practices are developed to protect soil, water, natural vegetation, and biological diversity. This has important implications for the conservation of plant genetic resources.

3. Through their daily work, rural women have accumulated intimate knowledge of their ecosystems, including the management of pests, the conservation of soil, and the development and use of plant and animal genetic resources.

4. It is estimated that up to 90 percent of the planting material used by poor farmers is derived from seeds and germplasm that they have produced, selected, and saved themselves. This means that small farmers play a crucial role in the preservation and management of plant genetic resources and biodiversity.

5. In smallholder agriculture, women farmers are largely responsible for the selection, improvement, and adaptation of plant varieties. In many regions, women are also responsible for the management of small livestock, including their reproduction. Women often have a more highly specialized knowledge of wild plants used for food, fodder and medicine than men.

The critical role which Indigenous women play in maintaining biodiversity, conservation, and promoting sustainable development is acknowledged in two international instruments and the action plan of the FAO. The Convention on Biological Diversity (1993) and FAO's *Global Plan of Action for the Conservation and Sustainable Utilization of Plant Genetic Resources for Food and Agriculture* (1996a) acknowledge the role played by generations of men and women farmers and by Indigenous communities in conserving and improving plant genetic resources.

Two key objectives of Chapter 24 of *Agenda 21*: *The Rio Declaration on Environment and Development* (UNCED 1992) are to promote the traditional methods and the knowledge of Indigenous people and their communities, emphasizing the particular role of women relevant to the conservation of biological diversity and the sustainable use of biological resources and to ensure the participation of Indigenous women and peoples in the economic and commercial benefits derived from the use of such traditional methods and knowledge.

The Convention on Biological Diversity and the FAO *Global Plan* also affirm the need for women to participate fully in conservation programs and at all levels of policy making.

Despite these legal pronouncements and the existence of other international instruments that specifically prohibit discrimination against women (such as the Convention on the Elimination of all Forms of Discrimination Against Women [CEDAW] and the Draft Declaration on the Rights of Indigenous Peoples), Indigenous women continue to be marginalized and excluded from policy making and program services.

FAO (1999) reports the following:

> … [L]ittle has yet been done to clarify the nature of the relationship between agro-biological diversity and the activities, responsibilities, and rights of men and women. Women's key roles, responsibilities, and intimate knowledge of plants and animals sometimes remain "invisible" to technicians working in the agriculture, forestry and environmental sectors, as well as to planners and policy-makers.
>
> The lack of recognition at technical and institutional levels means that women's interests and demands are given inadequate attention. Moreover, women's involvement in formalized efforts to conserve biodiversity is slight because of widespread cultural barriers to women's participation in decision-making arenas at all levels.
>
> Modern research and development and centralized plant breeding have ignored and, in some cases, undermined the capacities of local farming communities to modify and improve plant varieties. With the introduction of modern technologies and agricultural practices, women have lost substantial influence and control over production and access to resources, whereas men often benefit more from extension services and have the ability to buy seeds, fertilizers and the necessary technologies.

FAO's conclusions in this area are verified by the work of the LinKS Project in Africa:

> For a long time, despite an increased recognition at the international level, the importance of local knowledge and gender in agriculture has been neglected in policies and development programs related to agriculture and natural resource management. Modern research, science, and national policies undermine even further the capacities of local farming communities to sustain and manage agro-biodiversity and secure food production. In this context, contributions that bring farmers' perspectives, their practice and knowledge of biodiversity into focus are important for a constructive policy dialogue on sustainable management of natural resources.

It is clear that sexism, racism, and poverty operate in the United Nations System and broader civil society to marginalize Indigenous women. These negative forces need to be acknowledged and addressed as a matter of urgency and as a high priority because of the nexus between women's traditional knowledge and their role in maintaining biodiversity and ensuring food security.

IV. Countering Globalization

The foundation of globalization is and will continue to be the commercialization of knowledge and data and the commodification of knowledge and the life forms relating to that knowledge.

The primary elements of the information society are knowledge, information (data) and communication. Information and communication technologies (ICTs) are the transmission instruments used by modern technological states and corporations to further communication in all areas including economic and social development, health, education and security.

Traditional knowledge is the basis of all Indigenous cultures. Indigenous concepts and practices relating to knowledge have evolved for centuries and are defined by the socio-cultural environment of each distinct culture. In Indigenous cultures, gender roles and responsibilities determine who is the keeper of certain knowledge systems and how the knowledge is maintained and transmitted within specific cultural contexts. Most Indigenous cultures follow strict cultural protocols for the sharing and dissemination of knowledge and for communications in general.

In addition, there is a direct relationship between Indigenous knowledge and traditional land rights. The Forum Expert paper prepared by Marcos Alonso (2003) states:

> As for Indigenous Peoples, the generation, transmission, and preservation of knowledge is inextricably linked to their continuing relationship and interaction with knowledge from generation to generation in their own way.
> Traditional knowledge not only contains the history of a people, but also provides the basis for all customs, traditions, and practices like traditional agriculture or medicine. It is holistic in nature and sets a blueprint for proper relationships between humans as a well as between humans and non-humans, such as plants and animals. In summary, it is a core element of the identity of an Indigenous People.
> It is only through maintaining and strengthening their distinctive traditional relationship with their lands, waters, coastal seas, and related natural environments that Indigenous Peoples will be able to save their existing knowledge and to secure the flourishing of its development. Only then, Indigenous Peoples will be in a position to share their traditional knowledge on their own terms.

In Indigenous societies knowledge is carefully guarded and often considered "sacred, secret or gender bound." It is customary with Indigenous peoples who follow an oral tradition that the transmission of knowledge may require years of mentoring, as well as ceremonial undertakings. In Indigenous societies knowledge is the inheritance of the living and the legacy they will leave to further generations.

By contrast, knowledge in the globalized context, is viewed as a valuable economic commodity that should be freely available to anybody wishing to utilize or commercialize it. Western intellectual property law favours the practice of commodification, reserving exclusive use for a short period of 20 years. In the globalized world, the underlying practice is to view knowledge as a commodity in the public domain.

Given the situation, it is no wonder that Indigenous peoples are in conflict with and oppose state and private sector efforts to obtain traditional knowledge. Indigenous peoples often view scientific and economic research and development as the theft of Indigenous intellectual property and bio-piracy.

Indigenous peoples assert that their traditional knowledge systems are their cultural property and that they should have the right to control the use and application of their knowledge whether for commercial or non-commercial purposes. In addition, Indigenous people are undertaking efforts to establish *sui generis* systems for protection of their intellectual property while resisting efforts of transnational corporations-pharmaceuticals to copyright traditional medicinal knowledge and patent life forms. There are increasing examples of the unauthorized and inappropriate use of traditional knowledge and there is significant evidence that corporate and state actors are intent upon appropriating not only Indigenous knowledge but Indigenous sciences and technologies including human and other genetic resources.

IV. Globalization and Poverty

The privatization of life, through the western intellectual property regime has resulted in the earth's bounty being appropriated in the private property of a few individual shareholders and their transnational corporations. The result has been expanding poverty in all regions of the world and an extreme imbalance in the consumptive practices of the developed North. Today, the United State consumes 80 percent of the earth's resources including food, services, commodities, and natural gas and oil. In comparison the developing south, continues to live in extreme poverty and while supplying their natural resources, labor, goods and food to the north, this imbalance is maintained by the multilateral and bilateral trade regimes and international financiers such as the World Bank.

International efforts to address the phenomena of growing global poverty through the UN Millennium Development Goals (MDG) have proven ineffective because the standard of poverty is linked to the U.S. dollar. Under this approach, people live in extreme poverty if they earn less than $1.20 a day (USD). This standard ignores the fact that real poverty is measured by starvation, hunger, landlessness, ill health, and the inability of people and communities to access land and resources needed for their survival. Despite the fact that the UN Special Rapportuers on

Extreme Poverty and the United Nations Permanent Forum on Indigenous Issues have called for the definition of extreme poverty to be changed, no action has been taken by the UN System and states to change either the rule of globalized trade or the definition of poverty.

The gift economy provides a workable alternative to globalization and a realistic and achievable approach to poverty. Most importantly, the gift economy is people and community based (see Vaughan 1997). For the developed North it means that people can choose to change their consumptive practices, to do with less, and to boycott goods and products that do not meet the standard of fair trade. Our own consumptive practices drive the market economy and the phenomenon of globalization. By returning to gifting and practicing reciprocity between peoples and among nations, we will be able to significantly impact poverty in the South. Indigenous peoples have a role to play in this humanitarian undertaking. By sharing and gifting to others, our traditional knowledge relating to the sustainable use of the earth's resources and the application of culturally appropriate technologies and practices, Indigenous people can demonstrate to others the path of balance and equitable sharing

IV. Conclusion

If we are to press for a paradigm shift—towards the gift economy and away from market capitalism—we must be involved in and support the efforts of Indigenous women and their communities to protect traditional knowledge and Indigenous intellectual property and oppose the patenting of life forms. The copyrighting of knowledge privatizes the lessons learned and the benefits arising from that knowledge. The patenting of life forms means that a few will own the bounty needed to feed and cloth the world. The gift economy requires that the bounty be part of the commons of all human kind and that human beings, as the guardians of the earth and each other, must ensure the equitable sharing of benefits so that all may share in the gifts of the Creator.

Mililani Trask is a Native Hawaiian attorney with an extensive background on Native Hawaiian land trusts, resources, and legal entitlements. Her work has been cited by the Hawaii Advisory Committee to the U.S. Commission on Civil Rights and published by Cultural Survival *and* IWGIA *Magazines on issues relating to Native people and human and civil rights. In October 1993, Ms. Trask was invited to become a member of the prestigious Indigenous Initiative for Peace (IIP), a global body of Indigenous leaders convened by Nobel Laureate Rigoberta Menchu-Tum, the United Nations Goodwill Ambassador to the UN Decade on Indigenous Peoples. Since that time, Ms. Trask has worked in the global arena for passage of the United Nations Declaration on the Rights of Indigenous Peoples. In this respect, Ms. Trask attended and participated in the United National Global Consultations in Cairo, Beijing, Copenhagen and Vienna as a Pacific Delegate to the Indigenous caucus. She is a founding member and current Chair of the Indigenous Women's Network, a coalition of Native American*

Women whose work includes community based economic development, social justice, human rights, housing and health.

References

Alonso, Marcos. 2003, 31 October. Forum Expert Paper. Doc. WSIS.

Cohen, Alex. 1999. *The Mental Health of Indigenous Peoples: An International Overview.* Geneva: Department of Mental Health, World Health Organization. WHO/MNH/NAM/99.1.

Convention on Biological Diversity. 1993, 29 December. Online: http://www.biodiv.org/convention/default.shtml.

Food and Agriculture Organization of the United Nations (FAO). nd. *LinKS Project - Gender, Biodiversity and Local Knowledge Systems for Food Security.* Online: http://www.fao.org/sd/links/home/prima.html.

Food and Agriculture Organization of the United Nations (FAO). 1989. *Conference Resolution 5/89, 25ᵗʰ Session of the FAO Conference.* Rome, 11-29 November.

Food and Agriculture Organization of the United Nations (FAO). 1993. *World Watch List for Domestic Animal Diversity.* Eds. R. Loftus and B. Schert. Rome: Author.

Food and Agriculture Organization of the United Nations (FAO). 1996a. *Global Plan of Action for the Conservation and Sustainable Utilization of Plant Genetic Resources for Food and Agriculture* and *The Leipzig Declaration.* Online: http://www.fao.org/ag/agp/agps/gpaen/gpatoc.htm.

Food and Agriculture Organization of the United Nations (FAO). 1996b. *Harvesting Nature's Diversity.* Rome: Author. Online: http://www.fao.org/DOCREP/004/V1430E/V1430E00.htm.

Food and Agriculture Organization of the United Nations (FAO). 1999. *Women: Users, Preservers and Managers of Agrobiodiversity.* First version. Rome: Women in Development Service, FAO Women and Population Division. Online: http://www.fao.org/sd/nrm/Women%20-%20Users.pdf.

Goldschmidt, Walter Rochs. 1990. *The Human Career: The Self in the Symbolic World.* Cambridge, MA: Blackwell.

International Board for Plan Genetic Resources (IBPGR). 1991. *Geneflow: A Publication About the Earth's Plant Genetic Resources.* Rome: Author.

United Nations Conference on Environment and Development (UNCED). 1992. *Agenda 21: The Rio Declaration on Environment and Development.* New York: United Nations Department of Economic and Social Affairs, Division for Sustainable Development. Online: http://www.un.org/esa/sustdev/documents/agenda21/index.htm.

Vaughan, Genevieve. 1997. *For-Giving: A Feminist Criticism of Exchange.* Austin, TX: Plainview/Anomaly Pres..

CORINNE KUMAR

Supryia and the Reviving of a Dream

Toward a New Political Imaginary

1. Introduction

Let me tell you a story:
a story of women, of their creative survival,
a story of timeless care,
a story of the gift imaginary :

It is a story from Tagore on the *Riches of the Poor*.

Once upon a long ago and of yesterday
it was a *time of darkness*;
it was also a time of famine that was devastating the land of *Shravasti*
people gathered; poor people, hungry people:
Lord Buddha looking at everybody and asked his disciples
who will feed these people? who will care for them?
who will feed these hungry people?
he looked at Ratnaka the banker, waiting for an answer:
Ratnaka, looked down and said
but much more than all the wealth I have would be needed
to feed these hungry people
Buddha than turned to Jaysen, who was the chief of the King's army:
Jaysen said very quickly *of course my Lord I would give you my life*
but there is not enough food in my house.
then, it was the turn of Dharampal who possessed large pastures
sighed and said the *god of the wind has dried out our fields*
and I do not know how I shall even pay the king's taxes.

The people listened, and were so hungry:
Supriya, the beggar's daughter was in the gathering, listening too
as she raised her hand, she stood up and said
I will nourish these people: I will care for the people
everybody turned to look at Supriya:

how would she they thought do this? How will she, a beggar's daughter with no
material wealth, how would she accomplish her wish?
but how will you do this, they chorused:
Supriya gentle and strong looked at the gathering and said
It is true that I am the poorest among you, but therein is
my strength, my treasure, my affluence, because I will find
all this at each of your doors.

Supriya's words and actions come from *another logic*: she refuses the logic of property,
profit, patriarchy; inviting us to another *ethic of care*, of concern, of connectedness.
She sees the poor as a *community of people* with *dignity* in a relational way, not
as individual separate units; and speaks for the many all over the world who are
challenging the totalitarism logic of the master imaginary and trying to re-find
and re-build communities, regenerating people's knowledges and cosmovisions,
reviving the dream for us all.

2.

We live in violent times: times in which our community and collective memo-
ries are dying; times in which the many dreams are turning into never-ending
nightmares; and the future increasingly fragmenting; times that are collapsing
the many life visions into a *single cosmology* that has created its own *universal
truths*—equality, development, peace; truths that are inherently discriminatory,
even violent. Times that have created a development model that dispossesses the
majority, desacralizes nature, destroys cultures and civilizations, denigrates the
women. Times in which the war on terrorism a la Pax Americana brings a time
of violent uncertainty—brutal wars for resources—oil, diamonds, minerals: wars
of Occupation state terrorism going global, patented by the USA, franchised by
the CIA to nation states all over the world, times that are giving us new words:
*pre-emptive strike, collateral damage, embedded journalism, enemy combatants,
military tribunals, rendition;* new words: *words soaked in blood*. Times in which the
dominant political thinking, institutions and instruments of justice are hardly able
to redress the *violence* that is escalating, and *intensifying*; times in which *progress*
presupposes the *genocide* of the many; times in which human rights have come
to mean the rights of the privileged, the rights of the powerful; times in which
the *political spaces* for the other is diminishing, even *closing*.

The world, it would seem, is at the end of its imagination.

Only the imagination stands between us and fear: fear makes us behave like
sheep when we should be dreaming like poets.

Let me tell you another story, a story of horror and hope, a story of the missing,
the disappeared; a story so real, yet magical: a story from Lawrence Thornton in
Imagining Argentina (1987).

It is a story about Argentina under the dictators. The hero is a gentle person,
Carlos Rueda, an intense man who directs a children's theatre and is at home in

the world of children. During the time of the dictators, Carlos discovers that he has an extraordinary gift. He realizes that he is the site, the locus, *the vessel for a dream*. He can narrate the fate of the missing. From all over Argentina, men and women come to his home and sitting in his garden, Carlos tells them stories: tales of torture, courage, death, stories about the missing, about the *disappeared*.

One day the regime arrests his wife Celia, for a courageous act of reporting. The world of Carlos collapses till he realizes that he must keep her alive in his imagination.*Only the imagination, says Carlos, stands between us and fear; fear makes us behave like sheep when we must dream like poets.*

As the regime becomes more violent, it is the women who object. It is the women as wives, as mothers, as daughters who congregate in silence at the *Plaza de Mayo*. Silently, each carries a placard announcing or asking about the *missing*. The women walk quietly, sometimes holding hands.

It is not just an act of protest; it is *a drama of caring*; each listening to the other's story, each assuring the other through touch, weaving a sense of community.

The community grows as the men join them. All the while, through the window, the Generals watch them.

People realize that they cannot be indifferent observers, spectators, bystanders, *even experts*. The indifference of the watchers to the regime is not enough. One must be a witness. A witness is not a mere spectator. S/he *looks* but she also *listens*. S/he *remembers*.

Everything must be remembered. Nothing must be forgotten. We must retrieve history from memory

We must explore the new imaginary not as experts but as witnesses.

The Mothers of the Plaza Mayo, in Argentina express this new imaginary.

3.

Our imaginaries must be different. The new imaginary cannot have its moorings in the dominant discourse but must seek to locate itself in a *discourse of dissent* that comes from a deep critique of the different forms of domination and violence in our times: any new imaginary cannot be tied to the dominant discourse and systems of violence and exclusion.

This new imaginary will move away from the eurocentric and androcentric methodologies which only observe and describe; methodologies which quantify, percentify, classify, completely indifferent to phenomena which cannot be obtained or explained through its frames. We need to deconstruct the dominant mythology, disallowing the invasion of the dominant discourse; refusing the integration of the *South* into the agenda of globalization and the war on terrorism. The new imaginary invites us to create a new spectrum of methods which depart from the linear mode of thought and perception to one that is more *holistic, holographic*. It urges us to search more qualitative methodologies in oral history, experiential analysis, using fluid categories, *listening for the nuances, searching for the shadow*, in poetry, in myth, in metaphor. It invites us to a way of knowing that refuses to control and exploit Nature, but one that finds our *connectedness to Nature:* to place together these fragments, to discern the essence, to move into another space, another time, recapturing hidden knowledges, regenerating forgotten spaces, refinding other cosmologies, reweaving the future. It is here perhaps, that the notion of the sacred survives; it is here in the cosmologies and rootedness of cultures; here in discarded knowledges of peoples on the peripheries here in the silenced wisdoms of women that we must seek the beginnings of *an alternate discourse.*

It is not difficult to see that we are at the end of an era, when every old category begins to have a hollow sound, and when we are groping in the dark to discover the new. Can we find new words, search new ways, create out of the material of the human spirit *possibilities* to transform the existing exploitative social order, to discern a greater human potential?

What we need in the world today are new universalisms; not universalisms that deny the many and affirm the one, not universalisms born of eurocentricities or patriarchalities; but universalisms *that recognize the universal in the specific civilizational idioms in the world.* Universalisms that will not deny the accumulated experiences and knowledges of past generations and that will not accept the imposition of any monolithic structures under which it is presumed all other peoples must be subsumed. New universalisms that will challenge the universal mode—militarization, nuclearism, war, patriarchy. Universalisms that will respect the plurality of the different societies, of their philosophy, of their ideology, their traditions and cultures; one that will be rooted in the particular, in the *vernacular,* one which will find a resonance in the different civilizations, *birthing new cosmologies.*

We need to imagine alternative perspectives for change: to craft visions that will evolve out of conversations across cultures and other traditions; conversations between cultures that challenge and transcend the totalitarianism of the western logos; conversations that are not mediated by the hegemony of the *universal discourse.*

The new imaginary invites us to another human rights discourse; one that will not be trapped either in the *universalisms* of the dominant thinking tied as it is to a market economy, a monoculturalism, a materialistic ethic and the politics and polity of the nation state; neither must it be caught in the discourse of the *culture specific* but one that will proffer universalisms that have been born out of a *dialogue of civilizations.* And this will mean another *ethic of dialogue.* We need to find new perspectives on the universality of human rights: *in dialogue with other cultural perspectives of reality,* other notions of development, democracy, even dissent, other concepts of power (not power to control, power to hegemonize, but power to facilitate, to enhance) and governance; other notions of equality; equality makes us flat and faceless citizens of the nation state, perhaps the notion of *dignity* which comes from depth, from *roots,* could change the discourse: other concepts of justice—*justice without revenge,* justice with truth and reconciliation, *justice with healing* of individuals, of communities, because *human kind proffers many horizons of discourse* and because our eyes do not as yet behold those horizons, it does not mean that those horizons do not exist.

Take the *universal* discourse on *democracy*: the new magical word to *reform* the world, the Greater Middle East: the dominant understanding on democracy is tied to the notion of individual rights, private property, profit, the *market economy*; we are all equal we are told but the market works as the *guarantor of inequality*, of unequal distribution, of how only a few will have and how the many must not have. What shall we do with the rhetoric of political equality on which this democracy is built, while the majority are increasingly dispossessed, living below poverty lines? We must seek new understandings of democracy; that will include a concept of freedom that is different from that which is enshrined in the Enlightenment and its Market. There is an urgent need to reinvent the political; to *infuse the political with the ethical: the new political imaginary speaks to an ethic of care.*

In 1996, Madeleine Albright the then U.S. Secretary of State was asked what she felt about the 500,000 Iraqi children who had died as a result of U.S. economic sanctions (in the name of United Nations Security Council). In the context of the continuing war, was it a high price to pay? Was it worth it? She replied: "*yes, all things considered, we think that the price is worth it.*" Lives of children lost in wars are considered *collateral damage.*

In the world of rights we all are equal; each has the fundamental *right to life.* But what does the right to life mean to the genetically damaged children born all over the world because of depleted uranium? Depleted uranium that was used in wars in Bosnia, Kosovo, Afghanistan, and in Iraq for this generation, and for the generations to come.

The new political imaginary invites us to write another history: *a counter hegemonic history*, a history of the margins. It is a journey of the margins: a journey rather than an imagined destination. A journey in which the daily-ness of our life proffers possibilities for our imaginary, survival, and sustenance; for connectedness and community. For the idea of imaginary is inextricably linked to the personal, political, and historical dimensions of community and identity. It is the dislocation expressed by particular social groups that makes possible the articulation of new imaginaries. These social groups, the margins, the global South, *the South in the North*, the *South in the South*, are beginning to articulate these *new imaginaries.*

The peasants in Chiapas, Mexico, describing their *new imaginary* explain their core vision in their struggle for their livelihoods and for retaining their life worlds. And in their profound and careful organization, in their political imagining and vision do not offer clear, rigid, universal truths ; knowing that the journey is in itself precious, sum up their vision in three little words: *asking, we walk.*

The asking in itself *challenges master imaginaries, master narratives*, masters' houses, houses of reason; universal truths, of power, of politics, of patriarchy. The Zapatistas in offering another logic, draw the contours of this new imaginary.

The new political imaginary invites us to *dismantle the master's house*; and as the poet, Audre Lorde said, the *master's tools will never dismantle the master's house.* There is an urgent need to challenge the centralizing logic of the master narrative implicit in the dominant discourses of war, of security, of human rights, of democracy. This dominant logic is a logic of violence and *exclusion,* a logic of developed and underdeveloped, a logic of superior and inferior, *a logic of civilized and uncivilized*.

This centralizing logic must be decentered, must be interrupted, even disrupted. The new political imaginary speaks to this disruption; to this trespass.

4.

It is a disruption of the dominant discourse and the dominant politics of our times and Public Hearings, Peoples Tribunals, Courts of Women are all expressions of people's resistance: expressions of the new imaginary that is finding different ways of speaking *Truth* to *Power*, recognizing that the concepts and categories enshrined in the dominant thinking and institutions in our times, are unable to grasp the violence.

We must ask where can sovereign people go for redress, for reparation for the crimes committed against them? Where will the *people of Iraq seek the reparation* that is *owed* to them?

There are no mechanisms in the rights discourse (in its praxis or politics) where *sovereign people* can take sovereign nation states to task, locked as the discourse is into the terrain of the nation state: the states, on signing the International Covenants/Universal Declaration on Human Rights, become the *guarantor* of human rights and freedoms for their citizens; but what often happens is that the *state is the greatest violator*. We know that the International Criminal Court has been ratified by many countries but remains state-centric: the greatest violator, USA, refusing to ratify the Rome statute, continues to make bi-lateral treaties with other states assuring that the USA will not be prosecuted for war crimes that they will continue to commit with impunity.

So, where shall we find justice?

Perhaps, it is in the expressions of *resistance* seeking legitimacy not by the dominant standards, not from a dominant paradigm, not by the *rule of law*, but by claims to the truth offering *new paradigms of knowledge*, of politics: the Truth Commissions, the Public Hearings, the Peoples' Tribunals, the Courts of Women are movements of resistance that are *speaking to power, challenging power*, speaking truth to the powerless, *creating other reference points*; other sources of inspiration, speaking to the *conscience* of the world, returning *ethics to politics*, decolonizing our minds and our imaginations, moving away from the master imaginary, finding worlds that embrace many worlds.

The *South* has, for too long accepted a worldview that has hegemonized its cultures, decided its development model, defined its aesthetic categories, outlined its military face, determined its science and technology, its nuclear options and moulded its modes of governance through the modern nation state. For the modern idiom of politics is the eurocentric world of nation-states, centralized, bureaucratized, militarized, some even nuclearized. The nation state in its homogenization of the polity, has subsumed all cultural diversity, all civilizational differences, into one uniform political entity, which now belongs to the *New World Order*.

A cosmology constructed of what has come to be known as *universal values*; a cosmology whose philosophical, ideological, and political roots were embedded in the specific historical context of the culture of the west. What qualified it then to be termed *universal?* The vision of the world in which the centre of the world was Europe and later North America (West) encapsulated all civilizations into its own western frames: it reduced their cultural diversities into a schema called *civilization*; it made universal the specific historical experiences of the west. It announced that what was relevant to the west had to be a model for the rest of the world: what was good for the centre had to be meaningful for the periphery. *All that was western simply became universal.* Every other civilization, every system of knowledge came to be defined and compared vis-à-vis this paradigm submitting to *its insights as imposition, its blindness as values, its tastes as canons, in a word to its euro-centricities.*

The *Other* in this cosmology were the civilizations of Asia, the Pacific, Africa, Latin America, the Arab world. *Scarcely twenty years were enough to make two billion people define themselves as under-developed* (Illlich 1981) vis-à-vis the post war growth model, the market economy and the international economic order conceived of at Bretton Woods. It minisculed all social totalities into one single model, all systems of science to one mega science, all indigenous medicine to one imperial medicine, all knowledge to one established regime of thought, all development to gross national product, to patterns of consumption, to industrialization, to *the western self image of homo-economicus with all needs commodity defined*, and *homo economicus has never been gender neutral.*

This cosmos of values has determined the thought patterns of the world, as also the world's ecological patterns: indicating its scientific signs, giving it the development symbols, generating the military psyche, defining knowledge, truth: *universal truths which have been blind, to cultures, race, class, gender.* Universal *patriarchal* truths, whatever the cultural ethos, whatever the civilizational idiom.

5.

What is essential is not to develop new doctrines or dogmas, or to define a new, coherent political schema but, to suggest a *new imaginative attitude*, one that can be *radical and subversive* which will be able to change the logic of our development. Perhaps as the poet says we *should now break the routine, do an extravagant action that would change the course of history.* What is essential is to go beyond the politics of violence and exclusion of our times and to find *new political imaginations.*

An imaginary where people of the margins, of the *global South* are subjects of our own history, writing our own cultural narratives, offering new universals, imagining a world in more life enhancing terms, *constructing a new radical imaginary.*

We must seek new imaginaries from the South: the South not only as third world, as the civilizations of Asia, the Arab world, Africa, Latin America; but the South as the voices and *movements of peoples*, wherever these movements exist.

The South as the *visions and wisdoms of women.*

The South as the discovering of new paradigms, which challenge the existing theoretical concepts and categories, *breaking the mind constructs*, seeking a new language to describe what it perceives, refusing the one, objective, rational, scientific world view as the only world view. The South as the discovery of other cosmologies, as the *recovery of other knowledges* that have been hidden, submerged, silenced: the South as a *rebellion of these silenced knowledges*.

The South as history; the *South as memory.*

The South as the finding of new political paradigms, inventing new political patterns, creating alternative political imaginations: the South as the revelation of each civilization in its own idiom: the South as *conversations between civilizations:* The South then as *new universalisms.*

It invites us to challenge the master imaginary, to create a new imaginary, the South as new political imaginary (Kumar 2005).

6.

The Courts of Women are an articulation of the new imaginary. The *Courts of Women* are an unfolding of a space, *an imaginary*: a horizon that invites us to think, to feel, to challenge, to connect, to dare to dream.

It is an attempt to define a new space for women, and to infuse this space with a new vision, a *new politics*. It is a gathering of voices and visions of the *global south*. The Courts of Women reclaim the subjective and objective modes of knowing, creating richer and deeper structures of knowledge in which the observer is not distanced from the observed, the researcher from the research, poverty from the poor. The *Courts of Women* seek to weave together the *objective* reality (analyses) with the *subjective* testimonies of the women; the rational with the intuitive ; the personal with the political; *the logical* with the *lyrical* (through video testimonies, artistic images and poetry); *we cannot separate the dancer from the dance* .

It invites us to discern fresh insights, offering us other ways to know, urging us to seek deeper layers of knowledge towards creating new paradigms of knowledge.

The *Courts of Women* are public hearings: the *Court* is used in a symbolic way. The *Courts* are *sacred* spaces where women, speaking in a language of suffering, name the crimes, seeking redress, even reparation.

It is a rejection of the *silencing of the crimes of violence*. Silence subjugates; silence kills: breaking the silence signifies the point of disruption and of *counterhegemonic truth telling*.

While the *Courts of Women* listen to the voices of the survivors, it also listens to the voices of women who resist, who rebel, who refuse to turn against their dreams. It hears challenges to the dominant human rights discourse, whose frames have *excluded the knowledges of women*. It repeatedly hears of the need to extend the discourse to include the meanings and symbols and perspectives of women.

It speaks of a new generation of women's human rights.

The *Court of Women is a tribute to the human spirit:* in which testimonies can not only be heard but also legitimized. The Courts provide witnesses, victims, survivors and resistors not only the validation of their suffering but also the validation of their hopes and dreams that they have dared to hold. It speaks to the right of the subjugated and the silenced to articulate the crimes against them; it is a taking away of the legitimizing dominant ideologies and returning their *life worlds* into their own hands.

The Courts of Women celebrate the subversive voices, voices that disrupt the master narrative of war and occupation, of security, of justice, of patriarchy...

We need to find new spaces for our imaginations: gathering the subjugated knowledges, seeking ancient wisdoms, with new visions, listening to the many voices speaking but listening too to the many voices, unspoken; remembering our roots knowing our depths of wisdoms written on the barks of trees, written on our skins, as we search for the *river beneath the river*, listening to the different colors of the wind.

Supryia listens to this wind:
She offers another logic, another lyric,
lifting the human spirit, creating a new imaginary.
offering another dream.

Corinne Kumar is a poet, a dreamer leader, a visionary ... a pilgrim of life as she calls herself. With an abiding faith in women's knowledge and all vulnerable wisdoms, she is a woman deeply committed to issues related to women and human rights, peace and justice. She has initiated and sustained groups at the local, regional, and international level, whose core is transformational politics that is rooted in a more caring and compassionate society in immediate, lived realities. These include the Centre for Development Studies (CIEDS), Vimochana, a forum for women's rights, both based in Bangalore, India and the Asian Women Human Rights Council, a regional network of women's and human rights organizations. For the past decade, she has been the Director of El Taller, an international NGO based in Tunis that through its perspectives and programs, including training programs for NGO activists, attempts to create spaces for constructive reflection and action on the important issues of our times and enables a South-South and North-South dialogue. Information on the World Courts of Women is available at: www.eltaller.org.

References

Illich, Ivan. 1981. *Shadow Work, Vernacular Values Examined*. London: Marion Boyars Inc.

Kumar, Corinne. 2005. *A South Wind Towards A New Political Imaginary: Dialogue and Difference*. New York: Palgrave Macmillan.

Thornton, Lawrence. 1987. *Imagining Argentina*. New York: Doubleday.

MARTA BENAVIDES

Reflecting on Gifting and the Gift Economy in El Salvador

I was born and raised in El Salvador. I have been through many exiles. Because of this I have learned so much, especially to appreciate diversity, the unity in diversity, the many cultures of the world, and the real meaning of solidarity and caring. Now I am back in El Salvador, and my work is with people of various political, ethnic, religious, social, and educational backgrounds. My sister Ana and I take care of our father, who is 96, and our mother, 86. It is both good and challenging and difficult.

I returned to El Salvador just before we signed the peace agreements in 1992. I thought then that the time had come when we could all do the things that we had been dreaming about as a nation. When we signed the accords, I expected us to be loving to each other, to start doing what we needed to do for the betterment of our country. Much of the urgent work needed was about taking care of Mother Earth and our Indigenous roots. Though I look European, I am, as are most of the people in my country, Indigenous and black. Some of us look white and thus some people refer to us as *mestizos*. This is a racist term, created by the colonizers to divide and more effectively conquer us. Our culture is mostly based on our Indigenous roots, in spite of the fact that the language and religion and many ways that we have to live by in the larger society are western.

After the peace agreements there was much conflict in the country, despite the progressive peoples' movement. And even progressive people wanted leadership positions, power. Today we are paying the price of divisiveness within the progressive movement, while a very close-minded government goes about its business, which has resulted in increasing poverty, repression, and hopelessness. Often we can be busy being the Left, but not busy enough in effectively supporting the work people must do in order to transform society to meet their needs and aspirations, and to become a nation of peace and justice for all, in a healthy, natural environment.

It is important to pay attention, and to be clear, that is why I am sharing this experience on how change is generated. My mother would reflect on our situation and say, "Well, things are the way they are, because that's where we [humans] have allowed them to get to." All of us participate in creating the reality/ies we live under. As an example, the peoples' movement lost the last presidential elec-

310

tion in El Salvador, though there was a good chance that we could have won. But the same situation that happened in the U.S. happened in my country: fear was instilled in the people. Many people voted for the government that is in power right now, which is not the Left (even though the Left was almost ready to win) because of fear. This fear is related to the well-known fact that more than one-fifth of the population of El Salvador is in the USA, a good number without documents, and these Salvadorians are sending remittances to their families at home that amount to one-third of the budget of El Salvador, even more than is exported annually.

Everyone in El Salvador was aware of this. The people in government and the people's movement knew this; there are a few in the middle who also knew this, but they usually vote the status quo anyway. The present government which acknowledges itself as the Right and those in the middle vote together all time, so it was hard for the opposition to win. There was a program of intimidation, of threatening that if the opposition won the election, the country would become like Cuba and in Cuba they are dying of hunger, with no jobs, no social services, and lots of people in jail. In the media, the leaders of the people's movement were shown with gangs burning and destroying properties and businesses, and so there was great fear. This is because when one does not have an education, and is not trained to think critically, then there are no parameters, no points or reference and therefore an inability to discern the truth, thus people only react in fear.

This is the trap of poverty and lack of education. Thus, this is one of the key gifts we must work for: to facilitate people coming of age so that they can carry out their own discernment. Critical thinking is a gift. For it is on this basis, with available resources, that we can figure out and decide the process for what is the best, for ourselves, for others, for future generations, and for the health of the planet.

In spite of all the propaganda, and the fear that was generated, about two weeks before the elections, it still it looked as if the Left might win, although the Left is not so Left any more, but much more to the Center. There is very little Left left—just like in the U.S.! But here is the key: we have to be smart and pay attention because we don't want to be back-pedaling—we must know now that the work is not going to be done by any political party, the church, or an NGO. The work for change is going to be done by us. We are the people, we are the community, and whatever we want and whatever we need is up to us. The party is just an instrument, a means to an end, and not an end in itself. This is historically true. If we take a good look, we can see that it is in the leadership of women, the people's movements, affirmed by Indigenous cultures, that change happens and is maintained. That is the way it has been throughout history. The pressure for change comes from below.

About two weeks before the elections the U.S. Undersecretary of State for Latin America arrived in El Salvador and he appeared in all the media, which in most countries, ours not the exception, is owned by the richest people. In interviews he was asked what would happen if the Left were to win and how would the country's relationship with the USA be affected. The U.S. representative replied that he could see there would be problems;that probably those Salvadorans living in the United States without immigration documents might not have their time extended, thus they would have to return, and even those legally in the U.S. might not be allowed to send the monthly help. Thus, fear was instilled as this situation would be an enormous problem for there are no jobs in El Salvador, and how could the country survive without the support the Salvadorans in the U.S. regularly send back home?

"Did you hear that?" the people were saying. Therefore, everybody voted for whoever they had to in order to maintain the status quo. Whole towns, even those with mayors of the opposition party, voted for the conservative party because of that fear.

Indigenous people in Salvador have a phrase that goes like this: "They have your tail under their foot." If somebody stands on a dog's tail, it cannot go very far, it cannot move. This is what colonialism has done, and today is a modern-day colonial practice.

Yet, it is here that we must remember we are beings that have the power to create. Even in Salvador we are thinking, "We have to take the power for ourselves." In this case, "taking the power" meant having everybody vote for the opposition, so that from the top down we can have the kinds of laws that will give justice and peace and freedom to the people—thinking that political power is the key.

I have come to understand that it doesn't work like that. We concentrate on taking, getting the power, and we maneuver and fight and struggle to do that. Even within the party itself people fight for control, because they see this as the way to have power. This I understand to be the wrong analysis, the wrong way of thinking. For we *are* power. We don't have to take over power because we *are* power. What we have to figure out is: why, if we *are* power, have we come to believe and understand that we don't have power, and that we powerless, and worse, we act that way.

We are the children of the universe. The universe has created all that we have and see, and much that as of yet do not see. Why then do we think that we are so helpless, and so powerless? We can create programs to empower people. If we work to empower someone, there is an important implication: that someone has power, is empowered, and that someone else is not. But if we start from the understanding that everything in the universe is power, and everybody in the universe, all human beings and all of nature *are* power, then we have a different way of working, because then it is about creating the conditions, together, for exercising or manifesting power to bring about those basic things that are our dreams and our aspirations, as persons and as humanity, and for the health of the planet.

When talking about reaching a state of wellness in society, people in El Salvador say, "Oh, but you're crazy, talking about that. It can never happen."

"You don't think it can ever happen?" I ask.

"Well, it might take a bunch of years," they answer.

"Like, how many years?" I respond.

"About 200, and then maybe we'll have what we have been dreaming about, but by that time I won't be around, so who knows?" is their response.

Conversations like this suggest we do not, cannot, create the future, and so we continue to allow our country, our nation, to be destroyed.

El Salvador is the second most environmentally destroyed country in the Americas. We continue to experience ever increasing violence that has made our country the most violent in the Americas because we continue to think it is not possible to be different due to the existing conditions. But it is up to us; *we* are the possibility. When we say that another, or many other worlds and better worlds are possible, they are! So we have to discern what world we want and what would make it possible, and start doing exactly that—intentionally and in real time, in community. We cannot wait for someone else to do it. That is a colonial mentality. We are human beings; we have the capability, we are pure potential.

What we are, and what we have to understand we are, is that we are *creators*. *We cannot escape that.* We come from the great Creator Spirit or force, Father-Mother, therefore we are creators. We must own this, and be responsible. We must figure out how to be responsible, intentional creators. That means we must develop a *conscious* culture, because what we have now is unconscious culture, unconscious practices. Culture is everything that we do, everything that we cultivate through our every day practices. But it must be an intentional, conscious culture. That means that every step we take, everything we do, has to be done with the consciousness of this totality, this wholeness, this oneness in diversity, consciousness of who we really want to be, and how we want the world to be.

So people kept saying to me, "Two hundred years for this or that, Marta!" And I respond, "Well, that would be the twenty-third century, right?" And they say, "Yes!" And I say, "Okay. So how about choosing to be the twenty-third century here and now?" What is stopping us from exercizing the future now?

Whatever our actions are today create the future even if we are not conscious of it. So we must use the gift of consciously and intentionally being the future in the here and now.

The way this is done is by practicing discernment, which is about figuring out what we want to manifest as an intentional choice, paying attention, and then creating a process together. Dis-cernment is a compound word. The preposition "dis" is a negative, and "cernir " is to spread out, as when one needs to sift flour, when you bring it together you are *discernimiendo*, and that is when one can proceed to make the bread. So this is the important thing: we must embrace the gift of taking the time to discern situations, our work, the future, and to develop such skills for ourselves and support others to do the same. We already have the power, because we *are* power itself. Now we must develop the skills to manifest the power that we are in a conscious, intentional way, and in community for the best results.

In what way can we do this, in a country like El Salvador? If we were to take the International Criminal Court (ICC) under the present cultural and political conditions, we could say that it is about 200 years away. Because this institution is an important deterrent against violations and crimes against humanity, we must be about creating the conditions for the society to support and press the government to adhere to and implement the International Criminal Court in our legal processes. Thus, we have created the Salvadoran Coalition for the ICC, and now we have the regional coalition, the Central American Coalition for the ICC. In this way we are creating a new environment not only for our country and the region but for the world.

We can figure out what the future will be like if we continue to move and be, as we are, and then figure out what best expresses the hopes and aspirations of our nation, a country of peace, justice, freedom, in a healthy environment. It is like visiting the future, then envisioning how to start manifesting it in the present, day in and day out. By doing so, we can change the past, have a different present, and arrive at the future we aspire to.

In colonial times, the colonizers in El Salvador would demand of the Indigenous peoples: "When I am talking to you, you look down. Don't look at me. And before I finish talking, you start running!" We were forced to learn those ways. Many people still do not look at someone eyes when they are talking, and then, before s/he is finished, they start running, but they are running in the same place. As I observe our society, I see that often we continue running in the same place. Then we feel like we cannot really move ahead, but we can. We must know what we want, though. It means that every day we say to ourselves when we get up in the morning, when we wake up, that we can. It means that everyday we remember to live with a thankful heart, because we know that everything has been given to us—the air that we need to breathe, the water, the earth, everything that we need to be alive has been given to us, as well as the power to create, the power to create and resolve everything in community.

So we must choose, every morning, to do this. There are times I don't feel like doing it, to tell you the truth, because the work is hard and very tiring at home. So I support myself. I have created a mechanism to give me the spark. When I wake up, and I don't feel like getting up, I breathe deeply, and since on purpose I leave my window open, I pay attention and listen to the birds sing, and then I say, "Oh, the whole universe is waking up and letting me know that everything is ready for me to go out to work," and then I start intentionally to give thanks. Then my heart opens up, and I begin giving thanks consciously, and yet naturally.

This is the thing. We must figure out how to live that. In El Salvador we are very ready to be in resistance, and in opposition. It's been more than 500 years of exploitation, and the oppression in our country is really terrible. Even now my parents become very frightened if I have not returned by 6:30 in the evening. They worry. My father, 96 years old, says, "Tita, you know that your mom is too old to go out of the country. We cannot travel!" He is making an allusion to a life again in exile. And I answer, "Si, papa." And then my mom says, "Your father is too old to travel, to live outside the country." And I answer, "Si, mama." I know that I cannot go into exile again, and besides, the purpose of life doesn't have to be to live in resistance, in opposition, or to be in exile, or to be fighting all the time.

Life is to be lived and so my work in El Salvador has to be to work with people to create conditions so that we don't live to work. This is what is happening in all of Latin America, in Africa, and all over. People are merely surviving, living to work. We must create conditions so that we live to enjoy life. Whatever we do we have to keep that in mind, because otherwise we end up living to work and that is not living.

When I witnessed all the fighting within the party and didn't want to go into the communities and work with the people, which was what we were supposed to do, I discovered that we all wanted to have peace, we wanted to have justice, we wanted to have freedom, but we wanted the revolution to give it to us. More than 80,000 Salvadorians gave their life for that, and many more were ready to also give their lives for that peace. All of us were living in a culture of giving. Our people have always given, helping and taking care of each other, many women especially as single heads of households, but we have been forced to give and to maintain the society through our giving. But the time has come that we must be choosy and give because we are willing to give, to give from our hearts. If we are willing to die for our aspirations—peace, freedom, and justice—why not live for them instead? This is a conscious way of living and giving. This is the gift we must give! It is easier sometimes to struggle and endure, but it's not about struggling, it is about being efficient so that we can really have what we dream about.

I found out that there is a qualitative difference between being a revolutionary to being the revolution itself. We must manifest it. There is a difference between building and constructing, defending and struggling for peace, and being peace. It's easy, and it's hard. It is being very mindful and intentional. So the work that we have to do is to be in this consciousness, and understanding how the universe works, be responsible and intentional about this knowledge.

For example, in El Salvador everybody says, "Oh, but look at all this violence! We cannot do anything about that, we cannot change that." The UN Economic Commission for Latin America-CEPAL has declared my country the most violent of the Americas. So people ask, "When is the violence going to stop?" Because we have at least a dozen terrible murders every day, and we have gangs and we have corruption, we become more militarized. Currently, the President of El Salvador has given us a "gift"—that is what he calls the "dollarization" of the economy. The President pushed for our national coin to be substituted by the U.S. dollar. His political party in the legislature, and the other political allies, approved it without discussion, but in violation of our constitution. This is legal, but it is illegitimate and immoral. The purpose of the legalization of the dollar for our economy was to support industry, commerce, and international investments in our country. This has made the cost of living go so high in El Salvador that today we are one of the most expensive countries on the continent.

The government of El Salvador has now given us another "gift" for security and against terrorism. El Salvador is the only country that has a contingent in Iraq. These soldiers have recently been honoured since they saved a U.S. contingent. Besides the medals the soldiers were given, we are reminded often of: "How brave you Salvadorians are and what great things you are doing!" The government declares, "We are fulfilling a commitment that we made to you when we were campaigning," and now we also have the Super Iron Fist Law.

That is its the real name: Super Iron Fist Law. It is a version of the U.S. *Patriot Act II*. It means repression, especially of the young people, and the poorest people. Many gang members have parents working in the United States, and these young people have been sent back to El Salvador because while the parents were working very hard to maintain the family, these kids were on the streets. These young people, back in El Salvador, are often in very violent gangs. The government now has an arrangement with the national police in each country of Central America to fight terrorism, to fight the gangs. But, in response to this, the gangs joined forces and are now organized throughout the whole region. Today, as per the arrangement of the governments, the police from any Central American country can run across the borders, persecuting the gangs, regardless of sovereignty, and the youth are doing the same. Violence and crime have increased as a result.

The people say, "What can we do?" It is a responsibility to figure out what to do. To do this is to practice governance, and to practice governance is a gift. We have to see what it means in each place. It might mean, for example in the little town where I live, to develop a team of people to meet even with the conservative mayor. I live in an Indigenous town of very impoverished people. I need to pause here to say something about language. Notice that I don't say "poor people." I use the word "impoverished" because there is the process of impoverishment and a process of enrichment. We have to pay attention to language. (Also, I never call the people of the United States "Americans." I call them "United Stateans," or *estadounidenses*, because all of the people in the Americas are Americans.) In my little town, the gangs and drunken men have taken over the public park so no one can use or enjoy the park. We negotiated with the mayor take the park back for the people. We proposed creating a butterfly garden in the park with his support. We would provide ten people to do the work, we asked him to provide another ten, including council members. We wanted the high school kids to come and work with us in the park, and we wanted him to provide the equipment we would need. We explained to him that this would be a way to save animal and plant species, the diversity. He had to be there and if possible work with us. He agreed.

And there we went: us and a very conservative mayor, working in the park together. The mayor with his team came, and the students, and the government-sponsored House of Culture, and the church came, and they witnessed how everybody was stopping to see what we were doing. Then we explained *Agenda 21*—the 1992 Rio Declaration for a healthy planet and a peaceful planet. We then took time to reflect on how by creating a garden together, we had practiced a level of governance, caring for the Commons, and making them safe for the townspeople, working on plant and animal biodiversity, the filtration of water, the purification of air, and how this is part of what we have to do at the national and international levels for a healthy planet, what *Agenda 21* is all about. And when we finished, everyone saw the beauty that we had been able to create together, in a collaborative way, in a short time, and even with a conservative mayor. People were pleased, and some people said, "And it was good."

Now we are creating new projects with the mayor for the benefit of the town and the safety of the people. The butterfly and humming bird garden is beautiful, and people are coming from everywhere just to stand and look at it. There are butterflies, birds, and flowers. We have claimed back the park.

I am giving these examples because this is what I am writing about: understanding globally and acting locally. In order to act locally, we must do it personally, with our families, and then we have to really involve all the stakeholders, including the decision-makers or facilitators, not necessarily the people who are the most powerful. It is important for people to know the power they are.

The best way to mount resistance is to have this intentional culture, this conscious culture, and to create whatever you have been dreaming about. It is not a matter even of believing and having faith; it is a matter of knowing that we are power, knowing and affirming that we are creators, knowing that we are always cause, and never effect. We need to be conscious that whatever we decide to do, at any moment, will have an impact on what happens and on what we do later, on the people around us, even to the seventh generation, and on the health of the planet. Thus, as women, we must choose intentionally what to give, how to give, to whom to give, and what to give, for we are power, creative power, and with our actions we create; we are always cause and never effect.

Marta Benavides is an educator, a theologian, and permaculturist who works on social transformation through culture, culture of peace, life-long learning. She is the International President of the Women's International League for Peace and Freedom (WILPF), and part of the United Nations and UNESCO Women, Sustainability, and Peace Caucuses. She worked for a political, peaceful, negotiated solution to the war in El Salvador in the 1980s. During the war, she also worked with Monsignor Oscar Romero, who was slain in 1980 in El Salvador, and together they established the first refugee centers in the country, and directed the Ecumenical Committee for Humanitarian Aid (CEAH). Marta's father rested on Earth Day, April 22, 2005, and her mother on April 19th, 2006. In their memory, on September 23, 2006, she and her sisters opened the Culture is Peace and the AHA Folk Arts and Cultures Museum in Santa Ana, the second city of El Salvador, for the purpose of promoting a culture of peace through social transformation and global and planetary citizenship.

References

United Nations Conference on Environment and Development (UNCED). 1992. *Agenda 21: The Rio Declaration on Environment and Development.* New York: United Nations Department of Economic and Social Affairs, Division for Sustainable Development. Online: http://www.un.org/esa/sustdev/documents/agenda21/index.htm.

PAOLA MELCHIORI

From Forced Gifts to Free Gifts

My contribution to this volume should not be considered a "paper" *per se*, but rather an ongoing dialogue with the living-thinking members of the Feminist Gift Economy Network and the ones whom we carry with us. I strongly believe in the power of presence, in its capacity to set in motion a different process of thinking and discovering. I am choosing this incompleteness, this particular kind of thinking that becomes alive when we meet as a group in order to make visible a feminist methodology of thinking and producing knowledge that has been my experience of our various conferences and network meetings to discuss the gift economy. As an incomplete dialogue it thus needs and responds to the others also collected in this volume.

Gifts and Paradigms

I see the gift as an epistemological tool, a paradigm in its most classic meaning: a concept which makes other ideas as acceptable, diverse ways of thinking as legitimate, thus opening a mental space to think differently, creating new imagination. When we say that a new paradigm has emerged, we mean that the basic thinking that allows us to "see" something has changed, providing us with the possibility to ask different questions, and to imagine different answers.

It is no accident that Genevieve Vaughan (1997) developed the gift paradigm within her feminist thinking. Feminism is already a fundamental change paradigm, able to shift our whole thinking. By making visible the lives and thoughts of women, their resistance to dominant paradigms, their knowledge-production processes, feminism makes visible other aspects of the entire social fabric of society, creating different links between phenomena and legitimizing different ideas of how knowledge is created. In this sense, the gift paradigm is one of the best examples of feminist knowledge: it changes our way of seeing the same things, it makes us see differently, and it lies at the junction of different disciplinary fields (economics, politics, psychology, and anthropology, at the least), making it impossible to choose one over the other. I see the gift paradigm as something that is able to "enlarge" the worldview we have developed through feminism, going more deeply and expansively from a theory of subjectivity toward a theory of economics and social bonds, obliging us to keep together the approaches that have been fragmented by patriarchal knowledge.

The first thing that the gift paradigm makes visible is women's invisible unwaged work. More importantly, it overthrows a basic assumption embedded in economic thinking, namely that of *homo economicus*, looking for a different, non-utilitarian paradigm, based on the anthropological structure of the human being. According to this perspective we do not live in a world of scarcity. Vaughan (1997) challenges the premise of current economic thought, and claims instead that we live in a world of abundance. Moreover, by showing that the market, in reality has a parasitic relationship to the gift economy, the gift paradigm goes further, asking all of us to imagine not only a different economy but also a different idea of what economy is.

I do not think it is by chance that evidence of the gift "being at work" rises to the forefront during extreme social experiences. In revolutionary times, in times of deep crises, when the normal rules of living and of economies are suspended, we can see the gift paradigm, the gift economy, at work, together with other invisible aspects of the human society and of human beings. Normally, this paradigm is not only invisible, but also considered meaningless. However, when the boat is sinking, when the system is collapsing, only a gift economy can keep the social fabric together, emerging behind and inside the barter and the other informal economies that come to light during times of crisis.

There are many examples of this and we might choose to interpret them in different ways. During these times of crisis, *real scarcity* makes visible what can be considered the *real abundance*, which is lost when the market economy "works well." Other possibilities come along, new ways of imagining relationships and the economy. In this sense, the situation of Argentina, where the economic system collapsed in 2001 as a result of an expropriation process which combined forced privatizations, export of capital, and massive corruption, was paradoxical and exemplar at the same time. The crisis was terrible, people were starving, but another economy was being discovered and used, awakening an enormous energy among people, developing what I would call a "healthy crisis" of the social imaginary. Other ways to survive, other social fabrics, became visible and imaginable.

We should ask ourselves what, hidden in the other economies, arises in times of extreme conditions, of catastrophes. What, hidden often within a barter economy, makes barter not a "primitive form" of the market but the anticipation of another scenario, where survival is linked to the capacity to preserve the social bond, as African societies keep telling us. What kind of strength is awakened by the capacity to share beyond promises of restitution? What kind of energy is awakened in the human being when s/he "gives" outside hopes or calculations of restitution? The key word here is: "passion for the social link." Jacques T. Godbout (1993) defines it as follows: "'giving' without any guarantee of restitution with the goal to create, nurture or re-create a social bond among people" (30, *my translation*). This social act works contagiously, putting into motion a whole series of other social acts. According to Jacques Derrida (1995), the gift is the only event that lies at the foundations of real democracy, "a democracy to come" that "opens community and democracy to a future that cannot be appropriated" (361, *my translation*).

The gift paradigm is not new. Marcel Mauss (1923-24), Jacques T. Godbout (1993), Alain Caille (1998), Georges Bataille (1997), Emmanuel Levinas (1961) and other anthropologists or philosophers have conceptualized the gift as the basis of the social bond and the economy. However, it is not without meaning that today this "other economy" is reawakening in the midst of political thinking. All these theories, from Mauss to Godbout, to, most recently, Derrida (1995), indicate the need to rethink the foundation and the complexity of the social fabric, the need for a vision that will allow us to get out from under an utilitarian anthropology, and away from a fragmented view of the human being. This means, also, rethinking a theory of the human subject.

This theory continues to be, and *cannot be*, nowadays, gender neutral. Yet, the research by male theorists stubbornly continues to be gender neutral. From Derrida (1995), to Godbout (1993), to Lévinas (1961), an idealized feminine is very present, as the "name" by which they try to imagine the absoluteness and purity of the gift: *philia*, the love for the affinity, *agape*, the spirit of absolute pure love. The more the *feminine* appears as a concept, the more *women* disappear. Even the more sociological analyses, like those by Serge Latouche (1991) for example, which provided inspiring visions of the only movement still active in the international scene, the anti-globalization movement, completely overlook the role of women in this respect. Amazingly, women are almost entirely absent from both the theoretical articulations and the descriptions of various exemplary experiences, even in situations where the presence of women is overwhelming. Sometimes there is a nod to the fact that, yes, strangely enough, in all the social struggles of the present times women are the majority, or the main leaders. And "another economy" is at work. This phenomenon, however, is not questioned nor further analyzed.

As a result of this general gender neutrality of male theorists, it is not surprising that their theories of the gift are literally "tortured" by the issue of reciprocity. Is the gift a free gift? How can the gift be a gift if not absolutely pure, or free? Are you waiting to receive something in return, or not? Mauss (1990 [1923-24]) has argued that the gift is in reality the worst compulsive social obligation. In Derrida (1995) the issue of the "purity" of the gift, without expecting anything in return, takes him very close to the Christian concept of pure self-sacrifice.

However, when they look for possible roots of human generosity, trying to solve the issue of reciprocity and pure other-oriented love, the only paradigm that comes to their mind, from Aristotle to Todorov to Freud, is the example of maternal love. Tzvetan Todorov (1992) has long worked on the roots of generosity in extreme situations such as in concentration camps. In his book, *Di fronte all'estremo*, he studied both the Nazi concentration camps and the gulags, interviewing people and trying to understand the root of self-sacrifice. Why is it that some people are able to share their last piece of bread, and some others are only able to hide it? Apart the self-sacrificing-for-the-glory-hero-model, Todorov concludes that the only other model he could refer to is the model of the mother, particularly the "thinking" of a mother. To provide an example he quotes, interestingly, not a *real* mother but a potential mother, a sixteen-year-old girl, Fania Fenelon. From a barrack in Auschwitz, while she looks at other prisoners during the night, she writes: "I look at them, and a deep tenderness is awakened in me, a protective tenderness which goes back to the depth of centuries. From where can it come to me, to me, the youngest among all of them?" (Todorov 1992: 196, *my translation*).

Recalling the example of maternal love and the importance of women as the subjects of this particular behaviour, which is at the basis of the gift economy, Vaughan (1997) highlights how in symbolic exchange, as in language, the relationship is not only economic or social, not utilitarian and based on exchange and expectance of reciprocity. It is based on the satisfaction of giving. The return is in the experience of giving. The energy awakened is the affirmation of the importance of the bonds with the others. It is impossible in this model to understand the issue of reciprocity as it has traditionally been conceptualized. In this perspective we overcome symmetry and reciprocity, because the obligation becomes desire, recognition of the importance of a relationship. This is the political meaning of the semiotic aspect of the gift. The gift implied in the linguistic exchange is the paradigm of the human relationship, the kind of act that lies at the foundation of the social bond, that bond which gives humans meaning, and pleasure. It also leads to a rethinking of the economic bond. Perhaps we might also have to reconsider that "oceanic sentiment" that Sigmund Freud (1978 [1930]) talks about, as the only emotion able to overcome, together with maternal love, the experience of ambivalence and the drive for pure survival. We need to be more careful in our studies of all those social areas where the connection between human needs and the public worlds, which have been built around these needs, hiding them, are still visible, as the mass experience.

Rethinking Motherhood

The mother as the anthropological basis for gift giving is at the core of Vaughan's (1997) theory. However, this paradigm of a human relationship should be carefully re-questioned and re-elaborated, because at the present time we are witnessing fundamentalisms and churches attacking women's advancement using precisely the values accorded to motherhood. It becomes therefore important to trace the difference between a forced and "natural gift" and a free gift. From abortion to assisted procreation, to women's role in society and family, we are facing what I call a *forced gift* economy to keep women in, or put them back into, their patriarchally-assigned place, socially, economically, culturally. We are at risk of having our values stolen, our rights taken away. It is easy to recognize that that one of the reasons for the recent Republican electoral victory in the U.S. was the capacity of the fundamentalist Right to advocate so-called traditional values, and to convince people to give away their rights in name of those values.

In 2004, the Roman Catholic Church issued a "Letter to Bishops on the Collaboration Between Men and Women," a very long and important document which talks directly to feminists, and which seems to take into consideration some feminist claims and finally gives them a death blow. Then Cardinal Ratzinger, now Pope, wrote this letter. Its significance should not be underestimated. In all religions today, including the Islamic religion, there are specific "schools" whose goal is to get women to conform to their patriarchally-defined roles. Ratzinger talks about this moment, this "difficult moment of history"—and he is not referring to current wars, global violence and poverty, and a certain model of masculinity that thrives on war and threats. He says, in this letter, that the real threat of these times is that women are abandoning their traditional role of being mothers and nurturing human beings, to "live by and for themselves." He adds: "...She [the woman] is abandoning her intuition, the deep intuition that the best of her life is the fact that all her activities are oriented to the awakening of the other, to the love of the other, to the growth of the other, the perfection of the other." This letter is a very refined document where women are strongly recognized, however within a fixed role of complementarity to men, prescribed not perhaps "by nature," or biology, but by God. In this order it is important to avoid competition between the sexes to achieve a "spousal" order made up by the complementarities between the sexes.

The document is so intriguing that even some strong feminists have been "lured" by it. This is because it recognizes and idealizes women's values and contribution to society to such an extent that it is difficult even for feminists to trace the limits between the feminist re-discovery and re-affirmation of the value of motherhood and the manipulation of the Catholic church. I don't know if we can all see the difficulty and danger this thinking poses.

We have to be able to articulate the difference of how gift giving, and mothering, which is the basis of the gift economy, is different from the patriarchal image of a mother and a woman, an image used today by all fundamentalists' attacks against women's only recently won freedom. It is important today not to be caught in the "forced gift economy," which has been the life of women, the only base of their importance and recognition, and still is, in the greater parts of the world. We have to be able to show that these gifts should be *free* gifts. In order for this to happen, we have to see that the gift paradigm is embraced by free women who *can* speak and live *also* for themselves. "The world needs the love of a free woman" not that of a *good* woman, says the poet Nan Peacocke.

Motherhood is a very good example of the difficult work done and to be done by feminists. It lies on the very edge of a fine line between the gift paradigm's power for liberation and orthodox religion's oppressive glorification of enforced female self-sacrifice (and enforced "mothering"). Men have recognized the gift, the maternal gift from women. What they cannot accept, as Cardinal Ratzinger tells us clearly, is women's free gift, their freedom to choose to give this gift, which is women's subjectivity and autonomy, women's representation as more than just mothers. There is a patriarchal mythology of motherhood where this ideology of maternal giving hides the slavery of women, the control of their bodies, sexuality, and lives. The motherhood that comes from *that* gift carries all sorts of frustrations, hidden returns and dark sides, which are the denial of the idea of the free gift we are talking about. There is a terrible market of suppression and returns, built on the negation of women's freedom but also on a false image of maternal power. We should also remember that in all religions and in all continents men are still wildly conflicting politically on the control of women's bodies (as is witnessed in abortion and assisted procreation debates), and we should also remember the "internationality" of violence against women, also a form control over women's bodies, from Sweden to Afghanistan.

The distinction between these two opposing and complex positions is difficult to see clearly because so much is involved in each. As emotions, dependency, and social bonds have been attributed historically to women, motherhood is still the place where women find and experience *at the same time* their power(s) and their slavery. Motherhood is still the most complex and unexplored human experience: the experience of the long dependence of one human being on another human being (*neotenia*), and the fact that this dependency is on the female sex, remains substantially unexplored. Only if we explore beyond any idealization of this human experience from both sides, from the mothers and from infants of both sexes, as feminism has started to do, can we constitute a different subjectivity, a real one, *"carved in"* between patriarchal idealization of motherhood and women's difficult struggle to define themselves liberated from the trap of idealization and devaluation.

The complexity of the definition of the work of *caring* is a good example of the difficulty of carving out a new image able to rescue the denial of the value of motherhood and, at the same time, not fall into the trap of a new idealization. The enormous amount of work embedded into caring is linked to the more fragile moments of the human condition, childhood, old age, and death, that have been hidden by men, in the undergrounds of history. Women, as caregivers, are reminders of this part of life. For those who want to externalize this evidence they become, alternatively, persecutors, angels or witches, whether they come out of the shadows as caregivers or as reminders of dangers of that need to be avoided. This immense work, in Italy, my country, today for example, when women are trying to get away from a self-sacrificing model, is being marketed and confined to other and new invisible women, the migrants. Here the market and the gift come together again. Here the market economy profits on the misery and impotence of the human condition, its material, often terrible, needs and on migrant women's poverty. It is obvious, especially today, that women's gift giving has to be cultivated and enforced by patriarchy, in order for patriarchy to continue to pillage, to plunder, for years to come, as it has always done. As long as they are successful in this, men will continue to hold onto their privileges, and continue to be cared for without any recognition of the caregiver. The most miserable parts of the human condition, where human beings are reminded of their fragility, of the futility of the monuments they have erected, must remain invisible in order for people not to truly see who they are. The idealization of women goes together with that. It keeps women where they are and takes them out of the shadow in a non-dangerous way. It is very hard for women to free themselves from this patriarchally defined role. There is a terrible internal conflict, profoundly felt, which makes it very difficult for a woman to conceive or define herself outside of the maternal framework. These are areas of painful research for women because motherhood is the only relative area of privilege and recognition they are allowed, in exchange for their total service. However, anti-market by definition, it is within this position that women bury the maximum of their feminine "spontaneous" culture of resistance, a culture rooted in their forced position but also prefiguring something new. Inside this position, with its closer relationship to life and death, lies also the possibility of a different notion of personal and social bonds.

We need to be very clear about the distinction between women's defensive use of motherhood and the possible invention it embeds: we need a feminist gift paradigm. The gift we are talking about is the gift that comes from a real motherhood, "rethought" and reinvented by feminists. It unmasks that "other motherhood" invented by men for their own interests. This motherhood is really "other-oriented" because it is done freely. It comes from a free subjectivity finally identified. It is not internally or externally enforced and requires compensation. This marks the difference between a culture of motherhood, which is just a culture of resistance, and a creative politically active culture of motherhood based on new feminine subjectivities.

This was made possible paradoxically when feminists "re-carved" the imaginary of motherhood, freeing it from the patriarchal dream of an eternal, but powerful, dangerous mother. Since then motherhood has been filled with the real experiences of real women, in all their ambiguity. With feminism, motherhood has perhaps been too quickly reclaimed. But it has also been exposed to the light, re-signified as a subject of autonomous desire rather than a subject of predetermined destiny. Throughout this voyage it has been necessary to travel through ambiguities, and pains. It is always like that when one leaves a condition that is oppressive but well-known, and secure in its aspects. New lives require losing identities, securities, known bonds. Rethinking motherhood means jumping away from the privileges of a bad "sacredness," made of illusory grandiosity and imaginary power. It implies engaging with history and its limits, with other women, and this is difficult for women too.

Only this painful process allows re-signification, builds other meanings, giving limited reality to dreams. It is important, in this perspective, to de-idealize motherhood as well as the gift, so that its importance in human relationships, its value, can avoid being pillaged again.

Perhaps the difficulties and splendours of the relationships that we have in the women's movement, so painfully shaped, allude also to new interpersonal and social paradigms. There is a lot of mothering there and here, and there is also very dark mothering at some moments, full of control and bad powers, because mothering in itself is not necessarily "good." But there is also a lot of caring and love and "good" mothering; many gifts, and many gift economies.

I think we can look at the practices we have developed in these years from this point of view and the different values that have emerged as different paradigms for beginnings of a real history of women, by women, for women.

I would like to finish with a poem by Nan Peacocke, a Caribbean writer and poet, and friend.

The world needs the love of a free woman

The world needs the love of a free woman
Not the love of a good woman
There's already too much
Of that good woman's love
Waiting in the bantustans
While her husband's soul is mined
Deep in South Africa.

Enough of the love of a good woman
Far in the dark city
At a high small window
Lying on a bed
Crying in her sleep
So she won't disturb the others.

The world needs the love of a freewoman
But early in the suburban gleam
Assisting the suds and cleansers at their chores
Is one whose dreams are?
Dried and stacked on immaculate shelves
Her mask now fixed
For the trick, the hoax
The stench of life's betrayal.

Poor bitch
Gnawing at the bars of your penalty
Your children know the love that
Cuts the heart of the holder
It's wild dishevelled madness.

The world has seen and seen the one
Who keeps these things in her heart
She kneels beholding
The bleeding feet of her boy
Blessed Art Thou Among Women
And never a nuisance.

The world needs the love of a free woman
Who forgives god

But doesn't ask him for an explanation
Of her brother's murder
Her daughter's rape
Her mother's unrepresented life.

She speaks loud
Naming lies
She moves
Clearing the piercing forest
Of guns and crosses held aloft
She works
Planting hopes
And fetching from the horizon
The thoughts of free women
Rising in millions
From this shantytown.
                        —Nan Peacocke, Barbados, 1986

For more than 25 years, Paola Melchiori has created, nationally and internationally, free spaces of critical thinking, teaching and learning, based on the model of the Free University in Berlin. She is the founder and president of The International Feminist University Network, an international think-tank for women's critical thinking and education. The university is committed to developing and making visible new paradigms of knowledge based on women's ways of knowing and learning and to make them available and meaningful for new generations of women leaders. She has written extensively on feminist theory, knowledge creation, and on interdisciplinary and relational learning and education. She is currently focusing on how to "pass on" experiences, memory, history, to young women and men, through written and visual texts.

References

Aristotle. *Ethica Nichomachea*. Vol. III.

Bataille,Georges. 1997. *Il dispendio*. Roma : Armando.

Derrida, Jacques. 1995. *Politiche dell'amicizia*. Milano: Cortina.

Freud, Sigmund. 1978 [1930]. "Il disagio della civiltà." *Opere*. Vol. 10. Ed. Cesare Musatti. Torino: Bollati Boringhieri.

Godbout, Jacques T. 1993. *Lo spirito del dono*. Torino:Bollati Boringhieri

Latouche, Serge. 1993. *Il pianeta dei naufraghi*. Torino:Bollati Boringhieri

Lévinas, Emmanuel. 1961. *Totalitè et infini*. La Haye : Nijhoff

Mauss, Marcel, 1990 [1923-24]. *The Gift: The Form and Reason for Exchange in Archaic Societies*. London, Routledge.

Todorov,Tzvetan. 1992. *Di fronte all'estremo*. Milano: Garzanti.

Vaughan, Genevieve. 1997. *For-Giving: A Feminist Criticism of Exchange*. Austin, TX: Plainview/Anomaly Press.

Ratzinger, Joseph. 2004. *Lettera sulla complementarietà dell'uomo e della donna*. Rome.

FRIEDA WERDEN

The Gift of Community Radio

Prologue

As Jane Jacobs observes in *Systems of Survival*, different sectors of society have different moral codes. She posits that hybridization of these codes can create moral monsters that have the vices of both systems and virtues of neither. In this paper, I observe the interactions of two moral codes in media, those of the exchange economy, and those of the gift economy. My understanding of the gift economy as a morally distinct economy that is often appropriated by the exchange economy is based on a long intellectual association and friendship with the philanthropist, semiotician, and economic linguist Genevieve Vaughan. Vaughan's work over more than 25 years on the concept of the Gift Economy has sparked an intellectual movement that includes academics, activists, and indigenous thinkers.[1] In the interests of full disclosure, I must say that Vaughan has supported my work and that of many others producing feminist media during more than 20 years.

Introduction

> In order to reject patriarchal thinking, we must be able to distinguish between it and something else, an alternative. (Vaughan 1997: 18)

I have been a community radio practitioner for more than 30 years, and during that time have observed several kinds of controversy and struggle erupting within the field. In this paper, I will examine radio and especially community radio in terms of gift economy concepts, and explore the hypothesis that much of the conflict that emerges within community radio can be seen as a conflict between a nurturing gift model and a hierarchical or patriarchal-exchange model.

Definitions and Discussion

First, how is community radio different from other kinds of radio broadcasting? In practice, the definition of community radio is inconsistently applied, and can overlap with other categories such as public radio, state radio, development radio, and association radio,[2] and even commercial radio—especially in countries that have no enabling legislation for community radio licenses. However, in December 2003, the World Summit on the Information Society (see Civil Society Initiative on Community Media) divided mass media into three recognized sectors: commercial media, public service media, and community media. Each of these sectors can be described in terms of a gift analysis.

Commercial Radio

Commercial radio is a radio station (or network) set up as a business. Its owners sell advertising to raise revenue, and a money bottom line is usually the prime driver. It is often said of these stations that in business terms the product is the audience, which is sold to the advertiser for a profit, and that the content of the station is simply a means to attract the audience so that the audience's attention can be sold. Station rankings are determined by surveying selected people from the potential audience to find out what percentage of "market share" each station has captured, in terms of gender and age and economic groupings. For example, males 18-34 living in families making more than $100,000 a year would be a pretty desirable demographic, because it is relatively easy to get them to spend money on advertised goods. It is also fairly certain that you can attract a sizeable amount of them with the right bait. The preference for a male demographic tends to skew broadcasting content towards lowest common denominator fodder for males, such as sports, smart-ass commentary (and on television, sex and violence).

In the United States, the Federal Communications Commission (FCC) formerly interpreted the *Communications Act* of 1937 to mitigate the commercial nature of broadcast media and require that it give something of value to the public.

> The policy ... that became known as the "Fairness Doctrine" is an attempt to ensure that all coverage of controversial issues by a broadcast station be balanced and fair. The FCC took the view, in 1949, that station licensees were "public trustees," and as such had an obligation to afford reasonable opportunity for discussion of contrasting points of view on controversial issues of public importance. The Commission later held that stations were also obligated to actively seek out issues of importance to their community and air programming that addressed those issues. With the deregulation sweep of the Reagan Administration during the 1980s, the Commission dissolved the fairness doctrine. (Limburg)

Congress passed a law in 1987 to try to restore the Fairness Doctrine by writing into law what had formerly been only administrative regulations of the FCC. However, President Reagan vetoed the bill, and other attempts have failed. Other obligations of commercial broadcasters that have been dissolved since the 1980s in the U.S. include obligations to air news and public service programming, to give a right of reply against attack,[3] and "to offer 'equal opportunity' to all legally qualified political candidates for any office if they had allowed any person running in that office to use the station" (Limburg). This final requirement was suspended for 60 days by the FCC, shortly before the 2000 election, and resulted in, for example, some Belo Corporation TV stations reportedly refusing to air Democratic Presidential Candidate Al Gore's ads.[4] The suspension of the equal time rule was supposedly in anticipation of a court ruling striking down the rule on grounds that it violated broadcasters' right of free speech; however, as of the present writing the courts have not definitively ruled on this matter.[5]

The rhetoric of the broadcast regulation that emerged in the U.S. from the 1937 *Broadcasting Act* turned upon the issue of scarcity. Because broadcasting spectrum was a scarce resource and was interpreted as belonging to the public, this supposedly justified putting requirements on broadcasters to meet community needs. In 1980, broadcasters were required to make an annual survey of nineteen categories of potential community needs and show how they responded to this with programming; by 2000, they were only required to keep a public file of any community issues and programs they aired. Within this time frame, the *Telecommunications Act* of 1996 changed the rules to permit the same owners to have almost unlimited numbers of radio stations. "Family owned" radio stations that might have some human ties to the local community have virtually disappeared, swallowed up and chased out by a very limited number of fiercely competitive conglomerates (Mills and Schardt 2000).

The commonly stated rationale for permitting these ownership changes is that with the availability of more kinds of media outlets (for example, cable TV and radio, satellite radio and netcasting), there is no longer a scarcity of media outlets. However,

> Since 1994, the Federal Communications Commission (FCC) has conducted auctions of licenses for electromagnetic spectrum. These auctions are open to any eligible company or individual that submits an application and upfront payment, and is found to be a qualified bidder by the Commission. (FCC "Auctions")

In effect, by permitting a few of the largest cash- and credit-rich companies free reign in enclosing the Commons, government is colluding in an artificially-enhanced scarcity of broadcasting spectrum. In the words of former Clinton-appointed FCC Chairman Bill Kennard: "Of course, spectrum has always been in short supply. But never in history have we seen more intense demands on the spectrum resource. We are in danger of suffering a 'spectrum drought' in our country."[6]

In the words of Bebe Facundus, who was forced by economics to sell the commercial women's radio station she had created in Louisiana, "Only three entities own everything [i.e., all the commercial radio stations] in the city of Baton Rouge, and that's happening throughout the country" (qtd. in Werden). These conglomerate owners could buy up the most powerful stations with the best reception and greatest audience reach; using economies of scale they could undersell her in advertising until they drove her out of business, and they (and the casinos) could hog and drive up the price of billboards used for radio promotion. Facundus tried to make her station both attractive and useful to women in her community—an example of how a commercial station that is locally owned can cross over category and be oriented towards meeting needs. She put a large amount of her own money into the station but was unable or unwilling to absorb a big financial loss as the conditions in the community changed. She also says about her experience that she had a problem with male investors, whom she had to buy out because "if men come in with any money they think they own everything" (qtd. in Werden).

The loss of local ownership and local accountability is now recognized by the public in the U.S., and has generated such a backlash against the FCC that in October 2003 the federal regulatory body created a "Localism Task Force":

> … to evaluate how broadcasters are serving their local communities. Broadcasters must serve the public interest, and the Commission has consistently interpreted this to require broadcast licensees to air programming that is responsive to the interests and needs of their communities. (FCC "Powell Statement")[7]

A North Carolina TV station's website contained this reporting about the FCC hearing in Charlotte, which was attended by Chairman Michael Powell and other commissioners:

> Powell, one of three Republicans on the commission who backed the new rules, has said he believes the issue of how broadcasters serve their local community should be addressed separately from the ownership rules. But he could not stop speakers from bringing up the ownership dispute at the Charlotte hearing. "To try to talk about localism without discussing media ownership is avoiding the issue," said Tift Merritt, a singer-songwriter from Raleigh who told the FCC members she was unable to get her songs on her local radio station. Her comment drew applause from the packed hearing. ("FCC Localism Hearing Draws Large Vocal Crowd" 2003)

In contrast to 1960, when "Payola" (companies paying to get their records played on radio stations) was a crime, today in the U.S.: "Listeners may not realize it, but radio today is largely bought by the record companies. Most rock and Top 40 stations get paid to play the songs they spin by the companies that manufacture the records" (Boehlert 2001). This affects not only local artists and the local audiences who would like to hear songs on the radio that reflect local culture, but they also shut out smaller and independent record-labels.

Several extreme failures by conglomerate radio stations to meet local needs were widely publicized and became one of the main reasons for the FCC localism hearings. For example:

In January 2002, a train carrying 10,000 gallons of anhydrous ammonia derailed in the town of Minot, causing a spill and a toxic cloud. Authorities attempted to warn the residents of Minot to stay indoors and to avoid the spill. But when the authorities called six of the seven radio stations in Minot to issue the warning, no one answered the phones. As it turned out, Clear Channel owned all six of the stations and none of the station's personnel were available at the time. ("#17 Clear Channel Monopoly Draws Criticism" 2004[8]).

And then there was the report, also from the North Carolina, that the *Bob and Madison Morning Show* on WDCG-FM had included a lot of hate talk directed at cyclists, including discussion of how much fun it was to run cyclists off the road. Cycling organizations' protests got the station to promise to run road safety announcements, but these public service announcements were reportedly also parodied and derided by the morning show hosts ("Poor, Poor Broadcasters Might Have to Endure Complaints at FCC Localism Hearings…" 2003).

So-called "shock radio" with hate elements, including sexism, has become standard fare for many commercial radio stations across the U.S., especially in the most widely listened-to time slots. Howard Stern, a shock jock syndicated by a CBS subsidiary, got away with advocating rape, among other things (Pozner 1999). According to the New York-based NGO Fairness and Accuracy in Reporting (FAIR), hate radio is political.[9] This assessment would seem to be borne out by the fact that Stern's show was cancelled from all the stations of the vast Clear Channel network in February 2004. While CNN reported that this was because Stern violated the FCC's new decency standards ("Howard Stern Suspended for Indecency" 2004),[10] Stern himself was widely quoted as saying that it was because "I dared to speak out against the Bush administration and say that the religious agenda of George W. Bush concerning stem cell research and gay marriage is wrong" ("Stern Feels Bush-Whacked, End is Near" 2004).

Hate radio for political purposes is far more widespread than just in the U.S., of course. According to Radio Netherlands (2004), "Hate radio killed more than 800,000 people in the last decade." They maintain regularly updated listings of examples of both hate radio and peace radio stations. Among the examples of hate radio they list:

Radio Télévision Libre des Mille Collines (RTLM) is the most recent and widely reported symbol of "hate radio" throughout the world. Its broadcasts, disseminating hate propaganda and inciting to murder Tutsis and opponents to the regime, began on 8 July 1993, and greatly contributed to the 1994 genocide of hundreds of thousands.

This hate radio station in Rwanda was succeeded in 1994 by two peace radio stations, Radio Agatashya ("the swallow that brings hope" in Kinyarwanda) and Radio Amahoro ("Radio Peace"). However, both these stations were short-lived as a result of funding shortages.[11] Since 1997, women's programming has also been used to promote peace.[12]

The association between women's radio and peace has a flip side in that shock radio, also described as "aggressive reality" radio, finds more of its listenership among males (Dietrich 2003). Not surprisingly, it is also understood to be a tool of a religio- Republican hierarchical ideology that has been struggling hard against feminism and environmentalism in the U.S. Patrick Burkart (1995) analyzed this phenomenon:

> Using Clinton's election in 1992 as a basis for a backlash, talk show programs directed momentum-building campaigns of mass fax and phone call petitions to national politicians, especially in response to changing federal policies towards abortion restrictions, discrimination against gays and lesbians, and strengthening national educational standards.

America's most ubiquitous talk radio personality, Rush Limbaugh, undermined the reputation of feminism by popularizing the term "feminazis." Referencing early studies of Nazi radio, Burkhart (1995) found that America's sneering right-wing talk-jocks follow the same model—being absolutist and programming to build a false sense of consensus. "Disagreement and dissent are programmed out," he writes, as a targeted marketing tool. Shows are "de facto ... reaching only those audiences with lifestyles that support consumption of this entertainment technology." My own informal survey in 2002 showed Limbaugh was on the air Austin, Texas, 34 hours a week.

Groups ranging from FAIR in New York ("Challenging Hate Radio: A Guide for Activists"),[13] to the Coalition Against Hate Radio in Portland, Oregon ("Groups Demand End to 'Hate Radio'" 2002), among others, recommend liberals to mount campaigns that include calling in to hate radio programs. However, Burkart explains that the shock radio programs today use technologies such as pre-screening callers and using a delay to allow editing calls even on live radio, in order to build up a picture of monolithic public opinion supporting the host's fascistic pronouncements. As Genevieve Vaughan writes in *For-Giving* (1997):

> An environment is created in which some ideas fit together and thrive because they are validated as permissible and respectable, while their alternatives are discredited. The so-called 'free market' of ideas, like the economic free market, often promotes the benefit of a (genetically superior?) few while appearing to be good for everyone.... Systems of ideas which have been taught us as the truth back up the political and economic systems of which they are a part. (19)

Burkart's (1995) analysis of right-wing radio is corroborative of that insight: "Shock radio is a technocratic forum, portraying its ideological perspective ... delivering daily, oracular, absolutist insights. Rush Limbaugh reminds his audience regularly that he is the only voice of the truth in 'the media.'"

Commercialism also has a role in less "mainstream" hate radio, whose purveyors simply buy time from commercial operators that exercise no control over the content. This, for example, appears on the website of famous Nazi sympathizer Ernst Zundel:

> With only a limited budget, anyone can buy airtime on hundreds of AM or shortwave stations throughout America. Almost everyone listens to the radio! Ernst Zundel urges his listeners to join the "Freedom Evolution" towards Truth and Justice, by participating in this bold new venture in mass communication.

Public Service Radio

Public service radio could mean many things,[14] but you can get an idea of the generally accepted range by looking at the membership of the European Broadcasting Union. Its members are radio and television companies, most of which are government-owned public service broadcasters or privately owned stations with public missions. Support and control relationships between public service broadcasters and governments vary. Stations and networks may be owned by the government like Radio Mozambique (TV Radio World). They may be owned by a foundation partly controlled by the government, like Swedish national radio (Ruhnbro 2004). Or, they may be owned by a state-initiated private company, funded by a dedicated tax and with nominal government control, like the BBC. In the case of National Public Radio in the U.S., you have a non-profit corporation indirectly funded by a line in the government budget, with the money laundered first through the Corporation for Public Broadcasting (a bipartisan politically directed body) and then through a network of member stations that are also listener-, donor-, and business-funded. Looking at these structures, you can infer that public service radio is intended to be for the public benefit, but not "by the people." In many cases, the government makes show of an arms-length relationship, but I think it is fair to say that these entities are expected to promote stability in the present system and cannot afford to be radical. It is a fact, however, that in the current climate of capitalist globalization even maintaining the status quo can become radical by default.

Remember that radio itself is only about 100 years old. In 1894, Marconi "made a bell ring using radio waves." In 1902 there was a "public demonstration of radio." Not until 1906 were the first radio set advertised and the first music broadcast on radio. Radio transmitters interfering with each other soon became an obvious problem. The first U.S. law to regulate broadcasters was passed in 1912 ("Radio Broadcasting History"). This was, incidentally, the year the Titanic sank, a ship that had a radio but couldn't reach anyone with it. The nearest ship did not have a 24-hour radio operator. It was also the period of the First World War, and governments could certainly see the building power of radio for war, not only at home but also in their colonies.

New Zealand passed the first law to require government licensing of radio, in 1903 ("A Brief History of Regulation of Radiocommunications in New Zealand, 1903-2003"), while it was still a British colony ("Timeline: New Zealand"). Private broadcasting was introduced in New Zealand in 1923, but in 1936 the 22 private broadcasters were nationalized to create a state broadcasting monopoly. In 1947, New Zealand became one of many colonies that gained full independence from Britain. Like other former British colonies (and most of the rest of the world) it retained monopoly broadcasting and looked to the BBC for ideas. However, the BBC's programming was supported by government-levied licensing fees for radio receivers, and New Zealand was too small a country to make much money that way; hence, they took advertising, with its attendant pressure to make programs attractive to wealthy businesses. They also bought the majority of their programs from BBC.

In the mid-1980s, a New Zealand Royal Commission "advocated a strong public service system with limits on advertising levels and a local program quota." But instead, national broadcasting was made into a state-owned enterprise that was supposed to return a profit to the government. Bids for programs the government wanted produced were let out for bidding to private companies. One big project the government funded was the medical soap opera *Shortland Street,* "NZOA's major prime-time vehicle for representing a changing national culture." *Shortland Street* is a wonderful example of how government-funded programs can be politically shifted. Watched by 700,000 people every weeknight, the show has been top-ranked drama in the country ever since its debut. But as its website describes, the program has changed:

> When Shortland Street began in 1992, "privatization" and "business practice" were the buzzwords of a health system reinventing itself. The direction of healthcare seemed to lie in the private accident and emergency clinics springing up around the country. The forward-looking clinic Shortland Street A&E Medical was the way of the future.
>
> Ten years later, faced with a decline in the demand for specialist private clinic services, Shortland Street has become a public hospital, funded by a district health board, and managed by a DHB-appointed CEO. Reflecting the heath services most in demand in the fictional suburb of Ferndale, it provides a 24-hour accident and emergency service, community services (including GPs and preventative health care programs), and elective surgery facilities.

The program had been initiated by the right-wing National Party during the Labour Party interregnum of 1990-1999, with the obvious political aim of normalizing privatized healthcare. Perhaps unfortunately for the Labour Party when it returned, it wasn't as simple to turn around broadcasting policy as it was to change content. In 1991, New Zealand under the National Party had dropped all restrictions on transnational ownership of broadcasting, and the results were disappointing to some:

Although the introduction of competition has significantly increased the number of television services available within New Zealand, there is heated debate as to whether it has extended the range of programming on offer. Critics of the reforms point to the cultural costs of the minimal restrictions on commercial operators, the intensified competition for ratings points ... the absence of any quota to protect local programming, to NZOA's inability to compel stations to show the programs it has funded in favourable slots; and to the marked increase in advertising time which gives more space to commercial speech and less to other voices. (Murdock)

The National Party had not only deregulated New Zealand's broadcasting sector, it had made a gift of it to the corporations and corporate-controlled states through the General Agreement on Trade and Services (GATS), an internationally negotiated trade pact.

New Zealand deregulated its broadcasting sector and listed it as a covered service under the GATS. It is thus constrained from reintroducing content quotas, despite a change in government and a clear public will to re-regulate the sector. ("Advancing Cultural Diversity Globally" 2003)

Most other countries have similar points of struggle to New Zealand's. There are governments that still maintain broadcasting monopolies, but far fewer now, even in Africa and Asia. Zimbabwe remains one of the few governments that maintain total monopoly over broadcasting. Recently a high-ranking minister in Zimbabwe cancelled the popular national anti-AIDS TV soap opera *Mopane Junction*, because funding had come from the Centers for Disease Control in the United States (Khumalo 2004).

Canada is a country that still has a major government-funded public service broadcaster. Through a combination of budget cuts and exponential growth of its competition, the Canadian Broadcasting Corporation (CBC) has lost ground in the ratings, but is still the major opinion-testing ground of the nation, and clearly courts more diversity of opinions than the U.S. commercial talk radio referenced in the beginning of this article. Canada also has stiff requirements for Canadian Content (CanCon) in the music played on its radio outlets; and the province of Quebec has additional quotas for playing songs that include at least some French.

With so much shared border and so much shared language between Canada and the economically and culturally aggressive U.S., the results of dropping Canadian cultural quotas and subsidies would be instantly noticeable and highly unpopular. Canada was one of the countries that brought the 2003 Free Trade Area of the Americas (FTAA) to a halt in the fall of 2003, largely over the issue of protection of cultural diversity. Other countries share Canada's concerns. The UNESCO Executive Committee recommended in 2003 that a Convention on Cultural Diversity be developed as a legally-binding international instrument, citing:

•There is a growing awareness that aspects of globalization are leading to cultural homogenization and increasing the difficulties for local and diverse cultural production.

•Bilateral and multilateral trade agreements make the situation worse by limiting the ability of nations to support their own artists, cultural producers and institutions. Trade in "products and services" of the "entertainment industry" is big business, accounting for an increasing share of the trade balance of several countries.

•"Exempting" culture from trade rules has been ineffective in preserving cultural sovereignty. WTO rules have been applied to cultural activities by trade panels. Cultural policies are increasingly made to conform to trade commitments. Developing nations cannot promote their own indigenous artists and cultural producers even when they have the capacity to implement appropriate policies.

UNESCO's General Conference Approved the Convention on the Protection and Promotion of the Diversity of Cultural Expressions on 20 October 2005.[15]

Sweden provides a tidy example of public service radio at the service of national policy (see Ministry of Culture). The current guidelines for Sweden's public service broadcasting were vetted by a committee appointed by the government that included members of all the parties in the Riksdag (Parliament). What they accepted includes this definition:

In general terms the task of public service radio and TV can be described as giving everyone access to a balanced and independent selection of high quality programs with no commercial advertising. Among other things this means that the broadcasts shall reach people throughout the country and that the broadcasts shall be so composed that it ranges from programs of general interest to the more specialized, at the same time as the citizens are given new and unexpected choices of programs and genres. The broadcasts shall be characterized by the fundamental democratic principles by which the state is governed and shall meet the requirements of impartiality, objectivity and independence of both state and private interests, and of political, economic and other spheres of authority. All programs shall be of high quality. Another important aspect is that the broadcasts shall reflect the country as a whole and that programs therefore shall be produced in different parts of Sweden.

One may note within the description above a number of phrases that are typically used for keeping station and programming decision-making within establishment boundaries, such as "of high quality," and "objectivity."[16] "Diversity," explicitly mentioned elsewhere in the guidelines, is largely described in terms of geography and alternative languages. But we also see, later in the same document, indicators that Sweden intends public service broadcasting should be something of a counterweight to private media consolidation:

> Public service radio and television enjoy high status and will become in-
> creasingly important when there is greater competition. The Government
> proposes that the fundamental principles for public service broadcasting shall
> continue to apply and considers that there is broad agreement on having
> well-established public service radio and television companies in Sweden in
> the future. Vigorous public service radio and television can provide a strong
> balancing force in a media landscape that otherwise risks being dominated
> by a few actors. (Ministry of Culture)

In early 2004, there was a conflict in the UK around the independence of the
BBC from government control. I had imagined when I began researching this that
BBC was a government entity that had been granted independence by sufferance,
but when I looked into its history, I found that it was actually a private-public
partnership from its inception in 1922:

> Though it was the Post Office that had initiated the meeting, it was the six
> main manufacturers of radio equipment (the Marconi Company, Metro-
> politan-Vickers, the Western Electric Company, the Radio Communication
> Company, the General Electric Company, and the British Thompson-Houstan
> Company) who were asked to form a committee to prepare the plan for
> broadcasting in Britain.

The formation of the BBC involved companies making a capital investment
for setting up transmitting stations that would reach all of Britain, thus creating
a demand for radio receivers. The "new BBC was to undertake to sell only Brit-
ish-made sets, to pay to the Company ten per cent of the net wholesale selling
price of all broadcast receiving apparatus." BBC was also forbidden to accept
money for carrying any message or music, except with written permission from
the Postmaster. In 1927, Parliament joined the troika with the Postmaster-General
and the corporate governors, and was nominally given "ultimate control" of the
BBC; but basically "broadcasting had become a monopoly, financed by licensing
fees on radio receivers, and administered by an independent public corporation"
("The Unofficial Guide t the BBC").

One of the stumbling blocks BBC had to get around when it began was opposition by the British newspaper industry. Initially the industry won a ruling
saying that the BBC would have to buy and pay for its news from existing print
news services. Before long, of course, it outstripped these other sources—it still
pays rather well, but has its own relationship with correspondents. Recently the
conflict between BBC and newspapers has heated up again, though, and the crux
of the matter is related to gift giving.

In August 2003, a headline appeared reading, "Dyke to Open Up BBC Archive."
Greg Dyke, Director General of the BBC, had announced that:

…everyone would in future be able to download BBC radio and TV programs from the internet. The service, the BBC Creative Archive, would be free and available to everyone, as long as they were not intending to use the material for commercial purposes….

"The BBC probably has the best television library in the world," said Mr Dyke, who was speaking at the Edinburgh TV Festival…. "I believe that we are about to move into a second phase of the digital revolution, a phase which will be more about public than private value; about free, not pay services; about inclusivity, not exclusion…. It will be about how public money can be combined with new digital technologies to transform everyone's lives."

Dyke's announcement of free content fell in the middle of a spate of decisions by other UK news agencies that they were going to start charging for content on the Internet. An analysis appeared on the University of Southern California's *Online Journalism Review*:

The BBC has the most popular British news website by far, with 16 to 20 million unique users per month. But it has pockets £2 billion ($3.32 billion) deep, filled with taxpayers' money. While it does not run advertising, most commercial newspapers believe that the BBC makes it harder to compete and survive because it poaches potential readers and subscribers.

The BBC response is to claim the public service defense. "We believe that the news we provide is a valuable service for the UK's license fee payers," said Pete Clifton, the newly appointed editor for BBC News Online. "It delivers to them, on an increasingly important platform, a rich source of BBC News content which they may have missed elsewhere. This content, paid for by them, covers news from local to international, and we feel it is right to make this available on the Web."

Newspapers are eagerly awaiting the British government's online review, which will report on the market impact of BBC's Web business next year. Many in the industry want curbs placed on the BBC Online; they hope the online review will make recommendations to that effect.

All of the United Kingdom's bigger online news operations are focused now on growing profits—and doing that is naturally more difficult in a market-place where one of your competitors is deeply subsidized and giving away top product for free. (Ó hAnluain, 2004)

This controversy reflects a very deep conflict in societies around the world between models of socially-provided goods and services that are collectively sup-ported for all, and individual payment on the barrelhead for everything (even essentials of life like water). In the case of public service radio in the UK, "free" access to information and entertainment was made possible by over-the-air broadcasting to all who have the receivers, and those who bought the receivers paid for this information through dedicated taxes. Now public access, to what is essentially collective wealth, is being vastly extended by the BBC's opening its archives to all who have sufficient Internet tool access, and this is considered an attack by those who need a condition of scarcity to help them make money on selling information.

It is important to note that the resemblance between the issue of information access and water access is not merely coincidental. Both are the subject of extremely heated trade negotiations, legislative activity, regulatory interpretations, and court fights all over the world, brought by a corporate sector that seeks to privatize valuable resources in both the material and the information commons. New laws formed in these arenas are extending copyrights, so that the products of creativity are not coming out into the public domain. They are newly criminalizing the copying of "intellectual property" even for individual use, research, or critical analysis. They are giving broadcasters and distributors new ownership rights over material that they did not create. And they are extending enforcement jurisdiction not only to those who actually copy or share protected intellectual property, but to those whose services or equipment designs are used in these newly illegal activities. That means Internet service providers (ISPs) and engineers being held liable for what might be done by others. ISPs in some places are being subpoenaed to provide the names of their users who might potentially be sharing music files, for example, and coerced to provide this information under penalty of law.[17] As pointed out by attorney Robin Gross (2003) of the organization IP Justice, these new laws and trade regimes contravene an international human right, Article 19 of the Universal Declaration of Human Rights, which states: "Everyone has the right to freedom of opinion and expression; this right includes freedom to hold opinions without interference and to seek, receive and impart information and ideas through any media and regardless of frontiers."

This brings us then to the final section of this article, and a discussion of community radio.

Community Radio

Community radio is the form most clearly concerned not only with people's ability to seek and receive information through media, but also with our ability to "impart information and ideas" to one another. As Genevieve Vaughan (1997) has pointed out, "'Co-muni-cation' is giving gifts (from the Latin munus—gift) together. It is how we form 'co-muni-ty'" (25-26).

Since the first community station started broadcasting to Bolivian miners in 1947, the movement's development has been uneven in both geography and time, but now it is growing fast. As of 2005, Jordan licensed what is probably the first community station broadcasting in Arabic. In 2006, both the UK and India finally opened to more than a few experimental licenses; and Nepal, where the monarch tried to suppress community news, had a revolution with community broadcasters as heroes. In 2006, Mexico, which had legalized community radio, illegalized it again by privatizing broadcast regulation; Indigenous communities have literally fought battles to remain on the air. In 2003, the World Bank announced it intended to put 100 community radio stations on the air in Africa, raising debates about what constitutes community radio, and whether it is distinct from "development" radio and other potentially donor-controlled models. There is no single exemplar by which community radio can be defined.

**Some stations are owned by not-for-profit groups or by cooperatives whose members are the listeners themselves. Others are owned by students, universities, municipalities, churches or trade unions. There are stations financed by donations from listeners, by international development agencies, by advertising and by governments. *"Waves for Freedom." Report on the Sixth World Conference of Community Radio Broadcasters, Dakar, Senegal.* ("What is Community Radio?")

The World Association of Community Radio Broadcasters (Association Mondiale des Radiodiffuseurs Communautaires [AMARC]), based in Montreal, promotes mutual support among community radios around the world. They organized the Dakar conference of community broadcasters referenced above, as well as eight others since 1983. AMARC has members that are licensed and members that broadcast illegally; members that are free-standing stations, members that do community radio in the permitted niches of state broadcasters, and members that share frequencies with stations that may have incompatible aims to their own. If you go to the AMARC website <www.amarc.org> and click on "What is Community Radio?" you'll find instead of one definition a series of quotes submitted by members in different regions. For example, from Latin America, where community radio stations are numerous and are often strongly linked to anti-oligarchical struggles:

Radio stations that bear this name do not fit the logic of money or advertising. Their purpose is different, their best efforts are put at the disposal of civil society. Of course this service is highly political: it is a question of influencing public opinion, denying conformity, creating consensus, broadening democracy. The purpose—whence the name—is to *build community life.* *"Manual urgente para Radialistas Apasionados."*

In Latin America, there are approximately one thousand radio stations that can be considered community, educational, grassroots or civic radio stations. They are characterized by their political objectives of social change, their search for a fair system that takes into account human rights, and makes power accessible to the masses and open to their participation. *"Gestión de la radio comunitaria y ciudadana."*

From Canada, where community radio is obligated by government to promote diversity and Canadian culture:

340

The tone of each community radio station is well modulated in the image of its listeners. The important thing is to seek out differences. Community radio is an element of closeness, a bridge, a step toward the other, not to make the other like us, but to have him become what he is. It is not a question of having more, but of being, that is the real mission of community radio stations in Canada. Isn't the most meaningful definition of culture the act of making people aware of the greatness they possess? *Alliance des radios communautaires du Canada (ARC) Canada.*

From France:

Free, independent, lay radio stations that are linked to human rights and concerned about the environment. They are many and pluralistic. They refuse mercantile communication. They scrupulously respect the code of ethics of journalists and work to disseminate culture by giving artists broader expression within their listening audiences. They have association status, democratic operation and financing consistent with the fact that they are non-profit organizations. They are solidary toward each other and constitute work communities that make it possible for each member to fulfill its mission to the utmost. *Charte de la Confédération Nationale des Radios Libres (CNRL), France.*

From the Philippines, where radio was very powerful in mobilizing People Power that overthrew the Marcos dictatorship:

Stations collectively operated by the community people. Stations dedicated to development, education and people empowerment. Stations which adhere to the principles of democracy and participation. *TAMBULI, Communication Project, Philippines*

From Africa:

The historical philosophy of community radio is to use this medium as the voice of the voiceless, the mouthpiece of oppressed people (be it on racial, gender, or class grounds) and generally as a tool for development. *AMARC Africa and Panos Southern Africa.*

A far-reaching example of community radio organizing, started by women, originated in Africa during the period when government-controlled radio was the rule across the continent. In 1988, the Zimbabwe chapter of the Federation of African Media Women (FAMW) resolved to get more rural women's participation into broadcasting, and came up with the idea for radio listening clubs (Matewa 2002[18]). These professional women communicators contacted women in rural villages, asked them to listen to the radio as a group, and then recorded the rural women's comments and questions. Next the journalists took the rural women's questions to public officials and asked them to respond. Programs combining these elements were aired on Zimbabwe Radio 4. The rural women listened to the programs, again responded, and the series went on in this vein. Eventually, having observed how little it took to make the recordings, the rural women asked to be given their own recording equipment, and told the professional journalists they were no longer needed during the discussions (Karonga 1999).

Radio listening clubs spread first to other countries in the Southern Africa Development Community (SADC) region, and then to other parts of the world. It became a model for other feminist and community media projects in film, video, and still photography. And it's been copied by governmental and non-governmental development agencies seeking to accelerate social change. In *Media and the Empowerment of Communities for Social Change,* Chido Matewa (2002) writes of radio listening clubs: "Grassroots participation is what sets this project design apart and distinguishes it from other rural radio which is in line with the agenda setting theory of McCombs and Shaw, i.e., that the media agenda (MA) leads to the people's agenda (PA)."[19]

According to Matewa, radio listening club membership declines when radio sets become more available in villages, so expansion has been in ever more remote areas. Another problem may be that the association of radio listening clubs with state radio, and the adaptation of the radio listening club model to the aims of development agencies change the experience from participatory to didactic, and reduces its value as a gift. One gets a hint of local contempt for such coercion in a speech delivered by Kate Azuka Omunegha (2003) at the World Forum on Communication Rights:

> One thing that seems to be glaring in Nigerian media is the near absence of women as newsmakers. One possible reason for this is the new news value, which privileges prominence, who is involved. Closely related to this again is the idea that Nigerian media seem to work with what we call the ideology of developmental communication. The media are seen as the mouthpiece of the government.

As more governments have opened up space for independent broadcasters, though, some community radio stations have been created that incorporate values from radio listening clubs and also consciously draw on the values taught by Brazilian popular educationist Paolo Freire, values such as starting with people's own lived experience, *concientizacion* (a word that is very popular in Latin America, but whose closest common North American equivalent is "consciousness raising"), and emphasis on dialogue that involves respect and working together.

There are community radios in Africa consciously promoting those values. The one I visited, Radio Ada, was first set up to serve the coastal fishing community of Ada, but because they could uniquely fill a need for local, participatory radio programming in the Dangme language, they ended up serving the entire region of about 500,000 Dangme-speaking people, half of whom are not literate. The station's mission as reported on the website of their funder, UNESCO, is "to support the development aspirations and objectives of the Dangme people, give a voice to the voiceless, sustain the growth of Dangme culture, and encourage, promote and contribute to informed dialogue and reflective action" ("Ghana: Radio Goes Up in the Air").

I visited Radio Ada in 2003, in the company of the coordinator of the Ghana Community Radio Network, and was fascinated by a description of how they work on reflective action in the public sphere. First, I was told, they ask the people what their problems are, then whose responsibility it is to deal with the problems. Then they go to those responsible, often public officials, and ask what they have done to meet their commitments around the problem. Then they give everybody time to think and work on the problem. This groundwork is done before beginning any recording, so no one is shamed on air before they've had a chance to improve their practice. I was told that this was normal procedure for all four stations in the Ghana Community Radio Network.[20]

Another African station that grew directly out of the radio listening club movement was Radio Mama, the women's station in Kampala, Uganda, regrettably shut down by the Ugandan government on January 8, 2004 (reportedly for not having paid its license fees) ("Mama FM Closes"). According to an interview I conducted in 2002, Radio Mama had been assigned a broadcasting frequency that could not be picked up on car radios, a staggering handicap for developing an audience. (Note: Radio Mama has re-opened!)

The issue of who is the audience, in other words, who is the recipient of the gift of radio, is a crucial one for community stations. To be community stations in the sense of "giving gifts together," the audience and the operators of the station should be interrelated categories.

Radio Ada co-founder and Deputy Director Wilna Quarmyne (2001) clearly subscribes to this view. She is originally from the Philippines, where she was also involved in the community radio and popular education movements. She writes that the approach to training in the station's activities was

…originally developed in 1997 for and at Radio Ada, the first full-fledged community radio station in Ghana. The approach is continually being enriched and has succeeded in enabling a group of volunteers with no previous training or experience in broadcasting to operate a full-scale, 17-hour-a-day service entirely on their own. Some of the volunteers have grown into trainers. The approach has also been extended with positive outcomes to other member stations of the Ghana Community Radio Network, as well as to a prospective community radio station in Ethiopia.

In some stations, the radio audience may be virtually coterminous with the presenters. The legendary Margaretta D'Arcy is an AMARC member who runs Radio Pirate Women in Galway, Ireland, a pirate (unlicensed) station that operates during periodic Women's Radio Festivals, using a transmitter small enough to fit in a purse. When asked how many listeners the station had, D'Arcy stated that listeners were completely unimportant—that what is important is that the women talk on the radio, they listen to each other, get all fired up, and then they go out in the street and they demonstrate!

Another type of pirate radio is represented by the movement of small, unlicensed radio stations that sprang up across the United States, mainly during the 1980s and 1990s. Often organized by young people under the philosophical banner of anarchism, some of these stations followed a model of open access, allowing all comers to express themselves without any restriction, with DJ's cursing frequently, while others, such as KIND in San Marcos, Texas, had the open blessing and participation of the local establishment (Pyle 2001; Markoff).[21] However, unlicensed radio stations are still proliferating in many parts of the world, such as Mexico (Calleja 2006) and Haiti, where community radio licensing is unavailable to local or indigenous communities. These stations' equipment is often seized or destroyed by authorities, as by virtue of its signal it is impossible for a broadcast station to be truly clandestine.

Larger and more permanent community stations around the world usually have doors open for volunteers but also have some kind of long term paid staff for facilities management, and may also have staff setting programming policies. To maximize the gift-giving potential of community radio, leadership should ideally be nurturing and give way (Vaughan 1997: 96) to the needs of the organization, promote horizontal giving, and promote "abundance through the cessation of waste" (Vaughan 1997: 98). However, most stations also exist in a context of patriarchal hierarchicalism that can be insidious. In the United States, for instance, the Corporation for Public Broadcasting gives money to noncommercial radio stations that meet certain criteria, which in recent years have included having not less than five full-time paid staff members. This can provide an opening for stratification, and be in conflict with the kinds of values that often emerge from collective activity, where paid positions are often part-time or rotating jobs that help subsidize people of small financial means who are also volunteers. Professional aspirations of staff to earn higher salaries without moving on can lead to cutting in other areas (Gerry 1998), and staff desires to minimize conflicts and hassles and streamline decision-making for themselves can lead to imposition of rules and loss of flexibility. Allowing breaking of rules so as to be flexible for some people and not others is then a likely source of cronyism and dissatisfaction.

Another entrée for hierarchicalism is provided by the "ownership structures" of most noncommercial stations. In order to qualify for noncommercial frequencies, receive public funds, and offer tax-deductible status to donors, stations generally have to have boards of directors. In the U.S., only one state, Wisconsin, even permits nonprofit organizations to have a cooperative structure, and even those have to have boards of directors (Stockwell 2000). Directors have the legal liability for the station, the rights to change its bylaws and approve its budget, and are in effect treated by the law as the owners of the station. (And as volunteers have sometimes found when they tried to go to court against boards of directors, "ownership is nine-tenths of the law.") A famous recent struggle within the five-station Pacifica network turned in part on directors' decisions to change the board from elected to self-selected, and a suggestion that they would change the bylaws to allow board members to make a profit from activities performed for the station. In both staff and board hierarchies, you can see a potential for imposition of one/many structures, where the one or ones who are staff or board substitute and take over from the many who are volunteers or listeners (or both). This pattern can be found not only in community radio, but in many kinds of nonprofit organizations. A corollary of such a development is that volunteer contributions are devalued and raising and spending money takes over as the dominant activity of the organization. In the case of U.S. community radio, the Corporation for Public Broadcasting promoted such substitution by changing the way it awarded public funds. Where formerly stations' "match" for public funds they received could include volunteer hours assigned value in monetary terms, this was changed so that stations had to raise actual dollars to match the federal dollars they might be given (Anonymous 1995). This discounting of volunteers' gifts of their labour and denial of economic means to support that work seems related to the following statement in Vaughan's book, *For-Giving*: "Free gift giving to needs—what in mothering we would call nurturing or caring work—is often not counted and may remain invisible in our society or seem uninformative because it is qualitatively rather than quantitatively based" (1997: 24).

Many community stations run on very little funding, but even they have financial needs for equipment, for electricity, for materials, and usually for at least some paid staff that can spend the concentrated time to coordinate volunteers and keep things running smoothly. Whether the funds come from NGOs, foundations, the government, or business advertiser/underwriters, they often come with some kind of mandate, pressure or temptation to modify or abandon a social change agenda. Even listener donations can tempt community radios to play to the richer elements of society. One of the most frequently heard debates within listener-supported radio is whether the value of the program should be measured by how much money is donated to the station when that program is on the air, and whether shows that don't raise enough money should be dropped, even if they serve a disadvantaged audience.

A related conflict is whether the value of a station can be measured by the number of its listeners. Commercial radio stations use commercial measuring services to come up with audience "ratings." The sample of people asked to give data on their listening habits is supposedly randomly selected from fixed demographic categories (e.g., males 18-34). Standings in the Arbitron ratings are used to rank stations in terms of "market share" both geographically and demographically, and these figures in turn are used by stations to set advertising rates. That is the process by which the invisible product of human attention to radio is made visible and sold.[22] Similar methods of audience measurement have been adopted by National Public Radio (NPR) in the U.S. Their audience surveys include asking whether their listeners use or buy long lists of products, but have little (usually nothing) about the listeners' social change activities. Starting in the 1980s, a well-publicized goal of their audience research department was to "double the NPR audience," and the announced plan for doubling the audience was to have stations program so that the same people would keep listening longer. This led to a conscious effort to program more for the well-off white male, the same demographic that commercial radio found most desirable. While some editions of *The NPR Audience* noted that older women are actually more generous and consistent listener-donors, they were considered a shrinking part of the audience, and of course they were less attractive to underwriters. (Underwriting is a form of quasi-advertising that NPR, PBS, and most U.S. public radio and television stations now pursue heavily.)

Within U.S. community radio, two divergent streams of thought emerged around the question of audience. One faction believed and promoted the concept that pursuing similar strategies to NPR's would be good for community radio and give it more listeners, more money, and greater stability. Their approach was to change stations so that there would be more paid programmers and hosts, a more consistent sound, and more mainstream kinds of music and information. This was similar to the usual public radio formula, and often included airing offerings from the major public radio syndicators, NPR and Public Radio International. Programs most likely to be cut included women's programs and other kinds of programs run by collectives or groups, the reason given usually being that shared responsibilities and changing hosts led to inconsistent air-sound. The other community radio faction, however, developed a very different self-identity, rejecting some of the advice that was being promoted to them through the collaborative efforts of the National Federation of Community Broadcasters (NFCB) and the Corporation for Public Broadcasters. In 1996, breakaway stations from NFCB created a new annual conference, the Grassroots Radio Conference (GRC), "as a reaction against the homogenization of commercialization of public radio." The founders of the GRC, Marty Durlin of KGNU in Boulder, Colorado, and Cathy Melio of WERU in Maine, wrote an article explaining their movement. I excerpt here from a version found on the web:

> You can recognize a grassroots community station anywhere in the country. There is a freshness you'll not hear elsewhere due largely to the variety of voices and connections the station has with its community.... Local programming is the backbone of community radio, [but] another element that connects grassroots stations are the independently-produced national programs many of us broadcast, including Alternative Radio ... WINGS (Women's International News Gathering Service), National Native News, and Making Contact.
>
> These national programs connect the grassroots stations, while our local programs ground us in our own communities.... Sometimes the performances of inexperienced programmers are rough...[but] those new voices

become competent and creative broadcasters before our very ears.... It is insulting the intelligence of people to think that they can not accept or appreciate variety of programming.... We believe in expanding the audience for the variety, not reducing the variety to expand the audience.... Important principles to maintaining a community involved grassroots station are: participatory governance, with active committees involved in decision-making, community and volunteer involvement in all major decisions, openness on the air (no gag orders!), elected volunteer representatives serving on the board of directors, open access to the airwaves, active recruitment and ongoing training of volunteers, commitment to diversity, consideration of those under-served by other broadcast media, and diverse programming. (Durlin and Melio)

The GRC has done much to strengthen the self-identity and resolve of community radio in the U.S., and its model has had a strong impact. Throughout the eight years of GRC conferences, it has also provided a national venue for the struggles of volunteers and listeners to reclaim the five-station Pacifica network from its runaway board. Many of the GRC stations were affiliates of the syndicated programming distributed by the Pacifica network, and organized among themselves to support striking Pacifica news reporters and withhold affiliation fees in support of the struggle. After the volunteer-listener victory and re-organization of Pacifica, GRC co-founder Marty Durlin was overwhelmingly elected to chair the reclaimed board of the Pacifica Foundation, in March 2004.

In 2002, at the World Social Forum in Porto Alegre, Brazil, Brazilian popular education activist Moema Viezzer took me to visit a special community radio station. It had been set up with city government support for the use of the youth at the conference. They were broadcasting primarily via loudspeaker to the youth camping area, and to a landless-persons' camping area nearby. The studio was a large log building with a packed earth floor, and inside were rows of computers, and a complete broadcasting studio. Over the microphone was a sign, which Moema Viezzer translated for me: "A microphone is not a piss pot."

What did this mean? I wondered. Finally, this occurred to me: radio is gift giving, and gift giving is transitive (Vaughan, 1997: 36).[23] When you speak into a microphone, you don't do it to relieve yourself. You do it to reach people with something that will meet their needs.

An earlier version of this article, "Gifts of Sound," appeared in The Gift/ Il Dono: A Feminist Analysis *(special issue of* Athanor: Semiotica, Filosofia, Arte, Letteratura 15 (8), *edited by Genevieve Vaughan (Rome: Meltemi Editore, 2004).*

Frieda Werden is the co-founder and producer of WINGS: Women's International News Gathering Service; the Spoken Word Coordinator of CJSF-FM, Vancouver; ice President for North America of AMARC and President of the International Association of Women in Radio and TV.

Notes

1   For examples of gift economy proponents, see the speakers listed on the website of the 2004 International Conference on the Gift Economy at <http://www.gifteconomyconference.com/>.

2   An example of an association radio station serving the community is, Meridien FM in Tema, Ghana, owned by an association of women journalists. An example of a station formally owned as a commercial licensee functioning as a community station is Radio Ammannet in Amman, Jordan, founded by Daoud Kuttab. Radio Ammannet is hosting the 2006 conference of the World Association of Community Radio Broadcasters

3   "Corollaries to the fairness doctrine—the 'personal attack' and 'political editorializing' rules—were thrown out in October 2000 by the U.S. Circuit Court of Appeals for the District of Columbia" (Lee).

4   See WINGS #4-01: "Revenge on Big Media: Dallas's Cat-Killers." Radio program produced by Mary O' Grady for Women's International News Gathering Service and released in 2001.

5   "Section 315 of the *Communications Act*—the section that imposes an equal time requirement for all broadcasts featuring candidates—may itself be unconstitutional" (Dorf 2003).

6   I am using the U.S. as my primary example because I am most familiar with the process there, and because the process of enclosing the commons there is very stark. However, as will be discussed in the section on government radio, there is more than one way to ensure control through scarcity. Genevieve Vaughan's (2002) theory of the gift economy posits that the creation of scarcity is one function of the exchange economy: "The exchange paradigm requires scarcity in order to maintain its leverage. In capitalism, when abundance begins to accrue, scarcity is artificially created to save the exchange-based system. Agricultural products are plowed under in order to keep prices high. Money is spent on armaments and other waste and luxury items, or cornered in the hands of a few individuals or corporations in order to create and maintain an appropriate climate of scarcity for business as usual to continue. These mechanisms have other advantages which also reward successful exchangers with social status and power and penalize gift givers by making their gift giving (in scarcity) self sacrificial. A context of abundance would allow gift giving to flower while a context of scarcity discredits gift giving by making it painfully difficult." (94).

For information on the technical feasibility of alleviating scarcity of broadcasting spectrum through new methods of spectrum-sharing see, for example, the New America Foundation's Wireless Future Program <http://www.newamerica.net/index.cfm?pg=sec_home&secID=3>.

7   Chairman Michael Powell is the son of the U.S. Secretary of State Colin Powell. To see what is the "community" of media owners in the U.S. (and transnationally) today, see the web page "Who Controls the Media?" maintained by the National Organization for Women, as part of their campaign against lifting media ownership restrictions (see <http://www.nowfoundation.org/issues/communications/tv/mediacontrol.html>).

8   Summarizes coverage by Jeff Perlstein from September 2002.

9   See collection of back articles from FAIR on http://www.fair.org/media-outlets/talk-radio.html. In 2005, the Canadian Radio and Television Commission (CRTC) opened the door to shocked broadcasters by licensing U.S.-based Sirius Satellite Radio. While

Canada's content standards are different from those imposed by the FCC, *The Howard Stern Show* likely offends both. For the broadcast industry interpretation of CRTC standards regarding ethics, violence and sex portrayal, visit www.cbsc.ca and click on "codes."

10   These new "decency standards" are also quite political, a reversal of the entire trend toward deregulation of media content pleasing to the fundamentalist sector of the U.S. political right.

11   Radio Netherlands describes the funding crisis of Radio Agatashya: "In June 1994 it was pledged a U.S.\$20,000 grant by UNESCO, which it never received, and turned down a French government gift of 250,000 French francs owing to the French military involvement in Rwanda. It was funded by the UNHCR, European Union and the Swiss government.... The radio has been off the air since 27 October 1996, mainly due to a funding shortage."

12   See Case Study 9: Rwanda – Urunana (Hand in Hand). Online: <http://www.comminit.com/pdsradiodrama/sld-9388.html>

13   "Call in to the show. Call the on-air line during the show and try to challenge the racism, sexism or homophobia calmly and directly. It often doesn't take much to demonstrate the absurdity of bigoted arguments. If several people call in, it can change the entire show" ("Challenging Hate Radio: A Guide for Activists").

14   In the U.S., the term "public service radio" is sometimes applied to emergency radio communications used by police and fire departments, and "public radio" is used for the noncommercial broadcast stations.

15   The press release with a link to the full text of this UNESCO convention can be found on the web. See <http://portal.unesco.org/culture/en/ev.php-URL_ID=11281&URL_DO=DO_TOPIC&URL_SECTION=201.html> accessed March 28, 2006

16   See, for an example of such discussion, Noam Chomsky's book *Objectivity and Liberal Scholarship* (1967), which discusses objectivity as an ideological mask for championing mainstream self-interest against mass movements for change.

17   Robin Gross, speaking at the World Summit on the Information Society 2003, can be heard in radio program WINGS #52-03 Copyright and Human Rights, streamable from web page http://www.cas.usf.edu/womens_studies/wings.html.

18   See Chapter 5: "Participatory and Development Communication in Zimbabwe."

19   I can't resist commenting that the "MA leads to PA" formula might be phrased in a more feminist manner: "MA leads PA."

20   N.B.: "We are not using the violent methods of the system but are looking for other ways to change it from within" (Vaughan 1997: 23).

21   The pirate radio movement in the U.S. was greatly diminished by the availability of low-power FM licensing for under-served communities, starting in the year 2000 (Sakolsky 2001). For more on low-power FM licensing today, see the Prometheus Radio Project's website, www.prometheus.org.

22   I should mention here that community broadcasters, including both FIRE (Feminist International Radio Endeavour/Radio Internacional Feminista, based in Costa Rica) and the great community station Bush Radio in Cape Town, South Africa, are coming up with new and appropriate ways of not only measuring but valuing their audiences.

23   Also: "[G]iving to needs creates bonds between givers and receivers. Recognizing someone's need and acting to satisfy it, convinces the giver of the existence of the other, while receiving something from someone else that satisfies a need proves the existence of the other to the receiver" (Vaughan 1997: 24).

References

"#17 Clear Channel Monopoly Draws Criticism." Online: http://www.projectcensored. org/publications/2004/17.html.

"A Brief History of Regulation of Radio-communications in New Zealand 1903—2003." Online: http://www.med.govt.nz/rsm/publications/pibs/radiohistory/footnotes. html#fn09. Accessed March 6, 2004.

"Advancing Cultural Diversity Globally: The Role of Civil Society Movements." October 1, 2003. Online: http://www.incd.net/Conf2003/INCD_papers2003_Convention. htm. Accessed March 10, 2004.

Anonymous. [Pacifica] Program Director Meeting (Part II). Albuquerque, New Mexico. February 28, 1995. Online: http://www.radio4all.org/fp/pdmeet1.html.

Boehlert, Eric. "Pay for Play." 2001, March 14. Salon.com. Online: http://dir.salon. com/ent/feature/2001/03/14/payola/index.html.

Burkart, Patrick. 1995. "Radio Shock: Talk Radio Propaganda." *Bad Subjects* 23 (December 1995). Online: http://www.eserver.org/bs/23/burkart.html. Accessed March 6, 2004.

Calleja, Aleida. 2006, April. AMARC-Latin America. Speech at the National Federation of Community Broadcasters, Portland, Oregon.

"Challenging Hate Radio: A Guide for Activists." Online: http://www.fair.org/activism/hate-radio.html.

Chomsky, Noam. 1967. *Objectivity and Liberal Scholarship*. Online: http://question-everything.mahost.org/Archive/chomskyspain.html.

Civil Society Initiative on Community Media. Online: http://www.worldsummit2003. de/en/web/229.htm. Accessed January 25, 2004.

Dietrich, Heidi. 2003, October 17. "Polite Market: Area Not Known for Shock Radio." *Puget Sound Business Journal*. Online: http://seattle.bizjournals.com/seattle/stories/2003/10/20/story3.html. Accessed March 6, 2004.

Dorf, Michael C. 2003, August 22. "Why U.S. Law May Keep the Terminator Stuff Off the Air Until After Election." CNN.com/Law Centre. Online: http://www.cnn. com/2003/LAW/08/22/findlaw.analysis.dorf.arnold/. Accessed March 5, 2004.

Durlin, Marty and Cathy Melio. "The Grassroots Radio Movement in the U.S." Online: http://www.morelater.com/kaos/forum/messages/43.html. Accessed March 16, 2004.

"Dyke to Open Up BBC Archive." 2003, August 24. *BBC News*. Online: http://news.bbc. co.uk/1/hi/entertainment/tv_and_radio/3177479.stm. Accessed March 12, 2004.

"FCC Localism Hearing Draws Large, Vocal Crowd." 2003, October 22. WRAL.com. Online: http://www.wral.com/news/2574901/detail.html.

Federal Communications Commission (FCC). "Auctions." Online: http://wireless.fcc. gov/auctions/. Accessed March 5, 2004.

Federal Communications Commission (FCC). "Powell Statement." Online: http://www. fcc.gov/localism/. Accessed: March 5, 2004.

Freire, Paolo. Infed Encyclopedia Archives, n.d. Online: http://www.infed.org/thinkers/et-freir.htm. Accessed March 22, 2004

Gerry, Lyn. 1998, May 26. "KPFK Programmers Ordered to Mainstream Content; Advocacy Journalism is 'Out.'" Online: http://www.radio4all.org/fp/mainstream.htm. Accessed March 16, 2004.

"Ghana: Radio Ada Goes on the Air." Online: http://www.fao.org/docrep/003/x6721e/x6721e30.htm. Accessed March 14, 2004.

Grassroots Radio Conference. 1996. Online: http://www.kgnu.org/grassroots6/. Accessed March 22, 2004.

Gross, Robin. 2003. Paper presented at the Community Media Panel on Intellectual Property Rights. World Summit on the Information Society, Geneva Switzerland, December 11.

"Groups Demand End to 'Hate Radio'." 2002, April 24. Posted by John C. Online: http://www.indybay.org/news/2002/04/124735_comment.php [DATE ACCESSED?]

"Howard Stern Suspended for Indecency." 2004, February 26. CNN.com. Online: http://www.cnn.com/2004/SHOWBIZ/News/02/25/stern.suspension/.

Jacobs, Jane. 1992. *Systems of Survival: A Dialogue on the Moral Foundations of Politics and Commerce*. New York: Random House.

Karonga, Elizabeth. 1999. Interview aired on radio program, *WINGS #44-00 Media for Women's Development*. Produced by Frieda Werden for Women's International News Gathering Service: www.wings.org .

Kennard, Bill. Online: http://www.ncs.gov/N5_HP/Customer_Service/XAffairs/Speech-Service/SS00-056.htm. Accessed March 5, 2004.

Khumalo, Musi. Private communication, February 2004.

Lee, Douglas. "Overview." First Amendment Centre. Online: http://www.firstamendment-center.org/Press/topic.aspx?topic=press_broadcasting. Accessed March 5, 2004.

Limburg, Val E. "Fairness Doctrine." The Museum of Broadcasting Communications. Online: http://www.museum.tv/archives/etv/F/htmlF/fairnessdoct/fairnessdoct.htm. Accessed March 5, 2004.

"MAMA FM Closes." Online: http://radio.oneworld.net/article/view/73528/1/. Accessed March 15, 2004.

Markoff, John. "Pirate Battles to Keep the Airwaves Open." Free Radio Berkeley. Online: http://www.freeradio.org/index.php?pagename=press/pirate_battles.html&subnav=press/subnav.html. Accessed September19, 2006.

Matewa, Chido E. F. *Media and the Empowerment of Communities for Social Change*. Unpublished Ph.D. dissertation, University of Manchester, 2002. Online: http://www.comminit.com/idmatewa/sld-6133.html. Accessed March 15, 2004.

Mills, Ken and Sue Schardt. 2000. "Listener Choice Radio Study 2000." *Essays: Broadcasting Shifting Landscape*. Online: http://www.listenerchoice.com/essays/BroadcastingShift.html. Accessed March 5, 2004.

Ministry of Culture, Sweden. "Public Service Radio and Television 2005." Online: http://www.google.ca/search?q=cache:mWfBSHFt2QgJ:kultur.regeringen.se/inenglish/pressinfo/pdf/Public_service_%2520eng.pdf+%22public+service+radio%22&hl=en&ie=UTF-8. Accessed March 11, 2004.

Murdock, Graham. "New Zealand." Museum of Broadcast Communications. Online: http://www.museum.tv/archives/etv/N/htmlN/newzealand/newzealand.htm. Accessed: March 5, 2004.

Ó hAnluain, Daithí. 2004. "Free Content Becoming Thing of the Past for UK's Online Newspaper Sites." *Journal Review* February 13. Online: http://www.ojr.org/ojr/business/1067472919.php. Accessed March 12, 2004.

Omunegha, Kate Azuka. 2003. "Women, Poverty and the Media." Paper presented at the World Forum on Communication Rights, Geneva Switzerland, December 11.

"Poor, Poor Broadcasters Might Have to Endure Complaints at FCC Localism Hearings..." 2003, October 23. Mediageek. Online: http://www.mediageek.org/archives/002169.html.

Pozner, Jennifer. 1999. "I'd Take Them Out with Sex: Journalists Trivialize Howard Stern's Advocacy of Rape as 'Insensitivity'." *Extra* (July/August). Online: http://www.fair.org/extra/9907/stern.html.

Pyle, Emily. 2001.The Death and Life of Free Radio." *Austin Chronicle* 22 June. Online: http://www.austinchronicle.com/gyrobase/Issue/story?oid=oid%3A82153. Accessed September19, 2006.

Quarmyne, Wilna. 2001, February. "A 'Kente' Approach to Community Radio Training: Weaving Training into the Community Empowerment Process." Online: http://www.comminit.com/africa/st2004/sld-1467.html. Accessed March 22, 2004.

"Radio Broadcasting History." Timeline, Online: http://senior.billings.k12.mt.us/otran-nex/history/radio.htm. Accessed March 6, 2004.

Radio Netherlands. "Counteracting Hate Radio." Online: http://www.rnw.nl/realradio/dossiers/html/hateintro.html. Accessed March 6, 2004.

Ruhnbro, Christina. 2004, March 15. Private e-mail correspondence.

Sakolsky, Ron. 2001. "The LPFM Fiasco." *LIP Magazine*, 17 January and 30 June. Online: http://www.lipmagazine.org/articles/featsakolsky 77.htm. Accessed September 19, 2006.

Shortland Street. FAQ. Online: http://shortlandstreet.nzoom.com/faq/. Accessed March 11, 2004.

"Stern Feels Bush-Whacked, End is Near." 2004, March 3. Online: http://www.fmqb.com/Article.asp?id=20252.

Stockwell, Norm. 2000, July 22. General Manager, WORT-FM, Madison, Wisconsin. Small group discussion.

"The Unofficial Guide to the BBC." Online: http://www.vaxxine.com/master-control/BBC/chapters/Bbc_form.html. Accessed March 11, 2004.

"Timeline: New Zealand." *BBC News*. Online: http://news.bbc.co.uk/1/hi/world/asia-pacific/country_profiles/1138430.stm. Accessed March 6, 2004.

TV Radio World. "Mozambique." Online: http://www.tvradioworld.com/region3/moz/. Accessed March 12, 2004.

Vaughan, Genevieve. 1997. *For-Giving: A Feminist Criticism of Exchange*. Austin, TX: Plainview/Anomaly Press.

Vaughan, Genevieve. 2002. "Mothering, Co-Muni-Cation and the Gifts of Language." *The Enigma of the Gift and Sacrifice*. Eds. Edith Wyschogrod, Jean-Joseph Goux, and Eric Boynton. New York: Fordham University Press, 2002.

Werden, Frieda. nd. "A Woman's Local Commercial FM Station." Women's Radio Fund. Online: http://www.womensradiofund.org/batrogue.htm. Accessed March 5, 2004.

Werden, Frieda. nd. Interview notes. Women's Radio Fund. Online: http://www.womensradiofund.org/femradio.htm. Accessed March 5, 2004.

"What is Community Radio?" Online: www.amarc.org/amarc/ang. Accessed March 16, 2004.

Women's International News Gathering Service (WINGS). Online: http://www.wings.org/2003.html.

Zundle, Ernst. "The Zundelsite." Online: http://www.zundelsite.org/english/catalog/audio_catalog.html. Accessed March 10, 2004.

RENEA ROBERTS

Gifting at the Burning Man Festival

The Burning Man Festival is an annual event that takes place in the week leading up to and over the Labour Day Holiday in September, in Nevada's Black Rock Desert. The festival creates an experimental community that encourages participants to express themselves and as a result of it's remote location also challenges participants to a degree that is not normally encountered in one's day-to-day life" (see www.burningman.com to learn more). The festival's humble origins date back to 1986 when Larry Harvey set out to burn a wooden stick sculpture in the figure of a man at Baker Beach in San Francisco. At the instant the eight-foot figure was ignited, others who were also on the beach that evening drew close to witness the burning. Strangers in a circle with fire-lit faces, they began to introduce themselves to one another and shared gifts of songs and stories. As they stood there in this circle with newfound friends, they were inspired to repeat the event the following year. That first year there were about 20 people present. Four years later, in 1990, the crowd attending the burn had grown so much that the organizers, Larry Harvey and Jerry James, decided to move the gathering out to the Nevada desert. As the number of people participating in the desert festival grew, so did the art installations, costumes, community services, theme camps and even villages organized by the participants for the participants. This festival, with its radical self-expression and radical self-reliance in a forbidding environment has grown to over 40,000 participants in 2006.

What I would like to share with you in this paper is what I consider to be the heart of the festival. While participants pay an entrance fee which offsets administrative expenses and the fees charged by the Federal Bureau of Land Management (the largest fee charged to anyone in the U.S.), organizers prohibit vending and any form of advertising and have rejected all offers of sponsorship. With no emphasis at all on buying or selling anything, the participants in the festival must rely on themselves and each other to fulfill needs whether for food or water, protection from the sun, or for help of any kind.

I first heard about the Burning Man Festival in a *Wired Magazine* article when I was finishing graduate school in Atlanta in 1998. I had completed a degree in community psychology and was interested in exploring the idea of alternative communities and the article had made an impression upon me. It wasn't until two years later though that two friends and I drove for 20 hours straight to spend two days and two nights at the Burning Man Festival. I was overwhelmed by everything: the art, the people, the conversations (the best gift!), the organization, the beauty, the laughter, the tears, and the striking contradiction to our consumerized world. I carried a camera with me but I never took a single picture that year and because my time there was so short, I wasn't able make a lot of deep connections. But I saw enough to know that something different, something very positive, was going on. I just didn't know what it was. Where did that magic and peacefulness with radical self-expression arise from? It was only in hindsight that I realized that the fruits of a gift giving culture, and the community these gifts sustain, were the very core of this event.

I had attended other alternative events, like the Rainbow Gathering, but none had the level of expression, freedom, creativity, and community that I glimpsed at Burning Man. I watched other documentaries after having gone that first year and felt none of them addressed the aspect that peaked my interest. Most coverage was sensational in nature. I wanted to produce something authentic to this community.

So I sent a proposal to Burning Man, explaining my desire to make a film that focused on the community aspects of the event, looking for patterns of contributions, and to explore what I considered then to be their barter system. My proposal was very well-received by the organizers who wrote back, "sounds like you're interested in the gift economy." That was the first time I had ever heard those words.

I was off to the desert with my camera, a one-woman film crew, to make my first film. I knew I would ask the people there about community, expression, and gifting, but I didn't know what I would find or what patterns would emerge.

From the moment I arrived, I was witness to unending acts of gifting. Some I caught on camera, most I did not. Everywhere I turned some sort of gifting was taking place and it wasn't just in the fabulous and engaging art that surrounds you at every turn. Neighbours greeted us our first morning with fresh brewed coffee. An artist explained his struggle to figure out how to fix a key aspect of his sculpture, which had just broken, when a stranger walking heard part of the story and happened to have the knowledge and the tools to help out. A shade structure was given to a camp that wasn't prepared for effect of 118 degree weather by another camp two blocks away, and it goes on and on. One year a participant came deliberately with nothing and called himself "the nothing camp." No tent, no sleeping bag, no clothes, no food, no water. As the days passed, he was given all the articles he needed to survive along with the non-material gifts that really make the heart of the festival.

It wasn't until that second year that I was truly able to see all the gifts that were unfolding every moment, and the enormity of the event I had witnessed became clearer as I began filming and later reviewing the footage.

Oddly, on my way out to the desert I worried about using the term gift economy, wondering if anyone would understand what I was referring to. But not once did

I have to explain these words at Burning Man.

After I got back and began editing the film, people would ask me what I was working on and over and over again I had to explain the concept of gift economy and work through people's preconceived notions and confusion with the barter system, as well as explain just how magical gifting can be. Spending day after day and month after month with the footage, a strong pattern emerged in the film confirming that a vital foundation of the power of the festival was the absence of commercialism and the ethics of a gift giving culture.

In 2002, I finished my documentary on the Burning Man Festival, which I called *Gifting It: A Burning Embrace of Gift Economy.*[1] It is a meditative piece that explores how a host of social elements are affected in an experimental community that embraces a gift giving culture. Burning Man allows a unique opportunity to experience the fruits of a gift giving culture as they happen within a particular time and space. And the documentary suggests that this altered reality may extend far beyond the festival's boundaries, and, in fact, it may be the hope arising out of its ashes that our world desperately needs.

Renea Roberts believes in an intimate approach when creating Feature length documentaries and shorts. She's also passionate about alternative energies, permaculture, and learning to garden organically in the high deserts of New Mexico. See www. giftingit.com for more information.

Notes

---

[1] A two-minute trailer that will give you a feel for the documentary can be found at www.r3productions.net.

BRACKIN FIRECRACKER

Activism

A Creative Gift for a Better World

Activism is derived from the word "action," and an activist is one who literally takes a creative and direct action to bring attention to an issue. Activism's gift for the world is to expose an issue or wrongdoing that will hopefully garner enough public support to then, in turn, bring about a social and political change for the betterment of all. The way I've personally been able to have hope in a world full of such fear, injustice, and despair is through activism. Of course there are as many kinds of activism as there are worthy and righteous causes. I ascribe to a form that I like to call creative activism. By using artistic expressions in the forms of street theatre, visual arts, dance, songs, and puppet shows and pageantry, the protest message can be translated to a larger audience. This type of activism is based in finding innovative ways to break down the gap between us (the protestors) and them (all other people). Creative activism can be seen in terms of the gift economy as an inspiring gift to both the movement itself by means of support and morale and to the general public as education and entertainment.

One such form of creative activism is called "radical cheerleading." In radical cheerleading there are no such things as "try-outs," and no one person can be a squad. In the spirit of teamwork, you must join in. To get into character, start by imagining yourself in your cheerleading suit of choice (it doesn't have to be a short skirt-unless of course you want it to be!) and then picture yourself with your squad unified against one common enemy.

Squad set, you bet!

Who let the bombs drop?
Bush bush bush
And who do we gotta stop?
Bush bush bush
And who funds Bin Laden?
Bush bush bush
Just like his daddy taught him
Bush bush bush
Who steals food from children?

356

Bush bush bush
In Iraq and Afganistan.
Bush bush bush
And who is a facist?
Bush bush bush
The worlds worst terrorist
Bush bush bush
Break it on down
Cops on the street yo
Threatening to beat you. Don't let them hurt you
Get rid of W. but don't just fight the symptoms tear down the system
Actualize solutions, global revolution!
(Cheer written by Valera Giarratano, Austin, Texas)

Of course, it's impossible to capture the spirit of a cheer when written on paper, however, the word "revolution" can sometimes arouse fear and bad connotations whether read to oneself or screamed aloud. In the context of the cheer, we are not advocating for a global revolution which takes up arms and instigates a world war. Revolution in this cheer means getting to the root of the issue (hence the word radical), acknowledging the problem, and then proposing proactive solutions for global radical change. For example, Bush merely personifies the problem at hand but really he is just a symptom of a much greater problem—the system itself—which is based on patriarchal capitalism, exploitation, oppression and greed. It is equally important to not only speak out against Bush and the system, but also to come together to devise a united revolutionary plan of action. The result of such strategies is a solution that can be actualized by providing an alternative model of what a different system could and does look like. Conferences such as the International Gift Economy Conference (Las Vegas, Nov 2004) allow us to be inspired to action by the fact that we can gather together, learn from each other and be consoled and unified in realizing that alternative systems to the patriarchal market economy do, indeed, exist. This creating and sharing of our visions of a what a radically different world looks like, is at its very essence creative activism.

What Connects Us?

We may all have different definitions of activism, but I think it is safe to assume that what most often connects us is the tremendous energy, hope, passion, and commitment that we share to create a more nurturing and just world. We may not even describe ourselves as activists, that may be to some an isolating term. We may feel more comfortable identifying as organizers, networkers, rebel rousers, lecturers, academics, teachers, professors, healers, bodyworkers, therapists, scientists, caregivers, builders, technicians, journalists, maids, maidens, mothers, and/or crones. Whatever our title, what connects us is that we are all gift givers. There is no way to either qualify or quantify our dedication, spirit, and love that we put into our, more often than not, unpaid work of promoting radical positive change. Our time and commitment to the cause, whether it be social, political, environmental, and/or even spiritual, is not valued in the capitalist market economy. That is why the work we do is a gift.

The Gift/Il Dono

Genevieve Vaughan (2004) sees activism as the defining of a problem and seeking solutions to it, not just for ourselves but the universe at large. In her preface to the article about the activist work of women in Argentina, she states:

> The problem solving of activism can be understood as the satisfaction of a social need, addressed with creativity and determination, individually and in community with others. The actual solving of the problem is a unilateral gift given by those who have dedicated themselves to doing it in spite of great difficulties. It is a gift to society as a whole.... I would even say a gift to the powers that be, because it has kept them from perpetrating yet another evil upon the people. Social activism can be thought of in this way, as gift giving to society. That is, the gift of social change is the most necessary gift in our times. It can have huge multiplier effects, by changing the system that is causing the needs, and by spreading the example and the hope that this can happen. (313)

I deeply connected with another article in the collected volume, *Il Dono/The Gift*, called "The Gift Economy in My Life." The author, Jutta Reid (Vaughan 2004: 301), narrates her whole entire life in relation to the gift economy. Until I read this article, I did not have a truly good understanding of the gift economy. For me, it took seeing someone else's life through the perspective of the gift economy to relate. Hopefully you will be able to do the same. I offer to you my life as I equate it to the gift economy.

Radical Cheerleading

Radical cheerleading is what gifted me my voice and shaped my path of activism over the last ten years. I happened upon radical cheerleading in January of 2007 in South Florida, when the initial bright idea was just being ignited. We started by out by reclaiming the American icon of the "cheerleader" and radicalizing it to fit our needs. We declared no try-outs and encouraged anyone that wanted to shake it for the revolution to participate. We also welcomed everyone to write cheers for whatever cause, action, or campaign that needed support and energy. Since then literally hundreds of cheers have been written regarding everything from pro-bike, pro-choice, anti-war and anti-globalization (to name only a few). It is easy to look back and see the gifts that were given and received through the process. Radical cheerleading gave the opportunity to be creative, dress up, coordinate routines, work cooperatively and form a nurturing community, while at the same time fostering an innovative way to speak truth to power. Radical cheerleading continued to serve its traditional purpose of providing morale, enthusiasm, and support but it took that role and elevated it to center stage instead of just the sidelines. Radical cheerleading gave fun and animation to the protest and captured the eye of the media allowing the protest message to be heard by the larger public. Even with very limited access to resources, we were able to give strength and excitement to many causes. I'm speaking in the past tense; when in reality, I should be speaking in the present or future for that matter. Since its inception, radical cheerleading has spread across the country, and now the world. Its unpredictable course has created its own movement. This movement was facilitated by the fact that radical cheerleading is based on the anarchist principle of autonomy. There is no one that owns the idea of radical cheerleading. As radical cheerleading spread and new squads were being formed, each new group of radical cheerleaders were independent in defining how they would be both individually and as a team and what issues stood out for them to cheer for and against. Today there are countless squads all over the world that have either existed and or are still in existence. There are also radical cheerleaders. like myself, that no longer practice cheerleading on a regular basis but put on the non-uniform and gather together a squad when the need for a cheer arises (which could be any moment!)

In terms of the gift economy, I've looked at radical cheerleading's gifts to both the movement and the greater public but it is also important to note the gifts I've received personally over the years. The gifts are many but what stands out for me the most is the radical community that I met through my extensive and adventuresome travels as a radical cheerleader.

The Rhizome Collective

While traveling to conferences and gatherings, I met many likeminded people who were also manifesting through art, puppetry, dance, and street theatre. Creativity abounded and many of us started thinking about using our creativity to not only protest what we were against but to demonstrate what we were for. We learned from the Zapatistas that as important as it was to travel and be a part of the global protests and mobilizations that it was equally important to foster something at home. Needing a base of operation lead to the fall 2000 planting of the Rhizome Collective in Austin, Texas. Over time and through many trial and errors, we developed our dreams into a collective mission that unconsciously resembles the gift economy. This mission agreed upon by the collective and articulated by Stacy Pettigrew, a co-founder of the Rhizome, is as follows: "In our worldview, the dominant values of competition, greed, and exploitation would be replaced with cooperation, autonomy, and egalitarianism. We believe that all struggles against oppression and for self-determination are connected, and that it is important to construct viable alternatives while simultaneously fighting for social justice." The Rhizome, in name, refers to both a consensus run member based organization as well as a 9400 sq. foot warehouse with an outside courtyard and gardens. The space itself was gifted to the Rhizome Collective as not only a low income space to live (a need for the people involved) but also as a place for various grassroots activists and organizations to work out of (a need of the community). In addition, the Rhizome is an educational resource center which provides for the needs of the public. Classes are free or sliding scale and focus on creative arts and activism as well as ongoing permaculture and environmentally sustainable projects. The Rhizome Collective also receives endless gifts from outside the market economy including but not limited to materials to build, seeds to plant, financial help, land, and hundreds of thousands of volunteer labor hours. This vast network of people who are involved in the Rhizome give meaning to the definition of the word—rhizome: *An expanding underground root system, sending up above ground shoots to form a vast network which makes it very difficult to uproot.*

Bikes Across Borders

Bikes Across Borders (BAB) is one of the organizations that took root in the early days of the Rhizome Collective. I mention BAB in particular because it serves as a prime example of the gift economy. A small group of us created Bikes Across Borders as a way to recycle the excess of capitalism. We started a bike shop inside the Rhizome where all the bikes had been either been found in the trash or gifted to us. We wound up with such a large number of bicycles that we realized that we needed to develop a program to fix them up and give them away. There was already a grassroots organization in Austin that was providing for the bike needs of the city so we looked elsewhere, this time south of the border. BAB became aquainted with a women led organization on the Mexico side of the border called the Committee for Border Workers (the CFO). They worked tirelessly to educate workers of their rights and fight for better conditions in the U.S. owned assembly plants (las maquiladores.) The CFO had put the word out that one of their needs was bicycles so they could have more autonomy in their daily transportation, thus an alliance between BAB and the CFO was forged. On our first organized trip to the border a group of BAB radical clowns rode their bikes from Austin to the border where we met up with them with over 80 bicycles. On this day, even after all our our experiences of protesting global trade organizations, we truly began to understand the consequences of "free trade." To bring the trailer full of bikes across the border we were told by government officials that we would have to pay a heavy tax that none of us on either side of the border could afford. In response and as advised by Julia, the director of the CFO, we spent all day riding each bike across the border one by one. It became apparent that NAFTA (the North American Free Trade Agreement) was created for big corporate businesses not for small grassroots organizations and everyday working people like ourselves. For the next two years we made a number of trips to the border not only providing bicycles and bike tools but also creative activism in the form of circus acts, puppet shows, visual arts and radical cheerleading. What we found is that through providing conscious entertainment we were breaking down both cultural and communication barriers. For-give me if I sound like we were doing all the giving. The CFO also used creative activism to share their message with us. They demonstrated how to use Theatre of the Oppressed as a fun and innovational organizing tool. But most importantly the Committee of Border Workers gave to us the gift of trust, which allowed us access to their homes and most personal experiences.

We were moved by their tireless passion for justice and inspired upon our return to take action. We brought their stories to life by translating them into various forms of creative activism. These puppet shows, comic strips, radical cheers and slide shows were used to educate people in the states about the struggles endured by the CFO and how to be in solidarity with them. Through this process, our project evolved to not be charity, but instead an organization based on solidarity and mutual aid. Mutual aid is *not* an exchange of a tit for a tat. Mutual aid is an example of gift giving. None of us on either side of the border were consciously counting gifts. It's only now through reflection that I understand that what we were sharing was much deeper than the exchange of money and material possessions. What we experienced was giving for the simple sake of giving, not for the sake of getting something in return. That in itself is radical.

Burn-out and How to Cope

As activists we often times give so much of ourselves that our vital flame inside us begins to be snuffed out. Burn-out is quite common in activism but very rarely discussed. We sometimes have very high expectations and become easily disappointed in ourselves and in others. There is always so much to do! How can we as one individual person be everywhere all at once? How can we keep up the same energy and passion we once had? How can we balance the amounts of gifts we give with the gifts we need to sustain ourselves? I, honestly, ask these questions for myself but feel that others can probably relate. We must remind ourselves and friends that "gift giving is not self-sacrificing" (Vaughan 1977).

In our creative endeavors to establish more radical models to live by, we must at the ground level establish better ways to communicate and support each other. We should also allow each other to take time to nurture ourselves without passing judgment for not living up to prior expectations. Taking a reflective break allows us time to self critique and redirect our activist work down new and innovative paths. By giving to ourselves, we can better be able to serve and give to others.

To avoid a complete burn-out, I have slowed my pace to a more sustainable speed. In this reflective phase, I'm trying to learn to say "no" when appropriate and take time for myself without guilt. For many years I lived off adrenaline. Now I'm taking the time to learn to be healthy by studying herbal medicine and bodywork. This healing time is balanced by working from home on two separate projects that document, archive and preserve inspiration stories. I'm co-directing the WINGS, Women's International News Gathering Service, archival project and also co-editing a book on radical cheerleading. The sharing of these herstories is a true gift for both present and future generations.

Organizations can also experience a burn-out. For the sake of sustaining the group it's imperative to have periodic assessments of what has worked and what hasn't over the long term. In Bikes Across Borders we realized that we did not have the same resources and time to do what we had done before. So after many years of intermittent travel and taking bikes and puppet shows to many parts of the U.S., Canada, Mexico, and Cuba, the members of Bikes Across Borders redirected their focus to be more locally based teaching bike maintenance, puppetry and arts in the public schools. BAB continues to send bikes to Cuba and Mexico through the more established connections of the Pastors for Peace biannual caravans. In our group's check in, what we recognized as a consistently positive aspect of our organization was our adherence to the principles of solidarity and mutual aid. Through cross cultural networking, we are presently able to provide housing at the Rhizome Collective for creative activists from four different countries.

By looking back over the last ten years of my life through the lens of the gift economy, I am able to honor the many gifts that I have been blessed. I am also able to recognize the gifts and experiences I shared, not as wasted time, but as time that was and still is validated in the gift economy. I say "wasted time" because that is what much of my family and old friends, indoctrinated by the capitalist system, thought I was doing. The question was always, "When are you going to get a job and stop all that protesting?" My answer now is that creative activism is my life's work and everything else is *lagniappe.* * I think it's important to recognize my first world white privilege in this equation. I was never forced to have to get a job and financially take care of anyone else but myself. I was able to commit myself wholeheartedly to my activism, because I was being supported by my community and the Rhizome Collective. Not having to pay high rents was a true gift. I did work an occasional freelance job, but it is true that I don't have much, monetarily speaking, to show from most of my adult life. However the gifts I do have are the skills and community that I acquired from my years of volunteer work. I now am lucky enough to work a job in the market economy that I like and even have enough time left over for my activist projects and sometimes for myself.

Conclusion

Once I was able to see the gift economy in my own life, I began to see it everywhere. For some, maybe we just knew and called it by some other name. It's more than likely something we have been practicing in some form or fashion all of our lives, especially if we have been socialized as women. By beginning to see activism as a gift, we are more able to equate value with the work we do for either low or no pay. Society at large doesn't honor our work so we have to take it upon ourselves to acknowledge each other. When we feel validated we live more meaningful and inspired lives. However, it's easy to get overwhelmed and let the system get us down. To counteract this feeling we should start by recognizing our many gifts within and then gather strength by reaching out to those friends that live by a respectful, nurturing, and compassionate worldview. Really the gift economy is simple: our work is to establish a radically different world that puts at its center the needs of the people and the planet before money. It seems easy; however, we must overcome thousands of years of indoctrination. It is our job as creative activists to break the curse of this outdated patriarchal consciousness and to generate creative ideas of how to "actualize solutions for a global revolution!"

To come full circle, I would like to end with an adapted version of one of the first radical cheers ever written. Since radical cheerleading was designed to speak to whatever issue is at hand, I thought it would be an appropriate gift to present a radical cheer to lend support, morale, and validation to the gift economy.

Squad set... you bet!

I don't want to work no more.
What did you say? I said
The capitalist system doesn't work no more.
That's what I said, now say,
The gift economy is what came before
What did I say? I said
The gift economy is what came before.
Yes that's what we say, now
Stomp dissolve the state, let's liberate
Patriarchy go to hell
Another woman to rebel!
Organize and raise some hell
Create something radical—REBEL!
(original cheer by Aimee and Cara Jennings, Florida, December 2006, adapted by Firecracker)

Creole dialect for extra or unexpected gift or benefit.

Brackin "Firecracker" Camp grew up in a small town in Mississippi and came of age in New Orelans, Louisiana. She has an extensive background in protesting, networking, traveling, interviewing, researching, radical cheerleading, circus performing, parading, bike riding, and organizing events/conferences throughout the U.S. and in various other countries. To support herself in the market economy, Brackin presently works as a personal care attendant/body worker as well as a puppeteer in the Austin public schools. In addition, Brackin is a board member of the Rhizome Collective and a member of the committee to free the Angola 3.

References

Vaughan, G., ed. 2004. *Il Dono/The Gift: A Feminist Analysis. Athanor: Semiotica, Filosofia, Arte, Letteratura* 15 (8). Roma: Meltemi Editore.

ANGELA MILES

Women's Giving

Feminist Transformation and Human Welfare

Genevieve Vaughan's (1997) theorizing of the gift paradigm provides essential support for feminists who know intuitively that the political, spiritual, economic, and environmental are connected and who are struggling to bring these together in our practice and in the world we want to build. The recognition that *giving* is an alternative paradigm to *exchange* and not just a different type of behaviour, is incredibly important.[1]

Understanding that *giving* relations (with each other and nature) are *both* the fullest expression of our humanity/spirituality *and* our greatest wealth reveals the self evident but currently hidden truth that economic relationships are human and social relationships. It allows us to know deeply and confidently that our world is a whole and that holistic politics, visions, and practices are both crucial and possible. So it invites, encourages, even requires, that each of us open ourselves to elements that have not hitherto been a feature of our work. This provides important ground for transformative feminists working in different communities around different issues to identify and build connections among our struggles in a way that deepens and broadens all our politics.

My sense is that the rich array of feminists all over the world who are drawn to the gift paradigm are attracted by just this promise of dialogue and solidarity across what have tended to be the spiritual, political, and economic solitudes of our movement. Here, we find longed for space to articulate the spiritual elements in our political and economic struggles and the political and economic elements of our spiritual struggles. In this way the International Feminist Network for a Gift Economy offers the vital opportunity for diverse transformative feminists to strategize and work together while retaining the autonomy and diversity of our practice.

The Network at this stage is essentially an e-list of individual Indigenous and non-Indigenous feminists from all regions with enormously varied priorities and histories, engaged with a broad range of issues at local, national, regional, and/or global levels. Many, though not all participants in the Gift Economy Network have met and dialogued with each other at conferences dedicated to exploring the gift paradigm and related matriarchal paradigms[2] and many have presented together and individually in other contexts.[3] For instance, the "Position Statement for a Peaceful World" which follows this article was presented at the World Social Forum in Porto Alegre in January 2002. The diversity of participants and the rich variety of their work and relationships to the gift paradigm are evident in *Il Dono/The Gift: A Feminist Analysis*, a collection edited by Genevieve Vaughan (2004).

The articles gathered in this new book are based on presentations at the second international conference on the gift economy held in Las Vegas in 2004. Indigenous and non-Indigenous feminists from Asia, Africa, Latin America, Europe, and North America shared information about important, hugely diverse struggles that illuminate and are illuminated by the gift paradigm. A powerful implicit theme was the common conviction expressed eloquently by Marta Benavides, that the *way* we move forward must be a central part of our Network's discussion and reflection:

> We must ... consciously and intentionally be the future in the here and now.... There is a qualitative difference between being a revolutionary to being the revolution itself. We must manifest it. There is a difference between building and constructing, defending and struggling for peace, and being peace. (page 315 in this volume)

The extensive testimony at this gathering to the practical relevance of the gift paradigm and our evident consensus on the importance of means as well as ends is exciting to me. It shows that when Linda Christiansen-Ruffman and others at the gathering speak of strengthening the feminist movement, they/we are looking for far more than mere alliances, or mere mutual agreement to collectively prioritize one issue at a time. We are not looking for a common political line or proposing a political orthodoxy. Rather we are seeking relationships, networks, and strategizing that connect us in the fullest most integrative sense.[4] Such relationships are only possible among those who share a critical and visionary perspective that is broad and deep enough to speak to all our struggles and move them all forward. The gift paradigm provides that perspective. It is clear from the articles gathered here that no one is going to drop what they are doing to work with the gift paradigm. Instead, this paradigm will allow each of us to more completely realize the potential of our specific and varied ongoing work.

In the rest of this article I will briefly outline a few of the most immediate ways I believe theorizing *the gift* contributes to my own understanding and, I think, to transformative feminism generally in Canada and globally.

Gender and the Gift

In patriarchal misogynist societies around the world transformative feminists do not base women's claims to equality, autonomy, and humanity simply on our similarity to men. We challenge not only women's exclusion from humanity, but the dominance of male-associated values and the androcentric definition of humanity itself. The Third World feminist network, Development Alternatives with Women for a New Era (DAWN), expressed this eloquently in an influential (later published) document they issued in preparation for one of the United Nations World Congresses on Women:[5]

> The women's movement ... at its deepest is not an effort to play "catch up" with the competitive, aggressive, "dog-eat-dog" spirit of the dominant system. It is, rather, an attempt to convert men and the system to the sense of responsibility and nurturance, openness, and rejection of hierarchy that are part of our vision. (Sen and Grown 1987: 72-73)

This spirit is evident, also, in the following feminist response to the Royal Commission Report on the Status of Women in Canada (1970):

> Our goal must be to obtain full human status for women in every area of human activity. And this is not to accept the present "human activity" realm of the male. Values in the male realm today are firmly rooted in the evils of power, dominance and oppression. We must look for a broader and deeper definition of human life. (Dorothy 1971: 3)

These transformative feminist challenges involve affirming women and women-associated work and values while resisting gender as a structure of hierarchy. The vision of a less fragmented and less "male" world in which characteristics, concerns, and values associated with women are the defining human values has been at the heart of transformative feminist practice in all regions for many decades. The following quotations from U.S. feminists Barbara Ehrenreich and Deirdre English (1979) and Indian feminist Vandana Shiva (1989) are just two eloquent articulations of this common feminist project:

> We refuse to remain on the margins of society, and we refuse to enter that society on its own terms.... The human values that women were assigned to preserve [must] become the organizing principles of society. The vision that is implicit in feminism [is] a society organized around human needs.... There are no human alternatives. The Market, with its financial abstractions, deformed science, and obsession with dead things must be pushed back to the margins. And the "womanly" values of community and caring must rise to the center as the only *human* principles. (Ehrenreich and English 1979: 342)

> The recovery of the feminine principle allows a transcendence and transformation of patriarchal foundations of maldevelopment. It allows a redefinition of growth and productivity as categories linked to the production, not the destruction of life. It is thus simultaneously an ecological and a feminist political project which legitimizes the way of knowing and being

that creates wealth by enhancing life and diversity, and which delegitimises the knowledge and practice of the culture of death as the basis for capital accumulation. (Shiva 1989: 13)

Affirming (female) gender *against* gender is a "contradiction" that many of us have necessarily been prepared to live with. I have written elsewhere that this is not a static linear contradiction, but a dialectical contradiction from which creative new possibilities emerge (Miles 1996). Still, we have not found words to adequately capture the substance of the human process we are engaged in. The project of "feminizing the world" can be misread as retaining the very gender definition of qualities and priorities we wish to generalize/humanize. The gift paradigm helps us in this quandary by theoretically clarifying how and why the feminist affirmation of women-associated characteristics, concerns, work, and values is a human struggle to move beyond a gendered world.

The gift paradigm shows us that giving is the defining quality/activity of *all* human beings, male and female; exchange behaviours and ways of being and seeing are departures from the human. "Masculation" is the term coined by Genevieve Vaughan (2004) for the process by which males in patriarchy were originally, and are still socialized away from giving into exchange behaviours and learn to base their claim of masculinity on their distance from their mothers and from giving. The female gender is, then, the residual human. Patriarchal dominance is at its root the dominance of exchange over giving. Even in modern urban contexts where women move also in the public world of exchange and market and have learned to see the world largely through the dominant exchange lens, they/we remain associated with and are necessarily still more grounded in giving. So we can see that when women affirm our experience, values, and responsibilities as formative of our struggle, we are affirming the human. In the non-patriarchal world we aspire to men will not be masculated; their maleness will be lived through and not against their giving human qualities.

"New Socialist Man" and the Gift

Understanding human beings as essentially giving creatures helps us see that we need not concern ourselves with the classic Left project of creating "new socialist man," that is, new human beings capable of living in a world without individualism, competition, or profit. Even today and even in the heart of hyper-capitalist globally dominant neo-liberalism we all feel best—most human, vibrant and alive—when we are giving and receiving in a human way. We don't need to be made human, we just need to be allowed to be human. So our challenge is to create a world in which we can be fully ourselves, not a world where we can be something else. The awareness that in our struggle we are working *with* our humanity and not against it is a significant shift of awareness for me. I find it a far more hopeful scenario.

Women's Leadership and the Gift

The gift paradigm also provides critical theoretical support for the feminist knowledge, gained from decades of political observation and experience, that women are playing a leading role in the struggle for change in all areas. Feminists have noted that women make up the majority of grassroots activists in the economic South and North—in their communities and in local and global campaigns and movements against poverty and mining, for the environment, for the Commons, for land, for human and community rights, health, peace, education, democracy, food security, and water among many others (Seager 1993; Marcos 1997; Mies 1998; Maathai 2004; Ackerley 2005). Women are disproportionately committed to the thankless long-term tasks of building relationships, knowledge and organizations with the capacity to confront power. And women have proven less likely to be sidetracked from long-term aims by offers of jobs or profit sharing or deals with colonizers (Brownhill 2006).

The central, even leading role of women remains largely unacknowledged except by feminists who have explained it in various social and structural terms. These include, for instance, women's more immediate responsibility for sustaining individual and communal life; their greater vulnerability to the harms of "development" and neo-liberal globalization; their necessarily less complete separation from nature and the body, their ultimate outsider status and consequent lack of access to the benefits of deals and power sharing (O'Brien 1981; Hartsock 1983; Aptheker 1990; Smith 1990; Agarwal 1992; Mies 1998; Collins 2000; Burack 2001; Higgs 2004). All these are obviously important factors that help explain women's leading activism. The gift paradigm takes us further by more fully revealing the deeper meaning and significance of this activism.

When we theorize giving as a different paradigm from exchange, giving becomes visible and we can see that at the deepest level, our movement is not simply about fairer exchange, less—or even no—exploitation, or more equality of condition, respect, and status; it is about creating a giving society and economy. The organic connections among all our many and varied issues and campaigns become clear and the underlying logic of the most progressive expressions of the feminist movement in all these areas is illuminated. We have new ways of thinking about and articulating our long-term dream of a world where women, women's work, and nature are valued. We have a new grasp of these as quintessential gifts and giving relationships; a more adequate understanding of women's reluctance to pursue or accept market measures of value for these things; and a deeper theoretical understanding of their human and political significance as central fields of struggle in our movement toward a giving society, economy, and world.

Women's Consciousness, Women's Liberation, and the Gift

Feminists worldwide are questioning everything, especially the models that are presented to us as the most advanced and the best for women. In the two thirds/

majority world feminists have for decades now been documenting and resisting the negative impacts of "development" on whole communities, especially the poor and the Indigenous, particularly women and children (Anand 1983[6]; Dakar 1982; Sen and Grown 1987; Tauli-Corpuz 1993; Tauli-Corpuz 2000). In the "developed" world feminist radicals have, since the 1970s, been drawing on their own experience to de-mystify false promises of "modernization" and "development" (Boston Women's Health Collective 1973). Indigenous feminists in their resistance in all regions are re-discovering, defending, and sharing the non-patriarchal traditional knowledge surviving (to greater or lesser degree) in their communities and among their peoples (Trask 1984; Allen 1986).

The gift paradigm strengthens us in all these stands inside and outside our communities. For instance, it exposes the continuity in the historical and current colonization of women, nature, land, and labour (Miles 2001). It also clearly shows that the modern urban educated "equal" woman isn't so advanced. Far from providing a model for women's progress, she is at risk of becoming purely a creature of exchange and forgetting she is a woman. This leaves her vulnerable to the domesticating mystification that her conditional privileges are the pinnacle of freedom for women everywhere (Rich 1986; Standing 2006-07).

Theorizing the gift helps feminists resist this false and divisive model of "liberation" which masks women's shared oppression and common strengths and undermines women's potential for mutual identification and solidarity across our hugely diverse circumstances. Seeing "giving" counters the male-identified ethnocentric, even racist, belief in the backwardness of "other" women that traps many well-meaning "liberated" women in the economic North in patronizing attitudes that render them incapable of respectful participation, and therefore acceptance, in the global feminist movement. The clear theoretical articulation of an alternative gift-based vision of women's liberation and future human society also strengthens in important ways the recognition, acceptance, and practice of "third world," marginal and Indigenous women's leadership. For traditional women-identification that persists more among these groups, and the holistic knowledge surviving in Indigenous communities are important and defining strengths. In a feminist movement that is seeking giving alternatives to exchange rather than escape from giving, remaining women's sub-cultures and matriarchal Indigenous cultures are honoured as essential precursors of a more human future, not dismissed as vestiges of the past.

Anti-Globalization and the Gift

Feminists have long known that using Gross Domestic Product (GDP) as a measure of well-being is a lie. For GDP measures only the value of market transactions and fails to take account of environmental and social destruction (Waring 1988; Shiva 1989; Isla 2007). Growth in GDP today comes mainly from enclosure and appropriation, that is, drawing non-market goods, services, land, resources, and labour into the market as new profit opportunities for the few—making these, at the same time and with devastating consequences, less available to the many. Neo-liberal globalization is the triumph of minority forces that benefit from this economic growth at the expense of the majority of the world's people and the environment (Miles 2001). Feminists have resisted this process of theft and destruction by insisting that the market cannot be the only measure of value, and by naming the harm and protecting the wealth that GDP discounts. This refusal of capitalist market measures is the ground on which we and other anti-globalization actors have attempted to exempt some areas (water, education, health, etc.) from pervasive and intensifying commodification, win more equal terms of trade, place limits on the environmental and social damage caused by essentially destructive forms of production, and protect people from the worst effects of enclosure and appropriation of common wealth.

The gift paradigm provides support for much more radical challenge and alternatives. Theorizing the gift goes beyond insisting that there is value outside the market, to showing that this is the only true wealth. For it demonstrates how exchange, the market, and trade (even fair trade) are parasitical on the gift, require and enforce scarcity, in their very essence interrupt our human relationships, reduce the wealth we can give each other and the abundance which could be ours. With this perspective, our aim is no longer merely to limit the damage of the market but to refuse the market itself and *all* commodification as we work toward our vision of a fully human future. This feminism resonates with and draws deeply on Indigenous relational and holistic worldviews and Indigenous and third world feminist leadership against colonization and neo-liberal globalization.

Women's Welfare and the Gift in Canada

Still, feminists need to deal in market and exchange contexts in our crucial struggle for money for women and children's immediate survival. I'd like to close by sharing one case where we in Canada are drawing on gift theorizing to deepen our demands and articulate them in terms of an alternative paradigm. We have overwhelming testimony from other articles in this book (Ana Isla, Claudia von Werlhof, Maria Jiminez, Linda Christiansen-Ruffman) that in this period, triumphant neo-liberalism is spreading poverty, violence, desperation, and destitution everywhere. Certainly this is true in Canada where social support and social services are being undermined at a great rate (Armstrong *et al.* 2004). It seems to many of us here that, at this time, the women's movement to be worthy of its name, has to make the fate of the most economically vulnerable women a central and pressing issue.

As part of this commitment about twenty women gathered in September 2004 in Pictou, Nova Scotia, representing national groups from across Canada and grassroots groups from the Atlantic region. We began by sharing our many and varied experiences campaigning against women's poverty and for economic support, social services, and labour rights for women. The notion of a basic income or annual general income (or as we preferred to call it, "guaranteed livable income")

Feminist Statement on Guaranteed Living Income[7]
Pictou, Nova Scotia, Sept 18-20, 2004

For millennia women's work, along with the free gifts of nature, has provided most of the true wealth of our communities. Women's work has been central to individual and collective survival. In all our diverse communities women can be seen to work on the principle that everybody is entitled to economic and physical security and autonomy and a fair share of the common wealth.

Women in every community, context and racial group are still denied our rightful political power over the economics governing these communities and our world. To paraphrase "A Women's Creed," for thousands of years men have had power without responsibility while women have responsibility without power. This situation must change.

Feminists insist that all activities of government and business in our nation(s) and our diverse communities should be assessed in the light of the prime value of sustaining life and the social priorities of universal entitlement, human security, autonomy, and common wealth. These must become the central priorities in social life and in public policy.

We refuse to accept market measures of wealth. They make invisible the important caring work in every society. They ignore the well-being of people and the planet, deny the value of women's work, and define the collective wealth of our social programs and public institutions as "costs" which cannot be borne. They undermine social connections and capacities and currency.

We reject policies that sacrifice collective wealth and individual security in the interests of profit for transnational corporations.

Women in Canada expect full and generous provision for all people's basic needs from the common wealth. Social and collective provision for sustaining life must be generous and secure in Canada and must be delivered through national mechanisms appropriately influenced and controlled by the women of our many specific communities.

We expect all people's full and dignified participation in society including full individual and social sharing of the work and responsibility of sustaining life that has so far been gendered. Men must share equally in this work within and beyond monetary measures.

We expect our rightful share of the wealth we have created. Women's work must be recognized and valued both within and beyond monetary measures. We expect sustained and expanding collective provision for people's needs.

Women demand an indexed guaranteed living income for all individual residents set at a level to enable comfortable living.

for all emerged as an important and positive way to respond to criminal decreases in welfare and the government's sharply diminishing resource commitments to women. We liked what we felt was the potential of this demand to shift the idea of poverty alleviation out of a charity frame and make women's demands general social demands. In this period of harsh government cutbacks we also welcomed the fact that this demand achieves this reframing without in any way absolving government of responsibility for individual and community well-being. Yet we were concerned that basic income has never been articulated in feminist terms. As it is generally conceptualized, it leaves women's disproportionate unpaid work invisible and does not contribute to a shift in this burden (Standing 2006-07). From these discussions we drafted a "Feminist Statement on Guaranteed Living Income," known as the "Pictou Statement," in which we (1) challenge poverty through an affirmation of the wealth women create and distribute, not in exchange terms but according to people's needs; and (2) demand that the whole of society adopt these gift principles. This Statement [see box] is just one specific example of the ways a gift perspective can deepen even struggles for money and more participation in the market in crucial transformative and feminist ways. Participants in the International Feminist Network for a Gift Economy share a myriad of such instances in their gatherings, their e-list, and their publications. Readers are invited to join the Network and share your reflections and experience.

Angela Miles is Professor of Adult Education and Community Development at the Ontario Institute for Studies in Education of the University of Toronto. She is committed to building and studying autonomous women's local and global activism and its genesis and significance in the current period of neo-liberal globalization. She is a founding member of Toronto Women for a Just and Healthy Planet, the Feminist Party of Canada, the Antigonish Women's Association and is a member of the editorial board of Canadian Woman Studies/les cahiers de la femme. Her publications include, Integrative Feminisms: Building Global Visions (Routledge 1996) and the co-edited collection Feminist Politics, Activism and Vision: Local and Global Challenges (Inanna/Zed 2004).

Notes

1   For sources, publications and information on the gift paradigm see http://www.gift-economy.com/.
2   These conferences include "A Radically Different World is Possible: The Gift Economy Inside and Outside of Patriarchal Capitalism" November 13-14, 2004, Las Vegas, Nevada; "Societies of Peace, Past, Present, Future," Second World Congress of Matriarchal Studies, September 29-October 2, 2005, San Marcos, Texas.
3   For instance, at World and Regional Social Forums in Porto Alegre (2002, 2003, 2004), Mumbai 2005, Mali 2006, Nairobi 2007; the International Interdisciplinary Congress on Women in Upsala 1999, Kampala 2002, Seoul 2005; European ATTAK Graz, Austria 2003; Semiotics Conferences in Finland, France, Italy and the U.S.A.; The Other Economic Summit (TOES); the International Association for Feminist Economics (IAFFE); the National Women's Studies Association in the USA.; the

Canadian Sociology and Anthropology Association and the Canadian Woman Studies Association, 2003; the UK and Ireland Women's Studies Association, Dublin 2004; "Spirit Matters: Wisdom Traditions and the "Great Work," Toronto 2004; American Association of Anthropology 2006; International Peace Research Association Calgary, Canada 2006; International Women's Peace Conference Dallas, U.S.A. 2006.

4   I use the term "integrative" feminisms and feminists to refer to feminisms seeking deep transformation with integrative/holistic practice that addresses the whole world and understands the integration of race, class, colonial, and patriarchal structures of power (Miles 1996).

5   A version of this statement was later published by Development Alternatives with Women for a New Era (DAWN) as *Development, Crises, and Alternative Visions: Third World Women's Perspectives* (Sen and Grown 1987).

6   While published by *ISIS* in 1983, this document was first written and circulated in 1980.

7   First published with an explanatory introduction and list of those present in *Canadian Woman Studies/les cahiers de la femme's* special issue on "Benefiting Women? Women's Labour Rights?" 23 (3,4) (Spring/Summer 2004).

References

Ackerley, B. A. 2005. "Women's Human Rights Activists as Political Theorists." *Feminist Politics, Activism and Vision: Local and Global Challenges.* Eds. L. Ricciutelli, A. Miles and M. H. McFadden. Toronto/London: Inanna Publications/Zed Books. 285-312.

Agarwal, B. 1992. "The Gender and Environment Debate: Lessons from India." *Feminist Studies* 18 (1): 119-58.

Allen, P. G. 1986. *The Sacred Hoop.* Boston, Beacon Press.

Anand, A. 1983. "Rethinking Women and Development." *ISIS*: 5-11.

Aptheker, B. 1990. "Imagining Our Lives." *Woman of Power* 16: 32-35.

Armstrong, P. *et al.*, eds. 2004. *Benefiting Women? Women's Labour Rights.* Special issue *Canadian Woman Studies/les cahiers de la femme* 23 (3,4) (Spring/Summer).

Boston Women's Health Collective 1973. *Our Bodies, Ourselves.* New York, Simon and Schuster.

Brownhill, L. 2006. *Land, Food, Freedom: Struggles for the Gendered Commons in Kenya, 1870 to 2006.* Unpublished dissertation. University of Toronto.

Burack, C. 2001. "The Dream of Common Differences: Coalitions, Progressive Politics, and Black Feminist Thought." *Forging Radical Alliances Across Difference: Coalition Politics for the New Millenium.* Ed. J. M. Bystydzienski. Lanham, Maryland: Rowman and Littlefield. 35-48.

Collins, P. H. 2000 [1990]. *Black Feminist Thought: Knowledge, Consciousness, and the Politics of Empowerment.* 2nd ed. New York: Routledge.

Dakar. 1982. "The Dakar Declaration on Another Development for Women." *Development Dialogue* 1 (2): 11-16.

Dorothy. 1971. "Position Paper of a Feminist on the Report of the Royal Commission on the Status of Women in Canada and the National Ad Hoce Committee on the Status of Women." *The New Feminist* 2 (2): 2-6.

Ehrenreich, B. and D. English. 1979. *For Her Own Good: 150 Years of the Expert's Advice to Women.* New York: Anchor Press.

Hartsock, N. 1983. *Money, Sex and Power: Toward a Feminist Historical Materialism.* New York: Longman.

Higgs, K. 2004. "The Bougainvillel Rebellion." *Women's Review of Books* 22: 8-10.

Isla, Ana. 2007. "An Ecofeminist Perspective on Biopiracy in Latin America." *Signs* 32 (2): 323-331.

Maathai, W. 2004. *The Green Belt Movement: Sharing the Approach.* New York: Lantern Books.

Marcos, Subcomandante. 1997, September. "The fourth world war has begun." *Le Monde Diplomatique-English Edition.* Online: http://mondediplo.com/1997/09/marcos.

Mies, M. 1998. *Patriarchy and Accumulation on a World Scale: Women in the International Division of Labour.* London: Zed Books.

Miles, A. 1996. *Integrative Feminisms: Building Global Visions, 1960s-1990s.* New York: Routledge.

Miles, A. 2001. "Womens Work, Nature and Colonial Exploitation: Feminist Struggle for Alternatives to Corporate Globalization." *Canadian Journal of Development Studies* 22: 855-878.

O'Brien, M. 1981. *The Politics of Reproduction.* London: Routledge.

Rich, A. 1986 [1979]. "What Does a Woman Need to Know?" *Blood, Bread and Poetry: Selected Prose, 1979-1985.* Ed. A. Rich. New York: Norton: 1-10.

Royal Commission on the Status of Women in Canada. 1970. *Report of the Royal Commission on the Status of Women in Canada.* Ottawa: Information Canada, Government of Canada.

Seager, J. 1993. *Earth Follies: Coming to Feminist Terms with the Global Environmental Crisis.* New York: Routledge.

Sen, G. and C. Grown 1987. *Development, Crises, And Alternative Visions: Third World Women's Perspectives.* New York: Monthly Review Press.

Shiva, V. 1989. *Staying Alive: Women, Ecology and Development.* London: Zed Books.

Smith, D. E. 1990. *The Conceptual Practices of Power: A Feminist Sociology of Knowledge.* Toronto: University of Toronto Press.

Standing, G. 2006-07. "Objections to Basic Income Not Based on Sound Reasoning. Basic Income Would Enhance Freedom and Individual Rights." *The CCPA Monitor Canadian Centre for Policy Alternatives* 13 (7): 34-36.

Tauli-Corpuz, V. 1993. "Keynote Address: First Asian Indigenous Women's Conference." *Change* 4 (1): 9-14.

Tauli-Corpuz, V. 2000. "The Indigenous Women's International Forum and Reflections on Beijing Plus Five." *Third World Resurgence* 120-21 (August-September): 57-59. Penang, Malaysia.

Trask, H. 1984. "Fighting the Battle of Double Colonization: View of a Hawaiian Feminist." *Critical Perspectives* 2 (1): 196-212.

Vaughan, G. 1997. *For-Giving: A Feminist Criticism of Exchange.* Austin, TX: Plainview/ Anomaly Press.

Vaughan, G. 2004. "Heterosexual Economics: Gift-Giving and Exchange." Paper presented at A Radically Different World View is Possible: The Gift Economy Inside and Outside of Patriarchal Capitalism, Las Vegas, November 12-14. Online: http://www.gift-economy. com/radicallydifferentmedia.html.

Vaughan, G., ed. 2004. *Il Dono/The Gift: A Feminist Analysis. Athanor: Semiotica, Filosofia, Arte, Letteratura* 15 (8). Roma: Meltemi Editore.

Waring, M. 1988. *If Women Counted: A New Feminist Economics.* San Francisco: Harper and Row.

Position Statement for a Peaceful World
Feminists for a Gift Economy

Presented at the World Social Forum in Porto Alegre, January 2002

From the dawn of time women's gifts have been creating and sustaining community, and we have struggled to make the world a better place. In recent years women have been articulating new forms of protest, refusing war and all forms of violence, protecting the environment and all life, creating new multi-centred and diverse political spaces and defining new politics of care, community, compassion, and connectedness.

Women, from both North and South especially from the margins of privilege and power, are creating alternative visions. Over the last decades the growing feminist movement has developed analyses, changed paradigms, built solidarity through listening to each other. We are rethinking democracy, creating new imaginaries, even reconceptualizing the foundations of political society.

The anti-globalization movement is grounded in the new political space women have created. The global dialogue and networking among men, so celebrated today as a new achievement, post-dates the growing global women's movement by many years. Yet this is rarely acknowledged and feminist leadership is seldom invited. Feminist perspectives remain largely invisible in the struggle against globalization, impoverishing not only women but the struggle as a whole.

We, women of many countries, believe that the death dealing elements of patriarchal capitalist colonial globalisation are rooted, not in unequal exchange alone but in the mechanism of exchange itself. The creation of scarcity, the globalisation of spiritual and material poverty, and the destruction of cultures and species are not failures of a wealth creating system. They are essential expressions of a parasitical centralizing system which denies the gift giving logic of mothering.

Traditional gift-giving societies integrated the logic of mothering into the wider community in many ways. Now socio-economic systems based on the logic of exchange degrade and deny gift giving while co-opting the gifts of most women and many men, dominating the gift givers and destroying the remnants of traditional gift giving societies.

Nevertheless, mothering is a necessity for all societies. Because children are born vulnerable, adults must practice unilateral gift giving towards them. Women are socialized toward this practice which has a transitive logic of its own. Men are socialized away from mothering behavior and towards a self-reflecting logic of competition and domination. The gift logic, functional and complete in itself is altered and distorted by the practice of exchange which requires quantification and measurement, is adversarial, and instills the values of self interest and competition for domination. Exchange, especially monetized exchange, the market, and the capitalist and colonial economies that derive from them are formed in the image of masculinist values and rewards. For this reason we can characterise capitalism as patriarchal.

In the present stage of patriarchal capitalism, corporations have developed as disembodied non-human entities made according to values of dominance, accumulation and control and without the mitigating rationality and emotional capacity a real human being would presumeably have.

Corporations have an internal mandate to grow or die. However, even simple market exchange superimposes itself on gift giving at all levels, cancelling and concealing its value and appropriating its gifts, renaming them as its deserved profits.

Women's free labour is gift labor and it has been estimated as adding some 40 percent or more to the GNP in even the most industrialized economies. The goods and services provided by women to their families are qualitative gifts that create the material and psychological basis of community. These gifts pass through the family to the market, which could not survive without them.

Profit is a disguised and forced gift given by the worker to the capitalist. Indeed the market itself functions as a parasite upon the gifts of the many. As capitalism "evolves" and spreads, its market becomes needy for new gifts, commodifying free goods which were previously held in common by the community or by humanity as a whole. The destructive methods of appropriation which feed the market also create the scarcity necessary for the exchange-based parasite to maintain its control. Since gift giving requires abundance, the parasite can only keep the gift giving host from gaining power by creating artificial scarcity through the monopolization of wealth.

Northern patriarchal capitalism has grown exponentially by invading the economies of the South and extracting their gifts. In the past whole continents have been appropriated, their territories and peoples divided into private property of the colonizers, their gifts commodified. Today, in a new form of colonization, traditional indigenous knowledge and plant species, as well as human, animal, and plant genes are being patented and privatized so that the gifts of the planet and humanity are passing again, at a new level into the hands and profits of the few.

The mechanisms of exploitation are often validated by the very institutions that are established to protect the people. Laws are made in the service of the patriarchal parasite and justice itself is formed in the image of exchange, the payment for crime. Apologists for patriarchal capitalism exist at every level of society from academia to advertising. The very language they use has been stolen, the common ground of its meanings distorted and co-opted in the service of the perpetrators of economic violence. Thus "free trade" apes the language of the gift and liberation while it is only short hand for more exploitation and dominance.

While fair trade seems to be better than unfair trade, it is not the liberating alternative we seek. Exchange itself and not just unequal exchange must give way to the gift. The answer to the injustice of the appropriation of the abundant gifts of the many is not a fair return in cash for the theft but the creation of gift based economies and cultures where life is not commodified.

While such a radical change may appear extremely difficult, it is more "realistic" than simply continuing in our attempts to survive and care for one another in the frighteningly destructive and increasingly toxic world we know today, for these attempts are doomed to failure in the long term.

Women have worked to transform political spaces and have made important, though fragile and highly contested gains in the last decades in affirming women's legal, sexual and reproductive rights, challenging fundamentalisms, opposing violence, and war, improving women's education, health and economic conditions. These struggles have broken new ground while remaining within the exchange paradigm. Our successes and failures challenge and inspire us to seek new terrain, recognizing that "the masters tools can never be used to dismantle the masters house" (Audre Lorde).

WE WANT A MARKET-FREE SOCIETY, NOT A FREE-MARKET SOCIETY

WE WANT:

A world of abundance where bodies, hearts and minds are not dependent on the market.

A world where gift-giving values of care are accepted as the most important, the leading values of society at all levels.

A world where women and men enjoy taking care of children and each other.

A world where everyone is able to express their sexuality in life-loving ways, where their spirituality is treasured and their materiality is honored.

A world where trust and love are the amniotic fluid in which all our children learn to live.

A world where boys and girls are socialized without gender limits as gift-giving humans from the very beginning.

A world where mother nature can be seen as the great gift giver, her ways understood and her infinitely diverse gifts celebrated by all.

A world where humans and all species can reach their highest potential in relationship rather than their lowest potential in parasitism and competetion.

WE WANT:

A world where money does not define value nor legislate survival.

A world where all the categories and processes of parasitism and hate - racism, classism, ageism, ablism, xenophobia, homophobia are regarded as belonging to a shameful past.

A world where war is recognized as expressing unnecessary patriarchal syndromes of dominance and submission in a ridiculously sexualized death ritual using phallic technological instruments, guns and missiles of ever greater proportions.

A world where the psychosis of patriarchy is recognized, healed, and no longer validated as the norm.

We will create the world we want while keeping intact our full humanity, humor and hope.

November 15, 2001

NB: This document is not patented, commodified or copyrighted. Anyone can use it. Please respect its integrity.

Index

Abercromby, John, 68
Aboriginal see Indigenous,
abortion, 35, 212, 321, 323, 332
abundance, 3, 8, 9, 28, 41, 50, 52, 58, 59, 61, 71, 73, 126, 134, 246, 319, 344, 348, 370, 376, 377
academia, 9, 11, 25, 26, 35, 376
academy, 8, 17, 31, 71, 73-81, 83, 258, 265, 283
Ackerley, B. A., 373
activism, 31, 63, 148, 245, 247, 259, 282, 350, 356-363, 368, 372
Agarwal, B., 373
Allen, Paula Gunn, 36, 373
Alonso, Marcos, 300
Anand, A., 373
ancestors, 72, 85, 88
Anders, Günther, 152
anti-war, 254, 358
Anttonen, Veikko, 68
Anzaldúa, G., 179
Anzaldúa, G. and A. Keating, 179
Aptheker, B., 373
Arawaks see Indigenous peoples
Arendt, Hannah, 152
Armstrong, P., 287, 373
assimilate, 187

Bahn, Paul G. and Jean Vertut, 94
Bakan, Joel, 82
Bakhtin, Mikhail, 119
Bales, K., 179
Batchelor, Stephen, 94
Battiste, Marie, 82
Beasley, C., 179

Bell, Diane and Renate Klein, 152
Bellezza, John Vincent, 94
Bennholdt-Thomson, Veronika and Maria Mies, 36
biodiversity, 160, 162, 177, 259, 279, 295-297, 316
Birnbaum, Lucia Chiavola, 94
bodies, 15, 27, 55, 90, 91, 93, 102, 113, 114, 127, 128, 148, 157, 158, 165, 167, 168, 172-175, 177-179, 322, 323, 377
Boehlert, Eric, 350
borders, see also transnational, 74, 165, 222-225, 227, 229, 316
Bourdieau, Pierre, 82
Bourdieu, Pierre, 36
Bracken, Christopher, 82
brothers, 47, 101, 154, 155, 182, 183, 225, 231
Brownhill, L., 373
Burack, C., 373
Burkart, Patrick, 350
Butler, Judith, 213

Caille, Alain, 36
Calleja, Aleida, 350
Canadian Charter of Rights and Freedoms, 257, 282
capitalism, 1-4, 6, 7, 9-11, 16-23, 25-27, 29, 32, 33, 36, 37, 68, 76, 81, 83, 111, 112, 115, 141, 147, 148, 151, 153, 157, 158, 169, 172, 199, 200, 203, 205, 209, 211, 213, 230, 232, 233, 243, 247, 248, 274, 282, 293, 299, 357, 360, 372, 374, 376
capitalist, 6, 14, 25, 29, 31, 54, 75, 77, 110-

112, 115, 139, 141, 143, 145, 147-151,
153, 172, 175, 200, 217, 218, 220, 227,
228, 232, 233, 333, 358, 362, 363, 367,
370, 375, 376
care, 4, 6, 7, 9, 15, 18, 27, 33, 35, 41, 46-48,
52, 64, 65, 88, 99, 103-105, 109, 116,
125, 146, 172-178, 182, 183, 185, 187,
217-219, 226, 227, 235-237, 255, 266,
293, 301, 302, 305, 310, 315, 334, 362,
363, 375, 377
caregiving, 16, 24, 200, 265
Caribbean Association for Feminist Research and Action, 234
Caribs, see Indigenous peoples
Chargaff, Erwin, 152
Chattopadyaya, Debiprasad, 152
Cheal, David, 36
Cheng, S. J. A., 179
Chief, see Indigenous
children, 6, 7, 10, 12, 15, 17, 24, 29, 32,
34, 35, 41, 42, 47, 65, 66, 72, 103-105,
107, 113, 122, 130, 139, 148, 154, 155,
157-159, 165-169, 171-177, 182-186,
189, 190, 200, 201, 206, 207, 217, 218,
220, 225, 227, 231, 232, 235-237, 242,
244, 261, 265, 269, 270, 274-276, 285,
302, 303, 305, 312, 325, 356, 369, 370,
375, 377
Chodorow, Nancy, 36
Chomsky, Noam, 152
Chossudovsky, Michel, 152, 197
citizenship, 317
Cixous, Helene and Catherine Clement,
36
class, 17, 19, 51, 62, 73, 76, 102, 130, 158,
161, 167, 168, 171, 188, 218, 233, 242,
246, 273, 278, 307, 320, 341, 373
classism, 11, 378
climate change, 157, 161
coalition, 282, 314
Cohen, Alex, 300
Cole, Douglas and Ira Chaikin, 82
Collins, P. H., 373
colonial, 8, 73, 75, 78, 125, 129, 161, 168,
312-314, 373, 375, 376
colonies, 125, 165, 234, 284, 333, 334
colonization, 3, 9, 18, 27, 52, 75, 80, 93,
140, 157, 182, 369, 370, 376
colony, 333

colour, 24, 50, 57, 77, 96, 204, 242
commodification, 30, 54, 75, 275, 297,
298, 370, 376
community, 2, 3, 9, 14-17, 19-22, 25, 27-
29, 33, 41-49, 52, 61-64, 66, 73-75,
86, 90, 92, 98, 99, 102-105, 114, 117,
127-129, 132, 141-143, 151, 154-159,
162, 164, 165, 168, 175, 177, 178, 181-
185, 189, 196, 204, 205, 207, 213, 218,
224-227, 229, 232, 238, 239, 241-245,
249-252, 257-286, 284-287, 293-296,
299, 300, 302-305, 311, 313-315,
327-331, 333-335, 337, 339-349, 351,
353-355, 358-360, 362, 364, 366, 368,
369, 371, 372, 375, 376
competition, 4-6, 8, 14, 16, 22, 26, 27,
32-34, 51, 52, 62, 66, 73, 112, 121,
124-130, 132, 133, 142, 199, 208, 209,
232, 233, 259, 268, 322, 329, 334, 335,
337, 359, 366, 367, 375
consciousness raising, 63, 342
Convention on the Elimination of All
Forms of Discrimination against Women
(CEDAW), 281, 283, 296
cooperation, 5, 16, 21, 27, 33, 42, 46,
51, 104, 125, 128, 133, 196, 197, 233,
248, 359
cross-cultural, 50, 59, 100
culture, 9, 20, 24, 27, 29, 41, 52, 55-58,
62, 66, 67, 71, 88, 91, 93, 102, 106, 107,
113, 114, 121-124, 130, 141-143, 147,
149-151, 165, 172, 175, 190, 212, 218,
220, 243, 255, 259, 260, 262, 264, 269,
274, 279, 280, 284, 294, 297, 304, 307,
310, 313, 315, 317, 330, 334, 336, 340,
341, 343, 349, 354, 355, 367
Czaplicka, M. A., 94

Daly, Herman, 169
Darwin, Charles, 123, 125-128, 134-135
Davis-Kimball, Jeannine, 94
De Camino, Ronnie, O. Segura, L. Arias
and I. Pérez, 169
Debold, Elizabeth, 135
debt, 21, 27, 157, 159, 163, 165-168, 184,
196, 205, 239, 240, 277, 285, 293
Deloria, Barbara, Kristen Foehner and Sam
Scinta, 82
Deloria, Vine, Jr., 82

Derrida, Jacques, 34,36, 319-320, 326

development, 30, 35, 66, 78, 85, 87, 99, 106, 109-112, 116, 118, 130, 140-142, 144, 148, 158, 159, 163, 168, 169, 186, 201, 203, 204, 208, 222-224, 226, 228, 234, 249, 258, 261, 263, 264, 271, 273, 275, 280, 282, 283, 284, 285, 286, 293-298, 300, 302, 304, 306, 307, 339, 341-343, 345, 369

Development Alternatives with Women for a New Era (DAWN), 234, 257, 276, 288, 366, 373

Diamond, Jared, 94

diaspora, 29, 47, 175, 231, 232

Dietrich, Heidi, 350

disadvantage, 101, 248

diseases, 32, 60, 166, 184

division of labour, 158, 165, 184, 199

Dorf, Michael C., 350

Durlin, Marty and Cathy Melio, 350

ecofeminism, 64

ecological, 10, 50, 56, 60, 62, 79, 134, 139, 157, 158, 307, 366

ecology, 41, 134, 148, 168

economic North, 277, 369

economic South, 277, 368

economics, 9, 10, 16, 21, 33, 36, 50, 52, 57, 126, 129, 130, 133, 230, 232, 250, 274, 318, 329, 371

Economy and Solidarity Network, 238

education, 35, 76, 78, 79, 81, 109, 129, 174, 184, 232, 235, 241, 242, 261, 264, 272, 277, 278, 297, 311, 341, 343, 347, 356, 368, 370, 377

Ehrenreich, B. and A. R. Hochschild, 179

Ehrenreich, B. and D. English, 373

Eisler, Riane, 36

elders, *see* Indigenous

Eller, Cynthia, 68

Ellsworth, Elizabeth, 82

employment, 131, 132, 158, 164, 173, 224, 272, 277

empowerment, 68, 132, 341

environment, 8, 20, 22-25, 42, 63, 71, 75, 112, 126-129, 140, 154, 167, 175, 184, 276, 277, 285, 294, 297, 310, 314, 332, 341, 353, 368, 370, 375

environmental, 8, 18, 21, 52, 139, 156, 157-159, 161, 163, 168, 188, 258, 276, 277, 296, 358, 364, 369, 370

equality, 38, 62, 99, 101, 210, 211, 258, 277, 281, 282, 283, 302, 304, 305, 365, 368

essentialism, 4, 6, 8

ethnic, 21, 109, 173, 230, 310

ethnicity, 19

Eurocentric, 64, 74, 76

exchange, 2, 3, 5-29, 31, 33, 34, 48, 50, 51, 54, 55, 59, 60, 62, 65, 66, 71, 77, 104, 106, 110, 112, 116, 127, 129-131, 147, 158, 165, 167, 196, 199, 204-213, 215, 218-220, 228, 233, 236, 239, 243, 245, 259, 267, 270, 274, 279, 283, 293, 294, 321, 323, 327, 348, 361, 364, 367-370, 372, 375- 377

exclusion, 11, 28, 43, 78, 204, 205, 266, 303, 306, 307, 338, 365

factory, 236

family, 5, 9, 17, 21, 27-29, 41-49, 63, 66, 82, 105, 115, 125, 127, 131, 132, 154, 158, 163-165, 173, 174, 176, 182-188, 190, 191, 197, 201, 202, 205-207, 211-213, 219, 222- 229, 231, 232, 236, 239, 241, 242, 244, 262, 265, 268-270, 272, 276-278, 293, 311, 316, 317, 321, 328, 362, 376

farm wife, 262

farmers, 3, 88, 161, 163, 276, 295, 296

female, 2, 11, 16, 26, 46, 51, 54-59, 62, 65-68, 72, 76, 84-93, 101, 142, 143, 154, 167, 175, 184, 199, 200, 205-207, 209, 212, 213, 251, 294, 367

femaleness, 45, 46

femininity, 68

feminism, 151, 168, 176, 212, 242, 245, 247, 257, 318, 324, 331, 366, 370; ecofeminism, 64; transformative, 365

feminist, 1, 2, 4, 8, 9, 18, 19, 21, 29-32, 35, 38, 50, 53, 55, 62-64, 66, 68-70, 76, 94, 95, 107, 119, 120, 135, 139, 141, 151, 153, 157, 159, 169, 170, 171, 177, 179, 180, 187, 188, 200, 212, 214, 234, 238, 239, 240-243, 246, 247, 249, 251, 252, 254, 257-260, 264, 266, 268, 269, 271-274, 277-286, 300, 318, 321, 322, 324, 326, 339, 342, 347, 349, 352, 363-

375, 378; Feminist Network for a Gift Economy, 364, 372; Feminist Statement on Guaranteed Living Income, 371, 372; theory, 151

feminists, Indigenous, 364, 365, 369

Feminists for a Gift Economy, 31, 375; Position Statement for a Peaceful World, 375

first world, 139, 153, 236, 333, 362

Folbre, Nancy, 36

food, 16, 27, 28, 42, 46, 49, 59, 85, 88, 93, 101, 104, 125, 126, 128, 141, 154, 155, 160, 177, 182-186, 191, 218-220, 235-237, 245, 253, 274, 277, 285, 294-298, 301, 353, 354, 356, 368

Foster, Bellamy John, 169

Foucault, Michel, 119

free trade, 75, 130, 174, 224, 335, 360, 377

Freire, Paolo, 350

fundamentalism, 29, 260, 285

Garfinkle, Yosef, 94

gay, 199, 331

GDP, 29, 131, 369, 370

gender, 6, 15-17, 19, 22, 23, 28, 33, 35, 45, 50-52, 54, 60, 64-66, 77, 99, 109, 146, 157, 158, 161, 168, 181, 184-186, 195, 199, 200, 202, 206, 207, 209, 210, 212, 218, 223, 253, 263, 294, 296, 297, 307, 320, 327, 341, 366, 367, 377

gendered, 50, 51, 62, 209, 217, 218, 273, 367, 371

genocide, 4, 32, 302, 331

Genth, Renate, 152

George, Bill, 135

Geyer Miller, Sandra, 68

gift economies, 3, 4, 6-9, 16, 22, 23, 30, 33-35, 159, 211, 324

gift economy, 1, 2, 4, 5, 7-9, 11, 12, 18-23, 25-33, 35, 36, 49, 55, 64, 93, 96-98, 106, 145, 159, 168, 187, 201-204, 207, 209, 211, 217, 218, 220, 222, 224, 227, 228, 230, 232-240, 242, 245, 247, 248, 254, 259, 273, 282, 293, 299, 313, 315, 317-319, 321, 322, 327, 348, 354-356, 358-360, 362, 363, 365, 378

gift giving, 2-31, 33-36, 43, 45, 47, 49, 53, 65, 81, 103, 106, 107, 115, 116, 142,

151, 159, 177, 199, 200, 202-213, 217-220, 222, 225, 227-229, 232, 240, 249-251, 253, 259, 319, 321-323, 337, 345, 347, 348, 354, 355, 361, 375, 376

gift paradigm, 1, 7, 8, 18, 20, 21, 25, 31, 35, 81, 101-103, 105-107, 142, 149, 210, 211, 230, 232, 233, 318, 319, 364-369, 372

Gilligan, Carol, 37

Gimbutas, Marija, 94, 152

Girard, René, 152

girls, 15, 90, 166, 167, 169, 212, 220, 244, 265, 377

giving, 2, 4-6, 8-16, 18-31, 33-35, 41, 48-51, 54, 56, 57, 59, 60, 62, 67, 68, 71-73, 75, 79, 84, 90, 92-94, 97, 98, 104, 107, 115, 116, 124, 128, 135, 149, 150, 177, 196, 199, 200, 204-211, 213, 217-219, 222, 224, 227, 228, 232, 241, 242, 244-250, 253-255, 258, 259, 281, 283, 285, 287, 289, 291, 302, 307, 314, 315, 317, 319, 321, 336, 338, 339, 341, 343, 344, 347, 348, 355, 361, 364, 367-369, 371, 373, 375-377

global, 8, 15, 25, 26, 31, 53, 63, 75, 77-81, 93, 106, 109-115, 125, 126, 129, 131-134, 139, 140, 148, 150, 157-160, 165, 167, 168, 170-172, 174-176, 193, 195, 222-224, 227, 228, 230, 232, 233, 240, 242-244, 248-250, 257, 259, 298, 299, 302, 305, 307, 308, 317, 322, 357, 359, 360, 363, 364, 368, 369, 372, 375

Global Fund for Women, 244

global warming, 53, 63, 159

globalization, 9, 26, 28-31, 34, 63, 74, 81, 105, 109, 110, 130, 131, 134, 140, 151, 193, 223, 229, 233, 236, 248, 260, 284, 297-299, 303, 319-320, 333, 336, 358, 368-370, 372, 375

Godbout, Jacques T., 33-34, 36, 319-320

Godelier, Maurice, 152

Goettner-Abendroth, Heide, 37, 68, 107

Goldschmidt, W., 300

Goux, Jean-Joseph, 37

Grande, Sandy, 82

grandmothers, 27, 48, 156, 182, 185, 219, 281

Griffin, David Ray, 198

Gross, Robin, 351

Guha, Ramachandra and J. Martinez-Alier, 169

Haavio, Martti, 69
Hall, Anthony, 82
Haramein, Nassim and Elizabeth Rauscher, 135
Harris, David R., 94
Harrison, Jane, 69
Hart, M., 179
Hartsock, N., 373
Hawthorne, S. and R. Klein, 179
Hecht, Susana and Alexander Cockburn, 169
Hegel, Georg Wilhem Friedrich, 119
Henderson, Hazel, 37, 135
Herman, Andrew, 37
Hesiod, 54, 55, 56, 65, 69, 70
heterosexism, 199, 200, 201, 203, 205, 207, 209-212, 213
heterosexist, 199, 202, 209
heterosexual, 28, 50, 203, 206
heterosexuality, 28, 199, 202, 206, 210, 213, 220
hidden alternative economy, 4
hidden economy, 6, 19
hierarchies, 18, 43, 51, 52, 73, 99, 104, 106, 127, 209, 212, 269, 345
hierarchy, 6, 14, 17, 232, 259, 366
Higgs, K., 374
HIV/AIDS, 27, 28, 166, 181, 184-186, 220, 335
home, 13, 15, 28, 29, 42, 85, 86, 115, 130, 169, 172, 174, 176-178, 182, 183, 185, 187, 188, 190, 191, 194, 203, 218, 224, 225, 228, 231, 232, 235, 254, 268, 270, 272. 302, 303, 311, 312, 314, 333, 348, 359, 361
homophobia, 11, 199, 349, 378
Hondagneu-Sotelo, P., 179
Honko, Lauri, 69
hooks, b., 179
household, 85, 101, 159, 172, 174, 181, 185, 186, 225, 241, 262, 295
housewife, 86, 273
housework, 24, 34, 115, 210, 273
Hughes, D., 179
human rights, 30, 93, 109, 155, 156, 164, 167, 222, 229, 235, 252, 283, 300, 302, 304-306, 308, 309, 340, 341
Hyde, Lewis, 37, 326

identity, 4-7, 11, 13-16, 19, 26, 34-36, 50, 62, 79, 109, 110, 113-118, 150, 190, 199, 200, 202, 204, 207, 209, 210, 297, 305, 324, 346, 347
Illich, Ivan, 309
immigrant, 27, 173, 222, 227
immigration, 173, 192, 223, 312
Indigenous, *see* also women, Indigenous peoples, 1-10, 12, 16, 20, 23, 25, 30-32, 34-36, 41, 42, 47, 50, 64, 68, 69, 71-83, 115, 128, 151, 159, 168, 181, 209, 213, 217, 231, 247, 254, 280, 293-300, 310-312, 314, 316, 364, 365, 369, 370, 374; Aboriginal, 79, 83, 94, 280; Chief, 201; elders, 44, 128, 155, 183
Indigenous feminists, 364, 365, 369
Indigenous peoples, 1, 4, 9, 10, 25, 30, 71, 73, 75, 76, 78-82, 128, 159, 231, 247, 293-295, 297-299, 312, 314; Arawaks, 231; Caribs, 231; Khoekhoe, 28, 217-220; Native Americans, 4; Sami, 23, 25, 57, 59, 64, 69, 71, 72, 81, 83; Syilx, 34, 41, 42, 49
Indigenous women, 23, 30, 64, 76, 81, 294, 295, 297, 299, 369
Indigenous Women's Network, 300
industrialized countries, 160
international conferences,
   A Radically Different Worldview is Possible: The Gift Economy Inside and Outside Patriarchal Capitalism, 1, 11, 23, 68, 260, 282
   United Nations Conference on Environment and Development (UNCED)· 157, 159, 295, 300, 317
International Criminal Court, 313-314
International Monetary Fund, 36, 130, 165, 166, 167, 172, 173, 193, 195
International Women's Day, 191
Irigaray, Luce, 82
Isla, Ana, 169, 374
Ismail, M., 179

Juuso, Inga, 83
Karonga, Elizabeth, 351
Kemppinen, Iivar, 69

Kennard, Bill, 351
Khoekhoe see Indigenous peoples
Khumalo, Musi, 351
King, Thomas, 83
Kiuchi, Tachi, 135
Kjellström, Rolf, 83
Klare, Michael, 152
Klein, Anne Carolyn, 94
Korpinen, Tuulikki, 69
Korten, D. C., 179
Korten, David, 69
Kramarae, Cheris and Paula A. Treichler, 69
Krogerus, Tuulikki, 69
Kumar, Corinne, 152, 309

labour, 6, 8, 10, 28, 33-35, 50, 51, 65, 113,
   147, 157-159, 171-174, 178, 181, 182,
   184, 209, 210, 218, 220, 223, 224, 237,
   264, 265, 270, 272, 274-276, 285, 298,
   345, 360, 369, 370, 376
Lakoff, George, 37, 214
Lakoff, George and Mark Johnson, 37
language, 16, 20, 22, 25, 26, 28, 34, 35,
   41-45, 48, 49, 72, 77, 78, 84, 100, 108,
   110, 116, 118, 187-189, 191, 207, 240,
   247, 293, 308, 310, 316, 321, 335, 342,
   376, 377
Lappé, Anthony and Stephen Marshall,
   198
Lappé, F. M. and A. Lappé, 179
Latouche, Serge, 37, 326
Lee, Douglas, 351
Lemke-Santangelo, G., 179
lesbian, 187, 256, 269
Levinas, Emmanuel, 119
Lewis, I. M., 94
liberation see also women's liberation , 7,
   29, 77, 184, 188, 192, 224, 260, 280,
   288, 368, 369, 377
location, 2, 353
Lönnrot, Elias, 69
Lorde, Audre, 69, 214
low income, 360
Loye, David, 135

Maathai, W., 374
Magat, I. N., 179
Mäkinen, Kirsti, 69
Malarek, Victor, 170

maleness, 31, 45, 46, 206, 207, 367
Mann, Barbara, 37
Mann, Charles, 37
marginal, 232, 369
marginalized, 71, 166, 252, 296
Marglin, Frederique Apffel, 94
Margulis, Lynn, 135
market, 1-19, 21, 23, 24, 27, 28, 31, 33-35,
   47, 77, 110, 112, 113, 124, 130, 137,
   147, 158, 160, 161, 163, 165, 199-206,
   208-213, 220, 223, 230-233, 236, 237,
   239, 240, 248, 250, 258, 269 270, 275,
   293, 299, 304, 305, 307, 319, 322, 323,
   327, 332, 338, 345, 357, 358, 360, 362,
   363, 367-372, 376, 377
market economy, 3, 7, 23, 47, 77, 158,
   209, 220, 230, 239, 240, 248, 258, 293,
   299, 304, 305, 307, 319, 357, 358, 360,
   362, 363
Marshack, Alexander, 94
Marx, Karl, 5, 6, 13, 16, 34, 37, 38, 151,
   159, 201, 209, 213, 214
masculinity, 22, 68, 200, 212, 322, 367
master imaginary, 25, 50-56, 59, 60, 62,
   64, 302, 306, 308
Matewa, Chido E. F., 351
matriarchal, 1, 2, 4, 5, 12, 26, 31, 33, 34,
   52, 56, 59, 61, 66, 68, 69, 85, 88, 90,
   93, 99-107, 139, 141-147, 149-151, 153,
   154, 212, 279, 364, 369
matriarchy, 27, 38, 53, 55, 62, 69, 70, 95,
   100, 102, 104, 139, 141-145, 147, 149,
   151, 153, 213, 247
Mauss, Marcel, 37, 326
McLaren, Peter, 83
McLaren, Peter, and Ramin Farahmandpur, 83
Mellaart, James, Udo Hirsch and Belkis
   Balpinar, 95
Meyer, Leroy N. and Tony Ramirez, 69
Mies, Maria, 37, 83, 152, 170, 272, 374
Mies, Maria and Veronika Bennholdt-
   Thomson, 37
migration, 112, 141, 183, 224, 229
Miles, A., 289, 374
militarism, 254, 258, 260
Mills, Ken and Sue Schardt, 351
mining, 154, 160, 161, 163, 168, 368
misogyny, 4, 260, 263

Monestel Arce, Yehudi, 170
mother, 6, 8, 13, 15, 16, 20, 24, 35, 45,
47-49, 52, 54, 57-59, 62, 66, 67, 72, 84,
85, 92, 93, 101, 103, 107, 116, 142-150,
154, 156, 178, 182, 183, 185, 188, 191,
196, 199, 200, 207, 209, 211, 212, 217,
219, 235, 236, 253-256, 260, 262, 310,
317, 320-322, 324, 325, 378
single, 207
motherhood, 172, 217, 256, 322, 323,
324
mothering, 4, 6-9, 13, 15, 16, 20, 22-24,
30, 33, 35, 36, 199, 200, 205, 206, 209,
211, 213, 217, 220, 228, 258, 273, 324,
345, 352, 375
mothers, 6-8, 12, 15, 16, 19, 24, 30, 35, 53,
92, 100, 101, 103, 143-145, 148, 154,
155, 171, 172, 174, 182, 184, 200, 235,
274, 303, 322, 324, 357, 367
multiculturalism, 79
Murdock, Graham, 351

nation, 5, 73, 74, 77, 106, 131, 158, 182-
185, 223, 257, 283, 302, 304, 306, 310,
313, 314, 335, 371
Native Americans, see Indigenous Peoples
Native, see Indigenous
nature, 1, 3, 9, 16, 20, 21, 24, 25, 27,
30, 50, 51, 53, 54, 56-60, 62-64, 66,
67, 74, 76, 79, 80, 85-87, 90, 91, 97,
99, 102, 103, 106, 111, 118, 121, 126,
129, 131, 140, 142, 143-147, 149, 150,
157-159, 161, 167, 168, 171, 172, 250,
261, 265, 272, 277, 279, 280, 283, 296,
297, 302, 312, 322, 328, 354, 364, 368,
369, 371, 378
Negri, Antonio and Michael Hardt, 214
Nenola-Kallio, Aili and Timonen Senni, 69
neoliberal, 50, 51, 62-65, 74, 75, 77, 140,
230, 232, 233, 248, 260, 277-279, 367,
368, 370, 372
neoliberalism, 177
networks, 28, 29, 105, 160, 223, 224, 233,
238, 239, 266, 268, 269, 272, 273, 278,
333, 365
Niemi, Irmeli, 69
Noble, Vicki, 95
nongovernmental organizations, 240, 309,
311, 331

non-white, 51

Ochs, Carol, 70
Odio, Elizabeth, 170
Omunegha, Kate Azuka, 351
oppression, 4, 5, 31, 158, 165, 166, 229,
233, 255, 256, 275, 285, 314, 357, 359,
366, 369
orientation, sexual, 19, 212
other-orientation, 18-19, 22, 34, 55
otherness, 26, 60, 79, 109, 114, 116, 117

paid work, 268, 269
parasite, 6, 8, 10, 199, 319, 376
parasitic, 7, 10, 11, 17, 149, 211, 273
Parreñas, R. S., 179
patriarchal, 1-11, 16-27, 29-36, 46, 50-59,
61-68, 72, 73, 75, 77, 78, 81, 93, 99, 100,
104-106, 115, 116, 139, 141-149, 151,
157, 158, 165, 172, 174, 175, 178, 181,
199-203, 209, 211-213, 232, 258-261,
264, 269, 271, 273-277, 279-284, 307,
319, 322, 324, 327, 357, 363, 365-367,
369, 372-374, 376, 378
patriarchy, 2-8, 10, 15-19, 22-27, 32, 37,
38, 46, 51, 53-56, 59, 62-64, 66, 70,
83, 93, 99, 100, 103, 104, 139-151,
153, 159, 170, 177-180, 187, 201-203,
206, 207, 211, 233, 243-244, 246, 247,
253, 255-256, 259-260, 262, 275, 280,
283-284, 302, 304, 305, 309, 323, 363,
367, 374, 378
peace, 8, 21, 30, 87, 96, 109, 139, 141,
194-197, 199, 204, 211, 235, 256, 258,
285, 302, 309, 310, 312, 314, 315, 317,
331, 365, 368
Peirce, Charles Sanders, 119
Perkins, John, 135
Petaja, Emil, 70
Petrilli, Susan, 119
Pettman, Jan J., 170
Phipps, William E., 70
Plumwood, Val, 70, 83
Polanyi, Karl, 152
policies, 30, 80, 130, 143, 149, 154, 155,
173, 187, 188, 193, 223, 224, 238,
271, 276-279, 284, 296, 332, 336,
344, 371
policy, 102, 125, 140, 188, 195, 223, 233,

243, 257, 258, 263, 274, 278, 282, 296, 328, 334, 336, 371
political action, 249
pollution, 60-62, 155, 159, 163
Porsanger, Jelena, 83
poverty, 19, 27, 28, 34, 48, 109, 139, 157, 158, 167, 168, 178, 182, 183, 185, 225, 235, 236, 271, 275, 276, 285, 296, 298, 299, 305, 308, 310, 311, 319, 322, 368, 370, 372, 375
power, 4, 10, 11, 17, 18, 24, 30, 31, 43, 51, 52, 54, 57-59, 61-63, 68, 73, 77-79, 90, 92, 98, 100-102, 105, 106, 118, 122, 124, 144, 156, 158, 159, 165, 167, 174, 175, 185, 187-189, 191-193, 196, 197, 202, 203, 206, 212, 213, 219, 233, 237, 239, 243, 245, 246, 249, 255, 256, 259, 261, 273, 274, 278, 282, 304-306, 310-314, 317, 322-324, 333, 340, 348, 349, 355, 359, 366, 368, 371, 373, 375, 376
Pozner, Jennifer, 351
practices, 26, 72, 75, 78-81, 87, 89, 91, 92, 109, 110, 113, 116, 151, 172, 173, 247, 255, 276, 294-299, 313, 324, 364
privilege, 43, 46, 51, 79, 206, 241, 242, 246, 323, 362, 375
profit, 6, 10, 11, 24, 29, 66, 77, 78, 80, 82, 103, 112, 113, 116, 140, 148, 150, 152, 158, 161, 165, 174, 197, 205, 208, 209, 227, 229, 239, 246, 252, 275, 293, 302, 305, 327, 333, 334, 339, 341, 345, 367-369, 371, 376
progress, 30, 51, 74, 109, 122, 130, 133, 140, 142, 143, 148, 150, 173, 241, 263, 284, 302, 369
prostitute, 93, 174
prostitution, 157, 165-166
Pyle, Emily, 352

Quarmyne, Wilna, 352
queer, 213

race, 11, 17, 53, 65, 88, 92, 132, 167, 171, 195, 205, 211, 242, 307, 373
racism, 11, 106, 168, 230, 296, 349, 378
racist, 256, 310, 369
Raddon, Mary-Beth, 37
radical feminist, 256
rape, 93, 188, 255, 325, 331

receiving, 3, 8, 10, 12, 14-16, 23, 30, 81, 96, 172, 200, 202, 204-206, 208, 213, 225, 232, 337, 349, 367
relationship, 16, 29, 42, 43, 71-73, 75, 76, 79, 81, 102, 111, 116, 122, 202, 222, 232, 239, 252, 280, 294, 296, 297, 312, 321, 333, 337
remittances, 15, 21, 24, 28, 30, 115, 171, 225, 227-229, 231, 232, 311
reproduction, 58, 73, 111, 201, 264, 266, 268, 275, 295
social, 111
research, 22, 50, 55, 56, 64, 73, 75, 81, 92, 93, 99, 100, 106, 107, 122, 123, 129, 135, 149, 151, 160, 168, 255, 257, 259, 260-262, 264, 277, 281-283, 285, 294, 296, 298, 308, 319, 320, 323, 331, 339, 346
revolution, 19, 21, 30, 73, 77, 85, 110, 122, 129, 187, 246, 249, 315, 338, 357, 358, 363, 365
Rich, A., 374
Rifkin, Jeremy, 153
Rosch, Eleanor, 214
Rossi-Landi, Ferruccio, 37, 119
Royal Commission on Aboriginal Peoples (Canada), 79, 83
Ruddick, Sara, 38
Ruhnbro, Christina, 352
Ruppert, Michael, 198
rural, 158, 165, 167, 181-186, 219, 262, 263, 277-278, 280, 295, 341, 342
rural women, 158, 165, 167, 183-185, 262, 280, 341, 342
Russell, Walter, 135

Sachs, Wolfgang, 170
Sage, Luis and R. Quirós, 170
Sahtouris, Elisabet, 135
Sakolsky, Ron, 352
Sami, see Indigenous, 23, 25, 57, 59, 64, 69, 71, 72, 81, 83
Sanday, Peggy, 38, 95
Sanday, Peggy Reeves, 38, 95
Saussure, Ferdinand de, 38
scarcity, 8, 9, 14, 21, 23, 26, 28, 35, 41, 59, 125-127, 134, 159, 164, 183, 184, 196, 212, 223, 275, 319, 328, 329, 339, 348, 370, 375, 376

Schrift, Alan D., 38
Seager, J., 374
Sebeok, Thomas A. and Marcel Danesi, 214
self-determination, 62, 359
self-interest, 4, 7, 11, 19, 52, 73, 79, 129-131, 160, 273, 349
Sen, G. and C. Grown, 374
sex work, 93, 166, 172, 174, 176
sex worker, 172, 174
sexism, 11, 106, 296, 331, 349
sexual orientation, 19, 212
sexuality, 55, 57, 172, 174, 176, 177, 322, 377
Shaw, Miranda, 95
Shiva, Vandana, 38, 170, 374
Shiva, Vandana and Maria Mies, 38
Siikala, Anna-Leena, 70
silence, 73, 76, 77, 193, 303, 304, 308, 309
Silko, Leslie Marmon, 83
single mother, 207
sisters, 30, 47, 154, 155, 168, 182, 225, 231, 243, 254, 256, 317
slavery, 19, 28, 87, 93, 96, 158, 167, 217, 220, 231, 236, 275, 280, 322, 323
slaves, 10, 76, 125, 174, 219, 236, 245, 275
Smith, D. E., 374
social change, 1, 4, 19, 21-24, 29, 31, 32, 115, 188, 199, 241-245, 248, 258, 340, 342, 345, 346, 358
social construction, 199, 209
social relations, 16, 111, 233, 240, 263, 278, 364
social reproduction, 111
Sohn-Rethel, Alfred, 214
solidarity, 19, 21, 23, 24, 29, 33, 75, 172, 194, 196, 230, 231, 239, 240, 247, 248, 310, 361, 362, 364, 369, 375
Sombart, Nicolaus, 153
spiritual, 9, 21, 25, 28, 49, 54, 58, 59, 62, 66, 72, 102, 103, 105, 106, 177, 218, 226, 243, 246, 275, 358, 364, 375
spirituality, 3, 28, 61, 62, 93, 106, 150, 217, 218, 243, 245, 364, 377
Spretnak, Charlene, 70
Standing, G., 374
Stiglitz, Joseph, 83

Stockwell, Norm, 352
Stone, Merlin, 70
structural adjustment programs (SAPS), 286
subordination, 80
subsistence, 28, 33, 105, 147, 157-159, 161, 163, 168, 171, 220, 238, 267, 273, 277
surplus value, 8, 10, 159
sustainability, 52, 62, 87, 139, 163, 224, 294
sustainable, 50, 52, 53, 62-64, 68, 72, 80, 131, 134, 157-160, 167, 168, 247, 294-296, 299, 360, 361
sustainable development, 157-160, 168, 294, 295
Sylix, see Indigenous Peoples

Tannen, Deborah, 38
Tauli-Corpuz, V., 374
Taylor, John R., 38, 214
technologies, 127, 133, 148, 149, 248-252, 278, 296-299, 332, 338
Temple, Robert, 95
theory, 18, 20, 23, 29, 61, 62, 67, 71, 76-78, 80, 81, 115, 117, 118, 124-126, 129, 130, 145, 159, 177, 195, 201, 222, 227, 230, 242, 244, 259, 283, 285, 286, 318, 320, 321, 342, 348; feminist, 151; third world, 157, 164, 168, 170, 235, 240, 248, 287, 307, 366, 369, 370, 373, 374; third world feminist, 366, 370
Thompson, Paul, 198
Thornton, Lawrence, 309
Torres, Sonia, 170
trade, 59, 65, 85, 105, 125, 127, 159, 166, 228, 231, 298, 299, 335, 336, 339, 360, 370, 377
trade unions, 339
traditional community, 43
traditional practices, 43
trafficking, 27, 172, 174, 244
transformative feminism, 365
transgendered, 203
transnational, see also borders, 140, 160, 171, 173, 175-177, 179, 193, 195, 224, 298, 334, 371; corporations, 140, 195, 298, 371
Uchatius, Wolfgang, 179

unemployed, 174, 185, 202, 276

United Nations, 30, 94, 129, 133, 234, 235, 283, 286, 294, 296, 298-300, 305, 315, 317, 331; Convention on Biological Diversity, 295, 300; Organization for Education, Science and Culture (UNESCO), 317, 335, 336, 343, 349

universities, 77, 78, 123, 269

unpaid work, 76, 159, 172, 257, 257-258, 264, 267, 268, 271, 273, 274, 283, 357, 372

urban, 122, 182, 262, 264, 367, 369

value, 2, 5, 6, 7, 11-17, 19, 23, 28, 34, 35, 51, 64, 67, 104, 105, 107, 113, 117, 122, 124, 133, 134, 145, 150, 154, 155, 196, 201-205, 208-211, 213, 236, 238, 239, 253, 257-259, 261, 269-271, 273-276, 278, 280, 281, 293, 295, 324, 328, 338, 342, 345, 362, 368, 369, 370, 371, 376, 378

values, 2, 5, 6, 7, 9, 10, 18, 19, 21, 29, 31-33, 50-53, 56, 64-68, 73, 74, 77, 78, 80, 81, 88, 106, 108, 109, 113, 124, 131, 181, 183, 184, 187, 194, 199, 203, 210, 228, 230, 233, 239, 240, 246, 259-261, 264, 267, 270, 277-279, 285, 293, 307, 321, 324, 342, 344, 359, 365-367, 376, 377

Vaughan, Genevieve, 38, 70, 95, 107, 115-116, 120, 135, 139, 153, 158, 170, 214, 220, 253, 256, 289, 300, 318, 327, 332, 352, 358, 364-365

Vernadsky, V. I. Vladimir, 135

violence against women, 17, 104, 323

Vizcaíno, Irene, 170

voluntary, 159

volunteer, 225, 250, 264, 265, 266, 270, 345, 347, 360, 362, 363

Vygotsky, Lev Semenovich, 38, 214

Wakernagel, Mathis and William Rees, 170

Walker, Barbara, 70

Wallerstein, Immanuel, 153

war, 11, 17, 18, 27, 52, 54, 61, 87, 88, 93, 105, 109, 111, 113, 130, 133, 139, 141-143, 149-151, 153, 157, 159, 189, 193-196, 211, 235, 240, 254, 302-307,
309, 317, 322, 333, 357, 374, 375, 377, 378

Waring, Marilyn, 38, 289

Warren, K. J., 70

water, 8, 9, 27, 67, 96, 140, 154-156, 160, 162-164, 177, 188, 191, 219, 226, 245, 273, 295, 314, 316, 338, 339, 353, 354, 368, 370

Watson-Franke, Maria-Barbara, 38

wealth, 8, 17, 61, 77, 93, 101, 102, 106, 123, 129, 130, 139, 141, 147, 148, 158, 165, 166, 193, 196, 222, 241-243, 250, 259, 269-276, 278, 280, 281, 283, 284, 301, 302, 338, 364, 367, 370-372, 375, 376

Weatherford, Jack, 38

Welby, Victoria, 120

Werden, Frieda, 352

Werlhof, Claudia von, 38, 153, 180

West, Martin Litchfield, 70

White, David Gordon, 95

Wolf, Doris, 153

women, European, 4, 167; Indigenous, 295, 297, 299; Indigenous Women's Network, 300; rural, 158, 165, 167, 183-185, 262, 280, 341, 342; young, 281, 282

women's liberation, see also liberation, 260, 368, 369

work, paid, 268, 269; unpaid, 76, 257, 258, 264, 267, 268, 271, 273, 274, 357, 372

World Bank, 36, 130, 134, 158, 165-167, 169, 170, 172, 173, 193, 195, 298

World Courts of Women, 306, 308-309

World Social Forum, 11, 31, 240, 347, 365, 375

World Trade Organization (WTO), 80, 130, 131, 193, 336

Wright, Kenneth, 38

xenophobia, 11, 378

Yeoh, B. S. A., S. Huang and J. Gonzalez, 180

youth, 44, 57, 184, 226, 243, 316, 347

Zarembka, J. M., 180

Ziegler, Jean, 153

Zundle, Ernst, 352